THE INDIVIDUAL AND TRADITION

THE INDIVIDUAL AND TRADITION

FOLKLORISTIC PERSPECTIVES

Edited by Ray Cashman,
Tom Mould, and Pravina Shukla

Special Publications of the Folklore Institute, no. 8
Indiana University Bloomington

Indiana University Press
Bloomington and Indianapolis

This book is a publication of

Indiana University Press
601 North Morton Street
Bloomington, Indiana 47404-3797 USA

www.iupress.indiana.edu

Telephone orders   800-842-6796
Fax orders   812-855-7931
Orders by e-mail   iuporder@indiana.edu

Manufactured in the United States of America

Cataloging information is available from the Library of Congress.

ISBN 978-0-253-35717-5 (cloth)
ISBN 978-0-253-22373-9 (paperback)

1 2 3 4 5 14 13 12 11 10 09

for

HENRY GLASSIE,

bright star in the folklore universe

CONTENTS

Introduction: The Individual and Tradition
Ray Cashman, Tom Mould, and Pravina Shukla   1

Entering Tradition: Kim Ellington, Catawba Valley Potter
Charles G. Zug   27

Delight in Skill: The Stone Carvers' Art
Marjorie Hunt   47

The "Talking Machine Story Teller": Cal Stewart and the
Remediation of Storytelling
Richard Bauman   71

Chief Ovia Idah: *Bricoleur* of Benin City and a
Star for All Times
Philip M. Peek   93

Place Matters: A Wooden Boat Builder in the
Twenty-First Century
Maggie Holtzberg   113

A Backdoor into Performance
Tom Mould   127

The Maintenance of Heritage: Kersti Jobs-Björklöf and
Swedish Folk Costume
Pravina Shukla   145

The World of Ogre-Tile Makers: The Onihyaku Line in
Hekinan, Japan
Takashi Takahara   171

Bringing Them Back: Wanda Aragon and the Revival of
Historic Pottery Designs at Acoma
Karen M. Duffy   195

Artistic Courage in Small Groups: Identity, Intermediality,
and Indian Country
Michael Robert Evans   219

CONTENTS

Navigating the Legends of *Treasure Island:* Narrative, Maps, and the Material
Greg Kelley 235

Fluid Identities: Madame d'Aulnoy, Mother Bunch, and Fairy-Tale History
Jennifer Schacker 249

Counting the Stars: The Study of Creativity on a Human Scale, or How a Bunch of Cajun and German Farmers and Fabricators in Louisiana Invented a Traditional Amphibious Boat
John Laudun 265

On Middle-Range Structures in Heroic Epic
William Hansen 287

The Role of Tradition in the Individual: At Work in Donegal with Packy Jim McGrath
Ray Cashman 303

Customizing Myth: The Personal in the Public
John Holmes McDowell 323

David Drake: Potter, Poet, Rebel
John Michael Vlach 343

The Mother's Voice: An Analysis of the Content of Turkish Lullabies
İlhan Başgöz 353

Contested Performance and Joke Aesthetics
Elliott Oring 365

Vernacular Interpretation in a Public Folklore Event: Listening to the Call of Florida Fiddlers, Three
Gregory Hansen 387

Georgia Decoy Maker Ernie Mills: A Folk Artist Defines His Work
John A. Burrison 409

Rapid Transportation
Lee Haring 429

Working Through Tradition: Rug Farming In Anatolia
George Jevremović   441

A Few of My Favorite Things about North Carolina Pottery
Mark Hewitt   455

That's Where I Came In: Henry and His Teachers
Robert Cochran   471

At the Black Pig's Dyke and Other Writing:
Crossing Borders of Art and Tradition
Vincent Woods   483

A Folklorist's Work: Henry Glassie's Life in the Field
Ray Cashman, Tom Mould, and Pravina Shukla   499

Acknowledgments   529

Tabula Gratulatoria   531

Contributors   533

Index   541

THE INDIVIDUAL AND TRADITION

David Stuempfle. Seagrove, North Carolina, 2004

Introduction:
The Individual and Tradition

Ray Cashman, Tom Mould, and Pravina Shukla

We are, all of us—whether storytellers, teachers, singers, scholars, poets, curators, painters, parents—individuals working within traditions that we shape and re-shape. We all use elements of the past to meet our needs in the present and our hopes for the future. In the process we make tradition our own, leaving our marks. These marks may be deemed art, craft, communication, performance, folklore, but they are all simultaneously autobiography, a reflection of the self as forged in the shaping and re-shaping of tradition. The relationship between the individual and tradition is central to the dynamic of culture, implicit in any study of humanity, and most explicit in the contemporary study of folklore.

As have generations before us, we folklorists study traditional, vernacular expressive culture—oral traditions, material objects, customs, rituals—performances all. We strive to approach, interpret, and appreciate forms of folklore on their own terms. Most often we seek through folklore an entry into values, beliefs, aesthetics, preoccupations, ideology—in other words, into the minds of others and sometimes of ourselves. Folklore scholarship, theory and practice—what Edwin Sidney Hartland called, in his late Victorian terms, "the science of tradition" (1968 [1899]:11)—is indeed our tradition, and our tradition necessarily begins with close attention to the words, actions, and creations of specific individuals. Accordingly, we understand ourselves to be practitioners of performer-centered ethnography, a tradition of scholarship nowhere better exemplified than in the work of Henry Glassie, the inspiration for this volume.

For over five decades and across five continents Glassie has stood side by side with artists, craftspeople, musicians, raconteurs, and star performers of many traditions, working to understand those individuals and traditions on their own terms, to bear honorable witness to humanity from many perspectives. Dialogue and apprenticeship with those individuals was the most productive route to hard-won knowledge. Through a handful of star storytellers on the Northern Irish border, for example, we come to understand the true nature of community and to comprehend how divided neighbors cooperate and prevail in a time of war (1976, 1982a, 1982b, 2006). Through specific creators—blacksmiths, weavers, carpenters, potters, and calligraphers—we learn about the living arts of Turkey, insiders' standards for excellence, and deep resonances between aesthetics and worldview (1993). Through an examination of the life history, visual style, and repertoire of one Nigerian painter—Prince Twins Seven-Seven—we see how art can be at the one time modern and traditional, a portrait of the individual and of the collective, a conjuring of the ancestral past and visualization of invisible spiritual realities (2010a).

In order to interpret and to generalize—to earn conclusions—folklorists gather information from specific individuals because tradition is enacted only through an individual's acts of creative will. This starting point— the study of tradition through attention to the individual—is not merely a methodological necessity (one must start somewhere), but more significantly a matter of philosophical conviction. One can declare an interest in the role of the individual in tradition—as did Stith Thompson as early as the mid-twentieth century (1953:592), as did several Russian folklorists beginning in the late nineteenth century (Baiburin 1983:70–71). But this formulation—the role of the individual in tradition—can too easily slide into misleading conceptions of tradition as mysteriously external, autonomous, and superorganic, and of individuals as merely bearers, carriers, and greater or lesser stewards and practitioners. The fieldwork experience in particular convinces us that there is no such thing as tradition without the individuals who enact it. Let us consider both concepts in turn—tradition and the individual—to better appreciate their interrelationship and mutual constitution.

TRADITION

Over time, tradition has been defined in many though not unlimited ways (see Hymes 1975, Ben-Amos 1984, Bronner 1998 and 2000, Glassie 2003 and 2007, and Noyes 2009 for some recent definitions). Here we will focus on two characterizations—tradition as process and tradition as resource. Tradition as process is, in Glassie's terms, "volitional, temporal action" and "the means for deriving the future from the past" (2003:192). Such a formulation foregrounds the agency of the individual and frees the notion of tradition from its associations with stasis. The antonym of neither change nor creativity, tradition as process depends on both and "flowers in variation and innovation" (Glassie 1993:9). In this first definition, we can view tradition as if it were a verb, a doing, but what people are doing is working with a collective resource, something noun-like, our second definition.

That is, in addition to tradition as process, we also need to be able to talk about tradition as the accessible raw materials, the handed-down knowledge and ways of knowing, with which an individual may go to work. If tradition is a process not unlike recycling, tradition as resource comprises those things available for recycling. Again, tradition does not force itself upon anyone—some will make more extensive or more competent use of the collective resource than others—but the resource is as pervasive as it is malleable.

As Glassie points out in his great work on Turkish traditional art, the English word "tradition" denotes, through its Latin etymology, a handing on of an object from one person to another (1993:529). This informs the problematic notion that any alteration in the object during or after the transfer amounts to tradition-breaking apostasy. If this were true, the individual could only choose between the faithful but repressive path of replication and preservation, or the liberating but irreverent path of rebellion and deviation. Many reject such a notion. For T. S. Eliot, tradition cannot be reduced to mindless repetition, nor is unprecedented novelty the highest goal; inspired creativity is only possible through working within a tradition, both a process and a resource that is not inherited but acquired only through great labor. The poet or artist serves as a catalyst introduced to established elements, recombining and transforming them in such a way that the existing order is altered, proportions adjusted, even if only slightly (1948). For Dorry Noyes, the work-around for the limiting implications of *traditio* is a reconsideration of what is handed from one generation to the next. The most important transfer is not of objects or property, but of responsibility, in conscious reference to Richard Bauman's concept of performance as assuming responsibility to an audience for a display of communicative competence: "That hand-to-hand transfer we may take as a metaphor for the transmission of metaknowledge along with the practice itself: what it means, how it is to be used, everything that is shaven off when it is packaged as a product or an entry in a database" (Noyes 2009:248). Here is a performance-inflected vision that reconciles tradition as process and tradition as resource.

Glassie would find both Eliot's and Noyes's formulations agreeable, but as usual he foregrounds those he meets in the field, allowing them to guide us out of the mire. In Turkey the word for tradition is *gelenek*, and when Glassie asked Turkish artisans how it works, they spoke "not of passing things along, but of breathing in the air." He continues, explaining their sense of tradition:

> You live in a cultural environment, and the air you breathe circulates through you to emerge in actions that are yours alone but can be called traditional because you created them out of the general experience of life in some place. Your works will be like those created by others who breathe the same air. Generally I find Turkish artisans acknowledging their masters reverently but saying they taught themselves, taking in the air of instruction, then exhaling in their own way, refining their art through self-directed practice. The Turkish concept feels freer, kinder to the will, being centered, not on the act of transfer, but on the act of creating unavoidably in the atmosphere of influence. (1993:529)

Inhaled, exhaled, and transformed, tradition is both a resource used by the individual and a process enacted by the individual. This begs the question, what, then, is the individual?

THE INDIVIDUAL

In this consideration of tradition so far, the individual is very like Claude Lévi-Strauss's *bricoleur* (1966), a crafty recycler who constructs new possibilities out of available handed-down raw materials, meeting present needs. In a very real sense the song does not exist without the singer and the singing; individuals shape tradition, performance by performance.

With both individual agency and the collective atmosphere of influence in mind, another conception of the individual we may wish to pursue is that of a proposed and performed subjectivity in contrast to the conception of the individual as a unified, natural, essential entity or category. In this conception of the individual, there is no self except in relation to others, to past precedent, and to ambient discourse. The individual self is a discursive construction subject to variation depending on context, a recursive but changeable negotiation that depends on handed-down resources and models for expression—texts and ways of creating texts, both verbal and nonverbal (cf. Sawin 2004:4–9). Just as we have come to appreciate that, say, ethnic identity or indeed gender is neither essential nor fixed but subject to ongoing negotiation through interaction, it follows that the performed self may be the only one there is and probably the only one any of us will ever get. The individual, then is itself a *bricolage,* an on-going assemblage of performances, an intertextual work-in-progress. Note that such a formulation does not challenge the centrality of individual agency. As Mikhail Bakhtin observes, our mouths are full of the words of others (1981:293, 337), but which words and how spoken, matter. It makes the greater or lesser difference between you and me.

While our present perspective is that tradition and the individual are inseparable, there have been periods in intellectual history when focus has shifted almost entirely to one side of the individual-tradition equation. Tradition, arguably the most fundamental concept in our discipline, has always been with us. Even when Dan Ben-Amos pointedly left tradition out of his definition of folklore as "artistic communication in small groups" this led not to the abandonment of tradition but to a more productive and astute redefinition of tradition as including innovation rather than opposing it. The fortunes of the individual, rather than tradition, have been more varied in our discipline's intellectual history. Structuralism, oral-formulaic theory, the historic-geographic method—none of these theoretical orientations necessarily or inevitably neglect the individual creator in favor of something like Francis Gummere's anonymous dancing throngs (1907:20ff.). But such orientations do invite and enable interest in patterns beyond the individual, sometimes overlooking the significance of not just biographical specificity but also other forms of context that make a difference.

Again, our experience of fieldwork with others attests to the centrality of individual agency, as much as our performance studies orientation is founded on and revolves around it. But here we are not making the case that the individual has never been the focus of folklorists until now, the more enlightened present. Previous pioneering work on the topic includes, for example, Joseph Jacobs's late-nineteenth-century plea for greater attention to the individual (1893), Linda Dégh's classic work dealing with the creative individual's transformation of the folktale (1969), Juha Pentikäinen's monumental investigation of worldview through an individual's repertoire (1978), and Edward D. Ives's exemplary book-length studies of the lives and worlds of folk composers and performers (1964, 1971, 1978, 1988). If we are not the first to look to individuals in the explication of tradition, we note that the intellectual history of our discipline has occasionally made pendulum swings between a greater emphasis on the individual—the concept and specific individuals—and a greater emphasis on a more anonymous and collective vision of tradition. We do not seek a swing back to the individual at the expense of tradition but rather a recognition that, because the individual and tradition are intimately bound, an either/or proposition is erroneous.

INTERSECTIONS OF THE INDIVIDUAL AND TRADITION

Having made broad claims about what tradition is, what the individual is, and how we can only understand one in relation to the other—the individual and tradition are inseparable and mutually constituting—we need to have a closer look at the details of how this relationship unfolds in everyday practice. Doing so—telescoping from broad dynamics to specific mechanics—means attending to, among other things, the workings of genre and performance, and the effects of attribution and intertextuality.

Shifting disciplinary interests and theoretical trends are not the only reasons that the attention of folklorists to the individual has waxed and waned at different times. Interestingly, there are aspects of the workings of folklore and culture more generally that would distract anyone, not just folklorists, from a full awareness of the individual's centrality in tradition. Faces and names from both the past and present may blur or be ignored in the process of enculturation—the informal way we learn the norms of the groups in which we live, play, and work.

We are born into the world as active learners of culturally appropriate ways to behave. We learn to express ourselves in practical and artistic ways. We dress our bodies, tell stories, and decorate our homes. The structures, forms, and rules we see enacted around us on a daily basis provide the means for our own creation. As folklorists, we recognize how these forms and rules may be used within a community as an identifiable genre of performance. The memorate, the song, the ritual, the dance, the mask—these are cultural forms defined by expectations, norms, and structures. Performance, facilitated and guided by genre, enacted by individuals, is shaped by past performances and contributes to future ones. Yet despite the integral role of the individual in performance, these generic conventions may be extracted from the specific event, internalized by performers, would-be performers, and audiences alike. In this synthesizing enculturation process, specific individuals may be forgotten, amalgamated, synthesized, rendered nameless. Rules, norms, values, forms, styles, structures: all are extracted for future use, future performance, at the expense—potentially—of attention to individuals.

When Glassie explored folk housing in middle Virginia, he came to articulate the unspoken rules governing competence within one genre of traditional creativity (1975). Through careful, methodical measurement, the rules that governed the building of these houses emerged, rules held in the mind, committed in wood. Those rules were neither arbitrary nor formally taught. Rather, builders employed a process of observation, trial and error, creativity, and the application of skills, knowledge, and competency drawn from the work of the past and their own work in the present. They realized, as did Glassie who followed in their footsteps as a careful observer, that with a stick and a set of formal principles and relationships, houses could be built, revised, and expanded upon through a creative but finite set of possibilities. It is the same process that Albert Lord and Milman Parry discovered in the epic poetry of modern Serbo-Croatian singers and, by extension, of Homer, the most famous bard of the classical world. With a set of formulae, rules, and structures, oral poets could create epic poems so long it took a week of performances late into the night to complete them (Lord 1960). While genres are ideal types and do nothing in and of themselves, shared, transferrable generic norms, expectations, patterns, formulae, and structures provide the individual with powerful tools for performance.

The metaphor of genre as tool, however, can be extended only so far. Individuals are rarely shackled by genre. The creative impulse finds many outlets and choices abound. Critique of the local government, for example, can be mounted through jokes, legends, and more overt polemic discourse. It can also be levied through parades and posters, broadsides and protest songs. Some genres will be more amenable to some topics and some styles of discourse than others, carrying with them their own ideological orientation (Cashman 2007). But even within a genre, there is room for innovation. Further, genres are hardly static, fixed forms. They can blur, bleed, or blend with others in a constant reorganizing of performance possibilities (Bakhtin 1986, Bauman 2004 chapter 2).

At the moment of contact when the creative act gains an audience—whether during the performance of a song or the handling and use of a rug—the individual is on display. The most competent individuals may linger in our minds long after the transitory performance, and even longer in the enduring object. But in time, even these individuals may fade from view. This process can be particularly unforgiving as audiences become artists, and these new performers internalize for themselves generic conventions for future performances in new contexts. The reason is simple. We learn the abstract structures of performance—the false sincerity of the tall tale, the symmetry of an I-house—from listening to hundreds of tall tales and living in a region of I-houses. However, if our focus shifts to the particular, the individual reemerges. In the particular performance, individuals attract our attention for retelling the old story a certain way or for throwing the familiar type of pot as only he or she could. The absurdist fantasy of a potato that grew so large it blocked the road may be remembered from a singular performance by a particular individual—in this case, by Hugh Nolan in County Fermanagh on November 28, 1972 (Glassie 1985:104–5)—distinguishable by name within a deep tradition of fantastical tales.

We may use the term "extraction" to name that generalizing process whereby individuals gradually comprehend then competently apply generic conventions in performance. Extracting such patterns over time from many observed performances may de-emphasize specific individuals and particular performances. But there is another equally forceful impulse in the act of performance—incorporation—that refuses to dismiss the individuals of the past, often prompting us to call them forth by name. This incorporating impulse is partly conscious, partly inevitable—inevitable because traditional art and practice calls attention to continuity in time and space, acknowledging that which is handed down and from whom. Incorporation unfolds in at least two ways: attribution and evocation.

One of the most common and easily recognizable ways we incorporate the individuals of the past into present performance is through attribution. While we may unintentionally and unconsciously strip away the individual from the abstract set of generic norms and rules we operate by, we are much slower to do so for the coherent text itself that is remade, retold, or reshaped: the design of an iron gate, the plot of a tall tale, the step of a dance, the refrain of a song. As often, we borrow whole cloth—gate, tale, dance, or song in its entirety. The process is dynamic; rarely is slavish duplication idealized or attempted. In borrowing, we revisit the past, the initially observed performer and performance. In time, we may claim the pot or story or joke for ourselves, and attribution dissolves. Different genres situated in different cultural and situational contexts will preserve or dissolve the identities of past performers or originators variously. Jokes rarely demand attribution, though their frame hints at past tellings—"Did you hear the one about. . . ." Legends, on the other hand, often require attribution, even if only to a friend of a friend, an attribution so common it has earned its own acronym. Narrators call forth these faceless and often nameless individuals to provide testimony to the truth of the event.

In some cultures and traditions, the concept of individual ownership shapes performance. In such cases, individuals are granted control over their tale, their design, their dance. The impulse may fit neatly into a Western tradition of copyright law and intellectual property rights that is slowly being adopted globally as communities watch while their images and traditions are adopted, adapted, and co-opted in ways that can be damaging, even dangerous, not to mention financially alienating and disenfranchising. However, this impulse to ownership is not inherently capitalistic. Rather, the ownership of a story or design is a recognition of the deep relationship between creator and creation, of the intimate enactment of identity through performance. Although people creating within such traditions sacrifice some of the casual, free flow of ideas in cultural creation, they gain the recognition and respect fostered for the individual creator, a respect many do not think twice about granting to Titian, Picasso, O'Keeffe, or Warhol but that some only begrudgingly offer to the vernacular artist immersed in local traditions among a community of artists.

Attributive reference can be explicit or implicit. As folklorists we have often relied heavily on the concept of intertextuality to identify and elucidate references between and across performances, but intertextuality in name as well as in application favors the text rather than the creator. Often the references performers make *are* to texts—whether in terms of form, content, or style—rather than to creators. Yet every such reference is a nod to an individual performer, who in his or her own time drew from past performances to shape present ones that carried forward into the future as both process and resource.

The combination of attribution and intertextuality can create a dialogue between artists. In narrative that dialogue can be explicit. When Choctaw storyteller Estelline Tubby recounts the prophecies she heard from her aunt and mother, who in turn heard them from her grandmother, Estelline does not merely attribute the story and then move to narration. Rather, she quotes these women, weaving their voices together with her own, distinguishing between the voices of these women now past, the content of the prophecy itself, and her own voice. The performance is heavily dialogic, all the more noticeable for the fact that Estelline does not fully agree with the interpretation of her female relatives (Mould 2003:93–100).

In material culture, that dialogue may be visual rather than verbal but no less explicit. Mark Hewitt draws his brush in serpentine motion down the side of an iced tea ceremony tumbler in conscious repetition of Michael Cardew. His conversation with Cardew—and with the Devon pottery tradition that Cardew referenced in turn—is at one and the same time formal, aesthetic, and personal. Mark Hewitt studied with Cardew and counted him as friend and mentor. In his essay "Mark in Place," Glassie explains that Hewitt, like his teacher Cardew and the potters who inspired Cardew—Bernard Leach and Shoji Hamada—all reached back in time and outward across space, incorporating traditions from England and Japan, mingling familiar and foreign technique, form, and design with local clay (2010b). Pottery allowed these men to connect to their past tradition and to foreign masters, while simultaneously situating themselves in their places. The same is true for the woman in India whose bodily self-presentation references a variety of artists: her mother and older sisters from whom she learned; the goldsmiths, jewelers, weavers, and tailors who supply the materials of her creation; and the merchants who advise her on the selection of the ensemble. Through the raw materials of silk, gold, cotton, she, like potters in North Carolina, connects to the natural environment. But, through her complete assemblage, she situates herself in a wide social spectrum that includes men and women of her contemporary and historical social setting (Shukla 2008:211–18). The same is true for Estelline Tubby whose evocation of her mother, aunt, and grandmother is personal as well as interpretive. Connection through attribution and intertextual dialogue between artists, past and present, can be deeply intimate and personal; it is also the driving force of tradition.

Vestiges of the misleading distinction between the traditional and the innovative lurk at the intersection of genre and the individual. Yet situated between the social sciences and the humanities, folklorists claim a privileged vantage point to explore this intersection. thinking as social scientists we are drawn to broad themes and patterns, noting them across a range of performers of a particular genre. Yet the humanistic orientation of the historian and art critic helps us recognize that patterns are not merely adopted and duplicated but created, re-created, and developed. Extraction is not the end of the story, nor does incorporation spiral into repetitive copying. It is not despite but precisely because of intertextual dialogue, attribution, and evocation that performers may cultivate a personal style.

Out of respect for one's peers and predecessors and out of a desire to situate oneself in time and place, individuals most fully enact tradition when they come into their own in unmistakable, personally characteristic ways. Appalachian storyteller Lee Wallin, for example, developed a rhythmic style of narrating folk tales immediately recognizable in performance. In the language of commercialism, Wallin developed a recognizable brand. The patterns of style developed by artists make it possible to walk into the

Pottery Center in Seagrove, North Carolina and know immediately which pot was made by Sid Luck, which by Ben Owen III, which by Pam Owens, without ever turning the piece on end to see the literal brand, the signature in clay. Forms, shapes, glazes, the turn of the handle, the dimple of the spout, all provide clues of authorship as tell-tale as genetic code. Prince Twins Seven-Seven, likewise, sings a song of the self in consistent, characteristic ways across genres and media. Not only in his artwork, but also in narrating his life, he employs sprung symmetry in form and moves thematically from bursts of joy to eventual disappointment, applying inherited means to personal ends, simultaneously embodying and shaping Yoruba perspectives on the world (Glassie 2010a:11–13, 32–36, 150–51).

With a broad focus on the group, generic patterns may engage the social scientist. But once we twist the lens to zoom in to the individual, new patterns emerge—idiosyncratic and every bit as integral to the artistic process and to the dynamics of tradition. Those who master the simultaneous expression of the self as both distinct individual and member of a collective are often the stars of their expressive traditions.

STARS AND THE ETHNOGRAPHER

If we accept that the individual and tradition are inseparable and mutually constituting, and if we embrace the tradition of performer-centered ethnography exemplified by Glassie's work, our version of the "science of tradition" necessarily begins with attention to individuals. But we should consider: which individuals and why? Every person in a given community or society has information to share and all people may serve as instructive examples. Yet not all the people the fieldworker encounters will receive full attention. After a period of general acquaintance, the fieldworker typically concentrates on a few exemplary individuals, chosen for their talent, perspective, or depth of information. In this unofficial categorization of extraordinary persons, there are two varieties—the star informant and the star performer.

The ideal situation in any ethnographic endeavor is to find persons who are knowledgeable, eloquent, and willing to help with the task of elucidating their culture. In *A Guide for Field Workers in Folklore*, Kenneth Goldstein describes these star informants as those who are motivated and articulate, have good memories, and are both cooperative and accessible to the researcher (1964:125). Star informants are useful to fieldworkers who are seeking information, and because star informants often occupy a somewhat distant or peripheral position in society, they are in a genuinely good position for detached observation. This peculiar social standing—their ability to be simultaneously members of and analytic observers of their communities—also motivates many star informants to seek and retain contact not only with fieldworkers, but also with patrons, journalists, the local elite, and representatives of museums, universities, or arts agencies. Folklorists have not created the phenomenon of the star informant. Rather, star informants are the local sociable personalities who are not only qualified but poised and ready to help those who come to learn about their culture.

Whereas star informants are judged as exceptional by outsiders, star performers are judged as exceptional, most crucially, by insiders. In his fieldwork guide, Goldstein specifies that the star performer is one valued by a community that judges him or her as excellent according to shared criteria for virtuosity, while the star informant is often considered by insiders an average or typical performer (1964:88). Both "star informant" and "star performer"—or just "star"— are social roles earned through interaction. One is useful to the outsider; the other is acknowledged by insiders as an intellectual and artistic leader within the community. Because the criteria for stardom differ by community—as Glassie teaches us, the term is an emic designation (2006)—an examination of a community's conceptions of stardom is particularly valuable for revealing vernacular criteria for excellence in a given genre or form of expression.

In Glassie's *Turkish Traditional Art Today*, we learn that in the ceramic center of Kütahya, the star artist is one who excels in this Ottoman tradition of underglaze-painted ceramics. The local term for a star is *son usta*, the great master. The *usta* epitomizes the local aesthetic criteria, for he or she is able to channel deep spiritual principles into art. The star's painted *çini* plates embody sincerity, soulfulness, and virtuosic craft. Part of the challenge of our ethnographic work is to be able to recognize who is a star informant and who is the local star. In Kütahya, a potter on the periphery, Mehmet Gürsoy, volunteered himself as Glassie's star informant, claiming the interest of the ethnographer. But the community agreed that the great master was Ahmet Şahin. In time, both cooperated with Glassie, for Gürsoy wanted to validate his work through Glassie, and Şahin wanted Glassie to record his work and his city's history, updating the scholarship on Turkish pottery beyond the sixteenth-century Ottoman zenith.

The concept of star performer, unlike that of the star informant, does not depend on the ethnographer, yet a star informant and a star can be the same person, and a star informant may become a star performer as a result of interactions with the researcher. Since the publication of *Turkish*

Traditional Art Today, which featured Mehmet Gürsoy on its cover, Gürsoy has become a star, having just been recognized by UNESCO as a living national treasure, and having his work endorsed by museum curators and government officials in Ankara and Istanbul. Gürsoy was not a master artist when Glassie encountered him in 1985, but he has since become one as a result of his dedicated effort, encouraged by the validation he has received in the form of the book and numerous exhibitions. While Gürsoy is a new star, the community still recognizes the now-deceased Şahin as the great master of its tradition (1993:425–562).

A star informant—by Goldstein's definition, average in talent but exceptional in knowledge—can become inspired by the attention of the ethnographer. Mehmet Gürsoy and İbrahim Erdeyer, another Kütahya potter, claim that the ambition that they have always had was encouraged by the external response; Erdeyer said that he never had as much respect for his own art as he did when he received the applause of the audience at the exhibition of his work that Glassie arranged at the Indiana University Museum of Art. Like the validation from the ethnographer, the validation from outsiders—Turkish government officials and American art lovers—can alert a star informant to the deep significance of his or her tradition, thrusting that performer forward, launching him or her as a star.

Another example from Glassie's work helps clarify the peculiar relationship between the star and the ethnographer. In the Irish community of Ballymenone, excellence in storytelling is characterized by the gifts of deep memory, sharp wit, and poetic genius. The community's own term for gifted narrators is "stars," and Glassie explains in his book devoted to the radiance of the old stars that it was their role and duty to create the community's art (2006:110–13). The brightest of the Irish stars was Hugh Nolan, locally revered for narrating the history of his place. Mr. Nolan, like some people we are lucky to encounter in the field, in fact combined both categories of star into one.

With Ballymenone as our example, we can identify another aspect of the role ethnographers play in the communities they study. In addition to validating the local star or encouraging potential stars, ethnographers can also fill an established position in the community when they become recipients of a tradition, pass it on, and keep it alive. In Ballymenone, tradition depended on old men who accepted young men as apprentices in the craft of historical narration, telling the whole story, keeping the truth. When Hugh Nolan was young, he learned from Hughie McGiveney; when Nolan was old, he taught Glassie (2006:77–99). The ethnographer, like Glassie in

Ballymenone, may naturally enter into a relationship with a star, accept the responsibility of preservation, and in that way, encourage the star performer as well as the star informant.

Consider the responsibilities of ethnographers at work with individuals and traditions. Our accountability to the star informants and star performers who guide our understanding of traditions is an ethical imperative. We must respect those who have helped us, making sure to do them no harm, while bringing them into the record, and to honor them through reciprocal action. We, too, have responsibilities to the traditions they enact, and our labors, also, make a difference. We document traditions through photography, audio, or video recordings, and we elucidate these traditions through scholarship and public programs—whether in the form of publications, museum exhibitions, archives, festivals, radio programs, websites, or CDs. This attention often encourages many performers to maintain their traditions even as our records help them to develop those traditions, as several essays in this volume demonstrate. Furthermore, scholarly interest may inspire some to self-consciously revitalize or traditionalize some aspect of their expressive culture, as other essays in this volume illustrate. Documentation and providing access are among folklorists's responsibilities because we are not merely observers of tradition; we are part of the process of its development.

We also have an obligation to do our jobs well. That is, our responsibilities to the traditions we study oblige us to be attentive enough to identify properly the collaborators who will best teach us. In *The Stars of Ballymenone*, Glassie says that we need two things—patience and time (2006:255). The most brilliant stars were not necessarily those he met on the first day but rather those like Hugh Nolan with whom he slowly developed, over a decade, a relationship of apprentice to master. We have a responsibility to be in place, focused long enough to recognize those the community acknowledges as stars, as well as those who are easiest and most informative in conversation. There is no better model for such a research methodology or tradition of scholarship than in the works of Henry Glassie.

THE STRUCTURE OF THE BOOK

Our book belongs to an old and sturdy tradition, created by folklorists who, in the manner of the art-historical monograph, have granted full treatment to creative individuals: to storytellers, to Natal'ia Osipovna Vinokurova (Azadovskii 1974 [1926]), Thomas Casey (Hyde 1939), Seán Ó Conaill (Ó Duilearga 1981 [1948]), Zsuzsanna Palkó (Dégh 1995), and Ray Lum (Ferris 1992); to singers, to Almeda Riddle (Abrahams 1970), John Maguire (Morton 1974), Archie Edwards and John Cephas (Pearson 1990); to craftsmen, to the chair-maker Chester Cornett (Jones 1989), the blacksmith Philip Simmons (Vlach 1992 [1981]), the stoneworker Virgil Boruff (Duffy 1996), the saddlemaker Don King (Evans 1998), the basketmakers William Houck (Glassie 1967) and Dwight Stump (Joyce 1989), the potters Cheever Meaders (Rinzler and Sayers 1980), Lanier Meaders (Burrison 1983), Burlon Craig (Zug 1986), and Haripada Pal (Glassie 1997); to painters and sculptors, to William Robbie (Goldstein 1962), Duga of Meko (Bascom 1974), Elijah Pierce (Davis 1994), Dorris Curtis (Cochran 2004), Mayer Kirshenblatt (Kirshenblatt and Kir-shenblatt-Gimblett 2007), Prince Twins Seven-Seven (Glassie 2010a), and A. D. Pirous (George 2010).

To strengthen and advance that tradition, our tradition, we have as-sembled this book, arranging the chapters that follow so that they can be lo-cated in the territory mapped in this introduction's previous sections. Each one expands our understanding of the relationship between the individual and tradition through case studies that bring us into close encounters with skilled and talented individuals from around the world. Unlike with many edited volumes, finding the common threads that tie the articles together has not been our problem. Instead, we face an abundance of connections and interrelations that bind these articles together in a web, making a single linear order difficult to establish. For the Internet surfer accustomed to hypertext, untangling may matter little, and the brief descriptions of the articles that follow may help identify those articles of most specific interest for a particular reader. But for those who appreciate a purposeful path, we have ordered the contributions in a trajectory that reflects the deepest con-nections we found among the articles.

We begin with an overture. Sampling from the major themes of the book, we have selected three articles that help us frame the entire book and provide a sense of scope for our collected endeavors. That overture begins, appropriately enough, with a study of material culture, where arguably the impact of Glassie's work on the intersection of the individual and tradition has been greatest.

In his book *Turners and Burners*, Charles C. Zug has written the story of North Carolina pottery, describing its historical cycles, peaks and valleys, bringing us to the end of World War II when the products of the Industrial Revolution largely ended the craft. After the war, one potter, Burlon Craig, kept at his wheel and gradually modified his output for a new clientele from outside his community: folklorists, museum curators, antique dealers, and collectors. In turn, Craig trained a whole new generation of potters who are flourishing today. In this chapter, Zug tells the story of this new generation by way of the development of a single potter, Kim Ellington. Initially trained as a studio potter, Ellington was so completely astounded by the skill and artistry of traditional Catawba Valley pots made one hundred and fifty years ago that he sought out master potter Burlon Craig and slowly but deliberately "entered" the Catawba Valley pottery tradition. In telling Ellington's story, Zug shows just how powerful the individual is in shaping tradition, and in turn, how powerful that tradition is in shaping the individual.

Kim Ellington, though born in the Catawba Valley was initially unaware of the deep pottery tradition of the area, but master stone carvers Roger Morigi and Vincent Palumbo were born into stone carving families, so immersed that Morigi describes stone carving as "in the air." Marjorie Hunt provides the space for Morigi and Palumbo to describe their personal involvement in what Glassie has termed an "atmosphere of tradition." In particular, Morigi and Palumbo explore craftsmanship as performance and artifacts as enactments of values. In doing so, Hunt highlights the productive tension between the collective and the individual, a theme that runs throughout this book. Because carvers must faithfully translate a sculptor's designs into stone, they have little freedom to alter basic form, and their personal creativity is always informed and sometimes constrained by collective aesthetics. As in many traditional arts, however, masters such as Morigi and Palumbo play expertly within these limits, in their case, crediting memory and tradition for inspiration, emphasizing the expressive power of technical excellence, and taking delight in skill.

In both Zug's and Hunt's chapters, it is a foregone conclusion that Burlon Craig, Kim Ellington, Roger Morigi, and Vincent Palumbo are stars of their respective traditions. Richard Bauman's contribution addresses the nature of stardom head-on as he explores the creation and construction of a star performer. Bauman considers the case of Cal Stewart, an early American recording artist, popular in the late nineteenth and early twentieth centuries, whose stardom owes everything to his adopting the persona of an old-fashioned country storyteller and his trading in traditional tales from a classic American repertoire. Stewart's body of work illuminates the process of remediation—the refashioning of earlier media forms in new ones—and particularly the process by which stardom in one medium may serve the creation of stardom in another. Stewart's career as "the talking machine story teller" has broad cultural significance in the history of modernity in that, ironically, his remediation of storytelling in phonograph recordings—seeming to preserve traditional storytelling while disseminating it to a mass audience—contributed to its decline by casting the traditional storyteller as anachronism and traditional storytelling as residual culture.

Taken together, these three articles provide a sampling of the articles that follow, addressing some of the dominant and recurring themes at the heart of our exploration of the individual and tradition: the deliberate, recognizable and laudable acts of individual artists; the negotiation of personal values and aesthetics with the expectations, norms, and patterns established over time in identifiable traditions; the expression of the self in tradition, and tradition in the self; and the social, cultural, historical, and personal dimensions of mastering tradition and achieving recognition.

Extending beyond our initial overture, we begin where Bauman leaves off, with the concept of the star. In the mid-1960s, Chief Ovia Idah rose to prominence in Benin City, Nigeria, as an artist who defied easy categorization. As a *bricoleur* he wove together the many traditions and experiences of his life to create art that was at one and the same time traditional art, contemporary art, and tourist art, challenging the validity of these categories altogether. In Chief Ovia Idah, Philip Peek finds an individual who *because* of his singularity, not despite it, served a critical link in the development of the traditional art in Benin City. Likewise, the power of a single individual to shape tradition is echoed in the work of Harold A. Burnham, a boat builder who has virtually single-handedly revived traditional boat-building in his home town of Essex, Massachusetts. Where Chief Ovia Idah challenged the boundaries of the arts traditions of his home as a way forward, Harold A. Burnham has returned to the traditions of the past and brought them into the present after a fifty-year gap. As Maggie Holtzberg reveals, the result is not mere recreation or replication, but rather a renewed and reinvigorated tradition that speaks to a contemporary context, so much so that it has been welcomed as a crucial piece of the regional cultural identity.

Both Chief Ovia Idah and Harold A. Burnham are stars. Both have achieved that status among multiple audiences—art collectors, tourists, and perhaps most importantly of all, among their neighbors and peers. Holtzberg outlines these contexts and communities that confer star status, making explicit the implicit assumptions of much of our work as folklorists. Tom Mould picks up this exploration of the creation of the star in his comparison of narrative traditions within and across cultures—in this case, the Mississippi Choctaw and North Carolina Latter-day Saints. While some traditions allow, even encourage the recognition of star performers such as storytellers Estelline Tubby, Rosalie Steve, and Billy Amos, others may intentionally obscure the role of the individual and the status that comes with honed competence and skill. These norms may vary within a single community, challenging the assumption that stars emerge in the same way in all genres, traditions, and cultures.

Having examined the concept of the star both implicitly and explicitly, in case study and in comparison, we shift to a more concerted focus on the various ways individuals engage with, carry on, revive, and ultimately create tradition. Kersti Jobs-Björklöf has devoted her life to the preservation of folk costume in Sweden. Her commitment is simultaneously familial, communal, national, and ideological. And yet as Pravina Shukla points out, external influences and agents have received a disproportionate share of credit and attention, overshadowing the insiders who labor within the tradition—a phenomenon all too common in the analysis of cultural revivals. In her own work, Shukla recalibrates the scales, attending to both insiders *and* outsiders but with a focus on those hard-working people at the center of the tradition.

The familial connection to tradition so important to Kersti Jobs-Björklöf is brought to the foreground in Takashi Takahara's analysis of the ogre-tile makers in Japan. At the center of this tradition is the Onihyaku family of ogre tile makers, four generations deep. Yet this story of family lineage is hardly as linear as one might assume, with the whims of human nature and personality reshaping and rerouting the tradition in new and unexpected ways. Less unexpected, but equally grounded in the familial past of artist ancestors, are the cyclical rhythms of the tradition of Acoma pottery studied by Karen Duffy. While revival can suggest discontinuity, in Acoma pottery it is a fundamental part of the historical and contemporary tradition. For star potter Wanda Aragon, the importance of family and the recognition of the recursive nature of the Acoma pottery tradition provide a system for the creation of a style at one and the same time unique to Wanda but deeply embedded in the designs of her ancestors.

While some artists such as Wanda Aragon, the Onihyaku family, Harold A. Burnam, Roger Morigi, Vincent Palumbo, and Kim Ellington remain faithful to their materials and media even as they innovate in style and design, others artists such as Chief Ovia Idah and Cal Stewart leap across genres and media, carrying ideas and aesthetics from one tradition into another. The dynamic work of boundary crossing is expected when moving across situational and cultural contexts, but less attention has been paid to those leaps across media. Like Bauman, Michael Evans explores the mass media as fertile ground for folkloric analysis as he considers how an individual—Paul DeMain—shapes the generic norms of newspaper editorial writing to courageously send his words into the world as part of a dialogue with an array of competing voices and agendas far removed from the confines of a co-temporal, face-to-face interaction. For DeMain, such efforts have come at great cost to his personal and professional life, highlighting the powerful repercussions of public performance where individual identities are inseparable from messages.

Greg Kelley also explores border crossings in genre and medium, this time in the work of Robert Louis Stevenson. In *Treasure Island* (1883), Stevenson builds on a nuanced understanding of oral storytelling and storytellers to offer an extended legend that fuses oral and print generic conventions. As treated by Kelley, Stevenson, rather than Jim Hawkins or Long John Silver, becomes the protagonist most worthy of our attention; he is a star performer working within a tradition of legend-telling while extending it into a new medium. Jennifer Schacker continues this exploration of boundary crossing not only across genres and media, but also across national borders, historical eras, and most significantly, imagined realities. In her analysis of the transformation of Madame d'Aulnoy from author of fairy tales in the courts of seventeenth-century France into folk character Mother Bunch of nineteenth-century English pantomimes, Schacker tracks the dramatic shift that blurs the lines between fiction and non-fiction, creator and creation, historical individual and stock character. In doing so, Schacker not only challenges the conventional history of the fairy tale, but also provides long overdue attention to the multidimensional individuals—real and fictional—integral to the formation of the genre.

Blurred by the passage of time, Schacker's subjects must be salvaged from archival records, rescuing the individual from oblivion. Such work is particularly important in a field that once assumed all traditions originate in collective anonymity. John Laudun is ideally positioned to challenge the old assumption, being present for the birth of a tradition when environmental challenges, economic opportunities, technical skill, and individual creativity merged. Individual stars can be identified and named—Tedmon Habetz, Harold Benoit, Gerard Olinger, Greg Frugé, Clayton Courville, Mike Richard, Kurt Venable, Henry Cormier, Jimmy Abshire, Dale Hughes, and Michael Quirk—but as Laudun argues, their work must be understood as part of a network of individuals joined in the common goal of developing increasingly effective and efficient ways of harvesting crawfish from the soggy rice fields of south Louisiana. While Laudun's analysis provides a rare and valuable glimpse into both the individual and collective origins of tradition, the maxim that ontology recapitulates phylogeny reminds us that the inventive acts of the individual working within a shared tradition can be glimpsed anew in every performance, not merely the first. This maxim also underlies William Hansen's structural analysis of the oral poetry of Homer. Taking the paradigm-shifting ideas of Milman Parry and Albert Lord as his point of departure, Hansen examines the process of individual creation and creativity in the act of performance. Hansen challenges the canonical tripartite system in oral poetry of formula, theme, and story pattern by identifying middle ground patterns, greater than theme but smaller than story. These "thematic complexes" suggest that the dynamic interplay between generic norms and individual creativity is more pervasive than generally thought.

The analysis undertaken in the preceding articles focuses primarily on the vital and integral role of individuals as the fundamental creators of tradition. Whether inventing, shaping, working within, or reviving tradition, individuals are the active protagonists without whom there could be no tradition. As important as individuals are, these studies have used the individual primarily as a lens through which to focus on tradition. This relationship can be profitably inverted, however, so that the tradition becomes a lens to understand the individual. In Ray Cashman's contribution, that individual is Packy Jim McGrath. Cashman looks to both the life stories and mythic narratives told by Packy Jim to explore the proposition that regardless of differences in genre and provenance, all stories in a person's repertoire are on some level instrumental in that person's self-conception. When considered in its performance context and in light of long association with the performer, a folklore text even as canonical as an account of the origin of the fairies can be appreciated as autobiographical. This case study suggests that tradition plays a role in the development of individuals as much as individuals play central roles in the development of traditions.

John McDowell maintains a focus on the personal as he challenges the staid notion that mythic narrative is impersonal and operates on the level of the collective and the universal. In the myths and memorates shared by Mariano Chicunque, María Juajibioy, and Francisco Tandioy of Colombia's Sibundoy Valley, and Luis Alberto Yamberla and Maruja Picuasi of Imbabura province in Ecuador, McDowell identifies deeply personal connections and autobiographical details conveyed through vicarious and virtual identification with mythic characters. In such cases, tradition can provide a medium for self-presentation through the personalization of collective narratives, as Glassie stressed in his analysis of the performance of myths in Bangladesh and Nigeria (1997:103–15; 2010a:57–61).

As with narrative, material culture provides a vehicle through which artists may express the self. In the case of David Drake, an enslaved man living in South Carolina during the nineteenth century, that vehicle is clay. Using historical artifacts as evidence, and benefiting from historians, museums, and the art market, John Michael Vlach examines the pottery that continues to speak for David Drake long after his death, revealing the layers of his identity as potter, slave, husband, father, and keen if ambiguous commentator on his own life and society. Vlach trains his lens on the individual rather than the tradition, reading the man out of the clay rather than the reverse. İlhan Başgöz attempts the same in his study of Turkish lullabies. Examining over three thousand lullabies, Başgöz draws the mother out of the lullaby, imagining the personalities, values, and beliefs of the women who sung their babies to sleep with these songs.

For Başgöz, the singers of these Turkish lullabies are unnamed, many long dead, unable to provide further clarification or interpretation of their tradition. Their art must speak for itself. Yet much of the work we do as folklorists involves fieldwork with living people who are often willing and eager not only to perform their traditions, but also to interpret them. Daniel and Diane both consider joke telling a part of their personal and ethnic identities and have thought critically about what makes a good joke. Encouraged by Elliott Oring, Daniel and Diane critique each other's performances of some of their favorite jokes. Their critiques—focusing on such issues as economy, repetition, diction, accent, intonation, and gesture—reveal their aesthetic choices and reflect fundamental differences in who they are and their conception of what a joke performance is intended to achieve. Three fiddlers gathered on stage together for the First Coast Folklife Festival in Jacksonville, Florida, also provide native exegesis of their tradition, sharing their views on the music that binds them together. Robert "Chubby" Wise, George Custer, and Richard Seaman all use personal experience narratives as illustrations of their individual interpretations of their shared tradition. The result is a presentation of the self as much as of the music. Likewise, John Burrison listens carefully as he explores the art of Ernie Mills, third-generation decoy carver, and finds that Mills's talk *about* art is as important and revealing a discourse as what the decoys themselves can convey. Appreciating that "ducks aren't art critics" Mills's first priority with working decoys is attention to form and utility, but he observes that capturing the essence of a real waterfowl in the abstracted form of a working decoy can be an even greater aesthetic achievement—and sense of accomplishment—than faithfully replicating a bird in detailed decorative sculpture. Combining utility and beauty, Mills's views and body of work echo Glassie's challenge to the false dichotomy of art and craft, an intellectual argument mounted most completely in *The Spirit of Folk Art*.

Yet another dimension in the relationship of the individual and tradition is the personal connection between fieldworker and artist that frequently erases the boundaries between observer and observed. Folklorists have frequently studied their own communities, often by stepping outside the group to gaze in. Lee Haring, however, participated fully in the Sunday afternoon gatherings of folk music revivalists in New York City's Washington Square Park. Here he recounts a story of three friends who were part of a crowd that did not want for individualism but nonetheless provided an early sensation of being enmeshed in community. Lee Haring focuses on his friends Erik Darling and Billy Faier, but Haring is never far away, providing a perspective both personal and analytical. Each individual eventually took a divergent path but shared in the development of an authentic alternative to mass culture, adding their bit to the folk music tradition of the United States. Comparably, the development of an authentic alternative to mass culture is at the heart of the work of art collector and dealer George Jevremović. Owner of the store Material Culture in Philadelphia, Jevremović has worked tirelessly with traditional artists around the world—including Prince Twins Seven-Seven, the star of Glassie's most recent book. In his contribution, Jevremović describes the role of an outside agent in pushing the tradition of Turkish rugs back to a higher standard of materials and innovative design by motivating the weavers to hold to their traditional methods of creation, processing of materials, and aesthetics.

Jevremović's chapter, and many others in this book, underscore the important intersection of the artist and the outsider in the interpretation, continuation, and development of tradition. In Mark Hewitt, the roles of artist and scholar are fused seamlessly, with no mediator or translator other than the artist himself. Mark Hewitt is a star potter in the North Carolina tradition. He is also an author and sometime curator who reflects analytically as well as aesthetically on the pottery tradition to which he has devoted himself. Here, Hewitt describes his personal connection to the local and traditional in North Carolina pottery—the materials, the old masters, and the local community of artists, scholars, and collectors. As Hewitt demonstrates, all the relationships forged among these men and women, who often serve in more than one role at a time, are integral to the creative process and to the viability of traditional arts.

As a star performer in multiple realms and contexts, Mark Hewitt provides a natural transition to the star at the center of this book. Consummate scholar, fieldworker, teacher, mentor, and artist in his own right, Henry Glassie provides us a model for understanding the individual in tradition, in his own considerable body of work. Each of the chapters of this book reflect Glassie's influence, which is acknowledged most directly in the final two chapters. Robert Cochran initiates our consideration of Henry as a shining star in the tradition of folklore studies. Citing parallels in his own career and that of other folklorists, Cochran traces Glassie's development as an ethnographer, growing in skill, seeking out "live guidance" to understand others on their own terms through their own creations. Lessons learned are rooted deeply in principles of neighborliness, loyalty, and devotion experienced in communities across the globe; such principles in turn serve as the foundation for responsible, exemplary fieldwork, that most intimate and social engagement with others to bear honorable witness. Intimate engagement is at the heart of playwright Vincent Woods's contribution, a memoir and performance in prose that is an artistic achievement in its own right. Woods weaves together his reflections on Glassie's influence on his own work—plays steeped in Irish culture and history, performed around the world—with his own experiences of tradition while growing up on the Irish border. Woods's chapter exemplifies the transformation of art into scholarship and of scholarship into art. It is a process that feels wonderfully familiar from reading Glassie's writing, where art and scholarship blend in topic and prose.

We close this volume with an essay detailing Henry Glassie's monumental contributions to folklore studies and a bibliography of his published works. For having recognized the bright stars in Northern Ireland, Turkey, Bangladesh, Yorubaland, and elsewhere we owe to Henry Glassie our understanding of the various traditions he has documented and analyzed by featuring key individuals, both star informants and star performers. We dedicate this book to Henry Glassie in part for his devoted attention to creative individuals, and indeed for being a star in our tradition of folklore scholarship.

References

Abrahams, Roger D. 1970. *A Singer and Her Songs: Almeda Riddle's Book of Ballads*. Baton Rouge: Louisiana State University Press.

Azadovskii, Mark. *A Siberian Tale Teller*. 1974 [1926]. Trans. James R. Dow. Austin: Center for Intercultural Studies in Folklore and Ethnomusicology, University of Texas.

Baiburin, A. K. 1983. The Problem of the Individual and Tradition in the Work of J. Pentikkainen. *Soviet Anthropology and Archeology* 21(4):69–83.

Baker, Ronald L. 2000. Tradition and the Individual Talent in Folklore and Literature. *Western Folklore* 59(2):105–14.

Bakhtin, Mikhail M. 1981. *The Dialogic Imagination*. Trans. Caryl Emerson and Michael Holquist. Austin: University of Texas Press.

———. 1986. *Speech Genres and Other Late Essays*. Eds. Caryl Emerson and Michael Holquist. Trans. Vern McGee. Austin: University of Texas Press.

Bascom, William. 1974. A Yoruba Master Carver: Duga of Meko. In *The Traditional Artist in African Societies*, ed. Warren d'Azevedo, pp. 62–78. Bloomington: Indiana University Press.

Bauman, Richard. 2004. *A World of Others' Words: Cross-Cultural Perspectives on Intertextuality*. Malden: Blackwell Publishing.

Ben-Amos, Dan. 1972. Toward a Definition of Folklore in Context. In *Toward New Perspectives in Folklore*, eds. Américo Parades and Richard Bauman, pp. 3–15. Austin: University of Texas Press.

———. 1984. The Seven Strands of Tradition: Varieties in its Meaning in American Folklore Studies. *Journal of the Folklore Institute* 21:97–132.

Bronner, Simon J. 1998. *Following Tradition: Folklore in the Discourse of American Culture*. Logan: Utah State University Press.

———. 2000. The Meanings of Tradition: An Introduction. Special issue: The Meaning of Tradition. *Western Folklore* 59(2).

Burrison, John A. 1983. *Brothers in Clay: The Story of Georgia Folk Pottery*. Athens: University of Georgia Press.

Cashman, Ray. 2007. Genre and Ideology in Northern Ireland. *Midwestern Folklore* 33(1):13–27.

Cochran, Robert. 2004. *Come Walk with Me: The Art of Dorris Curtis*. Fayetteville: University of Arkansas Press.

Davis, Gerald L. 1994. Elijah Pierce, Woodcarver: Doves and Pain in Life Fulfilled. In *The Artist Outsider: Creativity and the Boundaries of Culture*, eds. Michael D. Hall and Eugene W. Metcalf, pp. 290–311. Washington, D.C.: Smithsonian Institution Press.

Dégh, Linda. 1969. *Folktales and Society: Storytelling in a Hungarian Peasant Community*. Bloomington: Indiana University Press.

———. 1995. *Hungarian Folktales: The Art of Zsuzsanna Palkó*. New York: Garland.

Duffy, Karen M. 1996. The Work of Virgil Boruff: Indiana Limestone Craftsman. *Midwestern Folklore* 22(2):4–71,

Eliot, T. S. 1948. *Notes towards the Definition of Culture*. London: Faber and Faber.

Evans, Timothy H. 1998. *King of the Western Saddle: The Sheridan Saddle and the Art of Don King*. Jackson: University Press of Mississippi.

Ferris, William. 1992. *"You Live and Learn. Then You Die and Forget It All": Ray Lum's Tales of Horses, Mules, and Men*. New York: Doubleday.

George, Kenneth M. 2010. *Picturing Islam: Art and Ethics in a Muslim Lifeworld*. Chichester: Wiley-Blackwell.

Glassie, Henry. 1967. William Houck, Maker of Pounded Ash, Adirondack Pack-Baskets. *Keystone Folklore Quarterly*, 22(3):163–85.

———. 1975. *Folk Housing in Middle Virginia: A Structural Analysis of Historic Artifacts*. Knoxville: University of Tennessee Press.

———. 1976. *All Silver and No Brass: An Irish Christmas Mumming*. Bloomington: Indiana University Press.

———. 1982a. *Passing the Time in Ballymenone: Culture and History of an Ulster Community*. Philadelphia: University of Pennsylvania Press.

———. 1982b. *Irish Folk History: Texts from the North*. Philadelphia: University of Pennsylvania Press.

———. 1985. *Irish Folktales*. New York: Pantheon Books.

———. 1989, *The Spirit of Folk Art*. New York: Harry N. Abrams.

———. 1993. *Turkish Traditional Art Today*. Bloomington: Indiana University Press.

———. 1997. *Art and Life in Bangladesh*. Bloomington: Indiana University Press.

———. 2003. Tradition. In *Eight Words for the Study of Expressive Culture*, ed. Burt Feintuch, pp. 176–97. Urbana: University of Illinois Press.

———. 2006. *The Stars of Ballymenone*. Bloomington: Indiana University Press.

———. 2007. Traditional Art: A Theory for Practice. In Henry Glassie and Firoz Mahmud, *Living Traditions*, pp. 25–70. Dhaka: Asiatic Society of Bangladesh.

———.2010a. *Prince Twins Seven-Seven: His Art, His Life in Nigeria, His Exile in America*. Bloomington: Indiana University Press.

———. 2010b. Mark in Place. In *Mark Hewitt: Falling into Place*. Durham: Nasher Museum of Art at Duke University.

Goldstein, Kenneth S. 1962. William Robbie: Folk Artist of the Buchan District, Aberdeenshire. In *Folklore in Action: Essays for Discussion in Honor of MacEdward Leach*, ed. Horace P. Beck, pp. 101–11. Philadelphia: American Folklore Society.

———. 1964. *A Guide for Field Workers in Folklore*. Hatboro: Folklore Associates.

Gummere, Francis. 1907. *The Popular Ballad*. New York: Houghton, Mifflin and Company.

Hartland, Edwin Sidney. 1968 [1899]. Folklore: What is It and What is the Good of it? In *Peasant Customs and Savage Myths*, ed. Richard Dorson, 1:230–51. Chicago: University of Chicago Press.

Hyde, Douglas. 1939. *Mayo Stories Told by Thomas Casey*. Irish Texts Society. Dublin: Educational Company of Ireland.

Hymes, Dell. 1975. Folklore's Nature and the Sun's Myth. *Journal of American Folklore* 88:345–69.

Ives, Edward D. 1964. *Larry Gorman: The Man Who Made the Songs*. Bloomington: Indiana University Press.

———. 1971. *Lawrence Doyle: The Farmer-Poet of Prince Edward Island*. Orono: University of Maine Press.

———. 1978. *Joe Scott: The Woodsman Songmaker*. Champaign: University of Illinois Press.

————. 1988. *George Magoon and the Down East Game War*. Champaign: University of Illinois Press.

Jacobs, Joseph. 1893. The Folk. *Folk-Lore* 4:233–38.

Jones, Michael Owen. 1989. *Craftsman of the Cumberlands: Tradition and Creativity*. Lexington: University Press of Kentucky.

Joyce, Rosemary O. 1989. *A Bearer of Tradition: Dwight Stump, Basketmaker*. Athens: University of Georgia Press.

Kirshenblatt, Mayer, and Barbara Kirshenblatt-Gimblett. 2007. *They Call Me Mayer July: Painted Memories of a Jewish Childhood in Poland before the Holocaust*. Berkeley: University of California Press.

Lévi-Strauss, Claude. 1966. *The Savage Mind*. Chicago: University of Chicago Press.

Lord, Albert. 1960. *The Singer of Tales*. Cambridge: Harvard University Press.

Morton, Robin. 1974. *Come Day, Go Day, God Send Sunday: The Songs and Life Story, Told in His Own Words, of John Maguire, Traditional Singer and Farmer from Co. Fermanagh*. London: Routledge and Kegan Paul.

Mould, Tom. 2003. *Choctaw Prophecy: A Legacy of the Future*. Contemporary American Indian Studies. Tuscaloosa: University of Alabama Press.

Noyes, Dorothy. 2009. Tradition: Three Traditions. *Journal of Folklore Research* 46(3): 233–68.

Ó Duilearga, Séamus. 1981 [1948]. *Seán Ó Conaill's Book: Stories and Traditions from Iveragh*. Dublin: Comhairle Bhéaloideas Eireann.

Pentikäinen, Juha. 1978. *Oral Repertoire and World View: An Anthropological Study of Marina Takalo's Life History*, Folklore Fellows Communications 219. Helsinki: Suomalainen Tiedeakatemia.

Pearson, Barry Lee. 1990. *Virginia Piedmont Blues: The Lives and Art of Two Virginia Bluesmen*. Philadelphia: University of Pennsylvania Press.

Rinzler, Ralph, and Robert Sayers. 1980. *The Meaders Family: North Georgia Potters*. Washington, D.C.: Smithsonian Institution Press.

Sawin, Patricia. 2004. *Listening for a Life: A Dialogic Ethnography of Bessie Eldreth through Her Songs and Stories*. Logan: Utah State University Press.

Shukla, Pravina. 2008. *The Grace of Four Moons: Dress, Adornment, and the Art of the Body in Modern India*. Bloomington: Indiana University Press.

Thompson, Stith. 1953. Advances in Folklore Studies. In *Anthropology Today*, ed. A. L. Kroeber. Chicago: University of Chicago Press.

Vlach, John Michael. 1992 [1981]. *Charleston Blacksmith: The Work of Philip Simmons*. Columbia: University of South Carolina Press.

Zug, Charles G. III. 1986. *Turners and Burners: The Folk Potters of North Carolina*. Chapel Hill: University of North Carolina Press.

Entering Tradition: Kim Ellington, Catawba Valley Potter

Charles G. Zug

> Like traditional artists throughout the world, they have stepped out of the rush for modernity and returned reverently to ideas from the past. Acting in a spirit of revitalization, they resist the technological progress that divides people from the earth and separates the mind from the hands. . . . This mix of accommodation and resistance establishes a frame of adaptive revival within which forms and techniques hold steady but functions shift.
>
> —Henry Glassie, *The Potter's Art*

North Carolina possesses one of the largest, most diverse and enduring traditions of pottery making in the nation. In fact, in 1995 Pennsylvania potter Jack Troy declared that "If North America has a 'pottery state,' it must be North Carolina. . . . There is probably no other state with such a highly developed pottery consciousness" (1995:22–23). The major center of production is the Seagrove area, located almost precisely in the center of the state. Today, along the rural roads of southern Randolph and northern Moore Counties, there are over one hundred small, family-run shops in operation. Some of the potters trace their lineage back for five to ten generations, and many youngsters continue to follow their parents into the craft. And each year, tens of thousands of eager customers from across the nation regularly visit this area, filling the trunks of cars and bellies of buses with brightly colored wares.

Just one hundred miles due west of Seagrove is the Catawba Valley, which contains North Carolina's other great pottery tradition. During the eighteenth century, numerous families, most of German origin, made their way south down the Shenandoah Valley and settled in what is now Lincoln

The Ritchie family shop, Catawba Valley, c. 1914.
Photograph courtesy of Clara Ritchie Wiggs

Burlon Craig admiring a fresh crop of ware, 1978

and Catawba Counties in the western Piedmont. The Catawba River encircles this region, and its South Fork, which meanders through the heart of both counties, has provided superb clays for the potters' wheels. Historically, the Catawba Valley produced almost as many potters as Seagrove, but throughout the twentieth century it was widely ignored, even by North Carolinians (See Zug 1986:70–93). Perhaps because it lies closer to the major cities of the Piedmont, Seagrove has been the Mecca of pottery collectors, the place that most embodied historical continuity and native artistry. But over the last thirty years all that has begun to change.

The modern history of Catawba Valley pottery owes a huge debt to one man—Burlon Bart Craig (1914–2002) of Lincoln County. In 1928 at the tender age of fourteen, Burlon began an informal apprenticeship with his next door neighbor, James Lynn, and quickly learned how to make the traditional alkaline glazed stoneware of the region. Throughout the 1930s he worked as a journeyman in the local shops, turning the utilitarian forms needed in homes and farms. During World War II he served in the Navy and then returned home in 1946 to continue his craft. He purchased the pottery shop and kiln of one of his former employers, Harvey Reinhardt, but quickly discovered that his old world was gone. Demand for the old jars and jugs, churns and milk crocks, pitchers and flowerpots, had fallen off sharply, and potters had abandoned their wheels to work in textile and furniture factories. And so, Burlon worked on alone for decades, fully expecting that he would be the last in a long line of potters. But then his world changed once again. By the early 1970s, Americans were planning their Bicentennial and reflecting on the history of the nation. This, in turn, spurred interest in antiques of all sorts, folk art and all things "country," and the hand-made object. During the late 1970s, a new clientele began to appear at Burlon's kiln openings—collectors, antiques dealers, academics, museum curators—who valued his work not for its utility but for its historical significance and authenticity. Prices surged, and Burlon was widely acclaimed for his traditional skills, even winning the National Heritage Fellowship from the National Endowment for the Arts in 1984. Equally important, younger potters appeared, eager to learn the traditional forms, glazes, and technology that he alone possessed.

A Studio Potter

One of those young men was Kim Ellington, who was born in 1954 in the city of Hickory, only a short distance north of the rural district of Vale where Burlon lived. Kim grew up in a middle class home knowing nothing about the nearby Catawba Valley tradition. After completing high school and a stint in the Army, he spent some time searching for a meaningful career. Eventually he ended up at Haywood Technical College in the western mountains of North Carolina, planning to study horticulture. But then he discovered their program in production pottery. Almost on a whim, he recalls, "I signed up and thought, well, if it connects, it does, and if it doesn't, it doesn't. And it did connect" (January, 17, 2007). Even while a student he began filling orders and making tablewares for a local restaurant. And then, in 1982, he moved back to Hickory and set up his own shop.

For the next few years, Kim produced what any studio potter in the country might have made. "It was typically what you see if you go into any craft store up in the mountains or something, the coffee mugs and the teapots," "a good bit of custom dinnerware," "some lamp bases," and "little oil lamps. I made thousands upon thousands and thousands of oil lamps" [laughs]. Kim bought all his clay and used commercial glazes. And most of his pots were extremely modest in size. "I was making a lot of whatever I thought was contemporary, but it was all, nothing over ten inches tall." The only unusual feature of his business was that he quickly began wood firing his wares, not for aesthetic reasons but because "I didn't have the money for propane burners and shutoffs and filling up the gas tank." Hickory still had numerous furniture shops at the time, and "there were piles of wood everywhere, so I thought, well, why in the world not try to use some of this stuff?" Overall, Kim recalls, his business was at best a modest success. "I had a retail shop as well as doing wholesale to New Morning Gallery up in Asheville. . . . It was sustenance, that's what it was. There wasn't any profit involved, but it was enough to keep the doors open and keep me going at it" (January 17, 2007).

One Saturday morning, a year or so after his return to Hickory, Kim set up his pots at a yard sale at Shuford Mills, a local textile company. He'd just had a firing, and so he covered his table with "a lot of pieces with this dark, what I call the *Temmoku* glaze, which I'd learned in school." Kim was not optimistic about selling anything. His pots were black, coated with a classic Oriental glaze saturated with iron, whereas most people at that time wanted "bright pinks and blues and such, mauve as they called it." But one local woman walked up and began picking up his pots and studying them very closely. Then she announced, "Oh, this reminds me of what my granddaddy used to make." Kim was astonished, thinking "how could anybody around here be messing with this *Temmoku* glaze?" The woman introduced herself as Irene Reinhardt Gates, the daughter of Enoch Reinhardt, a well known Catawba Valley potter who had hired Burlon Craig as a journeyman during the 1930s. Surprised but still skeptical, Kim allowed that, "'that's just amazing. And oh, I wish I could have been a part of that or seen that or something.' She says, 'Well, do you not know Burlon Craig?' I said, 'Well, no, I don't know him.' 'So, well, you need to go see him, because he's still doing that kind of pottery'" (January 17, 2009).

Kim wrote down Burlon's name but didn't try to contact him. As he explains, "it seemed so far removed; I'd never heard anyone mention the guy or anything. And so I thought, well, I found it hard to believe. It didn't really connect." But two years later, something happened that forced Kim to make the connection. He went to a local display of old pots where "I finally saw my first five gallon Catawba Valley jug. And I went over there to pick it up, and when I picked it up, I almost hit myself in the head with it." Stunned by the lightness of this large form, Kim could only wonder at "the skill level that was involved in that." The simple act of holding one of these old pots forced him to reevaluate everything he'd learned about making pottery. "I thought I was on the cutting edge of things. And I was looking back at something made 150 years earlier that I could not even come close to being able to make. And there's a certain time when you have to swallow your pride, and that's where, usually, where gains can be made." And so Kim picked up the phone and called the Craigs to ask if he could come see their pottery. The day he arrived, Burlon happened to be firing his big groundhog kiln, and that proved the final catalyst. "When I saw that, everything blew out the window. . . . I'd seen these films of the Japanese potters with their big *anagama* kilns and all this. And I just went, 'Oh my God!' This is happening right here in front of me in Vale, North Carolina" (January 17, 2007).

From the mid-1980s into the early 1990s, Kim worked at making the transition from studio potter to traditional potter. This was a major change, one that he describes as a process of letting go or emptying out. "I basically had to forget everything I'd been taught. . . . I was turning sitting down! You know, *everything* is different. The kiln was different, the clay was different, the size was different. The main thing, I basically, like I say, had to forget everything I knew" (May 27, 1992). But Kim did not immediately abandon his dinnerwares and oil lamps and commercial clays. He simply couldn't afford to, and so for a number of years, he observes, "I was really kind of dancing in both worlds. . . . I would have changed overnight if I had been able to, but it was a simple matter of not having the ability to do that" (January 17, 2007). There was simply too much to learn about kilns, clays, glazes, and forms.

Entering Tradition

One of the first things Kim did was to begin helping Burlon fire his groundhog kiln. By this time Burlon was in his early seventies, and he needed help in loading his huge groundhog kiln with five or six hundred pots and then stoking the fireboxes with pine slabs for eight to ten hours. At first, Burlon's methods seemed totally foreign. He didn't use ceramic cones or a pyrometer to gauge the heat or time the firing cycle. Instead Burlon "had his wind-up Westclox. He'd get that thing out and count those hours off. And so, 'Well, I do this for this many hours.' And he started telling me about soot lines and all this stuff. And I was just totally lost" (January 17, 2007). As Kim would soon learn about clays and glazes, Burlon's teachings were pragmatic, not from the theoretical or scientific approach Kim had experienced in school. Soon he would understand that the black soot lining the interior of the kiln walls had to be gradually burned off to a whitish hue, indicating that the kiln was totally dry. Only then was it safe for the stokers to "blast off" the kiln to its maximum temperature.

After four or five firings, Kim was beginning to understand the traditional firing process, but even then, "it wasn't like anything I ever saw myself going into. I mean, this huge kiln. I didn't have any property, so that wasn't even an option" (January 17, 2009). But in 1987, Dr. Bob Hart walked into his shop one day and solved that problem. Hart was the owner of Hart's Square, a large, open air museum with seventy-five log buildings located about ten miles south of Hickory. He had watched Kim's progress with Burlon and wanted him to build a working groundhog kiln for the museum. Kim had built several smaller kilns by this time but nothing on the scale of a twenty-five foot long groundhog kiln. Hart would supply the bricks and materials, but it was Burlon who offered the knowledge of how to construct a proper breast wall, firebox, arch, and chimney. And to shape the arch of the kiln, Burlon lent a set of arch boards that had been used by potters across the area for 150 years. Recognizing that this was an extraordinary learning opportunity, Kim took on the challenge. He ended up with a kiln very similar to Burlon's, except that he added side walls to raise the arch slightly higher. He then fired the new kiln for the first time in the fall of 1987, with Burlon in attendance. The following year, he and his wife Betsy left Hickory and purchased a home in Vale in the heart of the old

Kim Ellington finishing the neck of a jug.
Photograph courtesy of Kim Ellington

Burlon Craig firing his groundhog kiln, 1980

pottery region. He immediately constructed a gas kiln on his property to continue his studio wares, but now he could easily access the big groundhog at nearby Hart Square to produce traditional forms. And he now lived only a few miles from Burlon.

Unfortunately, the first few firings at Hart's Square were not successful. As Kim recalls, "first firing [we] hauled everything all the way out there to Hart's and had to glaze out in the open and everything. Blew up half the firing, because we were loading it wet, you know, it had just been glazed" (January 17, 2009). Normally, a potter glazes and then lets the pots dry out completely before loading the kiln. But a much bigger problem was that Kim did not yet have the proper clay to make large Catawba Valley pots. "I had me some clay," Kim explains, "you know, the commercially-mined clay, and sure enough, I was turning five gallon pieces out of it. Hot damn! It all blew to hell in the kiln! [laughs] That clay just wouldn't work" (May 27, 1992). After that first firing, Kim took "all these messed up pots" out of the kiln and prepared to "just throw all this stuff in the ditch." But Dr. Hart stopped him and said, "'Sunday, we'll have a sale out here at my farm.' Says, 'I'm going to call everybody that I know.'" And on Sunday, "a bunch of people came out. And so I was going, oh gosh, let's see, if I get five dollars a pot, let's see, that'll be three hundred, four hundred bucks. Ah well, that'll pay my rent." But then Bob Hart stepped up in front of the crowd and announced that "'everyone will only be able to purchase one piece.'. . . . I was sitting in the back; my mouth just dropped, and I went, 'What in the hell is he saying?'" What happened next astonished Kim even more. "Sure enough, here everybody comes, and they start scrambling around, and they get their one piece. . . . Then he says, "OK now, whatever's left.' And by golly, people were buying stuff that was totally screwed up. And anyway, we sold it and made, instead of hundreds, we made a couple thousand dollars. . . . It was more than I'd ever made in a pottery sale before" (January 17, 2007).

This was Kim's first "kiln opening," a sales technique widely used by Burlon Craig and other North Carolina potters and one that he would soon adopt. As disappointed as he was with his own handiwork, Kim now recognized the latent demand for Catawba Valley pots. And there were a few successes in this first firing. He well remembers his wife Betsy's praise: "when I got that first nice jug out. She said, 'Now *that's* pottery!'" And Bob Hart was pleased too, "egging me on, you know: 'You need to keep going over to Burlon's, you need to get you some clay'" (January 17, 2007).

As a studio potter, Kim had relied exclusively on commercial clays and had never given any thought to digging it out of the ground himself. Now he recognized that he needed a clay that was plastic and would turn well; that was strong enough to stand up in large, bulbous forms; and that could withstand the extreme heat of the groundhog kiln. First he dug some clay on a friend's land: "it was the roughest, rockiest stuff you'd ever come across in your life, but by God, it turned and it fired." Finally, he decided, "OK, Burlon is the one, he knows this stuff. So that's when I really just went to Burlon." Burlon sent him down to dig clay in the old Rhodes clay hole along the South Fork of the Catawba River and offered to test whatever he brought back. "He'd look at it, and then one day he finally said, 'Let's put some in the [clay] mill.' Usually it was, 'Ah well, you're going to have to look.' Usually it was just some sandy mess." But Kim persisted until one day he brought in some clay, and Burlon asked, "'Where did you *get* this?' [laughs] And then I knew. Aha, now we're getting somewhere" (January 17, 2007). Altogether, it took Kim about five years to find a good source of local clay, but "it just changed everything I did." Reflecting on his earlier work, he allows that "if I was still doing that same kind of pottery out of those same bags out of that same clay, man, I wouldn't be doing it. I'd be burnt out" (May 27, 1992).

Mastering the groundhog kiln and finding local clay were probably the most difficult tasks that Kim had to face. By comparison, learning the local alkaline glaze was a breeze. For the first firing at Hart's Square, Burlon told Kim, "'Seven, five, two.' And he gave me a bag [of powdered glass] and said, 'Well, maybe this will get you on your way.' And it certainly did." The numbers Burlon provided represented the basic formula for the Catawba Valley alkaline glaze—seven parts sifted hardwood ashes, five parts powdered glass, and two parts clay slip, all mixed with enough water, as Burlon liked to put it, to produce the consistency of buttermilk. Kim didn't drink buttermilk, so he headed for his mother's house, "and I went straight for the refrigerator and got out the buttermilk. And the way I could tell the thickness was by sticking my fingers in it, seeing it drip. . . . And my mother said, 'What in the world are you doing with that buttermilk?' So I explained to her, that's how to mix my slip. She thought I was crazy." All this was totally different from what Kim had learned "in the school environment," where "I learned glaze chemistry and molecular equivalents and all that sort of thing." Under Burlon's regimen, the basic method was "make it and put it in there and see what you get" (January 17, 2007).

Perhaps the one useful skill that carried over from Kim's studio days was his ability to turn modest forms on the wheel. But even here he had to make some major adjustments. First, he had to learn to turn standing up rather than sitting down. Southern traditional potters stand so they can use the strength of their legs and whole body to pull up large forms. As Kim realized, "you're not going to make a five gallon piece sitting down." In addition, it is easier to view the overall form when standing, and it takes less time to cut the piece off the wheel and center a new ball of clay. Second, Kim had to master the technique of "capping," that is, making a tall piece in two or three sections. Five gallon jars are about eighteen inches tall (actually more when still wet). It is very difficult for the potter to reach inside to the bottom to remove excess water or trim the walls. So, the potter centers all the clay needed on the wheel (about twenty pounds for five gallons), then pulls up the top section and cuts it off. Next he re-centers the remaining clay, pulls up and trims the bottom of the pot, and then adds on the top and trims that. Akin to the Oriental technique of throwing off the hump, capping allowed Southern potters to turn large forms more efficiently and rapidly. Third, Kim had to learn to produce Catawba Valley swirl ware, a striped clay body made by combining light and dark clays. Again, there was nothing formal or academic about this. "Burl," Kim explains, "he isn't going to teach you anything, but if you watch, you're going to learn something. And I was over there one day, and he was making swirl. . . . I saw, well, that's how you do it. So I ran back to my shop at once. Been making it ever since" (May 27, 1992).

Altogether, it took about five years of hard work for Kim to make the transition from studio pottery to becoming a traditional Catawba Valley potter. It is difficult to define just when Kim achieved basic competence in his new craft, but he marks that moment as a day in 1993 when he received Burlon Craig's full recognition. Each time Kim unloaded the kiln at Hart's Square, Burlon would appear to appraise the new crop of pots. For Kim, "the more attention Burlon started paying to my pots, the more I realized I was on the right track. And then, I guess when I finally felt, well, I guess I finally made something, was when Burlon asked me if I would trade . . . for a five gallon face jug." Kim was "just like astounded" when Burlon made his offer. "I didn't even know how to answer him. It was like, what? Because he was getting all that money for his, and how come he wants to trade with me?" But Kim saved a jug that Burlon had admired and took it over to his house to make the exchange. He had no illusions that he was Burlon's equal, but he allows, "That's when . . . I felt like I had a chance" [laughs] (January 17, 2007).

A CATAWBA VALLEY POTTER

Given Kim's lengthy odyssey into the Catawba Valley clay, what is it that most drives a contemporary potter to enter tradition? Beyond the individual skills for producing the pots, Burlon's teaching provided a largely self-contained *system* of knowledge, one with clear working principles and a long history behind it. Appropriately, Burlon Craig's son Don, a close friend of Kim, explains the interlocking nature of each phase of production in the Catawba Valley. "What most people don't realize is the pottery, what you're turning out, has entirely all to do with what you're working with. . . . The kind of clay, the kind of kiln, the kind of wheel you turn on—all these things affect what you turn out. And most people will never have the resources. Because anybody can't just go out here and build a groundhog kiln. Or can't go out here and get [the local] Rhodes clay" (July 7, 1993).

It is this sense of logic and unity that has so appealed to younger potters like Kim and Don. Instead of an amorphous, national pottery as embodied in the pages of *Ceramics Monthly* or *Studio Potter*, the Catawba Valley tradition is tightly defined and offers the potters a clear path and purpose. And beyond the technology, the practical side, Burlon also provided a "history" of the tradition through his anecdotes about earlier generations, such as the epic laziness of his mentor, Jim Lynn, or the relentless perfectionism of Sam Propst. Burlon loved to talk about Sam Propst (1882–1935), who had lived just down the road when he was young. Always he praised Sam Propst as "'the best turner of all, as far as uniform [shape] and turning it out top to bottom the same thing. . . . He could turn out a board full of five gallon jugs or jars, and I'll bet you there wouldn't be more than a match stem difference in [height in], say, five or six.'" Burlon would tell stories about the older men he had known while he was firing his kiln with Kim and the other younger potters. And he would ensure that his account had meaning. Sam, he would say, "'was the kind of man that took pride in his work, a little more pride than some of them did'" (Zug 1986:253–54). Such tales served to humanize the Catawba Valley tradition, teach the qualities of the ideal potter, and provide a cohesive sense of style and region.

Beyond the legendary presence of the old masters, there are also huge numbers of old pots that they made that today's potters can pick up and handle and weigh in their hands. Kim, for one, owns a badly damaged, reconstructed five gallon jug made nearly a century ago by Sam Propst. Some friends had found it at the site of an old still, where presumably revenuers had smashed it against a tree. Kim calls this jug "my ghost pot, because it haunts me. It'll keep coming back whenever I'm making something. I'll think about how damned thin [walled] that Propst is." Precisely because it is broken, Kim explains, "You can see the cross section of this sucker. And there is not a single pot that I will make of five gallons that I don't

Kim Ellington's new groundhog kiln. Note the large loading port, the two stoke holes at the front, and the stoke holes to the left.
Photograph courtesy of Kim Ellington

Firing Kim Ellington's new kiln. The front doors are closed when the side holes are stoked. Courtesy Kim Ellington

see that this thing doesn't echo. . . . My god, the man set a standard that is unequaled." Asked whether he is as good as Sam Propst, Kim replies, "No—maybe on a really good day. Every now and then" (February 17, 2009). For Kim and his contemporaries, all of whom collect these old utilitarian vessels when they can afford them, these ghosts from the past continue to instruct and inspire—and also serve as the basis for future work.

Some of the potters in the Catawba Valley have been content to largely replicate the forms learned from Burlon, but Kim's goal is to carry this tradition forward. "I'm not trying to make reproductions," he explains. "I'm trying to make a continuum here and, you know, homage to the past and keep those skill levels intact. And the only way to keep those skill levels intact is to make those round, five gallon jars. But not like worship it or anything. Just move on" (January 17, 2007). Specifically, Kim affirms, "I've had more time to experiment with shapes and firing. I guess is what I've really changed more than anything is the firing, because I really haven't messed with the glaze all that much" (February 17, 2009).

Kim used the kiln at Hart's Square until 1998, when he constructed a modified groundhog kiln on his own property. In part, he did so because he grew tired of hauling fragile greenwares over to Hart's Square, but he also wanted to try out several new ideas. The new kiln has roughly the same sized setting floor as Burlon's, about twenty-one feet by ten feet, but it is much higher inside, about four feet rather than just thirty inches. The greater height allows Kim to load many more pots using ceramic shelves. In Burlon's kiln the pots were never stacked but simply set in one layer on the floor. The shelves also allow Kim to add a variety of smaller tablewares along with the larger forms common to the region. To compensate for the increased size of the interior, Kim doubled the height of the chimney to pull a strong draft through the kiln. Kim's second innovation was to add stoke holes along the sides of the kiln. The old groundhog kilns were fired from one end, meaning that the heat fell off steadily toward the chimney end. By adding side stoke holes Kim has ensured that the heat is much more even throughout the kiln. This, in turn, has doubled the firing time to about sixteen hours but has also allowed him to modulate the cycle of heating and cooling to produce unusual surface effects. Kim's general inspiration for the side stoke holes was the widespread Oriental chamber (*anagama*) kiln. Closer to home, he was influenced by the large kiln of North Carolina potter Mark Hewitt, which was modeled on a fourteenth-century kiln from Thailand.

The aesthetic appeal of Catawba Valley pots lies in their bold forms and their rich colors and textures. When he built his new kiln, Kim discovered that "that's when my glaze changed. I didn't necessarily change the glaze that much; it was the kiln" (January 17, 2007). Specifically, Kim has experimented with taking more time both to soak the pots in the kiln at high temperatures and to cool the kiln. The old utilitarian potters like Burlon wanted to fire their kilns as quickly as possible, usually in eight to ten hours. Their goal was to produce a mature, impervious glaze and then take out a saleable product. Kim, on the other hand, has found that what "changes the pottery more than anything is just the time allowed to the potter. . . . I figure, well, OK, you've spent three months working on this stuff. You've got it in the kiln. What's another four hours in the kiln after three months? . . . What's another six hours if you're actually going to get something different?" (February 17, 2009). This is not to say that Kim thinks he has tight control over what happens in his kiln. "'A force of nature is having its way with your pots in the kiln, and you don't know exactly what's going to come out'" (Hewitt and Sweezy 2005:175). But by extending his firing cycle and varying the kiln atmosphere he is producing "more variety of colors, more effects from the glaze" (January 17, 2007).

This conscious emphasis on visual appeal was clearly not a major concern for the earlier potters. And in conjunction with manipulating the groundhog kiln, Kim has also reinvigorated two old Catawba Valley glazing techniques: the addition of iron oxide and the use of broken glass. After Kim moved out to the Vale area, "'an elderly neighbor told me that the potters used to pay her and other kids twenty-five cents to collect a coffee can full of iron rocks—the hematite that's everywhere on the ground around here—to pound up for their glaze.'" The utilitarian potters felt that the iron created a tighter, denser glaze, and many admired the thick brown flows of iron down the sides of the pots. In adding iron oxide to the glaze, Kim has been able to create thick, often startling patches of color ranging from brown to yellow to brick red on the surface of his pots. He has also experimented in "brushing an iron wash under the glaze, and it brings out areas on some pots looking like what the Chinese called 'Hare's Fur' and 'Partridge Feather' glazes." While a great admirer of Oriental ceramics, Kim is quick to explain that "my aim is not to regain the Chinese glazes but to let this Catawba Valley glaze evolve in its own place—just let come out what comes out in these particular circumstances" (Hewitt and Sweezy 2005:188).

A second technique that Kim has adapted is the use of broken glass from old windowpanes or bottles. A number of the pioneer stoneware potters in the Catawba Valley, men such as Daniel Seagle and David Hartzog, set their

Planter by Kim Ellington with iron oxide wash
and glass runs. Courtesy Kim Ellington

Jar and jug by Daniel Seagle, c. 1850.
Ackland Art Museum, University of North Carolina, Ackland Fund

Greenware on the drying racks in Kim Ellington's shop.
Photograph courtesy of Kim Ellington

Buyers at a recent kiln opening at Kim Ellington's.
Photograph courtesy of Kim Ellington

glazed pots on the kiln floor and then carefully balanced shards of glass across the handle terminals and rims. The results were often striking—the glass would run down the sides of the pots in thick streaks of milky white and sky blue. Doubtless, the original purpose of the glass was to "glue" the handles to the body, but the lighter streaks contrasted to the darker alkaline glaze and created a powerful aesthetic effect. Burlon Craig revived this technique, and Kim refined it. Instead of merely balancing the glass, he began pressing smaller shards right into the soft clay body in geometric patterns, creating much more precise flows of glass. Other potters like Mark Hewitt have adopted Kim's innovation, thus continuing a nearly two hundred year old tradition in a slightly new form.

As Kim has enriched the surfaces of his pots, he has also developed a repertoire of classic forms to carry his textures and colors. His inspiration is clear: the work of Burlon Craig and the numerous earlier Catawba Valley masters, most of whom were capable of making jars and jugs in sizes ranging from five to ten and even twenty gallons capacity. What Kim sees in these forms is a universal appeal. "The reason I still adhere to some of the old shapes and stuff is, for one thing, they're just so resonant, not only with this community, which is number one, but also I find it resonates through the whole country. They see these shapes; I think they've been burned into people's brains for the past thousands of years. . . . I'm not trying to change anything. I'm just trying to expand, perhaps" (January 17, 2007). Kim is particularly renowned for his massive jar (or planter) forms, with their wide bellies or shoulders, neatly trimmed surfaces, and carefully attached handles. These mega-pots do resonate, most particularly with the work of Daniel Seagle (ca. 1800–67), a one-time resident of Vale who is widely considered to be the finest utilitarian potter who ever worked in North Carolina. Kim has also widened his output to include table wares, such as bowls, platters, canisters, and mugs. Such smaller forms were only rarely produced by earlier potters, but with shelves and kiln furniture in his new kiln, Kim can fire them much more efficiently. And part of his purpose in doing so is to go beyond "historic pots" and provide useful wares for contemporary homes.

Last Shards

Kim is well aware that the function of pottery today is greatly changed. As he very aptly explains, "it's gone from the springhouse to the big house. And what used to sit in the springhouse is now sitting on pieces of fine furniture, so you better smooth that bottom off, and maybe tuck it in a little bit and lift it up, get a little more presentation" (January 17, 2007). Where Burlon Craig was trained to knock out dozens of jars and jugs as fast as possible, Kim has to spend much more time on each individual pot, developing the form, trimming the walls, and attaching the handles. No longer filled with kraut and hidden away in the springhouse, they now sit in full view in people's homes and are judged for their formal beauty. And there is much more than that. These Catawba Valley pots embody hidden possibilities and meanings to their owners. In Kim's words, "pots are sought more as symbols of complexity and creativity than for practical purposes." They provide connections, first of all "to the natural world through clay and fire . . . because of the magic of transforming a bit of earth into such a beautiful thing." And then there is the sense of authenticity embedded in these native pots. Through their forms, glazes, and technology, "it's possible to feel kind of connected to people who made pots and lived with them over the past several thousand years." They function as a powerful "link to earlier times" (Hewitt and Sweezy 2005:181). Ultimately, Kim's pots appeal to contemporary buyers because they are not mass produced or standardized. In Susan Stewart's terms, his work constitutes "a nostalgia for preindustrial labor, a nostalgia for craft." His is "an antithetical mode of production: production by the hand, a production that is unique and authentic" (Stewart 1984:68). Kim himself recognizes that the way of working of academic and studio potters—"the one that I learned in school—is an offshoot of industrial technology. I call it 'noodling,' and I'd be bored to tears to go back to it" (Hewitt and Sweezy 2005:181).

In his long journey from studio potter to Catawba Valley potter, Kim has been triply blessed. He was extremely fortunate to discover a working pottery tradition in his backyard; to have found a mentor in Burlon Craig, the last of the old utilitarian potters in that tradition; and to be able to sell to a knowledgeable clientele that embraces wood fired, alkaline glazed wares. With his new status has come undeniable success. He holds three kiln openings per year—in the spring, late summer, and December—and attracts around one hundred people each time who willingly pay about $125 per gallon for his wares. (Burlon Craig made ten cents per gallon for decades; at the end of his life he received one hundred dollars per gallon.) In just three days Kim sells almost a full year's output. "It amazes me," he allows. "I'm totally amazed by it. I mean, I got people out here in my yard at nine o'clock in the morning ready to buy pots, rain, shine, cold, hot, whatever" (January 17, 2007). And over the last fifteen years he has been featured in exhibitions in galleries and museums like the North Carolina Pottery Center and the Mint Museum. In 2005–6 he was one of six featured potters in a major exhibition of old and contemporary forms, "The Potter's Eye: Art & Tradition in North Carolina Pottery," which was held at the North Carolina Museum of Art (Hewitt and Sweezy 2005:174–89). For all his success, Kim knows that his work is part of something larger. "I want people to see them as my pots primarily, but as Catawba Valley pots. And when I go out every now and then, maybe [to] go give a presentation somewhere or something, I always find myself saying, 'We.' I can't get up there and say, 'I do this and I do that.' And it's a 'we.' I'm not the first, and hopefully I'm not the last." Rooted in a sustaining, creative tradition, he knows that "my job is just to make the best pots I can" (January 17, 2007).

References

Craig, Don. July 7, 1993. Tape-recorded Interview. Bostic, NC.

Ellington, Kim. May 27, 1992. Tape-recorded Interview. Vale, NC.

———. January 17, 2007. Tape-recorded Interview. Vale, NC.

———. February 17, 2009. Tape-recorded Interview, Vale, NC.

Glassie, Henry. 1999. *The Potter's Art*. Bloomington: Indiana University Press.

Hewitt, Mark, and Nancy Sweezy. 2005. *The Potter's Eye: Art & Tradition in North Carolina Pottery*. Chapel Hill: University of North Carolina Press.

Stewart, Susan. 1984. *On Longing: Narratives of the Miniature, the Gigantic, the Souvenir, the Collection*. Baltimore and London: The Johns Hopkins University Press.

Troy, Jack. 1995. *Wood-Fired Stoneware and Porcelain*. Radnor: Chilton Book Company.

Zug, Charles G. III. 1986. *Turners and Burners: The Folk Potters of North Carolina*. Chapel Hill: University of North Carolina Press.

Roger Morigi, who worked at Washington National Cathedral from 1956 until 1978, poses with his gargoyle. Photo by L. Albee

Delight in Skill:
The Stone Carvers' Art

Marjorie Hunt

It has been thirty-one years since I met master stone carvers Roger Morigi and Vincent Palumbo, yet it seems like only yesterday. I vividly remember that summer day in 1978 when I first looked through the window of their small carving workshop in the shadow of Washington National Cathedral.[1] Vincent was working at his banker, carving a figure in limestone. The afternoon sun shone though the shop's many windows, dancing on the dust-covered walls and work benches and on the multitude of plaster models, stone carvings, and tools that filled the room. Solid and strong, Vincent leaned into his work, his massive hands deftly guiding a pneumatic hammer and chisel, sending chips of stone flying.

Looking up, he saw me standing there and waved for me to come in, greeting me warmly. As luck would have it, retired master carver Roger Morigi and another former Cathedral carver, Frank Zic, stopped by to visit Vincent that day. In only a matter of minutes, the three carvers seemed to forget that I was even there. They began to talk of stone and of tools, of great masters and beautiful work, trading stories of their apprenticeships and their work experiences. I was in awe, not only of the incredible depth of their working knowledge—their keen understanding of raw materials, tools, and methods—but also of their love for their craft and the sense of pride and satisfaction they derived from their work, their delight in skill.[2] I remember thinking, as I stood in their dust-filled workshop, that I was in the presence of rare individuals—artisans whose roots in the stone carving trade ran deep and whose knowledge, experience, and skill were unparalleled. And indeed it was true, for the Cathedral had gathered to it the few remaining master craftsmen who had the ability to carve the hundreds of ornamental and sculptural works that are an integral part of its fourteenth-century English Gothic style design. For me, it was one of life's transformative moments.

Over the course of two decades, I visited the carvers in their homes and at the Cathedral—in the carving workshop, up on the scaffolding, around the building site. I observed and documented their work techniques and processes, their skills and their stories. I interviewed them about their lives, their training, their aesthetic ideals, and their occupational traditions. Roger Morigi and Vincent Palumbo were my teachers; they guided me on a journey into their world of work, introduced me to a new realm of knowledge and experience, and inspired me with their dedication and their commitment to excellence. These great masters are gone now—Roger passed away in 1995, Vincent in 2000—but the spirit of creativity and excellence that infused their work lives on in a monumental legacy in stone and in the hands and hearts of the many carvers they trained.

Roger and Vincent viewed themselves as performers, as creative individuals engaged in the skillful act of interpretation. Through their knowledge, skills, and abilities, their judgment and care, they transformed designs on paper or in clay into lasting works of art in stone. In their work they were less concerned with design, with the creation of new texts, than they were with technique, with ways of working the stone. Their emphasis was on artistic action, on the process of creation.[3] What mattered was the performance of skill. Franz Boas recognized the aesthetic dimension of technique, writing, "Since a perfect standard of form can be attained only in a highly developed and perfectly controlled technique, there must be an intimate relation between technique and a feeling for beauty" (Boas 1955:11–19). Roger Morigi and Vincent Palumbo shared a deep appreciation for the aesthetic value and expressive power of technical perfection. They delighted in skill and found meaning and pleasure in the poetic qualities of workmanship—in their ability to manipulate the tools and materials of their trade and to create objects of beauty through their special "touch," through their mastery of technique. "You cut and cut and all of a sudden you see something grow," said Roger. "The more you work, the better it comes out. You feel good inside. You work, it gets brilliant, you see it move. I don't know, it fills you with some kind of emotion—such a sense of satisfaction."[4]

These master craftsmen found individual expression through the performance of skill, but they also worked within the boundaries of certain culturally determined rules of appropriate behavior and acceptable expression, balancing personal creativity with "group needs and received ideas."[5]

48

Vincent Palumbo
Photo by
Paul Wagner

The stone carvers' workshop, studio, and stone yard

Their work was shaped and evaluated by shared ideas of what good work should be like.

In the context of the workshop, surrounded by carvers of all levels of skill and ability, they continually watched one another, comparing individual styles and techniques, measuring themselves and evaluating the work of others, striving for the respect and recognition accorded to mastery.[6] "Between ourselves we knew," said Roger. "We recognized the one who was doing very good, and we would say it, 'Oh, you should see the beautiful work he's doing.' And you wanted that, to hear that, and you wanted to be one of them." Vincent put it this way: "First there was the challenge between the stone and myself and also there was the challenge to stay on pace with them [the other carvers in the shop] because they were old masters and they were to judge." Irish stone carver Seamus Murphy spoke for many when he described the thrill of watching a virtuoso performance in stone: "To see that man working was a treat. He made stone-cutting look simple and you wonder why the blazes you had to serve seven years to it. I don't know how he did it, but he had a system of working which left everyone standing" (Murphy 1966).

Stone carvers attend to craftsmanship: to systems of working and ways of touching the stone, to the selection and the use of tools and the treatment of raw materials, to the ordering of actions and the creative decisions and choices that are made as they transform a block of stone into a cultural artifact. In the end, the completed carving stands as an "emblem of the creative act," what Robert Plant Armstrong calls "an instance of incarnated experience" imbued with memories and meaning.[7]

This concept of craftsmanship as performance—as "cultural behavior for which a person assumes responsibility to an audience"—is crucial to understanding the stone-carving process and its meaning in the carvers' lives (Hymes 1975a:18). Like other stone carvers, Roger and Vincent had control over the process of creation, and thus the aesthetic possibilities of an object lay completely in their hands, not only in terms of their skill and ability, but also in terms of their attitudes and intentions. In workmanship we see both the communication of competence and, to use Kenneth Burke's phrase, the "dancing of an attitude"—an elaborate and carefully crafted performance of identity, experience, and values.[8] Taking my cue from the carvers, I looked to the expressive dimension of skill—to the ways in which Roger and Vincent communicated shared ideas, personal creativity, and cultural experience through workmanship.[9] I sought to understand the craft of stone carving from the perspective of the carvers. What did they know and value? How did they perceive themselves and their art? What were the underlying skills and aesthetic attitudes, the notions of beauty and excellence that shaped and gave meaning to their work?

Memory and tradition are critical factors in workmanship—as influential on the carvers' actions as events in the present (Glassie 1976:57). Folklorist Henry Glassie argues that in the quest for cultural meaning "what matters is not what chances to surround performance in the world, but what effectively surrounds performance in the mind and influences the creation of texts. . . . Learning what the artists know, learning their history and culture and environment, is one way to reconstruct invisible associations, to pump blood into dry texts" (Glassie 1982:521).

Tradition is an "actively shaping force," writes Raymond Williams, "powerfully operative in the process of social and cultural definition and identification" (Williams 1977:115). A dynamic and selective process, it has a strong incorporating power, bringing forward valued aspects of the past to serve in the present and shaping deeply felt human values into meaningful expressive forms.[10] For Roger Morigi and Vincent Palumbo, tradition played a critical role in the acquisition of skills and values, shaping their attitudes toward work, informing the way they defined and identified themselves, guiding the way they performed their craft.

Born and trained in Italy, Roger and Vincent were heirs to the accumulated knowledge of generations of stone workers in their families and local communities. "I was born into the stone," said Vincent. "I never had any concept to do anything else. I'm a descendant of that trade." When I asked Roger how he started in the trade, he replied, "It's got a lot to do with the section where you come from. Where I come from in the northern part of Italy, we have a lot of quarries, stone quarries. The main industry was stone, and most of the children would go for that. And another reason, the father would be in the stone business, and the children would follow the stone business. They would follow in their father's footsteps."

A fifth-generation stone carver, Vincent grew up steeped in the trade. Learning the craft came with being in the family; it was an integral part of everyday life and experience. "How I learn, I'm growing," he said. "I come from generations. My father was a stone carver. My grandfather was a stonecutter. So practically there was no apprenticeship for me. I was growing in the trade."

Vincent was nourished by a constant flow of ideas and talk about work; his education in the craft began, and continued to take place, in the home, in the discourse of daily life. "When you come from a traditional family," he said, "you learn from the talking. What happened to me, we was in that trade. We was talking about work anytime; at breakfast, dinner, supper, most of the subject was work. Think about this stone, how we gonna do this, who was gonna do that, we gotta use this trick. So you're growing, and you listen, and your mind, it gets drunk with all those things, and then, when it comes time, you remember."

Vincent grew up surrounded by the craft not only in the context of his own family, but also in the larger context of his local community. His home-town Molfetta, a fishing port on the Adriatic Sea in the province of Bari in southern Italy, was located near the Appian Way. There he encountered the rich material culture—Roman ruins, Romanesque churches, Renaissance villas—left behind by centuries of stone workers in his region.[11] Old forms on the land were not the only source of inspiration; there was also a vital living tradition. In Vincent's day, Molfetta was filled with men who "worked the stone." Stone formed a common bond, a unifying thread, a basis for social relationships and daily interaction. Indeed, Vincent came to see that the "stonemen" were held in high regard by their fellow townspeople—that his father and grandfather, as master craftsmen, were men of standing in the community, respected for their skill and knowledge. "In those days the men who work on stone, the stonemen, it was quite a respect," he said. "Everybody when they see on the street the stoneman, they say hello to him, they take off their hat. It was a trade that involved not the mechanical work but involved the art. Everybody knew what kind of working man was that. Some of the old men was so proud of their work. They was so precise. And everybody call him master because he was so good, so meticulous."

Inspired by his family, by the rich material legacy of the landscape, and by the long-standing occupational heritage of his local community, Vincent learned important notions of respect for good workmanship and responsibility to family tradition. He developed an occupational identity and pride in his heritage—attitudes and feelings that stayed with him and influenced him throughout his working life. "You've got to be proud," he said, "because, first thing, it's your heritage. It's been transmitted from the great-grandfather to the son and grandson. So you've got to be proud of that because, what happens, it begins to get in you. It's a part of you."

Roger Morigi's beginnings in the trade were in many ways quite similar. He was born in 1907, in Bisuschio, a village in the province of Lombardy in northern Italy that was in the heart of a major stone district. A second-generation carver, Roger also grew up immersed in the craft. Stone carving, he told me, was "in the air." As the dominant industry and economic

Outside the Palumbo family shop in Molfetta, Italy, an apprentice pulls the string of a drill for Vincent's father, Paul Palumbo, while he carves a marble statue, c. 1930.
Photograph courtesy of Vincent Palumbo

mainstay of his region, stone work touched every aspect of life in his community—molding the character of town, affecting the thoughts and actions of each generation—from the small children in school, to the young men in the workshops, to the old men on the bocce courts and in the piazzas. "Unless you left town," asserted Roger, "you worked in stone."

Reflecting on his background and training, Roger once commented that he learned to carve in "the traditional way." When I asked him what he meant, he answered in terms of the incorporating power of tradition, painting a vivid picture of the stone carving trade as an integral and sustaining part of life in his community: "What I mean by that, when we started in carving, that's all we dreamed about. That was it. You always was in the atmosphere of carving. The man who taught you, he was a carver. The man who taught you at night school, he was a carver. Then you went to all these little shops and learn. Actually, you were surrounded by it, see. And even when you, when people used to go to church, there was a plaza there, and the men would stop and blab their mouths, and that's all they used to talk about—carving. What this guy here was doing, what that guy over there was doing. You see, it was the whole atmosphere! The whole thing, you were so enthused about it. You hear all the old men talk, you listen, you try to emulate. And you say, 'Oh! I want to be just as good or better.'"

Henry Glassie notes in *Turkish Traditional Art Today* that Turkish potters speak of tradition in the same way—as an "atmosphere"; "they do not speak of passing things along, but of breathing in the air. You live in a cultural environment, and the air you breathe circulates through you to emerge in actions that are yours alone but can be called traditional because you created them out of the general experience of life in some place. Your works will be like those created by others who breathe the same air....The tradition that binds you is like the air around you, sustaining you, and life within it is comfortable and natural" (Glassie 1993:528–30).

For Roger and Vincent, to be a stone carver was to belong—to be connected to one's family, friends, and neighbors and to share common bonds of knowledge, skills, values, and heritage. Stone carving bound them to the past—to a rich tradition of craftsmanship going back generations in their families and communities—and connected them to the future through the creation of a lasting legacy in stone.

Family and community tradition played an influential role in the recruitment and training of stone carvers, but it was in the small world of the carving workshop—in close interaction with master carvers, journeymen, and apprentices—that the carvers systematically acquired their skills and knowledge, their standards of workmanship, and their aesthetic values and ideals. "The most important thing, where we learned an awful lot, we used to go to these shops when we were small—eleven, twelve years old—and there were other children there, so you compete," said Roger. "At that time, for the apprentice, it was much easier to learn because there were many jobs, many carvers," said Vincent. "So the apprentice, he goes from one place to another, and he learned all the tricks around. He had a chance to catch what was best for him, and he come up right away. That's the way a good carver comes up." As the carvers comments suggest, the skills of the trade were conveyed not by formal instruction, but by "precept and example" in the workshop (Thompson 1966:253).

"You don't teach anybody to carve," stated Roger. "You give them the fundamentals of carving, like you take a hammer and a point and you hit, you take a chisel and cut. But the main thing in carving, you *steal* carving. When I say steal, you see, like you're in the shop and there are seven or eight apprentice boys. One would be a little better than the other, and you have two or three carvers working in the same place, so you watch one, you watch the other; you steal a little bit from one, you steal a little bit from the other. Then you put it all together yourself. You develop your *own* technique."

Working side by side, in a setting in which their skills were open to the critical scrutiny and evaluation of their peers, apprentices continually measured themselves against one another, competing for the respect and recognition accorded to skill. "There was a tremendous amount of competition," stressed Roger. "When I as growing up, like I said, there were a lot of shops, and we talk, 'Hey, this man's really good.' The voice goes around. Between ourselves we knew, we respected, the one who was doing very good." The rewards for mastery were social and personal, as well as economic. Carvers admired and took pride in beautiful work.

Such competition was a key motivating factor in the acquisition of skill. "It drives you to learn," said Roger. Vincent expressed it this way: "What happens, you get in love with what you're doing because it's a challenging competition between [you and] the other apprentices. You see the other guys, how they're doing, and you start to get jealous because the other boy he might be doing better than you."

Vincent's grandfather would actively "push competition" between apprentices in an effort to instill in them the ambition to do good work. "My grandfather was some kind of character. He try to give us the strength, not the strength, but the ambition to do good work. In those days a lot of kids want to learn how to cut stone, and so it happened that we was five or six kids about twelve, thirteen, fourteen years old and trying to do different things. So my grandfather came to me, and he says, 'What the hell are you doing?' He says, 'You are the master's grandson, and you do the work worse than the other kids. Take a look at that guy; he's doing faster than you and better than you.' And so he push me to do faster and better. Then he goes to the other guy and tells him the same thing. 'Look, Vincent is doing better than you. Try and beat the grandson of the master!' And he give us that ambition to do faster and good and better. So, in other words, he push competition between us, not because he want more work from us, because we were just kids that were learning, but to do better one to the other one. That was the thing. That's the way in our life we find out to be a good carver, the best."

Vincent's story points to one of the central tensions of the trade—the need to balance production and excellence. Stone carvers are first and foremost production workers. Their craft is their livelihood, a full-time occupation. Thus, speed is a critical factor in workmanship.[12] But while speed and efficiency were highly valued, so was quality. For Roger and Vincent, to produce excellent work was to reap the respect and admiration of one's peers and neighbors, to earn a good name for one's family, and to bring honor to the shop. "It was a matter of pride," said Vincent. "Your reputation goes around, especially in a small town, you see, and people, even the town, they respect you, wherever you go. You go to the butcher, and you'd be surprised, people say, 'Oh, Master Anthony, please go in front of me.' You go to the store and everybody [says], 'How you doing?' And they take off their hat. They respect you because you earn that reputation."[13]

As apprentices, Roger and Vincent were taught to take pride in their work. "They wanted the best first," said Vincent. "In those days, if somebody wasn't good, they didn't hesitate to tell you to go clean the street." The best, the carvers soon learned, had as much to do with technical excellence as it did with artistic expression. Methods of instruction emphasized the perfection of technical form and the exactness of the work. "The most important thing in those days was to be precise," Vincent asserted. "My grandfather used to tell me, 'What's the use of you finishing this stone in one day and then I can't use it? Spend two or three days, but we can put this stone where it's supposed to go.'"

Thus Vincent and Roger began to discover the aesthetic principles that governed the way in which work was performed and evaluated. The good carver, they came to see, was one who produced quality work with speed, precision, and care; a craftsman who successfully balanced the need to "make more production" with the desire to do "the best first."

Roger Morigi and Vincent Palumbo brought these shaping principles—the respect for good workmanship and pride in their heritage, the importance of speed, accuracy, and excellence—with them to their work in the present. When Vincent carved, for example, it was his father's teachings and his vivid memories of the many years they spent working together that guided and inspired his actions. "When I was working with my father on a job," he told me, "we don't feel we were father and son, but just partners. We talk a variation of things—how to do the best. He always teach me the secrets how to give the master touch, how always he wants me—even if stone is a dead material—still he was telling me how to make that stone look like life, almost talk, look realistic . . . That was the best part. And I'm trying to do the best I can in his memory."

At Washington National Cathedral, Roger and Vincent were part of a close-knit community of workers, sharing common bonds of skill, values, and tradition. The carvers' workshop was the center of that community. It was not only the key context for work, but also for fellowship. "It was just like a family," Vincent told me. "We work and we laugh, we joke. Practically, it was not work what we was doing, it was just living, everyday living!" The workshop at the Cathedral was also the main stage for performance—a setting in which carvers assumed "accountability" for the display of technical mastery.[14] Here, work took on a strong aspect of performance, with carvers displaying their artistic competence before the ultimate critical audience—their fellow workers.[15]

At the Cathedral, stone carvers made a distinction between two different types of carving: "working the model," in which carvers carefully and exactly translated sculptors' plaster models into stone with the aid of a measuring device called a pointing machine; and "freehand carving," in which carvers could work more freely from architectural blueprints and patterns or from drawings and small maquettes to create imaginative gargoyles, grotesques, and other ornamental carvings. Methods of carving varied according to the type of carving, the kind of stone being worked, and, to a great degree, the individual techniques of the carver, each working within the traditions of craftsmanship passed down over generations in the various shops and locales where they learned their trade. "You learn the way in the particular shop where you are," declared Vincent. Irish stone carver Seamus Murphy notes of the old carvers who taught him the trade: "They had a way of carving all detail, a way they had inherited, and they would not tolerate any deviation from it" (Murphy 1966:10). John James, in his

The stone carvers' workshop, Washington National Cathedral

The stone carvers' workshop, 1980

fine study of the stone craftsmen who built Chartres Cathedral, writes that "the individual tended to remain within the mould that had formed him in his early years" (James 1982:140–41).

For stone carvers at the Cathedral, the carving process began, not with an idea in the mind of a carver, but with a design created by an architect. "The drawing is the most important thing," said Roger. "The architect makes the drawing, and you've got to go by that. You're not doing it on your own. Each stone has its own design. Each stone has to fit." The primary task of the carver, Vincent and Roger made clear, was to understand and to carry out the intentions of the designer—whether sculptor or architect. "The workman is essentially an interpreter," observes David Pye in *The Nature and Art of Workmanship,* "and any workman's prime and overruling intention is necessarily to give a good interpretation of the design" (Pye 1968:16). Roger and Vincent echoed this view. "When you work a model, you've got to pay attention to the form and get the form like the model," said Roger. "You have to put in not your idea but the idea of the sculptor. I try to understand and reproduce what is there; that's all. It didn't make any difference to me what it was; if it was upside down, but they put it like that, I'm gonna do it upside down. That's the way you like, that the way you get!"

Accuracy—in the sense of being faithful to the prototype design—was a major criterion for evaluating performance. Good carvers respect the integrity of the original text. "You have to have the ability to understand and interpret each different sculptor's style," said Roger. "You have to change your own technique to please the sculptor. I had to change my way of carving to interpret their way. And I have to reproduce *exactly* what they put there in clay. A lot of carvers let their own egos run away. They think, 'Well, I can do it better.' But that's not the idea. You've got to restrain yourself and be sure that you do what's in the model, that you copy the model to perfection."

Stone carving is characterized by what David Pye terms the "workmanship of risk."[16] For a carver striving to exactly reproduce a given form in a material that is hard and unforgiving, the danger of making costly mistakes—of breaking the stone or cutting too deeply—is a constant reality. "The sculptor with clay has the option to take off and put back," said Vincent. "The carver's got only one chance. It's got to be the right one. If he takes more than he's supposed to, he's ruined." Roger put it this way: "You can't stick the stone back like clay. You cut it one time, and that's it; it's down on the floor!" The high degree of risk inherent in their craft shaped the carvers' approaches and attitudes to their work, requiring not only great manual dexterity but also patience and care.

With the sculptor's plaster model beside him, Vincent Palumbo
uses an air hammer and tooth chisel to finish Frederick Hart's
statue of Saint Peter for the Cathedral's west facade. Palumbo
worked at Washington National Cathedral for thirty-eight years.

Stone carvers strive to perfectly translate a sculptor's model into stone; but make no mistake, they are not mere copiers. Carvers pride themselves in their ability to give life to the stone. In fact, carvers see themselves as performers, as artists engaged in the skillful act of interpretation. Vincent compared stone carving and the relationship between the sculptor and carver to a musical performance. "In other words, it's the same thing like the composer write the music. Let's say Beethoven writes a nice symphony, and it's great, but when the musicians play, if the musicians are no good, that beautiful music is worth nothing. So that's the same thing in carving. The sculptor makes a beautiful piece, but it's up to the carver to make the work on stone look really good or to ruin the thing because he doesn't know how to carve."[17] Through a carver's deep understanding of raw materials, tools, and methods, through his mastery of technique, the aesthetic potential of a work is realized.

There is a sense on the part of the carver that while the work of the sculptor is to create—to give birth to—an image in clay, the job of the carver involves not so much an act of creation as an act of resurrection, of giving new and lasting life to an image in stone. "The sculptor is the creator," said Vincent. "He creates on clay. And then when they cast on plaster is the death. And the carving is the resurrection. That's the motto of our branch of the stone business." The ultimate aim of the carver is to reveal, by chipping away all unwanted stone, the image that the sculptor created in clay, nothing more, nothing less. What matters is workmanship, the performance of skill. As Henry Glassie observes of Turkish potters, stone carvers seek not originality, but perfection.[18] In his seminal book *Primitive Art,* anthropologist Franz Boas writes, "We recognize that in cases in which a perfect technique has developed, the consciousness of the artist of having mastered great difficulties, in other words the satisfaction of the virtuoso, is a source of genuine pleasure" (Boas 1955:25). Roger and Vincent shared a deep "appreciation of the esthetic value of technical perfection" (Boas 1955:19). In Vincent's eyes, the carver's act of giving life to an image through the perfection of skill and knowledge was as important and satisfying as the sculptor's initial act of creation. "It's different credits," he said, "but they both have the same feeling good."

The form and content of a carving may belong to the sculptor, but the surface treatment, the expressive details, belong to the carver alone. The stone carver's touch is his or her signature—a mark of individuality and, for many, a sign of the attainment of the highest degree of technical and artistic perfection. "Two, three, four, five carvers can carve the same thing," explained Roger, "but every one of them would have a different touch, what we call a touch, you know, a certain technique that differentiates the one from the other one and the other one. It's just like you sign your own name." Vincent agreed. "And everyone can recognize his own style. Roger and I, we can recognize each other right away, just like that!"

"That's right," said Roger. "Like the time they was carving in Baltimore, the cathedral over there, ten or fifteen years ago. And I was over there on a Saturday with my wife, and the superintendent let us in. And I went up in the scaffold, and I told him who was working in every scaffold. I told him the name of the carver. And he said, 'But you don't work here.' I said, 'I know I don't work here, but I know. Bramanti works here. Servos works there.' And he said, 'Right! How can you tell?' And I said, 'Well I can read it. That's the handwriting right there.' You see, everybody has a certain technique. If you work with them for a while, you can pick it up. Oh yeah. You can tell—very easy. Just like handwriting."

Others speak of the distinctive style of individual carvers in similar terms. Seamus Murphy writes of his fellow Irish carvers, "they each had their own way of doing detail as individual as people's handwriting" (Murphy 1966:26). Art historian John James observes of the medieval carvers who built Chartres Cathedral: "The same hand could be seen carving in an unvarying style over very long periods of time. . . . Though the style of the period as a whole might be evolving slowly . . . among individuals there was often no change at all" (James 1982:140–41).

In addition to a personal style or touch, Roger and Vincent were quick to stress that within the basic progression of tools and steps of the process each carver has an individual technique of working the stone. "All carvers have a different way to work," said Roger, "and they have different tools they favor. You yourself, you have to decide what kind of tools you'll use for a certain thing. Another guy wouldn't use the same tools." Work technique, along with personal style, was a primary vehicle for personal expression.

An exchange between Roger and former Cathedral carver Frank Zic points to the distinctive touch of the carver and highlights the ways in which carvers continually watch, evaluate, and learn from each other's work technique.

"Technique is different one man to another," Roger said.

"In the end, I don't think there's any one carver that does the same as another carver," agreed Frank.

"Right," said Roger.

"They're all different," said Frank.

A grotesque on the Cathedral's west front depicts Vincent Palumbo, an air hammer in his hand. Photo by Robert C. Lautman

Detail of the Creation tympanum on the Cathedral's west facade, designed by Frederick Hart and carved by Vincent Palumbo with help from Patrick Plunkett, Gerald Lynch, and Walter Arnold. Photo by L. Albee

"All different."

"They all have a different style completely. Completely different style."

"Right," said Roger. "Like the time when we were carving the grotesques for the Rockefeller church on Riverside Drive—you know, the grotesques that went up on top of the door there, all the way up. And for some reason or another, the way he was touching it, his came out like that. 'Grrrh.' Wild, full of life! And mine, eh, they was all right, but they didn't have the life. I couldn't understand how the hell he does it."

"Who was doing this?" Frank asked.

"Scafaro."

"The one with chewing tobacco?"

"Yeah, one of the great carvers," said Roger. "You know, he used to come to work with eight or ten tools. If you took one tool, he had to go home because he couldn't work. So I watch him, and I see the tools he used to give a certain touch. And he went to the bathroom, and I went over and got the tools there, and I went over and touch mine like that, and that was it! And it was all broke up tools; I wouldn't use it, you know, I wouldn't use it to work, but they was the right tools for the certain thing.

"So, when he come back, he's looking all over, he's looking all over. And I forgot about that I took his tools. So when I saw him looking all over, I said, 'Oh, doggone it, Roger, you took his tools. Now he's looking for you.' So I went back and I presented them to him. I said, 'Mister Scafaro'—because at that time then, older carvers, you call them 'Mister'—I said, 'Mister Scafaro, is that what you're looking for?' And he could speak English perfect. You never thought he was Italian. You thought that he went to Oxford to learn to speak English, that's how perfect he used to speak. And he said, 'Yes.' And I explained why I took them. And he said, 'It makes my heart feel so good.' And I said, 'Why? I took your tools.' And he said, 'No, because you're so interested to see to make good work.' He said, 'Today, very few feel that way.' He said. 'To me, it make me feel good.'"

The stories that carvers tell—about learning and performing, about great masters and beautiful work, about experiences on the job and customs in the shop—are significant texts. Encapsulated in these occupational narratives are notions about correct behavior and appropriate form—attitudes, standards, and ideals that lie at the heart of who they are and what they do. They embody, as Henry Glassie writes, "the essence of right thinking."[19]

In Roger's story we see the emphasis that carvers place on ways of working the stone. We learn about the importance of knowing the right tools for the job and having the ability to use them effectively to give that "certain

Cathedral stone carvers Vincent Palumbo, Roger Morigi, Frank Zic, and Constantine Seferlis celebrate together in their workshop at Washington National Cathedral.
Photograph by Paul Wagner

touch." We see the respect given to old masters and to efforts to strive for excellence. Above all, Roger's story underscores the aesthetic criteria by which carvers evaluate each other's work. The great carver, as Roger said, is one who can give life to the stone.

"It's the small details that give a carving life," notes Vincent. "If you carve a rose, it's the color that makes it beautiful. When you do a rose on stone, you've got to give that exaggeration—what we call optical illusion—to make the rose, even though it's on stone, you gotta make that stone look like it's moving, make it look like real. And that's very difficult; not too many can give that touch on stone."

This aesthetic of realism—of striving to imitate reality and to give life to the stone—is beautifully illustrated by a traditional story, common among stone carvers, of a carver who pretends to have a terrible time carving flowers because they look so real that the bees keep landing on them. Often told as a personal experience narrative, the story has numerous variants. Vincent told the following version of the story to Roger, Frank Zic and Constantine Seferlis: "It was Constantine, Malcolm, and myself. You remember? We was carving those boss on the baptistery over there, and I was carving the flowers. I finished the flowers and all of a sudden—I was on the scaffold—I started going 'bam, bam, boom, bam!' [He waves his arms wildly.] Constantine said, 'What happened, Vince? What happened?' I said, 'The damn bees have come on my flowers!' You remember? Constantine says, 'Damn, Vincent, you make me scared. I thought you fell off the scaffold!' Next day, Malcolm, with yellow thread and black thread, he makes a bee and stick on my flower. Was good." This story serves as an emblem of the standard of perfection and realism that carvers strive to attain. To carve flowers that fool the bees is the ultimate achievement.

Though carvers have a restricted license to interpret, the great carver plays masterfully within these boundaries. Through what David Pye calls "controlled freedom in workmanship," Roger and Vincent created carvings of expressive power and life (Pye 1968:19). Working within set boundaries, they endeavored to faithfully translate a sculptor's designs into stone, but they controlled the methods. The outcome depended entirely on their intent and their skill—on their "will to excellence" (Glassie 1993:97). In the end the finished product represents what Henry Glassie calls "the enactment of values." What a stone carver beholds in a finished carving is a "picture of process" imbued with meaning, values, and associations, with memories of artistic action that go far beyond its apparent form and function.[20] "Each piece," Vincent said, "represents a part of my art, my tradition, my family."

Notes

1. I began my research with Roger Morigi and Vincent Palumbo and their coworkers at Washington National Cathedral—Frank Zic, Constantine Seferlis, John Guarente, and Patrick Plunkett—in 1978 while conducting fieldwork for the Smithsonian Institution's Festival of American Folklife.

2. John Ruskin writes of the importance of the artist's "delight in skill" in his essay "The Relation of Art to Use" (1996:141).

3. I am indebted to Henry Glassie for his insights on the meaning and value that traditional artists place on the process of creation.

4. Unless otherwise stated, all quotations from the stone carvers are from interviews I conducted during my fieldwork.

5. See Henry Glassie, "Folkloristic Study of the American Artifact: Objects and Objectives" (1983:381) and Ruth Bunzel, *The Pueblo Potter: A Study of Creative Imagination in Primitive Art* (1972:1) for illuminating discussions on the way traditional artists balance personal creativity and community tradition. I am indebted to Dell Hymes for his notion of "appropriateness." See *Foundations in Sociolinguistics: An Ethnographic Approach* (1974:94–95) and "Breakthrough into Performance" (1975a:16).

6. Stone carvers regularly engage in what Dell Hymes has termed "true performance," "the taking of responsibility for being 'on stage,' for presenting a genre under circumstances consciously open to evaluation" (1975b:352).

7. I am indebted to Henry Glassie for his concept that a completed work of art stands as an "emblem of the creative act" (1992:269) and to Robert Plant Armstrong for his concept of art as the incarnation of valued experience (1975:20).

8. See Kenneth Burke (1973:9). See Larry Gross (1973:115–41) for a discussion of the communication of competence.

9. I am indebted to Robert McCarl for his insights on the expressive dimension of work technique (1978:9).

10. I adapt words from Dell Hymes, "Folklore's Nature and the Sun's Myth" (1975b:346). "[F]olklorists believe that capacity for aesthetic experience, for shaping deeply felt values into meaningful, apposite form, is present in all communities." See also Raymond Williams's important discussion of the concept of "selective tradition" (1977:115–18).

11. Henry Glassie writes of the "handmade history book of the landscape" in *Passing the Time in Ballymenone: Culture and History of an Ulster Community* (1982:603).

12. For further discussion of the importance of speed in workmanship, see Glassie (1989:57) and Zug (1986:251).

13. For discussions about the respect and status accorded to mastery, see Sturt (1958), Murphy (1966), Thompson (1966:236–37) and Glassie (1993).

14. See Richard Bauman and Charles Briggs (1990:79). For other important theoretical writings on performance and communication, see Dell Hymes "Toward Ethnographies of Communication" (1974:3–27) and "Breakthrough into Performance" (1975a).

15. In *The Stars of Ballymenone* (2006:170), Henry Glassie notes Irish musician Peter Flanagan's belief that it is only his fellow musicians in an audience who have the knowledge and ability to truly appreciate the excellence he displays in performance.

16. For an in-depth discussion of craftsmanship as the "workmanship of risk," see David Pye (1968).

17. David Pye also makes the analogy between workmanship and musical performance in *The Nature and Art of Workmanship* (1968:4).

18. Henry Glassie, lecture on folk art presented at the Smithsonian Institution, Washington, D.C., November 11, 1990.

19. See Henry Glassie (1982:14) for an illuminating discussion of "significant texts."

20. My thoughts on the nature of the stone carving process have been greatly influenced by Henry Glassie's concept of the creation of artifacts as the "enactment of values" (1983:376–83). I am indebted to Henry Glassie for his evocative description of a finished work of art as a "picture of process."

References

Armstrong, Robert Plant. 1975. *Wellspring: On the Myth and Source of Culture.* Berkeley: University of California Press.

Bauman, Richard, and Charles Briggs. 1990. Poetics and Performance as Critical Perspectives on Language and Social Life. *Annual Review of Anthropology* 19:59–88.

Boas, Franz. 1955. *Primitive Art.* New York: Dover Press.

Bunzel, Ruth. 1972. *The Pueblo Potter: A Study of Creative Imagination in Primitive Art.* New York: Dover Press.

Burke, Kenneth. 1973. *The Philosophy of Literary Form.* Berkeley: University of California Press.

Glassie, Henry. 1976. *All Silver and No Brass: An Irish Christmas Mumming.* Bloomington: Indiana University Press.

————. 1982. *Passing the Time in Ballymenone: Culture and History of an Ulster Community.* Philadelphia: University of Pennsylvania Press.

————. 1983. Folkloristic Study of the American Artifact: Objects and Objectives. In *Handbook of American Folklore,* ed. Richard Dorson, pp. 376–83. Bloomington: Indiana University Press.

————. 1989. *The Spirit of Folk Art.* New York: Harry Abrams in association with the Museum of New Mexico, Santa Fe.

————. 1992. The Idea of Folk Art. In *Folk Art and Art Worlds,* eds. John Vlach and Simon Bronner, pp. 269–74. Logan: Utah State University Press.

————. 1993. *Turkish Traditional Art Today.* Bloomington: Indiana University Press.

————. 2006. *The Stars of Ballymenone.* Bloomington: Indiana University Press.

Gross, Larry. 1973. Art as the Communication of Competence. *Social Science Information* 12:115-41.

Hymes, Dell. 1974. *Foundations in Sociolinguistics: An Ethnographic Approach.* Philadelphia: University of Pennsylvania Press.

————. 1975a. Breakthrough into Performance. In *Folklore: Performance and Communication,* eds. Dan Ben-Amos and Kenneth S. Goldstein. The Hague: Mouton.

————. 1975b. Folklore's Nature and the Sun's Myth. *Journal of American Folklore* 88:344–69.

James, John. 1982. *Chartres: The Masons Who Built a Legend.* London and Boston: Routledge and Kegan Paul.

McCarl, Robert. 1978. Occupational Folklife: A Theoretical Hypothesis. In *Working Americans: Contemporary Approaches to Occupational Folklife,* ed. Robert Byington. Washington, D.C.: Smithsonian Institution.

Murphy, Seamus. 1966. *Stone Mad.* London: Routledge and Kegan Paul.

Pye, David. 1968. *The Nature and Art of Workmanship.* Cambridge: Cambridge University Press.

Ruskin, John. 1966. The Relation of Art to Use. In *Lectures on Art.* New York: Allworth Press.

Sturt, George. 1958. *The Wheelwright's Shop.* Cambridge: Cambridge University Press.

Thompson, E. P. 1966. *The Making of the English Working Class.* New York: Vintage Books.

Williams, Raymond. 1977. *Marxism and Literature.* Oxford: Oxford University Press.

Zug III, Charles C. 1986. *Turners and Burners: The Folk Potters of North Carolina.* Chapel Hill: University of North Carolina Press.

Cal Stewart in character,
a photograph taken in the last years of his life

The "Talking Machine Story Teller": Cal Stewart and the Remediation of Storytelling

Richard Bauman

In the galaxy of traditional singers and storytellers who have illuminated the world of folk expression, there is a select number of alpha stars who have played an especially prominent role in the work and imaginings of folklorists. From the Grimms' Frau Viehmann to Glassie's Hugh Nolan, the "star informants" and virtuoso performers have been good to think with on multiple grounds: first as copious sources of texts and especially apt personifications of what a true "folk" performer is supposed to look like, later as exemplars of individual artistry within the normative world of the collectivity, most recently as engaged partners in the dialogic construction of folkloric knowledge. Although the conferral of stardom may be grounded in the judgment of a traditional performer's own community, as it is in Glassie's Ballymenone (Glassie 2006:67–113), for the most part it is a tropic extension from celebrity in the mass media, where the star system is an engine that powers the commodity fetishism of commercial entertainment. Somewhere on the boundary between the two domains, however, are those star performers for whom the qualities of stardom in the community milieu of co-presence become a resource for stardom in the mass-mediated world of mechanical reproduction (see, e.g., Danielson 1997).

One fruitful way to approach this boundary phenomenon is to consider it as an aspect of remediation. Bolter and Grusin, the media scholars who coined the term, define remediation as "the formal logic by which new media refashion prior media forms" (Bolter and Grusin 1999:173). Certainly, the formal logic that shapes the recontextualization of a performance form from one medium to another is of fundamental importance in the remediation process. But remediation will also inevitably involve a refiguration of pragmatic factors as well, as performers adapt communicative forms and practices to the affordances, participant structures, sensory modalities, and other constitutive features of a new medium. Those factors in turn will have a formative influence on the process of symbolic construction by which stardom in one medium serves the creation of stardom in another.

As a point of entry into this broad arena of investigation, I will offer in this essay a preliminary exploration of one historical instance of the remediation of stardom, focusing on the performance career of Cal Stewart, one of the earliest stars of commercial sound recording in the United States.[1] Stewart's recorded performances in his adopted persona of Uncle Josh Weathersby of Pumpkin Center, a fictional small town in rural New England, were immensely popular from the last years of the nineteenth century through his death in 1919 and for some years thereafter.[2] What makes him especially germane to the interests of folklorists is that he identified himself throughout most of his recording career as a *storyteller*. The overwhelming majority of Cal Stewart's recorded performances as Uncle Josh are in narrative form, but for illustrative purposes in this brief essay I will focus on a single example that brings storytelling itself into relief, incorporating traditional tales from the classic American repertoire. I begin with an examination of the example itself and then broaden my scope to consider some of the larger dimensions of symbolic construction and cultural meaning surrounding Cal Stewart's career as "the talking machine story teller" (Stewart 1903:2).

"A Meeting of the Ananias Club" is a performative representation of traditional storytelling, a narrative account of a storytelling session in one of its most canonical American contexts. The country or village store was a privileged site of male sociability in rural and small town American life, a place where the men of a community could gather to exchange the news, talk politics, comment on community life and the condition of the world more generally, and tell stories (Bauman 1972). Prominent in the expressive repertoire of these male gatherings were tall tales and other forms for the exploration of the epistemological tension between reality and fabrication, truth and falsehood, verisimilitude and exaggeration. The tall tale is a narrative genre that derives its interpretive effect by being framed as true, but in which the circumstances of the narrated event are stretched by degrees to the point that they challenge or exceed the limits of credibility and rational understanding. Tall tales (and the metonymic condensations of tall tales that center on the core descriptive element) always make some claims on belief even as they exceed plausibility (Bauman 1986:78–111; Brown 1987; Thomas 1977).

A Meeting of the Ananias Club (Victor GP Disc 1476, January 24, 1907)[3]

Well, one day last summer we was all sottin' around Ezry Hoskins's grocery store,
    'n' we got to talkin' about echoes,
    an' one feller said down where he was born an' raised
    there was seven hills that sorta come together,
    an' you couldn't get out there an' talk louder'n a whisper on account of the echo,
    but a summer boarder said he wasn't afraid of any darned ol' echo that ever was created.
Well, sir, he went out there 'n' hollered just as loud as he could holler,
    an' he started an echo to goin',
    an' it hit one hill 'n' bounced off,
    'n' hit 'nother,
    'n' over onto another hill,
    an' back around till it got where it started from,
    an' hit a stone quarry,
    an' knocked off a piece o' stone an' hit that feller in the head,
    an' he didn't come to for over three hours.

[Laughs]

Well, nobody said anything for quite a spell
    'n' Jim Lawson said well, down where he was raised,
    there used to be a very peculiar echo,
    and it was funny how folks used it.
Jim said when he'd come home at night 'n wanted to get up the next mornin' at seven o'clock,
    he'd just put 'is head out the winder 'n' said, "Jim Lawson, seven o'clock, time to get up,"
    'n' he started that darned echo to goin',
    an' it didn't get around till the next mornin',
    and said that "seven o'clock, Jim Lawson, get up."

[Laughs]

Well, Ol' Deacon Witherspoon said he didn't know very much about echoes
    but he'd seen some mighty peculiar weather.

He calculated he'd seen it rain just about as hard as anybody'd ever seen it rain.
Then somebody says, "Well, Deacon, how hard did you ever see it rain?"
An' he said, "Well, one summer, down home it got to rainin'
     an' we had an old cider barrel layin' out in the yard
     had both heads out of it 'n' the bung hole up.
It rained so darn hard into that bung hole,
     water couldn't run outa both ends of the barrel fast enough that it
     swelled up and busted."

[Laughs]

Well, we thought that was pretty good for a Deacon.

Well, Ezry Hoskins said he'd never seen it rain very hard
     but he'd seen some mighty dry weather.
And somebody said, "Ezry, how dry did you ever see it get?"
He said, "Why, one time when I was livin' out in Kansas,
     it got so dry that fish a-swimmin' up the creek left a cloud 'o dust be-
     hind 'em."

[Laughs]

Well, Ruben Hendricks said he'd never seen it get very rainy nor never get
very dry
     but he calculated he'd seen as cold weather as any of 'em
     and somebody says, "Well, Ruben, how cold did you ever see it get?"
And Ruben said, "Well, one time when I was livin' down Nantucket way
one winter,
     it got so tarnation cold along about hog-killin' time
     we had a kettle o' bilin' water sottin' on the stove
     an' we sot it out of doors to cool off
     an' it froze so doggone quick the ice was hot."

[Laughs]

By gosh, that busted up the meetin'.

[Laughs]

"A Meeting of the Ananias Club" exploits two participation frameworks
commonly found in American traditional storytelling. One framework is
adapted to the performance of longer narratives, in the course of which the
narrator holds the floor for an extended period of time. The performer may
index the other participants by means of various metanarrational devices,

but audience participation is limited essentially to backchannel responses. "A Meeting of the Ananias Club" is a narrative performance of this type. Cal Stewart is the sole speaker, from beginning to end. He does make one indexical gesture toward evocation of a co-present addressee, in his use of "Well, sir," in line 7: "sir" is a conventional appellative of respect. The overall performance, though, is an extended, fluent, virtuosic, but essentially monologic production. This framework, involving a solo performer, is clearly well suited to commercial recordings, and it is the format that Stewart employed virtually throughout his recording career. I should note that very few of Stewart's recorded narratives involve what folklorists would recognize as traditional folktales.[4] In generic terms, the overwhelming majority of Stewart's stories are narratives of personal experience or accounts of humorous or otherwise reportable occurrences in Pumpkin Center. "A Meeting of the Ananias Club" exemplifies the latter type, while incorporating thematic elements from the American repertoire of tall tales.[5]

The second participation framework is more interactive and conversational, involving more turn-taking and collaborative co-production of the performance. The narrative events in which this second framework prevails are characteristically sociable encounters, that is, they are occasions on which participants come together for the pleasure of each others' company and of the interaction itself, for its own sake. An especially significant feature of such traditional storytelling is that it is richly contextualized, indexing antecedent stories and storytelling events, the characters, roles, and relationships of participants, the emergent unfolding of the event itself, and the conventionalized frameworks for participation, relating to genre, ground rules for interaction, and other like metapragmatic elements.

An account of one such storytelling session at the country store serves Stewart as a frame-tale for the representation of storytelling in its situational context in "A Meeting of the Ananias Club." In this recorded performance, Uncle Josh offers a detailed and culturally accurate representation of a sociable gathering at Ezra Hoskins's grocery store. The grocery store is the site of numerous such encounters in Pumpkin Center, bringing together the familiar cast of community residents that people Cal Stewart's recordings. In fact, Stewart was sometimes referred to in publicity materials as "The Corner Grocery Store Teller."[6] Stewart's resort, across recordings, to the same settings and dramatis personae establishes a web of intertextual relationships among the recordings that serves as a broader contextualizing framework for the individual performances.

Cal Stewart as Uncle Josh

The event proceeds in a fashion typical of such sessions: a conversational topic—here echoes—serves as a stimulus and point of departure for a tall tale, and ultimately for a chained series of tall tales, all drawn from the traditional American repertoire. Hence the title "A Meeting of the Ananias Club": Ananias was a member of the church at Jerusalem who died immediately after uttering a lie (Acts 5.5); the Ananias Club is thus a classic liars' club. The first tale, after an interval of silence that is another common feature of such events (Welsch 1972:11), prompts a second one on the same topic, told by Jim Lawson. The two echo stories set the tone and the narrative domain: extreme natural phenomena. Following Jim Lawson's story, Deacon Witherspoon links his turn to the preceding one by acknowledging the topic of echoes, disclaiming further knowledge of it, but offering a new topic construable as related, namely, torrential rain, another extreme natural phenomenon. The Deacon's suggestion that he knows something reportable about heavy rain serves as a tacit offer to relate what it is he knows, and with smooth uptake, one of the other participants asks him "Well, Deacon, how hard did you ever see it rain?" amounting to acceptance of the offer. Deacon Witherspoon then relates his whopper as an answer to the interlocutor's question. The other participants respond to the Deacon's account with a positive evaluation: "Well, we thought that was pretty good for a Deacon," a church functionary who is not supposed to lie, after all. The evaluation makes clear that these storytelling sessions at the store are performance events, occasions for the display of communicative virtuosity, subject to evaluation by an audience.

The exchange revolving around the Deacon sets the pattern for the next two rounds. The storekeeper, Ezra Hoskins, ties his tale to the Deacon's in a manner similar to the way that the Deacon related his story to Jim Lawson's: he offers topical discontinuity in regard to rain, but continuity in regard to extreme weather, with a shift to extreme dryness. Again, one of the participants accepts Ezra's tacit offer to tell about "mighty dry weather" he has seen by asking him about it, and Ezra follows with his account of fish stirring up dust as they swam upstream. And similarly with Ruben Hendricks's shift to extreme cold. Hendricks's account about the hot ice is the topper, serving as a warrant to bring the session—the meeting of the Ananias Club—to a close, in tacit acknowledgment that Hendricks's tale is the most outrageous of the lot.

Stewart's representation of a storytelling session is impressively true to the ethnographic evidence. The sequencing and turn-taking by which the event unfolds, including topical sequencing, intervals of silence, evaluative judgments of the performance, and termination all accord well with the accounts of such sessions as documented by folklorists and other firsthand observers (Bauman 1972; Thomas 1977; Welsch 1972). "A Meeting of the Ananias Club" is a metanarrative, a story about a performance event in which traditional storytelling becomes an object: the *narrated* event is a *narrative* event that took place "one day last summer" at Ezra Hoskins's store.

Uncle Josh delivers the story in his characteristic speech style: informal, vernacular, marked by stereotypically "rural" dialect forms, such as dele-tion of final "-g" from "-ing" endings, the prefix "a-" attached to the pres-ent participle, as in "a-swimmin'," the preterit form "sot" for "sat" or "set," "calculate" for "suppose," "expect," "intend," and so on. While Uncle Josh's speech displayed a few features that would have been recognizable indicators of New England dialect to those familiar with the region, he relied for the most part on thematic elements to ground the narrative in place. His overall speech style was an amalgam of phonological, lexical and grammatical ele-ments of relatively broad regional distribution in American rural vernacular speech that listeners throughout the United States would have recognized as a generalized "country" dialect, perhaps not precisely like the dialect of their own region, but with enough familiar elements to do the indexical work of establishing Uncle Josh as a quintessentially rustic figure.

If we examine the formal devices that Uncle Josh employs in recounting the meeting of the Ananias Club, we find this performance exhibits many of the common features of American storytelling—including tall tale—sessions, including prominently the following:

1. the use of "well" as an opening and subsequently as an episode marker;

2. the polysyndetic, additive chaining of narrative clauses;

3. the frequent use of quoted speech and taking on of voices as a means of characterizing *dramatis personae* and foregrounding clever, humorous, reportable talk;

4. the use of idiomatic intensifiers to amplify the remarkableness of the natural phenomena that are the focus of the tall tales, such as "darned ol' echo," "very peculiar echo," "mighty peculiar weather," "so darn hard," "mighty dry weather," "so tarnation cold," "so doggone quick." This usage is entirely consistent with the keying of tall tales, which trade in exaggeration, hyperbole, and a general stretching of the truth.

5. Uncle Josh's signature laugh, an exuberant cackle that signals the nar-rator's own amusement at the narrated event and serves as a functional substi-tute for audience response and as an episode marker, setting off the successive turns at talk in the narrated event, the tall tale session at the general store.

Our examination of "A Meeting of the Ananias Club," brief and summary though it may be, reveals Uncle Josh to us as a talented narrator, highly competent in the ways of American vernacular storytelling. He is fluent, funny, a master of conventional form, schooled in the traditional repertoire, adept at anchoring his stories in familiar discursive and situational contexts. He displays both a knowledge *of* traditional, vernacular storytelling and a knowledge of *how* to tell stories himself. We can easily see Uncle Josh as one of the stars of Pumpkin Center. But of course, Uncle Josh was not the star of anything. Pumpkin Center was a fiction, a representation of a small, rural, New England town created by Cal Stewart. Uncle Josh was likewise a creation of Stewart's imagination and artistic skill, a performative simulacrum of a traditional storyteller.

There is some evidence to suggest that Cal Stewart, like other performers on early commercial recordings (Cogswell 1984:38), was something of a star storyteller in traditional, face-to-face milieux. While we do not know much about his early life or his exposure to or experience in oral storytelling in traditional contexts, a brief autobiographical sketch, published in 1903, reels off an extensive list of work experiences that include well-documented venues of male sociability in which storytelling was a likely occurrence: riverboats, lumber camps, railroads (Stewart 1903:7–8). More explicit reference to his ability as a traditional storyteller occurs in Stewart's claim that "[I] have been a traveling salesman (could spin as many yarns as any of them)" (Stewart 1903:8). Recalling his years as a railroad man headquartered in Decatur, Illinois, Stewart casts himself as the star of the sociable gatherings in the railroad yard: "I was the principal comedian in an old box car down in the yards that served as a waiting room for the brakemen. I was leading man there during the last six years I was in Decatur."[7] In what is perhaps a more objective assessment of his early talent, a Decatur newspaper article of 1910 recalls, "When 'Happy Cal' lived in Decatur he was known among his fellow employees for his inimitable wit and his never failing good humor. . . . During the winter he used to entertain his comrades with funny stories at the old East Decatur station as they sat around the stove."[8] The internal evidence of his recorded performances certainly points convincingly to firsthand experience of traditional yarnspinning. By the evidence of Stewart's recordings in which Uncle Josh told traditional stories or recounted the storytelling of others, he was demonstrably familiar with and adept at the forms and practices of the traditional storyteller's art.

But Cal Stewart, the talking-machine storyteller, was a very different kind of performer than Uncle Josh. While he might simulate address to a co-present interlocutor or multi-party audience by the use of terms of address ("Well, sir," "you folks"), Stewart told his recorded stories not to a co-present audience, a gathered, immediate public, but to a dispersed, distant, mediated public, constituted by the distribution and circulation of his commercial recordings. Stewart, that is, created a constructed representation of the local star performer, to be conveyed primarily to audiences distanced from the kind of milieu he depicted in his recordings. In this effort, he was not unlike the folklorist, though his motivations and goals and representational epistemology may have been different. Stewart used his knowledge and ability of the traditional star performer to achieve stardom in a different sort of social, cultural, and performance milieu. What can we discover of how he achieved national stardom in the mass medium of commercial sound recording?

When Cal Stewart made his first reliably documentable Uncle Josh Weathersby recording in 1897, he was somewhere in the neighborhood of forty years old,[9] already an experienced stage performer in both dramatic and platform events. Stewart's biographers make much of his experience as an understudy to the popular actor, Denman Thompson, who played the rural Yankee character Uncle Josh Whitcomb in his enormously popular play, *The Old Homestead* (Bryan 2002:234; Gracyk 2000:333; McNutt 1981:22–27). The first notice of Stewart's budding career as a recording artist to be published in the *Phonoscope,* a trade journal devoted to the nascent recording industry,[10] observes that "Cal Stewart has been before the public for the past twenty-five years, as a character comedian and monologue artist," underscoring his extensive experience as a stage performer. While the article identifies him by reference to his established identity as a performer who objectifies and enacts a Yankee character—"a delineator of New England character" and "a representative 'Yankee' comedian"—it goes on to observe that "his Uncle Josh Weathersby records have made a decided hit," calling attention to his new medium of performance and thus marking a critical turning point in his career. A half year later, in February 1899, a full page advertisement in the *Phonoscope* once again identifies Stewart as a "delineator" of "the New England character," but the master heading of the ad is "Cal Stewart, The Yankee Story Teller," followed by the question: "Have you in your collection any of the Uncle Josh Weathersby series of stories?"[11] Here is Stewart explicitly in the guise of storyteller, in the Yankee persona of Uncle Josh, but foregrounding the collectability of the records, as durable commodified objects. Stewart's storytelling has migrated from oral tradition and face-to-face venues to the domain of mass-produced commodities, available for fetishized accumulation. The commercial appeal to accumulation was a recurrent theme in the promotion of Stewart's recordings, as, for example, in this 1909 blurb in the *Edison Phonograph Monthly*: "Thousands of Phonograph owners are acquiring a complete collection of the Uncle Josh Records, getting the new ones as fast as they appear."[12]

Stewart's fame and the popularity of the Uncle Josh recordings grew rapidly. By mid-1900, the editor of the *Phonogram,* another trade journal, could plausibly maintain that "Everybody knows Cal or ought to," as "the author of the quaint talks known to all talking machine enthusiasts as the 'Uncle Josh series.'"[13] No longer, then, is Stewart identified in terms of his theatrical roles. In two short years, his primary public identity had come to rest on his Uncle Josh recordings. And the grounding of Stewart's identity and celebrity as a performer in the phonograph and in records as his medium of performance remained a core element of his career for the remainder of his life. In newspaper advertisements, announcements, and accounts of his personal appearances, Cal Stewart is routinely characterized in relation to his phonographic celebrity. Here are some examples:

1. An article published on March 4, 1902, in the *Coshocton Daily Age,* of Coschocton, Ohio, says of Stewart "he is a pioneer of the phonograph's early days and is known in all parts of the country" (p. 1). Note that this is a mere five years after Stewart made his first known recording.

2. An announcement on November 27, 1902, in the *Fort Wayne Sentinel* of a personal appearance in Indiana later that year identifies Stewart as "the famous Yankee story teller, in his character sketch of Uncle Josh Weathersby, so well known to all lovers of the Gramophone" (n.p.).

3. A September 20, 1913, notice from the *Lincoln Daily News* of Lincoln, Nebraska, speaks of "Cal Stewart . . . who is known from coast to coast as the 'Uncle Josh' of the phonograph records," and is accompanied on the same page by an advertisement that identifies Stewart as the "man who talked in your phonograph" (p. 3).

4. An October 11, 1916, ad for a vaudeville performance in the *Stephen's Point Daily Journal,* of Stephen's Point, Wisconsin, identifies Cal Stewart as "the man who made millions laugh," "the Uncle Josh of phonograph fame," and "the man who made you Uncle Josh records for your phonograph" (p. 6). A closely similar ad on January 31, 1917, in the *Iowa Recorder,* of Greene, Iowa, suggests that these terms of identification were part of Stewart's stock publicity materials (p. 5).

It is worth noting that there was a reciprocal relationship between the trajectory of Stewart's career and the evolution of sound recording as a popular medium. Not only did the development of commercial sound recording provide Stewart with the defining basis for the realization of his performances and his career, but he was recognized as an agent of the burgeoning of the medium itself. Recall, for example, the first newspaper notice from 1902, quoted just above. Here, a scant four years after his first known records were issued, Stewart could already be identified as a pioneer of the industry, with a national reputation. Late in his career, a *Reno Evening Gazette* ad of December 2, 1918, announces his personal appearance in Reno, Nevada, claiming that Stewart was "the man who made the phonograph famous" (p. 8). Even allowing for the hyperbole of advertising and the vanity of self-promotion, the claim is not implausible. To summarize, then, Cal Stewart was clearly and decisively a man of the new communicative technology, whose celebrity was inextricably tied to the nascent mass medium of commercial sound recording. He was indeed "The Talking Machine Story Teller."

Notwithstanding the priority of sound recording in the making of Cal Stewart's celebrity, he did not at all give up live performance. Indeed, he capitalized on his popularity as a recording artist by giving performances and demonstrations all over the country, maintaining an active touring schedule to the very end of his career. These live performances provided opportunities for audiences who knew him first and primarily through his records to enjoy him in person. The recordings are the primary frame of reference; the live appearances were framed as secondary derivatives of the recorded performances. We take that relationship for granted today in popular music, but the career of Cal Stewart reveals it to us in its formative moment.

Because record-buying audiences knew Cal Stewart through his recordings, they experienced him as Uncle Josh's *voice,* as a performer to be *heard.* As the December 5, 1917, *Iowa City Citizen* frames this aural engagement, "We doubt if there was anybody in the house last night who would not have recognized Cal Stewart, the 'Uncle Josh of the Phonograph' the minute he uttered his first sentence" (p. 3). Advertisements for Stewart's shows, though, characteristically made a point of these live performances as occasions to both "see and hear" the popular performer, but they emphasize as well that this multisensory, unmediated engagement is the exception, a one-time, not to be repeated opportunity. One ad, from the November 10, 1911, *Stephen's Point Daily Journal,* proclaims, "You will never have but one chance to see and hear America's greatest rural story teller—the man who made you Uncle Josh records for your phonograph" (p. 6). Another, from the April 19, 1915, *Elyria Chronicle,* of Elyria, Ohio, suggests to readers that the show being advertised is "A treat you will never repeat seeing and hearing" (p. 4).

Iowa Recorder (Greene, Iowa),
Jan. 31, 1917, p. 5.

Advertisement for a performance
by Cal Stewart

Cal Stewart's ever-growing popularity as a recording artist and his orientation to a broad commercial public brought about a gradual shift in his public persona. While he never completely abandoned or lost his identification with New England and his image as a Yankee comedian, the regional grounding of his character gave way increasingly to a broader and more diffuse identification with American rural life at large. But from mid-career onward—say, after 1908—references to "New England" or "Yankee" fade away in favor of characterizations of Stewart as "unrivalled [in his] impersonation of country folk types," or as "the best liked and best known rural comedian of the country," or as "without peer in his creation of country humorist," and even, ultimately, as "America's greatest rural story teller."[14]

When Cal Stewart embarked upon his recording career at the turn of the twentieth century, rural life in America was the focus of intense scrutiny and critical assessment. This was a period of great change in the United States, and of public preoccupation with change, heightened by the *fin-de-siècle* reflexivity characteristic of such transitional moments. The two decades that spanned Stewart's active career as a recording artist represented a watershed period in the transformation of the American economy from predominantly agrarian to predominantly industrial, with a concomitant trend toward the industrialization and scientific rationalization of agriculture, a burgeoning of consumerism, an acceleration in rural to urban migration, and a massive increase in immigration from Eastern and Southern Europe. All of these factors challenged deeply rooted ideologies that located the founding essence of American republicanism in an agrarian way of life and identified the farmer as the quintessential American (Danbom 1979; Diner 1998; Hofstadter 1955). Within this broad arena of flux, the symbolic construction of rural America was an active and contested arena of cultural and ideological production as policy makers, reformers, economic entrepreneurs, and, of course, rural people themselves attempted to comprehend and shape the past, present, and future of agrarian life (Bowers 1974; Brown 1995; Danbom 1979; Danbom 1995:132–84; Diner 1998:102–24; Rugh 2001:181–82).

Uncle Josh's location in this cultural field is very complex, implicating an impressive array of features and factors. Constructed from its inception in the late eighteenth century as a vehicle for embodying social contrast and change, the Yankee rustic remained a durable symbolic figure into the early decades of the twentieth century. In the latter period, however, that is, in Cal Stewart's heyday, the rustic stereotype appears to have become more polarized, tending either toward benign nostalgia or burlesque ridicule. Although some of Stewart's earlier recordings cast Uncle Josh as a naïve, credulous, and burlesque bumpkin, baffled by the complexities of modern, urban life, Uncle Josh, played as a happy, sunshiny character, fell decidedly on the former side of the symbolic ledger. Stewart himself, as well as his record companies, cast Uncle Josh increasingly in a nostalgic and sentimental key. "In Uncle Josh," he suggested, "you have a . . . character chuck full of sunshine and rural simplicity." Indeed, the key throughout Stewart's career was nostalgic retrospection: notices and advertisements in newspapers and trade journals characterized Stewart's manner as "quaint," Pumpkin Center as "romantic," and the scenes depicted in the recorded stories as "old fashioned."[15] But overarching all of Uncle Josh's various alignments vis-à-vis the life of his time is his primary identity as storyteller. In Cal Stewart's construction of Uncle Josh, storytelling comes to the fore: it is emblematic of "country" life, its preeminent expressive form.

And here, I would argue, lies the primary significance of Cal Stewart's remediated stardom, from "leading man" in a sociable group of railroadmen to national celebrity as "the talking machine story teller": the promulgation of a popular image of storytelling as residual culture, a form of expression that was fated to decline with the social and cultural formations in which it was rooted. To be sure, by the time Cal Stewart came along, the casting of storytelling as a key element in a vanishing rural way of life was a long established element of modern social theory, dating back at least to the late seventeenth century (Bauman and Briggs 2003). But the writings of social theorists were produced by intellectuals for intellectuals and were based largely on the advent of modernity in Western Europe. Stewart, however, addressed a large popular audience, in terms that resonated with their own American experience. Or, more accurately, with the experience of that burgeoning population of urban, middle-class Americans.

During the first two decades of the twentieth century, the phonograph was a part of an emergent consumer culture, targeted at the urban bourgeoisie and the growing class of prosperous, mechanized farmers with sufficient money and leisure to expend on home entertainment. We may gain a sense of the demographic reach of Stewart's appeal from reminiscences of the period. Consider, for example, the report of Jim Walsh, one of the principal authorities on Stewart's career, that "a friend of mine in Decatur, Illinois, has told me that a certain outlying area there is known as 'Punkin Center,' because of the resemblance of its farm types to those in the Stewart records" (Walsh 1951b:22). Walsh's friend is reporting the view from the urban center, looking outward beyond the city line to an "outlying area," a rustic hinterland. It seems more than likely that a similar impulse would account for the several dozen other Pumpkin Centers (or Punkin Centers) that dot the American map (including two in my own state of Indiana). Another observer, from California, recalled, "We are reminded of a time we stood at a talking machine booth at a state fair and noticed that the farmers who paused invariably asked for 'Uncle Josh' selections. 'Uncle Josh' was manufactured in the city. He was the city man's idea of a farmer, a creation which the real farmer accepted as being exquisitely funny because it was so far removed from his own experience."[16] The state fair was a display event for modern, up-to-date farmers committed to the scientific improvement of agriculture, precisely the kind of farmers who considered themselves far removed from the old fashioned hicks of Pumpkin Center. Other country people found the humor of performers like Cal Stewart less amusing. Respondents to a national survey conducted by the Secretary of Agriculture in 1913–14 deplored the stereotypes that "rube" humorists purveyed to the general public. A farm woman from New York wrote that "The thing that seems to me to most need remedying is the attitude most town people have toward the farmer. He is represented either as a 'Rube' with chin whiskers and his trousers in his boots or as having several motor cars bought with his ill-gotten gains from farm products figured at the highest retail prices. One of these ideas is just as inaccurate as the other" (USDA Office of the Secretary 1915:24). A farmer from Ohio voiced a similar charge: "The farm folks are treated with contempt and ridicule. Scarcely a daily paper or periodical of any kind but caricatures and pictures the farmer as old 'Hayseed' with a make-up that is disrespectful and not true" (USDA Office of the Secretary 1915:24).

Now, consider the image of the storyteller that Cal Stewart offered to the audiences that listened to his records, a constellation of tightly integrated features that constructed the storyteller as an anachronism. I emphasize the element of *construction*. The aggregate image of the storyteller that emerges from what follows is, like all social stereotypes, grounded only partially and diffusely in empirical reality (whatever that is) and virtually every element of the stereotype has been qualified and nuanced by much critical research. And again, like all stereotypes, it is an ideological construction: positioned, interested, differentially valued, contested. Nevertheless, the principles and tenets that entered into the construction of the storyteller as a relic, both by direct attribution and by contrast with its ideological opposites, were widely held in the first two decades of the twentieth century and served as guiding principles for policy and practice.

First, Uncle Josh is a New Englander, though the Yankee component of his persona diminished—but never fully disappeared—over the course of his career. Rural New England, in Stewart's time, was widely recognized as a region in economic and demographic decline, its farms unsustainable in the modern agricultural economy and its population diminishing as the young people decamped for the city (Brown 1995; Wood 1997). The venue for Uncle Josh's storytelling is the general store, an institution also in decline, in the face of new models of retail commerce, such as mail-order, chain stores, or urban department stores (Marler 2003). The general store was the quintessential site of a form of male sociability in which storytelling was a privileged mode of communication. That form of sociability, in turn, was deeply dependent on the rhythms of rural life and upon the *gemeinschaftliche* social relations in which community members were closely familiar with each others' lives-in-common. Urban life was supposed to be different: mobile, rationalized, impersonal.

The storyteller himself, embodied in Uncle Josh, is an old codger, marked by manner and name—Uncle Josh—as belonging to a senior generation and to extended family relations; he is the uncle you left behind in the country when you moved to the city and drew your web of kinship relations inward to the nuclear family or the fictive "uncle" who was a respected elder back in your small town. He delivers his stories in a non-standard, vernacular dialect, dramatically contrastive with the standard English taught in the schools and held up as a requirement for social and economic advancement. His speech style is colorful, heightened, idiomatic, and personally distinctive, all expressive features that were likewise flattened out by standardization and disvalued by language ideologies that privileged unadorned, clear, logical, objective, propositional discourse over artistic, highly figurative, allusive, and personalized narrative.

What is especially compelling about Stewart's stardom, of course, given that it was so centrally grounded in his figuration of the old-fashioned country storyteller, is that it was equally strongly dependent upon the new medium of phonographic sound recording. New communicative technologies, such as the telephone and the phonograph, were also widely understood in Stewart's day, as now, to have a transformative effect on social life, introducing mediated, distantiated, and commodified modes of sociality that contrasted with, and to a degree, displaced, the immediacy of co-present, socially embedded, spoken interaction. Cal Stewart's star persona, the talking machine storyteller, is thus a hybrid construction: both an ultra-modern creation and a relic. He relied for his storytelling on one of the very mechanisms fated to render his favored mode of expression obsolete. But a hybrid construction is well suited to a state and a period of transition, as remediation is a necessary element of nostalgia. Stewart's media stardom prefigures the far better known rube characters of radio, film, and television, but none of them makes storytelling so central a part of the rube persona or goes so far in casting storytelling in the popular imagination as an outmoded relic of our social and cultural past. Seeming on the face of it to preserve traditional storytelling and, in the virtuosic performances of "America's best loved storyteller," to extend its reach to mass audiences, the remediation of storytelling on Cal Stewart's recordings served to intensify the conditions of its decline by casting it in the popular imagination as residual culture, at best an element of nostalgia, at worst a corny index of a historical past best left behind.

Notes

I would like to express my gratitude to Patrick Feaster, my guide in all things concerning Cal Stewart and much else in the world of early commercial sound recording.

1. For biographical information on Cal Stewart, see Bryan (2002); Feaster (2006); Gracyk (2000):332–28; McNutt (1981); Petty (1974); Walsh (1951a, 1951b, 1951c, 1951d).

2. Patrick Feaster (personal communication) points out that "at first, Stewart often presented his rube character not as a New Englander but as a New Jerseyite. He played an 'Original Jersey Farmer' . . . on the stage at Fort Wayne in 1892, and even some of his early recordings give Josh New Jersey origin . . . ." Nevertheless, the New England setting of Pumpkin Center and Uncle Josh's persona as a Yankee storyteller became solidified very early in his recording career and remained in play thereafter.

3. The original recording is accessible online, through IU ScholarWorks: "The Meeting of the Ananias Club," https://scholarworks.iu.edu/dspace/handle/2022/. In the transcriptions that follow, I have had two principal concerns in mind:

(1) I intend the transcripts to convey that they are representations of spoken language. The chief means I have employed to this end is non-standard spelling to capture features of pronunciation. I have not, however, resorted to eye-dialect.

One of the recurrent problems in transcribing oral speech, especially oral speech in non-standard, vernacular dialects, is the danger of making the speakers appear to be unsophisticated rubes. I should make explicit, then, what will be even more obvious in my paper, that those stereotypes are precisely what the *performers* are trying to convey, and if my transcriptions evoke them yet again, so much the better.

(2) I have endeavored to represent by graphological means some of the significant formal patterning principles that organize the performances. Line breaks mark breath units, intonational units, and/or syntactic structures, which are usually—though not always—mutually aligned. Indented lines mark shorter pauses. Double spaces mark episode breaks or changes of represented speaker in direct discourse.

4. I analyze another of Stewart's recordings that includes a traditional folktale in Bauman (2010).

5. Type 1920 Contest in lying (Baughman 1966:59); Motifs N520 Lies about mountains and hills (Baughman 1966:547); X1764 Absurd disregard of the nature of echoes (Baughman 1966:590); X1764(b) Echo sounds a long time after sound is made (Baughman 1966:590); X1764(ba) Bugler blows in exact direction to cause echo to return exactly 24 hours later. He is able to sleep late every other day (Baughman 1966:590); X1654.3.1(a) In hard rain, the rain goes into bunghole of barrel faster than it can run out both ends (Baughman 1966:575); X1643(d) Fish kick up dust in river during dry spell (Baughman 1966:572); X1622.3.3.1 Ice freezes so rapidly (from water or coffee) that it is still warm (Baughman 1966:564).

6. See, for example, *Daily Northwestern,* Oshkosh, WI, June 23, 1908.

7. *Daily Review,* Decatur, IL, December 14, 1902, p. 13; cited in Feaster (2006):214n.

8. *Daily Review,* Decatur, IL, April 8, 1910, p. 7; cited in Feaster (2006):214n.

9. Patrick Feaster, who has done the most exacting research on the matter, estimates that Stewart was born about 1860 (personal communication).

10. *Phonoscope* 2:7 (1898):12.

11. *Phonoscope* 3:2 (1899):6.

12. *Edison Phonograph Monthly* 7:4 (1909):19.

13. *Phonogram* 2:1 (1900):30.

14. See for example, *Edison Phonograph Monthly* 7:1 (1909):19; *Iowa City Citizen* May 10, 1917:5; *Iowa City Citizen* May 12, 1917:3; *Steven's Point Daily Journal* October 11, 1916:6.

15. See for example, *Edison Phonograph Monthly* 6:9 (1908):26; *Coshocton Daily Age* March 4, 1902:1; *Edison Phonograph Monthly* 7:1 (1909):18.

16. *Oakland Tribune,* Oakland, CA, April 2, 1926, p. 24; cited in Feaster (2006): 247n.

References

Baughman, Ernest Warren. 1966. *Type and Motif-Index of the Folktales of England and North America.* The Hague: Mouton.

Bauman, Richard. 1972. The La Have Island General Store: Sociability and Verbal Art in a Nova Scotia Community. *Journal of American Folklore* 85:330–43.

———. 1986. *Story, Performance, and Event: Contextual Studies of Oral Narrative.* Cambridge: Cambridge University Press.

———. 2010. The Remediation of Storytelling: Narrative Performance on Early Commercial Sound Recordings. *Telling Stories: Building Bridges among Language, Narrative, Identity, Interaction, Society and Culture.* Report of the Georgetown University Round Table Discussion on Languages and Linguistics,

2008. Eds. Anna De Fina and Deborah Schiffrin. Washington, D.C.: George-town University Press.

Bauman, Richard, and Charles L. Briggs. 2003. *Voices of Modernity: Language Ideologies and the Politics of Inequality.* Cambridge: Cambridge University Press.

Bolter, David and Richard Grusin. 1999. *Remediation: Understanding New Media.* Cambridge: MIT Press.

Bowers, William L. 1974. *The Country Life Movement in America, 1900–1920.* Port Washington: Kennikat Press.

Brown, Carolyn S. 1987. *The Tall Tale in American Folklore and Literature.* Knoxville: University of Tennessee Press.

Brown, Dona. 1995. *Inventing New England: Regional Tourism in the Nineteenth Century.* Washington, D.C.: Smithsonian Institution Press.

Bryan, Mark Evans. 2002. "Magnificent Barbarism": The Rube and the Performance of the Rural of the American Performance Stage, 1875–1925. Ph.D. diss., Ohio State University.

Cogswell, Robert G. 1984. Jokes in Blackface: A Discographic Folklore Study. 2 vols. Ph.D. diss., Indiana University.

Danbom, David B. 1979. *The Resisted Revolution: Urban America and the Industrialization of Agriculture, 1900–1930.* Ames: Iowa State University Press.

———. 1995. *Born in the Country: A History of Rural America.* Baltimore: Johns Hopkins University Press.

Danielson, Virginia. 1997. *"The Voice of Egypt": Umm Kulthum, Arabic Song, and Egyptian Society in the Twentieth Century.* Chicago: University of Chicago Press.

Diner, Steven J. 1998. *A Very Different Age: Americans of the Progressive Era.* New York: Hill and Wang.

Feaster, Patrick. 2006. The Man Who Made Millions Laugh. Unpublished manuscript.

Glassie, Henry. 2006. *The Stars of Ballymenone.* Bloomington: Indiana University Press.

Gracyk, Tim. 2000. *Popular American Recording Pioneers, 1895–1925.* Binghamton: Haworth Press.

Hofstadter, Richard. 1955. *The Age of Reform.* New York: Vintage.

Marler, Scott P. 2003. Country Store. In *Dictionary of American History,* ed. Stanley I. Kutler. New York: Charles Scribners' Sons.

McNutt, Randy. 1981. *Cal Stewart, Your Uncle Josh.* Fairfield: Weathervane Books.

Petty, John A. 1974. Cal Stewart: The Acoustic King of Comedy. *New Amberola Graphic* no. 11:1–7.

Rugh, Susan Sessions. 2001. *Our Common Country: Family Farming, Culture, and Community in the Nineteenth-Century Midwest.* Bloomington: Indiana University Press.

Stewart, Cal. 1903. *Uncle Josh Weathersby's Punkin Centre Stories.* Chicago: Thompson and Thomas.

Thomas, Gerald. 1977. *An Analysis of the Tall Tale Genre with Particular Reference to Philippe d'Alcripe's La Nouvelle Fabrique des Excellents Traits de Vérité.* St. John's, Newfoundland.: Department of Folklore, Memorial University of Newfoundland in association with the American Folklore Society.

United States Department of Agriculture, Office of the Secretary. 1915. *Social and Labor Needs of Farm Women.* Report No. 103. Washington, D.C.: Government Printing Office.

Walsh, Jim. 1951a. Favorite Pioneer Recording Artists: Cal Stewart I. *Hobbies* (January):20–22.

———. 1951b. Favorite Pioneer Recording Artists: Cal Stewart II. *Hobbies* (February):20–25.

———. 1951c. Favorite Pioneer Recording Artists: Cal Stewart III. *Hobbies* (March):19–23.

———. 1951d. Favorite Pioneer Recording Artists: Cal Stewart IV. *Hobbies* (April):20–24.

Welsch, Roger. 1972. *Shingling the Fog and Other Plains Lies.* Chicago: Swallow Press.

Wood, Joseph S. 1997. *The New England Village.* Baltimore: Johns Hopkins University Press.

Chief Ovia Idah, 1968
Photograph by Charles Eilers

Chief Ovia Idah: *Bricoleur* of Benin City and a Star for All Times

Philip M. Peek

Chief Ovia Idah was surely one of the most intriguing individuals of his time, or anytime. With his traditional status, individual creativity, and entrepreneurial spirit, he was a perfect focal point for the transitions the art world of Benin City, Nigeria, was experiencing in the mid-1960s. Palace upbringing, ebony carvings, Ulli Beier and Mbari/Mbayo, innovative terracotta plaques, contemporary Edo¹ painters and more—all were part of Idah's creative world of art. This essay will be an attempt to portray this exceptional artist.

As I begin to relate Idah's story, the account becomes autobiographical since I am also relating my own story, first as a Peace Corps volunteer in Nigeria and later as an academic—first recalling my experiences with Idah and then my attempts to communicate his special personality and artistry. And it is additionally autobiographical in its current context of a volume honoring an old friend and mentor.

Henry Glassie has recently written about Irish artists in *The Stars of Ballymenone* (2006), about those extraordinary folk who literally bring light to our communities, casting out their own luminescence as well as reflecting others' brilliance. Given my focus on Nigeria in the 1960s, when Idah was most active, this imagery also recalls one of my favorite literary works from the important Niger River market center of Onitsha: *The Adventures of the Four Stars* (c. 1970) by J. A. Okeke Anyichie, an extraordinary tale of the "radical stars" and the exciting life of Lagos youth just after Independence. As the author declares: "Once a star, always a star!" Indeed, whether in Nigeria or Ireland, "all them brilliant men all be wild" (Glassie 2006:110).

93

Idah's quiet smile and calm demeanor belied his constant energy and his infectious aesthetic eye. He was, as are great artists everywhere, "adrift in imagination" (Glassie 2006:III).

Several years ago I tried to capture Idah's persona by describing him via an adaptation of Lévi-Strauss's discussion, in *The Savage Mind,* of the *bricoleur,* the artisan handyman, one who uses devious means to accomplish diverse tasks and engages in purposeful yet unanticipated behavior. The *bricoleur* is never subordinate to materials or tools and maintains a "heterogeneous repertoire" from which to select whatever is necessary to accomplish the task at hand, to express the vision currently in mind.

African artists are continually working between complementary realms: it is they who are the interpreters between this world and that of the ancestors and deities; it is they who maintain a "moving equilibrium"—a flexible balance—between present and past, culture change and continuity; it is they who transform private visions into public terms. Indeed, artists can be seen as the embodiment of cultural mediation, as they have been given permission to determine and interpret the appropriate communication codes within the culture; thus, as translators, they occupy the loci of communication between worlds and among individuals (Peek 1985:54).

In a passage from *The Potter's Art,* Glassie takes us further along this path: "It is good to be a potter. At work, the potter manages the transformation of nature, building culture while fulfilling the self, serving society, and patching the world together with pieces of clay that connect the past with the present, the useful with the beautiful, the material with the spiritual" (1999:116).

The reference to clay is highly appropriate here given Idah's expertise in working with terracotta, but we will not yet turn to his works of art. On one hand we seek in such studies of *bricoleurs,* of artisans, to provide biographies, personal records and insight into those individual lives which give us so much. On the other hand we seek what Warren d'Azevedo terms "the loci of artistry": "The problem, rather than one of 'biography,' however is essentially one of identifying a type of individual behavior and a type of social action that can be designated as the loci of artistry" (1975:6).

What has always intrigued me is that, while artists are clearly central to any society, they are very often marginal. In West Africa there are even artisan castes which, in a sense, serve to exclude from the larger society the artist whom all still consider absolutely essential to social interaction and the proper expression of cultural values. Intriguingly, their liminality ensures their centrality. Again, we are reminded of commonalities here as Glassie speaks of Ballymenone's "stars": "Like artists everywhere, they stood aside, nearly outside, and used their creations to gain a central place in society" (2006:111). Just as artists challenge social categories while they uphold them in their artistic creations, they mediate in another manner—they can cross time zones. While this will be a major theme as we turn to Idah's life and works, it seems to be yet another generality about artists everywhere. Glassie has observed about Acoma potters of New Mexico: "At the same time, like traditional artists throughout the world, they have stepped out of the rush for modernity and returned reverently to ideas of the past" (1999:54). But these uses of the past are not rote repetitions nor blind following of tradition. They are, as we return to Lévi-Strauss's ideas, "new arrangements of old ideas" (Peek 1985). Thus, while we will now focus on Idah and a life well lived, as per the cliché, we will also be documenting the "loci of artistry," illustrating the "how" of artistry while recording the "what" and struggling to express the "why" of such a star's brilliance.

Idah's Personal History

Although Idah was a true individual, his history is very much embedded in the royal court life of Benin City.[2] The still vibrant dynasty ruling Benin traces its origins back to the twelfth century and at its height in the fifteenth century the Benin Empire controlled much of southern Nigeria. The Oba or king of Benin may rule over less territory today but he still has a complex court system to govern. Benin City was known to European explorers and traders from the sixteenth century, but it was not until the 1897 British Punitive Expedition that the extraordinary bronzes of the Oba's palace were recognized in Europe. These beautifully cast plaques and commemorative heads were produced under the control of the court; in fact, the artisan guilds responsible for the bronzes and ivory carvings considered themselves to be servants of the Oba. The main guild was Igbesanmwan whose members produced the major ceremonial carvings for the palace. The Omada, another group of palace artisans, were primarily royal pages, but they also carved decorative and more utilitarian items. They were permitted to be more innovative than the Igbesanmwan (Ben-Amos 1976).

Born in 1908, Idah was taken to the Oba's palace when he was seven years old. Given bronze anklets to mark his position as an *omada* (Ben-Amos 1975), Idah commented later: "Anybody see me, they respect me" (Dickerson 1979:47). Oba Eweka was an accomplished carver and shared his knowledge of carving in wood and ivory with the young Idah, and later taught him bronze casting (Dickerson 1979:48; see also Kennedy 1992). Idah would often recall his sleeping at the end of the Oba's bed and playing in the palace with the future Oba, Akenzua II, then only fifteen years old (Dickerson 1979:47). He began carving by the time he was eight years old, working initially on coconut shells, palm kernels, and calabashes. During this period, Idah did acquire some elementary school education. Marshall Mount was told that he exhibited his first carvings in Benin City in 1921 (personal communication 2006).

Idah was released from palace duties and moved to Lagos in 1923. He learned carpentry there and continued carving. During this time he also began to produce very innovative work in concrete, developing techniques he would later utilize in Benin City. The most important innovation at this time was that Idah began carving in ebony, the first Nigerian artist to do so. Ebony was not normally used by carvers due to its extreme density, but it was not under the restrictions of the Benin Court either. Ben-Amos also notes that as an *omada,* Idah was allowed some traditional leeway to innovate (1975; 1976). Thus, Idah was free to experiment with this "new" resource as well as the other "new" resource of concrete. Here we see Idah's initial shift in media and creative process to a different aesthetic than that which had governed him in Benin City. Working in ebony and cement, he signaled his willingness to work between local and European worlds. In fact, Idah recalled that he sold his first ebony carving to an American embassy official, Captain Robert, for one pound (personal communication, Marshall Mount, 2006). Due to this breakthrough with ebony carving, Idah came to be known as *onikaro,* "the one who came first" (Ben-Amos 1971:123). After working as a carpenter with the Public Works Department in Lagos, he was hired to teach art at King's College, the premier grammar school in Lagos. An art instructor, Kenneth Murray, who later became the Director of Antiquities and of the National Museum, was instrumental in getting Idah hired. Their relationship soured over the years, as I will elaborate upon later. Dickerson relates how fondly Idah remembered his bachelor years in Lagos when he had three motorcycles. He kept one at home, one at work, and one at the mechanic's shop (1979:48–49). He was definitely a "Radical Star" in those days!

Nevertheless, Idah eventually became a family man. His first wife died very young. Ulli and Georgina Beier recall that another wife became seriously ill and was not recovering through hospital treatment in Benin City. Idah took her from the hospital and carried her to a traditional healer far from Benin. In three weeks she was cured and they walked back home together (Ulli Beier, personal communication 2007). Eventually, Idah married several more wives and had twenty-eight children (Dickerson 1979:2). His last child was born only a few years before he passed away.

Due to a severe illness, Idah left Lagos and returned to Benin City twenty-seven years after leaving it. Once recovered from his illness, he re-entered the artistic life of the traditional court of the Oba in the regional capital of Benin City. Oba Akenzua II asked him to stay in Benin City and appointed him as a court sculptor, working not only in wood but in terracotta and ivory as well. Idah taught art at the Benin Divisional Council Secondary Modern School and later at the Benin Divisional Council Arts and Crafts School until his retirement in 1967 (Dickerson 1979:50). The Oba also appointed him to direct the Benin Carvers Cooperative (which existed under several different names; see Beier 1964 and Dickerson 1979).

Idah produced many important terracotta works for the palace of the Oba, most notably the statue of Oba Ozolua, an extraordinary warrior, and the plaques which still decorate the front of the palace over fifty years later. Here we find the creative genius of Idah at play. Building on what he had learned in Lagos, he developed a unique blend of the usual clays for terracotta sculptures with cement and laterite sand to create a reddish terracotta-like material which could survive outdoors, exposed to the heavy rains of southern Nigeria (Dickerson 1979:34). Idah's choice of Ozolua as the major figure for the front of the palace was determined when the warrior Oba appeared to him in a dream and demanded that Idah create a sculpture of him (Dickerson 1979:37). The statue remains the highlight of the front of the palace. Oba Ozolua also appears in several of the terracotta plaques on the palace walls.

Throughout the city of Benin one could find examples of Idah's artistic imagination. Among his most important works were the famous doors for the Benin Divisional Council which he carved in 1947 (Dickerson 1979:45; Beier 1964:14). In 1961, Marshall Mount photographed several other works—a concrete elephant in front of the Ministry of Social Welfare (done in 1957) and Chief Osudi's memorial (1960)—which have not been previously recorded. One of Idah's most important and innovative projects was aiding Oba Akenzua II in building the Holy Aruosa Church of Christ. This was a fascinating project in religious syncretism in which elements of Christianity and traditional Edo religion were brought together under the royal patronage of the Oba. The Church, located, ironically, on Mission Road, is still in use, and yet, as far as I know, remains an unstudied aspect of Benin City history.[3] For the Church's construction, Idah prepared molds which produced large concrete blocks impressed with a traditional

Edo decorative motif. The creation of molded blocks was a technique which Idah developed while in Lagos in the 1920s.

As chief of the Benin Carvers Guild, Idah often posed with his emblem of authority, an *ebere* sword. As is already evident, Idah was a multi-vocal specialist—on one hand he was the key traditional artist of the Oba's Court, and, on the other, a creative leader in the growing tourist art industry of Benin City and an innovator on his own. Additionally, especially in his role of introducing Europeans and Americans to both traditional and contemporary Benin, Idah was truly a cultural broker and moved easily among the various art worlds of Benin. In fact, as Dan Ben-Amos and Paula Girshick discovered, Idah proved of great aid to foreign researchers as well. I still recall spending one very long night with Dan while he recorded traditional songs at Idah's house.[4] These traditional, commercial, and entrepreneurial roles would be enough for most to establish a permanent position in the art history of Benin City, but it is in the area of his very personal arts that Idah is most significant.

His very uniqueness has raised questions among some—was Idah really such a unique character or was he only the result of a romanticizing European search for "the Artist" in the heart of Africa? Nevadomsky, also a member of that generation of Peace Corps volunteers who knew Idah in the 1960s, has suggested that "Idah's glory lies enshrined with them," with Peace Corps volunteers and other outsiders, and that, finally, Idah was "whimsical and erudite, but marginal and maverick, neither art historically mesmerizing nor locally memorable."[5] But it is clear that Idah's innovative works and independent perspectives long predated academic and foreign interest in him. Paula Girshick (1995:61) cites well-known Edo artists Festes Idehen and Felix Eboigbe as being influenced by Idah. And there is now testimony from contemporary Benin art historians that Idah did play an important role in encouraging young artists of the time (Okeke-Agulu 2007). Not only did Idah thrive as an intermediary, leading visitors around Benin City and exposing them to the arts, but in his own artistic works he brought European and African aesthetics together. Idah's sense of humor belied any manipulative attitudes towards foreigners. This was not an act for friendly Peace Corps volunteers or "art-minded" Europeans. He simply enjoyed people and art and bringing them together. He may have been a self-styled impresario of Benin City arts, but this was a role chosen out of love rather than commerce.

Idah's personal arts are his most important legacy to this day. When he returned from Lagos, he first sought to build a new house on Oba Market Road out of the old city walls that meander through the heart of this ancient

Chief Ovia Idah, Chief of the Benin Carvers Guild

The front of Idah's house

Chief Ovia Idah
Photograph by Marshall Mount

capital. While this was a bit unusual, Idah's actual intention was to build a house in the shape of an elephant or, as Dickerson records "a cave in the shape of an elephant" (1979:51). Needless to say, this concept was a bit too much for the town building council which was expecting a traditional Benin house with fluted walls, and they put a stop to his plans. Oba Akezua II came to his old friend's aid and allowed him to build his new home into the city walls. And Idah did, finally, agree to build a house which approximated a house in a European style; but, as he slyly revealed later: "I built it like an elephant inside!"

And, indeed, the interior was truly a labyrinth as one moved up and down small steps with no room on the same level as another. Actually, even before one entered Idah's magical house, there were clear indications that all was not "normal." One had to ascend a steep central stairway to enter the house seemingly on the second floor. Once atop the stairs, the elaborate porch decorations could be appreciated. Several elephants and various human figures served as a balcony railing with posts, while small bas-reliefs covered the outside walls, including a rendition of Oba Akezua's meeting with Queen Elizabeth in 1956. Entering the front door, one was immediately confronted with one's own reflection in a huge Victorian mirror.

Once inside the house, the most memorable room was the parlor, preserved only in a black and white photograph by Ulli Beier (1964:10). Many have described this extraordinary room, often providing slightly different lists of objects, or better, *objects trouvé.* Jean Kennedy described Idah's famous parlor with its supreme *bricolage:* "Inside [the house], the rooms contained a marvelous conglomeration of found items carefully assembled alongside Idah's works and those of other African artists. Idah created a kind of African Bohemia" (1992:31). Carvings and terracotta sculptures were carefully balanced on huge truck springs—one image of a woman even had a ritual Olokun pot balanced on her head. Deer antlers along with European postcards and a large calendar decorated one wall section. There were busts of Idah by Sara Dickerson and by George Idah (Idah's eldest son). Beier learned that Idah often attended auctions in Lagos of household goods of British and other expatriates when they left (1964:16). This could explain the large blue and white ceramic cooler, perched in one corner, along with several brass ash trays and pewter mugs, an old derby hat, and the gilded Victorian picture frames hanging about. There was a line of theater seats which were also from Lagos; but Idah had removed the original seats and carved more form-fitting wooden replacements (painted bright red) while retaining the art nouveau wrought–iron frames.

Idah also continued to celebrate traditional Nigerian arts by displaying Ekpo Society masks (performed in Edo villages outside of the capital) and Igbo Afikpo yam festival masks from eastern Nigeria. There was one room which seemed a virtual museum with shelves full of old and new works of art, mostly by other artists. During the 1960s, many Peace Corps volunteers visited Idah's house and museum, and, fortunately, a number shared their recollections with me. One old friend, Frank Starkweather, had noticed how many art works Idah displayed from different regions of Nigeria, so he brought him a goat mask by Chuku Okoro of Afikpo (an Igbo village group in eastern Nigeria). Later Frank happened to be going through a book on Edo masks and noticed that virtually all the horns seemed to be broken. He thought little about this until he returned to Idah's and noticed his small Afikpo mask hanging on the wall—but now the horns had been cut off, down to the stubs (personal communication 2007). Frank never found out why Idah did this, but it recalls an experience I had with Idah regarding Ekpo Society masks. When I first asked Idah to help me find "old" Edo masks, he insisted on adding his own painting decorations in bright red enamel to them since he felt they looked "too old." He seemed a bit offended when I insisted that I "wanted them that way." Luckily, I did acquire a few which he left unaltered. David Prichett, another old friend and former Peace Corps Volunteer who lived in Benin, had a similar experience with repainted Ekpo Society masks (personal communication 2007).

But Idah was not always trying to modify traditional arts. Starkweather recalls the time he brought along a copy of William Fagg's *Nigerian Images* while visiting Idah. They started thumbing through it:

> Then we got to the Benin bronzes. Idah was thunder-struck. He became very emotionally charged, unable to speak, and suddenly jumped to his feet and bolted out of the room with the book! I learned later that he had gone straight to the Oba, Akenzua II. Idah said he had taken it to the Oba, and they had gone through the Benin pages together, carefully noting the images, what was worn by whom, the iconography and all the details. Then the Oba announced that he was keeping the book as evidence of the things which the British had stolen from his grandfather! (personal communication 2007)

In one corner of the parlor stood one of his several non-working refrigerators (Peek 1985:56). When I knew him, he was fascinated by refrigerators and toy cap pistols. He always kept a tiny pistol near his bed—"for protection" he joked. The bed was also "guarded" by his painted self-portrait rising out of the bed on the wall at the head of the bed (Beier 1964:12). In addition to the fridges which were never plugged in, he had a toilet installed in the Guest House—but there was no plumbing attached.

Charles Eilers shared a wonderful story about Idah and a chandelier that typifies Idah's unique approach to the world. Idah had installed a gaudy ornate brass chandelier in one of the new apartment bedrooms, but it hung too low over the bed. Resolving the dilemma in true Idah-think fashion, Idah cut off the bottom tier of the chandelier with its elaborate scrolled strips and put it on top of his walking stick to make it look like a scepter (personal communication 2006).

The elephant, as a royal symbol of the Oba, was a life-long obsession of Idah's. While his vision of a house shaped like an elephant was never realized, he did produce a number of elephant sculptures. There was the one in front of the Ministry of Social Welfare and several on his elaborate house porch. A much larger elephant was begun in his front yard but was destroyed in order to put up apartment extensions on the main house. Idah built these for extra income. Towards the end of his life he did one last major terracotta sculpture of a life-sized elephant mauling a man. This huge multi-figured work was tucked in under one of the apartments he added to his house (see Peek 1985:58). By the time Idah had stopped adding to his amazing house, he had more than earned Ulli Beier's label of the "Nigerian Gaudi" (1964:21). He had produced a house like no other.

The house and compound were absolutely unique evolving projects with artistic creations scattered everywhere. A small terracotta plaque was stuck in the wall near the guest house. One reached the guest house along a path created by a huge python in the act of swallowing some poor fellow. Idah's front garden was extensively planted with trees and flowering shrubs—yet another unusual touch for Benin City.

The guest house, built in the mid-1960s, extended the sensibility of the main house with its various levels and additions. A curving stairway led to the main room while a ledge at the back connected to the kitchen. On the verandah, Idah added an iron ring so that Ulli and Georgina Beier could tie their monkey there when they stayed with him. In exchange for his kindness, Georgina painted a large abstract mural on its exterior wall. John Ojo aided her on the project. When the work was almost completed, Idah and an elderly guest came to see it. The elder studied her mural for a long time and then declared, "My grandmother painted like that." Later, Georgina observed, "It was a compliment of such depth, it was unimaginable. Of course, my painting was nothing like his grandmother's mural;

Carved plaque
by Chief Ovia Idah

Idah's Guesthouse decorated by Georgina Beier.
Photograph by Charles Eilers

but something must have triggered his imagination" (personal communication 2009).

My own story about Georgina's mural and Idah's response is far less profound but still of interest. One day as Idah and I admired the finished guest house now covered with Georgina's wonderful work, he asked me earnestly, "What does it mean?" I often relate this story of the "reversed" roles between "outsider" and "insider" concerning the meaning of art. It seems we all seek to find special meaning in others' arts.

In addition to the guest house, another building appeared in Idah's compound at about the same time: the Olokun Gallery. Olokun, the "god of the sea," is one of the most important deities in the Edo pantheon, so it was appropriate to honor Olokun with an art gallery. As well, Idah often displayed intricate Olokun pots made by an exceptional potter whose name I am still trying to recover. This gallery was also associated with the Mbari Mbayo art movement which sought to bring all Nigerian artists together. Ulli Beier, its major originating force, had encouraged Idah to allow this gallery to be built on his property. The Olokun Gallery was opened, as Beier recalls, on December 4, 1965, by Oba Akenzua II with an initial exhibition of young artists from the then Midwestern Region of Nigeria. The second exhibition was of works by Colette Omogbai, an artist from the Zaria group. It was opened by the Obi of Agbor on January 29, 1966 (Ulli Beier, personal communication 2007). Eventually the Department of Extra Mural Education took over sponsorship of the Gallery.

Idah had always promoted the arts of Benin City artists, whether through the Carvers' Guild or through his own shop, so hosting the Olokun Gallery was a logical extension of his patronage. He welcomed the opportunity for contemporary artists from Benin City to exhibit their works, but he once confided to me that he wished that they had come to greet him. Although a real iconoclast in many ways, Idah still honored tradition and felt that as a chief he was owed such respect. The Gallery's presentation of other artists' works was simply a continuation of what Idah had practiced for years by decorating his own rooms with many and varied artistic works from everywhere. At one point, I even brought in a few carvings by Eture Egbedi, an Isoko carver I had come to know who lived in the town where I taught, to exhibit in the Gallery (Peek 1985).[6] We became a bit distressed because all we could find for a display area for this premier showing of Isoko art was an old bench; but Idah never hesitated.

Sadly, none of these extraordinary endeavors in support of the arts brought sufficient income to Idah and he had to destroy his wonderful balconies in order to attach two small apartments to the front of his house for additional income. And, in the end, it was this eternal struggle for money that destroyed his wondrous home all together. Idah's sons, shortly after his death, decided to sell this valuable property. Although it was listed as a national monument, the magical house and sculptures of Idah were torn down in 1981 (Nevadomsky 1986). The loss of this Nigerian national treasure is truly tragic.

There was certainly never a question about Idah's self-awareness. Although a very quiet person, even seemingly shy, Idah was very self-confident. He was unusually comfortable with himself—he never had to prove anything. He was simply himself: unique. Perhaps Idah's charm and self-awareness were not expected given the still prominent stereotypes about self-styled European "Bohemian" artists and anonymous African "folk" artists. He proudly proclaimed himself and his creations. Different? Yes, but still within the framework of Benin City and its heavy court tradition as well as its growing tourist arts industry. This combination of influences is why I find the concept of *bricoleur* so appropriate: new arrangements of old ideas, devious means to accomplish diverse tasks, heterogeneous repertoire.

Not many artists, especially in Africa, create statues of themselves in their front yards so one can understand the questioning of Idah's motivations in this regard. In Ulli Beier's small book on Nigerian art and artists of the 1960s, there is a photograph of one of the animal and human groupings on the porch of Idah's house with a small sign: "Idah The Young Lion The Artist" leaning against a cement elephant. Charles Eilers took an excellent photograph of Chief Idah late in his life in which we notice written on the wall behind him: "The Great Idah." Despite his quiet smile and sad face, no shy retiring fellow this artist.

He was unique, but so are artists everywhere. My favorite story related to the topic of artist's recognition revolves around a terracotta plaque Idah made for me. Actually Idah had become very well-known for his terracotta and wooden plaques, a format he had first created for the front of the Oba's palace. He was preparing a small wooden box to protect the plaque. After he had finished the box, I joked that he had forgotten to sign the art work. We laughed about that because, of course, no one in Benin City could mistake his work for that of another; but, in a bow to Western tradition, he signed the box. The idea of literally signing works of art may be a "sign" of Western art traditions, but the "authorship" of works of art throughout the world is seldom in question locally. Glassie has elaborated on this point: "Works of art are never anonymous inside the community; they become anonymous when they wander. Within the community there is no need for signature" (1989:184).

In this context, the photograph of one of Idah's terracotta plaques on the Smithsonian Institution's official videotape box takes on even more significance. Surely, only a tiny fraction of the few who would even look at this container would recognize Idah's work. But to give an "unknown" artist such recognition, by placing it among artistic images from all over the world, would have delighted Idah I am sure. And he did have a wonderful sense of humor. As well, he was, in a sense, fearless—a radical star! Although he was deeply rooted in Benin City, I always felt he could have survived anywhere, even at the Smithsonian Institution!

While praising Turkish ceramic artists, Glassie offers the following which easily applies to Idah:

> That is one purpose of art. It brings confidence to its creators. Those who make things know who they are. They have been tested and found competent. Then art exhibits value. The artist's creations act in the world, embodying the complexities of culture and shaping relations among people, between people and the environment, between people and the forces that rule creation. (1999:89)

As noted initially, Idah came to the arts through his appointment as a palace page; it was not an inherited or even a personal choice. He never mentioned any other artists in his family although several of his sons practiced sculpture for a while. His senior son, George Idah, did some sculpture but went on to become an engineer. Omere was the most prolific sculptor in the family in the late 1960s (and I still have several of his carvings). Samuel, who worked for a time with the United States Information Service in Benin City, may have done some sculptures as well. Dickerson illustrates works by other sons, Henshaw and Thomas (1979:68–69). Joe Nevadomsky has rescued several carvings from the Idah family, but their exact authorship is unclear. What is clear is that Idah was a singular phenomenon in this regard, not coming out of an artistic family, nor creating any artistic descendents. In fact, as already noted, the members of the family never really supported their father's activities and sold the land to "developers" of a new apartment complex. Ironically, one of Idah's grandsons was recently appointed chair of the Benin City Traditional Council.

I have many vivid memories of Idah and his fabulous house—I even have acoustic memories. Next door was a slaughter house for pigs—a sound one never forgets. More pleasing were the cries throughout the night of the "watch nights" who patrolled the old city and called out periodically to signal that all was well. One always wishes for clearer memories of those wandering worldly conversations over bottles of Star beer but, alas, we never know to record such occasions until years later. My final contact with Idah was depressing. When I was leaving Nigeria in 1966, I gifted Idah several Yoruba bronzes—we bid farewell, and I was off to Lagos. But when I reached the Department of Antiquities to get my collection cleared, Kenneth Murray remembered—somehow—the two Yoruba bronzes and demanded that I retrieve them from Idah or he would confiscate my whole collection. With a day left before my flight to Cairo, I rushed back to Benin City and sadly explained to Idah what had happened. "That's all right, I know that man." That was the last time I saw Idah. A few months later, after I arrived back in the United States, I sent him a new chisel from Berkeley but I never learned if he received it.

Ulli and Georgina Beier shared the account of their last meeting with Idah. Their decision to leave Nigeria in December 1966, for New Guinea was made abruptly and they had no time to return to Benin City from their house in Oshogbo to bid Idah farewell.

> Idah arrived in Oshogbo. He had dreamt we were leaving. The people in our house told him that we were going to spend the night in Ibadan. After dinner at the West End Café, we arrived at the University of Ibadan; it was dark. As we entered Frank Speed's house, a figure emerged from the bushes and said to Georgina: "I greet you for your journey and for your child." Nobody else knew at the time that Georgina was pregnant! We celebrated that evening together! (Ulli Beier, personal communication 2007)

Chief Ovia Idah died suddenly on September 27, 1968, at exactly 3:45 A.M., as reported to Ulli Beier by Samuel Idah (personal communication 2007). His coffin was designed by the Carvers Guild and made of iroko wood which marked Idah's importance. Funeral ceremonies were held at the Holy Aruosa Church of Christ. An elder Benin chief declared that "Idah's name will be remembered a thousand years in Benin" (Dickerson 1979:96). Indeed, a few years ago at a conference on African arts, several Nigerian art historians spoke of Idah's impact on artists of all types in Benin City.

Idah was the *bricoleur extrodinaire*. Anything and everything was art to him. Once while he and I were walking down a street in Benin City, he stopped and picked up a small stone he felt was striking and gave it to me. On another day he spotted a bracelet my future wife Pat was wearing: "Oh, here, let me make that beautiful for you!" He took the bracelet and a few weeks later, a wonderfully carved bracelet was returned to her. Sadly, that bracelet was lost, but we have never lost our vivid memories of that extraordinary artist.

As Ulli Beier recently wrote:

> Frankly, I believe that Idah's life-style was his greatest art work. His original architectural ideas; his assembly and juxtaposition of classical Benin art, with his own works and the European curios he had collected in Lagos. The new techniques he invented: designs on the cement blocks he used to build a church; his mud/cement reliefs, etc. And the way he made all these ideas and objects live together harmoniously. (personal communication 2007)

Again, we find apt words from Lévi-Strauss as he discusses the concept of the *bricoleur:*

> Further, the *'bricoleur'* also, indeed principally, derives his poetry from the fact that he does not confine himself to accomplishment and execution: he 'speaks' not only *with* things, as we have already seen, but also through the medium of things: giving an account of his personality and life by the choices he makes between limited possibilities. The *'bricoleur'* may not ever complete his purpose but he always puts something of himself into it. (1966:21)

The metaphor of stars, be they radical or not, remains an apt designation for Idah, for it is in such a personality's brilliance that all of us see a bit more clearly. And it is in our memories of these stars that their brilliance continues to shine, keeping the darkness at bay.

Chief Ovia Idah joyously occupied his own world full of art and he invited all to join him in it. Some of us were lucky enough to be able to do just that.

Notes

1. Terminology can become a bit confusing here: Benin City is the capital of the Benin Kingdom; Edo identifies an ethnic group encompassing Benin City as well as the language spoken in Benin and throughout the Kingdom.

2. My brief summary of Idah's life draws on several basic sources, primary of which is the biography by Sara Hollis (then Sara Jane Hollis Dickerson, 1979). Ulli Beier wrote of Idah in several publications (1960, 1961, 1964) as did Paula

Girshick (then Paula Ben-Amos, 1971, 1975, 1976, 1995), Jean Kennedy (1992), who draws heavily on Dickerson, and my own work (1985). I have also benefited from a number of personal communications from former Peace Corps volunteers and Marshall Mount, who taught in Benin City in the early 1960s. An earlier draft of this essay was presented in the panel on the "Art of Benin in the Twentieth and Twenty-first Centuries" at the Fourteenth Triennial Symposium on African Art, University of Florida, March 28–April 1, 2007.

3. There is information on the Holy Aruosa Church at http://www.greatbenin. org/Aruosa.html along with other entries from the Institute of Benin Studies.

4. My recollections of that time are in "Who Was That White Man?" (Peek 1975).

5. As for the formal recognition of Idah by his contemporaries, a poster from those days has Idah posed as if working on a terracotta sculpture with a hammer and chisel! Maybe no artist is ever properly recognized.

6. Because he knew so many Peace Corps Volunteers, Idah often confused us; so he gave me the nickname of "Isoko Man."

References

Anyichie, J. A. Okeke. c. 1970. *The Adventures of the Four Stars*. Onitsha: All Star Printers.

Beier, Ulli. 1960. *Art in Nigeria 1960*. Cambridge: Cambridge University Press.

———. 1961. Contemporary Nigerian Art. *Nigeria Magazine* 68:27–51.

———. 1964. Idah—An Original Bini Artist. *Nigeria Magazine* 80:4–16.

Ben-Amos, Paula Girshick. 1971. Social Change in the Organization of Wood-carving in Benin City. Ph.D. diss., Indiana University.

———. 1975. Professionals and Amateurs in Benin Court Carving. In *African Images*, eds. D. F. McCall and E. G. Bay, pp. 170–89. New York: African.

———. 1976. 'A La Recherche du Temps Perdu': On Being an Ebony-Carver in Benin. In *Ethnic and Tourist Arts*, ed. Nelson H. H. Graburn, pp. 320–33. Berkeley: University of California.

———. 1995. *The Art of Benin*. Rev. ed. Washington, D.C.: Smithsonian Institution Press.

D'Azevedo, Warren L. 1975. Introduction. In *The Traditional Artist in African Societies*, ed. W. L. D'Azevedo, pp. 1–15. Bloomington: Indiana University Press.

Dickerson, Sara Jane Hollis. 1979. Benin Artist Idah: Court Art and Personal Style. *Interdisciplinary Studies*, 2(2). New Orleans: Southern University.

Glassie, Henry. 1989. *The Spirit of Folk Art*. New York: Harry N. Abrams.

———. 1999. *The Potter's Art*. Bloomington: Indiana University Press.

———. 2006. *The Stars of Ballymenone*. Bloomington: Indiana University Press.

Kennedy, Jean. 1992. *New Currents, Ancient Rivers: Contemporary African Artists in a Generation of Change*. Washington, D.C.: Smithsonian Institution Press.

Lévi-Strauss, Claude. 1966. *The Savage Mind.* Chicago: University of Chicago Press.

Nevadomsky, Joseph. 1986. The House that Idah Built. *African Arts* 19:2, 8.

———. 2007. Comments for the panels on "The Art of Benin in the Twentieth and Twenty-First Centuries," Fourteenth Triennial Symposium on African Art, University of Florida, March 28–April 1.

Okeke-Agulu, Chika. 2007. The Burden of Tradition: Modern Edo Artists and the Legacy of 'Benin Art'. Fourteenth Triennial Symposium on African Art, University of Florida, March 28–April 1.

Peek, Philip M. 1975. Who Was That White Man? *Folklore Forum* 14:47–48.

———. 1985. Ovia Idah and Eture Egbedi: Traditional Nigerian Artists. *African Arts* 28(2):54–59, 102.

———. 2007. Chief Ovia Idah and Benin City Art of the 1960s. Fourteenth Triennial Symposium on African Art, University of Florida, Gainesville, March 28–April 1.

Harold A. Burnham at home

Place Matters: A Wooden Boat Builder in the Twenty-First Century

Maggie Holtzberg

> It is hard to imagine a place on earth where shipbuilding is more deeply embroidered into the fabric of the community.
>
> —Harold A. Burnham

Henry Glassie's humanistic approach to the study of material culture and the role the individual artist plays in shaping tradition has had a profound effect on the field of folklore. Having spent a lifetime studying what art is to people in "other" cultures, Glassie observes that, in shaping their own styles, all cultures come to emphasize certain media. Spend enough time with people and they will lead you to the "robust centers of culture" where certain material forms or performances are imbued with beauty and power (Glassie 1989:36).

In Massachusetts, where successive waves of immigration have increasingly diversified the population, one finds many such centers of culture. Patronize Boston's Irish American neighborhoods and you will discover that creative genius thrives in the rhythmic drive and melodic variation of reels and jigs played at local pubs and dance halls. Fieldwork in the Polish and Ukrainian communities of the Connecticut River Valley leads to individuals who have mastered the art of *pysanki* (egg decorating) and *wycinanki* (cut paper). In parts of Boston and Springfield, one discovers that communities originally from the West Indies islands of Haiti, Trinidad, and Tobago spend months each year making *mas,* enormous sequined and feathered costumes for the annual Caribbean carnival. Within the Chinese community of Greater Boston, you quickly discern a deep appreciation for antiquity, which takes physical form in the graceful practice of calligraphy and the miniaturist art of seal carving. Irish reels, Polish *pysanky,* Caribbean carnival, and Chinese calligraphy are "robust centers of culture" that attract society's most gifted individuals or "stars."

Glassie introduced the concept of stars in his book *Passing the Time in Ballymenone,* an eloquently written ethnography that captures a way of life in a Northern Irish community during the tumultuous Troubles of the 1970s (Glassie 1982). Working in a rural place in Ireland, in which violence and deprivation were daily realities, Glassie discovered the social importance of verbally brilliant individuals. The "stars" of this community were modest farming folk with extraordinary prowess—tellers of tales, poets, and singers whose wit and wisdom delighted listeners while keeping historical truths alive. Glassie returned repeatedly over the next decade. By the time he gave us *The Stars of Ballymenone* in 2006, life in this southwest corner of Fermanagh had changed dramatically. By book's end, learning that this generation of stars has been extinguished, we realize the magnitude of what has been lost.

It is no wonder that within Massachusetts's coastal communities, boat building would attract particularly gifted individuals. The sea is integral to the history of Massachusetts. An abundance of fish has drawn people to our coastline for centuries. Immigrants from Europe, Asia, Africa, and other parts of North America have made their life and work by the sea: fishing, whaling, building boats, or passing the time through art and craft— carving scrimshaw on whale teeth, tying knots, or building ship models. Fishermen stake their lives on the skills of boat builders. "No other artisans . . . are entrusted with more of their community's faith than shipwrights."[1]

Although the maritime industry has declined in recent decades, it remains an important part of Massachusetts's economy and more importantly, its character. Today, more people flock to the seashore for leisure and heritage tourism than for employment. Regardless of changes in what the sea means to people in and outside Massachusetts, it continues to inspire skilled traditional artists.

If boatbuilding on Massachusetts's north shore qualifies as a robust center of culture, what are the criteria for being a star? It is not merely an individual's adherence to traditional techniques, repertoire, and attitudes, nor excellence in his or her artistry, although these things matter. The stellar artist's work exists in the context of community. Genuine star status is revealed in how someone is regarded by one's peers, such as by other practitioners. One has only to think of the saying, "He's a musician's musician." An insider can discern star quality in a way that an outsider may not. This essay focuses on wooden boat building's relatively young "star," Harold A.

Lane's Cove on a cold winter's day, Lanesville, Massachusetts

Grave marker in Fishermen's Rest, Beechbrook Cemetery, West Gloucester, Massachusetts

Harold A. Burnham wielding an adze

The Burnham shipyard and house, Essex, Massachusetts

Burnham, who, despite his youth (he was born in 1967), has earned a place in history as a master boat designer and builder. A continuum of individuals from knowledgeable insiders to enthusiastic spectators hold Burnham in high regard: fellow boat builders, clients, the Coast Guard, the publishers of *Wooden Boat* magazine, maritime museum curators, folklorists, journalists, and tourists all help define Burnham as a star.

This is the story of a happy confluence of place, tradition, family legacy, and individual skill. The Burnham shipyard is located on the banks of a tidal river where, for eleven generations, members of the same family have built and launched wooden vessels.[2] Harold A. Burnham encapsulates something profoundly central to the founding identity of his hometown of Essex: townspeople have been building ships here since the 1630s. By the late 1660s, shipbuilding had become an enormously important part of the town's economy and remained so for two centuries. In the 1850s, Essex supported fifteen shipyards and launched more than fifty vessels a year. The majority of these boats were built for the Gloucester fishing fleet—vessels that plied the North Atlantic for cod and halibut.

By the late 1940s, however, the shipbuilding industry in Essex collapsed. Wartime manufacture of steel ships had become so efficient that wooden vessels were soon rendered obsolete. Economically, Essex turned away from shipbuilding and toward clams, restaurants, and tourism. As a consequence, traditional woodworking skills largely fell out of use; most people assumed the town's active shipbuilding was over.

For the next fifty years, however, a few Essex shipwrights continued to build smaller vessels like lobster boats and pleasure crafts. It was in these small shops that traditional shipbuilding methods were kept alive. Harold A. Burnham spent his youth watching and learning from these shipwrights, including his own father who, despite his day job as an engineer in Boston, spent weekends and evenings in the boatyard. "When I was growing up, if I wanted to be with my father—if I wanted to see him at all—I had to go over and build boats with him" (Murphy 1998:77).

Harold did not set out to be a boat builder. He chose to go to sea by way of the Massachusetts Maritime Academy. After graduating, he spent five years as an officer on some of the nation's largest commercial vessels. Between trips, Harold built a small New England lobstering smack[3] and started a charter business. A turning point came in 1996 when Captain Tom Ellis commissioned him to build the *Thomas E. Lannon,* a Fredonia style (Grand Banks) fishing schooner. Ellis wanted to give the public a feeling for what it was like to sail on the great Essex schooners. Although Harold was originally hired as the builder, he soon became the designer by default. It was a huge undertaking. She was to be the first sawn-frame, trunnel (tree nail)-fastened vessel built along the Essex riverbank in nearly fifty years. Harold sought the advice of family, naval architects, historians, engineers, model makers, and local shipbuilding elders like Dana Story, whose collection of historic photographs was invaluable in helping Harold learn about long-dormant Essex shipbuilding techniques.[4] From the start, Harold A. Burnham was aware that the building of the Lannon belonged in some sense, to the larger community. He moved his shipyard across a thirty-foot-wide creek onto a piece of land that had been set aside by the town fathers in 1668 "to the inhabitants of Ipswich (now Essex) for a yard to build vessels and employ workmen to that end."[5] Harold writes, "Given the vessel's size, visibility, central location, and close proximity to the Essex Shipbuilding Museum, she drew thousands of people to witness her construction. For the most part, these visitors were not merely tourists and curiosity seekers, but people who were genuinely interested in learning about or remembering the town the way it had been . . . . Many younger people were witnessing for the first time why their town's [sports] teams were called 'The Shipbuilders' and why the town seal was made from a photograph of a vessel under construction on the same spot where the Lannon was being built."[6]

Since the *Thomas E. Lannon* commission, Burnham has gone on to complete *Schooner Isabella,* Chebacco boats[7] *Lewis H. Story* and *Fame,* and oversee the rebuilding of the bow on *Schooner Ernestina,* a National Historic Landmark. In all his work, Burnham holds true to traditional materials and techniques. Using hand tools familiar to a nineteenth-century shipwright, he works out-of-doors through New England winters, and launches vessels the old way using wedges, grease, and gravity:

> My adze says on it, "H. A. Burnham, 11 Burnham Court" on the handle. That's not me; that's my grandfather. The adze and axe are things you still need from time to time, particularly for the dubbing [the smoothing of the frames] so that the planks seat well on them. Using hand adzes allows you to stand back and look at what you're doing. It allows you to get into places that no power tool will let you get at. (Viator 2005)

Because few wooden ships are being built these days, there are also very few suppliers of ship timber. Therefore, Harold cuts much of the timber for his boats himself. Most of the wood—white oak and locust—comes from local sources, donated by two conservation organizations: the Essex County Greenbelt Association and the Trustees for Reservations. Logs suit-

Schooner *Thomas E. Lannon* under sail during the Gloucester Schooner Race, 1997. Photo by Lew Joslyn

Framing the *Lannon*. Photo by Lew Joslyn

able for masts are towed from nearby Hog Island. To get the best use out of the natural curves of the wood, Harold not only cuts his own timber, but he also mills it. "It takes two people to run the saw," he explains. "One is the sawyer, who feeds the piece, or the futtock, and the other one is the beveller, who stands beside the saw, tilting the table to the correct bevel as the piece gets fed through. It takes a little bit of skill because . . . as one is feeding, the other has to change the bevels" (Viator 2005).

In addition to his competence as a logger and sawyer, Harold relies on his skills as a loftsman, shipwright, mechanic, plumber, electrician, spar maker, sail maker, and rigger. But without question, his skills as a mariner that make his boats uniquely seaworthy. "Sea time is invaluable. You really shouldn't be designing boats until you have ten years of sea time. You can't learn it from books. You've got to land the boat at the dock, and you've got to watch it hit, and think about what you could do differently. You've got to feel that bottom coming up from underneath you. It's a horrible feeling. And when you've hit that a few times, then you know where to put the wood or how much to put in."[8]

What might come as a surprise is that a traditionally built wooden boat is still just as functional as one with a fiberglass or steel hull. "The problem," Harold says, "is that there are so few people that know how to build them. The thing about these traditional methods is that it's an art form. It's taken thousands of years to develop this art form and for people to get to the point where they understand it and can do it effectively."[9]

One of those traditional methods is the use of half models. Rather than use computer-aided design (CAD), Burnham works with a more tactile tool, the half model. Historian and ship modeler Erik Ronnberg Jr., who painted the scrollwork on the *Lannon,* explains the use of half models in wooden boatbuilding:

> Building a half model is a real American tradition. Building up a hull in layers with the use of wooden toggles or screws so it could be taken apart and traced was invented by shipwrights who had no training in drafting. The half-model style developed in Essex shipbuilding yards. While layers are fastened together, you shape the hull. You carve it and sand it. Before you take it apart, you mark where each frame is going to go. Those marks are drawn across each layer, called a "lift." Then using a carpenter's rule, you measure those width lines (half breadth lines). The measurements are scaled up to full size and put on paper. Then you go to the mold loft floor and lay out a grid, in order to reconstruct it.[10]

To understand half models it helps to watch someone work on one, take it apart, and then use it to draw lines. An opportunity arose to do just that in an artist demonstration at the National Heritage Museum in Lexington, Massachusetts. Burnham's half model of the *Thomas E. Lannon* was on display in the "Life and Work by the Sea" section of the exhibition, "Keepers of Tradition: Art and Folk Heritage in Massachusetts."[11] On a Sunday afternoon, a nice crowd of mostly middle-aged to older males gathered to watch and hear Harold talk about half-hull models as a design tool. He explained the process of sketching the half model out on a block of wood made up of lifts. The lifts come apart and represent sections of the hull. Once the model is chiseled and sanded to perfection, you basically have your design. Or as Harold put it, "The shape of the model *is* the shape of the boat."

The next step is to take the lifts apart and used them to express a three-dimensional shape on a two-dimensional piece of paper. "If you are an accomplished boat designer or have the experience studying these lines, you can read the lines plan and know what the lines are saying." (The process is not unlike a composer reading a score and being able to hear the piece of music in her head.)

During construction, Burnham had taken the lines of schooner *Thomas E. Lannon* from this half model and then drew them full-scale on the loft floor (the loft space above the shipbuilder's shop). Then he created patterns and used them to carefully select and mark the futtock.[12] Once marked, the futtocks were cut and beveled and then assembled into heavy frames on the floor of the boat shop. When two or three frames were completed, crewmembers worked together to carry them outside. Harold describes this as a particularly satisfying step, "When you stand the frames up on the keel, you're actually watching the boat take shape in front of you." Perhaps most dramatic is the application of the planking. If the frames are the ribcage, and the keel is the backbone, it is the application of the planking, or skin, that reveals the true form of the vessel.

Working through the winter and spring, Harold and a crew of six to eight members finished construction of the *Lannon* in June 1997. Local shipbuilder Dana Story was amazed at how Harold solved problems along the way. "The boat that he built is strong. He did things that we didn't do in the old shipyard—like put mortise-and-tenon joints on the forward cant frames, a stern is not an easy thing to build; building an oval transom is the thing that separates the men from the boys. Harold figured out how to do it, and he did a splendid job" (Murphy 1998:81).

It was time to get her in the water. Harold had his hopes set on a traditional "side launch." The symbolic event marking a vessel's completion is an art in itself. The vessel is leaned over on her side, her weight transferred to a greased skidway, and, with the help of wedges, gravity, and momentum, she is allowed to slide into the water. During the nineteenth century, thousands of Essex vessels were launched this way. "As the tide rises, the vessel's blocking is split out from under her keel. With enough of her weight resting on the greased slabs, the gravity pulling her down overcomes the friction holding her back" (Burnham 2000:36). The vessel launches stern first on her keel and leans perilously to one side before entering the water with a dramatic splash. Imagine a hundred tons of oak sliding on one side over smoking grease and you can understand why owner Tom Ellis was nervous about authorizing a side launch for the *Lannon,* so he had her lowered into the water. But Harold got his opportunity to reintroduce the old Essex way of ship launching with his next commission, the *Lewis H. Story* (a Chebacco boat built for the Essex Shipbuilding Museum) and again, in 2006, with the launch of *Schooner Isabella.* Each launch has drawn a crowd of nearly three thousand people—*twice* the town's population.

Why would the launch of a wooden vessel built on the banks of the Essex River be so powerful in the twenty-first century? In a world with increasing standardization, where the makers of things (objects, music, and food) are increasingly distanced from the users of things, the appeal of direct connection is powerful. We delight in the hand-wrought object, built using some techniques that date back to biblical times. Place matters—on this very spot, for eleven generations, members of the same family have built and launched wooden vessels. Materials matter—these functional and stunning vessels are made of locally harvested trees. Commitment to local heritage matters—when Burnham built the sixty-five-foot *Lannon,* she was the first schooner launched in Essex in half a century. Though wooden schooners are no longer the fisherman's vessel of choice, Burnham's boats are economically viable; they earn their keep as passenger-carrying charters for cultural heritage tourism.

Author and historian Joseph Garland, known for bringing alive the struggles of Gloucester men at sea in the era of fishing under sail, spoke to the power of seeing the *Thomas E.Lannon* at sea:

> Living as I have on the western shore of Eastern Point for more than 40 years, and having written copiously on the subject of Gloucester's great history of fishing in the age of sail . . . I can hardly convey the emotions evoked by the sight of the *Lannon* scudding across the harbor under a full westerly with a deck load of thrilled passengers, or easing so quietly along before our gaze, just off our shorefront, silhouetted against the sunset, as my wife and I sit down for dinner, entranced.[13]

Launch of *Schooner Isabella*

Burnham has essentially revived a once dormant shipbuilding technique and, in doing so, has reconnected a town to its own shipbuilding heritage. He is more than a revivalist serving a small market of wealthy buyers who romanticize the past; he is an innovative craftsman working fully (and successfully) within the local wooden boatbuilding tradition. Dana C. Henson of Mystic Seaport notes, "The fact that Harold can practice his craft in a commercial environment speaks volumes to his abilities as a crafts person and a communicator."[14] Retired shipbuilder Dana Story considers Harold's aptitude for shipbuilding incredible: "He creates solutions to construction problems we never recognized and he executes them with great skill, speed, and efficiency."[15] The common wisdom is that Harold A. Burnham is the most *intuitive* of all living wooden shipwrights today. "His command of the complicated process of transforming trees to ships is almost clairvoyant."[16] Of those who know him personally, most would agree that Harold A. Burnham is an old soul.

Truly great folk art is made with an awareness of and a connection to tradition, community, and place, as Burnham is fully aware. He credits place as much as family legacy for enabling him to do what he does. In his words, "Given that the shipbuilding industry has continued uninterrupted in Essex since the town's first settlement, the number of vessels built here, their average tonnage, and the town's relatively small population, it is hard to imagine a place on earth where shipbuilding is more deeply embroidered into the fabric of the community."

NOTES

1. Molly Bolster, Executive Director, Gundalow Company, from a letter in support of Harold Burnham for a National Heritage Fellowship, September 24, 2007.

2. In the index of Howard Chapelle's *The American Fishing Schooners: 1825–1935,* twelve Burnhams are listed, all of them shipbuilders.

3. "Smack" is the term for a small sailing vessel, commonly rigged as a sloop, and mainly used in the fishing trade.

4. The Story and Burnham families are recognized as "elders" in the community, their families synonymous with boatbuilding heritage in Essex. Arthur D. Story's shipbuilding yard is adjacent to the Burnham homestead. Dana Story was born in 1919, when his father, Arthur D. Story, was sixty-five. A. D. Story's yard was legendary, building more vessels than anyone else in the Essex tradition.

5. The Massachusetts Bay Colony Tertiary Commission erected a sign in 1930 that reads: "Shipyard of 1668. In 1668 the town granted the adjacent acre of land 'to the inhabitants of Ipswich for a yard to build vessels and to employ workmen for that end.'" The shipbuilding industry has continued uninterruptedly in Essex since that date.

6. Quote taken from Harold Burnham's application narrative for a Traditional Arts Apprenticeship, November 2004.

7. Chebacco is basically a place name. This type of broad-bowed schooner originated in Essex, which at the time of the Revolutionary war was called Chebacco Parish of Ipswich, Massachusetts.

8. From a tape-recorded interview conducted by Frank Ferrel on May 16, 2000.

9. From a tape-recorded interview by the author on May 26, 2006.

10. As told to the author in a phone conversation, November 8, 2007.

11. "Keepers of Tradition: Art and Folk Heritage in Massachusetts" was a collaboration of the Massachusetts Cultural Council and the National Heritage Museum. Curated by Maggie Holtzberg, the exhibition ran from May 18, 2008 through June 7, 2009.

12. Futtocks are the separate pieces of wood that, when joined, form a single frame in a wooden vessel.

13. Joseph Garland, November 27, 2000, in a letter of support of an Artist Grant application to the Massachusetts Cultural Council.

14. Dana C. Henson, Vice President for Preservation and Programs, Mystic Seaport, in a letter of support to the National Endowment for the Arts, September 27, 2007.

15. Quoted in an H. A. Burnham Boat Building & Design brochure.

16. Molly Bolster, Executive Director of the Gunalow Company, in a letter of support written to the National Endowment for the Arts, September 24, 2007.

REFERENCES

Burnham, Harold. 2000. Side Launching the Old Essex Way. *Wooden Boat* 154 (May/June):36–40.

Chapelle, Howard I. 1973. *The American Fishing Schooners: 1825–1935.* New York: W. W. Norton.

Glassie, Henry. 1982. *Passing the Time in Ballymenone.* Philadelphia: University of Pennsylvania Press.

———. 1989. *The Spirit of Folk Art: The Girard Collection at the Museum of International Folk Art.* New York: Harry N. Abrams.

———. 2006. *The Stars of Ballymenone.* Bloomington: Indiana University Press.

Murphy, Matthew P. 1998. "Go See Harold . . . He Can Do It": The Building of the *Thomas E. Lannon. Wooden Boat* 143 (July/August):76–85.

Viator, Albert. 2005. *Fame, The Salem Privateer: A Portrait of Craftsmanship and Patriotism.* DVD available from http://www.schoonerfame.com/store.html.

Estelline Tubby at home in the Pearl River Community, Mississippi, 1997.
Photograph by Allyson Whyte

A Backdoor into Performance

Tom Mould

In *The Stars of Ballymenone* (2006), Henry Glassie revisits the men and women from *Passing the Time in Ballymenone* (1982) to explore the concept of the star, a term used by men and women in this small community in Northern Ireland to designate people who can transform a dull evening into an entertaining one through their performance of story, song and music.[1] They are artists, their product art.

While "star" is an emic term, it is not unique to Ballymenone, either in terminology or in concept. Popular culture in the U.S. employs the same term for its top entertainers, though the criteria for what defines a star is culturally specific. In Kütahya, the stars of Turkish *çini* are called masters (Glassie 1993), another term widespread throughout the world, particularly in the material arts where apprenticeship models thrive. Stars and masters are found the world over as communities herald those men and women who have excelled in their craft.

Stars fit neatly into performance theory that dominates the field of folklore today. The idea of performance reorients analysis from the product to the process, from abstracts skills and competencies to application and praxis. Deeply embedded in the concept of performance is the recognition of cultural and situational variation. "The essential task in the ethnography of performance," Richard Bauman argues in *Verbal Art as Performance,* "is to determine *the culture-specific constellations of communicative means that serve to key performance in particular communities*" (1977:22; italics in original). The cornerstone of performance theory provides a mandate for emic analysis and the recognition of multiple, even infinite articulations of competent, artistic, transcendent performance. Stars will be judged according to criteria that shift from culture to culture; a star potter in Seagrove, North Carolina may not be recognized as a star in Kütahya, Turkey, except by the most culturally relative of viewers.

Along with the fundamental recognition of cultural variation across tradition, these early definitions of performance also contained descriptions of the performer that favored individuals who emerge in social contexts as stand out performers, people worthy of the socially loaded designation of "star." Two of these early definitions continue to inform studies in performance today. In developing the concept of performance in oral narrative analysis, for example, Dell Hymes argued that performance should be evaluated according to structural norms of the genre, as well as norms of performance that distinguish "report" from "performance." According to Hymes, report is marked by summary, excessive attribution as a means of distancing oneself, lack of any responsibility to the material, lack of emotional attachment, lack of obvious expression of belief, and ultimately, lack of adherence to the stylistic demands of the genre (Hymes 1981:81). To perform, on the other hand, is to adhere fully to these demands. That moment of immersion, responsibility, and skillful execution of generic demands signals what Hymes has called a "breakthrough into performance." The concept of the breakthrough and its attendant requirements are regularly recapitulated in current definitions of performance (Kapchan 2003:123). Richard Bauman's articulation of performance in *Verbal Art as Performance* also continues to serve as a common starting point for defining performance today. In his definition, Bauman highlights issues of responsibility and accountability to an audience, social appropriateness, and the "special attention" that invites evaluation of verbal skill and communicative competence rather than referential content alone (Bauman 1977:11). The intensity of this spotlight on the performer remains undiminished in Bauman's more recent definitions, as when he describes performance as "a mode of communicative display, in which the performer signals to an audience, in effect, 'hey, look at me! I'm on! watch how skillfully and effectively I express myself'" (2004:9).

These definitions of performance helped direct long overdue attention to the role of the individual in tradition. In particular, they encouraged a search for local star performers, those men and women heralded inside and outside their communities for achieving a level of competence worthy of attention and appreciation equal to the artists represented in the world's major museums. Yet training a spotlight on the individual in tradition can uncover as well as highlight, and the glare of attention can reveal ambiguities and tensions previously overlooked. In considering the role of the individual in the context of performance theory, of the star in the context of tradition, two potential problems emerge.

The first problem emerges in recognizing that the majority of folklore is shared by people who are not stars. Folklore is a democratic enterprise. It encompasses expressions of the majority rather than the minority. It recognizes art in daily acts. It pries the artistic impulse loose from the stranglehold of marbled museums. In order to expand the Western canon and draw attention to the communal artistic traditions, folklorists have found it useful to tackle entrenched divisions between fine art and folk art. The star can serve as a brilliant ambassador in the debate, calling attention to both individual artists and communal traditions. However, while the recognition of stars is widespread, it is not universal to all communities and in all genres of expressive culture. If performance theory as applied in analysis is trained upon the star, rather than the broad base of community participants, analysis risks ignoring valued and valuable traditions worthy of attention.

The second problem is that much of what folklorists study today is not called art by the people who perform within the tradition (Griffith 1988:5). Practical, social and spiritual dimensions of a tradition may eclipse artistic dimensions. In some cases as with many non-fiction genres, to presume an artistic element at all suggests a lack of truth. Definitions of performance that focus on explicit articulations of formal, structural and stylistic qualities can run counter to emic systems.

In my fieldwork with Choctaw people in Mississippi and Latter-day Saints or Mormons in North Carolina, I have encountered narrative traditions that chafe against these unnecessarily restrictive parameters. Among the Choctaw, prophetic discourse demands that narrators not just frame but deeply contextualize their own narrative with the narrated event when they first heard the prophecy. For prophecy that had already been fulfilled, only by *reporting* prophetic discourse, can a person *perform* prophetic discourse (Mould 2003:34). For unfulfilled prophecy, on the other hand, the ambiguous nature of prophecy demands a degree of tentativeness in performance, one based in possibility rather than certainty, again chafing against definitions of performance that require a degree of authority and responsibility.

Ambiguity and tentativeness are also hallmarks of the narrative style for memorates shared by Latter-day Saints. Further, the formal, stylistic and structural elements so crucial to evaluating verbal art through the lens of performance theory are secondary to criteria based outside the specific performance event. Individuals remain central, but less for what they do in the moment of performance than for the personal reputation they bring to bear.

Rather than assertive breakthroughs into performance, Choctaw narrators of prophecy and Latter-day Saint narrators of spiritual memorates take a more humble approach. They craft narratives that fully meet the norms for the genre as developed within their community, norms that demand attribution, negotiation, and humility. The result is that narrators may enter performance through the backdoor, refusing immersion into the glaring spotlight of the stage.

"Backdoor" performances may be fairly common. Further, they fit comfortably within performance theory in its fundamental focus on cultural variation. Work by Dell Hymes in his explorations of the ethnography of speaking both before and after his articulation of a breakthrough into performance reminds us of this focus and downplays the emphasis on what can appear an aggressive bid for attention implied by "breaking through" or being on stage. Major revisions to performance theory are clearly not necessary. Instead, I am suggesting merely a reorientation to its most basic and fundamental claims and tenets. In this reorientation, the individual emerges in greater variety and includes the star as well as the humble but competent practitioner.

CHOCTAW PROPHECY

As a major category of expressive culture, storytelling among the Mississippi Band of Choctaw Indians fits comfortably within traditional definitions of performance. "Star" storytellers—those men and women who know the old stories and tell them well—are recognized throughout the community and regularly "breakthrough" into performance by taking responsibility for their stories and for entertaining as well as educating their audiences. They meet community standards for competence in performance, excelling in the aesthetic dimensions of the genre in a way that is appreciated by their peers. Estelline Tubby was such a storyteller, well known and well liked throughout the community. She passed away on October 4, 2006, but while alive, was the foremost storyteller in Pearl River, and one of the most well known storytellers in the tribe. She is featured in the film *Stories of the Red Clay Hills,* which loops on a television screen in the Choctaw Tribal Museum. When Oklahoma Choctaw storyteller Tim Tingle visited Mississippi in 1993, he was directed immediately to Estelline (Tingle 2003:9). The same was true for me when I first visited Pearl River in 1996. In Bogue Chitto, I was directed to Billy Amos. In Tucker, to Rosalie Steve.[2] With the death of Estelline Tubby, Rosalie became the best known storyteller throughout the tribe, even making storytelling a side business for herself. She was often employed by the tribal school system to tell stories to the youth and a was regular fixture during the annual Choctaw Fair.

Before Estelline, Billy and Rosalie there was Billy's father Wagoner Amos—who told powerful stories of mythic origins and prophetic fu-

Rosalie Steve,
Tucker community,
Mississippi

Billy Amos, Bogue Chitto community, Mississippi.
Both photographs by Allyson Whyte

tures—and Jim Dixon—who not only told tall tales, but appears in them as a legendary figure, both consummate storyteller and local funny man.[3] There were generalists and specialists alike. Family and community memory herald others in the recent past—Baxter York, John Hunter Thompson, and Inez Henry—while the historical record reaches even farther into the past to reveal still others—Olman Comby, Isaac Pistonatubee, Simpson Tubby, Peter Pitchlynn, Ilaishtubbee, Ahojeobe, Heleema, and Pisatuntema. Whether these men and women were stars in their communities or simply willing to talk to white men is unclear. What is clear is that all were capable and competent storytellers.

Even for storytellers recognized by their peers as stars, the restrictive criteria that continues to be employed in distinguishing a breakthrough into performance risks excluding some of these storytellers when narrating certain genres. Sharing a legend or humorous story, Billy Amos disappears into the narrative, achieving a breakthrough into performance as described by Dell Hymes. Sharing a prophecy he heard growing up, however, his style changes. Generic norms demand different obligations. In his account of prophecies of electricity, running water, and television, he remains an observer, on the outside looking in. Stylistically, his performance resembles undifferentiated discourse. When folklorist Lisa Gilman played Billy's taped performance to her graduate folklore class, many students were disappointed, expecting a dramatic delivery to match the content. These expectations were based partly on the fact that while Billy's performance was stylistically undramatic, its structure was impressive in its rhythmic patterning. In order to argue for prediction rather than hindsight, fulfilled prophecy must be situated as a performance event in the past. Fulfilled prophecy has to be reported, with careful and repeated attribution. Billy Amos did this by expertly moving back and forth between past and present, between the time he heard the prophecy and the moment of its fulfillment. Billy's structural proficiency led students to assume stylistic proficiency was also an important aspect to the performance of Choctaw prophecy. Further, inadvertent ethnocentrism led them to assume that stylistic proficiency for Choctaw prophecy would be similar to their own stylistic norms for dramatic performance, an expectation borne out by their own attempts to perform Billy's narrative before hearing the audio recording.

Estelline Tubby also recounts prophetic narratives with careful and repeated attribution that extends throughout her performance, suggestive of report rather than merely initial keying formula of appeals tradition to frame the narrative (see Bauman 1977:16). In narrating *unfulfilled* prophecy, however, Estelline's narrative challenge is different from Billy Amos's. Rather than establish prediction, Estelline must interpret the prophecy's referents and meaning. Her task is one of interpretation rather than declaration. Estelline continuously references past storytellers, distinguishing between what they said and how she has interpreted their words. Rather than remain immersed in the story, Estelline regularly steps outside of it to comment on it, evaluate it, and interpret it. She is ambiguous about its meaning. And rather than averring authoritatively, she tentatively probes the story, laying bare her own interpretative process in dialogue as much with the voices of past storytellers as with her audience (see Mould 2003:91–99; 2004:170–71).

Attribution is particularly important for both fulfilled and unfulfilled prophecy since a narrator cannot simply assume the role of prophet. Interpretation is equally important since prophecy is often ambiguous, where images of the future may be metaphoric, incomplete or intentionally obscure. In this way, Choctaw prophecy as a narrative genre operates similarly to memorates, where encounters with the supernatural or divine may be ambiguous and belief open for negotiation. As Dégh and Vazsonyi argued over thirty-five years ago, legend performances are often about dialogic interpretation rather than monologic declaration (1971). If performance is truly to represent the "culture-specific constellations of communicative means" (Bauman 1977:22), it must include reported and non-authoritative texts as well. If not, communally recognized "stars" risk being dismissed as incompetent performers.

Latter-day Saint Memorates

"Star" storytellers can also be found in the Latter-day Saint narrative tradition. J. Golden Kimball is perhaps the most famous, and infamous, storyteller in LDS history, immortalized not only by the stories he told, but by stories told about him (Cheney 1974; Eliason 2007). No single figure alive today rivals Kimball as a star storyteller, though few would want to. The attention and ire that J. Golden Kimball drew during his life is hardly enviable in a church where quiet, humble service is respected above ostentatious individualism. The one person today recognized as a consummate though not controversial storyteller is the current President of the Church: Thomas S. Monson. His reputation precedes the office; the moment he became a member of the General Authority and began addressing Latter-day Saints across the country and the globe during General Conference meetings, people recognized an expert storyteller.

More common than a single star for all of Mormondom are local stars, although they too are not widespread. Storytellers may be recognized by their fellow ward members and regional neighbors for their verbal skill and humor, such as Petie Bishop, renowned for the humorous tales he shared among his fellow Scandinavian immigrant neighbors (Adams 1999). Recognition as an identifiable star derives from secular attributes of their stories, and primarily from the secular stories they tell. Tall tales, humorous anecdotes and jokes are comfortably viewed as entertainment, regardless of other functions they may serve. Viewed aesthetically, secular stories can be evaluated according to structural and stylistic elements, traits that tend to be viewed as secular rather than sacred in nature. Spiritual stories, however, require a different set of criteria for evaluation that may favor neither stylistic elements of narration nor the social designation of a stand out performer.

To be sure, most of the stories that President Monson has shared over the years have a spiritual dimension. Many are memorates of revelations received to guide him in his church calling and personal life. Yet when people comment on his talent as a storyteller, they reference secular rather than spiritual elements of his storytelling. They mention content—such as his regular cast of widows and orphans—or style and tone—including his ever-present wit and humor. Where most church leaders share stories from scripture or spiritual experiences from their own lives and the lives of people in their wards and stakes, President Monson fills his talks with folktales and secular anecdotes as well as spiritual and scriptural stories. The concept of a star storyteller is ultimately a secular designation for Latter-day Saints, and it references secular aspects of the narrative tradition.

The most common type of narratives shared in church, however, are spiritual memorates. Just as Choctaw prophecy demands a different set of performance norms from other narrative genres within the Choctaw oral tradition, so too do spiritual memorates among Latter-day Saints. As a lay church with no trained clergy, the LDS church relies on church members to provide religious instruction. Stories are regarded as a fundamental tool in giving these talks, whether during Sacrament meetings, Fast and Testimony meetings, Sunday School, Priesthood, Relief Society or any of a number of other church meetings and functions. Personal stories are valued far above second hand ones. Spiritual memorates in particular are useful as they combine the personal and the spiritual. They are shared to educate and edify, two functions intertwined intimately with one another as knowledge of church doctrine helps one move closer to God and attain spiritual edification.

For stories to educate and edify, they must be believed. While there are verbal strategies that can build trust between narrator and audience and encourage belief in the narrative, the most important criteria for evaluating the narrative generally and belief specifically come from outside the performance event. Even before a person begins his or her narrative, audience members have begun their evaluation, training their focus on the narrator rather than the narrative. Revelation comes to the righteous. Whether the audience believes the performance or not is often contingent on a person's reputation for being spiritual, an aspect fundamental to their social identity within the church.

"It all depends on, I think, that perception people have of that individual," explains Keith Stanley, member of the Burlington First Ward at the time and now bishop of the Burlington Third Ward. "If it's somebody that they really look up to, that they consider a spiritual person that they go to for advice," he says, "they tend not to doubt it." Keith points out this phenomenon is hardly confined to Latter-day Saints, or spiritual memorates. "I think that's true in any society. They would look at them [he turns his head and narrows his eyes suspiciously] and say, "What have you been drinking?" (March 19, 2007).

Of course, social identities are not static. Reputations are built through any of a number of encounters with one's peers, including the sharing of spiritual memorates. Performance can provide a forum for negotiating identity, not simply reifying it (see Bauman 2002; Butler 2002; Sawin 2002). However, performance rarely provides a clean slate; biographies accumulated outside a single performance event can exert great influence in ordering social relations and in guiding interpretation.

In the performance of spiritual memorates among Latter-day Saints, a poor reputation in church can undermine edification and education because of the assumed motive for sharing. Some people are perceived as too eager for attention. Church members comment on those people who seem to have a dramatic spiritual encounter every month. Rather than lift up their peers spiritually, such narrators are perceived as attempting only to raise themselves up socially. After all, it is the righteous who regularly encounter the Holy Ghost. To share spiritual memorates freely and regularly can be an aggressive declaration of one's own righteousness. The result is an undermining of one's believability.

A paradox emerges. Church members are expected to appear both humble *and* righteous. Choosing when, where and how often to share a story can help negotiate these opposing norms. Narrative patterns and rhetorical strategies are also employed, injecting ambiguity into the narrative and tentativeness into the performance (see Mould 2011). The pervasiveness of these "disclaimers of performance" (see Bauman 1977:16) risks pushing these narrations outside the scope of performance if defined restrictively according to the degree of responsibility claimed by the narrator. However, greater attention to the role of the individual both as performer within the performance event and as social being outside it can clarify meaning and validate performance.

For Latter-day Saints, discrepancies between those identities can be dramatic. The reputation of a person outside the performance event can weigh so heavily upon the evaluation of performance that it can make people question the truth of a story even when they feel the presence of the Holy Ghost. Brigham Young University English professor Richard C. Poulsen describes hearing a story shared by a fellow ward member who was "off the edge a little," and prone to hysteria. Yet despite feeling a sense of awe upon hearing the story, Poulsen "didn't strongly believe it" (Nielson 1990:10). A poor reputation can become an insurmountable obstacle not only to belief, but to edification. In this way, social reputation may be the most important factor of all in evaluating performance if it has the potential to remove the possibility of edification.

At the heart of this discrepancy lies a conflict between the structural and stylistic norms of a genre and its social, contextual norms. As with the evaluation of LDS spiritual memorates, Diane Goldstein found that the narration of spiritual experiences during church services at an independent, ecumenical church were evaluated primarily according to the social identities and motives of the speakers and the spiritual effects felt by the congregation, not by formal artistic elements:

> Though structural norms and rules for genre performance were significant among these variables, they were secondary to the determination of competence based on the congregation's knowledge of the individual speaker, the speaker's past and potential performances, indications of the Grace of God in emergent performance, and perceived motives of narration. (1995:32)

This gap between structural and stylistic competencies and social hierarchies and reputations again suggests greater attention must be placed on the individual, not just within a particular performance event but outside it. With social relations in flux and variable from group to group, a performance evaluated positively in one place at one time among one group of people may not be evaluated as positively under a different set of circumstances. While evaluation involves a constellation of factors, one variable is the relationship between narrator and audience. In some cases, the individual, not the performance, lies at the center of evaluation.

Performer-Centered Approach

In such cases, a performer- rather than performance-centered approach to analysis may be appropriate. Linda Dégh has been a proponent of such an approach, applying lessons learned from her mentor Gyula Ortutay and the Budapest School of ethnographic folklore to her studies of Hungarian narratives, particularly those of "star" storyteller Zsuzsanna Palkó (Dégh 1995a). In her book *Narratives in Society,* Dégh strove to redirect the trend in folklore studies towards performance and re-center analysis on the individual (1995b). By constructing interpretive frames through personal biographies and local cultural worlds, scholars might hope to approximate a native hermeneutic that a performer's local audiences might use. Similarly, Henry Glassie regularly provides deep biographies in addition to thick ethnographic description in order to understand and appreciate the individual both from a critical perspective as well as an ethical humanistic one.

A performer-centered approach moves analysis outside the boundaries of the performance event. Such a move is not uncommon in folklore studies; many post-colonial and post-modern theories, including feminist theory, use analysis of the structures of power negotiated in society—particularly according to class, race, ethnicity, politics, religion, gender and sexuality—to analyze individual texts. While all of these theories move analysis outside the performance event, none convey the focus on the individual except as a member of a particular demographic group.

A performer-centered approach that plumbs aspects of a person's personal life relevant to performance is hardly without its ethical dilemmas, however. For the LDS storyteller with an impressive command of verbal skills but a poor reputation in the community, an in-depth exploration of the intersection between personal life and social reception in performance would be painful and embarrassing for storyteller, author, and reader alike. Such an approach becomes even more difficult when people do not see themselves even as artists much less as stars.

Folklore without Art

A central assumption of folkloric analysis is the recognition of an aesthetic dimension to many forms of communication. In the past, that artistic element was used to define genres that helped in turn to define the parameters of the field. Today, folklore is viewed less a series of identifiable genres than as a particular approach to the study of expressive culture. While art and aesthetics remain central to the field, they may not be central to the people engaged in a particular tradition under analysis. Terminology that casts action, speech, and expressions of belief as art or performance, can alienate rather than give voice to an individual or a group.

This is not a new phenomenon, though a broadening of the field has made this breach of emic norms more relevant. From the beginning of folklore as a discipline, genres that folklorists studied as their mainstay were not always considered art by the people who performed them. American Indian creation myths, for example, formed the cornerstone of one branch of early folklore study developed by Franz Boas and his students (Zumwalt 1988). While the concept of "art" has been heavily debated in American Indian Studies (see Brown and Cousins 2001:61–81), referring to sacred narratives as "art" can be alienating to the people who believe them. Further, while verbal competency is a necessary component for many rituals to be effective, neither Navajo healers nor Catholic priests nor any of a number of other religious ministers would first and foremost consider their sacred rites with the language of "performance" and "art." However, neither would they deny the aesthetic elements of ritual. Catholic mass is heavily adorned with prayers, symbols, chants, and material objects that attract the senses as well as the Spirit. The same is true of Navajo healing rituals, where sandpaintings must be beautiful in order to be effective (Parezo 1983).

Divisions *within* expressive culture between expression generally and art specifically mirror divisions between expressive culture and instrumental culture at the macro level. The divide between instrumental and expressive culture is notoriously blurry, and is useful primarily as a heuristic model. Nonetheless, cultural products and performances may be categorized or conceived of within a culture as more clearly one or the other, depending on the context. A baseball bat to one batter may be primarily instrumental, but that same bat to the father who made it for his son, or to the team who nicknamed it Marissa and used it for good luck, may be regarded as more expressive.[4] While occupational culture is clearly instrumental, folklorists have found the workplace a rich area for the exploration of expressive communication. Religion does not fall neatly into one category of culture or the other, yet the expressive nature of worship has led to a wealth of scholarship both deep and broad in folklore studies. The study of material culture provides the most compelling evidence of a false dichotomy between expressive and instrumental culture, regularly revealing how utility is experienced and appreciated as an aesthetic element of an object.

Nonetheless, divisions between art and expression, instrumental and expressive culture can describe very real social categories within a culture. To call religious experience art, or worse yet, folklore, can violate culturally constructed divisions between truth and artifice, sacred and secular. In sharing and evaluating spiritual memorates, Latter-day Saints focus on elements of spirituality, truth, righteousness, humility, and sincerity. These qualities are evaluated first in the context of the speaker, second in the context of the specific performance. Sharing these stories is fundamentally a spiritual and educational endeavor, not an artistic one.

Folkloric study is not irrelevant or inappropriate, however. While the bulk of evaluation is centered on the spiritual and social, people also allude to formal, stylistic and aesthetic qualities that make a good performance. People laughingly complain about stories that wander all over the place, muddying the message and driving away the Spirit. Verbal incompetency can stymie spiritual edification.

In formal settings like testimony meetings, stories should be short and to the point and connections to church doctrine unambiguous. In casual settings, stories can be longer, developed with detail and personal significance, though the connection to doctrine should remain evident. The performance should also be sincere. People should not over-dramatize their narrative as it renders the experience less believable. Paralinguistic elements such as tears are common to performances, but are complex in how they are evaluated. Judged sincere, they bolster a performance considerably. Judged insincere, they undermine credibility. That judgment can have as much to do with an individual audience member's view of tears as with a performer's reputation and the performance itself. Again, individual personalities—both of audience and performer—heavily shape evaluation.

Sincerity is a major component of both belief and the aesthetics of performance, making it clear that while a gap can occur between the spiritual and the aesthetic, the two cannot be fully separated. The problem arises when aesthetics are defined in terms of the artistic, where art implies artifice. The competent performance of a spiritual memorate is one judged sincere by virtue of a lack of artifice (Eliason 1999). In this way, even considering the sharing of a deeply personal spiritual memorate a "performance" with secular artistic appeal rather than solely spiritual truth violates an idealized cultural norm. Spiritual edification can and should have an aesthetic dimension rooted in the Spirit—transforming people, filling them with hope, love, and joy—but a simultaneous aesthetic dimension rooted in the secular appreciation of verbal competency can make some people uneasy. The one cultural caveat is when verbal competency is recognized as a gift of the Holy Ghost. Church members frequently speak of being guided by the Spirit in church talks, teaching, and even informal counseling among friends. While the focus is on spiritual edification, there is a parallel recognition that the talk was both spiritually *and* verbally compelling.

The challenge, then, is not in addressing expressive (or instrumental) culture as if it lacked an aesthetic and artistic dimension, but in addressing cultural performance that is constructed either in opposition to art as artifice or with artistic elements marginalized to such an extent that significant attention can be uncomfortable and alien to people within the community. Both performer- and performance-centered approaches can be problematic in these cases by violating culturally constructed boundaries.

Conclusion and Compromise

The questions raised by these brief examples from Choctaw and LDS narrative traditions implicate both performance and the role of the individual in tradition. The trend in folklore studies to develop emic analyses from the perspectives of the people themselves is valid and valuable both intellectually as well as ethically. Initial definitions for what constituted a breakthrough into performance attempted to accommodate culturally specific norms, but nonetheless assumed a degree of authority claimed by a performer not always appropriate for a specific genre within a specific community. A definition of performance reoriented to emic criteria for what constitutes appropriate and competent expression can more accurately reflect the wide range of genres performed within a community, as well as a wider range of performers. Further, analysis that fully addresses multiple competencies in performance—verbal, social, spiritual—can provide a more nuanced understanding of how individuals can contribute to varying aspects of a particular tradition.

Commitment to emic analysis can conversely diminish the role of the individual in folklore scholarship by removing individual people from the center of analysis. By attending to community standards for humility and generic norms for evaluation that dismiss the artistic, folklorists may struggle with how to present the individual in tradition. One compromise is to focus on "the individual" rather than specific individuals. Such a compromise can seem regressive, folding the individual artist back into the undifferentiated collective. Yet this solution is a far cry from Francis Gummere's nameless, faceless dancing throngs (Gummere 1959) or superorganic forces operating without individual effort. Human agency remains at the fore, even as individual personalities so central to social life and the creation of tradition recede. Artistry, skill, and competency are assumed rather than highlighted. The collective claims credit for virtuosity split among individuals. Names are used, individual performances attributed, but each serves to highlight a thriving tradition rather than a particularly skilled artist.

The move outside the performance context demanded by the gap between structural and social competencies must therefore be centered on the *factors* that *contribute* to personal reputations rather than the personal reputations themselves. Positive reputations would seem to stand as the exception, but even these biographies may be disconcerting to men and women who value humility. Shifting the focus to the individual rather than specific individuals, whether within or outside the performance frame, can provide the comfort of emic recognition and the need in many cases for humility, while continuing to explore the creative dimension of culture in traditions that herald no stars.

Notes

1. I have drawn this summary description of the star from an interview with Henry Glassie (2006:67–70). His book *The Stars of Ballymenone* provides a far richer description, articulating multiple denotations (2006:67, 99), shared traits (2006:110–13), and shared biographies (Britain 2009). More importantly, Glassie provides rich portraits of individual stars, centering his analysis on the individual rather than a composite.

2. In my work with Rosalie Steve back in the late 1990s, she wrote her name for me as "Rosalee," which is how her name appears in *Choctaw Tales*. More recently, however, her name has appeared in the *Choctaw Community News* as "Rosalie." Her granddaughter Sonja Monk explained that the confusion lies in the fact that she has two birth certificates, one with "Rosa Lee Grant Wilson," the other with "Rosalie Wilson." During the years, she has used both, including the combination she wrote down for me. Before her death on June 10, 2010, the name she used most often was "Rosalie," which is how most people remember her.

3. The role of "funny man" is widely recognized and appreciated in the community, though the term is hardly codified and women can also fill this role. Such a person is expected to be skilled at *shukha anumpa,* an emic category of stories that can be translated as "hog wash" and includes tall tales, animal tales, humorous anecdotes and jokes. In Pearl River today, Hulon Willis is just such a funny man or, as he occasionally refers to himself, "a Choctaw comedian."

4. Marissa is a real bat, named and used by the Burlington Bonefish youth baseball team during the 2007 summer season. Bonefish player Britt Kaffenberger owns the bat. The story of Marissa and the Bonefish is beautifully told in the ethnographic film *You Win Some, You Lose Some* by Conor Britain (2009).

References

Adams, William Jenson. 1999. *Sanpete Tales: Humorous Folklore from Central Utah.* Salt Lake City: Signature.

Bauman, Richard. 1977. *Verbal Art as Performance.* Long Grove: Waveland Press, Inc.

———. 2002. Disciplinarity, Reflexivity, and Power in *Verbal Art as Performance:* A Response. *The Journal of American Folklore* 115 (455):92–98.

———. 2004. *A World of Others' Words: Cross-Cultural Perspectives on Intertextuality.* Malden: Blackwell Publishing.

Britain, Conor. 2009. *You Win Some, You Lose Some:* elondocs.

Brown, Joseph Epes, and Emily Cousins. 2001. *Teaching Spirits: Understanding Native American Religious Traditions.* Oxford: Oxford University Press.

Butler, Gary R. 2002. Personal Experience Narratives and the Social Construction of Meaning in Confrontational Discourse. *Journal of American Folklore* 115 (456):154–74.

Cheney, Thomas Edward. 1974. *The Golden Legacy: A Folk History of J. Golden Kimball.* Provo: Brigham Young University Press.

Dégh, Linda. 1995a. *Hungarian Folktales: The Art of Zsuzsanna Palkó.* Jackson: University Press of Mississippi.

———. 1995b. *Narratives in Society: A Performer-Centered Study of Narration.* Folklore Fellows' Communications 255. Helsinki, Finland: Suomalainen Tiedeakatemia.

Dégh, Linda, and Andrew Vazsonyi. 1971. Legend and Belief. *Genre* 4 (3):281–304.

Eliason, Eric A. 1999. Toward the Folkloristic Study of Latter-day Saint Conversion Narratives. *BYU Studies* 38(1):137–50.

———. 2007. *The J. Golden Kimball Stories.* Urbana: University of Illinois Press.

Glassie, Henry. 1982. *Passing the Time in Ballymenone: Culture and History of an Ulster Community.* Philadelphia: University of Pennsylvania Press.

———. 1993. *Turkish Traditional Art Today.* Bloomington: Indiana University Press.

———. 2006. *The Stars of Ballymenone.* Bloomington: Indiana University Press.

Goldstein, Diane E. 1995. The Secularization of Religious Ethnography and Narrative Competence in a Discourse of Faith. *Western Folklore* 54 (1):23–36.

Griffith, James S. 1988. *Southern Arizona Folk Arts.* Tucson: University of Arizona Press.

Gummere, Francis Barton. 1959. *The Popular Ballad.* New York: Dover Publications.

Hymes, Dell H. 1981. *"In vain I tried to tell you": Essays in Native American Ethnopoetics.* Philadelphia: University of Pennsylvania Press.

Kapchan, Deborah A. 2003. Performance. In *Eight Words for the Study of Expressive Culture,* ed. Burt Feintuch. Chicago: University of Illinois Press.

Mould, Tom. 2003. *Choctaw Prophecy: A Legacy of the Future, Contemporary American Indian Studies.* Tuscaloosa: University of Alabama Press.

———. 2004. *Choctaw Tales.* Jackson: University Press of Mississippi.

———. 2011. *Still the Small Voice: Narrative, Personal Revelation and the Mormon Folk Tradition.* Logan: Utah State University Press.

Nielson, Cheryl. 1990. Signs and Superstitions in Determining a Future Spouse. BYU FA1 1104. Harold B. Lee Library, Tom L. Perry Special Collections, Provo.

Parezo, Nancy J. 1983. *Navajo Sandpainting: From Religious Act to Commercial Art.* Tucson: University of Arizona Press.

Sawin, Patricia E. 2002. Performance at the Nexus of Gender, Power, and Desire: Reconsidering Bauman's Verbal Art from the Perspective of Gendered Subjectivity as Performance. *The Journal of American Folkore* 115 (455):28–61.

Tingle, Tim. 2003. *Walking the Choctaw Road.* El Paso: Cinco Puntos Press.

Zumwalt, Rosemary Lévy. 1988. *American Folklore Scholarship: A Dialogue of Dissent.* Bloomington: Indiana University Press.

Kersti Jobs-Björklöf

The Maintenance of Heritage: Kersti Jobs-Björklöf and Swedish Folk Costume

Pravina Shukla

In this volume inspired by the work of Henry Glassie, scholars and artists consider the creative individual, and his or her relationship to tradition, a concept easy to understand viscerally yet hard to define. The most graceful of the definitions of tradition—"the creation of the future out of the past"—we owe to Henry Glassie (2003:176). In his epilogue to the exhibit catalogue *Swedish Folk Art*,[1] Glassie expands on the notion of tradition: "Though a force for continuity, tradition is not the antithesis of change. Tradition lives only in individual minds as part of the adaptive process of daily life, so it exists in a steady state of change" (1994:252). He continues, describing the patterns of tradition, among these intentional replication and revival: "Since tradition is a temporal process, all creations result from selections made among precedents, so all are, in some measure, the products of revival" (1994:254). Tradition, as Dell Hymes tells us, can become self-consciously "traditionalized" (1975). Not all aspects of culture are purposely preserved, but some genres such as songs, recipes, dance, and costumes are often thought to contain the history, geography, identity—the essence—of the people to whom they belong, and folk costumes are frequently selected to represent *heritage,* understood to be those aspects of tradition that are designated as worthy of preservation.

In Sweden, Artur Hazelius, through his Skansen Open Air Museum, set the model for the preservation and exhibition of material culture by placing architecture, landscape and gardens, furniture and costumes in context with each other, displaying the country's heritage at the nation's capital. Costumes were an integral part of Hazelius's mandate to preserve *kulturarv,* cultural

Parish Church,
Leksand

The village of Tibble, Leksand, Dalarna, Sweden

heritage, presenting "folk life in living brushstrokes."[2] In modern Sweden, as in other parts of Europe, scholars are currently studying heritage, defined by Barbro Klein as "phenomena in a group's past that are given high symbolic value and, therefore, must be protected for the future" (2000a:25). Among Europe's recent immigrants, efforts at the preservation of heritage are essential for those displaced from their former homelands. (This is also the case in the United States among those of Swedish ancestry eager to "make heritage" in the diaspora.)[3] But within Sweden, the displacement of rural people is not geographic but temporal. In many parts of the country, people want to retain a connection to their past and their ancestors, fighting the influence of "others," not foreigners, but modern versions of themselves.

My desire is to understand what heritage means to the people who construct and enact it, not only to the scholars who study it. Heritage is self-consciously maintained by dedicated local insiders such as Kersti Jobs-Björklöf in the lovely and highly symbolic countryside of Leksand, in central Sweden. As Barbro Klein has written, Swedish scholars, once in the vanguard of the study of folklife, became fatigued with the study of peasant cultures, growing tired of what many considered to be frivolous aspects of society, weary of what many considered "pompom research"[4]—folklife studies that "celebrated trivial aspects of an agrarian society that was now gone forever" (2000b:171). While native scholars are less inclined to study peasant culture and its heritage, the people themselves are as engaged as ever in the preservation of this heritage. The next step is an ethnographic investigation of the maintenance of heritage, an analysis of how individuals actively engage in the creation, dissemination, and preservation of their own culture.

In my quest to learn about the living tradition of the Swedish folk costume, I went to the place where Artur Hazelius was first inspired—by the local folk costume—to devote his life to the preservation of Swedish culture: the town of Leksand in the province of Dalarna in central Sweden. Near Leksand, in the village of Tibble, lives Kersti Jobs-Björklöf.[5] Her farm has been in the family since the late sixteenth century. Kersti's father, Verner Jobs, was the mayor of Leksand from 1951 to 1972. Her maternal uncle, Knis Karl Aronsson, was the force behind the founding of the local ethnographic museum Leksands Kulturhus. He passed away before the museum was completed. Kersti was the first director of this museum, implementing her uncle's ideas, occupying the post from 1980 to 2002. Kersti's dedication to the preservation of her tradition is familial, communal, national, and deeply ideological. Most of her efforts at the maintenance of heritage are directed towards the beautiful folk costume of Leksand parish, one of about four hundred regional costumes in Sweden today, and one of the few to be worn well into the twentieth century (Berg and Berg 1975:11, 140, and Bergman 2001:3).

THE LEKSAND FOLK COSTUME

The Leksand male costume consists of chamois leather knee breeches, navy wool vest, and a navy wool, long military-style coat with embroidered medallions as faux epaulets low on the shoulders. The women's costume, following the common European style, has a blouse, a bodice, a skirt, an apron, a neck scarf, and, for married women, a cap. The costume of Leksand parish, like a few others in Dalarna, follows specific coded combinations which consist mainly of certain apron and bodice colors. These combinations are worn for different occasions and contexts, sending messages through the color and also the material quality of the cloth. The various ensembles fall into two main tones—red and black—as Kersti explained to me in her fluent English. There is a logical distinction that the people of Leksand made between clothes in the "black field," handmade from homegrown materials such as wool or linen, fabric that has been handspun, hand-woven and sewn at home, and the clothes in the "red field," those made from purchased material, such as Cambric cotton and silk, and often tailor-made.

Clothes in this black tone are worn during periods of fasting and mourning, solemn periods in the Lutheran church calendar as well as periods of personal loss, such as the death of a relative. This black group is signaled by the use of the black cotton bodice, laced up front, worn with a yellow wool apron, hand-woven with sparse horizontal black stripes. A heavy black wool skirt is worn with this ensemble. This is the proper attire at a funeral, and also what one wears to church on the three Sundays before Advent, the Sundays of Lent, and to the Good Friday church service.

The set of clothes in the red tone is more varied. In this cluster, one wears a red silk bodice, laced in the front, with embroidered medallions on either side upon the breasts. This bodice is also worn with the same black wool skirt, yet there are four aprons that signal different levels of auspiciousness in the event. The aprons, called *raskmajd,* are made of a light wool fabric, "glazed," shiny on the front (they used to be waxed). The aprons, all made of the same fabric, are ranked in order by their color: blue, red, green, and yellow, a ranking that reflected the cost and availability of dye materials. Thus, the blue apron was the most precious because indigo (or woad) was special; the red apron was highly ranked because of the scarcity

Sune Björklöf and Kersti Jobs-Björklöf

of madder root; and yellow was the color of the lowest ranked apron and also the color of children's dresses in many parts of Sweden since it was the easiest dye color to acquire, made from birch leaves and moss (Nylén 1949:26). Following this code of aprons, the most important celebrations—your wedding, Christmas day, Easter day, Midsummer Day—are observed in church, colorfully, in the blue apron and red bodice combination. For Midsummer, women also don a cotton neck scarf that is either checkered or printed with bright flowers.

This code of aprons and appropriate ensembles, while following an internal logical system, is complicated, and as Kersti said, "the knowledge was neglected or forgotten." Gustaf Ankarcrona, a painter from southern Sweden and a great patron of the traditional costume of Leksand, thought it a good idea to write down this code, documenting it before it disappeared. He asked his friend, the lawyer Albert Alm, to do it. After interviewing local elderly women who still wore the clothes for daily use, Alm published, in 1923, *Dräktalmanacka för Leksands socken*; Kersti calls it "a help for the memory," and a "costume calendar." Alm's almanac detailed the appropriate combination for every Sunday of the church year, guiding the villagers on what they should be wearing when they arrived at the parish church in Leksand aboard the famous church boats. Of all the costume almanacs in Sweden, the one for Leksand was the very first.[6]

The almanac was pivotal for the retention of the code of the Leksand costume, as Kersti explained to me: "This calendar was in a way a help, and also, it helped for the revival of using the different aprons and so on in church. Because what you had during the different occasions in life—like christening a child, or Confirmation, or a wedding—that was very well known and used." But, she continued, most people did not remember what to wear for the other, less auspicious events. The almanac reminded people that there was a code, and with it, a logical ranking of costume for the various liturgical celebrations, and the various personal celebrations. While most people then, and especially now, did not own all the items necessary to adhere to the code, knowing that a code existed served to remind people of personal and religious events, marking the familial/domestic and the official/communal passing of time, differentiating between ordinary days and ritual times. Today, the costume in Leksand still follows three different yet related temporal streams: the passing of the church year, the passing of the calendar year, and with it, personal rites of passage. The third stream is the one in which fashion, and therefore historical time, is marked by changing fads, something that has always caused the costume of Leksand—and most folk costumes—to continue changing slightly, adapting aesthetically to the current fashions. The general shift—in Sweden and in other parts of the world—from a self-sufficient agrarian economy to one reliant on industrial products has led simultaneously to change and to a renewed commitment to continuity.

Alm's 1923 Leksand book had been out of print for several years by the time Kersti and her mother, Karin Jobs, were asked to create another one, a commission sponsored by the Leksands Hemslöjdsförening, the handcraft association founded by the artist Ankarcrona. They published their book *Almanacka för Leksandsdräkten* in 1978 and, unlike Alm's book which contained only verbal descriptions, Kersti's calendar included colored drawings by David Tägtström that showed men, women, and children wearing full ensembles, complete with jewelry, shoes, and other accessories. Each Sunday of the church year has its own entry in this small book, and next to each description is a small color rendition of the specific bodice and apron to be worn on that particular day.

The book Kersti and her mother Karin compiled has also gone out of print. The code of bodices and aprons is now disseminated by the Leksand Handcraft store: the shop's vitrine displays the coming Sunday's complete ensemble, and the store's website carries this information (only in Swedish), so that parishioners may go online and check the virtual almanac when deciding on what to wear to church that weekend.

WEARING THE COSTUME

The costume code described in the almanac tells us what should be worn at church, but not what was (and is) actually worn by the people. Kersti explained that most of the folk costumes in Sweden today are "compositions from 1920 and till late days" and that the costumes in different parishes of Dalarna are different in form and history: "And here it has been used—and this is the only part of Sweden where it has been used in everyday life that long. And then in Rättvik, the men used the folk costume as late as the women did here in Leksand. In Mora it was gone earlier, and in Gagnef, there the women also were using the costume very late. I think the very latest, and the very last, was here—women—here in Leksand." The photographs in the local archives at Leksands Kommun capture people wearing the Leksand costume into the 1950s and 1960s.

Today in Leksand, the costume is seldom used for regular church service. Kersti is one of the few who wear their costumes on ordinary Sundays, though many come to Midsummer church service in folk costume. Kersti has worn her costume for most of her seventy years of church attendance: "And I think I have not been in the church without my costume ever, just twice or three times, when I have broken my arm and I couldn't dress myself. If I go to a service, I can't do anything but use my costume." Kersti is one of eight "church wardens," two of whom are on rotating duty every fourth Sunday. This pair must prepare the church for the Holy Communion, help dress the vicar, and take the collection, passing baskets for the offering. These wardens, men and women, are representatives of the church, and they appear dressed in folk costume. Kersti, and many others, wear the Leksand costume to church because it is the most beautiful garment they own; in answering my question, many placed aesthetics as the first reason, and adherence to tradition only second to the desire to appear attractive in church, dressed in beautiful clothes.

For a few people every Sunday, for many on special occasions, the Leksand parish church provides a location for wearing the traditional costume, but the costume's great moment comes in Midsummer. Then in every village, the fiddlers who march, the men who slowly raise the Maypole, and many of their neighbors, who assemble to listen and watch and dance, adorn themselves in the beautiful and costly costume.

Acquiring and Storing the Costume

Many people in Leksand have old costumes preserved in their family storage chests or storehouses. Others receive new pieces as gifts, or they may make, buy, or rent the costume. While Kersti's storehouse contains many garments from previous generations, all of her children were given their own costumes to be worn during Confirmation. Kersti's private stash of costumes includes some that are never worn due to their fragile condition; these are upstairs in the storehouse, a free-standing uninhabited building whose sole purpose is to hold the family's historical objects. The costumes that Kersti wears regularly are kept in a dresser in her bedroom. Another dresser in a large room in the adjacent guesthouse holds aprons, bodices, and skirts that are borrowed by visiting family members and even by neighbors and friends who have a need to wear the Leksand costume but who do not own their own. In this way, costumes may be the property of individual families, but they serve a communal function. Several costume pieces I saw were on "temporary loan," kept at the house of the current wearer, yet owned collectively by the family (the fact that many pieces have embroidered initials and dates makes it easy to identity its owner or source).

Raising the Maypole, Tibble

Sven Roos and his daughter, Kersti, lead the fiddlers to Tibble.
Midsummer 2007

Preservation

Preservation of the Swedish costume has three major components: the conceptual preservation of the idea of the costume largely through written accounts, paintings, and photographs; the physical preservation of the actual garments; and finally, the functional preservation of the use of the garments in social contexts.

While Leksand costume fragments have been found in excavated graves, the oldest book carrying images of the costume is C. Forssell's *Ett år I Sverge* ("A Year in Sweden"), a book published in 1827 and containing color plates of regional costumes, including four color illustrations of the male and female outfits of Leksand parish. Another mode of the conceptual preservation of costumes is through research, documentation, and presentation in scholarly mediums, especially museum exhibits and catalogues. This continues to be a principal goal of the Nordiska Museet and Skansen, following Artur Hazelius's example. There are picture books, such as *Folkdräkter och bygdedräkter från hela Sverige*[7] and *Sockendräkter i Dalarna*,[8] which are part encyclopedia and part how-to manual, featuring real people dressed in their own costumes. Costume books usually contain many historical and contemporary photographs of people wearing the clothes. And Kersti uses the photographs in her family album to remember and to teach about the Leksand costume as well as to demonstrate her family's long commitment to wearing their folk costume. Kersti spearheaded the project at the Leksands Kommun archives to gather binders full of local photographs. The images—in the binders and in electronic form—await captions supplied by knowledgeable visitors or family members. The medium, and metaphor, of photography to preserve and disseminate folk culture is indispensable. Artur Hazelius in his museum displays tried to create "'snap-shots' of traditional life" (Scheffy 2004:233). Orvar Löfgren argues that photographs, especially postcards that miniaturize the large world into a small, portable medium, allow one to return to "a mythical past or a more authentic existence."[9]

Like photographs, paintings have long proved useful in the maintenance of the idea of the regional costume, not just in Sweden, but in many parts of the world.[10] Artur Hazelius commissioned several paintings for the Nordiska Museet, including one depicting a wedding scene in Dalarna, to preserve visually the costumes, customs, home decorations—the folklife—of the peasants.[11] Many of Sweden's artists, such as Anders Zorn and Carl Larsson, summered in Dalarna, producing art that featured peasants and their costume, locking it into the consciousness of the people.[12] These paintings show idyllic scenes of country life, celebrating and romanticizing the Swedish peasant in a nationalistic spirit. While the costume details and ensembles are not always accurate, they attempt to document the past in terms of its material culture: architecture, furniture, and clothes.

Written descriptions and illustrations of the costumes, whether in published books, photographs, or paintings, all help keep the costume—aesthetically—in the awareness of the local people. Many of these renditions, due to their artistic nature, do not portray accurate details about the garment construction, materials, proper combinations, or use. For the costume tradition to continue, one needs more accurate texts: the tools and techniques of making, and most importantly, the garments themselves. Cutting and sewing, weaving, and embroidery are taught, and preserved, at women's study circles,[13] and craft classes are offered by the handcraft shop and especially by the college of handcraft, Sätergläntan. Knowledge of making is also preserved by individual people who know how to cut, embroider, and weave.

The actual costume pieces exist—nestled in acid-free paper, in dark, cold storage rooms—in the local ethnographic museum, the Leksands Kulturhus. These objects are well-preserved, but not readily accessible to the average museum visitor. (An extreme case is the massive costume collection at Stockholm's Nordiska Museet that is closed to researchers. While one may study illustrations of the museum's clothes in its many published books, knowledge about the garment construction and physical qualities cannot be gleaned from examinations of a photograph, a two-dimensional representation of a three-dimensional object.) Putting clothes on display is a useful compromise, for the garments are on mannequins and visually accessible, yet they continue to be cared for by museum curators and conservators, exhibited in cases that are sensitive to temperature, humidity, and light. As the director of the Leksands Kulturhus museum, Kersti mounted a permanent exhibition which showed all the varieties of the Leksand costume, illustrating the various aprons, scarves, bodices, and organizing them into clusters according to occasion of use. All the costume varieties—defined by ceremonial use, work, gender, age, and season—are displayed in a long corridor with mannequins in dioramas. In 1998, Kersti curated a special exhibition on dress and hosted an international conference on folk costumes. It was the most popular exhibit ever shown at the museum; the audience consisted mainly of local, elderly women who came to hear about their own traditions.

Costumes are preserved visually by artists and photographers, and they are preserved physically in the museum (and in family storage chests). The only way they can be preserved in social context—their meanings and communications still functional—is through actual use, and this is the last major component of the preservation of a folk costume, a goal to which Kersti Jobs-Björklöf is particularly committed. The costume almanac, as we have already seen, is a major force in documenting and disseminating the functional potential of different versions of the Leksand costume. But it is only a book (or website or store window display). It requires human actors to bring the costume code and performance into real life. Agents of the costume include the makers, wearers, and their beholders. Today folk costume is worn widely by musicians and folk dancers in Dalarna, as it is in many other countries of Europe. Kersti wears her costume, carefully enacting the code written down by Alm, to church every single Sunday of her life. By wearing the Leksand costume, and displaying its variety and ensemble combinations, she helps disseminate knowledge about the garments: visually, conceptually, and socially.

Those who wear the costume, at considerable expense and hassle, need positive feedback and appreciation from others, for this keeps the tradition going. Kersti's mother, Karin Jobs, always encouraged all those around her to wear the costume. Kersti recalled that her mother would request that in lieu of a birthday or Christmas gift, her family wear the Leksand costume to the gathering, that the sight of them in the Leksand folk costume was the best present she could receive. In 1954, when Kersti passed her school exams, she wanted a new outfit, as was the custom among her classmates. Her mother told her that she too would receive a new set of clothes, but requested that she wear the Leksand costume for the school ceremony. Kersti did this reluctantly, being the only one to wear the folk costume at the event. When she shook hands with the headmaster, who was also the headmaster at the time of her mother's exam, he told her that just that morning he asked his wife, "I wonder if Kersti will wear the costume like her mother did back in 1922?" Kersti said that she did not appreciate standing out in the 1950s, but in the 1970s, during the revival of folk costumes in Sweden, she liked it. She was living in Stockholm at that time, and proudly wore her Leksand costume, receiving much praise. Many people said to her "I envy you" for having a traditional costume whose use had been preserved throughout the years.

In preservation, there is a dilemma. One may choose to preserve the garment in a locked vault, keeping the fabric from deteriorating and the colors from fading. Or one may choose to wear the costume, keeping it circulating in the consciousness of the people, yet damaging it through use. If you keep it, the clothes are safe; if you wear it, the clothes are alive.

These two opposing angles on preserving the costume work against each other. The folk costumes at Stockholm's Nordiska Museet are safely locked in storage, preserved forever. Some of the Leksands Kulturhus costumes are on mannequins, displayed safely yet still compromised from the optimal flat storage in acid-free packing.

The main difference between costumes stored in a museum and in a family clothes chest is that museum pieces are never worn. Kersti is the custodian of a large collection of family costumes, stored in various places: in the storehouse, in a bureau in the guest house, in her own wardrobe. In reference to a set of her great-grandmother's aprons, I commented that it seemed like a family museum, and she agreed, elaborating on this concept:

> It is very difficult for me because when working in a museum, you know exactly how to handle things with conservation, with keeping it in boxes, with special silk paper. Using white gloves, everything.
>
> So I said to my mother, "Oh my God, we shouldn't use it, we shouldn't keep it like this." And she said, "It's not a museum. It's our family things. Go there, if there is something that can be used, use it. But you will tell your daughters that they must be careful, and try to tell them about my wonderful grandmother, and the stories about her. Just give them some nice stories."
>
> And therefore, it's hanging there, and it's not hanging well. I have this bad conscience for not caring about it and so on.

INNOVATION

Change is manifest in folk costumes in many ways: the creation of a brand-new costume; the creation of a new version of an old costume or even the revival of an old garment style; and the reinterpretation of the contexts of the costume's use. One way to control the costume, and discourage unnecessary change, is to impose restrictions on who can and cannot wear the costume, limiting the number of actors who might contribute to modifications. In Leksand, all pressures to change work counter to the self-conscious efforts at preservation of tradition. Efforts at innovation help keep the costume alive and relevant today while causing it to lose some of its social and aesthetic features.

Many of Sweden's folk costumes are recent creations, in contrast to the famous costumes of Dalarna, which are celebrated partly for their long history. But even within the province of Dalarna, there are certain areas that did not have a costume tradition, such as Sundborn, in the mining region of Falun.

The Sundborn costume, with its green vest, red apron, and striped skirt, was created by the city's famous residents, the artists Carl and Karin Larsson, in 1902 (Berg and Berg 1974:160). In fact, Carl Larsson, along with fellow artist Gustaf Ankarcrona, is credited with creating the Swedish national costume in the early 1900s, even though the garment is the invention of Märta Jörgensen, whose role in the costume is often downplayed.[14] The national costume is a woman's dress, with the bodice and skirt attached, much like the southern Vingåker costume. It is a blue dress worn with a white blouse and a yellow apron, in the bright hues of the current Swedish flag.

The instance of inventing a costume that never existed before, like the national costume, is rare. A more common practice is to make slight alterations to existing pieces, or to revive forgotten items. The folk costume is always changing slightly. Skirt lengths get longer and shorter depending on the current fashion.[15] Kersti told me that in the 1950s, the Leksand skirt got shorter and "wider" by the addition of several underskirts that functioned as petticoats and changed the silhouette of the costume, imitating the wide profile of Christian Dior's fashionable New Look.[16]

At the end of the eighteenth and the beginning of the nineteenth centuries, the red vest was made of shiny damask cloth, with a high collar and a rolled hem, allowing the expert to date this style. Similar dating details exist for most costume pieces: its fabric, form, or method of construction is in a state of constant, slight variation. Self-conscious revivals of old pieces can be seen as acts of innovation since they change the current costume repertoire. An example is the green pleated wool skirt, worn under the apron in place of the black woolen skirt. The green skirt, according to Kersti, stopped being used around 1860 and was revived in 1950. This skirt, when worn with the blue apron, warrants the wearer the use of red stockings, instead of the white stockings worn with the black skirt, since the red stockings were made of precious dye materials, madder root or even cochineal. The result is a celebratory mix of green, blue, and red. Paintings from Leksand depict this combination of clothing. A painting on display at the Leksands Kulturhus, dated 1811, shows this green pleated skirt. Another example is Hjelt Per Persson's 1846 painting of a wedding procession outside of the Leksands Kyrka showing the bridesmaids in green pleated skirts, worn under blue aprons with ribbon appliqué on the bottom hem.[17] They all wear red stockings, adhering to the aesthetic code. During the occasions on which the blue apron is called for, most women wear the black woolen skirt, while Kersti wears her green pleated one (one of three that she owns), communicating a higher level of connoisseurship. Kersti elaborated on the history of the recent revival of the green skirt:

A teacher, who was a colleague of my mother's, she wanted to marry and have a crown, and not the white cap, because she said that it's such a day to be a bride and I want to use the crown.

And so she was in discussion with my mother, and my mother said that in the old days when they were brides—and also for very special Sundays—they had a green skirt. "Shouldn't you have a green skirt?" Because when you combine the green with the blue it's much more beautiful than the blue to the black, and then you have red stockings.

And then she got interested. And she said, "Yes, I will."

And so she was dressed, a bride, I think it was '50, like that, in a green skirt, and the crown, and with the ribbons and these decorations.

In this case, the revival was motivated by aesthetics, for a bride wants to appear beautiful *and* special, in extraordinary attire. For Kersti's own wedding ten years later, her mother wanted to commission a special, hand-woven green skirt, prompted, once again, by beauty. This is the story Kersti told me:

And then there was an artist living here, and he was a textile man, and then my mother said, "You go up to this room where we keep our clothes, have a look at these old green ones, the ones used, from Anna, 1846, and the other one from Brita, 1870, and look what you think is the most beautiful color, and tell us what kind of color so that the yarn got the right green color together with the blue one."

So it was very much discussed between my mother—because she wanted a *beautiful* green color.

So, there was a lady, who had woven many meters of this. So, then, for my wedding, relatives, they had made for themselves a green skirt.

The revival of the green skirt was provoked by aesthetics, and inspired by old family pieces, continuing the family tradition while changing the course of the current fashion.

While the costume tradition, like all traditions, is flexible by definition, allowing for variation, it is a different matter when these variations are codified and made official—when they become heritage—as in the costume almanac. Kersti told me about a recent phenomenon that took place in Leksand, and stimulated much debate among the city's tradition brokers. According to the almanac one is to wear the "black tone" garments of black bodice and yellow apron at a certain time of the year; yet parents may schedule Confirmations for their children during this time of year. The dilemma is this: should parents be allowed to bypass the general somber tone of the church calendar for the celebratory tone of their offsprings' rite of passage, and wear clothes in the "red tone" instead? Kersti describes the current situation:

> And people, they go to the handcraft shop, and say, "We have seen in the calendar, and we can see in the window that we should have black, and I haven't got a black vest. I only have the red one because we use it for Midsummer, and weddings, and special occasions. What shall I do?"
>
> And they say, "As I haven't got that one, and this is a happy occasion—Confirmation for my child—and what shall we do?"

Many in the community have appealed to Kersti, the author of the last published costume almanac and a leader in these matters, to help revise the official code, to help persuade the church to change the costume rules. Kersti vehemently believes that people have the right to wear what they want to wear; the costume tradition continues because people wear the folk costume. But, she said, these kinds of decisions should not be made inside the institution of the church. Flexibility is built into the code, and changes designed to accommodate a limited wardrobe should not be codified. She concludes:

> This is the tradition. If you don't have it, then use what you have. Tell the parents that if they have a red one, then be happy with their children and use the red one. I am not going to blame them for not having—I am not a *police!* I think that it's better that they use it.
>
> I think it's up to anyone to do as they like, so they feel happy. I don't blame them. I'm happy if they like to use the folk costume.

Kersti's statements show that even the most consistent champion of the folk costume is adaptable, believing that the costume code can be broken, that what really matters is that the costume continues to be worn, and to be worn with pride and love. The desire to police the clothes, however, is integral to the discussion of the Leksand costume. Kersti said that when she sees someone wearing the costume inaccurately, for example, with the belt tied on the wrong side, she says nothing. But if she notices that others in church snicker and laugh, then she takes the person aside, and offers to help her, inviting the person to her house, where Kersti can instruct her, in private, about the costume. Kersti is not interested in policing outsiders, for the costume means something different to a tourist than it does to a Leksand native. The code applies only to those on the inside, for whom the costume is a manifestation of regional heritage.

This brings us to the question—what is a costume? Is the Leksand folk costume a uniform, a performance outfit, or festive dress? The answer depends on whom you ask, on the contexts of use and the functions of non-verbal communication. In our conversations, Kersti repeatedly told me that her costume is *not a uniform,* for a uniform is restricted in its form and use and restricted to certain people who are allowed to wear it. In talking about the varieties of the striped apron, for example, she said that now people follow one pattern, "keeping every millimeter" the same, changing the costume into a "uniform," something it never was, for it always existed in perpetual variation. (However, in the Swedish diaspora, among a population less familiar and comfortable with its heritage, many view the folk costume as a "uniform" as Lizette Gradén shows in Lindsborg, Kansas.)[18] Kersti, a true insider, is more liberal about the costume tradition than others are.

Conclusion: The System of Heritage Maintenance

Kersti, in speaking about the Leksand folk costume tradition, made this statement to me: "When my mother's generation are dead, I think that it's gone." Upon hearing this declaration, I was shocked and dismayed, until I understood what she meant by it. Kersti's statement can be understood as a hyperbolic rhetoric of preservation, not descriptive, but rather prophetic, a jeremiad.[19] Her subversive, critical opinion of the current state of affairs is meant to ensure the preservation of creativity for the future. She states hypothetically what she hopes to avoid in order to encourage those around her to work against this forecasted death of the Leksand folk costume. I asked two elderly sisters, Britta Matsson and Anna Halvares, if they thought the tradition of the costume (making and wearing) was dying. They responded, in unison, with emphatic cries of *"Nej, nej, nej, nej!"* Ulla Björklöf, Kersti's daughter-in-law and the niece of Britta and Anna, translated their subsequent statement: "No, not dying. They think it is going up and down. Now it is down."

The costume tradition in Sweden, like all traditions, has gone up and down. A balance of preservation and innovation is necessary to keep any custom alive, flowing along through history, like a stream, experiencing robust and lean moments. For a tradition to survive, such as that of the folk costume, it requires actors—ideological and visionary outsiders as well as motivated, dedicated leaders from within.

Mats Hellspong and Barbro Klein, in detailing the history of folklife studies in Sweden, generalize a pattern of outsiders' interest in the folk cultures of their country.[20] In the sixteenth century, the elite were attracted to folk customs in part to highlight for the rest of Europe the uniqueness of their Nordic culture. During the next century, Sweden experienced the glory of a superpower, taking pride in its antiquities, using archaeology and history as vehicles of propaganda for imperialism. In the eighteenth century, the country turned back once again into itself, with a renewed appreciation of its flora, fauna, and folk culture. Botanist Carl Linnaeus, among others, traveled the nation, documenting what he saw, including the life and customs of the common country people. It is during the next century, the nineteenth, that the age of romanticism inspired many to collect from the peasants their songs and tales, and Artur Hazelius launched his collecting of the material culture of the peasants—starting with costumes from Dalarna—for what would become his monumental and hugely influential museums: Nordiska Museet and Skansen. During the turn of the twentieth century, Hazelius and other members of the Swedish bourgeoisie held romanticized notions of the peasantry. In *Culture Builders,* Jonas Frykman and Orvar Löfgren provide the cultural context for the collecting, and valuing, of folk arts and lifestyles—an attempt to delineate middle-class identity in relation to both the "declining peasantry and the emerging working class" of Stockholm—giving us an understanding of the audience for Hazelius's museums (1987:165).

The sequence of outsiders who helped to further the costume tradition of the local farming people begins with scientists and scholars, Linnaeus and Hazelius, and continues with artists. Carl Larsson, influenced by William Morris and the Arts and Crafts Movement, wrote in *Ett Hem,* in 1899: "Therefore, oh Swede, save yourself in time. Return to simplicity and dignity. It is better to be awkward than elegant. Dress yourself in skin, fur, leather, and wool. Make yourself furnishings that suit your heavy body, and on everything put bright colors" (Lofgren 1992:viii). Through ideology, practice, and art, Larsson helped to bring the folk costume into the twentieth century. With his wife Karin, Larsson created the famous Sundborn costume. With artist Gustaf Ankarcrona (and Märta Jörgensen) he invented the national costume, worn by people who have no regional costume of their own and eminently displayed (since 1983) on the royal body of Queen Silvia (who was born in Brazil). Ankarcrona's tremendous contributions to the preservation of the Leksand costume continues today with the pivotal role the handcraft store (that he established) still plays in the dissemination and maintenance of the folk costume tradition. It was Ankarcrona who persuaded Albert Alm to document the folk costume code in the almanacs he created for the parishes of Leksand and Dala-Floda.[21]

Artists and scholars, such as Hazelius, Larsson, and Ankarcrona, all lived in or visited Dalarna, and while technically outsiders, they worked closely with the populace whose costumes they strove to preserve. Their efforts lead to institutional support for folk costumes through handcraft stores, craft study circles, colleges of handcrafts, and museum displays and collections. We can add another institution that has always played a role in the continuation of folk costume traditions—the church.[22] The Lutheran Church, with its historical mandates that parishioners attend service in folk costume, and with its almanac of acceptable coded ensembles, is a force whose rules are enacted and enforced by local people. Kersti Jobs-Björklöf, along with the other church wardens, actively influences costume use and restriction by her example, advice, loans of pieces, and active instruction on use. The example of the church shows that any institutional drive, for or against the costume tradition, must be furthered by local people.

Folk costume in Sweden experienced a great wave of revival in the 1970s, and it is now, according to many experts, in a low period. In this essay, I have argued that the main agents for the preservation of the costume are not outsiders, but rather, insiders. Our examination of the Leksand folk costume reveals that while Hazelius and Ankarcrona were crucial, their ideological mandate has become the political and aesthetic aim of Leksand locals long after these men have passed away. Studies of European folk costume credit influential individuals—kings, scholars, and artists. While folklorists such as Barbro Klein, Dorothy Noyes, Regina Bendix, and Thomas Dubois, call for an ethnographic study of identity and costume in Europe,[23] practitioners and leaders from within the culture remain anonymous in the scholarly record. The application of performance theory to the study of costume in Europe would reveal the willed decisions these insiders make in shaping their own heritage. We see that an important component in the preservation of heritage is the family unit. Kersti continues to work in the trajectory set by her uncle Knis Karl and her mother Karin. Her daughter-in-law, Ulla follows Kersti, working at the Fräsgården museum. Individuals, such as Kersti and her brother-in-law Sven Roos, a traditional fiddler—through their connoisseurship, dedication, and good taste—rescue old pieces from obscurity and wear them, helping revive some, keeping the garments fashionable, or at least visible.

In analyzing this system of heritage maintenance, we identify some actors as outsiders and others as insiders. How accurate a distinction is this? In the case of folk costumes in Leksand, we categorize as "outsiders" the artists and scholars from elsewhere. But many of them summered in Dalarna, including Artur Hazelius whose house in Ullvi is about two miles away from Kersti's farm Knisgården. Kersti and her uncle Knis Karl are considered "insiders," born and raised within the tradition, but both engaged in folkloristic scholarship and public programming, much like Haze-

Kersti's grandson, Elis Kröger, dressed for Midsummer

lius himself. There is a pattern, not just in Sweden, but in many other parts of the world: outsiders often respond to movements that have started on the inside. They choose a particular locale—in our case Leksand, Dalarna— because it contains a living tradition which attracts these outsiders in the first place. (It is not a coincidence that Hazelius, Larsson, and Ankarcrona all came to Dalarna.) So, outsiders help energize and mobilize the locals who get involved in carrying out the mandate of preservation and revival. This mandate starts from within, emotionally, and takes power from the intellectual and political aims of progressive artists and scholars. Revivals of folk traditions are mostly attributed to outsiders and their large institutions, but as we have seen, it is the insiders, the locals, who literally populate these institutions of museums, schools, and stores, who accept the responsibility of local action.

The example of the maintenance of the folk costume in Sweden has analogues in other folk traditions around the world, including those found in the ethnographic writing of Henry Glassie.[24] For example, in Ireland, the folk drama of mumming—a Christmas folk drama performed in people's homes—had largely died out in the early twentieth century. Both Henry Glassie and Alan Gailey documented the texts and costumes, searching in the archives and interviewing people who had once participated in the plays. Irish playwright Vincent Woods took the idea of the mummers—anonymous men in disguise—from Glassie and Gailey, and put them into his modern play about the Irish Troubles, *At the Black Pig's Dyke*. But it was a local man, Bryan Gallagher, who read Glassie's book and created the revival of mumming in County Fermanagh. He involved his students in the collection of mumming texts from their families, supporting the acquisition of the materials for the creation of the costumes, encouraging locals to perform, once again, the play of death and resurrection. Now the tradition flourishes, albeit in a changed format. Instead of performing in homes, troupes act in public places like schools, festivals, and bars, often collecting money for charity.[25] The tradition has revived, resurfaced, as it has in Leksand, by collaboration between scholars, artists, and local community leaders.

By giving the credit for a revived tradition to an outsider, we steal the power of the insider; in Leksand, we diminish the role of those who are actually making, selling, and wearing their costumes today, who are making willed decisions in the preservation of heritage.[26] Artur Hazelius helped his country resist international forces by celebrating the national. Kersti Jobs-Björklöf helps her community resist national forces by celebrating the familial, the local, the regional.

Kersti taught me generously about her folk costume tradition through long interviews while I was in Sweden, and through follow-up emails and explanations upon my return to the United States. She has been generous with me, but she places her hopes, and her tradition, in the hands of her granddaughter, twelve-year-old Anna. I am an outsider, a scholar of folklore and dress; I can write and teach about the tradition. Her granddaughter Anna is an insider; she can live it. Both of us are necessary for the survival of the costume tradition. We are both committed: my obligation is ideological, intellectual; Anna's duty is emotional, familial, personal.

Notes

I would like to thank Kersti Jobs-Björklöf and Kerstin Sinha for reading a draft of this essay carefully, for suggesting many useful changes, and for translating original texts into English for me.
    1. In the Swedish version of the exhibition catalogue, Beate Sydhoff, Director of Kulturhuset, acknowledges Glassie's book *The Spirit of Folk Art* for inspiring the subtitle of the exhibit, "All Tradition is Change." Sydhoff (1992:187–88).
    2. *Skansen* (2005:6). See Klein (2006:57).
    3. This is a reference to the subtitle of Gradén's book, *On Parade,* in which she analyzes the conscious efforts at the public display of Swedish heritage in Lindsborg, Kansas.
    4. The "pompom" reference comes from the little pompoms in the knee-breeches of the men's costume, signaling that the costume was no longer of interest to scholars of Swedish ethnology and heritage politics.
    5. The interviews with Kersti Jobs-Björklöf, many of them tape-recorded, took place between June 17 and June 30, 2007. Many emails were exchanged between us from June 24, 2006, to August 31, 2010.
    6. Kersti Jobs-Björklöf quotes Ingrid Bergman who was in charge of the costume collection at the Nordiska Museet. Personal communication, June 2008.
    7. The English translation of this book is *Folk Costumes of Sweden,* by Inga Arno Berg and Gunnel Hazelius Berg.
    8. This book is by Benny Norgren, Birger Persson, and Rune Österlund.
    9. Löfgren (1999:79). See p. 84 for a photograph of a model in Leksand folk costume. To read his argument in full, see the chapter "Telling Stories," pp. 72–106.
    10. Snowden (1979:7–8) argues in his introduction that artists and writers throughout Europe paid particular attention to dress and other aspects of peasant life in the Romantic Age, which in turn helped maintain the existing tradition of folk dress.
    11. For an illustration of this painting by Stikå Erik Hansson of a wedding scene in Mora parish, see Jacobsson's "The Arts of the Swedish Peasant World" in Klein and Widbom (1994:69).

12. For more on artists in Dalarna, see Klein's "Introduction to Part 4" in Klein and Widbom (1994) and Rosander (1986:115, 124, 125).

13. See Waldén, "Women's Creativity and the Swedish Study Circles" in Klein and Widbom (1994).

14. For a discussion of the national costume and its creation, see Hellspong and Klein, pp. 26–27 in Klein and Widbom (1994) and Berg and Berg (1975:44). Ingrid Bergman, the former curator of textiles at the Nordiska Museet, gives due credit to the costume's originator, Märta Jörgensen, in her 2005 article.

15. For more on the relationship between tradition and fashion, see Shukla, (2008), especially ch. 10–12, 16.

16. For more on Dior's "New Look," see Dior (2007) and Wilcox (2007).

17. This painting is illustrated in Svärdström (1975), plate 14.

18. Gradén (2003:192). On p. 103, she describes the spectacle of people parading together, looking like members of a sports team or an army, in matching uniforms. On p. 210, some refer to their costumes as a "monkey suit" or "circus outfits."

19. See Glassie (2006: ch. 8), for another example of a jeremiad—Hugh Nolan's hyperbolic prediction of the future for the sake of the conservation of tradition.

20. See the essay "Folk Art and Folklife Studies in Sweden" in Klein and Widbom, *Swedish Folk Art*. See also Thompson (1961).

21. Alm's almanac for the province of Dala-Floda was published in 1939.

22. To read about the role of the church in controlling the use of folk costumes, see Berg and Berg (1975:29–32).

23. Klein, "Swedish Folklife Research in the 1980s." Noyes and Bendix, "Introduction: In Modern Dress," and Dubois, "Costuming the European Social Body" both in Bendix and Noyes (1998).

24. For example, see two brand-new writings by Glassie (2010b) and (2010a), ch. 8 and 19.

25. See Cashman, "Mumming on the Irish Border: Social and Political Implications" and Mac Cárthaigh, "Room to Rhyme: Irish Christmas Mumming in Transition" both in Buckley, Ó Catháin, Mac Cárthaigh, and Mac Mathúna (2007).

26. Rosander (1986:135) argues that while outsiders—artists and scholars—have helped create the cultural identity of Dalarna, "Pioneers from among the province's own inhabitants" are also to be acknowledged for their efforts; Knis Karl Aronsson, Kersti's uncle, is singled out as one of these "pioneers."

References

Alm, Albert. 1923. *Dräktalmanacka för Leksands socken*. Oskarhamn.

Bendix, Regina, and Dorothy Noyes, eds. 1998. In Modern Dress: Costuming the European Social Body, 17th–20th Centuries. Special issue, *Journal of American Folklore* 3(440).

Berg, Inga Arnö, and Gunnel Hazelius Berg. 1975. *Folk Costumes of Sweden: A Living Tradition*. Trans. W. E. Ottercrans. Västerås: ICA Bokförlag.

Bergman, Ingrid. 2001. *Folk Costumes in Sweden*. Stockholm, The Swedish Institute.

———. 2005. När den första sverigedräkten lanserades i Falun. In *Dalarna 2005: Utgiven av Dalarnas Fornminnes och Hembygdsförbund*, pp. 195–204.

Buckley, Anthony, Séamas Ó Catháin, Críostóir Mac Cárthaigh, and Séamus Mac Mathúna, eds. 2007. *Border-Crossing: Mumming in Cross-Border and Cross-Community Contexts*. Dundalk: Dundalgan Press.

Dior, Christian. 2007 [1957]. *Dior by Dior: The Autobiography of Christian Dior*. Trans. Antonia Fraser. London: Victoria and Albert Publications.

Fryckman, Jonas, and Orvar Löfgren. 1987. *Culture Builders: A Historical Anthropology of Middle-Class Life*. Trans. Alan Crozier. New Brunswick: Rutgers University Press.

Gailey, Alan. 1969. *Irish Folk Drama*. Cork: Mercier Press.

Glassie, Henry. 1983 [1976]. *All Silver and No Brass: An Irish Christmas Mumming*. Philadelphia: University of Pennsylvania Press.

———. 1989. *The Spirit of Folk Art*. New York: Harry N. Abrams.

———. 1994. Epilogue. In Klein and Widbom 1994:247–55.

———. 2003. Tradition. In *Eight Words for the Study of Expressive Culture*, ed. Burt Feintuch, pp. 176–97. Urbana: University of Illinois Press.

———. 2006. *The Stars of Ballymenone*. Bloomington: Indiana University Press.

———. 2010a. *Prince Twins Seven-Seven: His Art, His Life in Nigeria, His Exile in America*. Bloomington: Indiana University Press.

———. 2010b. A Forward in Celebration. In John A. Burrison, *From Mud to Jug: The Folk Potters and Pottery of Northeast Georgia*, pp. vii–xi. Athens: University of Georgia Press.

Gradén, Lizette. 2003. *On Parade: Making Heritage in Lindsborg, Kansas*. Uppsala: Uppsala University Library.

Hymes, Dell. 1975. Folklore's Nature and the Sun's Myth. *Journal of American Folklore* 88:345–69.

Jobs, Karin, and Kersti Jobs-Björklöf. 1978. *Almanacka för Leksandsdräkten*. Stockholm: AB Sigma-tryckeriet for Leksands Hemslöjdsförening.

Klein, Barbro, and Mats Widbom, eds. 1994. *Swedish Folk Art: All Tradition is Change*. New York: Harry N. Abrams.

Klein, Barbro. 1986. Swedish Folklife Research in the 1980s. *Journal of American Folklore* 99:461–69.

———. 2000a. Folklore, Heritage Politics and Ethnic Diversity: Thinking about the Past and the Future. In *Folklore, Heritage Politics and Ethnic Diversity: A Festschrift for Barbro Klein*, ed. Pertti Anttonen, pp. 23–36. Botkyrka: Multicultural Centre.

———. 2000b. The Moral Content of Tradition: Homecraft, Ethnology, and Swedish Life in the Twentieth Century. *Western Folklore* 59 (Spring):171–195.

———. 2006. Cultural Heritage, the Swedish Folklife Sphere, and the Others. *Cultural Analysis* 5:57–80.

Lofgren, John Z, ed. 1992. *Carl Larsson: The Autobiography of Sweden's Most Beloved Artist.* Iowa City: Penfield Press.

Löfgren, Orvar. 1999. *On Vacation: A History of Vacationing.* Berkeley: University of California Press.

Norgren, Benny, Birger Persson, and Rune Österlund. 1973. *Sockendräkter i Dalarna.* Falun: Esselte-Herzogs AB.

Nylén, Anna-Maja. 1949. *Swedish Peasant Costumes.* Stockholm: Nordiska Museet.

Rosander, Göran. 1986. The "Nationalisation" of Dalecarlia: How a Special Province Becomes a National Symbol for Sweden. *Arv* 42:93–142.

Scheffy, Zoë-Hateehc Durrah. 2004. Sámi Religion in Museums and Artistry. In *Creating Diversities: Folkore, Religion and the Politics of Heritage,* eds. Anna-Leena Siikala, Barbro Klein, and Stein R. Mathisen, pp. 225–59. Helsinki: Finnish Literature Society.

Shukla, Pravina. 2008. *The Grace of Four Moons: Dress, Adornment, and the Art of the Body in Modern India.* Bloomington: Indiana University Press.

Skansen Official Guide. 2005. Uppsala: Sandvikens Tryckeri AB.

Snowden, James. 1979. *The Folk Dress of Europe.* New York: Mayflower Books.

Svärdström, Svante. *Dalmålningar i Urval.* 1975 [1957]. Stockholm: Albert Bonniers Förlag.

Sydhoff, Beate. 1992. *Folkkonsten: All Tradition Är Förändring.* Stockholm: Carlsson Bokförlag.

Thompson, Stith. 1961. Folklore Trends in Scandinavia. *Journal of American Folklore* 74:313–20.

Wilcox, Claire. 2007. *The Golden Age of Couture: Paris and London 1947–57.* London: Victoria and Albert Publications.

Woods, Vincent. 1998. At the Black Pig's Dyke. In *Far From the Land: Contemporary Irish Plays,* ed. John Fairleigh. London: Methuen Drama.

Ryoji Kajikawa

The World of Ogre-Tile Makers: The Onihyaku Line in Hekinan, Japan

Takashi Takahara

I, myself, did not know the Japanese word *Oniitashi*. Most Japanese people do not know it either. Even if they were born and raised in Japan, the term would be unfamiliar. The word *Oniitashi* carries a special atmosphere. People might wonder if *Oniitashi* is the title of a tale of the fantastic, or the name of a master of an art described in the tale. However, *Oniitashi* people do not operate secretly. They are ordinary Japanese citizens.

Oniitashi people do not look different from others, but they have peculiar skills which set them apart. They belong to a category of action, like baseball players or Kabuki actors who make a living by mastering a special skill or natural talent inherent in their body. Closest to *Oniitashi* are Kabuki actors. Both depend upon a hereditary system of the transference of skills between the generations. However, there is a big difference between the two: *Oniitashi* are almost unknown in Japan, whereas Kabuki actors and Kabuki itself are known to everyone.

The ways of knowing *Oniitashi* and Kabuki are reversed. Everybody knows about Kabuki from watching television, looking at magazines, or learning about Kabuki at school, though most people have never seen live Kabuki performance. Furthermore, most Japanese probably will never attend a Kabuki performance in their lifetime. The possibility is close to zero. On the other hand, though most people do not know about the *Oniitashi*, the things produced by *Oniitashi* can be seen everywhere all over Japan. People see them every day. In fact, it is impossible to not see them! Now, this sounds very strange, as though invisible *Oniitashi* people have been casting a spell over Japan, but it is a fact and continues to be the state of affairs. For several centuries, *Oniitashi* have been making things called *Onigawara*. *Oniitashi* are the artisans who make decorative clay tiles in the form of ogres for the rooftops of houses and temples all over Japan. The tiles are similar to the gargoyles that adorn buildings in Europe.

Today, most Japanese houses and almost all temples have *Onigawara* roof-tiles. About sixty percent of the Japanese ogre-tiles were produced in Takahama and Hekinan cities and their suburbs in Aichi prefecture, Japan. It is in keeping with Japanese culture for many *Oniitashi* to gather together to make a living. But, as the number of *Oniitashi* people is so small, the name, *Oniitashi*, is almost unknown in Japanese society. Yet, a typical Japanese house has at least two ogre-tiles at the ends of the roof-ridge. Performers are invisible and localized, but the results of their performance are highly visible and have become ubiquitous throughout Japan.

CLAY ROOF-TILES

Tiles are used for covering the roof of a house. In Japan, any reference to a roof naturally calls roof-tiles to mind. However, in truth, various other roofing materials, such as copper, sheet zinc, aluminum, plastic, slating, and cement, are used today. Then, were roof-tiles the main material for roofing in the olden-days? The answer is, "No." People used straw, planking, bark, shingles, stones and so on, according to the environment, local traditions, time period, social class, the structure's purpose, and other considerations (Mori 1986, 2001).

Today, the commonly held image of a Japanese roof includes clay tiles, but this image is relatively new. In 1720, Yoshimune Tokugawa, the eighth shogun of the Edo period (1603–1867), issued a proclamation encouraging the use of roof-tiles because of the many fires in Edo (now Tokyo), and roof-tiles started to become widespread among the common people. By the Meiji period (1868–1912), the use of roof-tiles had spread throughout the whole country (Komai 1963:22–29).

It is noteworthy that the tiles that came to dominance on the roofs of the homes of the common people after 1720 were different from those that existed before the proclamation. Roof-tiles made after 1720 were called *Sangawara,* and today are called *Wagawara,* meaning "Japanese-style roof-tiles." These tiles were invented by Hanbei Nishimura, a roof-tile artisan, in 1674. The proclamation and the invention made roof-tiles popular in Japan, and the conventional Japanese scenery of today was created. Before the invention of *Sangawara,* in bygone days roof-tiles were called *Hongawara.* Roofs were a combination of plain rectangular tiles with a channel tile. In those days, ordinary houses rarely had roof-tiles. Instead, a thatched or shingle roof was most common. Clay tiles were mostly limited to the roofs of temples and castles. From the time that roof-tiles were introduced into Japan in the sixth century, this custom continued for almost one thousand years (Fujiwara and Watanabe 1990:12–17). Clay roof-tiles came to Japan from the Asian mainland along with Buddhism. Today, Japanese people do not think of Buddhist temples as foreign. However, in those days, Buddhist temples were exotic, strange, and even modern in the eyes of the public. Thus, the tile roof that characterizes the Japanese landscape today has been *Japanized* rather recently when we consider the long history of roof-tiles in Japan.

The roofs of *Hongawara* did not disappear. You can see them still. Many temple roofs are made in the basic *Hongawara* style. So when we go to a temple today, we feel something strange in comparison with the ordinary scenery of daily life, and the *Hongawara* roof is one of the reasons. The Japanese roof-tile provides a good example of the slow cultural synthesis that yielded the Japanese environment. In the process, the conventional image of the Japanese landscape gradually emerged.

Ogre-tiles

When you look up at a roof, you will notice that there are both Japanese and European tiles. Japanese roof-tiles take the *Hongawara* and *Wagawara* forms, but European roof-tiles follow Spanish or French styles. These tiles cover the main body of the roof. However, Japanese roof-tiles are traditionally much more decorative than European roof-tiles, which are of a simple design and free of ornamentation. In Japan, the corners, the nooks, the ends, and the edges are covered by types of tiles that come in various forms and are usually decorative. In Japan, these tiles are called *Yakugawara.* Both ends of the roof's ridge are covered by a special type of tile. There are many names for these tiles, but the usual name is *Onigawara,* or "ogre-tile" in English.

The name, *Onigawara,* or ogre-tile, suggests an image of an *Oni* (an ogre). However, ogre-tiles on Japanese roofs have deviated from the original form of *Oni,* and today various kinds of ogre-tiles that do not resemble ogres can be seen. When I refer to *Onigawara,* I cannot help thinking of Akio Kobayashi, an ogre-tile maker who has studied ogre-tiles throughout his whole career. He is a creator and a scholar. His roof-tile factory is very close to the Kintetsu Nara station, and I visited him there. His office is like a roof-tile museum. All of the ogre-tiles are the original works of Ogre-makers from the past. His collection of ogre-tiles and roof-tiles is literally a collection of National Treasures. You can see photographs of some of the tiles in his books (Kobayashi 1981, 1982, 1985).

According to Kobayashi (1991), roof-tiles came to Japan through the Korean peninsula in 588. For about six hundred years, from the Asuka period (538–710) to the Kamakura period (1185–1333), the decorative roof-tiles at the edges of the ridge were called *Hun*. The function of *Hun* was to bring good luck or to invite a visit from an auspicious god. In the beginning, *Hun* was a flat sort of roof-tile. However, in Japan over the course of one hundred years, the *Hun* gradually developed into a three dimensional figure: horns were attached; the forehead, nose, and cheeks protruded; upper and lower canines were added, along with hair and mustache. At one point in this process, the current image of the ogre appeared and the *Hun* for auspicious gods was transformed into an *Oni*. That is to say, Ogre-ization occurred. According to Kobayashi, the first known decorative roof-tile to depict an *Oni* dates from 1363 (Kobayashi 1991:19–22). This was the birth of *Onigawara* in Japan.

The Ogre-ization of the *Hun* was a Japanese invention that changed both the form of the *Hun* and the way in which the *Hun* was constructed. The Hun was a *relief*, or a flat clay tile formed by pressing clay into a wooden mold. On the other hand, *Onigawara* is hand-made by modeling the features of the *Oni* onto the tile's surface. When I was in Korea from 2006 to 2007, I noticed that the tradition of *Hun* is still in use all over Korea. The difference between Korea and Japan in terms of the form and style of the decorative roof-tiles was distinctive. In Korea, the *Hun* remains flatter and plainer whereas the Japanese *Onigawara* is three-dimensional and highly decorative.

First, the Japanization of the *Onigawara* ogre-tile happened. Then about 311 years later, during the Edo period, *Sangawara* was born. The birth of *Onigawara* and *Sangawara* was the beginning of the unique Japanese style of roof-tiles. Once this happened, the use of roof-tiles began to spread from the temples to the houses of common people and *Onigawara* became a part of the villager's daily life. *Onigawara* was an awesome thing in those days. As long as *Onigawara* appeared in the precincts of the temple, there was no problem. However, once the *Oni* appeared in the space of daily life, people became afraid of the power of *Onigawara* and began to dislike the *Oni*. It was a kind of mass Oni-phobia. I am sure that *Onigawara* was not viewed as mere decoration. People actually believed in *Onigawara*.

Hun tiles from Korea,
Sinra Period

Onigawara,
Asakusadera Temple,
Tokyo, Japan

Onigawara with a fish (a Non-Oni *Onigawara*),
made by Ryoji Kajikawa

As a result, the second Japanization of *Onigawara* happened. *Onigawara* that do not look like *Oni* were created by ogre-tile makers to counter people's fearful emotions toward the traditional *Onigawara* in their living space. The people's feelings triggered the transformation of a tradition. Ogre-tile makers in those days could not maintain the older tradition because they could not ignore the reaction of the people. *Onigawara* lost its central figure, the *Oni* itself. We might say that the Ogres were killed by the people.

This event suggests patterns of influence in the creation of a tradition within the performance field. *Onigawara* was transfigured from *Oni* to Non-Oni by the force of the consumers, and a new *Onigawara* was created. However, and fortunately, the old tradition was not completely discarded. Instead, the *Oni* returned to its original place on the roof of the temple. Since then, *Oni* has continued to live in the sacred space of temple while the Non-Oni dominates the profane space of the domestic dwelling. As a result of this expansion, the tradition of *Onigawara* was enriched.

Ogre-tiles in Sanshu

Roof-tiles produced in Takahama, Hekinan, and the suburbs surrounding these cities are called Sanshu-roof-tiles. Sanshu is the name of the eastern part of Aichi prefecture, and it is the number one roof-tile production area in Japan. About four hundred and eighty million roof-tiles are produced each year in the Sanshu area. According to the *Industrial Statistical Table of 2005*, Sanshu roof-tiles comprise 55.8 percent of the market in Japan and the total production is valued at about $46 million. To cover a roof, decorative tiles called *Yakugawara* are needed for the nooks, corners, and edges of the roof. Since *Onigawara* is a kind of *Yakugawara*, the Sanshu area is home to many ogre-tile makers as well. As a result, Sanshu is also the leading area for ogre-tile production in Japan.

The exact date of origin for the ogre-tiles in Sanshu is uncertain. However, ogre-tile production has been flourishing for many generations in the Sanshu area, mostly in the Yahagi River Delta plain, which has been accumulating mud and silt for millions of years, providing a rich bed of clay for pottery. A major pottery town called Seto is located in the middle course of the Yahagi River; it has been an important center of ceramic production since ancient times. Ogre-tiles are a sort of pottery; the basic techniques and materials are the same. Though there is no record of the origin of Sanshu *Onigawara*, we know from the first Japanese-style *Onigawara* tile that the techniques for making Japanese *Onigawara* appeared around 1363, so we can assume that the pottery industry and the *Onigawara* industry have been flourishing side-by-side in the Yahagi River Delta for many centuries.

The Sanshu *Onigawara* industry began in 1720 as a result of Yoshimune Tokugawa's proclamation encouraging the use of roof-tiles. Once the demand for roof-tiles appeared in the Edo market (the capital of the Tokugawa period, now known as Tokyo), the world of *Onigawara* also came to life. The Tokugawa family home was in the Sanshu area, so many Sanshu products were sent to Edo by ship, including roof-tiles. Therefore, we can assume that many ogre-tile makers were working in Sanshu during this time. There are also records that show many artisans left Sanshu and traveled to other districts to make ogre-tiles. The ways of transporting roof-tiles were limited. The roads were not good, so artisans began to travel to other towns and districts to make roof-tiles and ogre-tiles. This situation continued until the end of World War II (Nagano Municipal Museum 1998:4–5; Sugiura 1983:41–46). With the development of highways and commercial trucking, the migration of artisans became less common.

Today there are thirty-seven companies in Sanshu that produce ogre-tiles and decorative clay tiles for roofs (Takahara 2002, 2003). I have been visiting them since 1998 to study the world of the ogre-tile makers. The companies are clearly divided into two groups, similar to the medieval system of craft guilds. One group is called Kuroji (Black Guild). Kuroji produces ogre-tiles mainly by hand. The other group is called Shiraji (White Guild). Shiraji produces ogre-tiles mainly by machine, in a process of mass production. Kuroji has eighteen companies; Shiraji has nineteen. The companies in the guilds do not produce regular roof-tiles but produce the decorative tiles called *Yakugawara*. Among *Yakugawara, Onigawara* is the most decorative and the largest. In this article, I will focus on a group of *Oniitashi* or Ogre-makers within the Kuroji division to illustrate the role of the individual artisan in this long-standing tradition. The name of the group is Onihyaku.

THE ONIHYAKU LINE

Each company of ogre-tile makers has artisans, their number usually ranging from one to ten people. I chose the Onihyaku line because this group maintains the tradition of handmade ogre-tiles at the highest level in Sanshu. Furthermore, in Onihyaku, I could trace the depth of a tradition that has been passed from generation to generation. As a result, the group offers a good opportunity to consider the relationship between a tradition and its individual creators. The Onihyaku line has three companies, but I will present only two of the companies here because these two are the core of this group and the third company is not directly related by blood.

Onihyaku Core Company

The Onihyaku line's core company is called Onihyaku. The first generation of Onihyaku was its founder, Hyakutaro Kajikawa. Kajikawa was born in 1872 and passed away in 1909. He was an artisan working at Yamakichi. Yamakichi was the oldest company of *Onigawara* in Sanshu in those days. Yamakichi's master was Kichibei Yamamoto, whose name is still famous even today in Sanshu. In those days, if a company owner had no sons, it was common for the family to adopt the best artisan in the company and marry him to a daughter of the family. As Hyakutaro was an excellent artisan, he was adopted into the Yamamoto family and married Kichibei's daughter. The couple had three children. However, one day, Hyakutaro left the Yamamoto family, leaving his children and taking another of Kichibei's daughters with him. He became independent from Yamakichi and founded a new company, called Onihyaku. Following is the true story of the origin of Onihyaku. This case helps us think about the role of the individual in the continuation of the Japanese artisanal tradition.

Hyakutaro was a skillful workman in the Yamakichi shop. So the master of Yamakichi, Kichibei, decided to adopt him as a son-in-law for the purpose of inheriting Yamakichi's tradition. But Hyakutaro fell in love with Kichibei's other daughter, Otake. Since he could not continue to live with his wife, Hyakutaro, he and his sweetheart, Otake, left Yamakichi together. If Hyakutaro had not done that, the Onihyaku line would never have existed on the earth. The event itself was providential, but in those days people must have considered Hyakutaro's and Otake's action to be immoral. Because this incident happened, however, the most important family line of ogre-tile makers came into the world. The creation of a new tradition arose from love.

The sons from Hyakutaro's first marriage were left at Yamakichi, but did not inherit Kichibei's legacy as an ogre-tile maker. Yamakichi was dissolved after Kichibei's death. Yamakichi's tradition was passed through Kichibei's second daughter to the Onihyaku line. The line of the *Onigawara* tradition in the most famous company in Sanshu had shifted and broken, while the love between Hyakutaro and Kichibei's other daughter, Otake, created a new tradition in the world of the ogre-tile makers.

Life, however, was not easy for Hyakutaro and Otake. Hyakutaro passed away in 1909 when he was thirty-seven years old. Fortunately, he fathered two sons with Otake, but they were still quite young. So Hyakutaro's company, Onihyaku, could not survive. The equipment and artisans went to another company, called Onihukuyogyo. However, when Hyakutaro's son, Kenichi, was old enough to become an apprentice (at around twelve years old), he was invited into Onihukuyogyo where Hyakutaro's former artisans were now working. Kenichi became an apprentice in the company.

When Kenichi was in his twenties, he became independent from Onihukuyogyo and restored his late father's company, Onihyaku. There was a discontinuation of the family business between the time of Hyakutaro's death and the time that Kenichi reestablished the company, but Kenichi was trained at Onihukuyogyo, where the artisans trained by Hyakutaro were working, so Hyakutaro's tradition was passed to his son, Kenichi, through these artisans. Thus Kenichi became the second generation of Onihyaku through an indirect transfer of his father's knowledge and skills.

Kenichi was an excellent ogre-tile maker. He had seven children, and three of his sons became ogre-tile makers. I think that handing the tradition down to his sons is one of Kenichi's great contributions to the world of handmade *Onigawara* because the number of artisans is declining these days. However, Kenichi was a scary father to his sons. According to the fifth son, Tsutomu, his father was violent. Tsutomu and his brothers were often beaten by their father instead of being scolded. Kenichi was a strong-minded person who hated to lose and liked to dress up. Yet, Kenichi was bashful in public and was not good at doing business with merchants. No businessman, he was a real artisan. Whenever he got an idea about *Onigawara,* he immediately went to his workshop and tried to make it, whether it was night or day.

Kenichi introduced modern ideas into the world of traditional ogre-tile making in Sanshu, bringing about a technical and artistic revolution in the tradition of Onihyaku. This is his second great contribution to the world of handmade *Onigawara.* Modern sculpture in Japan developed from French inspirations, particularly from Auguste Rodin (1840–1917). Kenichi made the acquaintance of two modern sculptors, Sotaro Mitsueda and Sotaro's pupil, Chōko Kato. The historic meeting of an excellent artisan and a famous modern art sculptor and his pupil took place in Sanshu. The sculptors gave Kenichi instruction in sculptural techniques and aesthetic sensibility in the use of clay. Through Kenichi, the decorative art tradition of *Onigawara* in Onihyaku and that of French modern art merged. This was the moment when a new tradition in Onihyaku and *Onigawara* was created.

Kenichi's sons Morio, Tsutomu, and Ryoji all became ogre-tile makers. Morio, the eldest, began his training in 1939 at the age of fourteen. Ogre-

Hyakutaro Kajikawa

tile making is not learned in class, but in a job with a company. Craftsmen learn how to make *Onigawara* while working in the company's workshop. However, Japan was at war during this period. Kenichi's company had fewer and fewer orders; there was little demand for the work. The family could not make a living from *Onigawara,* so Morio went to work for a war factory in Toyota. After World War II, Morio returned home to work with his father, but there was still little demand for *Onigawara* during the 1940s. So Morio lost a very precious period in the training of an ogre-tile maker. It is said that the best period for learning the techniques of ogre-tile making comes when the artisan-to-be is in his teens. When Morio was in his teens, there was almost no demand for *Onigawara* in Japan. He lost the chance to become an ogre-tile maker because of the social turmoil of those days. A good seed failed to drop on fertile soil.

That loss, in fact, caused a trauma in his mind. When I interviewed him, Morio told me that his life was miserable. He can make a certain level of ogre-tile but cannot make a superb one. That gap engendered a psychological distress that oppresses his mind all the time (personal communication, March 9, 2003). If he had been born into another *Oniitaya,* another ogre-tile company, he would not have endured such torment. But he was born into the third generation of the Onihyaku tradition and was the legitimate successor of the Onihyaku line. Onihyaku's selling point as an *Oniitaya* was the high quality of their ogre-tiles. As a result of the gap in his training, Morio was given a name that means "the clumsy person" among his family.

Kenichi's fifth child was Tsutomu. He was born in 1932, whereas Morio was born in 1925. The difference in their years of birth was crucial. When World War II ended, Tsutomu was thirteen years old, the perfect time to begin his training. According to Tsutomu, he started to work at Onihyaku after World War II. For a while, the company made charcoal stoves from clay instead of *Onigawara,* but gradually orders for *Onigawara* increased. Once Tsutomu started to make *Onigawara,* he could manipulate an *Onigawara* spatula almost at once, just like his father, Kenichi. Tsutomu told me that he grew up watching his father work and he inherited his dexterity. When Tsutomu was twenty-three years old, Kenichi passed away. While his father was ill, Onihyaku got an important order from Tenrikyo, a new religious sect in Nara, for some very large ogre-tiles. Tsutomu became the leader among his brothers for making these tiles. When Kenichi saw the completed ogre-tiles, he said, "Tsutomu, you will be able to do [this business]." Tsutomu said, "I had never made such a large ogre before that time, though. My father said that, looking at what I made."

Tenrikyo also had ordered the same kind of ogre-tiles from two other companies. Before the ogre-tiles were put on the buildings, they were exhibited in the field in front of the temples. Tsutomu was told by Tenrikyo, "Onihyaku's ogres are the best." Tsutomu said, "At that time, I gained confidence from that comment. . . . I'd never made such a thing before. Moreover, the other ogre-makers were called 'Master of Onigawara' in those days. However, I was the only one who was praised like that. That's why I gained confidence" (personal communication, February 20, 2000).

When the master of Onihyaku, Kenichi, was passing away, he acknowledged Tsutomu's skill. At that moment Onihyaku was transferred to the next generation. It was a turning point in Tsutomu's life. He had received two great acknowledgments: one from his father, a master of ogre-tile making, and another from a customer who praised Tsutomu in public. We can see this as a case of the succession of tradition, or it can be interpreted as a Hero's Journey. A novice, unacknowledged in the world of traditional *Onigawara,* went on a journey to pursue a goal. In the process of accomplishing his task through various trials, he was transformed. When he returned home, he was acknowledged by the people as a hero: A new master of the tradition was born. Tsutomu expresses his psychological transformation again and again in his comment, "I got confidence."

Although Tsutomu gained confidence from Tenrikyo's evaluation, he told me that, as soon as he heard the words of praise, "I thought that [my success] was due to Mr. Chōko Kato" (personal communication, February 20, 2000). Kenichi's relationship with the sculptor Chōko Kato had already brought a distinguishing trait to Onihyaku's *Onigawara* that other ogre-tile makers lacked. When he was nineteen, Tsutomu began to visit Chōko Kato, when Chōko was established as an artist of the Japan Fine Art Exhibition. Tsutomu recalled, "I started to make Onigawara when I was fifteen, or sixteen, [so] two or three years had passed since I began making ogre-tiles. Mr. Chōko Kato told me that I should do it [study sculpture]. [He said], 'It's good for you'" (Tsutomu Kajikawa, personal communication, February 20, 2000). So, Tsutomu became Chōko's pupil; Chōko chose Tsutomu. It was not at Tsutomu's request, but Chōko's desire. In this way, a master chooses his pupil. A master appears when a person is ready.

Tsutomu was fortunate because Chōko lived in Onihyaku's neighborhood. Tsutomu began to receive lessons from Chōko who encouraged him to put his work on exhibit. Tsutomu said, "I did not actually become his student, but just visited him with my work. He looked at it and corrected it." According to Tsutomu, the lessons were what he calls, "clay dessin." Dessin is the French word for drawing, for design. Chōko would look at Tsutomu's work and modify it in the way that drawing teachers often correct their pupils' work. Sometimes Chōko would break the thing Tsutomu had made. In this way, Tsutomu learned. Chōko said to Tsutomu, "You do not need to be a sculptor. It's good to be an artisan. Studying sculpture will be useful for you. So study!" After a while, Chōko's teaching was realized in Tsutomu's own experience. "After one year, when I made something, I could distinguish that this was better than that." Then, Tsutomu said, "If people in Takahama want to make a living by handmade Onigawara, they should study sculpture like I did" (personal communication, February 20, 2000).

Tsutomu developed his artistry further by studying the Buddhist sculptures of the Kamakura period (1185–1333). What Tsutomu told me recounts the story of the birth of an *Oniitashi* (personal communication, March 8, 2003):

> When I look at old ogres of the Kamakura period, there are poor ones, though. In those days, sculptors of Buddhist art were working, weren't they? I can see evidence that some people [in the Kamakura period] received training from those sculptors. When I look at such a good Onigawara, I think, 'Oh, this is not from Oniitashi. This piece shows the flow of the sculptors of Buddhist art.' In fact, there is an extremely nice piece showing the traces of this influence.
>
> Long ago, you see Horyuji, for example. There are ogres that were put on the temple. Those who made them, I think, were influenced by sculptors of Buddhist figures. I really think so. I cannot think of other possibilities. No question! If they were like me, [when I] studied by myself, I think it would be impossible to make such an ogre. (personal communication, February 20, 2000)

Horyuji, a seventh-century Buddhist temple in Nara, is the oldest wooden building in the world. Over the years, during many phases of restoration and reconstruction, ogre-tiles by many different ogre-makers have been put on the building. The Kamakura period was a time when Buddhist art was flourishing, especially in sculpture. According to Kobayashi (1991), the first known *Onigawara* showing an *Oni* was made in 1363, not so long after the Kamakura period (1185–1333). Thus, ogre-tile makers could have benefited from Japan's Golden Age of Sculpture. Tsutomu's comment on the ogre-tile makers in the Kamakura period becomes very suggestive when we consider how *Onigawara* was created in those days.

Tsutomu's own story reflects a relationship between ogre-tile making and the sculpture of the Kamakura period. Tsutomu says that before learn-

Tsutomu Kajikawa making a *Shishi*

Ryoji Kajikawa making *Onigawara*

ing sculpture, he was just "clay-modeling." He learned to discriminate between the ogre-tiles made by ordinary craftsmen and the ogre-tiles made by artisans under the influence of the Buddhist sculptors only after studying sculpture under Chōko Kato. I think that Tsutomu's idea about the relationship between ogre-tile makers and sculptors of Buddhist images came about because of his own experience of being just an ogre-tile maker who learned about sculpture. This is why he can discriminate among the ogre-tiles on the temple roof and see the hidden inscriptions left by the sculptors of the Kamakura period in some of their works. In this way, Tsutomu attained a higher level as an ogre-tile maker. As Tsutomu points out, the meeting of *Oniitashi* with modern sculpture is not a new thing, but a recurrence of a tradition within the development of an authentic *Oniitashi*. The mingling of Onihyaku's ogre-tile techniques and styles with that of sculptors, which began with Tsutomu's father Kenichi, brought a unique aesthetic sensibility to Onihyaku's ogre-tiles. One could say that this is a form of transcendence in craftsmanship that set Onihyaku apart from other lines.

Oniryo

The youngest son among the three brothers to become an *Oniitashi* is Ryoji Kajikawa. He was born in 1938. After his father, Kenichi, left this world, Ryoji worked together with Morio and Tsutomu at Onihyaku. However, when Ryoji married in 1968, he left Onihyaku and founded a new *Oniitaya*, called Oniryo, a word derived from Onihyaku. This was the moment of the reinvention of an older tradition by an individual. Oniryo is located in Nishibata, Hekinan, about five minutes by car from Onihyaku.

Ryoji's career followed a different course from that of his brothers. In 1945, when the war ended, Ryoji was seven years old. Morio was twenty-one years old and Tsutomu was thirteen years old. They are brothers, but, as I mentioned before, the war years caused a big difference in their circumstances, especially between Morio and the other two brothers, Tsutomu and Ryoji.

Ryoji attended an evening class at Hekinan High School. While he was still at the school, Ryoji started to work at Onihyaku. He was only fifteen years old. For two or three years after World War II, there was no demand for *Onigawara,* so Onihyaku made charcoal stoves and other products from earthenware. Now, Onihyaku needed Ryoji's participation because the demand for *Onigawara* was growing. It took four years for Ryoji to graduate from the evening school. Ryoji told me he also mastered the basics of ogre-tile making during the period. He said, "The best period to become a good artisan is when a person is in the teens. People say that it is too late to become an artisan after the age of twenty years old. I think that is correct" (personal communication, March 13, 1999).

Ryoji's statement about the ideal age for becoming an artisan lends support to Morio's complaint about his inability to bridge the gap between his ideas and his technique. In the same conversation, Ryoji identified another important factor in becoming a good artisan. He said, "We can do well at what we like." When he was at Onihyaku, he exhibited extraordinary enthusiasm for making ogres. When he saw a good piece made by Kenichi or Tsutomu, he made the same thing in the evening, trying to imitate their techniques. He told me that he did this many times in those days. However, Ryoji was a man of spirit who refused to yield even to Kenichi and Tsutomu, who were his masters.

Tsutomu told me about the days when he taught Ryoji how to make ogre-tiles, illustrating the process of how a basic tradition is transferred from a master to a pupil in the world of the ogre-tile makers (personal communication, March 8, 2003):

> We put our working tables together like this, when doing a job. I taught him from the beginning. First, without any exception, when an ogre-tile maker makes one thing, he always makes another identical thing. Now, when I made something, I said, "Ryoji, try to make this." Well, it is impossible for us to teach [each person] one by one taking [him] by the hand, isn't it? Our job is inevitable—a pupil only has to imitate what I am making while watching me.
>
> Then, gradually he will learn how to make things on his own, I think. Well, surprisingly, he [Ryoji] was clever with his hands. As soon as I taught him, he made an exact likeness to mine. He was a dexterous person. Hum. After three years, he was able to make almost anything.

Tsutomu's statement corresponds to what Ryoji told me. It is a sort of endorsement from Tsutomu. This skill and training caused Ryoji to say that he graduated to an artisan's level when he was nineteen years old. But Ryoji's training was not over. The next stage of training is what Tsutomu calls "Technique and Sense," meaning a harmonious combination of skill and aesthetic sensibility. He says that, once a person masters the techniques, he needs to assimilate them into something greater. Ryoji remembers that time clearly. "I was nineteen years old. When I started to learn sculpture, I was nineteen years old" (personal communication, March 13, 1999). His brief statement suggests that there was a palpable distinction between his work before and after learning sculpture.

Tsutomu introduced Ryoji to Chōko Kato, but Tsutomu and Ryoji quarreled. According to Tsutomu, Ryoji liked drawing pictures. Ryoji once told Tsutomu, "I dislike sculpture. I will become a painter. I will do a picture." But Tsutomu persuaded Ryoji to go and see Chōko. Later, Ryoji often grew angry with Tsutomu, saying "You forced a person who wanted to be a painter to become a sculptor." Tsutomu told me about that time while laughing loudly (personal communication, March 8, 2003).

Still Ryoji began to visit Chōko Kato at Tsutomu's insistence, Ryoji told me about his training with Chōko:

> When I began sculpture, I continued to make only heads. Whenever I made a head, it was broken down. . . . What I made was broken, though. My teacher made a face for me, again. Then, I took another head with the face on which I put an expression. He broke it again. It continued like that again and again. As a result, it was a *dessin of space*. (personal communication, March 13, 1999)

Chōko often said to Ryoji: "You probably do not understand what you are doing, though. [Your work] will be the foundation of Onigawara." This is a very interesting statement because Chōko was teaching Ryoji not how to make *Onigawara,* but how to make sculpture. Ryoji describes this work as a "dessin of space." Ryoji started to walk along the way of *Oniitashi* and the way of sculpture at the same time. Before long, the two worlds began to resonate with each other. That is to say, "Technique and Sense," in Tsutomu's words, creates resonance. Then, a new world opens up. This is a special moment that touches the heart. Ryoji experienced it with his body. It was not an intellectual interpretation, but a physical insight gained by means of repetitive physical performances. He said:

> Once you start to do sculpture, you will notice a place that you had never noticed before. The way of thinking completely changes. This sense cannot be understood without doing it for oneself. It is hard to explain in detail, though. The power of observation will transform. (personal communication, March 13, 1999)

Ryoji Kajikawa's firm is called Oniryo, and he is called Oniryo as though he embodied his shop and his shop were an extension of him—an apt ambiguity and identification, fit to the tradition of the atelier (Glassie 1989:95–104), that permits us to say that Oniryo's work is excellent, praising correctly the man in particular and his shop, with its several workers, in general. Sculptural technique is basic to Oniryo's excellence, and in 2009 I asked him again what changes when an ogre-maker learns sculpture. Oniryo's ogre-making is acknowledged as superior, but the shop's customers do not know why. Even the other ogre-tile makers do not have a clear idea of the reasons for Oniryo's superiority. This is probably because Oniryo's sculptural tradition has been hidden from the public. It is a matter of private training and study carried on while *Onigawara* work continues in the shop. People have not seen the sculptural activity in the workshop, and I did not have a chance to see it for a long time. Ogre-makers do not conceal their activities. It is just that their task is to make *Onigawara,* and sculpture is a private thing done after the big jobs, often at night. Several years ago, Ryoji first answered my question by saying, "It is different to convey the sense in words."

Since 1998, I have often visited him and we have frequently discussed questions of the sort. Recently, Ryoji answered me as follows:

> What does it mean by doing sculpture? I answered it before, though. I'd like to say that the [artist] becomes able to understand, *Space Beauty,* [or] *the beauty of space* . . . something like that. Once you get this sense, you begin to leave the world of technique in which an artisan follows the way and form of the Sanshu tradition for the purpose of making the work pretty. But, using a spatula, an artisan tends to make [the image] much as the spatula hits the clay. It can be easy to [apply] the spatula to the clay well when [the surface] is flatter than [when it is] round. As a result, the line will be dull. So [if you study sculpture] you will leave that kind of thing. You will naturally leave it. You will try to express something different from that.

Ryoji then added more explanation:

> One is able to say that one's attitude toward seeing changes. Sculpture is about how to express various things based on images. Onigawara is the same as sculpture. Looking at *Onigawara,* an ogre-tile maker decides that it should be like this, this part should become this way, this space is much prettier, or this space should be kept open. This sense also can be mastered through making sculpture.
>
> There is a line which looks beautiful. It is a decisive position. A sculptor chooses it when making a form. I think our world is the same as that of the sculptor. I think it is impossible to discover this without the acquisition of sculptural experience. (personal communication, January 12, 2009)

Now, a new generation has come to the Oniryo workshop. Shunichiro Kajikawa is the son of Ryoji, and he represents the fourth generation in the Onihyaku line. Shunichiro studied sculpture at Nagoya Art University and began working at Oniryo in 1994 when he was twenty-four years old. Shunichiro is an artisan of *Onigawara* and also a sculptor who has been actively involved in the Japan Fine Arts Exhibition. His workshop reveals Shunichiro's two-fold identity. The first floor is the place for making *Onigawara*. On the second floor is his atelier for making sculpture. Most people do not know of its existence. I myself did not know until recently. On March 25, 2009, Shunichiro welcomed me into his atelier. He was immediately transformed into an artist in that room, creating sculpture in front of me while I was taking pictures and talking with him. The tradition has been passed down through Hyakutaro, Kenichi, Morio, Tsutomu, Ryoji, and now to Shunichiro, literally from generation to generation in the Onihyaku blood line. Furthermore, the tradition of *Onigawara* itself has been evolving through the hands of each successor, while keeping the tradition of the Onihyaku line intact.

Conclusion

Onigawara are pieces of artistic work crafted by one artisan; however, when an *Onigawara* is placed on the roof of a house after leaving the hands of its creator, the *Onigawara* takes on another meaning. It creates a beautiful aspect for the house itself. The house is not cut off from the world. On the contrary: in Japan, it is common for similar styles of houses to come together in the same location, lending a local character and a local aesthetic to the *Onigawara* on each house, and becoming part of a local tradition that brings harmonious beauty to the entire region. This beauty repeats in other regions to effect a congruent multiplicity of form.

I have not described an event of simultaneity, such as an inter-communicative transaction between performer and audience, but rather an evolutionary process over a long stretch of time. In this process, communication, or even a mutual awareness between performers and audiences, is not always present. Performers do not know their audiences, and audiences do not know the performers. The name *Oniitashi* is not known to the public, although *Onigawara* are seen everywhere in Japan. But, performers and audiences connect through a regionalism based on place and daily life (Takahara 1990, 1995). This localized intercommunication in the world of *Onigawara* is not temporary, but enduring, carrying forward from generation to generation. Old performances and new performances resonate with each other in space; people and things communicate with each other in

Shunichiro Kajikawa making a large *Onigawara*

constant encounter. From this ceaseless interaction, comes the living local tradition that forms the identity of the people in place.

Ordinal events are usually bound by a time sequence in which the interaction among performers, audiences, and occasions can be easily determined. However, in the case of ogre-tile making, there is rarely any such inter-communicative interaction. The process of the creation of a tradition and a cultural identity is disconnected and invisible to outsiders because of the time lost between making and seeing. But the insiders, who share the tradition and live through time's passing, see the inter-communicative interaction as a whole. The scenery is not static; it has been changing dynamically through time while the tradition of the region has been kept intact by the people who share a place of life and work.

The case of the Onihyaku line illustrates the integration of the tradition of *Onigawara* and its individual performers. Even a love affair causes the appearance and disappearance of a tradition. Yamakichi, the company with the oldest tradition of *Onigawara* in Sanshu, disappeared because of the unexpected love affair between the adopted son-in-law, Hyakutaro, and Otake, the other daughter. The destruction of tradition and the creation of tradition were correlative. Later, the tradition of Onihyaku was renovated by their son Kenichi. Then, the fortuitous meeting of Kenichi and Sotarao Mitsueda resulted in the introduction of Western sculpture into the tradition of *Onigawara*. When Kenichi recognized and experienced the importance of learning sculpture, a new sensibility was assimilated into the Onihyaku line.

Onihyaku introduced this new aesthetic to the Sanshu tradition, as well as establishing a new sequence in the Onihyaku line. The meeting of artisan and sculptor began a synthesis of Sanshu *Onigawara* and Western sculpture, though Kenichi's path was not new at all. It was the recurrence of an earlier encounter between *Oniitashi* and the sculptors of Buddhist images during the Kamakura period (1185–1333), and that encounter was a revolutionary event that probably laid the foundation for the creation of Japanese *Onigawara*. Kenichi's encounter with Mitsueda can be seen as the moment of origin recaptured for our time. I am sure that Kenichi did not know about the event in the Kamakura period. This insight came from Tsutomu's meditation on the significance and meaning of the introduction of Western sculpture into Onihyaku. However, as a result of this synthesis, Onihyaku could establish a new tradition that extended the horizon of beauty in Sanshu *Onigawara*.

The *Onigawara* tradition has its origins deep in the past. However, the tradition is also infused with a new and contemporary spirit because of the

A house with *Onigawara* by Ryoji Kajikawa

Ogre in progress in the shop of Ryoji Kajikawa

individuals who replace the old generation with a new one. When we consider the meaning of *Onigawara* and *Oniitashi* in the history of Japan, we can see that the Onihyaku line represents an exemplary case history of the role of the individual in maintaining and bringing new life to an honored tradition.

REFERENCES

Fujiwara, Tsutomu and Hiroshi Watanabe. 1990. *Wagawara no hanashi*. Tokyo: Kashima Shuppansha.
Glassie, Henry. 1989. *The Spirit of Folk Art*. New York: Harry N. Abrams.
Kobayashi, Akio. 1981. *Onigawara*. Nara: Daizokeizai Shuppan.
———. 1985. *Ikiteiru Onigawara*. Kozu: Amex Kyohan.
———. 1991. *Zoku Onigawara*. Nara: Shikaban.
Kobayashi, Akio, and Mitsuyuki Nakamura. 1982. *Oni Onigawara*. Tokyo: INAX Shuppan.
Komai, Konosuke. 1963. *Nendogawara Dokuhon*. Tokyo: Shokokusha.
Mori, Ikuo. 1986. *Kawara*. Tokyo: New Science Sha.
———. 2001. *Kawara*. Tokyo: Hoseidaigaku Shuppankyoku.
Nagano Municipal Museum. 1998. *Yanegawara wa kawatta*. Nagano: Nagano Municipal Museum.
Sugiura, Shigeharu, ed. 1983. *Takahamashi shiryo (VI)*. Takahama: Takahamashi.
Takahara, Takashi. 1990. The Image of the City in Bloomington, Indiana. M.A. thesis, Indiana University.
———. 1995. The Visible City and the Invisible City: Toward a Postmodern Folklore of Place. Ph.D. diss., Indiana University.
———. 2002. The World of Ogre-Tile Makers—Tradition and Transformation of Sanshu Onigawara. *Bunmei* 21(9):227–47.
———. 2003. The World of Ogre-tile Makers—Kuroji: Yamamoto Kichibei Line (2). *Bunmei* 21(11):81–132.

Wanda Aragon, 1998, holding a jar she made and painted
in a design from the 1880s. The design is her favorite.

Bringing Them Back: Wanda Aragon and the Revival of Historic Pottery Designs at Acoma

Karen M. Duffy

In constructing tradition—"the creation of the future out of the past," as Henry Glassie writes (2003:176)—people necessarily engage in the construction of continuity. To be deemed successful by artists and audiences alike, performances of key cultural expressive forms must effect a convincing sense of connection with the past, one that provides a satisfying experience of linking with one's predecessors.[1]

Of special concern to me here is how such connection might be achieved in instances of revived tradition, where gaps of time, knowledge, and practice must be overcome in order to forge the desired link. Community artists, who bear the burden of accomplishment, would surely agree with Brynjulf Alver that these traditions "are more complex and problematic than we as scholars can probably ever realize" (1992:65).[2] Revival's complexity is evident to them at every turn in re-creation, from finding suitable texts for models, to understanding them through study and analysis, to attaining competence in their composition while facing practical and emotional barriers raised by their anonymity. If the impulse to connect is not thwarted by all this, it might be stopped cold by the fact that works of revival so often remain suspect, their authenticity questioned or their aesthetic found wanting (see Rosenberg 1991, 1993)—doubts that can trouble traditional audiences just as they do us, and cause them to reject the works altogether. Yet despite its challenges and risks, revival is undertaken regularly by art-

Acoma Pueblo

Acoma Valley, looking toward Acoma Mesa

ists in many cultures, including ones with thriving traditions offering less demanding ways to link with the past.

Wanda Aragon is such an artist. Her place, Acoma, New Mexico, is one of a group of traditionally oriented Native American communities in the Southwest—the Pueblos—where the art of pottery is of high importance. While methods of making Pueblo pottery have long been stable, styles of painting it have long been prone to variation and change. Revival has been a recurrent mechanism for that change; indeed, with design revivals known to have occurred extensively within Pueblo communities at least three times in the twentieth century[3] and "hundreds of times" over the course of earlier centuries (Dittert and Plog 1980:135), revival truly marks "a major theme" in the history of Pueblo pottery (Brody 1990:10). Working in this recursive vein, Wanda Aragon endeavors to bring back into currency a set of designs from the late 1800s that had been virtually forgotten at Acoma until she began using them some twenty-five years ago.[4] In detailing her efforts—her early motivations, her ongoing procedures, and her ensuing constructions of continuity—I seek to provide one example of how revival, and traditionalization more broadly, are perceived and experienced by those who enact them. My choice to present this example biographically has been guided by the many performer-centered studies by folklorists that examine individual artists' lives for their personal associations and experiences with art. Each such study offers an irreplaceable "subjective revelation" (Glassie 2010:7): one artist's intimate understanding of the "emotional core" of his or her art, without which our own understanding of the art remains incomplete (Abrahams 1970a:148). In that spirit, I relate Wanda's story much as she does, emphasizing throughout the traces of social bonding and the possibilities for connectedness that are entailed in pottery, ideas that arise repeatedly in her remarks on her life and work.

Growing Up at Acoma: The Presence of Elder Kin

Wanda Aragon was born in 1948 to Frank and Frances Torivio, the seventh of eight children. The family lived in McCartys, one of several scattered farming villages on the Acoma reservation below Acoma Pueblo, the ancestral village on Acoma Mesa. As is common in Native American communities, their immediate family circle was enlarged by regular, frequent interaction with additional relatives, particularly older adults who played important roles in the youngsters' upbringing. Even today Wanda speaks of these relatives with great affection and respect, demonstrating the bond she felt with them and the value she attaches to their formative influence on her.

The primary set of such relatives for Wanda was Frances's five sisters, several of whom lived, with their own families, as the Torivios' nearest neighbors in houses clustered loosely along the road in McCartys. Sharing maternal identity within the Eagle clan, all these aunts and cousins (and their husbands or fathers who had married in) were an integral part of one another's daily lives.[5] As the children helped in group tasks, they learned from a range of adults at once.

Among the women's favorite and most frequent joint activities was pottery making. Three sisters in particular—Frances, Mamie Ortiz, and Lolita Concho, all "very close," Wanda says—were productive, accomplished potters who gathered for company and mutual aid during the many stages of their work. Digging the clay and grinding it on metates; mixing it with water and ground potsherds for temper; forming the pots by coiling and scraping; slip-coating the pots with a white-clay solution and polishing them with smooth stones; painting their designs onto the white background with mineral colors they mixed and yucca-leaf brushes they made; and finally, firing the pots in kilns they built outdoors, letting the fire enrich and enliven the pots' colors. Exposed early to all these steps of the traditional process, young Wanda looked upon the actual making of pottery (preparing and shaping the clay) as "too much work" and "too dirty" to want to do it herself, but painting was another matter. From the start she was fascinated by her mother's and aunts' skillful use of the yucca brush and by the colors going onto the pots in striking designs, predominantly geometric.

At some point, Wanda says, she began to notice that each woman painted in a distinctive style marked by such features as different types of designs, amount and kinds of detail, and ways of using color. Mamie preferred balanced, often circular designs full of small details. Frances liked dynamic diagonal designs, which she sometimes painted within three stacked horizontal bands and generally left plain, unadorned by detail. Lolita was adventurous in her use of color, finding the most unusual shades of natural paint she could and using them to great effect. The women's designs were compatible with one another, falling clearly within the larger category of allover geometric patterns—from near the pot's base to its rim—painted at Acoma throughout the twentieth century, yet each potter's skills and preferences shaped her characteristic repertory and made her particular work unique (see also Abrahams 1970b). Learning to recognize her mother's and aunts' styles by watching them closely as they worked, by "really studying their

198

designs," Wanda learned about personal expression in traditional art and the freedom potters enjoy at Acoma to exercise it. She understood that creating a distinct pot—one imbued with the potter's own spirit and embodying in every stage of work her vision of the earth's inner beauty—was each potter's aim. And she saw that Acoma's traditional designs afforded a wide choice of means for rendering that vision in paint, making earth's beauty "show out" arrestingly on the pot's surface in unique, if sometimes subtle, variations.

Another set of relatives extended these lessons for Wanda, giving them dimension in time. These relatives were two of her father's aunts, Juana Louis and Maria Vicente. Both women were called by the Torivio children "grandmother," a term used at Acoma not only for one's mother's mother and father's mother but for their sisters as well (Garcia-Mason 1979:465, fig. 19); additionally, Wanda says, it is used as a matter of courtesy when addressing any older woman in one's clan. Of all the grandmothers in Wanda's life, Grandma Juana and Grandma Maria were most important, for her parents' mothers had both died before she was born and these two "stepped in" to fill the void.[6] Embracing fully their special familial role, they showered the children with affection, encouraged their good behavior and best effort through playful teasing,[7] and often took over their care, especially in the summertime when their parents were engaged in seasonal tasks of small-scale farming. Since Juana and Maria were active potters, many of Wanda's experiences with them involved pottery.

One of those summertime pottery-related experiences, which continued over several years, gave rise to Wanda's earliest memories of time spent with these grandmothers. When she was only three or four years old, she says, the women began taking her with them to "the highway"—U.S. Route 66, which lay along the northern boundary of Acoma reservation land. There, under a brush-covered shelter, they sold their pots to travelers along the road, as Acoma potters did from the time of the route's opening in the 1930s until its closing in the late 1950s. Wanda's deepest impressions are of long pleasurable days with her grandmothers and huge quantities of their pottery spread out on blankets for display. The pottery was mostly small cheery souvenir items, the likes of three-inch-high water jars, sheep and turkey figurines, ashtrays and twisted-handled "baskets" with modeled birds' heads at each side. All Juana's work was painted with a bright, sunny orange in simple designs, usually the terraced triangles called "steps" and occasionally the double-headed eagles called "thunderbirds." As Wanda noticed, those same designs and color were favored by many potters of Juana's generation who came of age in the early twentieth century. The observation com-

Frances Torivio, 1989, selling her pottery at Indian Market in Santa Fe with two of her grandchildren and one great-grandchild: Heather Aragon, Clarice Aragon, and Nishelle Torivio

One of Wanda's first pots, c. 1966, painted in a simple, linear, allover design; it blew apart in firing

prised Wanda's first rudimentary historicization of pottery. Likewise, her observation of the highway forms led to her later understanding of pottery's subjectivity to historical circumstance, its styles shifting not only with the generations but with the concerns, conditions, and events of their times.

Beyond these realizations, Wanda's interest in history and historical pottery remained latent. Her grandmothers did not, she says, speak to her in much detail about the past, even their own childhoods. But they and the other nurturing adults who surrounded her did speak often about the people of the past—previous generations of relatives, her ancestors, whether recently or long deceased—included in the extended family of which they were part. Though no longer living, these generations were understood to be spiritually available, present in the greater scheme of existence. Wanda was told to think of them daily, to seek their help, and to express in quiet internal talk her indebtedness to them: they had made her own life possible by their care for the land and one another, and by their prayers for the continuance of their people (see Ortiz 1992:5, 1993:32–33, 1998:xii). Developing respect and gratitude toward her ancestors, she eventually began to wonder what their lives might have been like. When she did, she wondered especially about a generation she knew must have been a special one—her great-grandmothers, who had raised the grandmothers she knew and loved. Again, pottery provided the context for her experience (this time, an inner experience), which occurred once she had learned the art and extended her social ties further through years of its practice.

Becoming a Potter, Finding a Personal Style: The Search for the Old Pots

In her teenage years Wanda moved from watching her mother make pottery to actively helping her, a move that initiated her informal apprenticeship as a potter and caused her childhood aversion to working with clay to fade. She had long helped in small ways, as all the children did—chewing yucca leaves to soften them before their mothers shaped them into paintbrushes, for example, and joining the adults in "picking" (gathering) potsherds for temper. But their handling of pots-in-the-making was rare until they reached adolescence. Then Wanda and the other girls were bid to assist directly in basic tasks of the women's art, first polishing the white slip with stones, later "filling in" (painting the solid areas of) the designs their mothers outlined in black paint. Wanda thinks now that the hands-on closeness to her mother's pottery, the sheer enjoyment of the fun and sociability of helping, and the opportunity to wield the yucca brush at last, all sparked her desire, at about eighteen, to learn the art of pottery in its full scope. Soon, under her mother's watchful guidance, she was making and painting pots of her own.

At first Wanda's designs were simplified versions of Frances's. As she gained skill and confidence with the yucca (which unlike commercial brushes is pliable along its entire length), and as Frances encouraged her to paint "just whatever you want to paint," she tried other designs in the Acoma repertory, experimenting for a number of years with a wide variety she had seen used by potters both within and outside her family. By the time she was in her mid-thirties she was, as she puts it, challenging every design that came her way. At that point, she was painting regularly and selling her pots at markets and to dealers to help support her new family: her husband, Marvis Aragon, and their children Marvis Junior, Clarice, and Heather. Independent as a potter and mature as a woman, she was ready to choose and develop a personal style of painting,[8] one that would absorb her completely and allow her to apply her artistic sensibilities in ever more interesting ways to the potter's charge of revealing earth's beauty, hidden in clay and minerals until their transformation at the potter's hands.

For a while Wanda joined her contemporaries at the pueblo in painting a set of designs called the fine-lines, or simply "the lines," which seemed to offer great promise as a vehicle for personal stylistic development. These black-on-white patterns are painted in grid-based allover formats such as starbursts and labyrinths to create pots of startlingly modern, eye-dazzling impact. Stimulated by the many models she saw, Wanda tackled the challenges of planning, laying out, and painting the lines' intricate arrangements. She achieved a level of competence with them that pleased her, and they sold well, apparently pleasing her customers, too. Yet before long she found the designs "too easy" and began to tire of them. Composed only of "straight lines and square blocks" and dependent largely upon an exacting technical proficiency, they left her with little aesthetic pleasure or personal fulfillment. Furthermore, Wanda was bothered by the fact that there was "too much of that work." The fine-lines were beginning to dominate other styles at Acoma, limiting the variety that befitted her artistic tradition as she had always known it.

It was then that Wanda, dissatisfied with familiar styles of the present, became curious about unfamiliar ones from the past. When her curiosity surfaced it did so in personal, familial terms consistent with her experience of expressivity in art. One evening in the mid-1980s, as she sat working on pottery at home with Marvis, she spoke aloud the question that had been increasingly on her mind: "I wonder, what kind of pots would my great-grandmothers have been making? What would *their* designs be like?" No pots from that era, eighty to one hundred years before—the 1880s and 1890s—remained at the pueblo; as Wanda knew, all had long ago been sold out of Acoma family collections into museum ones, to early researchers who wanted to save the old pots as examples of what they believed was a culture doomed to extinction. To see those pots now and to answer the question that gripped her, Wanda would have to visit the museums to which they were taken. She would, as she accurately assessed, have to "start doing the research myself."[9]

Tracking down her great-grandmothers' art, Wanda went first to two cultural institutions in state with sizeable holdings from Acoma: the School of American Research (recently renamed the School for Advanced Research) in Santa Fe and the Maxwell Museum of Anthropology in Albuquerque. Although she discovered that neither held as many late-nineteenth-century pots as she had hoped, most having been taken east before these institutions were established, she found them well worth visiting, not only for the old pottery she did see but for what she learned about how to conduct museum research. At both places, she made appointments with curatorial staff to escort her into restricted storage areas where she could handle and closely examine the pots that attracted her. She obtained copies of accession records, made sketches, and took photographs, later organizing the documentation in binders at home for study and reference as she worked. All these practices became standard in her future visits to museum collections.

Meanwhile, two pottery dealers, themselves admirers of the old pots and anxious for variety in contemporary work, encouraged Wanda's interest and responded to her requests for help.[10] One sent photographs of about a half-dozen pots from early Acoma collections housed at the Smithsonian Institution; another sent books with color images of older Acoma pots and a subscription to *American Indian Art Magazine,* which often features historic work. These resources provided Wanda with many models from which to paint. Even more critically, they inspired her to keep searching for the old pots themselves, to see and touch them in order to appreciate their subtle qualities and true colors, consider them from all sides, and understand the structural systems of their designs.

Sometime around 1986, at a Native American art show in Milwaukee, Wanda met a Seminole beadworker and appliqué artist who, like her, was trying to locate the old designs of her people. As the two shared stories of their common desire, the woman urged her to persist and offered important practical information: federal funding, she told Wanda, was available to Native artists for museum research.

It took her several years to do so, but with the assistance of a niece who worked in Washington, D.C., Wanda obtained and submitted the application forms; subsequently, she received the award. In 1992, accompanied by her mother and sister Lilly Salvador—also a talented potter—she headed to Washington to the Smithsonian, to see firsthand the pottery collected at Acoma a century earlier, in 1879 and again in the 1880s, including those whose photographs she had been sent. Of all her museum visits before and after, Wanda says, that was "the Big One."

For all three women, the encounter with the great-grandmothers' pottery was overwhelmingly emotional. As Lilly recalled it for me, once they were given permission to touch the pots, they did not hold back. "We *went* for it," she said. They brushed their fingers over the pots' outer forms, felt all around their insides, and spoke to them softly in Acoma Keresan, voicing consolation for being far from home and reassurance that they were in a good, safe place. So approaching the pots as if relatives long held captive in strange surroundings, the potters communicated with them—and by extension, their makers—in deeply satisfying ways, through touch and talk in their native tongue. "We *really* let it out," Lilly told me. "Tears were flowing."

In turn, the pots communicated in their own way, effecting in Wanda a transformative aesthetic experience. "It just changed me," she says. From her very first view of the old pots, she was amazed by their beauty and the artistry of their makers. Looking back, she recalls her response:

> The designs were just so *different,* and *beautiful.*
> I thought, "These are *beautiful* designs."
> And the ladies that painted them on had *so much* talent. These were *their* designs at that time, and it was a shame to lose them.

Sad that the designs were no longer used "for people *now* to enjoy," regretting that they had been "lost," Wanda resolved then and there, in the storage rooms of the Smithsonian:

> I thought, "These are beautiful designs. They are too pretty to lose."
> And so I decided to bring them back.

Studying the Old Pots: Beauty and Challenge in the Old Designs

The designs that amazed Wanda were indeed different from the ones with which she was familiar. Studying the old pots in the museum and in photographs at home, she determined that the late-nineteenth-century designs have four primary distinctive features: they are big, full of curves, deep in color, and placed centrally on the pot with much open space above and below. These features set them apart clearly from their twentieth-century successors, the smaller, linear, generally lighter-toned patterns that cover the pot nearly entirely (and which became increasingly fine and complex over the century's course). Certainly when they came into vogue around 1900, the new designs, even in the simple versions Juana painted, initiated a change that was sweeping. By the time Ruth Bunzel did her fieldwork for *The Pueblo Potter* in the mid-1920s, the old style—predominant only fifty years earlier—had, like the old pots themselves, completely vanished from Acoma ([1929] 1972:36).[11]

To Wanda's eye, the characteristics of the old style are points of great beauty; they are, she often tells me, what captures her attention and holds her interest in these designs. At the same time, as an artist her appreciation of the traits is inextricably tied up with her knowledge of the processes underlying them. Aware that each point of distinction involves a particular difficulty or set of difficulties in execution, she sees and is drawn by both at once: by the challenges these designs pose and by the beauty they possess. The integration in her mind of beauty and challenge is evident in the way she discusses the four stylistic attributes in turn, each of which represents a new step toward understanding her great-grandmothers' bold artistry, bringing her closer to her goal of "feeling what they felt" as they painted.

First, she says, the large size of the designs makes them beautiful because it causes them to "stand out," as Acoma designs are meant to do. But it also magnifies any mistakes the painter might make in rendering the designs, whose formal elements and stylistic traits (including the ones Wanda stresses) are unfamiliar to the modern potter. Trouble in drawing these designs begets more trouble: whereas errors in the smaller designs can easily go unnoticed and so are sometimes left as is, correcting a mistake in a big design, where it "shows out" glaringly, is nearly mandatory, and there is only one way to do it. Using a damp cloth, the potter must, Wanda says, just "wash the whole design and start over." The very prominence of the old designs makes them terribly risky.

Then, she says, the old designs' curviness is beautiful because it gives them grace; they bend and bow pleasingly. But as every potter knows, painting curves is not as easy as it looks, and the longer they are, the harder they are. One difficulty is technical: the potter must apply an even pressure with the yucca brush (which must hold neither too much nor too little paint) so that the line be smooth and flowing along the whole long course of the curve.

Water jar by Wanda Aragon, 1987.
Late-nineteenth-century style

Water jar by Frances Torivio, 1980.
Twentieth-century style

Another difficulty is judging the curve's best trajectory: while there is only one straight line possible between two points, there are many curved ones; the question is, which will convey the most grace and avoid awkwardness or stiffness? A final difficulty—which, according to Wanda, is even greater than the other two—is the designs' *overall* curvilinear nature: being based thoroughly on curves, the design layout lacks a grid and is therefore hard to plot on the surface of the pot, confounding the potter accustomed to working from clear-cut, even divisions. As she comments, "When you have a design that has just straight lines, it is *much* more easier to section it off than these that curve." The elegance of the old designs makes them quite tricky.

Next, Wanda addresses her favorite characteristic of the old designs— their color, beautiful for its rich depth. Two factors, she says, account for this. For one, there is, quite simply, more paint on the old pots. The designs' large size calls for coverage of broad expanses: to fill those adequately, paint has been applied in multiple coats, not just the one or two typically used for the modern designs. As a result, the old pots have a lavish appearance. The challenge in achieving that, Wanda explains, is that the potter must sustain patience, since each layer of color, carefully laid on, must dry thoroughly before the next application begins; the potter must wait, resisting the temptation to rush the work or skip the extra coats.

The other thing that makes the old pots' color so deep is the nature of the hues themselves. They are, Wanda says, darker—more richly saturated— than those seen on twentieth-century pots: the old orange approaches burnt sienna, the red is near maroon. But the pigments from which those colors were made are hard to come by today because knowledge of their location was forgotten after the old style lost popularity around the turn of the century. Though Wanda looks everywhere and occasionally discovers small deposits, she has yet to identify bountiful sources. Not only, then, can the old designs' rich color be laborious to paint, it can be difficult even to find.

Last, Wanda speaks of the central placement of the old designs and the importance of the white slip around them. Spacious and open, with no framing lines to hem them in, these designs seem particularly light, as if they float on the background. In fact, instead of eclipsing that ground as the modern designs tend to do, the old designs use it effectively to set off their other distinctive properties: their rich colors, graceful curves, and large patterns. The use suits Wanda's taste perfectly. More importantly, it suits, in her opinion, the Acoma aesthetic, for, as she states, "I think to have a design *stand out* you want *space* around it, is how *I* feel about it." The increasingly crowded compositions on contemporary pottery represent, to her, a move in the wrong direction. Yet the spaciousness that Wanda admires poses a great challenge for her as a modern potter: its correct proportion—the proper balance of painted and unpainted areas—is difficult to judge because it is determined by rules of ratio utterly different from those governing the style in which she was trained. As is true of all artists, the sense of proportion she holds is so deeply ingrained as to be almost instinctual; to paint these designs, she must uproot this fundamental sense and supplant it with one that is unfamiliar. The openness of the old style can be more than a little mystifying.

While Wanda focuses on those four points as the style's defining aesthetic characteristics, she also notes that the old pots tend to feature a special subject matter: "You know," she says, "they're just more of nature." Life forms—birds, leaves, vines, berries, and flowers—are abundant in the old designs; although highly stylized, they can easily be spotted there amidst more purely conceptual shapes. Wanda believes these abstracted life forms are based on the old potters' direct observations of their natural surroundings; whatever their source, the subjects have been imaged in geometrized patterns rather than realistic pictures, in accordance with longstanding cultural preference.[12] The bird and plant forms complement the period style well, Wanda points out, since they are full of long, lithe curves and lend themselves to strong, layered color.

Throughout her work of studying the old pots—an effort that is continual for her—Wanda muses repeatedly on the artists who painted them. What, she wonders, do the many birds and plants and other distinctive designs reveal about these women? What do they tell about the lives they led, and the kind of people they were? Contemplating their pottery, Wanda focuses on the most outstanding qualities she sees in the pots and then relates them directly to the personal qualities of their makers. Above all, she says, they loved and valued beauty, nature, and color—signs of vibrant, lush life arising from Mother Earth to make possible continued human existence at Acoma. Sharing those values, seeing them as prime ones of her culture, Wanda cannot help but admire these women as she admires their art and dedicates herself to its revival.

Getting to Know the Old Potters: Connecting through Art

Wanda's practice as an artist—her committed study of the old designs and her work to acquire competence in painting them—has thus allowed her

A water jar, outlined by Wanda in a nineteenth-century
parrot design, alongside her source, a photograph in J. J.
Brody's *Beauty from the Earth*

to come to know the old potters generally, as a generation of artists themselves. Yet it has done more. It has, she is certain, allowed her to identify a few individuals within that generation as distinct from one another in their personal styles as were her mother and aunts.

There is the woman, she proposes, who sometime in the 1890s painted two versions of a design that, while firmly rooted in the old style, anticipates in important ways the new: her unusual composition combines old-style curves and leaves with squares rising diagonally, somewhat like the turn-of-the-century steps that Grandma Juana used to paint.[13] On one of the two versions, scallop-trimmed triangles edge the tops and bottoms of the stepped squares; on the other they edge their sides. Because other aspects of the design are the same and qualities of the pots' workmanship correspond, Wanda concludes that both examples can be attributed to the one inventive person. The slight variation between them can be explained by the potter's desire to try out different possibilities for her design, Wanda says, a desire that is familiar to her and to all Acoma potters she knows.

Another woman working about ten years earlier likewise made, in Wanda's judgment, two versions of a striking design she probably devised.[14] This woman is of special interest to Wanda, for hers is the design that she favors herself, of all the ones she paints. It involves a complex type of symmetry Wanda finds thrilling, one in which the elements are formally transposed in a staggered, alternating sequence along a curved band encircling the pot. Both versions of this particular composition render the band as a wide strip of fretwork that highlights the design's interrelatedness. Both have large, dark spreading motifs attached to the fret from both sides in a series of arcs. Both feature as well a third main motif, a medallion with leaves inside. But for a fourth main motif that alternates with the third, one version uses a medallion complementary to (though different from) the first medallion, while the other version uses only a plain triangle, lacking any interior elaboration. Furthermore, the latter version has far less detail overall, not only within the motifs but beside them and at the rim. Comparing the two versions, Wanda finds the plainer one to be disappointing—too empty and not well thought out, since, to her eye, its alternating motifs (the medallion and the triangle) relate only loosely to one another, breaking the design's rhythm. So different are the two versions that Wanda initially assumed they were made by different potters. Now, however, she thinks the same woman made both; having studied them carefully, she has found close resemblances in shape and color. How, then, does she account for the woman's great, almost extreme, simplification of design on one of her pots?

Once again Wanda draws an explanation from her own experience as an Acoma potter, an experience she believes would have been shared by potters of the past. This time, sympathetically posing a good reason for the potter's lesser performance, she reveals a marvelous ability to conceive of the woman personally in a particular, all-too-human moment: "Maybe," she suggests, "she was rushing. Time might have been catching up with her for, maybe, one of the ceremonial dances. And then she just put that big design there instead of, you know, putting all this other." The pressure to meet scheduled obligations is one Wanda knows well. On the one hand, she feels it from her community's annual rituals, those times when potters provide large numbers of pots for gifts and religious purposes; on the other, she feels it from the cycle of events like Santa Fe's Indian Market, when she and many other potters bring in a significant portion of their family's yearly income. While the nineteenth-century woman was spared the demands of the latter situation, she would still have felt those of the former, and so be as likely as anyone else to need, on some occasion, to hurry a piece of work.

As Wanda becomes acquainted with such potters through their designs, she enjoys thinking about her own possible relationship to them. "Might it be a great-, or a great-great—I don't know how many greats!—grandmother, either on my maternal or paternal side, maybe?" she wonders. "That *had* that design, or painted that design?" Although purely speculative, the musing nevertheless augments her sense of affiliation with the potters she is getting to know, and contributes emotional depth to her appreciation of their art. At times she even calls them all "the great-grandmothers I never knew," extending the term beyond her closest relations as a respectful form of address, just as she was taught to do with "grandmother." Whether or not these women are kin to her, she says, they are her teachers, enriching the lessons she learned from her mother, aunts, and grandmothers, allowing her to cross those generations in order to access these elders' own special vision of the earth's beauty.

Even with all her study and close attention, Wanda finds that it is not always easy to paint the great-grandmothers' designs. Often, she needs to call upon them for help. This most spiritual level of connection is effected in two ways, depending on Wanda's immediate circumstances. When she is lucky enough to have one of the old pots before her as she does in a museum, she achieves her connection by touch—not, as she once told me expressly, feeling for *how* the pot was made, but reaching for the *hands* that made it. The encounter is direct and real to Wanda because, as a potter herself, she knows the potter's spirit inheres in her work: all her emotions, com-

Wanda Aragon painting with a yucca brush, 1996

municated through her hands to the clay in the creative moment, remain available to anyone who would sensitively touch her pot thereafter.[15]

When Wanda is at home, though, with only her photographs and book illustrations for study, she uses a mediated method: in the absence of the actual pot, she touches its image, tracing her finger over the design with a prayer that it might "come into" her by the aid of the potter, whose hand she reaches for even in the photo. Her prayer takes the form of the quiet inner "talk," informal and intimate, that Wanda was taught as a child to use when addressing her ancestors. It goes, she explains to me, more or less this way:

> In my mind, I would talk to the artist that this design belonged to. "Whoever you are, come help me with this design." You know, spiritually: "Come and help me.
> "I want to paint your design on my pottery! Help me to revive it.
> "I want to bring it back," you know, "so people can enjoy it," is what I tell her.
> And that helps. Uh-huh, that helps. Yeah.

If Wanda is having an especially hard time with a design, she will continue her talk even as she struggles: "'How in the world did you ever *do* this?' You know, I would be talking to the *picture* and trying to connect somehow!!" Laughter punctuated Wanda's report, but her words about the results of such talk with the old potters were decidedly serious:

> And then, after I've painted it, I feel closer to that potter. You know, that they actually *helped* me. She, whoever painted that design, you know, *did* help me to figure it out.
> So, you know, you *do* connect, in some way. Yeah.

By putting her mind to the artist's mind, her hand to her hand, Wanda feels what the artist felt. Through the contact that she makes, the difficulties that confront Wanda as she paints are eased, and her work made pleasurable. At this point, the connection between herself and the original artist is complete. That connection—at once personal, spiritual, emotional, and aesthetic—is, Wanda says, altogether amazing to her, and makes the long effort she took to achieve it worthwhile. She only hopes that the deep satisfaction she finds in her finished pot is shared: that people today will enjoy the old designs again, and that the old potters will be happy to see them doing so. In that case, she hints, her art might bring, not only enjoyment to viewers and happiness to early artists, but perhaps even other possibilities she articulates in her prayerful talk: a flow of life-enhancing ancestral blessings to her, her family, and her people as a whole, carrying them into the future.

For Wanda, re-creating the old works is ultimately a matter of re-imagining the old artists. Bringing back their designs, she brings back an ineffable sense of the artists themselves—their standards of beauty and value, their engagement in creative challenge and play, their stunning successes and everyday accomplishments. With their art as her medium, she builds a smooth conduit for continuity between them and her, between then and now, based on the model she learned from her beloved elders. Although such work as she undertakes, reaching over stretches of time to revive expressive forms of the past, is not the usual course of tradition, its repeated occurrence throughout the world stands as pointed testimony to tradition's power in the human heart.

Notes

1. Among many folkloristic writings on tradition, I rely in particular upon those by Dell Hymes (1975), who formulated the concept of *traditionalization;* Dan Ben-Amos (1984), who contextualized it; and Richard Bauman (1992, 2001) and Henry Glassie (2003), who have refined it. I also appreciate studies by my colleagues in Native American folklore, especially Jason Jackson (2003, 2008), on Yuchi ideas about tradition as *work,* and Tom Mould (2005), on critiques of modernity implicit in Choctaw and other cultural notions of *the traditional.* In my essay here, I highlight the emotive character of the belief in tradition's "continuity," focusing on it as a motivating force for the artist engaged in revival. I fully agree with Mould that such belief acknowledges and comments critically upon harsh realities of cultural disruption. For precisely this reason, the "continuity" stressed by many traditional practitioners may be better understood as "connection," the term Wanda Aragon uses, since it does not imply a wholesale or permanent state.

2. Alver speaks exclusively of *revitalization,* using that term for traditions "already gone or about to disappear" (1992:65). Preferring to distinguish between those two types, I use *revival* for "dead and gone" traditions (such as the designs discussed in this essay) and *revitalization* for "alive but weak and dying" ones. It is not my purpose here to mount an argument for these definitions, but only to be clear about my own use. The terms are applied variously by folklorists; Neil Rosenberg, for example, uses them interchangeably (1991:221).

3. Twentieth-century design revivals include most notably ones initiated by Nampeyo of Hopi, Maria Martinez of San Ildefonso, and Lucy Lewis of Acoma, each of whom introduced a radical change into the contemporary repertory of her pueblo by drawing upon earlier models no longer in use. While scholarship on these three potters often argues vehemently about the extent of outsiders' roles

in prompting the revivals and so reveals a persistent tendency to question the potters' creative initiative (Frisbie 1973), it generally recognizes that for the potters and their predecessors who engaged in revival, such work likely represented "an important affirmation of their past" (Dittert and Plog 1980:135).

4. For an extended version of this essay on Wanda Aragon's revival project, see Duffy (2002:181–283). Folkloristic writings on Wanda and her work include Duffy (1995) and Glassie (1999a:48–56, 1999b:66–74). Her work appears in many art and art historical publications on Pueblo pottery, most importantly Dillingham (1992). See Duffy (2002:379–81) for further references.

5. Acoma clans, based on matrilineal descent, establish local residence to promote ongoing interaction and mutual support. The writer Simon Ortiz, one of Wanda's cousins in the Eagle clan, says, as she does, that their maternal family in McCartys was "close" and held a strong "connectedness" among themselves (1992:6). Many of his poems and essays concern his childhood in McCartys during the 1940s and 50s (e.g., Ortiz 1992, 1993, 1998).

6. Juana and Maria's actions fit Edward Dozier's account of the role of paternal relatives in the western pueblos, including Acoma: "The father's relatives, . . . particularly father's mother and father's sisters, . . . exert little authority and do not discipline [the child], but they provide love, comfort, and aid during crucial and anxious periods of his life" (1970:138).

7. For examples of cross-generational teasing at Acoma and discussions of its functions, see White (1943:320–21) and Duffy (2002:188–89).

8. The desire of Pueblo potters to paint in individually recognizable styles is neither new nor rare. We know from Ruth Bunzel that in the 1920s potters insisted they never copied one another's work but instead came up with their own design arrangements ([1929] 1972:51–53). Although she noted that many potters were in fact stylistically conventional, she found "a goodly sprinkling of artists of marked individuality" and acknowledged that there were no doubt more than she could recognize (68). In his late-twentieth-century study of Acoma pottery, Rick Dillingham wrote that finding a personal style is considered to be "part of a potter's artistic development" (1992:108). My research indicates that this stage usually comes in early to middle adulthood after a period of wide experimentation, as it did for Wanda.

9. Anthropologist Anne Fienup-Riordan calls such work "visual repatriation," a reclaiming, not of artifacts, but of cultural knowledge embedded in them (2005:280–89).

10. These were, respectively, Richard Howard, a retired National Park Service archaeologist who collected and sold Native American art, and Rick Dillingham, a ceramic artist who collected and dealt in Pueblo pottery. Wanda credits both for their longtime support and encouragement. The niece in Washington, D.C., was Louann Tenequer.

11. Bunzel ([1929] 1972) contrasts the two styles, noting that they are based on "entirely different principles," (36–38, 81–82; see also plates xi and xiv). Although she found no trace of the older style at Acoma in the 1920s, she knew it from her fieldwork preparations, having visited the Smithsonian to study and photograph

its pottery collections—including the very ones Wanda saw in 1992—in the weeks before she went to the Southwest (Hardin 1993:261).

12. These designs first appeared on Acoma pottery in the mid-1800s. Rick Dillingham believes they were inspired by floral and faunal images on Euro-American household items that belonged to neighboring colonists or arrived in New Mexico on the Santa Fe Trail (1992:142–46). Henry Glassie argues that historical connections alone do not adequately explain the enthusiastic acceptance of such images by folk cultures, including Acoma's. Instead, he credits the powerful aesthetic attraction these images hold for many of the world's traditional peoples by virtue of the balance the forms strike between geometry and realism (1989:147–66). For a comprehensive examination of geometry in art, see Hagen (1986).

13. Because its motifs are large and its white background prominent, this design clearly belongs to the old type. Nonetheless, a combination of new- and old-style elements such as it bears is rare. As Bunzel noted, the two styles were not developmentally continuous; they overlapped temporally for a brief period, but the new represents a break with the old rather than an evolution from it ([1929] 1972:81–82). The design under discussion here may be as close to a transitional one as exists. See Toulouse (1977:26, bottom) for a photograph of one of the two 1890 versions; see Dillingham (1992:84, fig. 5.1) for Wanda's rendition.

14. The two versions are presented in Dillingham (1977:47, fig. 5) and Howard (1987:49, fig. 6); Wanda uses the former as a model. While the type of symmetry these pots bear was applied in other patterns by many nineteenth-century potters, this pair is exceptional in its combination of motifs, particularly the large spreading forms hooked onto the fret. Wanda's rendition is shown in a photograph that appears in Glassie (1999a:118, top, and 1999b:224, bottom), taken by him at the same time that I took the photograph I include in this essay.

15. Like Acoma potters with whom I have spoken, Santa Clara potter Nora Naranjo-Morse speaks of the release of the potter's emotions via touch into the clay. Further, she specifies that the potter's consequent sense of connection with her work has a strong traditional base (Abbott 1994:201–2).

REFERENCES

Abbott, Lawrence, ed. 1994. *I Stand in the Center of the Good: Interviews with Contemporary Native American Artists.* Lincoln: University of Nebraska Press.

Abrahams, Roger D. 1970a. *A Singer and Her Songs: Almeda Riddle's Book of Ballads.* Baton Rouge: Louisiana State University Press.

———. 1970b. Creativity, Individuality and the Traditional Singer. *Studies in the Literary Imagination* 3:5–34.

Alver, Brynjulf. 1992. The Making of Traditions and the Problem of Revitalization. In *Tradition and Modernisation,* ed. Reimund Kvideland, pp. 65–71. NIF Publications No. 25. Turku: Nordic Institute of Folklore.

Bauman, Richard. 1992. Icelandic Legends of the *Kraftaskáld*. In *Rethinking Context: Language as an Interactive Phenomenon*, eds. Alessandro Duranti and Charles Goodwin, pp. 125–45. Cambridge: Cambridge University Press.

———. 2001. Tradition, Anthropology of. In *International Encyclopedia of the Social and Behavioral Sciences*, eds. Neil J. Smelser and Paul B. Baltes, 23:15819–24. Amsterdam: Elsevier.

Ben-Amos, Dan. 1984. The Seven Strands of *Tradition:* Varieties in Its Meaning in American Folklore Studies. *Journal of Folklore Research* 21:97–131.

Brody, J. J. 1990. *Beauty from the Earth: Pueblo Indian Pottery from the University Museum of Archaeology and Anthropology*. Philadelphia: The University Museum of Archaeology and Anthropology, University of Pennsylvania.

Bunzel, Ruth L. [1929] 1972. *The Pueblo Potter: A Study in Creative Imagination in Primitive Art*. New York: Dover.

Dillingham, Rick. 1977. The Pottery of Acoma Pueblo. *American Indian Art Magazine* 2(4):44–51.

———. 1992. *Acoma and Laguna Pottery*. Santa Fe: School of American Research Press.

Dittert Alfred E., Jr., and Fred Plog. 1980. *Generations in Clay: Pueblo Pottery of the American Southwest*. Flagstaff: Northland.

Dozier, Edward. 1970. *The Pueblo Indians of North America*. Prospect Heights: Waveland.

Duffy, Karen M. 1995. Narrator Style and Purpose in a Story's Crafting: Two Tellings of a Tale from Acoma. *Journal of Folklore Research* 32(3):221–66.

———. 2002. Carry It On for Me: Tradition and Familial Bonds in the Art of Acoma Pottery. Ph.D. diss., Indiana University.

Fienup-Riordan, Anne. 2005. *Yup'ik Elders at the Ethnologisches Museum Berlin: Fieldwork Turned on Its Head*. Seattle: University of Washington Press.

Frisbie, Theodore R. 1973. The Influence of J. Walter Fewkes on Nampeyo: Fact or Fantasy? In *The Changing World of Southwestern Indians: A Historic Perspective*, ed. Albert H. Schroeder, pp. 231–44. Glorietta: Rio Grande Press.

Garcia-Mason, Velma. 1979. Acoma Pueblo. In *Handbook of North American Indians, Volume 9 (Southwest)*, ed. Alfonso Ortiz, pp. 450–66. Washington, D.C.: Smithsonian Institution.

Glassie, Henry. 1989. *The Spirit of Folk Art: The Girard Collection at the Museum of International Folk Art*. New York: Harry N. Abrams.

———. 1999a. *The Potter's Art*. Bloomington: Indiana University Press.

———. 1999b. *Material Culture*. Bloomington: Indiana University Press.

———. 2003. Tradition. In *Eight Words for the Study of Expressive Culture*, ed. Burt Feintuch, pp. 176–97. Urbana: University of Illinois Press.

———. 2010. *Prince Twins Seven-Seven: His Art, His Life in Nigeria, His Exile in America*. Bloomington: Indiana University Press.

Hagen, Margaret A. 1986. *Varieties of Realism: Geometries of Representational Art*. Cambridge: Cambridge University Press.

Hardin, Margaret Ann. 1993. Zuni Potters and *The Pueblo Potter:* The Contributions of Ruth Bunzel. In *Hidden Scholars: Women Anthropologists and the Native American Southwest,* ed. Nancy J. Parezo, pp. 259–69. Albuquerque: University of New Mexico Press.

Howard, Richard. 1987. How Old Is That Pot? *American Indian Art Magazine* 12(4):46–49.

Hymes, Dell. 1975. Folklore's Nature and the Sun's Myth. *Journal of American Folklore* 88:345–69.

Jackson, Jason Baird. 2003. *Yuchi Ceremonial Life: Performance, Meaning, and Tradition in an American Indian Community.* Lincoln: University of Nebraska Press.

———. 2008. Traditionalization in Ceremonial Ground Oratory: Native American Speechmaking in Eastern Oklahoma. *Midwestern Folklore* 34(2):3–16.

Mould, Tom. 2005. The Paradox of Traditionalization: Negotiating the Past in Choctaw Prophetic Discourse. *Journal of Folklore Research* 42(3):255–94.

Ortiz, Simon J. 1992. Introduction. In *Woven Stone,* pp. 3–33. Tucson: University of Arizona Press.

———. 1993. The Language We Know. In *Growing Up Native American: An Anthology,* ed. Patricia Riley, pp. 29–38. New York: William Morrow.

———. 1998. Introduction: Wah Nuhtyuh-yuu Dyu Neetah Tyahstih (Now It Is My Turn to Stand). In *Speaking for the Generations: Native Writers on Writing,* ed. Simon J. Ortiz, pp. xi–xix. Tucson: University of Arizona Press.

Rosenberg, Neil V. 1991. "An Icy Mountain Brook": Revival, Aesthetics, and the "Coal Creek March." *Journal of Folklore Research* 28(2/3):221–40.

———. 1993. Introduction. In *Transforming Tradition: Folk Music Revivals Examined,* ed. Neil V. Rosenberg, pp. 1–25. Urbana: University of Illinois Press.

Toulouse, Betty. 1977. *Pueblo Pottery of the New Mexico Indians: Ever Constant, Ever Changing.* Santa Fe: Museum of New Mexico Press.

White, Leslie. 1943. *New Material from Acoma.* Anthropological Paper No. 32, Bureau of Ethnology Bulletin 36, pp. 301–59. Washington, D.C.: Government Printing Office.

Artistic Courage in Small Groups: Identity, Intermediality, and Indian Country

Michael Robert Evans

Every act of art is an act of courage. As Henry Glassie has noted on numerous occasions, all works of art are autobiographies; they reflect the artist's vision, the artist's condition in the world, the artist's soul. In his latest book, Glassie quotes Seamus Heaney: "All art is . . . 'a revelation of the self to the self'" (2010:6). And in an older book: "The values in the pot are the values in the man" (1999:47).

As autobiographies, works emerge from the artist into the world as vulnerable objects of critique. They can be reviewed, printed words responding to crafted creation. They can be rebuffed, ignored by all but the artist's closest circles. And they can be refuted, challenged by counterpoints offered in the same and different media. Discussing oral literature, folklorist Elliott Oring notes that "all stories are constructions and invite commentary" (1990:172). Folklorist Ray Cashman put it well: "Stories provide a vehicle through which personal and shared orientations may be passed on, instilled, or indeed critically evaluated and reconsidered" (2008:1). When they are supported and applauded, the artist might feel a sense of relief, of euphoria, of boldness to continue. When they are derided, assaulted, or dismissed, the artist may feel a sense of anger, of resignation, or of determination to insert another communication into the debate. Either way, the very act of shaping something inspired by one's own mind and soul and thrusting it into a social landscape peopled by critics and rivals requires immense reservoirs of courage, faith, and hope. It is the act, as Glassie has described it, of embedding art "in life's thickness" ([1982] 1995:xiv–xv).

219

These artistic dialogues pass among media: poetry responding to painting, pottery responding to dance. The business of art, as Coomaraswamy reminds us, is "to grasp the primordial truth . . . to enunciate the primordial word" (1956:11). In this artistic enunciation, the discussion is intermedial, reverberating from one medium to another in a ceaseless conversation whose ultimate topic is the eternal. Art, as Glassie tells us, "is judged philosophically, the object's worth lying in its ability to provoke and sustain argument" (1999:18). Art communicated through intermedial dialogue—including such mass-mediated forms as books, newspaper articles, and websites—is judged and valued in no less profound ways.

Intermediality is not a new term. It has been used in art history for quite some time to refer to an artist's expression of vision in multiple media. It has been used in education to mean the presentation of ideas in various mediated forms, a process that is accelerating with the explosion of online media into the classroom. But for the purposes of the present discussion, I would like to extend those uses into the realms of communication and performance. In these realms, *intermediality* can be used to refer to the carrying on of a dialogue not through direct interaction but rather through mediated utterances that are released into the world at large. The utterances have multiple intended audiences: the person or group engaged in debate, the immediate audience that might be expected to receive the communication (visitors to a museum, shoppers at a gallery, readers of a book), other practitioners of the artist's mode of expression, critics or reviewers who might consider the work from an analytical perspective, and historians and future generations who might embrace the work in emerging contexts. "Stories make contexts for each other," Glassie writes. "Meanings open between stories" (2006:255).

Any act of performance requires courage because of the constant possibility of refutation; one account of how something happened—in legend, myth, or other forms—could be countered by another, sometimes at great personal and social cost to the first performer. Sometimes, the debate centers on the competence of the performer, the critic arguing through direct attack or through the presentation of an opposing example that the teller failed to relate the story with fidelity. Using Richard Bauman's terms, this level of critique corresponds to both the "story" and the "narrative event"; the critic addresses the tale as it was told under the circumstances of its telling (1986:2).

Other times, the critique focuses on the validity of the facts that unfold within the story, the "narrated event" in Bauman's breakdown (1986:2). Tellers sensitive to such critiques often draw from a set of arguments or claims that are designed to strengthen the veracity of the account. Oring notes the wide range of "strategies for making narratives appear true," pointing to an array of "authenticating devices," to use Bennett's term, that are intended to reinforce the credibility of the tale (Oring 2008:129). One of the strategies described in Oring's "rhetoric of truth" involves an appeal to the authority of the source (131–32) and sometimes specifically the authority of a mediated source: "a written account, the printed word, or some other communicative medium" (132). In many cases, intermediated discourse becomes intertwined and self-referential. Writers may quote other mediated discourse to shore up their own arguments in the same way that people often claim authority for their views by noting "I read it in *The New York Times*" or "I saw it on TV."

At stake is the difference between legend and news. Oring notes that legends require skepticism, at least on the part of the folklorist (1990:165). Somewhere within the embrace of a legend lies the possibility that the story is false; otherwise, the story is presented as factual, as simply real, as journalism (165). This tension between news and legend (not between fact and fiction, but between *accepted* and *contested)* offers a battlefield for persuasion. If I can persuade you of the validity of my views, I can get you to move my claims toward "news," which in turn forces my opponent's views toward "legend," complete with the skepticism the genre implies.

Intermedial dialogues engage in that struggle, bringing into play their own traditions, their own styles, and their own aesthetics. Often, the aesthetics and traditions of journalism are deployed in an effort to increase credibility. By presenting claims in the seemingly neutral and unbiased tones of modern journalism—journalistic rhetorics of truth, as Oring put it (1990:166)—participants in intermedial debates can imply possession of the kind of accuracy and impartiality that journalists profess to hold dear. This use of tone as a claim to authenticity is not new. Storytellers often use anachronistic or archaic language to invoke the authority of ancestors. Similarly, the positions staked out in intermedial debate often use journalistic language to invoke the authority of news organizations respected for their thorough fact-checking. Indeed, part of the art of debates in the journalistic realm involves limitation. In some kinds of folktales and other forms of oral literature, authenticity lies with accuracy in reproduction; if a teller conspicuously alters a tale, others in the audience might protest that he "got it wrong." In journalism, authenticity lies with accuracy in representation. Acknowledging that no two people will see or remember an event the same way, journalists nevertheless try to "get it right" by teasing something like the truth out of generally agreed-upon facts. As Glassie once mentioned, the art of non-fiction storytelling lies in the teller's ability to create something relevant, profound, and beautiful using the unchangeable facts gathered through research (1996).

These intermedial dialogues serve the purpose of positioning the performer in relation to other performers, to the past, to society at large, and to possible future shifts in thinking. One common aim in intermedial communication involves the dictation of history; by producing utterances that depict a particular way of viewing a set of circumstances, the performer vies for dominance in the debate over how those circumstances will be evaluated and interpreted. *The Journals of Knud Rasmussen* (Kunuk 2006) and *Bury My Heart at Wounded Knee* (Brown [1970] 2007) are but two examples of efforts by Native people to address and correct depictions offered by journalists, explorers, authors, and missionaries.

Essential in this intermedial debate is the "creation of coherence," to use sociolinguist Charlotte Linde's term. In discussing life stories, Linde argues that people develop and adjust their own life stories to create coherence even in the midst of the absurd chaos of the human condition (1993:6). Similarly, contenders engaged in intermedial debate struggle to create a coherent view of the world that supports the positions they hold. To be persuasive—to maintain credibility and achieve potency in the intermedial realm—stories must make some kind of sense out of the facts that they relate. Connections drawn between the information conveyed in the stories and information reported in the media can strengthen this claim to coherence, to rationality, and to authenticity.

This kind of intermedial struggle goes on around the world, with positions staked out and defended, with aggressive moves aimed at preemptive positioning, with the casting and recasting of history in ways that suit present and future strategies. Many histories, for example, are published in an effort to cast politicians, generals, and other figures in either positive or negative lights; the litany of books published about the George W. Bush administration—both vacuously positive and shallowly negative—can be seen as salvos in an intermedial contest over that president's legacy.[1]

One arena in which this kind of intermedial skirmishing is especially pointed is Indian Country. For generations, stories have staked claims to history, to land, to authority, and to identity, each tale emphasizing its own particular views at the expense of competing interpretations. In recent decades, oral storytelling has broadened to include mediated forms of expression that reach wider audiences: radio, television, the Internet. That broadening has served to extend and amplify intermedial discourse, with radio hosts countering newspaper articles and books lining up against movies.

One highly charged case underscores the power that intermedial communication is given and the heightened role it plays in the battle for interpretational dominance. The case of Leonard Peltier is well known among those familiar with Indian Country; one of the reasons it is so familiar is that it has been fought—and continues to be fought—in intermedial space.

The incident that made Peltier an icon for American Indian activism occurred on June 26, 1975, during a gathering of Native people at the Jumping Bull compound outside Oglala, South Dakota, on the Pine Ridge Reservation. The gathering, organized largely by the American Indian Movement (AIM), aroused the concerns of the FBI, the South Dakota State Police, and local law enforcement officials. These forces surrounded the compound and set up roadblocks, staged roundups and arrests, and questioned Native people in an effort to find out the purpose of the congregation. Tensions ran high on both sides, and both sides were heavily armed.

Details of the incident are in dispute, but the general chain of events looks something like this: A Native man named Jimmy Eagle was accused of getting involved in an altercation and possibly stealing a pair of cowboy boots. Two young FBI officers, Jack Coler and Ronald Williams, believed they saw Eagle and decided to apprehend him on those charges. They pursued Eagle in their unmarked cars; Eagle was driving or riding in a red vehicle—reports describe it as either a pickup truck or a van—that was headed back to the Jumping Bull compound.

The compound, a ranch owned by Harry Jumping Bull and his wife, Cecelia, was accessed via a road that wound up the base of a canyon. The compound consisted of several houses and outbuildings, many of which lined the rim of the canyon overlooking the road. The entrance to the compound was marked with signs that warned trespassers—white people and the FBI in particular—to stay away or risk being shot. The red truck roared into the compound, toward the safety that the large group of Native American warriors would provide, and Agents Coler and Williams drove in behind it.

Some accounts say the agents entered the compound with guns blazing; others say the Native Americans shot first (Trimbach and Trimbach 2007). What is clear is that the agents' arrival triggered a stormy response by the Native Americans gathered at the compound. The warriors opened fire from the outbuildings, shooting the agents' cars numerous times.

When the shooting stopped, both agents were alive but seriously injured. As they lay on the ground, unable to mount a defense, one or more persons approached them and shot them each in the head. Both died instantly.

The shooting triggered the largest manhunt in FBI history. Joined by state troopers and local police officers, FBI agents tore through the region, looking for the killers. Many of the people involved in the shootout had vanished into the South Dakota hills, but the agents and officers rounded up every Native American person they could find for questioning, detention, and often arrest. Ultimately, four people were charged with the murder of the agents: Bob Robideau, Dino Butler, Leonard Peltier, and another man who was later released for lack of evidence.

Peltier fled to Canada and fought extradition, which proved to be a tragic mistake. Robideau and Butler were tried and acquitted on the grounds of self-defense. The jury acknowledged that they were merely returning fire after unknown assailants in unmarked cars began shooting at them. That left just one person to blame for killing the agents—Leonard Peltier—and law enforcement officials began extradition proceedings to force him to face trial in the United States.

Peltier's extradition from Canada is one of the rallying points for the "Free Leonard Peltier" movement. For Canada to extradite someone to the United States, enough evidence must be presented to convince a judge that if the case were held in Canada, the prosecution would have a reasonable chance of success. The evidence against Peltier was thin. He could be placed at the compound at the time of the shooting, and some evidence surfaced that suggested the agents had been killed with a gun belonging to Peltier, but the prosecution had nothing concrete with which to pursue extradition. Then a woman named Myrtle Poor Bear signed an affidavit testifying that Peltier was her boyfriend, that she was with him at the time of the shooting, and that he was involved. Poor Bear later recanted that testimony, saying that she was pressured by the FBI to sign a document she hadn't read. Nevertheless, armed with that signed document, the FBI was able to gain Peltier's extradition to the U.S.

At his trial, Peltier pleaded not guilty and expected that he would be acquitted on grounds of self-defense, as were Butler and Robideau. But Peltier's verdict was different: He was found guilty on both counts of murder and condemned to two consecutive life sentences in a federal penitentiary. He has been behind bars ever since, except for the short time he was free after escaping from the federal penitentiary in Lompoc, Calif., on July 20, 1978. Seven years were added to his double-life sentence for the effort.

Peltier is a Lakota and Ojibwe man who grew up on the Turtle Mountain reservation and lived in Montana, Washington State, and elsewhere before centering much of his life in South Dakota. He views the American Indian Movement not just as a modern organization but as an activist impulse that dates back to Columbus's arrival and that can be seen as embodied most fully in the characters of Crazy Horse and Geronimo.

Peltier's extradition, conviction, and double-life-term sentence have outraged many in Indian Country, and his story has served as a rallying spark around which anger about the unjust treatment of Native peoples has radiated. The fury settles around four distinct arguments, each with its own logic and support:

- Peltier should never have been extradited from Canada. The affidavit from Myrtle Poor Bear was coerced, and the FBI should not have been allowed to pursue the case because of that misconduct.

- The guilty verdict was based primarily on the fact that Peltier was the only one left to accuse, not because the case was convincing. The previous two defendants were found not guilty by reason of self-defense, but Peltier—for no reason other than the fact that he came last—was not allowed that argument.

- Even if Peltier did shoot the FBI agents, he should not be forced to spend his life behind bars. The Jumping Bull compound at the time was a war zone, with two armies facing off over the rights of Native peoples in this country. People get shot in a war zone; it is wrong to blame one man for "murder" when bullets were flying in all directions. At the very least, Peltier should be treated as a prisoner of war, not a common criminal.

- The agents had it coming. They drove past signs warning that white people and FBI agents in particular would be shot on sight. They fired their guns first, provoking the counter-attack. (Hence the self-defense verdicts for the first two defendants.) The FBI and other law-enforcement personnel had surrounded the compound and were harassing the Native people camped there despite the peaceful nature of the gathering. The representatives of the United States were the aggressors, and Peltier and the other Native Americans were merely responding to the agents' provocation.

In his loose autobiography, *Prison Writings: My Life is My Sun Dance* (1999), Peltier insists that he was not involved in the shooting in any way. In

225

Paul DeMain, editor of *News from Indian Country*.
Photograph by Kimberlie Acosta

his version of events, he was asleep in the compound's tent city when the shooting began. Rather than run toward the conflict, Peltier says he tried to protect the women and children in the camp, ultimately ushering them away from the shooting and toward safety. He insists that he has been singled out because he was a high-ranking officer of the American Indian Movement, and so he serves as a trophy for the FBI and a martyr for his people.

Prison Writings represents just one entry into the intermedial dialogue about Peltier, the shootout, and the larger conflict between the American Indian Movement and the FBI. Long before that book added its voice to the debate, a young editor named Paul DeMain launched a newspaper designed, in part, to contribute to the mounting pressure to free Leonard Peltier.

News from Indian Country began as a local newspaper for the Lac Courte Oreilles reservation of the Ojibwe Nation, just outside of Hayward, Wisconsin. Originally called the *LCO Journal American,* the newspaper was one of many tribally owned publications created to keep people informed about tribal activities and defend tribal actions, programs, and officials. Paul DeMain worked at the paper for a while in the 1970s and 1980s before being hired by Wisconsin governor Anthony Earl to serve as the liaison between the state government and the eleven Native nations within Wisconsin's boundaries. DeMain held that job throughout Earl's four-year term, ultimately stepping down when Tommy Thompson defeated Earl and became the state's next governor.

After the election, DeMain returned to the Lac Courte Oreilles reservation and took some time off, trying to decide what to do next. In his absence, the newspaper had dwindled to an irregularly published newsletter about the tribal government; housed bureaucratically under the auspices of the tribal radio station, the paper was nearly defunct, with no prospects for revival.

Ultimately, DeMain bought the newspaper, changed the name to *News from Indian Country,* and broadened the intended audience to include Native people coast to coast. The circulation grew, and *News from Indian Country* has become a significant voice in the Native American mediascape.

No stranger to politics and controversy, DeMain staked out a clear stance for the newspaper in favor of Peltier's freedom. His editorial voice joined the voices sounding in other media, including news programs, talk shows, documentaries, fictionalized films, and publications protesting the railroading of Leonard Peltier. These voices were countered by FBI officials and others—in much the same media—who insisted that Peltier was guilty.

This intermedial debate went on for two decades, with the Leonard Peltier Legal Defense Fund, *News from Indian Country,* and others voicing opinions and staking positions in the landscape of the dispute. Robert Redford produced a film, *Incident at Oglala,* that depicted the shootout in a way favorable to Peltier's case (1988). Peter Matthiessen published *In the Spirit of Crazy Horse: The Story of Leonard Peltier and the FBI's War on the American Indian Movement* ([1983] 1992), a book of more than six hundred pages that sets the stage for the shootout, analyzing the events and offering conclusions that support Peltier's claims. In 2007, Joseph H. Trimbach and John M. Trimbach published a book titled *American Indian Mafia: An FBI Agent's True Story about Wounded Knee, Leonard Peltier, and the American Indian Movement (AIM)* (2007), offering a different view and inciting further responses from Indian Country. Associated Press journalist Carson Walker wrote about a host of related cases and stories, at times angering people on both sides of the divide. And Peltier himself granted interviews for use in documentaries, televised news programs, and other media products.

At *News from Indian Country,* DeMain applied his substantial skills as an investigative journalist to the mission of unraveling the FBI's case against Peltier. He published articles and editorials revealing information he had gathered from formerly classified FBI documents, transcripts from related court cases, and other material. He filed numerous requests under the Freedom of Information Act, amassing boxes full of redacted FBI files, affidavits, and an array of other documents.

It takes courage to openly challenge the FBI, especially in Indian Country. The FBI has a long history of aggressive and at times abusive treatment of Native Americans, often assuming the role of enforcer for the Bureau of Indian Affairs and the federal government. DeMain knew people who had been harassed and arrested by the FBI, primarily at AIM takeovers of Alcatraz; the courthouse at Custer, South Dakota; and the BIA offices in Washington, D.C. At times, the standoffs grew deadly; more than a dozen people, for example, were killed during the AIM takeover of Wounded Knee. DeMain knew that his challenge to the FBI could make life difficult for him, but he considers himself a serious investigative journalist, and he is willing to place truth ahead of personal convenience or safety. He published his articles and his editorials, filed his FOI requests and dealt with mountains of other bureaucratic paperwork designed to obfuscate the truth, and published his paper regularly, building a solid subscription base.

As he gathered ammunition in the fight to exonerate Peltier, however, DeMain began to feel his courage tested on another front. He became troubled that Peltier, in his various mediated interviews, offered differing explanations of his whereabouts during the Jumping Bull shootout. In his book and in many other outlets, he insisted that he was not involved in the shooting at all, that he was back in the tent city when the fusillade began. Peltier describes the morning as calm and pleasant—at first.

> But suddenly this beautiful and peaceful morning was cut short by the staccato sound of gunfire. It seemed far off, and at first I dismissed it as someone practicing in the woods. Then I started hearing the screams. My heart nearly leaped out of my chest. Our spiritual camp had abruptly become a war zone. . . . I ran over to the little shack next door [to the main house], where I heard children's voices wailing out in fright. Bullets snapped at my heels as I ran, barely missing me—just the way you see it happen in the movies. . . . I called out to the young ones that it was time to be brave, time to be warriors. "Get under the bed! Stay there until we come get you!" I shouted, then I made a beeline out of there to draw the gunfire away from the house and the kids inside it. (1999:123–25)

But in various interviews, DeMain says, Peltier offered different stories, his location and participation in the shootout varying from telling to telling. DeMain, in his journalistic quest for the truth, began to wonder which version of Peltier's story was accurate. He also wondered why the story was changing, if indeed the original version were true. His support for Peltier began to wane.

Then came testimony in a related case, testimony that shattered DeMain's certainty in the innocence of Leonard Peltier. Darlene "Kamook" Nichols, testifying under oath in the murder trial of a man named Arlo Looking Cloud, described Peltier's apparent confession to the murder of at least one of the two FBI agents. According to Nichols, she was riding with Peltier and several others in a recreational vehicle lent to the American Indian Movement by the actor Marlon Brando. She described how she was involved in a conversation with some of the other people; Peltier alternated between sitting at the motor home's table and standing in the aisle. Then, according to Nichols's testimony, Peltier started talking about the events of June 26—the shootout with the FBI at Jumping Bull's compound—and he described how he had walked up to the agents after the shooting had stopped, heard one of the agents plead for mercy, and then killed him. In Nichols's testimony, Peltier's exact words were "the motherfucker was begging for his life, but I shot him anyway" (Nichols 2004).

That testimony, from a source DeMain trusts, was the last straw. In 2004, he published an editorial in *News from Indian Country* that opposed his previous stances: He declared his belief that Peltier was guilty.

This shift in the intermedial dialogue shook Indian Country. DeMain received hate mail and death threats, often from anonymous senders but sometimes from people he knew and considered friends. He received emails, letters, and phone calls from people vowing to shut down the newspaper and burn down its offices. He was sued by Peltier, who accused DeMain of libel.[2] DeMain was called a traitor to Native causes, accused of being an FBI informant, and described as an "apple" (red on the outside but white on the inside).

And the circulation base of *News from Indian Country* dwindled quickly. Many of the people who wrote angry letters to DeMain insisted that their subscriptions be canceled. A few people chose to subscribe in light of the bold new position that DeMain was asserting, but far more people abandoned the newspaper when its editorial stance shifted into something they found disagreeable.

In performance, the goal is rarely to alienate an audience. The performer might intend to disturb, unsettle, and even offend, but the ultimate goal is usually the advancement of a dialogue, the provocation or furthering of engagement with audiences over fundamental human issues. Outrage is not always an unwelcome response, but empty silence is a sign of disaster. After his editorial proclaiming his new view that Peltier is guilty and deserves to spend the rest of his life in prison, DeMain found himself on the receiving end of outrage and protest. Once the howls of anger died down somewhat, he found himself struggling with the obscurity that forced marginalization brings.

But he remains committed to the truth as he sees it. That commitment stems in part from DeMain's role as "Skabewis." *Skabewis* means messenger, and it is a title given him by an Ojibwe elder many years ago. The role carries with it serious connotations; as DeMain sees it, a *Skabewis* is obligated to ferret out the truth and share that truth with others, even at the risk of social ostracism or personal danger. Because of that title, and the honor and burden it carries with it, DeMain feels bound to pursue the truth and publish it—even if death threats come through the mail, even if circulation dwindles dramatically.

DeMain's voice, as has been mentioned, is just one of many taking part in this intermedial debate. Dennis Banks, once the head of the American Indian Movement, has published an autobiography titled *Ojibwe Warrior: Dennis Banks and the Rise of the American Indian Movement* (2004). Another AIM leader, Russell Means, wrote an autobiographic book titled *Where White Men Fear to Tread* (1995). Leonard Crow Dog, the AIM spiritual leader, published *Crow Dog: Four Generations of Sioux Medicine Men* (1995).

John Trudell has published several books about his life and views. He served AIM in many capacities, including chairman and information officer, and he has an active singing career; he has released more than a dozen albums of music with a Native theme. He also has a movie out titled *Trudell* (Rae 2005). Trudell's books include *Lines from a Mined Mind: The Words of John Trudell* (2008). These entries into the intermedial dialogue stake out positions that reflect the perspectives of their authors.

With the advent of the Internet, intermedial conversations can happen more easily and more often than ever before. Anyone with computer access can create a blog, post to listservs, and create websites designed to advance a particular point of view. The debate over the Leonard Peltier case is no exception, with Peltier's own website being joined by the website for the Leonard Peltier Legal Defense Fund, the website for *News from Indian Country*, websites for Trudell's movie and CDs and Trudell himself, and other entries into the digital current of intermedial discussion. As computer and Internet access continues to increase, the number of voices entering this intermedial debate will expand rapidly.

To create something in performance—a pot, a dance, a string of words on an editorial page—and thrust it out of one's own mind and into the world of imperfect forms takes extraordinary courage. It is the act of a loving parent, who prepares his children as well as he can and then trusts, alongside the alternate trust of prayer, that they will fend for themselves well in the world beyond his protection. Entries into the intermedial dialogues that surround us can bring joy, pain, fear, and the frustration of empty silence. Paul DeMain is wrestling with the reactions his words have brought. Other members of the American Indian Movement are crafting their own performances and hurling them outward in an effort to swing the debate. Leonard Peltier puts his book, his website, and his interviews into the whirlwind, letting them shape the debate in ways that he hopes will be beneficial to him.

When the events in question are open to debate, stories inch toward legendry as doubts are raised about the reliability of the information. Oring notes that legends encompass the unnatural, the unknowable, and the unlikely (1990:164), the *un-* prefixes admitting doubt into the information. For DeMain and others surrounding the Peltier story, the debate falls into the realm of the unknowable; the "truth" is unknowable because the facts have been so thoroughly contested that it is impossible to tell which claims are valid, which story reflects news. The truth also becomes unknowable because the people who do know are either dead or silent. In addition, the truth becomes unknowable because the credibility of the people involved has been shredded by self-interest. Credibility could be restored through confession, but to date everyone is clinging to versions that present themselves in optimal light. DeMain and others frame their arguments in modern-day rhetorics of truth: eyewitness accounts, evidence presented and refuted, appeals to logic.

Like others, Henry Glassie pursues his own writing, his own entries into intermedial space, with the deliberate intention of changing the dialogic landscape. "I had learned from my writings and the writings of friends . . . that scholarly books can benefit their subjects, encouraging them to keep at it and bringing them, through serious attention, financial gain" (Glassie 2010:5). He chose one recent project, a book about the artist Prince Twins Seven-Seven, "hoping it would help Prince during his struggle in my difficult country, knowing it would help me" (2010:5).

All of it is courage. All of it is hope. And everyone involved has a vision of the future that undoubtedly will be shaped in new and unexpected ways by the supportive, contradictory, or tangential efforts of others. "What we call folklore (or art or communication) is the central fact of what we call culture, and culture is the central fact of what we call history" (Glassie ([1982] 1995:xiv).

NOTES

1. Among the many available examples: *The Bush Tragedy* (Weisberg 2008); *Family of Secrets: The Bush Dynasty, the Powerful Forces That Put It in the White House, and What their Influence Means for America* (Baker, 2008); *The Prosecution of George W. Bush for Murder* (Bugliosi 2008), *After Bush: The Case for Continuity in American Foreign Policy* (Lynch and Singh 2008), *The Faith of George W. Bush* (Mansfield 2004).

2. The suit was ultimately settled when DeMain agreed to publish a clarification stating he had no reason to believe that Peltier was involved in the murder whose trial produced the testimony from Nichols. DeMain's assertion that Peltier was involved in the murders of the FBI agents remains unretracted.

REFERENCES CITED

Baker, Russ. 2008. *Family of Secrets: The Bush Dynasty, the Powerful Forces That Put It in the White House, and What Their Influence Means for America.* New York: Bloomsbury Press.

Banks, Dennis, with Richard Erdoes. 2004. *Ojibwa Warrior: Dennis Banks and the Rise of the American Indian Movement.* Norman: University of Oklahoma Press.

Bauman, Richard. 1986. *Story, Performance, and Event: Contextual Studies of Oral Narrative*. Cambridge: Cambridge University Press.

Brown, Dee. [1970] 2007. *Bury My Heart at Wounded Knee: An Indian History of the American West*. New York: Henry Holt and Company.

Bugliosi, Vincent. 2008. *The Prosecution of George W. Bush for Murder*. Cambridge: Vanguard Press.

Cashman, Ray. 2008. *Storytelling on the Northern Irish Border: Characters and Community*. Bloomington: Indiana University Press.

Coomaraswamy, Ananda K. 1956. *Christian and Oriental Philosophy of Art*. New York: Dover Publications.

Crow Dog, Leonard, and Richard Erdoes. 1995. *Crow Dog: Four Generations of Sioux Medicine Men*. New York: Harper Perennial.

Glassie, Henry. [1982] 1995. *Passing the Time in Ballymenone*. Bloomington: Indiana University Press.

———. 1996. Personal communication. Bloomington, Indiana.

———. 1999. *The Potter's Art*. Bloomington: Indiana University Press.

———. 2006. *The Stars of Ballymenone*. Bloomington: Indiana University Press.

———. 2010. *Prince Twins Seven-Seven: His Art, His Life in Nigeria, His Exile in America*. Bloomington: Indiana University Press.

Kunuk, Zacharias. 2006. *The Journals of Knud Rasmussen*. Igloolik Isuma Productions.

Linde, Charlotte. 1993. *Life Stories: The Creation of Coherence*. New York: Oxford University Press.

Lynch, Timothy J., and Robert S. Singh. 2008. *After Bush: The Case for Continuity in American Foreign Policy*. Cambridge: Cambridge University Press.

Mansfield, Stephen. 2004. *The Faith of George W. Bush*. Lake Mary, Florida: Charisma House.

Matthiessen, Peter. [1983] 1992. *In the Spirit of Crazy Horse: The Story of Leonard Peltier and the FBI's War on the American Indian Movement*. New York: Penguin Books.

Means, Russell, with Marvin J. Wolf. 1995. *Where White Men Fear to Tread*. New York: St. Martin's Griffin.

Nichols, Darlene. 2004. Testimony in the trial of Arlo Looking Cloud, Feb. 3. Accessed at http://www.jfamr.org/doc/kmtest1.html. Last accessed on Aug. 26, 2009.

Oring, Elliot. 1990. Legend, Truth, and News. *Southern Folklore* 47(2):163–77.

———. 2008. Legendry and the Rhetoric of Truth. *Journal of American Folklore* 121(480):127–66.

Peltier, Leonard. 1999. *Prison Writings: My Life is My Sun Dance*. New York: St. Martin's Griffin.

Rae, Heather. 2005. *Trudell*. Appaloosa Pictures.

Redford, Robert. 1988. *Incident at Oglala: The Leonard Peltier Story*. Miramax Films.

Trimbach, Joseph H., and John M. Trimbach. 2007. *American Indian Mafia: An FBI Agent's True Story about Wounded Knee, Leonard Peltier, and the American Indian Movement. (AIM).* Parker, CO: Outskirts Press.

Trudell, John. 2008. *Lines from a Mined Mind: The Words of John Trudell.* Golden, CO: Fulcrum Publishing.

Weisberg, Jacob. 2008. *The Bush Tragedy.* New York: Random House.

Navigating the Legends of *Treasure Island:* Narrative, Maps, and the Material

Greg Kelley

In the composition of his best-known work, *Treasure Island,* Robert Louis Stevenson drew upon an extant print tradition framed as non-fiction, and he created a fictional narrator immersed in a world of stories and storytellers. The novel unfolds as an emergent first-person account of the adolescent Jim Hawkins, in whose adventurous tale Stevenson demonstrates an implicit and nuanced understanding of the dynamics of oral narration—in particular, legend narration. In Jim, Stevenson creates so convincing a narrator that the audience is tempted to overlook the text's status as fiction—to read *Treasure Island* as historical. The entire novel can be viewed as a sort of extended legend telling, in fact, with some of the typical markers of legend encounters: assertions of truth and verisimilitude, temporal and spatial specifics, and communal narration, for example. Moreover, we see in the novel a fixation on material reality, with details that situate the narrated events specifically in time and place—like the legend—and evidentiary appeals that employ physical objects. These components all combine to enhance the novel's impression of authenticity.

The blending of fiction and non-fiction is an earmark of the literary sources that inspired Stevenson, and it is an important facet of the novel's legacy as well. *Treasure Island* presents us with literary ambiguity as it keys at least two print genres: the novel (specifically, the boy's adventure story), realistic but patently fictional; and the first-person travelogue, enhanced by the fact that Stevenson originally published the novel in serial form in the boys' periodical *Young Folks* under the pseudonym Captain George North. Stevenson consciously mined source material from *A General History of the*

Pyrates (1724), whose authorial status is still contested among eighteenth-century scholars: very little is known about the writer, Captain Charles Johnson, for a time believed by some to be a pseudonym for Daniel Defoe.[1] Compiled from numerous news reports, merchants' letters, communications of private trading companies, as well as second and third-hand oral accounts, rumors, and even court testimony (as many pirates ended their careers early at the gallows), the two-volume *General History* became enormously popular. Part historical journalism, part literary history, the book has been labeled by editors as a "creative reconstruction of dim events elevated at times to dramatic universality" and an "imaginative source of piratical lore" (Schonhorn 1999:xl; Cordingly 2001:195, n.10). By the time Stevenson was penning *Treasure Island* in 1881, Johnson's work stood in the popular English consciousness as the most comprehensive record of eighteenth-century piracy. In his preparations, Stevenson requested it as "the best book about the Buccaneers that can be had" (Booth and Mehew 1994–95:225, vol. 3);[2] the *General History* became an essential resource for him as he gleaned from it character prototypes and reputed real-life piratical exploits.[3] But more importantly, Stevenson's generous borrowing from Captain Johnson, and his assuming a Captain's pseudonym himself, placed his own novel squarely in a tradition of presumed authority regarding the life and times of notorious pirates, and, I would argue, in a tradition of legend telling as well.

Squire Trelawney, the bombastic financier of the treasure hunt, and Dr. Livesey, the avuncular guardian who accompanies Jim on the expedition, are effectively the instigators of the narrative: from the outset they have already requested that Jim relate retrospectively "the whole particulars about Treasure Island, from the beginning to the end, keeping nothing back but the bearings of the island."[4] The action begins for us, then, as we enter this storytelling event *in medias res,* and Jim delivers a protracted command performance that proves to be a narrative masterpiece. Even when Jim (temporarily) cedes this role, the interlude serves only to reinforce the authority of his perspective and the reliability of his reports. Dr. Livesey assumes the position of first-person narrator for a brief three chapters, relating events to which Jim had not been privy at the time, but the episodes are complementary to those told by Jim, serving essentially as corroborative testimony bolstering Jim's primary account. The doctor's collaborative narration functions to avert possible doubts of listeners (readers) who might question the veracity of extraordinary occurrences. This negotiation of the narrative among different participants is a common feature of the legend (Oring 2008:143; Dégh and Vázsonyi 1976:101ff), as are the overt and im-

Robert Louis Stevenson
Courtesy of the Beinecke Rare Book and Manuscript Library, Yale University

plied claims to truth, which become especially deliberate at choice moments in the novel when Jim disrupts the line of his own narration in order to announce evidentiary support.

For instance, when the pirate Black Dog first confronts his old mate Billy Bones at the Admiral Benbow Inn, a ruckus soon erupts (over the map of the island) and with drawn cutlass Billy Bones chases Black Dog from the premises. As Jim recalls the fray, "Just at the door, the captain aimed at the fugitive one last tremendous cut, which certainly would have split him to the chin had it not been intercepted by our big signboard," to which he strategically adds, "You may see the notch on the lower side of the frame to this day." Moments like these, in which Jim perceptibly breaks from the narrated events of the past into the present narrative moment, are infrequent in the novel, whose plotline is mainly single-stranded and chronologically unidirectional with few disruptions of narrative time—but they are always significant in that they reference a present material reality that is observable, tangible, and presumed certification of everything else he has related.

We find another example later in the novel when the action has shifted to the island itself. Held as a hostage by a few of the pirates, Jim witnesses an uprising against Long John Silver, a formalized ceremony of grievance among buccaneers in which they deliver to the defendant what is known as the black spot, a small scrap of paper with a darkened circle on one side. Silver nonchalantly tosses the paper towards Hawkins, saying "Here, Jim—here's a curiosity for you" (p. 178). As before, precisely at this point, Jim interrupts his past-tense narrative thread in order to furnish attestable evidence in the present: "I have that curiosity beside me at this moment," he says, "but not a trace of writing now remains beyond a single scratch" (178). This posture mirrors a common device of legend narrations, as storytellers who wish to be believed structure their accounts "with the precision of courtroom testimony" (Bennett 1988:16). In *Treasure Island,* the visible chink in the old placard and the scrap remnant of the black spot are held up by Jim as exhibits A and B—physical markers in service of what Elliott Oring (2008) calls the "rhetoric of truth" (see esp. p. 151). We are urged to accept the credibility of Jim's narrative by the proffered evidence.

There is in the novel a layering of legend elements, and the larger plot is driven by another internal legend, the story of Captain Flint and the legacy of his treasure. Fragmentary allusions to Flint abound among the seamen and citizens in and around Bristol. Although Jim admits he is unfamiliar with the name of Captain Flint, he observes that it is "well enough known" among locals and that it "carried a great weight of terror" (p. 30); from the youngest hand on the *Hispaniola* (the ship outfitted for the treasure hunt) we hear, admiringly, that Flint was "the flower of the flock" (p. 67); from the castaway Ben Gunn, "he was the man to have a headpiece, was Flint! Barring rum, his match were never seen. He were afraid of none, not he." (113); from an unnamed pirate on the island, "Dead—ay, sure enough he's dead and gone below . . . . but if ever sperrit walked, it would be Flint's. Dear heart, but he died bad, did Flint!' (p. 191); from another, "He were an ugly devil . . . blue in the face, too!" (p. 192); and even John Silver, who seldom displays trepidation, says "By thunder, if it don't make me cold inside to think of Flint . . . . praise your stars he's dead" (pp. 190, 92). Commenting on *Treasure Island* in 1911, Richard Middleton observed accurately that "the lesser ruffians of [the novel] fall to talking of him when they want to make our flesh creep. Their villainy is merely a shadow of Flint's" (n.p.). Such impressionistic allusions to Flint are truncated fragments of fuller stories circulating about the infamous Captain. A composite version of Flint's legacy would include details of his bloody exploits, the accumulation of his vast fortune (£700,000), the mysterious circumstances surrounding his burying the treasure, which led to six murders and left no eyewitnesses, and his agonizing death by rum poisoning in Savannah, which compelled him in the eleventh hour to hand over the map of the treasure's location to Billy Bones in 1754. A narrator might even amend the story with his own speculations on the *post mortem* superstition that Flint's unfriendly ghost guards the treasure. This is the back story of *Treasure Island,* and most of the characters seem to know a good deal of it. Jim learns more of the particulars soon after he meets Billy Bones, whose death in the Inn fortuitously brings the map into the boy's hands. At first, neither Jim nor the reader is in a position to understand the magnitude of the map's value, but as Jim imparts his story, embedded with the reports of others, we are carried into the general whisper about the emblematic map and its creator—and the novel moves forward accordingly as an adventure testing the veracity of the legend of Flint.

Within the frame of Jim's story, Billy Bones, Ben Gunn and John Silver command the most narrative authority—because they all have direct experience that places them in Flint's company. They were all aboard his ship *The Walrus* when he secreted his treasure on the remote island, and their first-hand accounts of Flint's brutality and the vastness of his treasure entice others to commit to the pursuit. Silver, for instance, in his beguiling campaign for mutiny, is overheard claiming to have personally seen Flint's ship "amuck with red blood and fit to sink with gold" (p. 67). Even the less nefarious characters have their claim to Flint. Dr. Livesey, preparing to open the packet containing the map (in the chapter titled "The Captain's Papers"), asks Squire Trelawney if he has heard of Flint:

"Heard of him!" cried the squire. "Heard of him you say! He was the bloodthirstiest buccaneer that sailed. Blackbeard was a child to Flint. The Spaniards were so prodigiously afraid of him, that, I tell you, sir, I was sometimes proud he was an Englishman. I've seen his top-sails with these eyes, off Trinidad, and the cowardly son of a rum-puncheon that I sailed with put back—put back sir, into Port of Spain." (pp. 41–42)

Like others, the squire maneuvers for credibility here by invoking the authority of the eye-witness account, which does seem to have more narrative clout among the observers than the doctor's prosaic response: "Well, I've heard of him myself, in England." Stevenson is dutifully attentive to the varying degrees of narrative distance that raconteurs assume with regard to their subjects. As Georgina Smith has noted of real life narrative situations, legends can be "incorporated" as first-person accounts, "semi-incorporated" by their attachment to "a relative, named friend, or local character," and "detached" without attribution (1981). The assorted narrators in *Treasure Island* represent all of these narrative stances. To the point here, as Oring observes, "distancing directly relates to the authority of the narrator" (2008:133). So, Trelawney and Livesey are clumsily jockeying for credibility by (artificially) narrowing their narrative distance from Captain Flint.

All of the seafarers in the novel, pirates and gentlemen alike, share a common frame of reference that provides fertile soil for the legends about Flint to take root. The mere mention of Flint's name or an oblique reference to the map functions as what Bill Ellis calls a legend metonym, reducing narrative to the level of simple allusion and thus "[recalling] the whole story simultaneously present in the minds of the group's members, without interrupting the present topic of conversation to replay it" (1989:40). Such legend metonyms, Ellis observes, are "opaque to outsiders," and only when new members are being added to the group does the narrative revert to its "finished form." This social dynamic explains why in *Treasure Island* the fullest details concerning Flint are given only when the conversation is directed at Jim, initiating him into this exclusive club of treasure hunters. To the others, however, simply intoning Flint's name rhetorically cues a full-blown narrative about him.

Long John Silver's parrot plays a part here as well. Close to two hundred years old, according to Silver, the parrot appears to have an illustrious piratical history of its own: aboard with the famed pirate Captain England, the parrot had been to Madagascar, Malabar, Surinam, Providence, and was present at the lucrative retrieval of the silver laden Plate Fleet, Spanish galleons that had wrecked in the gulf of Florida during a hurricane in 1714. On top of that, the parrot presumably had witnessed all of the exploits of *The Walrus*. Silver speculates that perhaps only the Devil himself had seen more wickedness than his darling parrot (p. 64). As a mimicking bird, the parrot contributes its own parlance to the story, imitated speech that is an additional link in the chain of oral retellings. Throughout, the parrot utters its signature phrase: "pieces of eight! pieces of eight!" It is another recurring metonymic reference to the treasure, and as such, a reminder of the full back story of the Captain's hoard that motivates the plot. Stevenson makes the connection transparent with the parrot's moniker—Captain Flint—a sort of avian reincarnation of Flint that squawks for his forgotten treasure and nudges the surviving pirates toward their objective.

If narratives themselves are verbal icons of the events they recount (Bauman 1986:5)—sometimes keyed by their own abbreviated verbal metonyms—there exist also non-verbal, purely material indexes of narrated events. Beyond metonymy, a particular narrative may be signified emblematically by an object rather than a word or phrase. We see an occurrence of just that with the map in *Treasure Island*. Showing the way to the immense cache, marking the place and date of its creation, inscribed by the captain, and attested to by Billy Bones, the map is another piece of concrete evidence giving credence to the told tales; conversely, to know the significance and value of the map is to know the legendary circumstances that led to its inception. So, like Linda Dégh's famous cracked red goblet, which she and Vázsonyi regard as the "source and bearer" of a legend (1978:258), the treasure map becomes the material expression—the embodiment—of the legend of Flint.

It appears that Stevenson was mindful of this interrelationship between story, object, and narrative authority as he wrote *Treasure Island*. In an essay titled "My First Book," he explained the process by which he conceived and composed the novel. "A lucky set of accidents," he writes, the novel began as entertainment for his twelve-year-old stepson Lloyd one August afternoon in 1881. Lloyd "had no thought of literature," but he loved to paint and sketch. Stevenson joined in occasionally, and on that day at the easel he serendipitously initiated his most inspired project:

> I made the map of an island; it was elaborately and (I thought) beautifully colored; the shape of it took my fancy beyond expression; it contained harbours that pleased me like sonnets; and with the unconscious of the predestined, I ticketed my performance "Treasure Island."

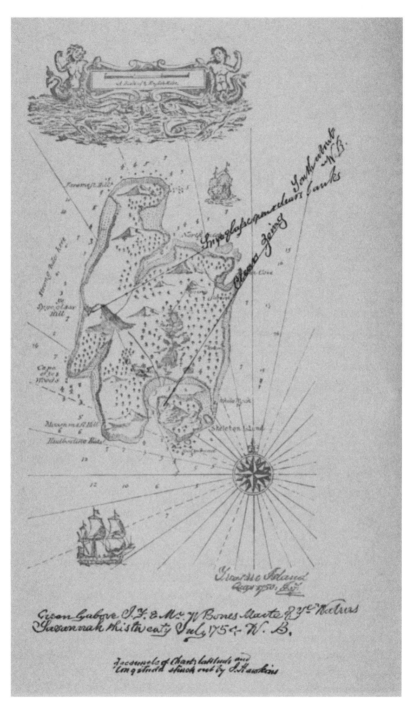

Stevenson's Map

Poring over the map, Stevenson imagined the future characters emerging visibly among imaginary woods. "Their brown faces and bright weapons peeped out upon me from unexpected quarters," his recollection continues, "as they passed to and fro, fighting, and hunting treasure, on the few square inches of a flat projection. The next thing I knew, I had some paper before me and I was writing out a list of chapters."

Though the map preceded his writing, Stevenson remembers that it embodied for him almost the entirety of the plot, and that he wrote *Treasure Island* "up to the map." As he saw it, the map itself had a story to tell and the task fell to him to put into words a narrative "pre-scribed" by the artifact. He seems to have intuited what Henry Glassie has convincingly demonstrated: an artifact, like a story, is by all rights a *bona fide* "text, a display of form and a vehicle for meaning" (1999:46). As inspiration and vehicle, Stevenson's sketch became the material expression of a larger story—anticipating the role that the map would play *within* the novel as well. In fact, the notion of "map as embodiment" is suggested in the text when the map is first uncovered in Bristol. Billy Bones's papers were in a bundle sewn together, and in order to get into them the doctor cuts through the stitches with a pair of medical scissors from his instrument case—performing what amounts to an exploratory surgery on the body of papers, and retrieving from it the sealed map. As with this striking image from the story, the map itself is the heart of Stevenson's enterprise.

Stevenson was determined to include his original sketch with the book's first edition, and he suffered much distress when the map was lost in the mail. By that time, Stevenson was wholly committed to the novel's projection of realism; so, with great care and a compass, he meticulously imitated the original drawing for the frontispiece, going as far then in the interest of verisimilitude as having the signature of Captain Flint and the sailing directions of Billy Bones "elaborately *forged*" by his father (Stevenson 1923–24:II, xxx, ital. in original). He also delivered precise instructions to the publisher on using red ink and various degrees of blackness to distinguish the separate signatures (*LET*:IV,151). These devices transmuted the fictional characters into actual personalities with real-world exploits—in effect recasting plot elements as reported legend.[5]

In the novel, the map points to both the story of Flint and to the treasure itself, and in a sense it comes to stand for both: the map is a material index to the legend, an artifact of the captain's legacy bearing his own inscription. One pirate calls the map "Flint's fist" (p. 36), referring ostensibly to the handwriting on it but also invoking the notion of a lingering, fragmented physical connection to the deceased Captain. (Suitably, the word "fist" conjures images of Flint's infamous tyranny or perhaps his fingers clutching a last handful of doubloons.) Furthermore, the map is a compelling substitute for the treasure itself, in a connection more emblematic than material. Characters behave as if possession of the map is *de facto* ownership of the treasure, and in the circuitous chase the map changes hands at least five times along the way. Once the pirates get a hold of it, Jim recounts,

> They leaped upon it like cats upon a mouse. It went from hand to hand, one tearing it from another; and by the oaths and the cries and the childish laughter with which they accompanied their examination, you would have thought [that they were] fingering the very gold. (p. 177)

Sadly for them, that is as close as the pirates get to any treasure.

Stevenson's tactics of verisimilitude were convincing: some enthusiastic readers, persuaded that the story of *Treasure Island* was rooted in real events, sought to pinpoint the date of the treasure voyage and to locate the precise bearings of the eponymous island. Even the internal legend of Flint found its real life adherents—as a function of tourism at the Pirate's House restaurant in Savannah, Georgia. The restaurant is part of a larger structure, the oldest building in Georgia, built in the 1730s. The house is aptly named, for in the 1800s it was a tavern serving the roguish tastes of buccaneers who frequented the Savannah coast. It is not out of the question that there may have been a real historical pirate captain (by whatever name) who died drinking rum in Savannah—and if he had done so, chances are that it would have been at the very same Pirate's House Tavern that today serves up an all-you-can-eat seafood bar. But because Savannah is mentioned specifically in *Treasure Island,* the restaurant has commodified that association, claiming to be the very location where Flint inscribed the map and subsequently died of rum. They say that Captain Flint's spirit troubles the building (just as he is reputed by the pirates in the novel to haunt the site of the buried treasure); and the restaurant even printed a version of the ghost legend on the menu. The "History" link of the restaurant's web page states that *"Even now, many swear that the ghost of Captain Flint still haunts The Pirates' House on moonless nights"* (www. thepirateshouse.com/history.html). Most of the alleged ghost sightings are said to have taken place in two smaller dining rooms that have been dubbed, appropriately, "the captain's room" and "the treasure room." As an apparent material reiteration of the oral reports, the proprietors have displayed conspicuously on the wall a framed title page from a first edition of *Treasure Island* and, it should not surprise us, a first edition frontispiece of Stevenson's sketched map. This invented touristic legend developed logically by its link to the novel, which Stevenson couched in the realm of the plausible with legend components.

Treasure Island points up a rich confluence of legend, literature, and material culture—and its prefatory map is the conjuring force. Stevenson's friend and editor, W. E. Henley, once recounted a vignette of a Professor Beesley,[6] discovered by his family while alone in his study, "his history books thrown by . . . his Herbert Spencer all forgotten, sunk to the throat in 'Treasure Island'. He had a magnifier at his eye, and through the magnifier he was (historian-like) a-studying the map of Captain Flint, tracking the bloody course of John Silver" (in Maxner 1981:142). And so it is with many readers of *Treasure Island,* captivated by Flint's enigmatic map, which is both an end and a means, a symbol and the thing itself. It charts a course through, at the same time that it authenticates, the remarkable narrative that is the novel.

Notes

I wish to thank Henry Glassie, who through the years has offered me inspiration, encouragement, and unfailing support. He generously guided me into many discoveries in folklore and its literary relations. And I remember fondly our frequent conversations about Shakespeare, Swift, Faulkner, and Stevenson—among my warmest memories of graduate school.

An earlier version of this essay was presented as part of the double panel on genre at the annual meeting of the American Folklore Society in Atlanta. Richard Bauman's insightful comments as panel discussant inform my current version. Heartfelt thanks also to Jennifer Schacker for her helpful feedback and to the editors—Ray Cashman, Tom Mould, and Pravina Shukla—for spearheading this project and diligently seeing it through.

1. The theory that Defoe had authored *A General History of the Pyrates* under the pen name Captain Charles Johnson originated in 1932 with American scholar John Robert Moore, who published his strongest rationale in *Defoe in the Pillory and Other Studies* (1939). Moore's position was the accepted scholarly view for fifty-years until largely discredited by P. N. Furbank and W. R. Owens (1988). Still, for the scant biography of Captain Johnson, there remain many questions regarding the authorship of this influential book.

2. Subsequent references abbreviated *LET.*

3. The most thorough study of Stevenson's sources is Harold Francis Watson's *Coasts of Treasure Island* (1969).

4. This quote, from p. 20, and all subsequent references are taken from the 1998 edition of Robert Louis Stevenson's *Treasure Island,* edited by Wendy R. Katz.

5. Similarly, Stevenson playfully touts his invented sea shanty "dead man's chest" as "a real Buccaneer's song, only known to the crew of the late Captain Flint" *(LET:*III, 225).

6. Henley is referring most probably to Edward Spencer Beasly (1831–1915), Professor of Latin at Bedford College from 1860–93.

References

Bauman, Richard. 1986. *Story, Performance, Event.* New York: Cambridge University Press.

Bennet, Gillian. 1998. Legend: Performance and Truth. In *Monsters with Iron Teeth: Perspectives in Contemporary Legend III,* eds. Gillian Bennett and Paul Smith, pp. 13–36. Sheffield: Sheffield Academic Press.

Booth, Bradford A. and Ernest Mehew, eds. 1994–95. *The Letters of Robert Louis Stevenson.* New Haven: Yale University Press.

Cordingly, David, ed. 2001. *Treasure Island.* New York: Modern Library.

Dégh, Linda, and Andrew Vázsonyi. 1976. Legend and Belief. In *Folklore Genres,* ed. Dan Ben-Amos, pp. 92–123. Austin: University of Texas Press.

———. 1978. The Crack in the Red Goblet or Truth in Modern Legend. In *Folklore and the Modern World,* ed. Richard M. Dorson, pp. 253–72. The Hague: Mouton.

Ellis, Bill. 1989. When is a Legend? An Essay in Legend Morphology. In *The Questing Beast: Perspectives in Contemporary Legend IV,* eds. Gillian Bennett and Paul Smith, pp. 31–53. Sheffield: Sheffield Academic Press.

Furbank, P.N. and W.R. Owens. 1988. *The Canonisation of Daniel Defoe.* New Haven: Yale University Press.

Glassie, Henry. 1999. *Material Culture.* Bloomington: Indiana University Press.

Johnson, Captain Charles. 1724. *A General History of the Pyrates.* London: Printed for C. Rivington, J. Lacy, and J. Stone.

Maxner, Paul. 1981. *Robert Louis Stevenson: The Critical Heritage.* London: Routledge and Kegan Paul.

Middleton, Richard. 1911. *Treasure Island* as a Book for Boys. *The Living Age,* October 28.

Moore, John Robert Moore. 1939. *Defoe in the Pillory and Other Studies.* Bloomington: Indiana University Press.

Oring, Elliott. 2008. Legendry and the Rhetoric of Truth. *Journal of American Folklore* 121(480):127–66.

Schonhorn, Manuel, ed. 1999. *A General History of the Robberies and Murders of the Most Notorious Pyrates.* New York: Dover.

Smith, Georgina. 1981. Urban Legend, Personal Experience Narrative, and Oral History. *ARV: Scandinavian Yearbook of Folklore* 37:167–73.

Stevenson, Robert Louis. 1923–24. My First Book. In *The Collected Works of Robert Louis Stevenson*. Tusitala Edition, eds. L. Osbourne and F. Van de G. Stevenson. London: Heinemann.

Stevenson, Robert Louis. 1998 [1883]. *Treasure Island*. Ed. Wendy R. Katz. Edinburgh University Press.

Watson, Harold Francis. 1969. *Coasts of Treasure Island*. San Antonio: Naylor.

MARIE CATHERINE LE JUMEL
DE BERNEVILLE.
Comtesse d'Aulnoi.
Morte au Mois de Janvier 1705.

Madame d'Aulnoy: Marie Catherine Le Jumel de Berneville,
Baroness d'Aulnoy, a portrait engraved by Pierre-Françoise
Bason after a sketch by Elisabeth Sophie Chéron

Fluid Identities: Madame d'Aulnoy, Mother Bunch, and Fairy-Tale History

Jennifer Schacker

For more than two centuries, discourses around the fairy tale have been preoccupied with the narration of origin stories and tales of authorship. Although related, these two forms of critical "storytelling" are distinct from one another: the first involves conjecture about the origins of oral traditions and of specific tales, the other fixates on the individual genius and his or her creative process. Scholars have thus established narrative traditions of their own—what Elizabeth Harries has referred to as "fairy tales about fairy tales" (see 2001:19–45)—each drawing selectively (as would any skilled storyteller) to delineate boundaries around the "usable past," by necessity marginalizing, obfuscating, or overlooking some details in favor of others (see Glassie 1995:395). I am fascinated by the history of the fairy tale in England precisely because it is complicated, and resistant to easy narration—a history characterized by the repeated blurring of the borders of languages, national and local traditions, genres, disciplines, audiences, and communicative forms. Nevertheless, many variants of the genre's historical metanarrative have privileged metaphysical and transcendental rhetoric, framing the fairy tale as "timeless" and "universal"—with the unfortunate consequence of generating mystified and often oversimplified reworkings of that history. In this essay, my broad concern is with the place of the French fairy tale tradition (the literary *contes de fées* of the late seventeenth century) in Victorian popular culture, but I would like to focus attention on the tangled stories of two individuals whose legacies cross historical periods, narrative forms and national boundaries: those of the French writer Marie-Catherine d'Aulnoy (generally known as Madame d'Aulnoy) and the legendary English folk

figure of Mother Bunch. Although both names have faded into relative obscurity for English-language audiences, they were once well known and frequently referenced—each name carrying with it a complex (and sometimes
self-contradictory) set of associations likely to be lost on the modern reader.
I suggest that narratives about each of these two figures are highly relevant
to the history of folklore; analysis of their forays into adjacent traditions—
those of the literary fairy tale, popular print culture and theater, to name but
a few—foreground the complexity of the discursive field within which our
own disciplinary tradition emerged.

In an earlier attempt to contextualize the emergence of folklore as a discipline and popular discourse in nineteenth-century England, I found myself
contributing (inadvertently) to the solidification of one part of a conventional narrative: I set the early Victorian fascination with oral traditional
"popular tales" in opposition to extant editions of fairy tales imported from
France, about which English commentators had become increasingly critical. Nineteenth-century criticisms of French tales on the grounds of their
artificiality, superficiality, and decadence have long been attributed to
the fact that in translation the texts had been "progressively infantilized,
stripped of subtext and innuendo until they indeed appeared to be the
'artificial' and empty extravagances" disdained by a new wave of folklore
enthusiasts (Schacker 2003:7). English editors' use of "Mother Bunch" as
d'Aulnoy's posthumous *nom de plume* has generally been taken as a sign of
this trend towards infantilizing a sophisticated imported literary tradition
(see, for example, Verdier 1996; Blamires 2008; Jones 2009), but very little
consideration has been given to the complex intertextual field within which
the name of Mother Bunch was circulating in the eighteenth and nineteenth centuries. Expanding my perspective to include English popular theater, I would suggest that conventional understandings of the role of French
literary *contes de fées* in Victorian culture can be challenged, complicated,
and enlivened by attending to Christmas pantomime—one of the most
significant and enduring means by which fairy tales have been transmitted. D'Aulnoy's tales have a significant place in the pantomime tradition,
as David Blamires's recent case study of "The White Cat" in both print
and theater cultures (2008) has demonstrated, but the figure of Mother
Bunch—to whom d'Aulnoy's tales were frequently attributed in English
books—also makes many curious and heretofore unexamined appearances
on the Victorian panto stage. Before I turn to the complex and intersecting
histories of these two individuals, I would like to introduce two of the traditions within which their stories unfold.

The British Pantomime Tradition

Pantomime has very recently received some increased critical attention, in terms of its place in Victorian children's culture (Gubar 2009), its intertextual relation to modernist writing (Martin 2006), and its modern performance conventions (Taylor 2007), but it has generally been overlooked in histories of folklore and of the fairy tale. Although "panto" (as it is generally called) is relatively unknown in the United States, in the United Kingdom it has remained a vibrant performance tradition—with several "classic" French tales serving as panto standards.

Much of the appeal of modern panto resides in its structural and narrative predictability. As theater historian Peter Holland has noted, the performances are expected to include a "succession of conventional moments, without which the audience would feel cheated." These include an opening chorus of peasants or townspeople—the honest, humble setting from which our romantic leads usually emerge; "an introductory scene for a comedian telling jokes and throwing sweets to the children in the audience"; at least one of several conventionalized routines of slapstick or physical comedy, including the Mirror Sketch (featured in the Marx Bros' "Duck Soup," but dating back to the mid-nineteenth century), the Kitchen or "slop" scene, the Balloon Dance, and the Undressing Scene; and a final musical "walk-down," in which characters reappear, in pairs, dressed in the production's flashiest costumes, and culminating with the reappearance of the principal boy and girl in wedding dress (Holland 1997:195).

English pantomime has undergone some significant changes and adaptation since it emerged as a distinct form of performance three centuries ago. The roots of panto as a "distinctly British form" of entertainment (O'Brien 2004:xiii) can be traced to Italian commedia dell'arte, introduced to the English court under Charles II in the years following the Restoration. Pantomime in early eighteenth-century England combined music, dance, and the highly stylized gestures of the commedia tradition. Early English productions also united the basic story of a popular tale or Classical myth (the basis for the first part of the panto) with the stock masks of commedia dell'arte, namely the lovers Harlequin and Columbine, Clown, and the rival Scaramouche. Characters from the opening would be magically transformed into these commedia figures by a good fairy (known in panto as the benevolent agent) and a chase scene—highly physical, acrobatic, wordless—followed. This sequence of several scenes came to be known as the Harlequinade.

The Theatre Licensing Act of 1737 played a role in the rise of pantomime in English popular culture, granting a select number of theater houses—the so-called "patent theatres"—an absolute monopoly on spoken drama. This situation necessitated tremendously "creative" readings of the law on the part of minor theater owners who could acquire only a burletta license for the staging of both the comic operettas signaled by the license's title, and any other performance that refrained from sustained use of spoken dialogue. It was in this context that many relatively unregulated forms of performance flourished—including early pantomime, which emerged by century's end as a significant outlet for topical humor, both social commentary and political satire (Mayer 1969:7). With the relaxation of the Theatre Licensing laws in 1843, panto ceased to be marginalized, and soon highly-profitable Christmas-season pantomimes were appearing at both the patent theaters as well as the minor houses. As panto entered the mainstream of mid-nineteenth-century theater, it retained its extensive use of music, dance, and physical comedy but the former emphasis on up-to-the-minute topical humor increasingly shared center stage with elaborate set and costume design, mechanics, showiness, and spectacle—anything that might prove a box-office draw.

The fit between the fairy tale, popular theater, and the Christmas season may seem self-evident: magic in the narrative can be translated, on stage, into musical comedy with crowd-pleasing effects (of set, props, and costuming)—all framed and grounded by a familiar romantic storyline derived from or, in most cases, grafted onto a traditional tale type. Tales such as d'Aulnoy's "Yellow Dwarf" and "The White Cat," and Perrault's "Little Red Riding Hood," "Cinderella," and "Sleeping Beauty," emerged as panto favorites—loosely adapted—just as a set of recognizable conventions of Victorian pantomime production, performance and characterization were being renegotiated (see Mayer 1969:309–27). Simultaneously, Christmas was in the process of being reinvented, drawing together a bricolage of regional European customs to form a modern, industrial festival of sentimentality and materialism which has proven to have global reach (for example, see Golby and Purdue 1986; Belk 1987; Miller 1993; Nissenbaum 1997). The emergent association of French literary tales with these profit-driven seasonal theatrical productions resonates, as we will see, on the stage—as a form of metacommentary spoken by the dramatis personae—and in Victorian commentaries on both English panto *and* the French *conte de fées*.

THE FRENCH FAIRY-TALE TRADITION IN ENGLAND

Victorian folklorists sought to distance themselves from the fairy tales of Old Regime France (see Schacker 2007)—many of which had become integrated to the panto repertoire, their transnational histories downplayed or, in many cases, rescripted. It is one such form of discursive manipulation I will focus on here: the metamorphoses of Madame d'Aulnoy. At the turn of the eighteenth century, D'Aulnoy was one of a group of aristocratic women and one notable member of the Académie, Charles Perrault, for whom the salon recitation and publication of *contes de fées* served as means to refine rhetorical skills and articulate subversive ideas (including indirect criticisms of Louis XIV). As scholarship of the past twenty-five years has demonstrated, the fairy tale was often associated imaginatively in this context with culturally marginal groups—women, children, servants, peasants— associations sometimes reinforced in illustration, where the source of tales could be imagined as a sylph at a writing desk (as it was in some French editions of Madame d'Aulnoy's tales) or an elderly peasant at fireside (as in the famous frontispiece to Charles Perrault's collection)—either way a woman who might seem to be removed from concerns of the court. And yet, as French fairy-tale scholars have suggested, one ought not to take such associations at face value. The *contes de fées* of d'Aulnoy, Perrault and their contemporaries were shaped by a shared stylistic ideal that was understood as aristocratic and refined: *négligence*—a discursive register associated with a conversational but sophisticated "naturalness of expression." As Lewis Seifert explains, writers of this era refer often to this style as *"naïveté, simplicité,* and *enjouement"*—a style understood to give the appearance of being at once "innate, effortless, and aristocratic" (1996:185). Simplicity in the conteuses' narrative style was associated with salon conversation and thus with a form of orality, but it indexed a radically different class context in late seventeenth-century French texts than it did in the folklore books so popular in later English print culture. Importantly, in the former context *négligence* was understood as an artistic achievement, and one that stood in opposition to dominant neo-Classical aesthetic and ideological frameworks within which women's writing was often trivialized.

Critiques of artifice and excess in *contes de fées* date to the early decades of its literary history. For instance, in an oft-cited treatise from 1699, the Abbé de Villiers declared that "la plûpart des femmes n'aiment la lecture, que parce qu'elles aiment l'oisiveté & la bagatelle; ce n'est pas seulement dans la Province, c'est aussi à Paris et à la Cour qu'on trouve parmi elles ce goût pour les Livres frivoles [. . .] elles s'amusent d'un Livre avec la même esprit dont elles s'occupent d'une mouche ou d'un ruban"(1699:286–87). (Most women enjoy reading only because they enjoy laziness and the trivial; not only in the provinces, but also in Paris and at the court one finds among women this taste for frivolous books [. . .] they amuse themselves with a book in the same way they play with a fly or a ribbon).[1] Villiers asserts that literature has been sullied by the presence of women writers and readers, and feminine sensibilities in the literary marketplace: "qui ne se persuade pas que les Livres sont une marchandise qui change de mode comme les garnitures & les habits?"(1699:278–79). (Who is not convinced that books are now a modish merchandise like accessories and gowns?). Christine A. Jones notes that the conteuses strategically recast notions of elegance, frivolity, and triviality, "reclaiming a charged discourse that had long been used against women tellers and innovative thinkers" (2003:58). In fact, d'Aulnoy's tales are saturated with sartorial detail—but it is not a fly nor a ribbon, but rather the poised pen that serves as the most striking visual symbol of her efforts.

D'Aulnoy's approach to the *conte de fées* is obviously different from that later valued by the Grimms and the folklorists they inspired. Rather than emulate popular oral storytelling, d'Aulnoy inscribed the dynamics of salon conversation into her fairy tale writing, embedding tales into her novels (see, for example, Stedman 2005) or framing and linking individual tales with playful repartee, dialogue, and debate, often between aristocratic women. Her tales extend from and are framed by representations of a distinctly aristocratic mode of oral storytelling, characterized by a narrative voice that repeatedly breaks frame to comment on both the action within the tale and on the conventions of the genre—what D. J. Adams has called a persistent "self-questioning" (1994:20) or even "burlesque self-mockery" (21) that serves to foreground the artificiality and the absurdity of the fantastic. These narrational asides, Adams suggests, "hint at a sophisticated complicity expected from at least some readers" (21)—stylistic features that resonate with conventions of pantomime performance.

D'Aulnoy and Mother Bunch

D'Aulnoy's name had become well-known in eighteenth-century England, as her novels, her accounts of European travel and court scandal, and especially her intricate, highly self-aware, self-referential and influential fairy tales were translated and adapted for English audiences—resonating in the work of Ann Radcliffe, Maria Edgeworth, Anne Thackeray Ritchie, and many others.[2] In fact, the term "fairy tale" entered English parlance in 1699 when d'Aulnoy's *Contes des Fées* was first translated. As Jones has demonstrated (2009), early translations of d'Aulnoy situated the author as a great wit and bourgeois genius, but by the turn of the twentieth century her name had been all but forgotten—not only because adaptations of her fairy tales ceased to be fashionable but also because d'Aulnoy herself had been subsumed by the English figure called "Mother Bunch," to whom translations of her tales were first attributed in the Newbery edition of 1773 and with whom they were repeatedly associated in decades to come. David Blamires cites six Newbery editions of *Mother Bunch's Fairy Tales* extant by 1779 (2008:69), and Jones has traced the predominance of this attribution in editions from the 1790s through the early decades of the nineteenth century (2009:253–54).

Who is Mother Bunch, and why should she be chosen posthumously as d'Aulnoy's alter ego? Mother Bunch's varied guises have been undertheorized, even dismissed; when meriting any mention at all in the history of the fairy tale, this figure has been assumed to represent one of several generalized English peasant-woman storytellers. For example, in the *Oxford Companion to Fairy Tales,* Mother Bunch does not earn an entry of her own, but is dismissed as one of many "representation[s] of the motherly, lower-class storyteller" (Zipes 2000:325)—considered suitable as a children's author, but a far cry from d'Aulnoy's representations of herself as a sophisticated and fashionable woman writer addressing a "feminine, aristocratic listening audience" (Harries 2001:56). For Elizabeth Harries, the erasure of the tales' origins in a specifically French, aristocratic, literary context is energized by the association of Mother Bunch with orality, specifically women's storytelling. Marina Warner has offered an extended analysis of the most durable of these English figures—Mother Goose, to whom Perrault's tales were sometimes attributed (a connection encouraged by his 1697 subtitle, *Contes de ma mere l'oye,* and in illustration)—but Warner dismisses Mother Bunch as just another of the "beldames of folklore," one of "Mother Goose's counterparts" (1990:13). Similarly, Blamires notes only that Mother Bunch was "knowledgeable in English folklore" and a presence in English writings from the sixteenth century onwards (2008:75). Neither Warner nor Blamires give much consideration to Mother Bunch as a distinct figure, with a distinct but quite complicated history in print and on stage. This is a history Margaret Spufford mentions in her important study of popular seventeenth-century fiction (1982) and one that has received more recent attention, most notably from Pamela Allen Brown (2003)—but it has not, to date, been extended to the nineteenth century nor has it been brought into sustained dialogue with fairy-tale studies. As we will see, by the 1770s Mother Bunch had a complex history of her own, and although the name signaled legendary verbal skill, Mother Bunch was *not* associated with the circulation of fairy tales before this point in time. Moreover, the complex set of associations Mother Bunch carried with her in the late eighteenth century was not eclipsed by her new role in the history of the fairy tale, as is especially evident if we consider her many and varied appearances on the English panto stage.

Mother Bunch appears as a character in many nineteenth-century pantomime treatments of French fairy tales and takes a variety of forms, but none of these includes her better-known role as d'Aulnoy the writer. In fact, Mother Bunch appears more often in panto renditions of Charles Perrault's tales than those of d'Aulnoy. For example, the 1822 Covent Garden production of "Harlequin and the Ogress; or, The Sleeping Beauty of the Wood" features three "mothers" of panto fame—Mother Goose, Mother Shipton, and Mother Bunch—as does E.L. Blanchard's "Mother Goose and the Enchanted Beauty," some sixty-five years later (1880). "Beauty and the Beast; or Harlequin and Old Mother Bunch" likewise situates Mother Bunch in an adaptation of a French tale, Jeanne-Marie La Prince de Beaumont's "La Belle et la Bête." In some cases, Mother Bunch shares the stage with characters who *are* of d'Aulnoy's creation (recontextualized, in panto fashion, to other tales). This is the case in William Walton's 1897 "Sleeping Beauty and the Mystic Yellow Dwarf." Here, Mother Bunch is not a speaking part but one of five cross-dressed "mothers" who support the malevolent actions of Old Mother Baneful. Alternately, Mother Bunch can sometimes serve the role of the good fairy or benevolent agent, as she does in Charles Rice's "The Babes in the Wood and the Great Bed of Ware" (1874), and George Conquest and Henry Spry's "Mother Bunch, the Man with the Hunch, the Reeds, the Weeds, the Priest, the Swell, the Gipsy Girl and the Big Dumb Bell" (1881).

In the latter example, Mother Bunch is the most prominent of four witches (Mothers Goose, Shipton, and Hubbard being the others) who embody the spirit and energy of pantomime itself. The performance opened with Mother Bunch's meta-pantomimic reflection—set in an elfin library of "tales [. . .] often told"—on her responsibility to an audience of "little dears" eager for a yearly treat (1881:7). Presented with possible subjects for the Surrey Theatre's 1881 pantomime, this Mother Bunch requests something not so familiar and "well worn" as Aladdin, Sindbad, Red Riding Hood, Cinderella, Bluebeard or the Yellow Dwarf—all of which entered the canon through translation from the French. And yet, on this stage such tales are declared by Mother Bunch herself to be "quite used up, in present form at least," leaving her "in despair about [the Surrey's] Christmas feast"

(1881:8). By 1881, adaptations of the work of Antoine Galland, Perrault, and d'Aulnoy had been so thoroughly naturalized, domesticated, and embraced by English audiences that the character of Novelty can, in this opening scene, contrast such tales (now classics of the English panto repertoire) with an exciting alternative: "Suppose we boldly trench," suggests the embodiment of Novelty, "On foreign ground—suppose we say the French?" In unison, the three mothers exclaim "Oh, that's very new and novel!" and Mother Bunch prepares to welcome a new "little stranger" (Victor Hugo's *Hunchback of Notre Dame)*: "though from *abroad,* pray make yourself *at home.*/ You'll be our honoured guest, so happy be you/ As long as folks will pay their cash to see you" (1881:8). In the conventional panto role of benevolent agent, Mother Bunch is responsible here for supporting the unfolding of the plot as it moves towards its desired and expected conclusion in romantic pairings-off, but she is also responsible to the audience (seeking novelty and diversion) and the theater (generating cash).

This example of a panto Mother Bunch is rich in itself, but what struck me most as I began to take stock of the figure's varied appearances on the Victorian stage was just how multi-valenced she was at this point in time—serving as much more than the generalized figure of peasant storyteller. By the late nineteenth century, Mother Bunch carried with her a wide range of intertextual and cultural associations on which dramatists could draw—still powerfully connected to the genre of the fairy tale, and specifically a tradition of French tales-in-translation.

How can one make sense of the transmogrification of the French aristocratic writer Madame d'Aulnoy into the specific form of Mother Bunch, this English folk figure who predates d'Aulnoy by nearly a century? In my own previous account of this bit of history, I echoed (rather uncritically) claims that have been made about d'Aulnoy's posthumous recasting as "Mother Bunch"—namely, that this maneuver signaled the trivialization and infantilization of her work by the English reading public (2003:7). In fact, Mother Bunch would appear to be a highly unstable cultural icon, both before and after her association with d'Aulnoy's fairy tales. She is a figure who is certainly not associated with the salon, but variously with the alehouse, the marketplace, open fields, as well as the theater. Nevertheless, there are points of resonance between d'Aulnoy's persona and those associated with Mother Bunch that render evocative what might otherwise appear to be a very odd pairing.

The Oxford English Dictionary offers two definitions for Mother Bunch: "strong ale (as proverbially served by Mother Bunch)" and "a stout, untidy, or awkward-looking woman or girl." These lingering associations of Mother Bunch with ale, on the one hand, and a specific body type, on the other, have their roots in her first significant appearance in English book history: *Pasquil's Jests and Mother Bunch's Merriments*. This jest-book was published in 1604, more than 150 years before Mother Bunch became associated with d'Aulnoy, and it remained in print throughout the nineteenth century (see Hazlitt 1864). This Elizabethan collection of bawdy anecdotes, jokes, and tall tales depicts Mother Bunch as an alehouse keeper and masterful storyteller. Pamela Allen Brown notes that in this volume Mother Bunch's own body "sometimes attracts satire" (2003:77), producing laughter and flatulence, inspiring both "terrour" and "amazement" as the "wind in her belly, and one blast of her taile [. . .] blew down Charing-Crosse, with Paul's aspiring steeple." All in all, this Mother Bunch is "an excellent companion, and sociable; shee was very pleasant and witty, and would tell a tale, let a fart, drink her draught, scratch her arse [. . .] as well as any Chymist of Ale" (reprinted in Hazlitt 1864:112–13). Powerful and carnivalesque, this Elizabethan figure is a far cry from d'Aulnoy's self-representation as an aristocratic woman and sophisticated writer. And yet, like d'Aulnoy, this Mother Bunch is a highly self-aware and skilled orator. Brown argues that although Mother Bunch is "laid open to laughter she is strikingly unscathed by it, flourishing as a seller of ale and teller of tales, both of them salable and appetizing commodities" (2003:77). In contrast to Marina Warner's characterization of Mother Bunch as a woman whose "clowning camouflages [her] power" (1990:13), Brown suggests that Mother Bunch's jests—remembered, recounted, collected, repeatedly consumed—comprise a form of social power.

Mother Bunch's power is infectious, and as producer and dispenser of the strong ale that bears her name, she is rumored to have had the most profound effect on her female patrons. With a masterful hand on the ale tap faucet, Mother Bunch "raised the spirits of her spigot to such a height, that Maids grew proud, and many proved with childe after it, and being asked who got the childe, they answered, they knew not, only they thought Mother Bunches Ale, and another thing had done the deed, but whosoever was the father, Mother Bunches Ale had all the blame" (reprinted in Hazlitt 1864:10). As Brown comments, the Elizabethan Mother Bunch is striking in her ability to "flout all rules" (2003:78), including social conventions and restrictions on women's speech, women's economic independence and women's bodies—her own as well as those of her patrons. The cultural "life" of the Elizabethan Mother Bunch overlaps with that of Mother Bunch the fairy-tale narrator, creating an intertextual field that is far more complex than earlier accountings have suggested. Reprinted at least seven times in the seventeenth century, *Pasquil's Jests* remained in print throughout the nineteenth century, revived and reprinted in 1864 by William Hazlitt as one of the jest-books on which Shakespeare would have drawn. Hazlitt notes that this alewife's "celebrity was, doubtless, extreme," and that "subsequent book-makers did not scruple to trade upon it." The result, in Hazlitt's view, is the proliferation in popular print culture of *"pseudo-Bunchiana,* to wit: 'Mother Bunch's Golden Fortune-Teller,' 'Mother Bunch's Closet Newly Broken Open,' and the like, the chronology of which publications is rather dubious, from the persistent absence of dates" (Hazlitt 1864:5).

In fact, we do have a sense of the publishing history of some of the *pseudo-Bunchiana* to which Hazlitt refers: *Mother Bunch's Closet, Newly Broke Open* is a collection of stories of romantic and sexual mishaps, about which the thrice-wed and newly-widowed Mother Bunch offers practical advice and tips for divining fortunes. This text was printed in numerous cheap editions between 1685 and the mid-nineteenth century, and was reprinted both in 1885 by folklorist George Laurence Gomme (in his *Chapbooks and Folk-Lore Tracts)* and then in 1889 by Robert Hays Cunningham *(Amusing Prose Chapbooks, Chiefly of Last Century). Mother Bunch's Closet* begins with the anonymous speaker recounting the "story of an old woman" well known both for her fortune-telling abilities and, along the lines of the classic pantomime dame, her voracious sexual appetite. Readers are introduced to Mother Bunch as an "old woman" who has "newly buried her husband, [and] was taking a walk in the fields, for the benefit of the air, sometimes thinking of the loss of her husbands, for she had had three, yet had a great desire for a fourth" (1685:1–2). She encounters a series of pretty maids, and a few young men, offering them divination tools and sexual advice (in language "thick with innuendo," as Margaret Spufford notes [1982:63–64]). Classified retrospectively (by an 1860s commentator) as one of the "useful" variety of chapbooks, *Mother Bunch's Closet* offers stories of advice sought—simultaneously dispensing advice to readers. With its focus on seeking spouses and sexual fulfillment, *Mother Bunch's Closet* is defined—like d'Aulnoy's corpus of tales—by a largely if not exclusively homosocial communicative frame (see Spufford 1982:61) in which closets are burst open, secrets revealed, and the private made public.

In both of these cases—the jesting alewife and the sexually experienced fortune-teller—Mother Bunch entertains and profits from her verbal skills. It is worth noting that d'Aulnoy (like her fellow *conteuses)* was publishing fairy tales in France at a time when the social status of the professional writer was increasing and gaining "acceptance and a certain respectability" (Hannon 1998:165). Nevertheless, the presence of professional women writers like d'Aulnoy in the world of letters was controversial and perceived to be potentially transgressive (see Hannon 1998:164–78). It is precisely the act of inscription, of speaking to and writing for a predominantly female public that is emphasized in d'Aulnoy's paratextual materials (prefaces, frontispiece illustrations, etc.). This is symbolized visually by the open inkpot and especially by the poised pen: in one early frontispiece to d'Aulnoy's *Contes Nouveaux,* a woman "in the flowing robes and turban usually associated with a sybil" is pictured in the act of inscribing the title of one of d'Aulnoy's tales in a book; in another, a woman wearing a winged helmet writes with a quill as a predominantly female audience sits rapt at her feet (see Harries 2001:52–56).

This iconography seems to have no bearing on the English figure of Mother Bunch: despite her shape-shifting capacity, Mother Bunch was never associated with the act of writing. Rather, Mother Bunch's associations with the genre of the fairy tale (in print and on stage) are generally described in fanciful and corporeal terms—she is seen as both the transmitter and the embodiment of fairy-tale magic. For example, in an 1822 *London Magazine* review of the season's pantomimes, the periodical's (adult) readership is instructed to recall childhood debts and thus to "cherish Mother Bunch, Mother Goose, and all those old enchanting mothers, who suckled us with fairy milk" (The Pantomime 1822:134). Although Mother Bunch is not connected to potential transgression via ink, she is, as we have seen, associated nevertheless with a number of other densely symbolic fluids that threaten (or promise) to obfuscate boundaries, that intoxicate, impregnate, and nourish, that defy efforts to contain them—ale, semen, and now breast milk.

The universalizing and allochronic dimensions of such discursive constructions is striking: d'Aulnoy's specificity as a talented, influential, innovative woman writer is erased in this fantasy of Mother Bunch's body as a wellspring of liquid enchantment. These fantasies take a slightly more solid form in an 1831 article from *The Edinburgh Literary Journal,* where Mother Bunch figures as a source of nourishment and rejuvenation for grown men, more powerful than time itself: "In the Christmas week we think of nothing [but pantomime]. We dream of the pantomime; we breakfast, dine, and sup on the pantomime; we give up all our ordinary pursuits, and do not care one farthing for the state of Europe [. . .]. [F]or five blessed hours, what looks of rapture! What peels of merriment! What thrillings of delicious emotions! 'Time! Time! Time!' how thou dost change all these things!—but, thank Heaven! 'Mother Bunch' is greater than thou, and when she comes to our aid, we defy thee, wrinkled cynic!" (The Edinburgh Drama 1831:17). Here pantomime is said to satisfy hunger, the longings of the body, the desire for diversion, the thirst for the extraordinary; it defies temporality; and it is represented by the figure of Mother Bunch. To the catalogue of cultural functions Mother Bunch has served, we can add one more: she has served as the embodiment of apolitical, ahistorical, romantically nostalgic fantasies in which complicated histories of literary and theatrical production—censorship, translation, adaptation—matter not at all.

And yet, if one resists the "rapture" promised by such invocations of Mother Bunch's name, if her varied and competing appearances in popular cultural forms from the seventeenth through the nineteenth centuries are brought into view, then such references emerge as far more complicated than they might otherwise appear. The points of resonance between Mother Bunch's various personae and that of d'Aulnoy suggest that the history of the *conte de fées* in England is anything but an uncomplicated trajectory towards simplistic fantasy, and then obscurity. Interwoven with the threads that comprise the histories of folklore study, print culture, and popular theater, this chapter of fairy-tale history promises to yield many more surprises and delights.

Notes

Henry Glassie's scholarship, advice, and insights have had a profound impact on my research and writing – keeping me grounded in the history of folklore, even as I have ventured into adjacent disciplines – and I am deeply grateful to him. For their invaluable comments on earlier drafts of this paper, I would like to thank Christine Jones, Greg Kelley, and Danny O'Quinn. Finally, Ray Cashman, Tom Mould and Pravina Shukla have been a pleasure to work with, and I thank them for the opportunity to contribute to this volume.

    1. Translation of passages from Villiers are from Harries (2001:25–26).

    2. On d'Aulnoy's influence on English fiction and English print culture, in general, see Adams (1994) and Palmer (1975).

References

Adams, D.J. 1994. The "Conte des Fées" of Madame d'Aulnoy: Reputation and Re-evaluation. *Bulletin of the John Rylands University Library of Manchester* 76(3):5–22.

Belk, Russell. 1987. A Child's Christmas in America: Santa Claus as Deity, Consumption as Religion. *Journal of American Culture* 10(1):87–100.

Blamires, David. 2008. From Madame d'Aulnoy to Mother Bunch: Popularity and the Fairy Tale. In *Popular Children's Literature in Britain,* eds. Julia Briggs, Dennis Butts, and M.O. Grenby, pp. 69–86. Aldershot: Ashgate.

Blanchard, E.L. 1880. *Mother Goose and the Enchanted Beauty.* Souvenir script, Theatre Royal, Drury Lane. Petingell Collection, University of Kent, Canterbury.

Brown, Pamela Allen. 2003. *Better a Shrew than a Sheep: Women, Drama, and the Culture of Jest in Early Modern England.* Ithaca: Cornell University Press.

Conquest, George and Henry Spry. 1881. *Mother Bunch, the Man with the Hunch, the Reeds, the Needs, the Priest, the Swell, the Gypsy Girl and the Big Dumb Bell.* Souvenir script, Surrey Theatre. Pettingell Collection, University of Kent, Canterbury.

Cunningham, Robert Hays, ed. 1889. *Amusing Prose Chapbooks, Chiefly of Last Century.* London: Hamilton, Adams & Co.

The Edinburgh Drama. 1831. *Edinburgh Literary Journal* 112: 17.

Glassie, Henry. 1995. "Tradition." *Journal of American Folklore* 108(430):395–412.

Golby, John M. and A. W. Purdue. 1986. *The Making of Modern Christmas.* London: Batsford.

Gomme, George Laurence, ed. 1885. *Mother Bunch's Closet Newly Broke Open, and the History of Mother Bunch of the West.* London: Villon Society.

Gubar, Marah. 2009. *Artful Dodgers: Reconceiving the Golden Age of Children's Literature.* New York: Oxford University Press.

Hannon, Patricia. 1998. *Fabulous Identities: Women's Fairy Tales in Seventeenth-Century France.* Amsterdam: Rodopi.

Harries, Elizabeth Wanning. 2001. *Twice Upon a Time: Women Writers and the History of the Fairy Tales.* Princeton: Princeton University Press.

Hazlitt, William Carew. 1864. *Shakespeare Jest-Books.* London: Willis and Sotheran.

Holland, Peter. 1997. "The Play of Eros: Paradoxes of Gender in English Pantomime." *New Theatre Quarterly* 13(51):195–204.

Jones, Christine A. 2003. The Poetics of Enchantment (1690–1715). *Marvels & Tales: Journal of Fairy-Tale Studies* 17(1):55–74.

———. 2009. Madame D'Aulnoy Charms the British. *Romantic Review* 99(3–4): 239–56.

Martin, Ann. 2006. *Red Riding Hood and the Wolf in Bed: Modernism's Fairy Tales.* Toronto: University of Toronto Press.

Mayer, David. 1969. *Harlequin in His Element: The English Pantomime, 1806-1836.* Cambridge: Harvard University Press.

Miller, Daniel. 1993. A Theory of Christmas. In *Unwrapping Christmas,* ed. D. Miller, pp. 3–37. Oxford: Clarendon.

Nissenbaum, Stephen. 1997. *The Battle for Christmas.* New York: Vintage.

O'Brien, John. 2004. *Harlequin Britain: Pantomime and Entertainment, 1690–1760.* Baltimore: Johns Hopkins University Press.

Palmer, Melvin D. 1975. Madame d'Aulnoy in England. *Comparative Literature* 27(3):237–53.

The Pantomime. 1822. *London Magazine* 5:183–84.

Rice, Charles. 1874. *The Babes in the Wood and the Great Bed of Ware.* Souvenir script, Theatre Royal, Covent Garden. Pettingell Collection, University of Kent, Canterbury.

Schacker, Jennifer. 2003. *National Dreams: The Remaking of Fairy Tales in Nineteenth-Century England.* Philadelphia: University of Pennsylvania Press.

———. 2007. Unruly Tales: Ideology, Anxiety, and the Regulation of Genre. *Journal of American Folklore* 120(478):381–400.

Seifert, Lewis. 1996. *Fairy Tales, Sexuality, and Gender in France, 1690–1715.* Cambridge: Cambridge University Press.

Spufford, Margaret. 1982. *Small Books and Pleasant Histories: Popular Fiction and Its Readership in Seventeenth-Century England.* Athens: University of Georgia Press.

Stedman, Allison. 2005. D'Aulnoy's *Histoire d'Hypolite, Comte de Duglas* (1690): A Fairy-Tale Manifesto. *Marvels & Tales: Journal of Fairy-Tale Studies* 19(1):32–53.

Taylor, Millie. 2007. *British Pantomime Performance.* Bristol: Intellect Books.

Verdier, Gabrielle. 1996. Comment l'auteur des "Fées à la Mode" devint "Mother Bunch": Métamorphoses de la Comtesse d'Aulnoy en Angleterre. *Marvels and Tales* 10(2):285–309.

Villiers, Abbé Pierre de. 1699. *Entretiens sur les Contes des Fées et sur Quelques Autres Ouvrages du Temps pour Servir comme Préservatif contre le Mauvais Goût.* Paris: Jacques Collombat.

Walton, William. 1897. *The Sleeping Beauty and the Mystic Yellow Dwarf.* Souvenir script, Theatre Royal, Edinburgh. Pettingell Collection, University of Kent, Canterbury.

Warner, Marina. 1990. Mother Goose Tales: Female Fiction, Female Fact? *Folklore* 10(1):3–25.

Zipes, Jack, ed. 2000. *The Oxford Companion to Fairy Tales.* New York: Oxford University Press.

The Olinger brothers, Dale and Gerard, at their shop in Louisiana, 2009

Counting the Stars: The Study of Creativity on a Human Scale, or How a Bunch of Cajun and German Farmers and Fabricators in Louisiana Invented a Traditional Amphibious Boat

John Laudun

The study of creativity is a vast enterprise. Within it, there must be a place for individuals whose eminence is bounded by locale, either by preference or by providence. Such individuals give us a glimpse of the nature of the creative act in a very immediate and intimate fashion. That is, within a definable horizon the creative act reveals the competence of the individual in the very moment of performance. Folklorists have long studied creativity, even if we were sometimes discerning its shape by its shadow, alongside other humanists, but in the last few decades we have been joined by an increasing number of scientists who, whether interested in the mechanics of the brain or in the way markets respond to novelty, work under the collective umbrella of creativity studies. A few initial forays into embedded, or contextual, studies of creativity—labeled case studies—within the larger field have been assayed, but it is early in their development, and I believe folklore studies stands to make a ready contribution to their efforts, offering as we can our decades-long refinement of the ethnographic study of creative moments.[1]

The trick, of course, is to study human beings as they are, always caught between being "free and stuck in the world" as Henry Glassie once observed (1982:15). Absolute freedom is where the humanities have tended to focus their attention, on artists who, alone in their studios or garrets, are able to explore the furthest reaches of what it is possible to imagine and then realize it in some fashion without concern for audiences or markets. At the other end of the spectrum, are those we imagine who are so stuck within the confines of everyday existence that they cannot see anything else, let alone accept any novelty, whether it be intentional or random. Glassie's ethnographic study of an Irish community revealed that there was plenty of middle ground, that there are folks within a community who stand out more than others, while remaining firmly a part of the dense web of community relations and ideas. Glassie came to adopt the local term for such individuals, stars. He notes: "The star stands at the center. Any consideration of a work of art, a story or song, in Ballymenone leads you to an exceptional individual. . . . The District's culture is not something apart from the particular individuals who are the force of its coherence, the reason for its existence" (1982:681). For Glassie, the older Irish men telling stories about saints in the past, who journeyed across the same landscape as men in a present filled with bombs and bullets, revealed how it is people get along in a world filled with others who may or may not be to their liking.[2]

Passing the Time in Ballymenone is filled with thousands of performances, some verbal and some material, all conscious manifestations of seemingly simple country folk living their lives year by year. What Glassie found amongst the poor farmers of Ballymenone was a constellation of stars, and it was this dense network of people and ideas that beckoned me when I began my own study of creativity on a quite different landscape, one filled with water and thus requiring a special machine to traverse it. I knew, too, that I wanted to address directly the antipodal anchors of creativity studies, the starry-eyed dreamer or the bloody-eyed laborer, and so I found myself drawn to an extraordinary artifact whose very realization screamed creativity and yet whose natal scene was grimy, noisy, and as modern as one could imagine it.[3]

The machine in question is known as a crawfish boat, a modern-looking thing with its metal hull and drive unit, hydraulic hoses and rams, and small-bore engine. Despite its rather homely appearance, it has a hidden virtue: it can go on land and water.

The crawfish boat is indigenous to the landscape it works, handmade in the area in a variety of shops and sheds on the Louisiana prairies. Some of the machine shops specialize in fabrication, some in agricultural equipment repair, some in welding, and some are simply the equipment sheds of farmers. The brief history of the crawfish boat that follows reveals that an

A crawfish boat, parked next to a rice field,
has its front wheels all but hidden from view

An irrigation riser floods a field that has
had its levees pulled up for rice cultivation

extraordinary imagination did not exist within one individual but existed across a network of individuals. Just as importantly, the network had, and has, no central node, and thus it is harder to argue that any node is more, or less important, than any other. Rather, each individual contributes some piece to the larger puzzle until, just like a constellation, enough pieces fall into place that we glimpse a larger structure.

The individuals involved have names that, in fact, locate them on the landscape: Tedmon Habetz, Harold Benoit, Gerard Olinger, Greg Frugé, Clayton Courville, Mike Richard, Kurt Venable, Henry Cormier, Jimmy Abshire, Dale Hughes, and Michael Quirk. Habetz and Olinger are names long associated with areas settled by Germans in the late nineteenth century. Many of the other names are obviously drawn from the region's most renowned group, the Cajuns.

How their ethnic heritage affects their individual perspectives is for another time. To understand the minds of these makers, we must first understand the landscape on which they work, followed by an examination of one particular set of mechanics, hydraulics, with which they approach problems. With the landscape and machines before us, we are prepared to glimpse the birth of the crawfish boat as it slowly develops into its current shape. That development is a function of men operating in loose networks of both discursive and material exchange that overlap and change shape over the course of the boat's thirty-year history. Our understanding will be based on a close examination of the thing itself, and from that, we may be able to glimpse how the minds of these men work. Of course, they understand themselves simply to be solving obvious problems posed to them by the constraints that we all face: the place in which they live and the time in which they live. We begin with their place.

LANDSCAPE

The Louisiana landscape can be a confusing one to behold.[4] Returning to Louisiana in the 1980s to film a documentary about "Cajun Country," Alan Lomax imagined he was weaving his way through marshes as he traveled the two-lane highways between Mamou and Eunice: "I want to share with you one of my most extraordinary experiences: driving down a misty road, past shining silver marshes that are so typical of that area. Of course, it's all low-lying. You're always draining water so you can farm. It's a rice area." There are, in fact, a few marshes sprinkled about the area, but they are small and infrequent. Instead, what Lomax found himself walking on was the northernmost portion of the West Gulf Coastal Plain, which runs from the Texas-Mexico border to the Mississippi River. The land was once prairies of tall grass only broken by tree-lined bayous.

These prairies could not have been more stereotypically American if they had been captured on film by John Ford. Long the province of Native American groups that enjoyed the area as a rich resource of game and fish, Louisiana's prairies were first colonized by Acadians (Cajuns), who ranched it extensively, replacing the native buffalo with European cattle. In some cases, especially along the coasts, they practiced a tradition they had brought with them of building levees around marshy land made marginal by saltwater intrusion and draining the fields off when they were flooded by rain. This practice of reclaiming marsh land for grazing by cattle continues to this day.

The real agricultural revolution came to Louisiana with the third wave of German settlement toward the end of the nineteenth century and the realization that the thin top soil, with a firm clay pan beneath, and relatively flat land could be turned to advantage by flooding it for rice cultivation. Rice is water tolerant and flooding the fields in which it is planted is an effective form of weed and pest control. Between the two systems of land use, draining a field to graze cattle on it or flooding a field to cultivate rice, the operative pairing in south Louisiana is not wetland or dry land but whether you are "pumping on" or "pumping off" water.

Water is managed by pumping into an established network of levees that, in the rice producing prairies, twist and arc across fields. The levees manage the landscape of the prairies, which has gentle drops of only tens of feet over a mile or more. There are a few places where one can glimpse the terracing that is, quite literally, all around, but for the most part it appears to the casual observer as simply a series of ponds. When the rice is high, the levees practically disappear and only a trained eye noticing the difference in vegetation textures can discern them.

The levees are "pulled up" in the fall, usually after soybeans have been harvested, and they divide fields into a series of "cuts" within which a farmer either seeds rice or crawfish. The cuts are imagined as a series, moving water from the highest point to the lowest point. The goal is to limit the difference between the high side of a cut and the low side to being less than an inch. Despite what some may think about abuse of water, or the spill off of agricultural chemicals, farmers do not like to pump a single gallon more of water than they have to, nor do they want to lose one ounce of any pesticide, herbicide, or fertilizer they have applied. In both cases, it is money lost.

By late July, the rice turns golden and the levees re-emerge as striking, bold green lines. All the drains and curtains are pulled, and farmers hope for a few dry weeks so that they can put combines in the fields to harvest the rice. Farmers generally prefer that the ground either be fairly dry or "sloppy wet." In both cases, it is easy to get a combine through a field. The worst case is when the topsoil appears to be relatively firm and can be easily walked upon, or driven upon by light gear like a pickup truck, but sticks to the wheels of a combine as it tries to ply its way through the thick mud. It makes the large vehicles hard to steer, causing them occasionally to slip off course, and the engine has to be run harder to make it through each pass. Under such conditions, it can take more time, which may or may not be available, and more fuel to complete a harvest. Both are costly.

Hydraulics

In some ways, hydraulics is at the center of this history. Pumping water onto fields, pumping it off. Pulling levees up to hold water and plant rice. Pulling them down for better drainage for soybeans. Certainly one dimension of hydraulics is simply about moving water around. Another dimension is the pooling and channeling of water into canals so that it will power machines: water's motion is converted into energy. There are no water wheels in south Louisiana; its relatively short topography does not provide on a regular basis the kind of pressure behind water flows that can produce reliable power.

Water under pressure is a poor transmitter of energy anyway. It transforms too readily from one state to another: apply too much pressure and it turns to steam. It doesn't help that water and steel, the chief structural material of our time, also have a rather tempestuous relationship: the iron in the steel is all too happy to pass its electrons to the oxygen in the water and become ferrous oxide, more commonly known as rust. Because of this, almost all modern devices use some form of oil in their hydraulic systems. Hydraulic machinery is, of course, all around us. Almost anytime heavy lifting needs to get done over a relatively short distance, it will get done by a hydraulic ram (sometimes also called a piston). Rams raise and lower the blades of bulldozers and power the movements of backhoes. Rams are the hidden power behind most elevators. (Contrary to popular belief, elevators powered by wires and winches are usually reserved for buildings of five floors or more.)

If you were to walk around a combine, the first thing that would strike you is its massive front wheels, which are taller than your head and so thick that were you try to hug a tire and reach for the rim, you would probably not be able to do so. Big tires for a big machine that gets heavier as it moves around a field, gulping great draughts of grain as it goes. Surely there must be a huge engine driving a massive transmission to power such a hungry beast. There is, but it is ten feet up in the air. And there is no transmission of the kind we find on cars and trucks, and even on other tractors. Instead, the engine drives a pump, which feeds the hydraulic motor that drives the wheels. (For those unfamiliar with hydraulic motors, simply imagine a turbine driven by oil instead of steam.) Hydraulic machines for a hydraulic landscape.

Hydraulic connections abound, too, on most tractors, powering front-end loaders, backhoes, as well as the great variety of equipment farmers pull behind them—harrowers, cultivators, plows, almost all of which have "wings" that are lifted when the unit is moved from one field to another, or passes down a two-lane highway, and then lowered when it is time to get to work. Indeed, when it is time to get to work, the device is usually lowered by raising the transport wheels up into the carriage, somewhat like landing gear raised up into an aircraft. All of this raising and lowering, digging and smoothing, is guided by hydraulics.

A substantial advantage to hydraulic systems is that they are closed: all oil pumped out to a piston or motor is driven back by leftover pressure into an oil reservoir from which the pump will draw when more work needs to be done. In order to do that work, the oil is pumped out under a great deal of pressure, which means the seals that keep the system closed must be extremely rugged and operate with reasonably small tolerances. A leak means a loss of power, as well as a loss of the very thing that conveys that power. It is the sealed nature of the system that brings us to the advent of the crawfish boat.

Water is the enemy of steel, but corrosion is a slow enemy. Abrasion is much faster, and grit comes in many forms. Most commonly it can be found in the small particles of clay or sand that are the inorganic constituents of topsoil. It can be picked up by the wind as a plow works the ground or churned up in water, but no matter how it rises up, it finds its way into every opening until it manages to get trapped somewhere. If nothing is moving, then all it does is build up. But if movement is involved, then the failure of some part is inevitable, if only through the slow careful grinding of one piece of grit on one small spot.

Every maker of machines knows this and everyone who maintains machines know it as well. In rice country, grit blows in the air as it does elsewhere, but it also hangs in the water. To keep the grit at bay for as long as possible, to delay the inevitable wear, and to make every piece of equipment last as long as it can, incredibly small tolerances are needed between parts of a machine. These kinds of precision are required of hydraulic systems. It was thus inevitable that hydraulics would find their way onto a vehicle that was slowly emerging onto the landscape, the crawfish boat.

History

As the commercial market for crawfish expanded through the 1970s, it became increasingly clear that there was room for more producers. The market had been dominated by crawfish trapped in natural habitats like the Atchafalaya Basin, but as the decade wore on, more and more farmland was being turned to crawfish production, either full-time or seasonally. All a landholder had to do was not drain a field after the autumnal rainy season or flood it back up after rice harvest—strategies varied depending on extant land use. Some fields could produce a crawfish "crop" all on their own: the animals are indigenous to Louisiana and practically omnipresent in any wetland area as well as those regions adjacent to wetlands. They live readily in roadside ditches and near the many irrigation canals and coulees that form an almost continuous web of water across the Louisiana landscape. If crawfish do not simply turn up by holding water on the land, then they are easily seeded.

Unfortunately for farmers, rice fields are not like swamps, which usually have channels through which one can run a boat with a conventional outboard motor. Rice fields are wide, flat, and very shallow. They are perfect for placing traps throughout the entire field, but walking in a flooded field is a tiresome affair, since booted feet plunge not only into water but into several inches of sticky mud. Farmers had to content themselves with working the edge of the fields, placing traps around the perimeter, and accessing those traps by walking along the rice levees with a five-gallon bucket, or two, in hand. Their routine was to empty the traps into one bucket and then re-bait the traps from the other bucket, returning to a provision point when either the crawfish bucket was full or the bait bucket was empty.

But everyone could see all that unused area in the middle of the pond just begging for traps to be placed in it. A few hardy individuals put some traps down and worked their fields by pulling washtubs or toddler splashing pools behind them: if it floated and could hold crawfish reliably, it was worth trying. Some truly hardy individuals pulled or pushed johnboats—

light aluminum-hulled scows sold widely and cheaply throughout the United States for use as fishing boats—through the fields. There is even documentation of one farmer hitching his boat to a horse. No matter what other equipment went into a field or pond, the farmer followed and waded until either all his traps were empty, all his sacks were full, or all his energy was gone.

As productivity in these fields rose and demands for a commercial crop rose, there was clearly a need for a way to move more easily and more quickly through the traps. Normal outboard motors simply could not operate in the shallow waters of flooded rice fields. A few farmers tried the newly-manufactured Go-Devils, a kind of outboard motor that was the pre-cursor to the modern surface-drive motors also manufactured in Louisiana. Even shallow-drive outboards like the Go-Devil proved hard to use in rice fields, where the draft can be as little as eight to twelve inches. What everyone wanted was a machine that could make its way through the field at something like a man's pace.

As luck would have it, the very first idea was the right one, but its appearance would spur a period of wild creativity in which any number of possibilities were tried out. Some took lawn tillers and hung them off boats; others built custom gear reductions or used a system of belts and pulleys in an attempt to take the high RPM of most small bore engines and tie them to some sort of steel driving wheel. But everyone was essentially trying to replicate what Ted Habetz and Harold Benoit had simultaneously arrived at as the solution, though Habetz was the first to demonstrate the power of the idea.

Habetz's boat premiered in the fall of 1982, at a field day hosted by Louis Kramer. The day was designed to mimic those held by local agricultural centers that had not yet turned their attention to the growing interest in commercial crawfish production. Kramer was someone who always kept the big picture in mind, and so he was simultaneously interested in growing the market for crawfish and making sure to attend to expanding local production capacity. Kramer had invited folks to come out to talk and compare notes. His plan was to have Amos Roy of Beaumont, Texas, demonstrate a harvesting machine. And certainly the buggy, which looked a bit like the lunar land rover set down in the middle of a muddy Louisiana rice field, got people talking, but it appears to have been eclipsed that day by a johnboat-come-lately that was built by Tedmon Habetz, who wasn't entirely sure what he had just gotten himself into.

The Habetzes are a German family from "the Cove" as Roberts Cove is known among its denizens, but Ted Habetz did not grow up there. Instead, his father farmed near Loreauville, which is something of a center for boatbuilding in south Louisiana. It is the home of a number of boatyards, none of which have anything to do with the current story — though it is interesting to note that neither the crawfish boat nor the surface-drive motor were produced by dedicated boat builders. Habetz's role as the man credited with inventing the modern crawfish boat began in 1964, when his father decided not to drain one of his fields that had been flooded by Hurricane Hilda (which perhaps hammers home better than any analytical flourish the idea that Louisiana natives understand the landscape differently). Instead, his father started crawfishing it. In the years that followed, the Habetz family crawfished it like everyone else, using set traps and working from lightweight johnboats pulled or pushed through the water.

In the fall of 1982, shortly before Kramer's field day, Habetz's brother Bruno built an eighteen-foot boat. It was pulled through the water by a spoked wheel turned by a worm drive pulled from a combine. Ted Habetz built a somewhat smaller boat with a chain drive. When Bruno received an invitation to the field day, he suggested that his younger brother should come along and bring his boat, too. In the period between the invitation and the day itself, Ted, ever the engineer, decided to take out the chain drive and install a hydraulic system. On the day of Amos Roy's demonstration of his crawfish buggy, Harold Benoit remembers seeing what he called "the first combine that anybody had ever seen." Admiring what Habetz had done, Benoit turned to his friend Lawrence Adams and said, "Look, it's my boat."

Working entirely independently, Benoit had arrived at much the same conclusion as Habetz, though he had not yet figured out how to get his boat down to a workable speed. As soon as he had done so, a number of Benoit's friends and acquaintances immediately pressed him into making them boats. And Habetz reluctantly founded Crawfish Combines, Incorporated, which would go on to make three hundred boats over the next ten years.

Neither Benoit nor Habetz intended to become manufacturers of crawfish boats, but a revolution had begun and they found themselves to be leaders, or at least suppliers. Over the next two decades, others joined them. Some were welders, like Greg Frugé of Eunice and Clayton Courville of Kaplan. Others were fabricators like Kurt Venable of Rayne and Mike Richard of Richie. Others, like Gerard Olinger of Robert's Cove or Jimmy Abshire of Kaplan, were makers and/or repairmen of agricultural equipment. And thanks to vocational agriculture programs still active in area high schools, a large percentage of farmers were able to weld together the necessary parts to turn a fishing boat into a crawfish boat. Within a few years, it became a common sight to see a farmer sitting in a boat being pulled by its own front-wheel drive.

But almost all modern crawfish boats are rear-wheel drive, a change that occurred around 1985 when one maker, Gerard Olinger, responded to increasing complaints by farmers about the difficulties they were having crossing levees with the front-wheel drive boats. The problem was twofold: first, most of the boats were using fairly lightweight engines and wheels, in part to keep costs down because no one was sure if anyone would pay more, and, second, there is the impossibility of the physics of pulling a boat across a levee from a wheel attached to its bow as the bow noses up into the air. There is just not much traction on air. A lot of farmers had working solutions, but they mostly involved driving a post in at a crossing point and winching the boat across.

Working with a farmer, and friend, Jerry Heinen, Olinger put the driving wheel in the back of the boat, creating a boat that could crawl over levees. Unfortunately, the power delivered to the rear of the boat crushed the lightweight johnboat hulls everyone had been using. Olinger's solution was to build hulls of a similar size, but made of thicker aluminum sheets and with much more bracing. The durability of the custom hulls combined with the ease of use of the rear-wheel-drive boats proved popular. In part, they were popular because farmers were driving the boats faster, covering more ground in a day, making more money. Driving fast in a boat which sat a little low in the back thanks to the drive unit wasn't a problem: the bow of any scow will tend to push up a little bit as speed increases. Turning fast proved to be something of a problem though: water was slipping over the top of the boat's side at the back of the boat. Olinger's initial solution was simply to raise the sides of the boat at the back. His more enduring solution was to widen the boat to make the boat more stable and more buoyant, and thus less prone to swamping.

It wasn't long before he and fellow boat makers such as Mike Richard and Kurt Venable took advantage of their custom handwork to build hulls better suited to the task, and so they used wider sheets of aluminum to build five- and six-foot wide boats that could carry more crawfish and had greater stability while being pushed through the water.

FORM

There were more innovations to come, as will be discussed below, but with this one revision, the moving of the driving wheel from the front of the boat to the back, the basic form of the crawfish boat was established. This was the form that Mike Richard used when he began building boats in the late eighties and the one that Kurt Venable adopted when he began building in the early nineties. Between the two of them, they have become the most prolific of the builders. Richard produces on average two dozen boats a year. Venable slowly ratcheted up production, and he now regularly turns out seventy boats a year.

But what is a crawfish boat? How to describe an object that seems like something imagined by Rube Goldberg? It is clearly a boat, and yet it did not arise out of a maritime tradition. It is a boat made by farmers and metal workers who refer to the bow as the front and the stern as the back. With the exception of Venable —who used an entire vacation to study traditional boat building —none of these men have any interest in boats apart from getting in one to go fishing. And some not even that.

Still, the crawfish boat is undeniably a boat, and any account of it would be remiss if it did not take up the boat portion of the vessel, which is, in form, a scow with a square bow and transom. While the transom stretches across the entire width of the boat, there is typically about a foot of taper from the standard width of the boat to the tip of the bow: five-foot-wide boats taper to four feet at the bow, six-foot boats to five, or, in other words, about six inches on each side. The gentle curve up from the bottom of the hull to the bow typically stretches across the same three foot length as the narrowing taper, reducing the depth of the hull from eighteen inches just in front of the front wheels (more on these in a moment) to three inches at the nose. At the stern, the transom is vertical for the top two-thirds and then breaks between six and ten inches from the bottom to rake forward. This cut to the transom keeps the rear edge of the boat from digging into the earth like a bulldozer blade as the boat portages from one field to another.

Early boats by Olinger had a few thwarts, structural members that cross the width of a boat, or a few braces, which can be placed anywhere, while he experimented with ways to control and contain stress to the hull. Venable maintains thwarts in some fashion with his use of small, one-inch by two-inch aluminum I-beams that run across as well as fore and aft in his boats to strengthen and rigidify his hulls—the structural network is hidden by plywood sheets that make the boat's deck. In contrast to Venable's decked hulls, Richard, and now Olinger, prefer an open plan, depending upon the steel bench that holds the engine and the operator and which sits athwart the hull a few feet ahead of the transom as the principal lateral brace. The sides of all the boats flare only a little, a few inches of difference between the edge of the bottom sheet of aluminum and the edge of the gunwale rail that all the builders use to cap the narrow sheet of aluminum that forms the side of the boat.

The hull is thus made up of only a few sheets of aluminum, a five by fifteen-foot sheet that lays flat, starting at the transom until it curves up to the bow. On top of that is welded two fourteen-foot-long by eighteen-inch-high sides, which taper at one end to help form the scow bow. The transom is the width of the boat and a little bit taller than the sides when it is first cut out. The extra height accommodates a forty-five degree bend that, by clipping the trailing edge of the boat a bit, makes it easier to cross levees. The final main piece of aluminum sheet is the bow deck, which is attached to the tip of the bottom hull sheet as well as to the side sheets, wrapping back to form the boat's nose and giving the bow structural stability and strength.

All this strength is required of a vessel that regularly crashes into a levee, bellies onto and over it, and then heaves itself from its beached state into the next field. To do so requires a great deal of power and an extremely robust yet incredibly articulate channel for that power. Every modern craw-fish boat has a steel arm that holds in its grasp a cleated steel wheel. The arm is hinged to move up and down in order to allow the wheel to float, in the mechanical sense of that term, so that it may find the bottom of a flooded rice field but later swing up, in relation to the thrust line of the boat, when the hull angles up over the levee. The arm must swing down again when the boat clears the levee but the arm itself has not. It is usually at this moment that the operator uses a hydraulic ram to push the arm down to force the wheel to get traction. Another ram swings the boat from side to side, but how that turn is accomplished varies from maker to maker. All the arms are, on average, about six feet long, and they hold wheels that are anywhere from two and a half feet to three feet in diameter. Mike Richard's arms are hinged at the very back of the boat; Gerard Olinger's arms are hinged just ahead of the fork that holds his twinned wheels; and Kurt Venable's arms turn the wheel itself. While both Olinger and Venable use rectangular tubing to fabricate the arms of their drive units, Richard uses three-quarter-inch-thick flat steel bent somewhat like a "P", not only to put the wheel on center with the arm itself, but also to give the flat bar greater rigidity to prevent it from twisting.

The hull is a big aluminum box to which the steel drive unit is attached. The problem for each builder is that the drive unit is so powerful it is quite capable of taking the hull and crumpling it much like you or I might do in

One of the early crawfish boats built by Harold Benoit.
Photograph courtesy of Harold and Juanita Benoit

An Olinger boat fron the late 1980s or early 1990s,
with a custom hull and a rear drive

discarding aluminum foil. The marriage of the two parts is further fraught because aluminum and steel cannot be cemented to each other through welding but must be attached through some other arrangement, usually bolting. Both Richard and Olinger use braces; Venable has cleverly adopted the use of a pod, an aluminum box welded into the structure of the hull itself and onto which he bolts his drive unit.

All of this engineering is required in order to accommodate the demand placed on the boats to be able to power through any situation. In almost all cases, this involves muddy water and muddy land and quite often someone trying to get the job done as quickly as possible since crawfish season begins in winter when there is a great deal of wind that cuts all the more sharply as it races across mile after mile of cold, flooded fields.

All the boats are powered by small-bore engines running at a high, fixed RPM. The two engine makers who dominate this particular market are Kohler and Honda, though Yamaha, Vanguard, and Kawasaki are popular elsewhere in the region, and they are regularly used in surface-drive boats. The engines drive a pump that simultaneously feeds three hydraulic circuits: the drive wheel, the steering ram, and the ram that raises and lowers the drive arm. The operator of the boat sits in the rear on the right-hand side and controls each of these three circuits by operating a collection of valves, though each builder places the valves —sometimes clustered together, sometimes not —in different places on the boat. Immediately in front of the operator is a sorting table onto which he, or she, dumps the contents of a crawfish trap.[5] He then simultaneously sorts the keepers into sacks hanging off the table, dumps the small fry as well as any debris in the trap back into the water, and then re-baits the trap, all in time to stick it in the ground just ahead of the next trap, which he then plucks out of the water. He does all this while operating a set of rocker pedals at his feet that steer the boat left or right through the field. Steering is an important part of the rear-wheel drive boats: when the drive wheel is in front, the boat simply follows it. When the drive wheel is in back, the boat is always seeking some direction and must be more actively steered.

The cleated steel wheel at the end of the steel drive arm has been a part of the crawfish boat since its inception in 1983. The size and the width of the rim, the number and placement of the cleats, and the angle at which the cleats are affixed to the rim, have changed over the twenty-five years of active production, with makers staking out certain ideas as their own, which may or may not be adopted by others. One example is illustrative and recalls a point made earlier in this essay about the matter of abrasion and wear on metal parts.

While the cleats look like paddles, they are best thought of as treads, and in some ways they are clearly related to the old steel tires once used on tractors—sometimes called moon tires locally, perhaps in reference to the steel tires that made it possible for the lunar rover to navigate the thick dust of the moon's landscape. Because the entire drive unit is hinged so that the wheel will drop to the bottom of a field, the cleats are pronounced in order to give the boat traction through the soupy mud. As the cleats push along, they are ground down by the sand and clay grit in the mud, and in some areas it is not unusual for a three-inch-tall cleat, typically made of a one-quarter-inch-thick steel plate, which has been cut into a rectangular shape and then welded directly onto the rim, to be worn down to a one-inch nub within a few years. Such wear results in the wheel being brought back to a maker for repair, which means the old cleats must be cut off with an acetylene torch so that new ones can be welded on, or the cleats must be cleaned up enough so that the new ones can be welded onto them. One maker, Kurt Venable, grew tired of the constant repair work and decided to weld a length of steel rod along the entire width of his cleats. It worked. More importantly, not only did it reduce the wear on the cleats, it also gave the wheel better traction and, many farmers felt, lessened the damage the wheels did to fields. (Every trough that a boat makes in a field is one that will be met later on a tractor when the field is drained and plowed for rice or soybeans.)

FLUIDITY

A decade before Venable's innovation Gerard Olinger had been the first to equip boats with rear wheels. Like Venable, Olinger was in search of a solution to a problem he was facing: farmers were wearing out the hulls of their boats all too quickly. One farmer after another would bring in a boat whose hull needed patching. He finally asked and learned that they were driving their boats from one field to another, instead of, as had been the practice, of trailering them. Sometimes they even drove their boats down a gravel or paved road. His response was simple: "I thought as long as they were going down the road, they might as well have wheels."

To Olinger, the idea was a commonsensical response, but the effect in 1985 was to turn the crawfish boat into a full-fledged amphibious vehicle. As the boats matured during their first decade in production, so did the business of making boats, always with about a half dozen builders actively

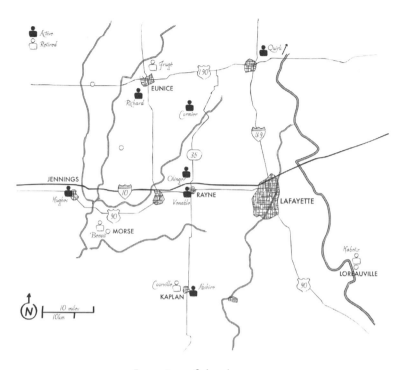

Location of the shops

producing craft. The first two, Benoit and Habetz, eventually left the business, and others, like Greg Frugé and Clayton Courville, manufactured for a time and then left the field as well to do other things. The current makers are Kurt Venable of Rayne, Mike Richard of Eunice, Dale Hughes of Jennings, and Michael Quirk of LeBeau. Mike Cormier and his son always build a few extra boats each year to sell to neighbors and acquaintances. Jimmy Abshire and his brother Robert build a boat now and then in their shop down in Kaplan, and Gerard Olinger continues to keep his hand in the game by making the occasional boat, as well as doing a lot of maintenance and upgrading of boats.

All the men are familiar with the work of the others. With a stable form and individual innovations often quickly adopted by others, it would seem that all the boats must surely look alike, and perhaps to an outside eye they do. But to eyes adjusted to the landscape and adapted to seeing the differences that matter as well as the commonalities that bind everyone together, each boat readily reveals its maker, or makers.[6]

Perhaps the place where each maker's signature is most clear is in the drive unit itself. Gerard Olinger has long preferred two wheels permanently welded into pairs and driven by two hydraulic motors. The steel arm of his drives slopes gently up to a hinge point that comes just ahead of the fork that holds the two wheels. Such a hinge placement means that his boats turn differently from Mike Richard's boats, whose drive arms hinge right at the back of the boat and hold a single, massive steel wheel that is driven by a single hydraulic motor. Richard feels confident that this is sufficient power for his boats, which are clearly designed to be much lighter in weight and more flexible in structure than those of Kurt Venable, who incorporates a significant number of structural elements in his hull, which is driven by a single wheel driven by two motors. A Venable boat turns at the wheel, which is held in place by a vertical fork that comes from above, thanks to a z-bar drive arm. Hughes models his boats after Venable, and Quirk models his after Richard. All of these are different from a Cormier boat or a Courville boat, as well as those boats made by the Abshires.

There are only a few manufacturing secrets here and there that each man possesses because everything there is to know is in the boat. Every hard won idea must manifest itself in steel or aluminum where it is available for all to see, analyze, and judge. And there is almost no end to the discussion of who makes a better boat or whose boat is best suited for which soil or terrain. The makers themselves are judged for the quality of their boats, their willingness to customize a boat, and their willingness to repair or modify a boat made by someone else.

The crawfish boat is the *nonpareil* of an imagination that is not anxious about the transmutation of land and water. If, for the rest of us, there is some lingering concern about contamination, that land made wet can never be trusted as land again, then the people living in south Louisiana do not share it. Wetlands are drained. Prairies are flooded. And then drained. And then flooded again. A rolling landscape is terraced to hold rice and crawfish, and low-lying fields are leveed to graze cattle.

Most importantly, an amphibious vehicle has arrived that allows farmers to become trappers, catching crustaceans that feast on last year's crop and selling them to an ever-expanding market. Within this ecosystem exists a machine that fully participates not only in the natural landscape but also in the cultural landscape. There are, for example, no patents on any part of the crawfish boat. This is not because the men who make them are not fierce competitors, nor is it because they are unaware of intellectual property laws or contemporary trends in patents and copyrights. In addition to his boat business, Kurt Venable mills a variety of custom parts for other manufacturers using his own CAM system. Gerard Olinger orders parts from his shop in the middle of Roberts Cove via his satellite service. Both of them are fully aware of the full force of the contemporary legal apparatus surrounding technology. On more than one occasion, Olinger has remarked that local fabricators always fill niches perceived as too small or unprofitable by large manufacturers. Both of these men, and any of the others, are fully capable of pursuing the legal steps necessary to mark some facet or another of the crawfish boat as belonging exclusively to him.

And yet no one does. As far as each maker is concerned, their reputations as builders, and the reputations of their boats—obviously, the two are intertwined—are well known throughout the community.[7] Venable prides himself on making the strongest hulls, Richard on flexible hulls, Olinger on his dual-wheel drives. Each has also borrowed ideas from the others. Such borrowing is not always from direct observation; it can often come in the form of indirect reporting: a farmer admires something on another farmer's boat and then requests that it be added to his own boat. Sometimes the addition catches on more broadly; sometimes the logic of the addition or emendation is obvious to the maker in a way that leads to further innovation.

Creativity draws from the deep well of common knowledge and experience. Farming, like any other activity, presents a series of problems to be solved, but how those problems are solved is largely determined by how they are framed or understood, and that understanding is itself a function of individual and collective experiences that are constantly being negotiated, not only in terms of content but also in terms of context. Thus, the framework for any solution, and thus the solution itself, is really a function of which individuals within a community are involved, which individuals have contributed, and who has accepted their contribution.

Each of the individuals in a community has to be understood as someone, not only with particular abilities and self-perceived roles—only a farmer, a farmer who occasionally fabricates something when he needs it, a farmer who actively fabricates for himself and others, a fabricator who farms, or strictly a fabricator—but also in term of personal proclivities. For example, one fabricator is a tinker by personality, another is a born competitor and must win in whichever domain he enters, and yet another is a raconteur of exceptional abilities. Together they make up, not a homogeneous community, not even a cohesive one, but rather a loose network of individuals who, through their presence, maintain a network of ideas that have evolved over time. Those ideas are, of course, situated in a value matrix that has remained fairly stable for at least three decades, and it is reasonable to assume the stability extends further back in time.

It is an ecology, and there could be no more striking example of the creativity of such an ecology than a modern metal machine gracefully wending its way through the water to the clatter of its small bore engine and then lunging itself onto dry land, where it blithely rolls down the road to the next bit of water. This complex story of simultaneous invention and diffuse experimentation is itself set in a larger, unfolding social and economic matrix that is at the heart of modern American farming, where farm subsidies and price supports for crops are part of growing rice but not of trapping crawfish.

The crawfish boat is an artifact born of modernity, but it realizes a number of traditional ideas within its various contexts. Traced through these various contexts, the artifact, be it a story or a boat, reveals that it is always more than a thing. It always expresses something about the individual who made it and the individual who uses it. When those two individuals are part of a larger group with shared ideas, the artifact cannot help but express something of that culture as well as the landscape on which the group resides and the artifact operates. It is the peculiar charm of the crawfish boat that its destiny was to be born on an ambiguous landscape. Its mobility, no matter the circumstance, allows us a glimpse into how creativity has been practiced in a particular place at a particular moment in time. Perhaps no more, but certainly no less.

Notes

1. Robert Sternberg's *Handbook of Creativity,* although ten years old now, offers a nice survey of the various approaches within the larger field of creativity studies. Very near to folklore studies, and to me, is a wonderful essay by my colleagues Carmen Comeaux, Janet Schexnayder Elias, and Subrata Dasgupta, which, while arguing for the rarity of the "highest form of creativity," do so within contexts akin to those to which folklorists are accustomed: storytelling or the making of artifacts. Their "cognitive case study" method is easily adapted to folkloristic uses, and I have deployed some of the case study tropes here. (For more of this kind of work, see Nersessian's study of a research laboratory [2006].)

2. Previously, in his native Virginia, Glassie had turned to the testimony of houses to begin to discern how a given group of people on a given piece of land on this small planet of ours could find themselves so divided. *Folk Housing in Middle Virginia* is famously devoid of people, focusing instead on a large collection of houses and the permutations of their spaces, but Glassie was clearly not interested only in

the houses: the diagrams that bedevil so many readers reveal that the houses are both projections of, and shells for, human imagination. That true object of his study is revealed in the opening and closing of the book: descriptions of a land of increasing alienation. At the beginning, a photograph centers on a sign for a Klan rally (1975:4), which is explained at the end of the book: "Unsure of his situation, [the white farmer] and his neighbors build identical houses with floor plans that suggest withdrawal and facades that suggest impersonal stability. Personal energies are removed from the immediate community and invested in abstract ideals, such as racial superiority, nationalism, or artificial, symmetrical order" (190).

3. Better documented in the larger project upon which this essays draws is the fact that the crawfish boat is not the first boat to be imagined as amphibious. The pirogue, first adapted from the local indigenous peoples' dugouts and later planked in the late nineteenth century, is a boat often said to be able to "glide on the dew." The crawfish boat itself comes on the heels of the beginning of what is now known as the "surface drive outboard" industry, which began in the late 1970s in Louisiana. For more on the early history of boats in Louisiana, see Malcolm Comeaux's survey (1985). For an example of the amphibious boat as imagined, see George Reinecke's translation of "A Louisiana Black Creole Version of 'The Land and Water Ship'" (1994).

4. On the second anniversary of the storms, reporting on the current state of things in New Orleans, a *National Geographic* article led off with: "The *sinking city* faces *rising seas* and *stronger hurricanes,* protected only by *dwindling wetlands* and *flawed levees.* Yet people are trickling back to the place they call home, *rebuilding in harm's way*" (Bourne 33; emphases in the original). Those five adjective-noun pairs beginning with "sinking city" and "rising seas," build to a kind of apocalyptic inevitability. The contradictory nature of the gerunds—first "sinking" and "rising" and then "dwindling" and "rebuilding"—underlines the absurdity of living on, or in, an ambiguous landscape. The nouns tell much the same story: city, seas, hurricanes, wetlands. *National Geographic* is not alone in seeing absurdity in living in, or on, wetlands: theirs was simply the most compressed, the most poetic.

5. Since its inception, the modern crawfish industry has been a family affair with women, whether they are wives or daughters, playing as much a role as husbands and sons in gathering, sacking, and selling the crawfish. Like other agricultural contexts where women are typically less involved with farm equipment and more involved in the business of the farm, women have played less of a role in the formal development of the boat, but it should be noted that Cheryl Venable, herself a Leonard from Roberts Cove, is an integral part of Venable Fabricators and her contribution and those of other women is one yet to be fully understood.

6. Few boats, except when brand new, survive in the field exactly as they were when they left their makers' shops. All farm equipment breaks under regular use and is often repaired, and perhaps modified, in the field by farmers themselves, many of whom are quite handy with a welding rig. (To be sure, almost all of them

use the much less expensive stick welders, and so their welds tend to be revealed by closer inspection.) It is also the case that boats made by one fabricator will be brought to another for repair and/or modifications. I have seen Olinger drive units on Venable hulls, and Richard-style sorting tables on Cormier boats.

7. Reputation systems are commonly discussed within the context of online communities or domains, where the automated systems are subject to scrutiny for their vulnerability to attack. But a peopled system is a much more complex and interesting affair, and recent scholarship has explored how such systems, and their peopled networks, might lead to more humane economies (Benkler and Nissenbaum 2006).

REFERENCES

Benkler, Yochai and Helen Nissenbaum. 2006. Commons-based Peer Production and Virtue. *The Journal of Political Philosophy* 14(4):394–419.

Bourne, Joel. 2007. The Perils of New Orleans. *National Geographic* (August):32–67.

Comeaux, Carmen, Janet Schexnayder Elias, and Subrata Dasgupta. 2006. Creativity, Cognition, and the Case Study Method. In *Frontiers in Cognitive Psychology,* ed. Michael Vanchevysky, pp. 105–25. Hauppauge, NY: Nova Science Publishers.

Comeaux, Malcolm. 1985. Folk Boats of Louisiana. In *Louisiana Folklife: A Guide to the State,* ed. Nicholas Spitzer, pp 160–78. Baton Rouge: Louisiana Folklife Program.

Glassie, Henry. 1975. *Folk Housing in Middle Virginia: A Structural Analysis of Historic Artifacts.* Knoxville: University of Tennessee Press.

———. 1982. *Passing the Time in Ballymenone: Culture and History of an Ulster Community.* Philadelphia: University of Pennsylvania Press.

Lomax, Alan. 1992. *American Patchwork: Cajun Country.* Pacific Arts Video.

Nersessian, Nancy. 2006. The Cognitive-Cultural Systems of the Research Laboratory. *Organization Studies* 27(1):125–45.

Reinecke, George. 1994. A Louisiana Black Creole Version of "The Land and Water Ship." *Louisiana Folklore Miscellany* 9:19–29.

Sternberg, Robert (ed). 1999. *Handbook of Creativity.* Cambridge: Cambridge University Press.

On Middle-Range Structures in Heroic Epic

William Hansen

INTRODUCTION: FORMULA, THEME, SONG

Much scholarly attention has been given to understanding how oral poets compose, or recompose, epic songs of substantial length in performance. To this end Milman Parry and his student Albert Lord distinguish in their individual publications three levels of compositional organization in oral poetry: formula, theme, and song (see Parry 1971; Lord 1960).

The singer's formulaic diction facilitates the production of metrical lines at a rapid pace, while composition by theme (or typical scene or type-scene) and composition by song (that is, song-type or story-pattern) refer to the production of narrative under the pressure of performance.[1] Composition by theme signifies the singer's employing conventional ways of handling brief events and ideas that recur in epic song. Themes or scenes may be nameable, such as dressing, arming, bathing, inviting, eating, sending a message, and holding a council, or they may be made up of elements that lack a necessary or predictable connection with one another and so are less easily labeled as well as less readily perceived.

Composition by song-type refers to the singer's producing whole songs after one of several conventional patterns that are found in his singing tradition. According to Lord, "the singer thinks of his song in terms of a flexible plan of themes, some of which are essential and some of which are not" (1960:99). For example, Return Songs in the South Slavic tradition are generally made up of a string of twelve themes: Capture of the Hero, Capture of Radovan, Conversation between Radovan and Hero, Shouting in Prison, Bargaining for Release, Preparation for Journey Home, Journey

Bust of Homer. A Roman copy of a lost Hellenistic original
of the second century B.C. British Museum, London

Home, From Arrival in Home Country to Arrival in Own House, Arrival Home and Recognitions, Return to Enemy, Settlement, and Sequel (Lord 1960:121–23, 242–59; see also Foley 1990).

Parry's and Lord's formula, theme (or scene), and song became, and have remained, standard tools of analysis for scholars of oral poetics. Writing at the end of the twentieth century, nearly forty years after the publication of Lord's seminal *Singer of Tales,* John Miles Foley employs the canonical triad unchanged in his presentation of the oral-poetic technique: formula; at a higher level, theme; and at the highest level, story-pattern.[2] These levels of organization may be adequate for understanding the composition in performance of epic songs such as those typical of the South Slavic tradition studied by Parry, Lord, and Foley. But what of the composition of oral-poetic songs of much greater magnitude such as Homer's *Iliad* and *Odyssey?* To put the matter into perspective, Serbo-Croatian songs appear to range typically from around 1000 to 3000 decasyllabic verses in length. The average length of the songs in the first volume of Parry's and Lord's *Serbo-Croatian Heroic Songs* is 1,012 decasyllabic lines, which is equivalent to about 675 Homeric hexameters, not much more than the average length of a single book of Homer's *Iliad* (654 lines) or *Odyssey* (505 lines). In terms of length you could fit approximately ten such South Slavic epics into one Homeric epic.[3]

Although in the realm of narrative Lord limits his nomenclature to theme and song, in practice he acknowledges the existence of other levels of narrative organization, in particular a level or levels greater than that of the theme but smaller than that of the sequence of themes that makes up a whole song.[4] He refers to these configurations in different ways, most often in terms of multiple themes; thus, "some themes have a tendency to cling together, held by a kind of tension, and to form recurrent patterns of groups of themes" (Lord 1960:112). Elsewhere we hear of a "complex of themes" (p. 96), which may be held together by a "tension of essences" (p. 97) or a "thematic complex" (p. 160) or "thematic repetition" (p. 173), in addition to terms such as "pattern" and "story pattern" (p. 160) and "multiform" (p. 169). Just as Lord recognizes large sequences of themes that define a particular category of song, so also he perceives smaller sequences of themes that define a particular "thematic complex" or the like, amounting to a middle-range narrative such as an episode or smaller story within the larger story. Officially, then, oral poets rely upon a tri-level technique of composition (formula, theme, and song), whereas, unofficially, there are poets who control at least four levels.

Taking Homer's *Odyssey* as representative of oral-poetic songs of substantial length and narrative complexity, let us consider the presence in it of levels of narrative organization higher than the theme but lower than the song itself.[5]

A Straightforward Case

Lord himself calls attention to such a thematic complex in Homer's *Odyssey* (1960:65–69). In Book 4 Menelaos consults the prophetic Old Man of the Sea, Proteus, on the advice of the nymph Eidothea, and subsequently, in Books 10–12, Odysseus consults the seer Teiresias on the advice of the nymph Circe. Lord lists four "points of coincidence" between the two stories: (1) the hero is detained on an island; (2) he is advised by a nymph to seek information from a particular seer; (3) he must perform a particular ritual in order to do so; and (4) the seer informs him why he is having trouble with the gods and what to do about it, and he prophesies how the hero's life will end (1960:165).

Lord's four points of coincidence certainly understate the extent of the narrative patterning shared by the two episodes, which perhaps explains why Lord does not feel the need to recognize in them a distinct level of compositional organization. Here is a fuller accounting of the parallels (though, for the sake of space, still abbreviated), arranged in the order in which the events appear in each narrative. On the first day (1) the hero (Menelaos/Odysseus) or his crew wishes to continue their journey home. (2) The hero encounters a nymph (Eidothea/Circe) and (3) asks her help. (4) She directs him to consult a particular seer (Proteus/Teiresias). When (5) the hero anticipates a difficulty in the task, (6) the nymph reassures him and (7) gives him detailed instructions on how to proceed. On the second day, (8) as the hero sets out with his companions, (9) the nymph provides them with certain objects for the task ahead. (10) The hero digs a lair or trench, whereupon (11) throngs of seals (or ghosts of the dead) gather about; then (12) the seer himself appears and (13) asks the hero why he has come. (14) The seer explains that the hero has offended a god, and (15) advises him what to do to reach his home. (16) The hero goes on to learn of the unhappy fates of three of his former comrades-in-arms at Troy, after which (17) he and his companions return to their ship and pass the night. On the third day, (18) after performing certain rites, including building a barrow for a deceased comrade, (19) they continue their journey, which the gods help by sending a favorable wind.[6]

290

These two episodes manifestly share an extensive pattern of events, which are distributed identically over a three-day period. The episodes can only be different realizations, or multiforms, of the same underlying sequence of narrative ideas, which I call the Conference Sequence since the events are organized around a conference between the protagonist and another figure, in this case an exotic seer. The passages are too long and varied to be reasonably or usefully called themes or type-scenes (the Menelaos episode consists of 236 lines of hexameter verse; the Odysseus episode, 898 lines) and of course far too short to coincide with the *Odyssey* as a whole song, and, as such, they furnish a clear instance of oral-poetic composition at an intermediate level, one lying between theme and song.

A More Difficult Case

In an article published in 1969 the classical scholar Mabel Lang points to a number of similarities between Odysseus's experiences among the Phaeacians, recounted in Books 5–12 of Homer's *Odyssey,* and his subsequent experiences on Ithaca, told in Books 13–23.[7] Odysseus arrives at an island kingdom (Phaeacia/Ithaca), where a young royal (Nausikaa/Telemachos) facilitates his dealing with the locals.[8] In time he proceeds to the palace and wins the goodwill of a powerful queen (Arete/Penelope). On Phaeacia an insult leads to Odysseus's joining and winning a discus competition, while on Ithaca an insult precedes his joining and winning an archery competition. In both episodes music and dancing follow. On Phaeacia Odysseus reveals his identity and then gives the Phaeacian court a detailed account of his fantastic adventures, just as on Ithaca, after his recognition by Penelope, Odysseus gives her an abbreviated account of his adventures. Lang calls attention to a number of minor correspondences as well. Secrecy characterizes Odysseus's arrival on Phaeacia, just as disguise does on Ithaca. On Phaeacia Odysseus arrives at a spring and shrine of Athena, and prays that he be received well; on Ithaca Eumaios and the disguised Odysseus arrive at the spring and shrine of the nymphs, where Eumaios prays for Odysseus's safe arrival. As Odysseus enters the Phaeacian palace, where he encounters metallic dogs of gold and silver, he marvels in much the same way as he does later when he enters the Ithacan palace and comes upon his old dog Argos. In both episodes Odysseus remarks on how shameless the belly of a hungry man is, and both episodes feature a recognition scene involving garments.

Other scholars, notably D. Gary Miller and Steven Lowenstam, add to and systematize Lang's miscellany of parallels, strengthening the case for a close relationship between the two episodes (Lowenstam 1993:207–28; Miller 1982:61–68; Reece 1993:101–21, especially 113–21). Bruce Louden adds a third narrative to the group, Odysseus's experiences on Aiaia, Circe's island (1993, 1999). Louden describes the shared narrative pattern that he perceives:

> Odysseus, as earlier prophesied, arrives at an island, disoriented and ignorant of his location. A divine helper appears, advising him how to approach a powerful female figure who controls access to the next phase of his homecoming and pointing out potential difficulties regarding a band of young men. His identity a secret (as approach to the female is perilous), Odysseus reaches her, finding a figure who is initially suspicious, distant, or even hostile toward him. She imposes a test on him, whereupon Odysseus, having successfully passed the test, wins her sympathy and help, obtaining access to the next phase of his homecoming. Their understanding is made manifest in her hospitable offer of a bath. Furthermore, Odysseus is now offered sexual union and/or marriage with the female. However, conflict arises between Odysseus and the band of young men. The young men abuse Odysseus in various ways and violate a divine interdiction. The leader of each band has the parallel name of Eury-; the band's consequent death, earlier prophesied, is demanded by a wrathful god. A divine consultation limits the extent of the death and destruction. (Louden 1999:2, original is in italics)

Overall, these scholars make a persuasive case that the Aiaian episode, the Phaeacian episode, and the Ithacan episode (to take them in the order in which they appear in the Odyssey) are three different realizations of the same action-sequence.

There is disagreement about the implications of this finding. On the one hand, Lang calls attention to oddities in the Phaeacian episode, such as that the Phaeacian queen is unusually powerful and that the otherwise hyper-civilized and hospitable Phaeacians are reputedly so hostile that Odysseus's presence among them must initially be concealed for his own safety. These aspects of the Phaeacian episode have also troubled other critics. Lang notices that narrative ideas corresponding to these appear also in the Ithacan episode, where they are not troublesome: on Ithaca it is unremarkable for Penelope to be the central figure in the palace in the absence of her husband Odysseus, and it makes perfect sense for Odysseus to make his approach in disguise there because of the presence of the hostile suitors and their supporters. Lang accounts for the presence of these themes in the Phaeacian episode by supposing that the Ithacan episode served as its model. Over time the oral bards borrowed motifs from the one and creatively adapted them for use in the other such that the Phaeacian sequence, although it appears earlier in the song, came to be a re-creation of, or variation upon, the Ithacan sequence. The Phaeacian narrative has "enough of the familiar to give comfort and reassurance and enough of the different to provide wonder and excitement" (Lang 1969:168). Many scholars agree, holding that the Phaeacian episode has been generated from the Ithacan and that aesthetically it serves as a prelude to it by offering similar and contrasting material.

On the other hand, J. B. Hainsworth points out that in an oral-poetic *Odyssey* it is unnecessary to propose that either the Phaeacian episode or the Ithacan episode is modeled on the other. Rather, the two episodes should be understood simply as different realizations of the same sequence of themes in accordance with the usual compositional method of oral singers, and similarly the minor incongruities in the episodes are of the sort commonly encountered elsewhere in multiforms of the same oral-poetic material (Hainsworth in Heubeck et al. 1988:290–91). Lord and other scholars have shown how oral poets do not always adjust a theme fully to a particular narrative environment, resulting in a narrative awkwardness or inconsistency.[9] The episodes of Menelaos and Proteus and of Odysseus and Teiresias, discussed above, contain several instances in which an utterance or the like in one episode would make better sense in the other (Lord 1960:165–69; Hansen 1972:8–19).

Louden's position is a mix of these views, combining the perspectives of the literary critic and the strict oralist. He holds that the narrative pattern observable in the Aiaian, Phaeacian, and Ithacan episodes exists to facilitate oral composition, but he also believes that it is consciously manipulated by the singer, who composes with an awareness of it (Louden 1993:32). For Louden the Aiaian episode and the Phaeacian episode are "rehearsals or anticipations" of the Ithacan episode, which is the goal, the episode in which the events unfold at greatest length (1993:7).

However that may be, in an oral poem we should treat repetition as a fundamental stylistic feature of the art form rather than assign repeated passages a relationship of model and copy, of early and late, as philological Homerists commonly did before the work of Parry and Lord, and for the same reason we should understand minor incongruities as normal byproducts of oral-poetic composition rather than explain them as unique byproducts of borrowing.[10]

What is the Pattern a Pattern of?

A question arising from the scholarly literature on the Aiaian, Phaeacian, and Ithacan episodes is the nature of the underlying pattern itself: just what is it a pattern of? The scheme that Louden perceives in these episodes has the form of a story: Odysseus arrives at an island in a helpless state, he is advised how to approach the powerful female character who dominates the place, he succeeds in winning her over, and complications arise, but they too are dealt with. The pattern is mostly Homer's but partly Louden's. When Homer presents an element out of chronological sequence, Louden puts it back. Thus the initial feature of Louden's pattern incorporates a prophecy: "Odysseus, as earlier prophesied, arrives at an island, disoriented and ignorant of his location." In the actual chronology of events the prophecy is made before Odysseus's arrival, but Homer informs his listeners of it later. Louden inserts it here at the head of the events where it would be if Homer recounted it in chronological sequence, which he does not.[11] Miller's and Lowenstam's lists of parallel traits similarly strive to capture a story, as a consequence of which they also give some items out of the sequence in which Homer presents them (Miller 1982:62–66; Lowenstam 1993:208–9). Does the singer generate these narratives from a story template in his mind, whether it is a conscious one (as Louden supposes) or not?

To answer this question I give a third instance of middle-range structuring in the *Odyssey*. The two episodes are recounted in the portions of the poem devoted primarily to Odysseus's son Telemachos, which are known as the Telemachy. The Telemachy is, as I argue elsewhere, made up of three consecutive realizations of middle-range structure, each featuring a consultation or conference. In the first, Telemachos travels to Pylos to consult Nestor (Books 1–3); in the second, he goes on to Sparta to consult Menelaos (Book 4); and in the third he returns to Ithaca, in the course of which he passes again through Pylos, where he engages in a spontaneous conference with a seer, Theoklymenos (Book 15). Here are the parallel events in the first and third journeys, labeled here Telemachy 1 and Telemachy 3, given in the order in which the singer presents them.[12]

Telemachy 1	Telemachy 3
	First Day
Athena goes to Ithaca.	Athena goes to Sparta.
Telemachos sits, fantasying his father's return.	Telemachos lies awake, anxious for his father.

294

Athena bids him ask the suitors to go home; he himself should go to Pylos and Sparta to consult Nestor and Menelaos about news of Odysseus. She departs.	Athena bids him urge his host Menelaos to send him home. She departs.

Second Day

Telemachos calls an assembly and bids the suitors return to their homes; if they do not, he will ask Zeus for just retribution.	Telemachos goes to Menelaos and bids him send him home; he wishes that Odysseus were home so that he might tell him of Menelaos's hospitality.
A omen (two eagles) appears. The assembly is amazed.	An omen (eagle and goose) appears. The onlookers rejoice.
An old man interprets: Odysseus may already be near, planning death for the suitors.	Helen interprets: Odysseus may already be home, planning death for the suitors.
Telemachos and his crew embark and sail all night.	Telemachos and his companion depart by chariot and pass the night in Pherai.

Third Day

They reach Pylos and join Nestor and the other Pylians on the beach.	They reach Pylos, where Telemachos's companion drops him off at his ship on the beach.
Telemachos prays to Poseidon.	Telemachos prays to Athena.
Nestor asks who they are and what their mission is.	A stranger, Theoklymenos, approaches Telemachos and asks who he is.
Telemachos explains who he is, saying that he has come after news of Odysseus.	Telemachos explains who he is, saying that he has come after news of Odysseus.
Nestor relates that he himself sailed from Troy to Pylos, escaping the wrath of Athena; but he knows little of Odysseus.	Theoklymenos explains that he himself has fled from Argos to Pylos to avoid his angry kinsmen.

295

Telemachos asks Nestor to tell him of Agamemnon and Menelaos.	Odysseus asks Eumaios to tell him of Antikleia and Laertes.
Nestor tells of Agamemnon's murder and Menelaos's voyage.	Eumaios tells of Antikleia's death and Laertes's suffering.
Nestor invites them to stay with him in his palace.	Theoklymenos asks whether he should go on to Telemachos's palace to lodge.
Telemachos's companion (= Athena in disguise) replies that he himself cannot stay but Telemachos should do so	Telemachos replies that he should rather go to the home of one of the suitors, although a disaster may come before any wedding takes place.
Athena departs in the form of a sea-eagle.	An omen (hawk and dove) appears.
Nestor interprets: The gods are your escort, for that was Athena!	Theoklymenos interprets: That was an omen—there is no more kingly family in Ithaka than yours!
Nestor leads the party to his palace.	Telemachos walks to Emaios's hut.

The extensive parallels between Telemachies 1 and 3 as well as their identical distribution over a three-day period show that these two episodes are forms of the same narrative pattern. More precisely, they are multiforms of the Conference Sequence, constituting, by virtue of their especially close parallelism, a subgroup within the larger family of such multiforms, just as the episodes of Menelaos's and Odysseus's consultations of a seer constitute a subgroup of their own.

Three of the episodes—Menelaos's consultation of Proteus, Odysseus's consultation of Teiresias, and Telemachy 1—show the same underlying story: the hero has a problem, a supernatural being advises him to go to a particular place to consult a particular being, the hero goes, the two confer, and after some additional inquiries the hero departs. The conference, whether it proves to be successful or not, is the event of central interest in each of these multiforms. What is striking about Telemachy 3 is that, unlike the foregoing episodes, the events are not all linked by cause, setting, or character to the actions that precede and follow.

For example, in Telemachy 1 Athena instructs Telemachos to go to Pylos and consult Nestor; he goes to Pylos, finds Nestor on the beach, and consults him. But in Telemachy 3 the same goddess instructs Telemachos to return home; he travels via Pylos, and while he is on the beach a seer, Theoklymenos, suddenly appears as if out of nowhere, and they confer. Although no consultation is planned, one happens anyway, and in the same position in the narrative as in Telemachy 1. The pattern of consultation found in the other multiforms is present, but not the narrative logic.

A second instance is more drastic. In realizations of the Conference Sequence the conference theme is often followed by a theme of intermezzo: business having been taken care of, the conversation turns to updates about old friends or family.[13] So in the Menelaos episode the hero asks Proteus about his old comrades at Troy, and Proteus informs him about the sad fates of three of them. In the Odysseus episode the hero, who is visiting the death realm at the time, directly questions three of his old comrades about their fates, and they respond or not. In Telemachy 1 the hero asks Nestor about two of his comrades at Troy, and Nestor informs him of their fates. But in Telemachy 3 the singer now dismisses Telemachos and company, and *changes the scene from Pylos to Ithaca,* where he presents a conversation between Odysseus and the swineherd Eumaios. In a truly remarkable instance of the persistence of narrative pattern, Odysseus asks Eumaios about his (Odysseus's) mother and father, and Eumaios informs him of their unhappy fates (see the italicized passages below); after the intermezzo theme the narrator returns to Telemachos:

Nestor relates that he himself sailed from Troy to Pylos, escaping the wrath of Athena; but he knows little of Odysseus.	Theoklymenos explains that he himself has fled from Argos to Pylos to avoid his angry kinsmen.
Telemachos asks Nestor to tell him of Agamemnon and Menelaos.	Odysseus asks Eumaios to tell him of Antikleia and Laertes.
Nestor tells of Agamemnon's murder and Menelaos's voyage.	Eumaios tells of Antikleia's death and Laertes' suffering.
Nestor invites them to stay with him in his palace.	Theoklymenos asks whether he should go on to Telemachos's palace to lodge.

Whereas the pattern of individual themes is maintained, the causal connections between them are not.

A comparison of Telemachies 1 and 3 shows therefore that the shared narrative pattern need not be story-dependent. By nature, then, the pattern is not, or need not be, a story. The crucial configuration is that of the events in the order of the singer's presentation, whether they are individually connected or not.

Conclusions

I have considered here four realizations of the Conference Sequence, consisting of a subgroup featuring Menelaos or Odysseus as protagonist and a subgroup featuring Telemachos; and three realizations of a narrative sequence that I will call the Powerful-Female Sequence, which features Odysseus as protagonist. Although these four episodes differ in magnitude, all of them exceed what can reasonably be thought of as a theme, while at the same time each amounts to only a fraction of the whole *Odyssey.*

I draw two conclusions. First, middle-range structures are found extensively in Homer's *Odyssey* and constitute an important level of narrative organization for the performer. Parry's and Lord's canonical three-level model of oral-poetic technique, developed to describe composition in the South Slavic tradition, must be modified to (at least) a four-level model—formula, theme/scene, sequence, and song—in order to deal adequately with the *Odyssey,* if not also with other large-scale epics.

Second, regarding the nature of these middle-range structures, it is incorrect, or not quite correct, to imagine that the pattern stored in the singer's mind and accessed by him to facilitate composition necessarily has the form of a story. As the four examples show, the elements of a patterned sequence of events can be connected closely or loosely, or not connected at all.[14] A conference may be planned or may occur by chance. The intermezzo may be a continuation of the central conference or may be unconnected with it. What is constant is merely a sequence of motifs.

Nevertheless, the episodes do usually reflect a story, showing themes connected with one another by character, scene, and/or cause. Accordingly, we should acknowledge two kinds of pattern: discourse pattern, that is, the narrated events taken in the order of the singer's presentation, whether they are related chronologically or not and whether they are connected causally or not; and story pattern, the chronological and more-or-less causal sequence of events pertaining to a character who attempts to solve a problem.

Discourse pattern is the template of the singer's immediate composition; story pattern must be more remote.

Discourse pattern and story pattern, as defined here, must then correspond more-or-less to surface structure and deep structure, respectively. We discern in the *Odyssey* two deep-structures, that which underlies the Conference Sequence, in which the protagonist's counterpart is a male, and that which underlies the Powerful-Female Sequence, in which she is a female. In the male pattern, the hero faces a problem, is advised by a supernatural female to consult a particular male being, does so, and departs. In the female story, the hero has a problem, is advised by a supernatural being how to deal successfully with the locally-dominant female, does so, and departs. These two deep-structural patterns are not greatly different, which suggests that ultimately they are forms of a single story. This is perhaps the *Odyssey* at its deepest level.

Historically, classicists and folklorists have been inclined to tug at their materials in different directions with regard to tradition and originality. Classicists have honored personal creativity in the poets they study, and have been slow to accept the role of tradition, whereas folklorists have long appreciated tradition and only recently honored personal creativity. The art of oral song depends crucially upon both tradition and creativity. Individual performers create pathways for recounting new stories, as any storyteller does, and in the aspect of the art form considered here, exceptional performers make the creative leap of decoupling discourse and story, freeing themselves, not of course from tradition, but from the literalism of story pattern.

Notes

1. "Theme" is Parry's and Lord's preferred term. The common designations "typical scene" and "type scene" derive from Walter Arend's monograph, *Die typischen Scenen bei Homer* [Typical Scenes in Homer], published in 1933. All these terms, along with "motif," are commonly found in subsequent scholarly literature. See also Edwards 1992.

2. Foley 1997:151–59. Matthew Clark, in a recent essay on the oral-poet's craft (2004:136–37), mentions formulas, type-scenes, and "larger narrative components," but not songs.

3. I draw the data on verses from Miller (1982:95). According to Miller the Oxford Classical Text edition of Homer's *Iliad* has 15,693 verses, and the *Odyssey* has 12,110 verses (99).

4. See also Foley (1990:241–46), who mentions middle-range structures in his writings.

5. The present essay does not aspire to identify all techniques used by oral poets to compose large-scale epic songs, only levels similar in nature to, but different in scale from, theme and song-type. For other kinds of structure see Tracy (1997).

6. The points of comparison are extracted from Hansen 1972:8–19; see also Plass (1969), Powell (1970), Fenik (1974:120–26), and Miller (1982:70–79).

7. Lang 1969:162–68. Similar ideas have been proposed independently of Lang; see, for example, Austin (1975:179–238), Krischer (1985), and Rutherford (1985).

8. Although probably most readers think of the land of the Phaeacians (which Homer calls Scheria) as an island, it is uncertain from Homer's *Odyssey* whether it is so or not. For clarity's sake I treat the place as an island and refer to it as Phaeacia.

9. In previous work, I have brought together several examples from Lord and others (Hansen 1972:2–7).

10. Cf. Fenik 1974:133–34. Homeric analysts attempted to account for the similarities in the episodes of Menelaos/Proteus and Odysseus/Teiresias in terms of model and copy (Plass 1969:105 n. 2).

11. Louden acknowledges the tension between the presentational and chronological sequences (1999:138, n. 8).

12. Hansen 1972:34–47; Hansen 1978:20–22. It goes without saying that as in the foregoing instances only parallels are extracted; intervening material is passed over.

13. For the term "intermezzo" see Page 1955:34, also, 32-35 and Hansen 1972:16–17, 41–42.

14. Telemachy 3 is not unique in this respect, but limitations of space permit only one example.

References

Arend, Walter. 1933. *Die typischen Scenen bei Homer.* Problemata, 7. Berlin: Weidmann.

Austin, Norman. 1975. *Archery at the Dark of the Moon: Poetic Problems in Homer's Odyssey.* Berkeley: University of California Press.

Clark, Matthew. 2004. Formulas, Metre and Type-Scenes. In *The Cambridge Companion to Homer,* ed. Robert Fowler, pp. 117–38. Cambridge: Cambridge University Press.

Edwards, Mark W. 1992. Homer and the Oral Tradition: The Type-Scene. *Oral Tradition* 7:284–330.

Fenik, Bernard. 1974. *Studies in the Odyssey.* Hermes Einzelschriften, 30. Wiesbaden.

Foley, John Miles. 1990. *Traditional Oral Epic: The Odyssey, Beowulf, and the Serbo-Croatian Return Song.* Berkeley: University of California Press.

———. 1997. Oral Tradition and its Implications. In *A New Companion to Homer,* eds. Ian Morris and Barry Powell, pp. 146–73. Leiden: Brill.

Heubeck, Alfred, Stephanie West, and J. B. Hainsworth, eds. 1988. *A Commentary on Homer's Odyssey, Vol. 1: Introduction and Books I–VIII.* Oxford: Clarendon Press.

Hansen, William F. 1972. *The Conference Sequence: Patterned Narration and Narrative Inconsistency in the Odyssey.* University of California Publications: Classical Studies, 8. Berkeley: University of California Press.

———. 1978. The Homeric Epics and Oral Poetry. In *Heroic Epic and Saga: An Introduction to the World's Great Folk Epics,* ed. Felix J. Oinas, pp. 7–26. Bloomington: Indiana University Press.

Krischer, Tilman. 1985. Phäaken und *Odyssee. Hermes* 113:9–21.

Lang, Mabel. 1969. Homer and Oral Techniques. *Hesperia* 38:159–68.

Lord, Albert B. 1960. *The Singer of Tales.* Harvard Studies in Comparative Literature, 24. Cambridge: Harvard University Press.

Louden, Bruce. 1993. An Extended Narrative Pattern in the *Odyssey. Greek, Roman, and Byzantine Studies* 34:5–33.

———. 1999. *The Odyssey: Structure, Narration, and Meaning.* Baltimore: The Johns Hopkins University Press.

Lowenstam, Steven. 1993. *The Scepter and the Spear: Studies in Forms of Repetition in the Homeric Poems.* Lanham: Rowman & Littlefield.

Miller, D. Gary. 1982. *Improvisation, Typology, Culture, and the "New Orthodoxy": How "Oral" is Homer?* Washington, D.C.: University Press of America.

Page, Denys. 1955. *The Homeric Odyssey.* Oxford: Clarendon Press.

Parry, Milman. 1971. *The Making of Homeric Verse: The Collected Papers of Milman Parry,* ed. Adam Parry. Oxford: Clarendon Press.

Plass, Paul. 1969. Menelaos and Proteus. *Classical Journal* 65:104–8.

Powell, Barry B. 1970. Narrative Pattern in the Homeric Tale of Menelaus. *Transactions of the American Philological Association* 101:419–31.

Reece, Steve. 1993. *The Stranger's Welcome: Oral Theory and the Aesthetics of the Homeric Hospitality Scene.* Ann Arbor: University of Michigan Press.

Rutherford, R. B. 1985. At Home and Abroad: Aspects of the Structure of the Odyssey. *Proceedings of the Cambridge Philological Society* 31:133–50.

Tracy, Stephen. 1997. The Structures of the *Odyssey.* In *A New Companion to Homer,* eds. Ian Morris and Barry Powell, pp. 360–79. Leiden: Brill.

Packy Jim McGrath, 2007

Packy Jim McGrath, 2009

The Role of Tradition in the Individual: At Work in Donegal with Packy Jim McGrath

Ray Cashman

Traditions do not exist but for the individuals who enact and develop them. This is the conceptual basis of and motivation for performer-centered ethnography, a tradition of folklore scholarship nowhere better exemplified than in the work of Henry Glassie. Indeed, Henry's tremendous body of scholarship inspires and guides me as I begin work on a new project with one storyteller in Ireland, a place Henry knows intimately. The methodological arguments that follow are not one-size-fits-all answers to questions about how to approach one individual working within and shaping a tradition. But focusing on one case study, my exercise in close details should speak, in turns, to the big-picture relationship between the individual and tradition, while demonstrating the necessity for grounding any consideration of tradition in close attention to the individual, and vice versa. "And vice versa" is not an empty phrase here. While most contributions to this volume focus—for good reason—on how certain individuals play central roles in the instantiation and cultivation of particular traditions, I would like to consider the reverse: how traditional resources, texts, or genres play a role in the construction and development of an individual.[1]

Like tradition, the individual is best understood not as a bounded, natural, static entity but as an on-going work-in-progress—enacted, maintained, and revised through performance, recursive and changeable over time. Every individual is a *bricoleur* in Lévi-Strauss's memorable term (1966), the agent who recombines inherited raw materials at hand—in other words tradition-as-resource—to meet present needs or desires. At the same time, every individual is a *bricolage,* the product of ongoing creative recycling—in other words, a product of tradition-as-process.

If we begin with a conception of the individual self as a proposed subjectivity—performed and re-performed through various forms of expression—it follows that there is no self except in relation to others, past precedent, and ambient discourse. In other words, the individual is in a very real sense a discursive construction subject to influence and variation over time depending on context, needs, and available handed-down materials and models for expression—texts and ways of creating texts, both verbal and nonverbal (cf. Sawin 2004:4–9). The individual, then, depends on tradition as much as tradition depends on the individual. With that in mind, I am interested in the role that tradition-as-resource plays in the individual-as-process.

But declaring an interest in exploring how a given person reuses various elements of tradition in the construction of self and society is one thing. Deciding which individual to attend to is yet another. Whom should we pick from the multitude for study? Henry's answer is "the star." Exemplary *bricoleurs,* masters of a given tradition, stars are lauded by their audiences as exceptional bearers of truth. Allied with Dégh (1995), Henry seeks out the exalted curators and bold innovators of tradition, those who have the greatest lasting influence—the likes of Hugh Nolan or Zsuzsanna Palkó. In my field experience, no one better approaches the model of the curator-innovator, master *bricoleur* than my star Patrick James McGrath—Packy Jim—of County Donegal, Ireland. Better appreciating this individual will set tradition in relief as much as tradition will set in relief this individual. Ultimately it does not matter whether one looks first to the role of the individual in tradition, or to the role of tradition in the individual. In the end, the quarry is a better understanding of both the individual and tradition by exploring their interrelationship.

Packy Jim McGrath

Packy Jim lives in the same nineteenth-century house where he was born in 1934, and he puts one in mind of Henry David Thoreau's *Walden* persona: a bachelor proponent of simple living who revels in his solitude but occasionally travels to town for news or to join others for a holiday meal. A self-sufficient, sociable hermit, if you will, Packy Jim says his motto is: "love many, trust few, and always paddle your own canoe."

Living on a secluded one-time smuggling route between the Republic of Ireland and Northern Ireland, Packy Jim grew up hearing news, songs, and stories from the men and women who stopped to pass the time until the cover of darkness allowed the border's unofficial economy to resume. Packy Jim says that in his early years he was all ears during these almost nightly *ceilis* with near and far neighbors, but now is his turn to talk.

Indeed, he is an imaginative, often animated teller of jokes, tall tales, local character anecdotes, and especially historical and supernatural legends, the largest portion of his repertoire. He also has a wonder tale, a couple heroic stories of Finn McCool, and several ballads and lyric folk songs. Add to this resumé his dressing in the dark suits and Wellingtons of a 1940s country farmer, living without electricity or running water, and cooking over an open hearth fueled by turf he cuts and dries himself. One may be forgiven the initial impression that Packy Jim is the salvage ethnographer's dream informant, a holdover from years past, a keeper of relics.

My intention, however, is neither to celebrate Packy Jim as ur-folk, nor to present him as the typical Irish countryman, Conrad Arensberg's archetype in the flesh (1937). He is, like all of us, both typical and unique, or as he says himself, "I suppose I must be a person that, in some fashion or another, I'm very much like the thousands around me, and in other ways I must be very different." As a novice fieldworker when I first met Packy Jim in 1998, I was elated to find his everyday conversation embellished with stories of ghosts and fairies, outlaws and powerful priests—the stuff we folklorists traditionally seek. But my interest in Packy Jim has matured through greater familiarity and friendship to focus less on the stuff, the lore, and more on the uses to which he puts it. That is, I have come to better appreciate that as a storyteller Packy Jim uses narratives from various traditional genres to comprehend and critique his own society, while at the same time seeking to articulate and project a coherent moral self. He is as much an individual working within and instantiating a tradition of Irish narrative we may wish to appreciate in its own right, as he is a *bricoleur* using traditional texts and communicative resources to construct a distinctive integrated self.

Such an observation does not come immediately, nor does it come fully formed, to me anyway. I have had to work up to it, tacking back and forth between my fieldwork records and recent models of folklorists approaching single individuals and their creations. Sawin (2004) and especially Henry's treatment of Haripada Pal (1997) and Prince Twins Seven-Seven (2010) have been particularly helpful as I confront a very basic question: given an exemplary artist or storyteller and an interestingly complex individual, such as Packy Jim, where and how should a folklorist begin? Elsewhere I have argued that one answer is life stories (2008a). But here, with limited space,

I will touch on only the highlights of this argument and its application to Packy Jim in order to leave room for developing further an understanding of the relationship between the individual and tradition.

WHERE TO BEGIN

Dialogic, discursive, recursive, constructed, performed, revised—the individual may be subject to continual negotiation, but this is not to say that there is no such thing as consistency or at least the drive toward a sense of stable individuality. Charlotte Linde observes that in the face of constant negotiation and revision there is typically both a personal and collective desire for coherence in any representation or self-representation of an individual (1993). The individual self as construction then is analogous to Robert Frost's idea of the poem as "a momentary stay against confusion" (2002[1939]:440). Of course we are not all poets, but many of us—perhaps most of us in individualistic Western societies—are inveterate tellers of life stories, personal anecdotes of the self with lasting reportability. Although the life story is not a universal genre or concept,[2] Linde focuses her attention on the life story as one crucial arena in which many individuals typically express a coherent sense of self, negotiating that self in relation to others, both present and not. Likewise, Amy Shuman has demonstrated how life stories are a vehicle for shaping an integrated self out of the fragments and inconsistencies of real thoughts and behaviors. Life stories invent rather than reflect the coherence we seek in our own self-image and in our presentation of self to others (2005:58–59). Sawin, Linde, and Shuman then are engaged to a greater or lesser extent in what Sawin terms "the ethnography of subject formation," something I, too, am interested in pursuing here. But investigation need not nor should not end with life stories. As we will see, the consummate *bricoleur* does not always limit him- or herself to one particular type of available raw material

My proposition is that life stories—first-person, autobiographical stories that express a sense of self—offer us an ideal source for conceptualizing and organizing a study of one person and his or her wider repertoire or body of work. There are, of course, many past precedents by folklorists to consider. Abrahams (1970), Jones (1989), Porter and Gower (1995), and Mould (2004), for example, use autobiographical narratives as one source in their introductions of tradition-bearers, and in the Irish context Séamus Ó Duilearga's *Seán Ó Conaill's Book* (1981) provides the clearest example of an established model in which the study begins with a biographical statement about the tradition-bearer followed by documentation and annotation of that person's repertoire, organized by genre. This established model is based on the reasonable assumption that beginning with biography orients the reader and helps illuminate the texts that follow, whether the texts be ballads, customs, or costumes. Ó Duilearga's book, and others of similar conception, serve as extremely valuable historical records, collections that are indispensable for comparative research. But there is an alternative to this model that subordinates life story to the contextualization of a tradition-bearer's lore, as a means to an end.

Recognition of the dialogic and recursive nature of life stories has led some folklorists, notably Sawin, to reverse the earlier emphasis on how a life illuminates folklore by focusing on how folklore (including personal narratives) illuminates a life. Whether a life is used to illuminate folklore or the reverse, there is room and need for both approaches, but the latter is not yet fully explored and may offer new room for maneuver.

Starting with life stories to privilege an individual's self-construction as an organizing principle in a one-person study is one unambiguous way to pursue the role of tradition-as-resource in the individual-as-process. Characterizing life stories as traditional may seem at first odd, but these stories are folklore subject to the dynamics of tradition as much as Mexican corridos or Georgian ugly jugs. As Sandra Stahl (now Dolby) has observed about personal experience narratives in general (1989), life stories may not be traditional in content (where we view tradition as a limited number of handed-down ideas and texts), but despite idiosyncratic content they are traditional in construction when viewed as examples of a conventional discourse genre and shared resource for social interaction.

The value of attending first to an individual's life stories is that it alerts us to patterns in that individual's typical moves in proposing coherence. The preoccupations and themes that emerge and re-emerge can and perhaps should guide the representation of an individual on that individual's own terms. For the folklorist, study cannot end here, but building on this foundation, the folklorist's review of that individual's entire repertoire can then proceed along those thematic lines, those typical moves, while often identifying others. Life stories suggest a thematic organization for a study that proceeds from a person's self-conception rather one that repeats the older biography-plus-repertoire study, arranged in chapters by genre.

In some respects life story is not just the opening chapter but the whole project. To be clear though, only some of the relevant self-revealing, self-constructing texts will be life stories told in first-person; the fact is, all the stories an individual allows or wants you to record are inevitably involved in that individual's construction of self. From life stories to jokes to myths, these narratives are not just an amalgam we lump together conceptually as repertoire then split apart practicably to satisfy the needs of a book divided into chapters. Regardless of differences in genre and provenance—and even if they come with identifiable tale types and motif numbers—all stories in a person's repertoire may be on some level instrumental in that person's self-conception. Or to put it more loosely, every story one internalizes or generates plays some greater or lesser role in the intertextual bundle that fills the person-shaped hole. On some level all expression is autobiographical.

Packy Jim, Life Story, and Traditional Idiosyncrasy

Let us turn briefly to how these propositions apply to Packy Jim and his repertoire. In over forty hours of recorded sessions since 1998, he has told and re-told several life stories that emerged naturally enough in our conversations. They are the sort of stories typically exchanged during the getting-to-know-you phase of any relationship, and they revolve around, in Linde's words, "'what events have made me what I am' or, more precisely, 'what you must know about me to know me'" (1993:20). Even after we came to know each other fairly well, Packy Jim continued to tell this type of autobiographical story to amplify rhetorical positions or offer glosses on particular threads of conversation.

The first thing to note is that, perhaps surprisingly, there are not that many of them. I identify only ten first-person life stories that he has repeated to me or to others in my presence with some frequency. Of course these are not the only personal experience narratives Packy Jim is capable of generating. On any given day he may narrate an account of being surprised at rising costs in a local shop or of being caught in an unexpected rainstorm. Such anecdotes contribute to conversational give and take, but they may never again require recall. The told and re-told stories I am focusing on here are those that seem to be polished set pieces—what Linda Shopes has termed "iconic stories" (n.d.)—that are part of Packy Jim's core repertoire and sense of self.

The relatively small number of life stories is not necessarily idiosyncratic. In my experience on the Irish border, life stories can be elicited. But they are not as common in everyday interaction because people place a premium on modesty and are cautious about seeming to reflect brightness on themselves (Cashman 2008b:138; see also Glassie 1982:59).

Packy Jim usually limits his life-story-telling to these ten narratives in part because most of them are appropriately modest. In fact, some do not portray him entirely in the best light. Moreover, they are not entirely about him. These life stories often focus on the behavior of others, and they frequently prompt lectures in which Packy Jim does not hesitate to mount passionate, well-considered critiques of local culture and Irish society at large. For example, one of Packy Jim's most frequently-told life stories details his confrontation with a smart aleck in a pub who made fun of him for remaining a bachelor, questioned his sexuality, and treated him as a foolish country rube. The theme of pride and condescension raised, Packy Jim added the following coda to one version of this story:

> I'd be a shy person by nature, and like, that old remarks or drawing attention at people, you can be made shyer, you understand. And if you're foolish you can be made foolisher.
>
> It's like what the man said—about the road down there—that had a son that used to work for this other man, periodically, on the land. And they were discussing the son going to this neighbor's house and back again.
>
> "Well," he says—the father had been about the house, too, and half reared about the house when he was a young lad, eighty years ago or more—"Well," he says, "If you went to that house with little wit, you *left it with a bit less,"* do you understand?
>
> The Irish personality is, if you're a wee bit simple, they'll try and make you worse. Or a bit foolish, they'll try to make you foolisher. They play on what they think would be your weak point. That's the Irish, do you understand. And the Irish, even though you're *not* a fool, in every locality there's somebody, and they're a *scapegoat,* do you understand.
>
> That's, as far as I know, one of the tricks of the Irish. It's not nice, but it's something that's ingrained in our personality.
>
> Every Irishman's not like that, now. But there's a quantity of them that's mostly like that.

As appropriately modest as most of Packy Jim's life stories are, through them he still offers a presentation of self, making a bid for coherence. Through life stories he makes a series of direct and indirect statements about being one sort of a person, not another sort, bothered by some things and not others. Yet he is not proposing too neat an image of a person who is consistently this or that, whether consistently a victim or consistently virtuous. His coherence proceeds not from a fixed essence, but rather from a core dynamic—that is, he presents himself as a person caught between certain extremes, animated by certain irresolvable tensions.

For example, on the one hand Packy Jim presents himself as a maverick who guards his autonomy jealously. He illustrates this with an account of how he would not be ruled over by his cousins after his parents' deaths. Furthermore, he says he would not be too "near-be-going." In other words, he does not feel obligated by principle to follow rules and laws. Smuggling and moonshine are not crimes; they are survival skills. "Wasn't it Saint Augustine himself who said stealing a loaf of bread is no sin when you're a starving man?" To quote one of Packy Jim's aphoristic pronouncements: "No, I tell you, it's a bad thing to be, what you may call, too scrupulous."

On the other hand, some rules are sacrosanct. For example, Packy Jim is absolutely scandalized by the fact of adultery and will have nothing to do with marriage, in part, because of it. Moreover his own early foray into rule-breaking—playing hooky—was nothing short of traumatic, and his accounts of this experiment in truancy are consistently the longest in his repertoire of life stories. As he characterizes his overwrought twelve-year-old sense of guilt and paranoia:

> The crime that I had committed was damnable, do you understand. . . .
> Oh LORD, if I had a done the wildest deed—if had picked up a gun and
> shot ten—that couldn't have been worse in my mind nor that simple little
> deed.

So perhaps Packy Jim is not entirely secure as a scofflaw either, and despite his talk in praise of autonomy and independence, he is also adamant that were his parents still alive he would be more than content to hand them back the reins to his life.

Recapping so far: through life stories, Packy Jim constructs a self, one that is deeply concerned with acting justly but not at all concerned with following rules for the sake of following rules. He represents himself as deeply moralistic, yet also deeply relativistic. He is a maverick, but within certain limits, never crossing certain lines. These are core tensions that animate the self he has represented in narrative, and the tensions rather than consistencies are what make possible another of Packy Jim's aphoristic pronouncements: "I'm my own man, like, but I play by the rules."

Of course these tensions are not the only thematic points that can be gleaned from Packy Jim's life stories. Others include his commitment to simple living and his revulsion to pride, pretension, and any form of uppity presumption. There are other themes to consider as well, but for now a larger methodological point is clearer. Starting with life stories is perhaps the best way to discern an individual's system for constructing a coherent self; it provides a glimpse into worldview. The exercise will certainly highlight inconsistencies and foreshadow tensions—this is the nature of constructed selves and of life story-telling—but the themes that emerge can and perhaps should guide how we approach the rest of the subject's repertoire. In other words, it may be more faithful to your subject's perspective and conceptual world to organize his or her repertoire, not strictly by genre—first a chapter on myths, then legends, then folktales, etc.—but rather by aspects of the self-image that individual has taken great care to present to you.

In Packy Jim's case, we note in life stories a preoccupation with the tension between autonomy and submission, or between independence and rule-following. That tension then becomes a natural theme for a chapter. However, while this chapter must certainly review the relevant life stories, it should also take into account narratives from other genres that speak to this same theme. This will include, for example, both a ballad about a girl who disobeys her father and anecdotes about local smugglers. In fact, the narratives through which Packy Jim offers his most elaborate meditations on the issue of rules are not life stories but rather his legends about the local eigtheenth-century outlaw Proinsias Dubh, doing the right thing by breaking the law.

People do different things through different genres (Cashman 2007, Seitel 1999), but perhaps when approaching one storyteller, all stories revolving around a particular theme or tension need to be explored together, just as they are in conversation. Perhaps we need to rethink what a repertoire is, and we need to do this from the self-possessed perspective of a storyteller rather than from the perspective of a folklorist tasked with sorting narratives into orderly chapters.

Life stories may be a natural starting point for discerning an individual's sense of self, but of course we must also review that individual's entire repertoire. Other aspects of an individual's personality, intellect, and perspective will emerge, and they may be more firmly rooted in and expressed through genres other than life stories.

Packy Jim, for example, thinks deeply about theology, ontology, teleology, and eschatology. His life stories tip us off to this fact, but he does not fully explore these matters through life stories. Here certain narratives concerning wraiths, ghosts, and fairies, come into play. Such stories are widely considered canonical in Irish tradition—Seán Ó Súilleabháin's *Handbook of Irish Folklore* (1942) anticipates all of them—and indeed Packy Jim is a worthy steward of this tradition. But these handed-down stories are also core to Packy Jim's individual project of coming to terms with the nature of things while simultaneously conceiving and projecting a coherent self.

Packy Jim, Myth, and Personalized Tradition

For a case study in the role of tradition in the individual, consider Packy Jim's version of the origin of the fairies—seemingly as traditional a story as Packy Jim's life stories are idiosyncratic. Of the three versions I have recorded, the following from July of 2002 offers a good starting point:

> Well, the story goes that God got lonely.
> And He decided to make himself some company.
> And He created what they call the Angelic Creation: angels.
> And there was nine lots of them, called "nine choirs" of angels.
> And when He made the angels, He made a place to hold them to, a home for them we call Heaven.
> But these angels were placed outside of Heaven on a probationary period.
> There was no two angels exactly the same. From the greatest to the least there were a big, big variation.
> But the greatest and the most intelligent of all the angels was an angel called Lucifer.
> And that was said to be the first sin committed, against God, if you like: the sin of pride, committed by an angel called Lucifer.
> So Lucifer got the idea in his head, to put it the best way I can, that he was as good as God. And a whole lot of angels sided with him, took his side. And there was what they called the Angelic Rebellion.
> And at that point in time, Hell was made. And the bad angels was put into Hell for to suffer there for their sin, and they're known now as the devils.
> Well then there was a considerable amount of angels, a vast amount of angels, that didn't take God's side in the rebellion, nor they didn't take the Devil's side in the rebellion—they were neutral.
> And when the thing was over, then, God made this material creation—the world, and the sun, and the earth, and all the rest of it—and these angels that were neutral were condemned till spend their time on this earth here. And they are known as the Fallen Angels or the fairies—the neutral angels that didn't take God's side in the rebellion, nor didn't take the Devil's side, they took no side.
> And they didn't get into Heaven.

God then took in the angels—the angels that took God's side were headed by an angel called Blessed Michael the Archangel, who was supposed to be the greatest angel in Heaven—and they were taken into Heaven, then, to their places in Heaven—there was a place in Heaven, as we're told, for every angel. And the angels were that many that they were numberless, they were millions of billions, maybe mightn't be the right way to term it.

So then there was a big space then, left, in Heaven, a vacancy left in Heaven, according to what the Catholic Church tells us, and I suppose the Protestant churches, too.

So God got the idea, then, of making another type of a creation, a material creation, and another type of beings, so that, as time would go on, succeeding generation after generation of them would move towards Heaven, when they would have their time spent here, and gradually that Heaven would be filled. And when Heaven would be filled this creation that we know now would cease, and that would be that.

We are supposed to be here for till take the place, if we're good, to say it that way, to fill those places in Heaven, that them bad angels left vacant.

I think that's the story of all Christian religions, as I was taught, I think Master Cunningham taught me that, and my mother who knowed a lot, taught me that about the same time or maybe earlier, but that's the story!

In this version from 2002, Packy Jim covers all the main points, in the same order, as two other versions I recorded in July 2000 and August 2007. In fact, many of the images and phrasings are similarly constructed in the 2000 and 2007 versions, in some cases word for word:

God made Heaven and he made nine batches of angels, and they were termed "nine choirs." (2000)

So God got lonely and desired company, so he made this big tribe of angels, and they were divided into nine lots called 'nine choirs.' (2007)

And there was no two of them the same. There were a difference between them like the stars in the sky. (2000)

And there was no two of them exactly the same. (2007)

He was so great, he was so powerful, that he took it in till his head that he was as good as God. (2000)

But the Devil seemingly thought he was as good as God. (2007)

And then this universe was made, and human beings were made—Adam and Eve to start off with. The human race were made, and then they were to [. . .] increase and multiply, and then when your station on this earth was over, you went into Heaven. And that was to go on, and on, and on, and on, and on, and on until Heaven was again full, that there was every place in Heaven occupied. And then, at that point then, everything finished then. This place come till an end. That's the story. (2000)

> The human race is supposed to last until such a time that all them seats left vacant in heaven is filled. And when heaven is filled completely, the human race is going to be finished off. It's going to be, I'd say, it ends. That's the story. That's the story: it ends then, when heaven's filled. (2007)

In addition to the consistency between Packy Jim's versions of the origin story, there is consistency between his versions and others recorded in Ireland. The idea of fairies as fallen angels—motifs F251.6 and V236.1 in Stith Thompson's and Tom Peete Cross's motif indexes—is widespread not only in Ireland and areas of Irish emigration, but also farther afield in other Celtic and Scandinavian regions.[3] The idea became popular in Ireland during the Middle Ages[4] for resolving tensions between pre-Christian and Christian cosmologies. Casting the fairies as fallen angels preserved some elements of native tradition by reading between the lines of Christian scripture (Isaiah 14:12 and Revelation 12:7–9) and giving the fairies a place in Christian cosmology and eschatology. Moreover, the resulting syncretism offers an opportunity, depending on the telling, to explore the nature of humanity through contrast with an antecedent but co-existing other. The only major element in other recorded versions missing from Packy Jim's is an explanation of fairy abductions of and intermarriage with humans. In many recorded sources, the fairies hope to increase the amount of human blood in their veins in order to secure some chance at salvation on Judgement Day.[5] While this is missing from Packy Jim's origin story, he nonetheless recognizes the fairies' occasional harassment of humans as jealousy that we still enjoy the possibility of redemption.

Whereas recorded versions have this or that element—Ó hEochaigh's version emphasizes the War in Heaven, Ó Duilearga's version highlights the fairies's hope for salvation, Lady Wilde emphasizes their residual powers and envy of humans—Packy Jim's version is a masterful synthesis of the many images, ideas, and motifs handed down to him. As a *bricoleur* of inherited narratives and fragments Packy Jim does more than account for the existence and nature of the fairies; he marshals traditional materials to define the human individual's ontology and teleology, articulate a charter for moral behavior, and explain the origins, workings, and eventual end of the world. Few stories could offer better material for an examination of collective belief, morality, and worldview.

Still, Packy Jim, an individual working within an established oral tradition, makes it his own in many ways. All three versions display the hallmarks of Bauman's conception of performance as an acceptance of responsibility to an audience for a display of communicative competence. In each, Packy Jim draws attention to his breakthrough into performance (Hymes 1975), signaling in effect "I'm on" (Bauman 2004:9), through various keying devices identified by Bauman (1977): *figurative language* (e.g., "There were a difference between them like the stars in the sky" [2000] and "But the devil seemingly thought he was as good as God [. . .] that's the stool that he fell over" 2007]); *parallelism,* (e.g., the ninth and tenth sentences of the 2002 version ending with emphasis on "an angel called Lucifer" and "to go on, and on, and on, and on, and on, and on" [2007]); *appeals to tradition* (e.g., "I think even a Protestant theologian—any Christian theologian—will tell ye the same thing as I'm telling you. But my mother Maggie Gallagher was the first that I heared at that, and I think Master Cunningham was the next that I heared at that, too. Oh, that's going till the root of the faith" [2000] and "Well, that's the story at the root of all Christians: Protestants, Orthodox, Roman Catholics, the whole damned lot, probably the Jews. [2007]); *paralinguistic features* (these are quite numerous, including several mimetic hand gestures, and regular rhythms established through speed, volume, pitch, and tone, then broken for dramatic emphasis).

As Packy Jim assumes responsibility through performance for tradition—in terms of both content and communicative convention—he also reveals much about his personal storytelling style and his individual subjectivity. Packy Jim's use of figurative language in the origin story, for example, reflects his broader preference for expression through analogies, similes, and metaphors that cast even spectacular events in ordinary, familiar terms. Note how he refers to the Devil committing the original sin of pride— setting in motion our very creation—as tripping over a stool. Likewise, Packy Jim depicts the gaping absence left in Heaven after the rebellion in everyday terms: "Then there was a big, big vacancy. It would be like maybe nine or ten people in the chapel and the rest of the chapel empty" (2007).

His matter-of-fact delivery and everyday imagery often serve as understatements for effect, but they also underscore a certain way of thinking about language, reality, and the problem of representation.

In all three versions of his origin story—and throughout his repertoire as I have recorded it—Packy Jim continually punctuates his descriptive prose with habitual phrases such as "to say it that way," "I'll put it that way," and "to put it the best way I can." These phrases tend to presage or mark a moment that advances plot as he makes a bid to represent something in a certain way: "as if." In part, these phrases put the communicative act on display as is common in performance. More to the point, such interjections are fundamentally metacommunicative. They acknowledge and illustrate that storytelling is going on here, that this is a process of representing a reality through the indispensable but ultimately limited faculty of language. Especially when discussing ultimate realities and nonmaterial beings that are completely other, Packy Jim is keen to indicate his awareness that language at best affords us analogies and metaphors rather than a transparent, one-to-one replication of actuality.

> Well, you have to chat about it this way, you know. You don't think about spirits in the way like you think about humans—chatting about an angel "thinking" or a devil "thinking"—but that's the way you must express it. We don't know whether angels or devils or things like that can think, but we must put it that way anyway. (2007)

> This is the curiosity about religion, what religion has to say. I suppose we need not liken angels to humans, but we must, as the saying goes, for to put the point over, I must say it this way: he took it in till his head that he was as good as God, do ye understand? (2000)

> So then, God took it in till his head—I'm putting it the rude way again—that it would be too bad for to have your place... the place not half full. "I'll go about it again and I'll make another creation, but it'll be a different creation." (2000)

Laying bare the mechanics of storytelling, highlighting the limitations of language, Packy Jim keys performance while making a bid to express his intellect, dispositions, and personality. Likewise, he regularly tacks back and forth between taking responsibility for the traditional materials at hand, and making more direct pronouncements about himself and the world around him. Just as his life story about confronting the smart aleck in the pub led to a short lecture on scape-goating, Packy Jim's story of the fairies' origin stirs him to comment on the state of the world today and how it relates to the sacred framework established in the beginning:

> But then, I suppose, if you're prepared to believe what we're taught, like the human race, I'm afraid that there's more of them going to Hell nor's going to Heaven at the present time. Barring that there's something in it that I don't understand, Satan's still getting his quota. (2000)

Ours is a fallen world—he uses the Biblical allusion "a valley of tears" in his 2000 version—and widespread wickedness delays Heaven's completion and the end times. Springboard for social commentary and moral proclamation, index of his predispositions or orientations to the world, Packy Jim's versions of this story do much more than explain the origin of the fairies or offer us another instantiation of tradition that can be dated, located, and archived. He has mastered the narrative—having arranged the handed down parts, having thought deeply about its implications—to articulate a coherent eschatology and a comprehensive cosmology that nonetheless leaves room for mystery. As Packy Jim declares in a coda to his 2002 version:

> All we know about it is that there's some kind of another side, some way or another, that you go till and nobody, as they say, has come back to tell it. But it's there, and I suppose you had better be a good boy as a bad boy, you'd fare better and have less to worry about. But I suppose if you're made to be a bad boy—that's the mystery of life—if you're made to be a bad boy, a bad boy you must be. That's the whole of that. It has to be that. Aye, I think so.

But neither the discussion nor the recording ended there. With his body tense and agitated, his brow knitted, Packy Jim became louder and quickened his pace:

> And there's another thing about it that the bad people, whatever's about it—some instinct sometimes can tell them when there's a good body, as the saying goes, in their presence. And many a reasonably good body or near perfect body—there's none of us a hundred percent, I'll say it that way—but many a time you've got insulted and belittled simply because I think the Devil's at the back of it propping them up to try to shame you, to try to and hurt you. Simply because the Devil in some shape or fashion lets them know: there's a person that has lived a good life, no mortal sin never in their life. "I'll hurt 'em, I'll belittle 'em, I'll take 'em down!" That's the Devil's way, it's said, when he has had contact with people, is to try to take you down. Aye. To belittle you, hurt you on your, on your good and religious points. Like your man. . . .

He began to segue into what I feel sure would have been another telling of his confrontation with the smart aleck in the pub, or a similar story, but much to my regret, I interrupted with another question about fairies, thinking I suppose that he was veering off-track. Obligingly Packy Jim answered my stuff-oriented, salvage ethnographer's query, then the conversation shifted elsewhere. It is only in retrospect that I understand that he was not off track at all.

This origin story is not just about cosmology and eschatology, belief and theology. Nor is it merely a handy reflection of Packy Jim's personality as an individual or his style as a storyteller. At least in this instance, he was trying to talk about himself: a reasonably good body confronting no less a figure than the Devil, the Angel of Pride, propping up some uppity pub-lounger to belittle him, to make him out the fool and scapegoat once more. The life story is not the only genre through which we hope to invent the coherence we seek in our own self-image and in our presentation of self to others. No less weighty a genre than collective, sacred myth can play a central role as "stories make contexts for each other" (Glassie 2006:255), making meaning through relation.

Stepping back to view a larger picture, we see that Packy Jim's versions of the origin of the fairies offer a clear example of the individual actively engaged in tradition as process, taking responsibility for and molding tradition to present needs. We also observe an equally clear example of tradition as resource playing a central role in the construction and articulation of self. Packy Jim as *bricoleur* masters this story because he needs this story. The slings and arrows of this world—from fairy mischief to hateful neighbors—have a primal sacred origin. Tradition provides Packy Jim both an explanation for evil in the world and a charter for his own moral behavior, helping him comprehend injustice and have faith that in the end the deserving will triumph.

Like the early Christian scribes who found a place for the fairies in the master narrative of scripture, Packy Jim finds through this story a place for himself in this life and, he hopes, the next. Though not a first-person story of experienced events, this collective origin myth is no less personal, immediate, or useful. Inserting himself imaginatively into this story-world of the Angel Rebellion and its aftermath, Packy Jim is in no way neutral. Here there is no tension or suspension between binaries of letter-of-the-law rule-following and spirit-of-the-law morality to dramatize. Here is something to latch on to, something of which to be sure. As it was in the beginning, some will not be allowed into the Kingdom, but unlike the fairies or the Devil's cohort, Packy Jim has reason to hope for salvation. Or as he demures, "I guess that's all we can ask right now is a sporting chance."

Conclusion

Engaged in our own tradition of performer-centered ethnography, attending to how individual stories are used by individual storytellers, we cannot but find fewer meaningful differences between such apparently divergent genres as collective myth and individual life story. Both genres and certainly others play crucial roles in the construction of self and society. In a performer-oriented ethnography of subject formation, what matters is how the stories are told, to what ends, and what "meanings open between stories and proliferate when stories are performed together" (Glassie 2006:255). We would do well to be quiet and listen.

To be clear, though, in pursuing something like the ethnography of subject-formation—or the role of tradition in the individual—I am not interested only in writing better biography, no matter how interesting the individual (to be fair, neither is Sawin). Better biography may be a happy by-product, but the ultimate goal is a better appreciation of the concept of the individual as it sets tradition in relief and the concept of tradition as it sets the individual in relief. Along the way other key concepts arise and beg further consideration—repertoire, worldview, identity, the star, among them. But let it not be said that privileging one individual as a focus for study is too small a scale, the details too microcosmic, the stakes too low. The individual and tradition: in a very real sense, one does not exist without the other. Moreover, as things-to-believe-in both are in one sense completely inaccessible. We cannot witness, characterize, or perhaps even approach such things as the individual or tradition (or poetry, or love, or God) except through their instantiations, and we cannot appreciate either the individual or tradition without fully grasping their interdependence.

Notes

In addition to the people named throughout, not least Henry Glassie, I owe a debt to several others for helping to shape my thinking here. The most important help is always that which comes at the beginning when the wheels spin but traction is limited. Lorraine Walsh Cashman pushed me out of several initial ruts, and was particularly helpful in thinking through the nature of the individual as performance and process. In addition, several of my Ohio State colleagues—Barbara Lloyd, Pat Mullen, Dorry Noyes, Kate Parker, Cassie Patterson, Amy Shuman, and Sabra Webber—have offered me generous and very productive advice on a previous draft. Co-editors, Tom and Pravina, have helped me better clarify with each step of revision. All shortcomings and failures to heed good advice are my own.

1. I am not the first to explore this issue. Most notably and recently, Michael Owen Jones conducted fieldwork with a particular individual, Gary Robertson, to explore how an individual may choose from among traditional resources to actively shape his or her "virtual identity," a person's perceived or aspired-to identity (2000). Jones's work rightly emphasizes that individuals need not passively follow tradition; rather individuals have the agency to choose from among traditions and handed down raw materials—alternative behaviors, activities, and objects—in order to construct an identity. My one slight reservation is that Jones's model of the individual as an agent picking that which he or she fancies from an international array of choices is conspicuously consumerist, seems less than universal, and may be most relevant to contemporary life under global capitalism. My work on the power of genre to shape ideology (2007) together with Bourdieu's notion of *habitus* (1977:72–94)—which consists of durable, transposable dispositions acquired in response to objective conditions, and contributing to social reproduction—may help to complicate and extend Jones's model. *Habitus* and genre suggest extrapersonal, pre-reflexive elements of culture that may circumscribe pure agency and shape something like consumerist desire, following Jones, in the arena of identity construction.

2. H. David Brumble, for example, discusses how traditional Native American conceptions of the self did not give rise to personal narratives of the kind expected by European American editors seeking to publish as-told-to Indian autobiographies in the twentieth century. According to Brumble, the resulting life stories must be read as bi-cultural documents (1988:11).

3. For illustrating texts and discussion of the fairies as fallen angels in Ireland see Christiansen (1971-1973:96–97), Lysaght (1996:44), Ó Duilearga (1981:253), Ó hEochaidh (1977:35), William Wilde (1972[1852]:125), Lady Wilde (1888:37–38), and Wood-Martin (1902:5–6). Rieti (1991:21–24) notes the belief in Newfoundland, a place of significant Irish immigration, while Evans-Wentz notes the belief in Celtic regions beyond Ireland, particularly Scotland and Wales (1990 [1911]:85, 105, 130, 154, 205, 241). Christiansen (1971–73) discusses variations on the idea of the fairies as fallen angels farther a field in Europe, especially in Scandinavia.

4. Ó hOgáin cites fifteenth-century manuscript evidence for the connection between fairies and fallen angels (2006:208), and William Wilde specifies the ninth-century *Book of Armagh* and the fifteenth-century *Book of Lismore* (1972 [1852]:125).

5. For examples, see Ó hEochaidh (1977:35) and Ó Súilleabháin (1967:83).

REFERENCES

Abrahams, Roger, ed. 1970. *Almeda Riddle: A Singer and Her Songs.* Baton Rouge: Louisiana State University Press.

Arensberg, Conrad. 1937. *The Irish Countryman: An Anthropological Study.* New York: Macmillan.

Bauman, Richard. 1977. *Verbal Art as Performance.* Long Grove: Waveland Press.

———. 2004. *A World of Others' Words: Cross-Cultural Perspectives on Intertextuality.* Malden: Blackwell Publishing.

Bourdieu, Pierre. 1977. *Outline of a Theory of Practice.* New York: Cambridge University Press.

Brumble, H. David. 1988. *American Indian Autobiography.* Berkeley: University of California Press.

Cashman, Ray. 2007. Genre and Ideology in Northern Ireland. *Midwestern Folklore* 33(1):13–28.

———. 2008a. Life Story, Coherence, and the Moral Self, unpublished paper presented at the American Folklore Society, Louisville, Kentucky.

———. 2008b. *Storytelling on the Northern Irish Border: Characters and Community.* Bloomington: Indiana University Press.

Christiansen, Reidar Th. 1971–73. Some Notes on the Fairies and the Fairy Faith. *Béaloideas* 39–41:95–111.

Cross, Tom Peete. 1952. *Motif-Index of Early Irish Literature.* Bloomington: Indiana University Press.

Dégh, Linda. 1995. *Narratives in Society: A Performer-Centered Study of Narration.* Bloomington: Indiana University Press.

Evans-Wentz, W. Y. 1990 [1911]. *The Fairy Faith in Celtic Countries.* New York: Citadel Press.

Frost, Robert. 2002 [1939]. *The Robert Frost Reader: Poetry and Prose,* ed. Edward Coneery Lathem and Lawrance Roger Thompson. New York: Henry Holt.

Glassie, Henry. 1982. *Passing the Time in Ballymenone: Culture and History of an Ulster Community.* Philadelphia: University of Pennsylvania Press.

———. 1997. *Art and Life in Bangladesh.* Bloomington: Indiana University Press.

———. 2006. *The Stars of Ballymenone.* Bloomington: Indiana University Press.

———. 2010. *Prince Twins Seven-Seven: His Art, His Life in Nigeria, His Exile in America.* Bloomington: Indiana University Press.

Hymes, Dell. 1975. Breakthrough into Performance. In *Folklore: Performance and Communication,* ed. Dan Ben-Amos and Kenneth S. Goldstein. The Hague: Mouton.

Jones, Michael Owen. 1989. *Craftsman of the Cumberlands: Tradition and Creativity.* Lexington: University Press of Kentucky.

———. 2000. "Tradition" in Identity Discourses and an Individual's Symbolic Construction of Self. *Western Folklore* 59(2):115–141.

Lévi-Strauss, Claude. 1966. *The Savage Mind.* Chicago: University of Chicago Press.

Linde, Charlotte. 1993. *Life Stories: The Creation of Coherence.* New York: Oxford University Press.

Lysaght, Patricia. 1996. *The Banshee: The Irish Supernatural Death Messenger.* Dublin: The O'Brien Press.

Mould, Tom. 2004. *Choctaw Tales.* Jackson: University Press of Mississippi.

Ó Duilearga, Séamus, ed. and trans. 1981. *Seán Ó Conaill's Book: Stories and Traditions from Iveragh*. Dublin: Comhairle Bhéaloideas Éireann.

Ó hEochaidh, Seán, Máire MacNeill, and Séamus Ó Catháin. 1977. *Síscéalta ó Thír Chonaill / Fairy Legends from Donegal*. Dublin: Comhairle Bhéaloideas Éireann.

Ó hOgáin, Dáithí. 2006. *The Lore of Ireland: An Encyclopedia of Myth, Legend, and Romance*. Woodbridge: The Boydell Press.

Ó Suilleabháin, Seán. 1942. *A Handbook of Irish Folklore*. Dublin: Educational Company of Ireland Ltd.

———. 1967. *Irish Folk Customs and Belief*. Dublin: The Three Candles, Ltd.

Porter, James and Herschel Gower. 1995. *Jeannie Robertson: Emergent Singer, Transformative Voice*. Knoxville: University of Tennessee Press.

Rieti, Barbara. 1991. *Strange Terrain: The Fairy World in Newfoundland*. St. John's, Newfoundland: ISER Books.

Sawin, Patricia. 2004. *Listening for a Life: A Dialogic Ethnography of Bessie Eldreth through Her Songs and Stories*. Logan: Utah State University Press.

Seitel, Peter. 1999. *The Powers of Genre: Interpreting Haya Oral Literature*. New York: Oxford University Press.

Shopes, Linda. n.d. What is Oral History? At http://historymatters.gmu.edu/mse/oral/oral.pdf.

Shuman, Amy. 2005. *Other People's Stories: Entitlement Claims and the Critique of Empathy*. Chicago: University of Illinois Press.

Stahl (Dolby), Sandra. 1989. *Literary Folkloristics and the Personal Narrative*. Bloomington: Indiana University Press.

Thompson, Stith. 1955–58. *Motif-Index of Folk-Literature: A Classification of Narrative Elements in Folktales, Ballads, Myths, Fables, Medieval Romances, Exempla, Fabliaux, Jest-Books and Local Legends*. 6 vols. Bloomington: Indiana University Press.

Wilde, William. 1972 [1852]. *Irish Popular Superstitions*. Shannon: Irish University Press.

Wilde, Lady Jane. 1888. *Ancient Legends, Mystic Charms, and Superstitions of Ireland*. London: Ward and Downey.

Wood-Martin, W. G. 1902. *Traces of the Elder Faiths of Ireland: A Folklore Sketch*. Vol. 2. London: Longmans, Green, and Co.

Customizing Myth: The Personal in the Public

John Holmes McDowell

> The psychology of artistic production and consumption involves identification processes at every turn.
>
> —Kenneth Burke (1973:227)

On the surface of the matter, it would seem that mythic discourse is a quintessential form of what Basil Bernstein terms "public language," that is, "a language which continuously signals the normative arrangements of the group rather than individuates experiences of its members" (1960:181). This assumption is amply reinforced by the important community work attributed to myth in the many definitions and roles devised for it by scholars over the centuries. Any folklorist could assemble a list of impressive public or communal duties assigned to myth in the last century or two, a list that might include (among other entries) Max Müller's ideas about "mythopoeic thought," G. L. Gomme's tidy characterization of myth as "the science of a pre-scientific age," Bronislaw Malinowski's thesis that myth establishes a charter for social institutions, and Claude Lévi-Strauss's notion that "myths operate in men's minds without their being aware of the fact" (1969:12). Whatever formulation is chosen, we find ourselves in a discourse that would seem to largely exclude the personal in favor of the impersonal, the communal, and the collective. Practical facts conducive to personalization of the narrative, such as the age of the storyteller, the composition of the audience, the occasion for the storytelling event, are a matter of indifference in these frames of reference.

This trope of impersonality clashes with what we know from innumerable ethnographies of speaking, that circumstantial factors condition every performance of traditional material. We have on our hands a collision between conflicting paradigms, one that argues for the impermeable character

323

of mythic discourse—as a public language, charged with weighty social functions, it cannot succumb to the merely fortuitous—the other arguing for the impact of situation on all performances, including those that feature mythic narrative. How are we to resolve this impasse? We can take note, at the outset, that the first of these paradigms operates at a level of considerable abstraction whereas the second paradigm is lodged in specific community events and actions. This distinction between angles of vision helps account for difference in conception, but it does not resolve questions about the fundamental character of myth. We are still obliged to ask, is myth, after all, a public language impervious to the incidental and the personal, or is it a permeable discourse open to personal influences?

To be sure, ethnographers of mythic narrative discourse as it occurs in its human settings have anticipated the response I will propose to this question. A classic case is the argument Dell Hymes made about the poignancy of the shining, destructive object in "The Sun's Myth," that this tale, for Charles Cultee, might well have been about "assimilating the disaster to his people through the genre of myth" (1975:360). Later, Ellen Basso (1990:8) formulated the consensus that mythic narratives derive from and exemplify "interactive, transactive processes" with a "metanarrational" character in that they are "formed from interpersonal processes that emerge from oral performance: shared imaginative intimacy or dialogicality."

What I propose to do here is extend this line of thought by isolating a set of individualizing maneuvers carried out by storytellers I came to know well as I experienced and documented the mythic narrative traditions of Andean peoples in Colombia and Ecuador. It has been my privilege to witness among the native peoples of Colombia's Sibundoy Valley, and among Quichua Runa in the vicinity of Otavalo, Ecuador, the workings of a living New World mythology. In the course of recording these mythologies, I found ample confirmation of the public-discourse paradigm, when my indigenous friends pointed to the myth plots as fundamental to understanding their collective identity. In the Sibundoy Valley, the myths stand as an account of the arrival of civilization; stories told in its two indigenous communities, the Kamsá and Inga, about the first people are foundational to the local ethos. In the Otavalo vicinity, mythic narratives about mountain and lake deities locate the Quichua in their corner of the cosmos. In both settings, mythic narratives rehearse a model of the civilizing process that sustains contemporary social relations and defines contemporary relationships with the spirit world. These are hardly tales to trifle with, given their association with the well-springs of these Andean communities. Those who perform such stories engage in a particular species of cultural transmission, that of conveying eternal verities from one moment, and one person, to another. Normally, they are elders or established members of the community, and by invoking the deeds of the ancestors, they cloak their own words in the trappings of authority.

Given this tendency in mythic narrative towards fixed and stable narrative armatures, the trick for our present purposes is to identify the spaces within this public discourse that are open to the incidental, the accidental, the personal. I explore here, in a preliminary fashion, the scope for customizing, for personalized shaping, of the shared mythic material. I view the mythic discourse of Andean communities in Colombia and Ecuador as a trove of communal narrative that is filtered through the minds and repertoires of individuals and that is, to a surprising degree—but of course, subject to limits—adapted to the orientations and concerns of the people who work these resources into actual narrative performances. In order to accomplish my purpose, I must introduce a handful of friends and associates who have regaled me over the years with their tales of mythic ancestors and other spirits: Mariano Chicunque (now deceased), María Juajibioy, and Francisco Tandioy of Colombia's Sibundoy Valley, and Luis Alberto Yamberla and Maruja Picuasi of Imbabura province in Ecuador.

Inspection of key mythic narratives I recorded from each of these individuals demonstrates that the mythology of a community, though remarkably persistent in its plot structures, is in many ways a very personal affair. I can detect in these tales a variety of methods for personalizing the public discourse of myth, each based on a process of identification linking the storyteller to a specific story protagonist. I want to distinguish kinds and levels of identification at work in this customizing process. One is *vicarious*, wherein the storyteller identifies with but remains distinct from the tale protagonist. These stories are set in third-person discourse and they preserve the distance between narrative frame and narrated event. Here I will draw on three Sibundoy examples: Mariano Chicunque and María Juajibioy tell stories that feature the wisdom and prowess of story protagonists who share their (the narrators') social positions; Francisco Tandioy also identifies with a story protagonist, and in his *"Shulupsimanda Parlo"* ("Story of the *Shulupsi* Bird"), this vicarious identification impels him to foreground the plight of the young man whose mother interferes with his courtship plans.

Myths are customized, I will argue, through a second type of identification, what I will call *virtual* identification, when the attraction between storyteller and story protagonist becomes so strong that the storytellers insert themselves into narratives imbued with a mythic consciousness. These tales

Mariano Chicunque, Kamsá storyteller, and Justo Jacanamijoy

Maria Juajibioy with her mother, Concepción

abandon the distancing of third-person discourse to settle in the immediacy of first-person narrative. If they necessarily separate themselves from ancestral times, they acquire in compensation the thrill of lived experience. To illustrate virtual identification I will sample gripping memorates performed for my benefit by two Quichua Runa friends from the area around Otavalo in the north of Ecuador. Maruja Picuasi and Luis Alberto Yamberla place themselves at the center of dramatic narratives evoking mythical scenarios. I should note that my choices of illustration here should not be read as stipulating tendencies inherent in Sibundoy as opposed to Quichua Runa mythologies. Both kinds of identification occur equally in both places.

Indeed, a subsidiary feature of my argument here is to assemble the genres of mythic narrative and myth-inspired tales of spiritual encounter into a larger category of narrative marked by mythic consciousness, which I define as an ability or tendency to perceive and articulate a spiritual substratum to everyday experience, often guided by a set of traditional mythic plots but fluid and adaptable to the vagaries of the mundane. Granted, mythic narrative and memorate can be juxtaposed to one another on formal and functional grounds, but my work in these Andean communities has convinced me that these narrative genres tap into a common fund of imaginative potential. For the Kamsá mythic narratives to be examined in what follows, what is of interest is the way personal orientations figure in the choices made by storytellers as to what they will narrate and how they will position specific actors in the stories. With regard to the Runa memorates, the intrusion of the personal is to be expected; what is of interest there is the way accounts of personal experiences are shaped by the communal contours of Runa mythic narrative. The clearest marker of this continuity in Runa mythic consciousness is the presence of Taita Imbabura, the spirit of the volcano, in both myth and memorate—in the former, he is a prime actor in Runa cosmogony, while in the latter, he is the principal source of spiritual strength when people are afflicted with spirit sickness through encounters with malevolent supernatural agents.

In every case the narrated events remain faithful to communal prototypes, yet the storyteller manages to cast the story in such a way as to highlight a personal connection, either indirectly, through vicarious identification, or more directly, through virtual identification. Clearly, these processes of identification animate these performances and give them much of their power, both for the storytellers and their audiences. I'd go so far as to say that this vested performance confers the spice and piquancy that is too often missing in scholarly treatments of myth's public persona.

Vicarious Identification among the Sibundoy

As I came into contact with Sibundoy narratives and narrators, I noticed a tendency for people to tell stories featuring a protagonist with whom they shared at least one important characteristic, especially age-rank or gender. A good illustration of this principle is the storytelling of Mariano Chicunque, the most prolific of my Kamsá consultants. Over a period of three months in 1978, I recorded quite a few mythic narratives from this amiable and knowledgeable elder. Typically, his stories featured the exploits of knowledgeable old men, whose application of wisdom to complicated situations generally moved things to a successful conclusion. It dawned on me that Mariano was, to a degree, telling stories about himself, or at least, about people in his social category—older men with a thorough mastery of local tradition. In one of these tales, *"Shatxetemunga,"* "The Red Dwarfs," an elder is brought in to figure out how to rid the population of small, reddish creatures who were harming the people around them with something like "electricity." The elder knows to use a certain wood for purposes of smoking the red dwarfs out of their caves. In the story's aftermath, Mariano reflects back on its meaning, and he exclaims, in Kamsá, *achka kulta bngabe tangwanga!* "So wise were our elders!," a salute he might well be making to himself.

Let's follow this process of identification into another realm of Kamsá mythic narrative. I argue elsewhere that the theme of paradise forestalled is perhaps the central thread of Sibundoy mythic narratives (McDowell 2007). A cluster of tales much savored by Kamsá and Inga audiences features an animal suitor, either male or female, seeking access to a human family. These suitors appear to be human in some ways but they maintain aspects of their animal identities—the owl-man, for example, pecks about for snails and is always scratching his hair. The suitor typically secures the loyalty of an intended spouse and enjoys a period of trial marriage, but in the end cautious members of the intended spouse's family take note of peculiarities and send the suitor away. The cosmological significance of these episodes becomes clear when we learn that the animal suitor possessed fabulous powers that might have mitigated the hardship of human life—the *shulupsi* bird-woman, for example, could brew a whole barrel of maize beer from just three kernels, while the owl-man could clear a thicket and plant and harvest crops just through a series of shouts. The elders lament these losses but I would surmise, taking in the whole sweep of these animal-suitor tales, that such gifts had to be rejected in order to secure a safe zone where human civilization could flourish without the destabilizing effects of rampant spiritual potency.

Now let's consider how two storytellers find ways to personalize tellings within this mythic narrative cluster. María Juajibioy was my hostess and surrogate mother—she called me her *wakiña mayor,* oldest child, during the year that I lived with her, her husband Justo Jacanamijoy, and their four boys still at home at that time, Juan, Angel, Lucho, and Gabe. The daughter of a distinguished community leader, Bautista Juajibioy, who had been *gobernador* of the Kamsá community six times, María was in many ways an exemplary Kamsá woman and mother. She was a skilled weaver, an excellent cook, and she possessed a good hand for planting corn. In short, she had all the female virtues and none of the vices—when people invited her to drink maize beer during the many festivities at her home, she would demur, saying, "Who will look after the children?"

Among her many talents, María was in those days a fine performer of mythic narratives. The story I focus on here, *"Tobiaxbe Parlo,"* "The Young Woman's Tale," belongs to the cluster of stories focused on animal suitors. This tale was told in Kamsá: I present here my transcription of the Kamsá and my translation of that text into English.

I

Kanye tobiaxe inashjango bobonsbiamaka.
A young woman arrived at the home of a young man.

I ch wamben mama jaboknán ibojauyan.
And that intended mother-in-law said to her:

"Xkatjesaboye jenaxaka."
"Come plant *barbacuano* seed."

I ch bebinkwa jabokná ibnetsjwañe:
And that intended daughter-in-law answered her:

"Xwatsetsejaja jomuxenaka."
"I myself will become *barbacuano.*"

Asna: "Bibiaxá xmetsabojeka."
Then: "Plant some *achira* for me."

Inye chká jatjwañana: "Xwatsetsejaja bibiná."
Again she responded like that: "I myself will become *achira.*"

I nye ndoñese juwenan ntxam tbojtserwanka?
And she just wouldn't listen, how could she beg her?

II

Chorna ch wamben mama jabokná inetsoñe jawashuntsam.
Then that intended mother-in-law went out to plant corn.

Inetsashuntsañokna santopeso ibninyenaka.
Where she was planting corn she found a centipede.

I as cha chuwashuntsantxeka ibnetsutsjanganja.
And then as she was planting corn, she struck it with her digging stick.

Nye natjumbañe inetsashuntsañe.
She just calmly continued planting corn.

Yojabuchoká orna yojtá tsoy.
When she finished she returned to the house.

Chorna ibninyen ch bebinkwa jabokná impasajem.
Then she found that intended daughter-in-law in bad shape.

Intsatotebemañe betxaxena txa lisianajem,
She was sitting there with her head all banged up,

umochkwanajem ibojinyem.
she found her with her head covered.

III

Chorna ch wamben mama jabokná ibojatjay:
Then that intended mother-in-law inquired:

"Ndayek sobrená chká biyatsmanaka?"
"Why, Niece, are you like this?"

Chorna ibojojwá: "Ndoñe kach batá chká xkondwabonaka?"
Then she answered: "Didn't you, Aunt, do this to me?"

Chorna ibojauyán: "Ndayentxe chká tkunbjamaka?"
Then she said to her: "Where did this happen to you?"

Chorna ibnojwá: "Ndoñe ch jajoka jenantxeka xkonjutsjanjanaka?"
Then she responded: "In the garden, didn't you strike me with the digging stick?"

Chorna ibnojwá: "Jenantxeka ndayá santo pesontxe chká tijutsjanganja.
Then she responded: "I struck a large centipede like that with my digging stick.

As ak ndoñe krischian nkondimunaka," ibnauyanaka.
Then you are not a human being," she said to her.

IV

Nye nyetxá sindutatxumbo.
That's all there is just as I know it.

This tale conforms to the paradise forestalled paradigm—the centipede-woman had the power to create food from her own body, but she had to be rejected from the human family to avoid the complications of unchecked spiritual potency. What I wish to highlight here are the continuities between the heroine in the story, the older woman who unmasks the animal suitor, and the performer of this tale, María Juajibioy. Both are mature women who know how to provide food for their families. Both are handy with the digging stick, the instrument used by women for opening the earth to insert seeds. María, in almost all ways a modest person, would brag to me that she had a good hand for planting. In the Sibundoy Valley, women are the planters of seed, and they have their hands cured by the native doctors to insure a good hand for planting. This curing entails hosting a ceremony featuring the ingestion of *ayahuasca,* the medicine vine (McDowell 1998). The result of such curing is a hand that is spiritually protected, which means that the seeds it handles will not be bothered by birds and insects and will instead grow to yield a substantial crop.

María's *"Tobiaxbe Parlo"* is a story of cultural preservation wherein an exemplary protagonist plays a key role in deterring the intended transgression of an animal suitor. María, an exemplary Kamsá woman in her own right, performs a tale of a mythical ancestor who resembles her in every way. In the maintenance of this story in María's repertoire, in her readiness to perform it, and in the slanting of the narrative to feature the heroic actions of its female protagonist, we see the workings of a process of identification linking narrator to story protagonist. Whether consciously or otherwise, María had good reason to tell this tale and tell it in this fashion: she is telling a story about herself.

Francisco Tandioy is a remarkable ambassador for the Inga community, carrying Inga language and culture first to the provincial capital city of Pasto, where for many years he taught Inga at the Universidad de Nariño, and later to the distant Midwest of the United States, where he currently teaches his language and culture to students and faculty at Indiana University. Turning now to his telling of *"Shulupsimanda Parlo,"* "The Tale of the *Shulupsi* Bird," we will see with greater clarity how this process of

Francisco Tandioy, Inga ambassador, with his mother, Margarita

María Juajibioy
working with a digging stick

identification can shape not only repertoire choice but also the weighing of different story components. *"Shulupsimanda Parlo"* is another member of the paradise forestalled cluster. It concerns a young woman who comes to the home of an eligible bachelor and is asked by the young man's mother to prepare maize beer for thirsty field workers. When the older woman returns from the fields, she finds the young woman combing her hair and the raw material for the beer, three barrels of corn cobs, still apparently just as she had left them. This woman becomes angry, and without looking to see if the beer had been made, she scolds the younger woman severely. As it happens, the maize beer had been made—the young woman possessed the uncanny ability to make a barrel of maize beer from just a few grains of corn. But the younger woman is so incensed at her treatment that she turns into a *shulupsi* bird, dips into the maize beer, and flies away. As with the centipede woman, the marriage deal is off; the boundaries of the human community are protected, but at the cost of rejecting a gift of knowledge that could have greatly reduced the human work load.

The core theme of paradise forestalled is made explicit in Francisco's performance. The *shulupsi* bird utters, in Inga, some parting words:

> *Kawachispaka, nirkasi: "Kunauramandaka, kimsa saparuwaka suglla mangallami aswankangichi."*
> Showing her the maize beer, she said: "From now on, with three baskets you will make only one barrel of maize beer."

Francisco's version of this story is unique among a dozen or so tellings in my possession for the epilogue he inserts, a dialogue between the mother and son. Here is the relevant text, in Inga and my English translation.

> *"Mana mamata nirkaiki, ama iapa mandapuakungi?*
> "Didn't I tell you, Mother, not to be ordering her about so much?

> *Ianga kawapuangi, kam mama mana uiangichu.*
> You see it's in vain, you, Mother, don't listen.

> *Kam tukui nukapa warmikunatami, chasa mitikuchipuangi, di rabumanda.*
> You make all my women leave like this from anger.

> *Chimandami ñujpa kawanga tiá, nispami piñanga tiá.*
> Because of that next time one must look, then one must scold.

> *Mama mana chasa piñapuangima, chi warmita, ñami nuka kasarani.*
> Mother, if you hadn't scolded that woman so, I would already have married.

I tukui warmikuna ñami, kimsa muru sarallawa, ñami aswankuna, sug manga junda.
And all women would already use only three kernels of corn to make a full barrel of maize beer.

Tukui warmikuna, manami iskunakurshangichi, kaituku achka sara, sug manga aswangapaglla."
All women would not have to shuck so much corn to make only one barrel of maize beer."

This epilogue underscores the high price paid when the *shulupsi* woman takes her leave. In addition, it features an extended rant by the young man, who accuses his mother of consistently ruining his romances by making heavy demands on the young women he brings around. It is this last detail, the son's recrimination, that is distinctive in Francisco's shaping of the story. Francisco, a young man himself at the time of this telling, gives vent to a feeling of outrage that works perfectly well within the confines of the story but seems, in its extension and vehemence, to transcend it to some degree. One suspects that Francisco is giving voice to an endemic complaint males among the younger generation launch against their seniors, that their mothers place obstacles in the way of their securing mates. And indeed, in anecdote and conversation, the exploitation of daughters-in-law does surface in the Sibundoy Valley (as elsewhere) as a major point of social tension.

What we see here is that even fixed story plots offer multiple interpretive options for storytellers. *"Shulupsimanda Parlo,"* for example, features three main protagonists: the young woman, the mother, and the young man. The storyteller can locate the narrative in the experience of any one of these; Francisco's version, as we have seen, places the experience of the young man in the foreground, at least in its concluding passages. This selection of focal point is another facet of the identification process linking narrators to story protagonists. As does María, Francisco chooses the character that most closely resembles him—in this case, the young man—as his narrative focal point. And by inserting the epilogue, Francisco opens an ample space for personalizing the story, for making it pertinent to his own concerns. Indeed, he stretches the story nearly to a breaking point, since had the son prevailed and the mother not intervened, the young woman would have successfully entered the family, thus violating the proscription entailed in the paradise forestalled paradigm (see McDowell 1994, 2007).

What we have in these three Sibundoy cases—Mariano Chicunque's, María Juajibioy's, and Francisco Tandioy's—is a sympathetic vibration that draws the storyteller to the story on the basis of vicarious identification. In each case the storyteller shares salient social characteristics with a main protagonist in the tale. For Mariano and María, the plot elements cast a favorable light back on the storyteller—the elders are wise, as is Mariano, and María has the good hand for planting and strives to assure the well-being of family, just as the mother does in *"Tobiaxbe Parlo."* Francisco's tale takes us a bit further in the direction of customizing myth—his vicarious identification with one of the three main protagonists in his tale causes him to spin out a facet of the story that remains minimal in other tellings.

It seems to me that the most important dimension of this identification dynamic we witness in these performances is the prior impact of the story on the storytellers themselves. It is reasonable to suppose that each of these storytellers finds the story inhabitable; the commonalities of social identity in each case create a comfortable match between storyteller and tale. These storytellers can try on these stories and sense their power and veracity; they can readily picture themselves in the starring roles. And this prior act of self-persuasion leads to a subsequent act of public persuasion when the stories are related to an audience, all the more convincingly because the performers can inhabit their tales.

Virtual Identification among the Quichua Runa

Is it fair to say that the memorate, the first-person narrative of spiritual encounter, is a customizing of myth? Perhaps not in all cases, but when the memorate coexists in a tale community with a living mythology, then I think the case can be made. Certainly, such tales evince, at the least, an intimate engagement with mythic thought. Quichua Runa are accustomed to hear and tell stories about spiritual actors who roamed their territory in ancestral times, setting the parameters of lived experience in our days. For example, *wando rumi,* a large stone lying part-way up the slopes of Taita Imbabura, Father Imbabura, the volcanic peak that rises above Ilumán and Peguche and Otavalo itself, is said to have arrived at that spot when Mama Cotacachi, a mountain that rises across the valley, threw it at her former lover, Taita Imbabura—she sought to strike his head with it, but her shot fell short of that mark. Another set of tales stresses the presence of spiritual actors in more recent times. A traditional Runa tale featuring Our Lord, for example, concerns an elderly, beggarly man who arrives at a sumptuous hacienda and asks for a piece of bread. Not only is he rejected, but the owner turns loose his attack dogs on the humble visitor. The first sign that something unusual is afoot comes when these vicious dogs catch up to the elderly man and start licking his hand. That night, rains come and persist until the hacienda and its owner are engulfed in the rising waters.

In this context of mythic consciousness, it is not difficult for contemporary Runa to push identification to its limits by locating themselves as protagonists in mythic encounters that resemble the tales they have heard over the years from their elders. I heard two such tales from my compadres in Ilumán, Luis Alberto Yamberla and Maruja Picuasi, when a session devoted to reciting superstitious beliefs evolved into a performance of memorates confirming the spiritual substrate implied in the belief statements. First, Luis Alberto told us the story of his encounter with a *sombra,* a spirit that interposes itself in human affairs to derail human endeavors. Luis Alberto was able to extract himself from the clutches of the *sombra* when he recalled the Runa belief that *sombras* must be struck only with the left fist. Following this account, his wife Maruja related a layered narrative with multiple episodes, the gist being that through her capacity to work with spiritual remedies, she was able to extract her neighbor, and then herself, from the grip of a life-threatening spiritual attack.

Granted, neither of these Runa narratives follows precisely a pre-existing script familiar from the collective mythology of the community. But this capacity to project oneself into a mythical framework insures that the mythic consciousness pervading the tales of the ancestors will not atrophy or become vestigial since it is re-enacted in the experience of today's living people. Here the process of identification, the ability of the storyteller to connect with the tale protagonist, reaches an apotheosis—the storyteller becomes a protagonist in a tale resembling the tales of old, and third-person discourse yields to the first-person mode of personal experience. But this process of virtual identification shares an important feature with the vicarious identification we observed in the Sibundoy texts—here, too, the storyteller assumes the role of cultural conservator, fending off against impertinent incursions from the spirit realm. Like María Juajibioy and Mariano Chicunque, Luis Alberto and Maruja shine forth in their stories as exemplary tokens of their community. The difference is that in the vicarious mode of identification, the light that shines is an indirect one, dependent upon the listener making the connection between tale teller and tale protagonist; in virtual identification, the illumination is direct as tale teller comes to equal tale protagonist.

Let's contemplate a key episode from each of the sample Runa texts. Luis Alberto is an entrepreneur of Runa culture, an emissary of its music and handicrafts, who has established a foothold in Madison, Wisconsin,

Luis Alberto Yamberla, Quichua Runa leader, with his wife, Maruja Picuasi
Photograph by Patricia Glushko

Wando Rumi
Photograph by Patricia Glushko

from where he wanders the Midwest attending fairs and visiting universities. He is a founding member of the Centro Cultural Inti Raymi, composed of several families interrelated through marriage, and a mainstay in the very successful musical troupe Inti Raymi, which has performed at, among other venues, the Lotus Festival in Bloomington, Indiana. Intelligent and forthright, Luis Alberto has been able to navigate in North American culture and he has had a positive impact on his community. Recently, the home that he and Maruja have created has become a destination for groups of university students doing tours of indigenous Ecuador.

Luis Alberto's tale of fighting off the *sombra* or shade that came upon him in a creek bed is a gripping tale of bravery and good thinking under the most difficult of circumstances. Attacked in a creek bed while in transit to his home in the wee hours one morning, Luis Alberto has the presence of mind to recall that evil spirits are to be repelled with a blow from the left, not the right, fist, and once that wisdom enters his mind, he is able to fend off the evil spirit and make his way home. As I have dealt elsewhere with Luis Alberto's tale (see McDowell 2010), I will convey, in brief detail, his wife Maruja's tale of the evil spirit that attacks her neighbor through his beautiful black dog. Maruja is a leader among the women in her extended family. She is known for the fine gardens she cultivates and for the maize beer she prepares for the Inti Raymi celebrations in June. She also possesses the ability to cure people who suffer from spiritual afflictions. Smart and capable, it seems that no task lies beyond her abilities.

Maruja's tale, told in Spanish, begins with her neighbor and compadre, Enrique, falling sick just as he is on his way to Quito early one morning. These neighbors have a strong and healthy black dog, but as Enrique sets off before dawn for Quito to purchase wool for weaving, the dog begins howling and dashing around in circles, and Enrique stumbles back to the house, deathly ill. Enrique's wife comes to Maruja in a panic, alerting her that her husband is sick, vomiting, his skin is cold, and he is barely breathing. Luis Alberto is traveling, but Maruja agrees to help and immediately draws on her store of traditional knowledge to assess the situation.

Y allí le digo: "¿Sabes qué?
And then I tell her: "You know what?

Yo le llego.
I will come to him.

Dele aguita caliente,
Give him a little hot water,

un arco le hizo mal el estómago."
a rainbow has damaged his stomach."

Maruja here makes reference to the Runa belief that the rainbow can work harm on a person, if there is a coincidence between the colors in the rainbow and some item of clothing a person is wearing. She then gathers some curing materials—cigarettes, hen's eggs, and a coin—and goes to the aid of her neighbor and compadre, Enrique. She learns that he spoke of a *sombra,* a *mal espíritu,* that attacked the black dog in front of the house and then struck him and sent him back to his front door, barely able to move. *"Un mal espíritu,"* he had said, *"me cruzó,"* "a bad spirit crossed my path."
Maruja continues:

Yo vengo,
I come,

cojo huevos, chicos, esos que hay aquí,
I grab eggs, little ones, those we have around here,

ya y yo así parece, increible, yo
then, and I, it appears, incredible, I

yo digo, rezando, "Diosito mío
I say, praying, "Dear God of mine,

y quita de ese malino
take away this evil,

quítale todo eso."
take all of this away from him."

Maruja knows the prayers to recite in these circumstances, and she calls on God and Taita Imbabura to release this man from his suffering. She also knows to rub his body with hen's eggs, and then with a coin, so that the evil influence will depart Enrique's body and soul.

But at this juncture events take a turn for the worse—the evil is too strong, it bursts the eggs, and when Maruja rubs the sick man's body with a coin, the healer herself is attacked. Suddenly, she finds that she cannot raise her own arms, and she is on the verge of vomiting. At this tense moment, she utters her fear:

"¿O sea que me gana el diablo pues,
"Could it be that the devil is getting the better of me,

me gana a mi mismo?"
that he is beating me here?"

Like her husband Luis Alberto at the bottom of the creek bed, Maruja has now entered her darkest moment:

Ya la cara pálida
Now with my face pale

no sé cómo me siento,
I can't say how I feel,

me seguía poco a poco.
it came at me little by little.

Yo digo, "Dios que está allá," digo, "ya me cuida."
And I say, "God who is up there," I say, "cares for me now."

At this point Maruja does something that is, by community standards, quite unusual and truly heroic, and indeed, worthy of the myth protagonists— she takes two eggs and begins to rub her own body!

Yo misma, yo también me voy, agarro, cojo dos huevos.
I myself, I also go and grab them, I grab two eggs.

Yo, a mi hija, no más, ya estaba corriendo a colegio,
I, to my daughter, just like that, she was running off to her high school,

yo digo: "Pásame dos huevos."
I say: "Hand me two eggs."

The struggle with the spirit of the *sombra,* the *mal espíritú,* is fierce; the evil has passed into Maruja as she cured her neighbor, Enrique, and it has hit her with even more force. She is seated in the bathroom of her house, she nearly succumbs, but at last through valiant effort, she vanquishes this spirit. Both Maruja and Enrique recover, but the black dog perishes at the end.

In these dramatic tales of life-and-death encounters with *sombras,* Luis Alberto and Maruja muster the spiritual strength to resist the onslaught of sinister spirits. They draw on knowledge that lies at the core of their community's intellectual heritage, and they call on the Christian God and on the beneficent spirit of Taita Imbabura to come to their aid. The cosmic moment of these anecdotes is modern, not ancient, and derivative, not formative. But the forces that shaped the land and charted human society in ancient times are still active, and now, as then, those on the good side of cosmic history must gather useful knowledge and act appropriately, if civilization is to be saved. The larger lesson, for the Runa and the Sibundoy alike, is that by following in the footsteps of the ancestors, by applying the knowledge they left behind, the modern people can conserve the precarious perch that was established for them in ancestral times.

Conclusion

I argue that myth, though inherently a public discourse, is prone to customization through processes of identification that connect storytellers to story protagonists. In one mode of personalization, vicarious identification, storytellers perform narratives that highlight their own positive attributes as mirrored in tale protagonists; we see this most clearly in the texts from Mariano Chicunque and María Juajibioy. In some cases, as we see with Francisco's *"Shulupsimanda Parlo,"* this vicarious connection can skew the perspective of the narrative. A different mode of identification, I propose, virtual identification, occurs when storytellers inject themselves into narratives pervaded with mythic consciousness. Luis Alberto Yamberla and Maruja Picuasi perform myth-like narratives with this feature, narratives that portray them in mortal combat with evil spirits operating in the modern world.

Recognizing these spaces for the personalization of myth helps resolve the clash of paradigms alluded to at this essay's outset. We can affirm from this vantage point that myth does indeed evince a collective persona, as many mythographers have detected over the years. At the same time, we find that those who tell the tales that compose a mythology find ways to make their personal imprint on the stories, and indeed, at times to insert themselves into comparable stories. Returning to the wisdom of Kenneth Burke (1973:296), we can avow that verbal art performances, whether spoken or written, are "proverbs writ large," that is to say, expressive forms shaped to label a situation from a specific angle of vision. The speaker's investment in what is spoken cannot be neglected if we are to obtain a secure purchase on even this most public of performance genres, the telling of mythic narratives.

References

Basso, Ellen. 1990. Introduction: Discourse as an Integrating Concept in Anthropology and Folklore Research. In *Native Latin American Cultures through Their Discourse,* ed. Ellen Basso, pp. 3–10. Bloomington: Special Publications of the Folklore Institute.

Bernstein, Basil. 1960. A Review of *The Lore and Language of Schoolchildren,* by I. Opie and P. Opie. *British Journal of Sociology* 11:178–81.

Burke, Kenneth. 1973 [1941]. *The Philosophy of Literary Form: Studies in Symbolic Action*. 3d ed. Berkeley: University of California Press.

Hymes, Dell. 1975. Folklore's Nature and the Sun's Myth. *Journal of American Folklore* 88:345–69.

Lévi-Strauss, Claude. 1969. *The Raw and the Cooked*. Trans. John and Doreen Weightman. New York: Harper and Row.

McDowell, John. 1994. *"So Wise Were Our Elders": Mythic Narratives from the Kamsá*. Lexington: University Press of Kentucky.

————. 1998. Native American Traditions (South). In *Translating Oral Tradition*, ed. John Miles Foley, pp. 162–73. New York: Modern Language Association.

————. 2007. Paradise Forestalled: Animal Suitors in Sibundoy Myth. *Midwestern Folklore* 33:3–36.

————. 2010. Rethinking Folklorization in Ecuador: Multivocality in the Expressive Contact Zone. *Western Folklore* 69:181–210.

David Drake:
Potter, Poet, Rebel

John Michael Vlach

David Drake was known by several names: Dave Pottery, Dave of the Hive, Dave the Potter, Dave the Slave. It was not until the end of the Civil War that he was recognized by his given name when he was listed in the federal census of 1870. His date of birth was never recorded but is assumed to have been in 1800. The year of his death is similarly vague but it is known from census records to have occurred in the 1870s since he was not counted in the 1880 census. His reputation as potter of inordinate strength and skill is based not on any record of congratulatory praise but from what can be termed his artifact trail—a list of 169 pots of varying sizes produced between 1829 and 1864 (Goldberg and Witkowski 2006:67–70). These works form the spine of his biography as a potter.

Drake, while born a slave, had the good fortune to be associated for a short time with Dr. Abner Landrum who was not only an original investor in Pottersville, a site of pottery production just one mile from the Edgefield County seat, but also the publisher of a newspaper called *The Hive*. Drake's owner was Landrum's nephew, Harvey Drake, and because of Landrum's various enterprises David Drake was exposed not only to ceramic production but also to the processes involved in operating a printing press. It is likely, then, that the commerce of words that he experienced at the print shop gave rise to Drake's ability to write and his proficiency with language (Todd 2008:44–45). While he never was assigned to set type, he did learn to read and write on his own—probably by witnessing the various processes associated with the operation of a printing press. Evidence of Drake's learning process, which involved careful observation and clandestine experimentation, was recently found at the pottery site just a mile outside of Edgefield where in the ruins of an old kiln a brick was found with the inscribed date: "April 16" (Todd 2008:45). The lettering, a clear match with the distinctive script also seen on Drake's pots, suggests that he had practiced in private in order to learn how to read and write. Many years later the matter of Drake's surprising virtuosity with language was extolled in a story published in the *Edgefield Advertiser* in 1863. The paper's editor described a friendly encounter with Drake when he chanced upon him in town: "Observing an intelligent twinkle in his eye, we accosted him with one of his own set speeches: "Well, uncle DAVE, how does your corporosity seem to sagatiate?" (Goldberg and Witkowski 2006:87)˙ The editor's essay was clearly aimed at showing that, even in the midst of the bloody Civil War, some slaves would remain loyal to and respectful of their masters. It is clear, however, that Drake used his verbal skill not merely to be entertaining but also to enhance his social position. While he may have been someone's property, his vocabulary was surprisingly rich. In his conversations he would readily throw out unusual terms that could catch his white superiors off guard. Moreover, it appears that he was able to shape the conversation in ways that suggested his somewhat eccentric and unusual terms were a feature of his usual light-hearted comic banter. But through his displays of humorous repartee, he was also demonstrating a mastery of language that was not expected of African-American chattels. By his humorous verse, Drake was able to offer a necessarily indirect critique of slavery. The system of bondage that was designed ultimately to make black people into property—goods that could be purchased, sold, or rented as it pleased a given owner—was, for a moment, challenged by Drake's humorous turns of phrase. While white people were evidently entertained by Drake's verbal dexterity, he had deeper motives of his own.

Laws prohibiting slave literacy in South Carolina were initiated as early as 1740. Those masters who allowed their slaves to read and write—if found out—were compelled to send those people out of the state (Monaghan 2005:243). But in Drake's case the statute was not enforced; largely, it would seem, because his pots were needed by local planters who had to feed the hundreds of slaves who produced the huge crops of cotton fiber that were the backbone of the local economy. Huge stoneware pots, the very type of vessel that appears to have been Drake's specialty, were exactly the kind of containers that planters needed to store and disperse the standard pork ration that they provided for their enslaved field hands. Edgefield County planter James Henry Hammond, the master of Silver Bluff plantation,

The largest stoneware jar made by David Drake is dated May 13, 1859 in his hand. It carries two names: Dave, the Potter, and Baddler, who was likely the turner. The letters "LM" are the initials of their owner, Lewis Miles. The pot is in the collection of the Charleston Museum. It is 29 inches high, 26 inches wide. On the opposite side is a short poem "Great & Noble Jar / hold sheep goat and bear."

This pot, standing 21 inches tall, is signed "Dave, LM November 9, 1860." It is inscribed on the opposite side: "A noble jar. For pork and beef—then carry it a round to the indian chief."

staged a food distribution ritual every Saturday during which he demanded that all the heads of slave households clean themselves up and gather at the plantation commissary where they would receive a week's worth of salted pork. To complete this weekly food distribution he needed many storage jars of the sort that Drake and other local potters regularly produced (Faust 1980:88). One wonders if the field slaves understood the words that Drake had scratched into the surfaces of his pots. Some of them surely must have marveled that a slave could read and write and probably garnered a bit of hope from the example of his skill in such a specialized craft.

Some of Drake's pots, like the one made in 1858 and dedicated to a Mr. Segler, carry lengthy messages: "This jar is to Mr Segler who keeps the bar in orange burg for Mr Edwards a Gentleman—who formly kept Mr thos bacons horses" (Goldberg and Witkowski 2006:87)· In other cases only a single polysyllabic word is used like "Concatination" or "Ponderosity." To-day his pots are much sought after by antique collectors; especially those vessels inscribed with his intriguing verses that are usually structured as rhymed couplets. Indeed, the couplet was Drake's primary format over the course of almost three decades. The largest of Drake's pots stood slightly above two feet in height and had holding capacities that approached forty gallons. Such vessels also bore inscriptions that commented upon the likely contents of Drake's huge pots: "A very large Jar which has 4 handles, pack it full of fresh meats—then light candles" (1858), "Good for lard—or holding—fresh meets / blest we were—when peter saw the folded sheets" (1859), "made at stoney bluff, for making or adgin [ageing] enuff" (1859), "A noble Jar. For pork or beef—then carry it a round to the indian chief" (1860). In one instance Drake even commented on his own captivity when he wrote in 1840 "Dave belongs to Mr. Miles, where the oven bakes and the pot biles" (Todd 2008:241, 245, 246, 248). While there is no surviving nineteenth-century commentary about Drake's poems, it is useful to ponder what he might have been thinking. He certainly knew that at some point his actions could have serious consequences since local laws promulgated in the 1830s not only forbade slave literacy but also required that literate slaves be sold out of the state. But since there is no record of any protest by planters or other local businessmen in the Edgefield District, it seems that Drake's behavior was overlooked because of his highly valued skill or his entertaining way with words or both.

Perhaps the greatest tragedy of David Drake's life occurred in 1833 when his owner Harvey Drake died. Being a highly prized artisan, David Drake was quickly sold to Lewis Miles while his wife and children were purchased by Harvey Drake's brother Reuben. David Drake's family was then taken five hundred miles west to northern Louisiana where Reuben Drake believed that he would not only find great reserves of high quality stoneware clay but also be able to evade the competition among Edgefield's numerous pottery shops. From David Drake's perspective the heart-rending separation from his family was a terrible blow. While he could do nothing about the financial objectives of his owner's family, two decades later he would fashion a pot inscribed with the following poem: "I wonder where is all my relations / Friendship to all—and every nation" (Koverman 1998:91). While the second line of the couplet offers an expression of optimistic partnership, the poem does not mask the abiding sense of loss that Drake must have felt. In 1843 David Drake entered a seven-year period of what might be termed "graphic silence" during which he inscribed no poems, names, or other messages on his pots. While the reasons for the cessation of inscriptions remain unknown, the overwhelming feelings of loss and abandonment that he must have experienced during that time provide the most plausible motive.

In the 1850s Drake once again resumed his habit of inscribing messages on the sides of his pots. Having become by then the property of Lewis Miles, he was sent to work at a new pottery site in the eastern portion of Edgefield County known as Stony Bluff. There Drake would produce his largest pots. Not only were they some of the biggest ceramic containers ever made in the entire history of Edgefield pottery, the messages that he wrote on their outer surfaces present a wide spectrum of topics ranging from moral philosophy ("I made this Jar for cash / though its called lucre Trash" [1857]) to observations on feminine wiles ("a pretty little Girl, on a virge / Volca[n]ic mountain, how they burge" [1857]) to the virtues of financial prudence ("This noble Jar will hold 20 / fill it with silver then you'll have plenty" [1858]) to statements linking his pottery skills to moral consequences ("I, made this Jar, all of cross / If, you dont repent, you will be, lost" [1862]).[1] Drake's time in the eastern portion of the county proved to be his most prolific period for poetic inscription. Of his last twenty-nine verses, twenty were inscribed onto pots made at the Stony Bluff pottery site located in the Horse Creek Valley.

Drake's largest, and consequently his most visually impressive storage jar was made at the Miles pottery on May 13, 1859. Assisted by a fellow slave named Baddler, who probably turned the potter's wheel, Dave produced a vessel capable of holding more than forty gallons. Its walls flare upward from the pot's base to a wide shoulder, then turn slightly inward, and end with an everted rim that encircles the wide mouth of the vessel. With a circumference measuring almost seven feet at its widest diameter, the pot appears as if it just might rise from the floor. Viewers today marvel at the vessel's impressive form in a manner that likely replicates the reactions of Drake's nineteenth-century customers. In this pot he had clearly pushed well beyond the usual expectations for a storage crock. Drake's personal pride in this vessel is signaled by the poem that he inscribed on the pot's shoulder: "Great & Noble jar / hold sheep, goat, and bear" (Baldwin 1993:77–78). Drake certainly knew that he had pushed the local limits of a pot's size and form to a new level.

The last of Drake's known pots was a modest fifteen-gallon vessel made in 1864 (Goldberg and Witkowski 2006:70). Given that there was a constant demand for storage crocks, he must have made many of these modestly sized vessels since they were considered an everyday necessity. The United States Census of 1870 recorded Drake as the seventy-year-old head of household No. 145, and it indicated further that he was still working as a pottery turner. The next line in the census taker's tally sheet indicates that living with Drake in the same household was another African-American man named Mark Jones who is also listed as turner. That Drake and Jones had known each other for some time is indicated by a stoneware vessel made in 1859 and signed "Mark and Dave" in Drake's distinctive hand (Koverman 1998:25). Clearly Drake, who had lost his family years earlier, was attempting to reconstitute a new family structure for himself by connecting with Jones, his wife, and their five children (Todd 2008:158). Drake's absence in the 1880 census confirms that he died at some time during the prior decade. Subsequently, his legacy as a potter was passed on to Mark Jones, who lived until 1910 when the Federal Census recorded him as a blind man who was then residing with his daughter Emma Adams. Jones's son Brister, who followed in his father's trade, seems to have perpetuated some attributes of Drake's style with a vessel on which he wrote the following inscription (Todd 2008:211):

Brister Jones
The maker
Sept the 6 1880
It Will hold
inny thing that
you can get in it

These lines mark the end of Edgefield County's long experience with ceramic pots inscribed with poems and other messages.

Jug by David Drake. The signature, date, and "LM" (for Lewis Miles) appear within an area of kaolin slip

The long list of stoneware vessels either signed by or attributable to David Drake is a proof of his prodigious talent and his industrious habits. He was probably able to endure slavery, in part, by finding himself a meaningful role within the given social order. While he was, for most of his life, a captive with no social option other than to serve his owners, he was clearly able to sustain his sense of personhood through various modes of what might be termed domestic or personal rebellion. It is apparent from the artifactual evidence provided by all of his surviving pots that he was a skilled artisan. Further, he was a craftsman who could be trusted to furnish the large ceramic vessels that were so essential to food storage and distribution on Edgefield County's numerous plantations. But even as he performed the tasks that were assigned to him, he also broke the laws of the state regarding slave literacy. In this way he may have reminded some South Carolinians of their constant anxiety over the possibility of a slave rebellion—a fear that traced back to an event that occurred on the outskirts of Charleston in 1739. There, along the banks of the Stono River, a group of twenty escapees, all of them hoping to reach the promise of freedom in Spanish-held St. Augustine, were quickly captured, decapitated, and their heads stuck atop poles at each mile marker as a warning against future uprisings. While the Stono Rebellion was a complete failure, South Carolinians, nevertheless, remained anxious over the threat of slave uprisings for the next two and a half centuries (Wood 1974:316–17). Certainly, in the plantation context where enslaved blacks outnumbered whites by a wide margin, blacks would have had the upper hand if they wanted to carry out a rebellion. In 1800 the General Assembly of South Carolina, fearing that literacy among slaves might allow them to share secret messages, passed a bill prohibiting black people from seeking any form of "mental instruction" that might give them the skills of reading and writing. Thirty-four years later the same body added harsher penalties to the extant prohibition on African-American literacy stipulating that any white person who taught a slave to read and write would be fined one hundred dollars and be imprisoned for six months. A free black person engaging in the same act was to be given up to fifty lashes and could also be fined up to fifty dollars (Williams 2005:207–8). Clearly there was a perceived link between rebellion and literacy.

While there are no records that indicate what David Drake's views on these laws might have been, clearly he was liable to serious penalties. While Drake was clearly anguished by the slavery system when his wife and children were taken away to Texas in 1833, he seems to have looked for ways to adjust to the indignities of bondage and thereby deflect, in some measure, the sorrow that slavery had inflicted on him. It is difficult to decipher completely what his intentions might have been in 1857 when he reflected via a poem on the loss of his wife and children ("I wonder where is all my relations") and ends with a seemingly hail-fellow/well-met response ("Friendship to all—and every nation"). One could conclude that he was attempting either to mask his anguish or trying to accept a fate over which he had no control. Since the historical record does not provide us with enough detail to know how he felt, we are left then only with his public performance as skilled artisan who produced the largest ceramic vessels ever made in the antebellum South. For that feat, Drake will forever be a pottery hero. His poems finally leave us with an array of questions about his deeper sorrowful feelings that he seems to mask with either the comedy of rhyme or his demonstration of bold, muscular, out-sized action.

NOTE

1. A full listing of Drake's poetic inscriptions can be found in Todd, *Carolina Clay*, pp. 232–51.

References

Baldwin, Cinda K. 1993. *Great & Noble Jar: Traditional Stoneware of South Carolina.* Athens: University of Georgia Press.

Faust, Drew Gilpin. 1980. Culture, Conflict, and Community: The Meaning of Power on an Antebellum Plantation. *Journal of Social History* 14(1):83–97.

Goldberg, Arthur F. and James Witkowski. 2006. Beneath His Magic Touch: The Dated Vessels of the African-American Slave Potter Dave. In *Ceramics in America,* ed. Robert Hunter, pp. 58–92. Milwaukee: Chipstone Foundation.

Horne, Catherine Wilson, ed. 1990. *Crossroads of Clay: The Southern Alkaline-Glazed Stoneware Tradition.* McKissick Museum, University of South Carolina.

Koverman, Jill Beute. 1998. Verses on Vessels Made by Dave. In *I made this jar . . . : The Life and Works of the Enslaved African-American Potter, Dave,* ed. Jill Beute Koverman, pp. 82–92. Columbia: McKissick Museum, University of South Carolina.

Monaghan, E. J. 2005. *Learning to Read and Write in Colonial America.* Boston: University of Massachusetts Press.

Todd, Leonard. 2008. *Carolina Clay: The Life and Legend of the Slave Potter Dave.* New York: W. W. Norton.

Vlach, John Michael. (1978) 1990. *The Afro-American Tradition in Decorative Arts.* Athens: The University of Georgia Press.

———. 1990. International Encounters at the Crossroads of Clay: European, Asian, and African Influences on Edgefield Pottery. In *Crossroads of Clay: The Southern Alkaline-Glazed Stoneware Tradition,* ed. Catherine Wilson Horne, pp. 17–39. Columbia: McKisick Museum, University of South Carolina.

Williams, Heather Andrea. 2005. *Self-Taught: African American Education in Slavery and Freedom.* Chapel Hill: University of North Carolina Press.

Wood, Peter. 1974. *Black Majority: Negroes in Colonial South Carolina from 1670 through the Stono Rebellion.* New York: W. W. Norton.

The Mother's Voice: An Analysis of the Content of Turkish Lullabies

İlhan Başgöz

The turn to performance, over the past half century, has charged folklorists with the obligation to record the ethnographic details out of which contexts can be constructed around texts to render them meaningful. These details concerning the interactional event and the biographies and attitudes of the participants are lacking in the older collections of folklore texts. But those collections remain rich resources from which folklorists—like archaeologists with their assemblies of unearthed fragments—can construct contexts through intertextual relations during their search for significant patterning in the cultures of the past.

My intention in this paper is to discover the voice of the mother in a collection of texts of lullabies. The lullaby exhibits the mother's social and psychological reality, her feelings and desires, and in it the mother's voice ranges across a wide variety of issues, including the structure of the family and the mother's values as expressed in her hopes and expectations for her children.

The data for analysis come primarily from Amil Çelebioğlu's *Türk Ninniler Hazinesi—A Treasurey of Turkish Lullabies*—a gathering of 3,089 lullabies published between 1892 and 1982. The mother who speaks in these lullabies is only a mother, any mother. No particulars are given about her, nor is the date of recording supplied, though that is an important variable in any study. The book provides only a location, a city, a town, a village.

I presume that the mother comes from a rural background, that she is slight in wealth and education, and I assume that the lullabies, taken as a

353

whole, represent the opinions and expectations of a generalized individual, the Turkish mother, of the earlier twentieth century.

Pertinent to my investigation is Çiğdem Kağıtçıbaşı's research, based on interviews and dealing with the issue of gendered roles and women's values concerning fertility and children in Turkey. Kağıtçıbaşı tells of the mother, her family life, and her expectations for her children. My examination of lullabies both squares with her findings and reveals dimensions untouched by her research. The methods of interviewing in the social sciences have their own problems. The respondent is apt to express a personal view that is socially acceptable. But the mother singing a lullaby beside the cradle, alone at night when no one is listening, feels no need to hide her deepest feelings. She can open her heart, and the information carried by her song is more trustworthy than the information given in an interview.

From Kağıtçıbaşı's research we learn that the mother expects from her children companionship and help during work, economic benefit in the future, and security in her old age. The lullabies reveal that the mother expects more from her male offspring:

1. I sing a lullaby so you should sleep. *Ninni diyem yatasın*
   You should grow quickly; *Hemincek boy atasın*
   When your father beats me, *Baban beni döğende*
   You should support me. *Bana arka çıkasın.*

The pain of the mother is manifold; it includes her husband's blows and a fear that the father will harm the baby, desert the family, or take a co-wife:

2. Dandily dandily, lamb with a toy, *Dandini dandini danalı kuzu*
   Lamb with hennaed hands and arms. *Elleri kolları kınalı kuzu*
   When your father comes in the *Akşam baban gelincek*
   evening,
   He will beat both me and you. *Hem seni döğer hem beni.*

3. Sleep my son, dear son, *Uyu oğlum can oğlum*
   My red coral son. *Kırmızı mercan oğlum,*
   If you father hears [your cries] he *Baban duysa öldürür*
   will kill you.
   Sleep my naughty son. *Uyu afacan oğlum.*

4. Dandily dandily, baby with a toy. *Dandini dandini danalı bebek*
   Pants at the bottom, vest at top, *Altta pantol üstte yelek*
   Never walks, this spoiled baby. *Hiç yaya gezmez bu nazlı bebek*

Sleep or your father will spank you.	*Uyu babandan yersin kötek*
Lullaby, my little one, lullaby,	*Ninni yavrum ninni,*
Your father loves someone.	*baban seviyor birini.*
5. Your worthless father left us and disappeared;	*Soysuz baban koydu kaçtı;*
Sleep, my little one, sleep.	*Uyu yavrum uyu.*
6. I went up on the roof to spread raisins,	*Dama çıktım üzüm sermeye*
Grandma comes to cuddle the baby,	*Nenesi geliyor çocuk sevmeye*
The dirty dog prepares to enter the bridal chamber.	*Dürzü köpek hazırlanmış güvey girmeye.*
Either give me my desire or take my soul.	*Ya ver muradımı yal al canımı.*
7. To the sky a ladder was built.	*Göğe merdiven kuruldu*
My son, your father entered the bridal chamber;	*Oğlum baban güvey girdi;*
My son, he showed us the road.	*Oğlum bize yol göründü.*

The mother's fear and anger can become so intense that she asks her baby to take revenge on the father:

8. I sing a lullaby and cry;	*Ninni diyem ağlayam;*
My heart burns.	*Ciğerimi dağlayam.*
Grow and take revenge on your father;	*Büyü hayfım al babandan;*
I rely on you.	*Ben sana bel bağlayam.*

The mother's complaints about her child's father can turn into a critique of her social conditions:

9. The fish in the skillet,	*Tavada balık*
Its tail is burned.	*Kuyruğu yanık.*
What a world!	*Bu nasıl dünyadır ki*
Your father sleeps, I am awake.	*Baban uyur ben uyanık.*

Her complaint about her world can also be addressed to God, the power of the Islamic world's ordering:

10. Trouble turns to tears,	*Derdi göz yaşı ettim hu*
I remained sleepless till morning.	*Figan ile sabah ettim*
What did I do to my God?	*Tanrı'ma ben ne ettim?*
Sleep, my little one, sleep.	*Uyu yavrum uyu.*

The baby's father, a guestworker in Germany, does not escape the mother's fury:

11. I sing a lullaby for my baby.   *Nenni dedim nesi var*
    My little one has a grandfather;   *Yavrumun dedesi var*
    In Germany, my son   *Alamanya'da oğlumun*
    Has an unfaithful father.   *Vefasız babası var.*

In the traditional Turkish family, it was the mother's responsibility to care for the children, day and night, to cook the meals and clean the house, to fulfill the household's responsibilities on hospitable and ceremonial occasions. Turkish lullabies, as a result, fill with complaints about exhausting work in the house and, along with the husband, work out in the fields. The lullaby, the mother's creation, provides a means of venting her feelings, and especially when the baby does not sleep at night, her sufferings rise to the surface, and her love for her baby converts into a complaint.

Her complaint can turn to the topic of violence. Turkish women were granted many social and political rights following the foundation of the Republic, but it is shocking to find that four out of ten women in Turkey report that they have been beaten by their spouses. Those are the results of a study, *Domestic Violence against Women in Turkey,* which provided the first official statistics on the matter. It is even more disturbing that the study reveals that nearly 90 percent of abused women do not seek help from an organization. "This is such a silent problem that most people don't believe you when you give them the numbers," said Henriette Jansen, team leader of the study, which was conducted by the Turkish General Directorate of the Status of Women (KSGM). "It shows how much women suffer alone and the huge stigma attached to violence against women." (http://www.globalpost.com/dispatch/turkey).

In this, Turkey is by no means alone. Violence against women exits in every country, often behind closed doors and rarely reported. The redress to the problem, however, must be tailored to the underlying causes. "In Turkey it's the patriarchal power relationship. When there is an issue of power in a family or relationship, violence will be in the middle," said Meltem Agduk, Gender Project Coordinator for UNFPA, Turkey. Now turn again to the lullaby texts:

12. Dandily dandily dandily,   *Dandini dandini dandini*
    Sleep, my little one, now hurry.   *Uyu yavrum artık haydini*
    Look, my knees are weary,   *Bak yoruldu dizlerim*
    My arm will break now.   *Kolum da kopacak şimdi.*

13. My baby is like honey,   *Balam bala dönüştü*
    Like butter and honey.   *Yağa bala dönüştü.*
    Singing lullabies all night,   *Layla layla demekten*
    My breast is like blood.   *Bağrım kana dönüştü.*

The mother's exhaustion causes her to curse her beloved baby:

14. Dandled dry stick, you sleep,   *Dandin daylak sen uyu,*
    Bark-butt, you sleep,   *Ensesi kavlak sen uyu,*
    Pot-bellied, you sleep,   *Küp karınlı sen uyu,*
    Cabbage-leg, you sleep,   *Lahana bacak sen uyu,*
    Ass-eared, you sleep.   *Carıt kulak sen uyu.*

15. Dandily, bottle plug,   *Dandini şişe tapası*
    You sleep, foal of an ass.   *Uyusana eşşek sıpası.*
    The dan-dandled baby   *Dan dan danalı bebek*
    Remained unsleeping, dog, son of   *Uyumadı kaldı köpoğlu köpek.*
    a dog.

16. I sing a lullaby to my daughter.   *Nenni dedim kızıma,*
    I said sleep, she didn't;   *Uyu dedim uyumadı,*
    A dog should shit on her   *Köpek sıçsın inadına.*
    stubbornness.

17. On a branch I put a swing,   *Asmaya kurdum salıncak,*
    And in his hand I put a toy;   *Eline de verdim oyuncak,*
    He did not sleep, the nasty scamp. *Uyumadı hınzır yumurcak.*

The joy of having and the sadness of not having a baby are both displayed in the Turkish lullaby. The legend called "The Stone Baby" provides a touching instance of the unhappiness of the childless wife. A woman who cannot give birth, and fears that her husband will divorce her for that reason, takes a stone, dresses it like a baby, and puts it in a cradle. Throughout the night, she sings lullabies to the stone and prays to God, to the Prophet, and to all the saints to give her a baby. When dawn breaks, the stone in the cradle cries. Many lullabies capture the mother's feelings of delight and despair:

18. If a seller of sieves comes and I buy *Elekçi gelse de bir kalbur alsam,*
    one;
    Crying and crying, if I sift soil [to *Uğrüne uğrüne höllük elesem,*
    place beneath the baby],

If I wrap my son in a mirrored cradle,
My God, have you no favors?

Aynalı beşiğe oğlan belesem,

N'olur kadir mevlam ihsanın yok mu,

Is there not a hand-sized piece of meat in your treasury?

El kadar et versen haznende yok mu.

19. I had mansions built of golden timbers,
I had tables set with honeyed pastries;
I did not sleep three nights beside a baby.

Konaklar yaptırdım altın direkli,

Sofralar serdirdim ballı börekli,

Üç gece yatmadım yanı bebekli.

20. In the small cauldrons, food is cooking.
I envy the children playing outside;

If I am barren, the son of a bitch will divorce me.

Küçük kazanlarda yemek pişiyor,

Oynayan çocuklara gönlüm düşüyor,

Doğurmazsam köpek beni boşuyor.

21. I cut out a shirt on the bias;
His gentle father comes from Van.
I love my baby
More than my mother and father.

Gömlek biçtim sana yandan.
Bey babası gelir Van'dan.
Ben bebeğimi çok severim
Hem anamdan hem babamdan.

22. Stars play in the sky.
My eyes never get enough of my little one.
Many others have kids but
Not the equal of mine.

Gökte yıldız oynuyor.
Gözüm yavruma doymuyor.

Ellerde yavru çok ama
Benim yavruma uymuyor.

23. They trimmed the rose bush
So the rose would bloom;
My God gave you to me
So I would forget every trouble.

Gül ağacını budamışlar
Gül ü reyhan bitsin deyi;
Tanrım seni bana vermiş
Her derdin unutsun deyi.

24. I have a little tambourine,
In my hand, I have an embroidery frame.
Today I cuddle my little one;
A small bit of joy is mine.

Bir küçücük tefim var
Elimde gergefim var

Bugün yavrumu sevdim
Bir parçacık keyfim var.

25. Spirit-lifting, my little one; Bağrımı kaldıran yavrum,
    Gloom-killing, my little one; Kasveti öldüren yavrum,
    In our house, Evimizin içinde
    My little one makes me laugh. Yüzümü güldüren yavrum.

Turkish lullabies help us understand gendered values. If there is discrimination against girls, it not shared by the mother. In all of these more than three thousand recorded lullabies, only one places high value on a male child:

26. The branches of the pines are Çamların dalları da ağır olmaz
      not heavy,
    Lullaby my lamb, Kuzum nen nen nen.
    The sons of others are not sons, Ellerin oğlu da oğul olmaz
    Lullaby my lamb. Kuzum nen nen nen.
    Not three girls or even five girls Üç kız değil de beş kız olsa
    Could take the place of one son, Bir oğlanın yerini tutmaz
    Lullaby my lamb. Kuzum nen nen nen.

But many lullabies value a girl:

27. Reeds grow in the gardens; Bahçelerde biter kamış
    They grow tall but bear no fruit. Uzar gider vermez yemiş.
    My daughter is like cast silver; Benim kızım dökme gümüş
    Lullaby to you, my pure silver one. Has gümüşüm sana ninni.

28. Horses in the vineyards Bağlarda atlar
    Graze side by side, Yan yana otlar.
    Ram-like young men Koç koç yiğitler
    All should sacrifice themselves for Hep sana kurban.
    you.

The voice of the mother in the lullabies reflects cultural tendencies with regard to the future occupation of the child. For boys the preferred profession is the military:

29. My son should go to the schools, Oğlum gide mekteplere,
    Develop a fancy for the military, Askerliğe heves ede,
    Become a dark-eyed officer, Sürmeli zabit ola,
    His pocket full of money. Cebi parayla dola.

30. He will sleep and become a man; Uyuyup da adam olacaak
    He will become a general officer. Paşa zabit olacak.

A Turkish mother: Aysel Öztürk and her daughter, Yasemin.
Karagömlek, Çanakkale, 1990

31. Cooks should prepare her food;   *Aşçılar aşını vursun*
    My daughter should sit on a balcony.   *Benim kızım sundurmada*
                                            otursun.
    My daughter's fiancée   *Kızımın nişanlısı*
    Should be an officer with a sword   *Yanı kılıçlı zabit olsun.*
    at his side.

Nearly a century separates the oldest and newest lullabies in Çelebioğlu's collection. That period, the twentieth century, was one of amazing change in Turkey; it cannot be assumed that the attitudes in the lullabies are attitudes to be found in Turkey today. The lullabies indicate a preference for military service, but when, in 2004, I asked forty mothers in the city of Van whether they wanted their boys to become army officers, very few did. Our lullabies provide historical information.

In the past, when a military career was favored, nationalism and national defense were also entailed:

32. I sing a lullaby, he should sleep;   *Ninni diyeyim uyusun,*
    He should sleep and quickly grow,   *Uyusun da hemen büyüsün,*
    Become a solider, and protect the   *Asker olup yurt korusun.*
    homeland.

Other futures are imagined in the lullabies. A boy might become a governor, a teacher, a scholar, a clerk, a shepherd, a pilgrim, a *hafız* (one who has memorized the Koran), and for one mother it is clear that it would be best for him to become a doctor. She tells her husband:

33. Sell your goods and property, his   *Malını mülkünü sat babası,*
    father;
    Make your son a doctor, his father.   *Oğlunu doktor yap babası.*

One mother even dreamed of a presidency for her baby in a lullaby that must have been composed after 1960, when a man with a rural background, Süleyman Demirel, was first elected president of the Republic:

34. The creek's pebbles;   *Derelerin çakıl taşları,*
    My son's penciled eyebrows.   *Oğlumun kalem kaşları,*
    My son will grow and study,   *Oğlum büyüyüp okuyacak*
    And become the president of the   *Olacak cumhurbaşkanı.*
    Republic.

The mother hopes her daughter will get an education, prospering as a weaver of carpets or even a teacher:

35. My daughter should sleep, lullaby,   *Benim kızım uyusun ninni,*
    Should sleep and grow, lullaby;   *Uyusun da büyüsün ninni,*
    My daughter should be a teacher,   *Kızım öğretmen olsun da*
    She should educate children, lullaby.   *Çocukları okutsun ninni.*

Çiğdem Kağıtçıbaşı's research suggests that mothers expect help during work and security in old age. Lullabies confirm her findings:

36. My son will grow;   *Benim oğlum büyüyecek,*
    Sleeping, he will grow.   *Uyudukça büyüyecek,*
    He will bring money home;   *Eve para getirecek,*
    He will free us from trouble.   *Bizi dardan kurtaracak.*

37. The lullaby I sing burns me.   *Ninni derim beni yakar.*
    From his lips honey runs;   *Dudağından ballar akar,*
    My little one will grow and take   *Yavrum büyür bana bakar.*
    care of me.

38. My son, my son, my little son,   *Oğlum oğlum al oğlum*
    Remain at the hearth, my son.   *Ocağında kal oğlum.*
    Your father is worn and weary;   *Baban kalan yoruldu*
    Take over the hard work, my son.   *İşe güce sal oğlum.*

39. The cattle in the byre: *Ahırdaki inekleri*
    He should tend them when grown.   *Büyüyünce bekleyesin.*

40. From the mountains, he should   *Dağlardan odun getirsin*
    fetch firewood;
    From the springs, he should fetch   *Pınarlardan su getirsin.*
    water.

In her lullabies, the mother reveals her choice of a future spouse for her child and her wishes for familial connection to a person of power—a *reis*, a chief (a chief judge, the chief executive officer of a business firm, the mayor of a city)—or a person of wealth:

41. Greet the chief;   *Selam söylen reise;*
    He should give his daughter to us.   *Kızını versin bize.*

42. Istanbul's governor   *İstanbul'un valisi*
    Should request my daughter's hand.   *Dünür gelsin kızıma.*

43. One hundred glittering pieces of gold   *Yüz tane yaldız altın*
    Should come as my daughter's bride   *Başlık gelsin kızıma.*
    price.

44. One thousand pieces of gold Should come as my daughter's bride price.	*Dizilmedik bin altın* *Başlık gelsin kızıma.*
45. Of age, my daughter; calm, my daughter; My daughter, the bride of the commander-in-chief.	*Erini kızım serini kızım;* *Seraskerin gelini kızım.*
46. To ask for the hand of my daughter, Men should come from places like Ankara.	*Yavruma dünürler gelsin* *Ankara gibi yerlerden.*

Turkish lullabies allow us to learn the mother's feelings about her rela-tives, her relations by blood and her relations by marriage. Her anger fre-quently rises against her in-laws, her relations by marriage, and contrasts with her affection for the people in the home of her birth, though her anger usually mixes with playful wit. The baby's paternal aunt, the father's sister, is *hela taşı,* a stone in the toilet; she is *yırtık donlu,* the one with torn un-derwear, or *yarım pabuçlu,* half a shoe, or *salya sümüklü,* a runny nose. *Çok söyler;* she is also a babbler. But the maternal aunt, the mother's sister, is *yüzük taşı,* a ring's precious stone; she is *tellice tellice,* dressed in cloth em-broidered with gold-wrapped threads, or *samur kürklü,* dressed in sable fur. She is *nazik hanım inci dizer fesine,* a kind lady with pearls on her fez—*cici cici teyzesi,* a cute auntie. The contrast, for the mother, between her family of birth and her family of marriage is clear:

47. I came and saw a crazy lineage; Filthy dirty paternal aunts, Maternal aunts with kohl-lined eyes, Maternal uncles with sable hair, Paternal uncles with big heads.	*Vardım baktım bir deli soy;* *Yalaşık bulaşık halalar,* *Sürmeli gözlü teyzeler,* *Samur saçlı dayılar,* *Koca kafalı amcalar.*
48. Come, his paternal uncle, come, A limping, bald uncle. Come, his maternal uncle, come, An uncle in a carriage like a gentleman.	*Gel emmisi gel emmisi* *Seksekli kel emmisi.* *Gel dayısı gel dayısı* *Atı arabası bey dayısı.*
49. The moon rises; The sun sets. His maternal uncle from Germany	*Ay karşıdan doğup gelir,* *Gün boynunu eğip gelir.* *Dayısı Almanya'dan*

Comes, counting [German] marks.	*Mark'larını sayıp gelir.*
50. My son should pick two watermelons,	*(Oğlum) iki karpuz koparsın,*
One for his mother, one for his father;	*Biri annesine, biri babasına,*
The rinds should remain for his paternal aunt.	*Kabukları kalsın halasına.*

We can imagine the perfomative scene. At home in the dark, the mother rocks her baby in a cradle hung from the ceiling. She sings repetitive verses to a repetitive melody, hoping her baby will sleep and grow and rise to success. I am not qualified to evaluate the therapeutic effect of the song on the mother or her child, but I am certain that the old collections of texts contain vast, unexplored riches for the folklorist in quest of an understanding of the world's variety of worldviews.

REFERENCES

Başgöz, İlhan. 2008. "Ninniler"in *Türkü*, pp. 63–76. İstanbul: Pan Yayınları.

Boratav,Pertev. 1969. *100 Soruda Türk Halk Edebiyatı.* İstanbul: Gerçek Yayınevi.

Çelebioğlu, Amil. 1962. *Türk Ninniler Hazinesi.* İstanbul: Ülker Yayınları.

Kağıtçıbaşı, Çiğdem. 1982. *Sex Roles, Family and Community in Turkey.* Bloomington: Indiana University Turkish Studies Publication.

Kunoş, Ignaz. 1925. *Türkçe Ninniler,* İstanbul: Hilmi Kitabevi.

Contested Performance and Joke Aesthetics

Elliott Oring

> When an artifact . . . represents the passionate union of the person with the materials—it is art.
>
> —Henry Glassie, *The Spirit of Folk Art*

Of all the aspects of humor that have been addressed by philosophers, scientists, and critics, the aesthetics of humor generally, and of the joke specifically, have perhaps attracted the least attention. The attention of philosophers to jokes has been directed to a narrow range of issues: the structure of humor and the ethics of joking.[1] Some philosophers do not regard jokes as art at all (Carroll 1991:294; 2003:358). Even Richard M. Dorson, a student of American folk narrative, was equivocal about the aesthetics of the joke: "Jokes seem so ephemeral, topical, and trivial that the literary and the folk critic may well be excused for scorning them" (1972:83).

For folklorists, art is the apprehension of extraordinary arrangements of words, gestures, sounds, colors, forms, textures, or ideas in relation to some ordinary unmarked background.[2] In the context of everyday speech, jokes are extraordinary arrangements of words and ideas. They are art—verbal art—as are folktales, ballads, toasts, proverbs, and jump-rope rhymes (Bascom 1955:245–52; Ben-Amos 1971:13). To call something "art" does not necessarily warrant its greatness, depth, or importance. It only presumes that for some period of time—brief or enduring—an arrangement calls attention to itself and is apprehended as somehow remarkable.

For the traditional verbal arts, there is no script, score, or artifact to peruse. The aesthetic qualities of these arts are manifested in their oral performance. Performance is an act of communication that is framed and displayed for an audience. Performers assume responsibility for their communicative skills, and they are assessed on their abilities to communicate

365

effectively and artistically. Every performance is a function of place, time, situation, and personnel. Performances emerge only within the field of dynamic interaction between these variables. Furthermore, performance is a reflexive activity. Performers must be able to see themselves not only as objects of direct contemplation, but through the eyes of their audience. Indeed, the notion of performance presumes the notion of feedback—the notion that auditory, visual, and even olfactory messages are constantly being received and shape what is being performed (Bauman 1992:38–49).[3]

What follows is a small study of folk aesthetics; an attempt to characterize the principles that inform the performances of two accomplished joke tellers based on their evaluations of one another.[4] While these tellers are in many ways socially and culturally similar, they operate with very different ideas of joke performance; with ideas that ultimately point to differences between their public personas and individual personalities.

This essay began with a dinner party. Two of the members of the party were enthusiastic joke tellers. Both—Daniel and Diane—had been at other parties, dinners, and get-togethers that I had previously attended, and both were known by their friends and acquaintances as dedicated joke tellers. All the members of this dinner party knew one another, and knew of Daniel and Diane's passion for joke telling. While the other members of the party could tell and occasionally would tell a joke, no other members of the party would have considered themselves—or would have been regarded—as possessing an extensive repertoire of jokes or as being virtuoso performers.

Both Daniel and Diane were in their late fifties or early sixties. Diane was the older and had recently retired. Both had been telling jokes since they were children. Both were Jewish, and while there is no empirical evidence to demonstrate that Jews tell jokes more frequently than non-Jews, or that they are in any way superior joke tellers, both tellers recognized joke telling to be an accepted, and even privileged, discourse in American-Jewish culture. Both grew up in kinship and friendship groups where jokes and witty repartee were appreciated and encouraged. Although Daniel and Diane were not religiously observant, neither were they ignorant of Jewish tradition and practice. Both frequently told jokes based upon Jewish characters and themes and rooted in Jewish custom. Both regarded joke telling as part of their personal as well as ethnic personas. They told jokes to friends and to strangers alike, and both had admitted to assessing people in terms of their liking for jokes and on the basis of their responses to particular jokes that they told.

The two joke tellers regularly told jokes to one another. They even shared some jokes by email, but both claimed that the great majority of the jokes that they received electronically from others were unappealing. Over the years, Diane had compiled lists on small bits of paper to remind her of jokes she knew and wished to tell again. Daniel employed no lists. He claimed that if he were asked to tell the jokes he knew straight out, he would be lucky to remember a dozen. He knew his repertoire to be much larger than that, but he said that he could only recall individual jokes in the context of specific conversations, interactions, or joke-telling exchanges. Most of his jokes needed situational triggers to be recalled to consciousness.

That these two individuals should wind up telling jokes at a dinner party was hardly surprising. Nor was it surprising that their joke telling became somewhat competitive, as this had happened many times before. What was surprising, however, was the criticism that each offered of the other's performances. When Daniel started to tell a joke, Diane interrupted to state that he was telling it wrong, and she went on to describe her objections. When Diane told a joke, Daniel offered his own critique. This exchange of jokes and critical commentary went on for perhaps half an hour. As is often the case with natural performances, there was no opportunity to record the exchange or even to write down what was being said. The best I could do was to arrange to have the two tellers together at dinner at my house a few weeks later where their jokes—and more importantly their critiques—could be elicited and recorded.[5]

Fortunately, at that preplanned dinner, they seemed to go at their joke telling and critique with the same gusto that they had at the earlier dinner party. The dinner began with normal conversation, but both knew they had been invited to exchange jokes. Once they were into their dinner, they both launched into joke telling and evaluation giving little thought to the tape recorder that sat on the table. A number of the jokes that had been told at the previous dinner party were re-performed and reevaluated. As far as I can recall, both the jokes and the evaluations recapitulated much of what had taken place at the dinner party a few weeks before. Some jokes that hadn't been told then were told now. Frequently both tellers interrupted one another in the middle of a joke to tell what they thought was wrong with it. This second dinner began with about fifteen minutes of general conversation. On two separate occasions in the midst of the joke telling, talk returned to non-humorous topics. However, thirty-five minutes of an hour's recorded tape was concerned with the performance, discussion, and the evaluation of jokes. The joke telling commenced with the following joke:

> DANIEL: An old Jewish man is walking down the beach in Tel Aviv, and he stumbles over something. He looks down and picks it up, and it looks

like an old artifact, a lamp-like thing, with some writing on it. And he starts to rub away the sand. And a genie appears. The genie says: "I'm the genie of the lamp and you can have any one wish that you want."

DIANE: Already I don't like it. Go ahead.

DANIEL: And the man says, [Yiddish accent] "Well, if I've one wish it's that there's been such strife in the Middle East with the Arabs and the Israelis, the shooting and the killing—it's terrible. Solve the Middle East problem." The genie says, "Well, you know this is a difficult process. It's been a long conflict—a hundred years we're talking about—that this has been going on. This strife and the animosity is so deep. If you have some other wish that, you know, you'd like me to take care of maybe, you know, that's equally important to you, maybe I'll do that." The guy says [Yiddish accent], "Well, all right. Every Friday [Diane laughs] night when I come home from work, I should like for my wife to give me a blow job." And the genie says, "What was that first thing again?" [Diane laughs] What don't you like about that? . . . Go ahead. . . .

DIANE: First of all, it should be a Jewish genie, 'cause I think that's funny in itself. [Yiddish accent] "Dank goodness you released me from this lamp. I've been in this lamp for thousands of years, but I'm a Jewish genie and you only get one wish, so make it good Buster!" It raises . . . the. . . . "Well, if I only had one wish, I got to make it good. Listen! Let there be peace in the Middle East. Arab and Jew, Palestinian and Muslim and Shiite, and all those guys, they should all get along they should live and be well." You don't have to call it this "animosity" stuff [Diane laughs].

DANIEL: You didn't understand the word [Diane laughs]?

DIANE: There's too many syllables. And he goes, the genie goes, "Whoa baby! You give me a tough one. I'll tell you what I'm gonna do. I'll give you another choice. This one's too tough." Then he says, not just on Friday nights but, "Every night I should come home I want a blow job." The genie sits for a minute, says, "Well, what was that first one again?" [Diane laughs].

DANIEL: I would say that when you make the genie a Jewish genie, you don't have any contrast in the speakers. You have two people speaking with a Yiddish accent so it doesn't highlight . . .

DIANE: But we're in Tel Aviv. What's he gonna . . .

DANIEL: He's a genie, a genie . . .

DIANE: The Patrick and Michael joke. Did I tell you that one? Yes I do. About they're cast adrift in a raft . . .

DANIEL: They wish for the ocean . . . ?

DIANE: And he finds a lamp and it's an Irish genie. So here he still only gets one wish. So without thinking he says, "I want the . . . ." So the Irish genie speaks with [Irish accent] a brogue, you know. So he gets one wish and he says quickly, "I want the whole ocean to turn into the finest brew." So the genie disappears. . . .

DANIEL: Why does the genie have to be Irish just because the protagonists are Irish, or the genie have to be Jewish because the protagonists are Jewish?

DIANE: Cultural continuity.

DANIEL: [disdainfully] Cultural continuity!

DIANE: Cultural continuity, that's my whole explanation.

DANIEL: There's no explanation.

DIANE: It also makes it easier because I don't have to switch brogues . . . and I'm good at the Yiddish one, and I'm good at the Irish one.

DANIEL: Yeah. But you could also do English.

DIANE: It's boring.

DANIEL: It's not boring if one of them is speaking in the accent. I mean, the genie says, "You only have one wish." [Yiddish accent], "One wish." There's contrast there.

DIANE: Then I'd make it a God-like one.

DANIEL: Yeah. You could change . . . you could make it a more imperious voice.

DIANE: I like the cultural consistency there. "It's a [Yiddish accent] Jewish genie."

DANIEL: Well, you've always told it that way. It doesn't necessarily make it a better joke.

DIANE: Oh yes it does.

There are several points about which Daniel and Diane are in agreement. Both regard jokes as objects that merit aesthetic evaluation and critical response. There are "good" and "bad" jokes, and for both of these tellers, the joke about the genie in the lamp on the Tel Aviv beach is one of the good ones; one worth telling and repeating. In fact, both said they had told this joke on many different occasions.

Not only do they feel that jokes merit aesthetic evaluation, but they are able to articulate this evaluation in abstract terms. This is not to say that they possess a systematized aesthetic philosophy or elaborate critical vocabulary. Yet the critical concepts and terminology they employ are more than mere assertions of preference or emotional resonance, and the criteria they invoke can theoretically be extended to very different examples and are, to some extent, empirically verifiable.[6]

Daniel, for example, emphasized notions of contrast. Characters should differ from one another. The genie should not speak with the same accent as the man on the beach.[7] Diane seemed insensitive to or uninterested in such contrast. She regarded the image of an Irish or Jewish genie as funny in itself. In her opinion, they enriched the joke.[8] She also found that making the joke characters of the same ethnicity created an opportunity for extended dialect performance—a type of performance at which Diane felt she excelled. When challenged by Daniel to explain why the genie and the man had to be of the same ethnicity, she came up with the term "cultural continuity." It was meant to sound authoritative, but it was a facetious term invented by Diane on the spur of the moment to justify her preference. Daniel dismissed it immediately, and Diane went on to explain that joke performance was easier when she did not have to switch dialects.

Daniel agreed that the idea of a Jewish genie was in itself funny, but he felt that the joke revolved around the dialogue between the genie and the old Jewish man. Giving a genie a Jewish (or Irish) accent, he thought, reduced the contrast in the exchange and weakened the joke. It called attention away from what the joke had to accomplish. Even if there were a joke in which a Jewish genie appeared, the humor of that image would depend on its contrast with the other characters. "Cultural continuity" was not something that Daniel wanted to establish in the joke.

Daniel also felt that some of Diane's language was protracted and excessive. He didn't see the need for the elaborated dialogue in which the genie expresses his relief at being released from the lamp, his challenge to the man to make his single wish a good one, or the elaboration of the problems that plague the Middle East through the enumeration of various ethnic and religious groups. For Daniel, they seemed to lengthen the joke without contributing significantly to its point—to its punchline.

In another joke that was told that evening, the question of contrast arose again. In this case, both tellers formulated their jokes in terms of contrast, but they developed the contrast differently.

DIANE: This guy gets thrown in jail, and it's on a minor real estate deal, but he gets thrown in a really bad . . . I don't remember this joke [laughs]. I'm faltering. And he gets . . . his cellmate becomes this huge black guy, and his name is Bubba [Diane laughs]. He says [black accent], "While you is in here," he says, "you is either gonna be the man—the husband—or you're gonna be the wife." He says [no accent], "You make your choice right now. . . . Honky [Diane laughs]" I remember now. "Well, I guess I want to be the husband." See, there's a change there. [Black accent] "Well, come over here and suck your wife's dick."

DANIEL: Now, see the way I told it, there was this Jewish guy who got caught—accountant who got caught—embezzling and sent to the state penitentiary.

DIANE: I wouldn't make him Jewish.

DANIEL: And he was very, very nervous. On the first day he comes in, they give him his uniform, they give him his blanket, and the guard leads him up to his cell, and they close the door.

DIANE: That's good.

DANIEL: And he's standing in there. There's this huge guy, bald, hairy chest, huge prison muscles . . .

DIANE: Is he black?

DANIEL: No. And tattoos. And he sorta nods, the Jewish guy nods to him. And the guy says [slow gruff voice], "One thing we got to get straight in here. You gonna be the husband or you gonna be the wife?" The accountant thinks about it for a few seconds, he says, [higher quivering voice] "Well, if it's a matter of choice, I think I'd like to be the husband." He says, "Fine! Get over here and suck your wife's dick."

DIANE: [Laughing] It's a great joke. No matter. You set the scene better. I haven't told it in a while.

DANIEL: I think the Jewish works better because, you know, you got this frail guy, you know, he's scared. All that comes through.

DIANE: Woody Allen!

DANIEL: Yeah. You get this Woody Allen kind of picture, so the contrast is between this guy in the cell and this accountant guy.

Both tellers recognize the need for contrast in this joke. Diane frames the contrast between the characters as one between a "huge black guy" and a presumably white guy, who is sent to jail for some white-collar crime. In the joke, she calls the black guy "Bubba." When Diane told this joke at the dinner party, Daniel challenged her on the name Bubba, as it wasn't a black, but a redneck, name. Another guest at the party—who did not particularly like the joke—nevertheless agreed with Daniel that "Bubba" seemed inappropriate.[9] Diane owned up to its inappropriateness. However, when she told the joke again at the dinner where she and Daniel were recorded, she continued to use the name "Bubba." Diane liked the way "Bubba" sounded, even if it was unsuited for the joke character it designated. For her it was a triumph of sound over sense.

Daniel said that he recast the character in the joke as a Jewish accountant. He had not heard it that way. In fact, he thought—although he was not certain—that he first learned the joke from Diane. He felt that the contrast between a timorous Jewish accountant and a hairy, muscle-bound, prison hulk served to polarize the characters better than a mere opposition between white and black figures could. This was a contrast that Daniel felt had to be developed, and could not be carried by a mere labeling of ethnic or racial differences. To some extent, Diane seems to have agreed with him as she admitted that Daniel "set the scene better."

DIANE: What's the other one I liked so much? Oh, that's the one. It came from you, but I think I tell it good. It's about the German soldier coming into the French village. . . . That's a fine joke. . . . This German soldier comes into the French village and finds the French maiden hiding in the barn. And he has his way with her. And as he's zipping up his pants he says [German accent], "And if in nine months a beautiful Aryan child should emerge from this union, you might call him Fritz." She says to him [French accent], "And if in a couple of weeks some strange spots come up on you private parts, you might call it measles." That's a good one.

DANIEL: First of all, I set it in World War I, not World War II.

DIANE: I didn't set it in World War . . . I didn't say that.

Daniel: Well, you did. But you did when you said a "beautiful Aryan child." That makes it World War II.[10]

Diane: Ahhh. That dates it. Oh, silly *moi*.

Daniel: So I make it in World War I. I have him come across her in the field. He throws her down and has his way with her. And he says [accent], "And if in nine months you bear a child you may call him Fritz, if you please." And she says, "And if in three weeks you find a rash all over your body, you may call it measles if *you* please."

Diane: Private parts. I like private parts.

Daniel: It doesn't matter. I think the important thing is the "If you please." In fact, it doesn't end with "You may call it measles"—stop. I think the "if you please" adds something.

Diane: Oh, I don't. I don't because I think it matches what the German has said. "You might call him Fritz."

Daniel: So does this. He's also said, "You may call him Fritz, if you please."

Diane: Oh, he said "If you please"? Oh, I never, after a rape like that . . .

Daniel: So there's a balance, a parallelism.

Diane: That's incongruous. Would you put your panties down?

Daniel felt that reference to an Aryan child relocates the joke from World War I to World War II. As he later revealed, this second war was too close and too sensitive for the setting of a joke that involves a rape. Diane seems to agree with him, although when she was re-recorded almost three months later, the reference to an "Aryan child" was retained in her performance.

In evaluating this joke, both tellers address the issue of parallelism in expression. What the French maiden says to the soldier must be similar to what the soldier said to the maiden. Both Daniel and Diane value such parallelism. This is a joke in which retribution is revealed in the formulation of a verbal expression. Daniel, however, prefers a parallelism that extends to the phrase "If you please," while Diane finds the courteous phrase implausible in the context of the rape.

When asked about it later, Daniel characterized the phrase as consistent with the patronizing demeanor of the soldier. He felt that the seeming courtesy was mere arrogance, and it was fitting that the maiden's retaliation should be couched in the very same terms. Daniel further insisted that it was a matter of meter. The "if-you-please" extension sounded right. He felt that Diane's version ended too abruptly. The three-word extension gave each of the character's expressions a metrical momentum that intensified the parallelism and heightened the sense of revenge.

Matters of contrast and parallelism figure centrally in Daniel and Diane's evaluation of the following joke.

DIANE: Sir Francis Drake in the Golden Hind? I must have told you.

DANIEL: No. I don't think so.

DIANE: Sailing the seven seas, and they look on this man as a noble, wonderful leader. And the modus operandi on the ship is that when the guy in the crow's nest sees an enemy sail, he screams out, "Enemy sail off the port quarter!"

DANIEL: Oh!

DIANE: The first mate goes down. . . . You know this?

DANIEL: Go ahead.

DIANE: Goes down to the captain's cabin and says, "Captain Sir, [low class English accent] "we spotted an enemy sail." And Sir Francis emerges from the cabin, and he's the picture of nobility and calm. And he comes on the deck and routinely says, "Glass!" And he pops [claps hands] the glass in his hand, and he studies the sail, and he pops [claps hands] the glass closed, and he hands it back to his first mate. And invariably he'll ask, "Bring me my red cape." And he swirls into this red cape, and he leads them into battle, and they fight like fools for him. Never get a scratch and never lose a battle. One day they were sailing along and the first mate says [accent], "Meaning no disrespect sir," he says, "why is it when we go into battle you always wear that red cape?" And Sir Francis strikes a pose of nobility, and he says [upper class English accent], "Should I shed blood in the course of the battle I wouldn't want our crew to fight with less valor that they need to conquer our foes." So now they think he's God-like, awesome leader. So one day they're sailing along and, a little historic license, but the guy in the crow's nest looks, and they're surrounded by the Spanish Armada. Three hundred and sixty degrees of enemy sail closing in. And he fast loses it. And the crew sees they're in deep trouble. And the first mate as always runs down, but he's so excited he can hardly get it out. "Sir Francis Drake." And he emerges, and just at the mere sight of him on deck the crew starts to settle down because things are in hand. Comes up on the quarter deck and says, "Glass!" Pops the glass in his hand and does a three-sixty of all these enemy sail, really closing in now. Pops the glass closed, and he hands it back to the first mate and says, "Bring me my brown pants."

Daniel then delivered his version of the joke.

DANIEL: In the days of the Barbary pirates, an American man-o-war was patrolling in the Mediterranean. One day the first mate comes running up to the captain yelling, "Captain, captain! Pirate ship off the starboard bow." The captain says to the mate, "Fetch me my telescope." The mate fetches the telescope, and the captain looks through it, and sure enough, there is a pirate ship off the starboard bow. He commands the mate, "Call the men to their battle stations, and bring me my sword and my red cape." The mate gives the order to battle stations, and fetches the sword and cape. The captain dons his cape, and the ship engages the enemy, and they are victorious. The next day as they are sailing along, the mate runs up shouting, "Captain, captain! Pirate ship off the port bow." Captain says, bring me my telescope." The mate brings the telescope. The captain peers through it, and sure enough, there's a pirate ship off the port bow. The captain says, "Bring me my sword and my red cape." The mate fetches them, they engage the pirates and are again successful. After the battle is over, and the smoke clears, the mate comes up to the captain and says, "I understand why you call for your telescope, and I understand why you call for your sword, but why do you call for your red cape?" The captain says, "Because, if in the course of battle I am wounded, my blood will not show, and the men will not become demoralized." The mate nods and goes about his duties. The next day the mate comes running up, "Captain, captain! There's a pirate fleet off the starboard bow." The captain says, "Bring me my telescope." The mate brings him the telescope. The captain looks through the telescope and sees a pirate fleet bearing down on his ship. He looks at his mate and says, "Bring me my sword and my brown pants." I think the sword works well. You don't use the sword.

DIANE: I don't. No.

DANIEL: Why not?

DIANE: It's a waste. I mean a battle's a battle.

DANIEL: It's not a waste.

DIANE: Of course they're gonna use weapons, but you don't have to say it. It's implied.

DANIEL: No it's not.

DIANE: Gestalt.

DANIEL: Bullshit! Stop making up terms to explain your failure to include the sword [both laugh]. . . . He's going into battle. He wants his sword and his red cape. . . . And you don't set the three-fold pattern in that joke. You only do it once.

DIANE: Well, I only have limited time when I'm giving my talk, and it's very efficient to tell it that way. Keeps their attention . . . ."[11] "Bring me my sword and brown pants." It just loses the meter of . . . "bring me my brown pants."

DANIEL: No. It doesn't. No. "Bring me my sword" because it sets up the we're going to engage in battle, and my brown pants, this time I'm gonna shit. It seems to me that the sword really helps. Instead of just dumping them with the brown pants.

DIANE: I've told this joke for years.

DANIEL: So have I.

DIANE: Same joke, again and again.

DANIEL: So have I, so have I.

DIANE: And just in terms of stress, and then I work it into my. . . . I've never had a sword in it once.

DANIEL: But this works too. I mean. . . .

DIANE: I feel like it's got to be in small, neat packages.

DANIEL: "Bring me my sword" doesn't substantially enlarge the joke.

DIANE: But the focus to me is on the cape.

DANIEL: And the three-fold pattern focuses still upon the cape, because the mate is willing to put that focus on the cape. He's gonna ask the question, "I understand why you bring—why you ask—for your sword, but why the red cape? 'Cause if in the course of the battle I'm wounded, you know, blood won't show and my crew won't become depressed.'"

The fact that the tellers set the joke in different centuries and different seas is not a matter of real concern to either of them. The dispute between them focuses upon issues of contrast and meter. Daniel does not like the fact that Diane's rendition lacks the three-fold structure with the ship first encountering an enemy vessel on the right, then on the left, and culminating in a confrontation with an entire fleet. Daniel feels that the pattern of asking for the sword and cape needs two repetitions to be effectively established (see Olrik 1965:133). Diane is satisfied that a pattern can be established in a single scene. She claims this is more efficient—although her rendition of the joke was not shorter than Daniel's.

Daniel also emphasized the importance of the captain asking for his sword *and* his red cape. Daniel explained that the sword and cape characterize the captain as man of action and valor, although the valorous significance of the cape has to be explicated in the joke text. The sword and cape come to complement one other. In the punchline, this association is disrupted when the switch from red cape to brown pants reveals the captain to be a coward. Daniel also felt that the meter was better with the incremental repetition of "sword and red cape," "sword and red cape," and "sword and brown pants," while Diane felt the meter was better when the cape and pants stood alone.

The point is not really to assess which joke versions or performances are better. The point is to try to understand why Daniel and Diane—two accomplished joke tellers—develop and prefer the performances that they do, and to grasp something of the aesthetic criteria they employ in the evaluation of jokes. Many of the differences in their approach to the joke texts and performances reported here seems to revolve around a single comprehensive difference: the difference between narrative and theater. Diane's jokes are theatrical. Diane employs changes of voice, dialect, and mimicry to a very high degree. When telling jokes she invariably employs exaggerated facial expressions, gestures, and pronounced bodily movements. For example, in the joke about Sir Francis Drake and the Spanish Armada, Diane did not merely describe the figure of Sir Francis Drake; she acted out the part. When Sir Francis emerges on the deck of the ship cool, calm, and collected, Diane moves her body to portray the character she is describing. She flutters her eyelashes, turns her neck slowly from side to side, and puts up her hands to frame her face and head as though a glow emanated from it in order to convey Sir Francis's calm and self-possession. When Sir Francis pops the telescope open and shut, she claps her hands in accompaniment. She pretends to bring a telescope to her eye to scan for enemy sail. She makes the appropriate motions when Sir Francis swirls into his red cape. She employs high- and low-class British accents to distinguish the speech of Sir Francis from his first mate.

Daniel does little of this. What he conveys he conveys in words. Almost everything is encoded in the joke text. It seems that he stresses the importance of the sword in the joke, because the sword represents the captain's courage and martial spirit. This signification is magnified in the explication of the reasons for the red cape. Sword and red cape serve as a formula for courage and intrepidity. The captain's final request for his sword once again would signify these traits, but in the climactic shift to brown pants, the captain's heroic posturing is undone.

Diane does not need a sword because she employed many words and gestures to characterize the nobility and vainglory of Sir Francis. For her, the brown pants alone can serve to shatter her elaborately crafted persona. As Daniel employs no verbal or body language to create the image of a brave or noble hero, the audience's impression of the captain heavily depends on his calling for his weapon, his ordering an attack on the enemy, and his explication of the red cape. No total persona has been created. There are only the captain's words and his reported actions.

Diane seems to remember and favor jokes that provide latitude for histrionic treatment. Each of the eleven jokes that she told or commented on during the dinner when she was recorded, were told with dialect or some other pronounced vocal or bodily mimicry. For Diane, a joke is a vehicle for a theatrical performance. Daniel, while not avoiding dialect and gesture, employs them much more sparingly. He used a low gruff voice and a higher, tremulous voice to emphasize the difference between the Jewish accountant and his prison cellmate. He also used a Yiddish accent for the man on the beach who releases the genie from the lamp. But dialect, mimicry, and gesture primarily served to accentuate the structure of the joke and to heighten its surprising effect. Daniel prefers jokes that are clever, that is, that depend on an abrupt and unexpected shift in conceptualization. Jokes for Daniel are not primarily theatrical performances but intellectual puzzles that have to be solved. The art of the joke for Daniel would seem to be the delineation of a puzzle with an unexpected, elegant, though immediately accessible solution.[12]

This difference in approach was actually articulated in the course of their dinner conversation. Daniel had finished telling a joke about clergymen and miracles. Diane agreed that it was a wonderful joke. Then Diane brought up a joke about a hunter. Daniel had learned that joke from Diane, and he said he had told it on a number of occasions. He recalled telling it during deer-hunting season to some friends who lived in the country. At that point, Diane started to repeat certain lines from that joke; lines that, even Daniel admitted, demanded vocal and behavioral mimicry if the joke were to succeed. Daniel agreed with Diane that it was a "good joke," but he immediately qualified his praise with, "but you know, it's not a clever joke." Referring back to the joke he told about the clergymen and miracles, he continued, "That's conceptually a brilliant joke."

As feedback is a critical force in artistic performance, it seems necessary to ask how much Daniel and Diane's criticisms ultimately affected the other's performances. After all, Daniel agreed with Diane that the idea of a Jewish genie was an idea with good comic possibilities. He was also impressed with her rendition of the captain and his first mate in high- and low-class British accents. Likewise, Diane admitted that there might be some problem in employing the name "Bubba" for the black cellmate and that Daniel had "set the scene better" in that joke. She acknowledged as well that referring to the "Aryan child" in the joke about the German soldier and French maiden might be questionable. How did the criticisms and these admissions affect their subsequent joke telling behaviors?

As far as I can tell (I have since had a number of opportunities to observe, since at the time of this writing it is some years since the original dinner party), their joke telling was not affected at all. Daniel never gave the genie a Jewish accent, nor did he try to employ dialect in the joke about the captain and the pirates (which also would have required a switch from an American to a British scenario). Diane did not set the joke up with a frightened Jewish accountant, and she continued to characterize the cellmate as black and to name him "Bubba." (She said she liked the sound of the name and the way she vocalized it in the joke.) Nor did she remove the reference to the Aryan child from her joke about the German soldier and the French peasant girl.

This unwillingness to respond to the critique of the other may be rooted, in part, in the competitive nature of their joke telling. For either Daniel or Diane to respond to the other's criticism would be something of an admission of defeat. It would, in effect, establish the other as a superior joke stylist. But it is the fundamental differences in their styles that stand as the greatest impediment to change in performance. These styles are not purely matters of disinterested aesthetic intention. Daniel and Diane are two different personalities, and their joke aesthetics are an extension of their personalities.[13]

Diane performs almost everything. Her performed expressions occur in virtually all situations and venues from meals to movies to social encounters. At a meal, for example, those around will be sure to learn of her evaluation of the food, not merely as a verbal statement but as a performed expression. Prolonged "ahs" and "hmmms" can mark the tasting of each and every dish. At movies, sighs, groans, and laughter leave those around her with little doubt as to her opinion of that segment of the film. In meeting new people—waiters, clerks, or even people on the street—she will often engage them comically in a loud voice that others in the shop, restaurant, or on the street corner can overhear. She creates a situation in which she is in control of a comic scenario.

She seems unable to resist this role. Once after she underwent a serious surgery, the surgeon told her she needed to rest and not move about. Nevertheless, she insisted on being the center of attention for those who were visiting her, jumping up from the floor to engage in some mimicry or other comic antic until one of her guests actually yelled at her to sit down and remain still as the surgeon had instructed. She was only able to follow that instruction for a short while before she was again engaged in some performance with full bodily involvement.

Daniel, no less than Diane, has a comedic persona. Humor is as central to his sense of and presentation of self as it is to Diane. But unlike Diane, he does not attempt to hold the center of attention on a full-time basis. He seems to prefer to hang back and let others hold the floor until he can deliver a comic line of appropriateness and force. He is more distant and aloof. Daniel reported that in his youth he was always coming out with one-liners from the back of the classroom. All through school, he liked sitting in the back of the classroom because he could see everything yet not be seen. He envisioned his comic interjections at school as emanating from a "disembodied voice," although he was well aware that everyone in the class knew who made them. Daniel's humor puts an emphasis on the verbal and serves more as a commentary on what is going on than as the driving force of the social action. Even Daniel's tellings of canned jokes tend to be triggered by an association to or commentary on the ongoing social interaction.

Daniel is more of a jester while Diane is more of a clown. Like a jester, Daniel listens to what others are saying and then offers a humorous remark or retort. Diane, however, is more likely to be the entire act. Like a clown, she employs an array of verbal, vocal, and kinetic techniques to create a scenario that can stand on its own. She is both the performer and the performance. So when it comes to joke telling, the joke narrative itself is only a facet of a more comprehensive comedic expression.

This is largely why their criticisms provoked no changes in the other's performances. Their joke telling performances are expressions of their comedic personas and ultimately their personalities. They are no more likely to change their styles of performance then they are to change from being right-handed to left-handed. One changes handedness in the event of some trauma that renders the preferred hand unusable. What might make Daniel and Diane change their joke-telling styles would be the trauma of repeated joke-performance failure. But, because Daniel and Diane tell jokes frequently and regularly receive positive feedback from their audiences, neither is likely to change a performance strategy that has proven successful *and* seems so much a product of who they are.[14]

Philosopher Noël Carroll believes jokes to be less than art because there is so little room for interpretive play in them: "The organization of the joke is . . . so parsimonious that any attempt to reflect upon the text and its interpretation for any period of time is likely to be very unrewarding. Jokes are not designed for contemplation—one cannot standardly review them in search of subtle nuances that inflect, enrich, or expand our interpretations" (1991:294).[15] In fact, the minutiae of joke construction and expression are precisely what Daniel and Diane argue about. For these performers, "subtle nuances" are at the core of joke aesthetics. Both feel that a word, an intonation, a repetition, a parallelism, or a heightened contrast makes a joke succeed or fail. The change of a word or inflection can, in fact, radically alter the interpretation of a joke and the ability to articulate what its message might be (Oring 2003:27–40).[16] Of course, Carroll has considered the joke as a type, not as an individual expression. The interpretative possibilities of a novel, poem, or painting might look equally limited were the genres themselves the objects of contemplation rather than particular novels, poems, or paintings. The formulation "initial situation, complication, resolution" might appear as thin a basis for an aesthetic evaluation of the dramatic novel as "incongruity resolution" might for an aesthetic evaluation of the joke. When philosophers seek to write about jokes as art, perhaps it would be a good idea to base their reflections on joke performances—that is, the observation of real joke tellers telling real jokes in real joke telling situations—rather than contemplate formulations of what jokes are supposed to be.

Notes

1. See for example, Morreall (1981:55–70), Martin (1987:172–86), Cohen (1983:120–36; 1998), Gaut (1998:51–68), and Carroll (2003). While these concerns have also been

of interest to scholars in other disciplines, they have not been generally conceptualized as aesthetic issues.

2. This view would be close to the notion of art as "significant form" (Bell 1958:19), but it does not presume that the aesthetic experience is purely a formal one. Form is what characterizes something as art. It is what provokes aesthetic attention. The aesthetic experience, however, depends upon the interrelation of form and content and their resonances for the individual—including purely subjective factors. The parts, the ideas and values connoted by the parts, their emotional valences, and their organization, mutually influence one another and bear upon this experience. The experience is a synthetic one.

3. I have no problem with the notion that a performer's audience may on occasion only include himself, as when a magician, mime, or dancer practices a routine alone in front of a mirror.

4. Folk aesthetics deals with the principles that govern aesthetic expression and reception in particular social or cultural groups. I use the term here to refer to any native aesthetic, even if only ascribed to a single individual. See Michael Owen Jones, "The Concept of 'Aesthetic' in the Traditional Arts," *Western Folklore* 30(1971):77–104.

5. This was the creation of an "induced natural context" (Goldstein 1967).

6. This is different from the kinds of evaluations that, for example, Michael Owen Jones heard from the chair makers that he studied in Kentucky (1971:96–99) or that Kenneth S. Goldstein was able to elicit from his own Anglo-American informants over a period of some forty years (1991:164–78).

7. Conforming, it would seem, with Axel Olrik's "Law of Contrast" for characters in a folk narrative (1965:135).

8. We might refer to this as *comic embedding;* the embedding of humorous images and phrases in a joke that are not essential to the success of the punchline of the joke.

9. "Bubba" is a Southern nickname derived from the word "brother" that is generally applied to elder brothers. It is often attached to large men of intimidating mien. Often a white—indeed "redneck"—sobriquet (Jenkins 1993), it is also applied to and used by blacks: William "Bubba" Paris, Charles Richard "Bubba" Wells, Daniel Lamont "Bubba" Franks, and Richard Stephen "Bubba" Crosby. It is also the name of Forrest Gump's black friend—Benjamin Buford "Bubba" Blue—in the film *Forrest Gump* (Zemeckis 1994).

10. Actually, "Aryan" was a recognized term for a racial category in the nineteenth century. It was employed as part of theories of history before World War I, most notably in the works of Houston Stewart Chamberlain. It was most frequently contrasted with "Semite." The politicization of these racial distinctions during the Nazi period gave the term a greater association with World War II.

11. Diane had said that she used this joke to open the workshops that she gave on stress management. She characterized it as a "stress joke," and she would tell

her audiences that she hoped that their levels of stress did not require a change of costume. Daniel claimed never to have heard Diane tell this joke before. He was surprised that she knew it. He had learned his version many years before, and was surprised that he had never told it to Diane.

12. Although I have no reason to believe that the differences between Daniel and Diane are attributable to their genders, it has been remarked that the differences between male and female comedians in Tubetube in Milne Bay Province, Papua New Guinea seem to turn on just such differences (Macintyre 1992:142).

13. I have not subjected either Daniel or Diane to any standardized personality assessment protocols. The differences I note are based on my own long-term, personal observations. For an example of such protocols in the analysis of jokes, see Burns with Burns (1976).

14. For another comparative assessment of joke performance which seems to depend on a difference in the personalities of the joke tellers see Bronner (1984:18–36).

15. I do not understand why art demands "contemplation"—a position that even Glassie would seem to endorse (1989:86). The contemplative response seems to limit art to the domain of Western fine arts and museum and gallery experience. That is why Robert Plant Armstrong tried to replace the term "art" with "affecting presences" (Armstrong 1971).

16. Richard Raskin holds that some jokes are open to multiple interpretations. He also holds such jokes to be aesthetically superior to "closed" jokes, but there is no reason to accept his view on this point (1992:25, 30–32). Carroll also recognizes the possibility of multiple interpretations of jokes (2003:359).

References

Armstrong, Robert Plant. 1971. *The Affecting Presence: An Essay in Humanistic Anthropology.* Urbana: University of Illinois Press.

Bascom, William. 1955. Verbal Art. *Journal of American Folklore* 68:245–52.

Bauman, Richard. 1992. Performance. In *Folklore, Cultural Performances, and Popular Entertainments,* ed. Richard Bauman, pp. 41–49. New York: Oxford University Press.

Beardsley, Monroe C. 1958. *Aesthetics: Problems in the Philosophy of Criticism.* New York: Harcourt Brace.

Bell, Clive. 1958 [1913]. *Art.* New York: Capricorn.

Ben-Amos, Dan. 1971. Toward a Definition of Folklore in Context. *Journal of American Folklore* 84:3–15.

Bronner, Simon J. 1984. "Let Me Tell It My Way": Joke Telling by a Father and Son. *Western Folklore* 43:18–36.

"Bubba." n.d. *Wikipedia.* s.v. "bubba."

Burns, Thomas A. with Inger H. Burns. 1976. *Doing the Wash: An Expressive Culture and Personality Study of a Joke and Its Tellers.* Norwood: Norwood.

Carroll, Noël. 1991. On Jokes. *Midwest Studies in Philosophy* 16:280–301.

———. 2003. Humour. In *The Oxford Handbook of Aesthetics,* ed. Jerrold Levinson, pp. 344–65. Oxford: Oxford University Press.

Cohen, Ted. 1983. Jokes. In *Pleasure, Preference, and Value: Studies in Philosophical Aesthetics,* ed. Eva Schaper, pp. 120–36. Cambridge: Cambridge University Press.

———. 1998. Jokes. In *Encyclopedia of Aesthetics,* ed. Michael Kelly, 3:9–12. New York: Oxford University Press.

Dorson, Richard M. 1972. *Folklore: Selected Essays.* Bloomington: Indiana University Press.

———. 1976. *Folklore and Fakelore: Essays towards a Discipline of Folk Studies.* Cambridge, MA: Harvard University Press.

Gaut, Berys. 1998. Just Joking: The Ethics and Aesthetics of Humor. *Philosophy and Literature* 22:51–68.

Glassie, Henry. 1989. *The Spirit of Folk Art: The Girard Collection at the Museum of International Folk Art.* New York: Harry N. Abrams.

Goldstein, Kenneth S. 1967. The Induced Natural Context: An Ethnographic Folklore Field Technique. In *Essays on the Verbal and Visual Arts.* Proceedings of the 1966 Annual Spring Meeting of the American Ethnological Society, pp. 1–6. Seattle: University of Washington Press.

———. 1991. Notes towards a European-American Folk Aesthetic. *Journal of American Folklore* 104:164–78.

Jenkins, Dan. 1993. *Bubba Talks of His Life, Love, Sex. Whiskey, Food, Foreigners, Teenagers, Football and Other Matters That Occasionally Concern Human Beings.* New York: Doubleday.

Jones, Michael Owen. 1971. The Concept of "Aesthetic" in the Traditional Arts. *Western Folklore* 30: 77–104.

Macintyre, Martha. 1992. Reflections of an Anthropologist Who Mistook Her Husband for a Yam: Female Comedy on Tubetube. In *Clowning as Critical Practice: Performance Humor in the South Pacific,* ed. William E. Mitchell, pp. 130–44. Pittsburgh: University of Pittsburgh Press.

Martin, Mike W. 1987. Humor and Aesthetic Enjoyment of Incongruities. In *The Philosophy of Laughter and Humor,* ed. John Morreall, pp. 172–86. Albany: State University Press of New York.

Morreall, John. 1981. Humor and Aesthetic Education. *Journal of Aesthetic Education* 15:55–70.

Olrik, Axel. 1965 [1909]. Epic Laws of Folk Narrative. In *The Study of Folklore,* ed. Alan Dundes, pp. 129–41. Englewood Cliffs: Prentice-Hall.

Oring, Elliott. 2003. *Engaging Humor.* Urbana: University of Illinois Press.

Raskin, Richard. 1992. *Life is Like a Glass of Tea: Studies of Classic Jewish Jokes.* Aarhus, Denmark: Aarhus University Press.

Reid, Louis Arnaud. 1931. *A Study in Aesthetics.* New York: Macmillan.
Zemeckis, Robert. 1994. *Forrest Gump.* Prod. Steve Tisch, Wendy Finerman, and Steve Starkey. 142 minutes. Paramount, videocassette.

Jim Quine, Robert "Chubby" Wise, George Custer, and Richard Seaman at the First Coast Folklife Exploration, Jacksonville, Florida

Vernacular Interpretation in a Public Folklore Event: Listening to the Call of Florida Fiddlers, Three

Gregory Hansen

Presenting folklife to audiences outside of academe offers opportunities and poses challenges unique to public folklore programming. In public folklore, the folklorist may develop and coordinate a wide array of presentations, ranging from producing studio recordings of traditional music, designing exhibits of folk art, coordinating educational programs in schools and community organizations, producing radio shows, and directing folklife festivals (Baron and Spitzer 1992; Belanus and Hansen 2000; Feintuch 1998; Hufford 1994; Jones 1994; Kurin 1997; Wilson and Udall 1982). The distinctive venues all provide new opportunities for folklorists to teach the wider public about both the content of folklore and the discipline of folklife studies. Folklorists working in the public and private sectors, however, face major challenges in finding effective modes of cultural interpretation within these non-academic settings, thereby managing a disputed distinctions between academic and public discourses (Kirshenblatt-Gimblett 1992:32). Simply stated, the approaches and formats used in public programming are different from those found in scholarly books and articles. Academic theories and esoteric interpretations have little currency among those attending public folklore events, and public folklorists have to avoid overly arcane cultural interpretations as they coordinate their public presentations of folk culture. These presentations generally must develop the interpretation outside the frame of scholarly conventions. Rather than citing scholarship and making theoretical arguments, folklorists have to take different approaches in crafting public presentations for non-specialized audiences. Public folklorists must synthesize what they know about the specific cultural tradition with their broader understanding of folklore by crafting presentations that are accessible, engaging, appropriate, and effective to a wide and diverse audience (Kurin 1997:14–20).

The enterprise of public folklore is not always fully embraced by folklorists. A common critique is that public folklore frequently provides an unnatural, even distorted, context for highly esoteric forms of cultural expression (Bauman 1992:106). Some critics argue that the staging of folk expression fosters a celebratory view of culture that blunts the critical edge of those engaged in cultural critique (Kirshenblatt-Gimblett 1992:44). Others focus on the apparent lack of theoretical sophistication in public programming (Ben-Amos 1998:268). Another common critique is directed specifically at public folklore and more generally at folklore as a discipline. Richard Handler argues that bracketing particular forms of culture as "folklife" in a public program creates a highly romanticized and distorted representation of culture, and his critique fits with broader concerns about the historical roots of romantic nationalism in folklore as a discipline (Handler 1988:63; see also Abrahams 1994:79 and Cantwell 1993:151). Articles and monographs delve into problems inherent in knowing that those participating in public folklore events as performers, artists, or raconteurs may have very different ideas about the tradition and its place within the event than the folklorists who coordinate the presentations (Bauman, Sawin, and Carpenter 1992). The list of critiques could continue, but it is important to realize that public folklorists themselves are engaged with challenges of this kind as they reflect on their work and evaluate, critique, and reconceptualize their approaches (Green 2001:153–54, Hawes 2008:129–33). Criticisms offered by academic folklorists and within the sphere of public folklorists alike have led to new ways of thinking about folklore, but there tends to be something lost in the sometimes cacophonic dialogue about public folklore. Namely, in valorizing the voice of the critical folklorist, we tend to ignore the vernacular theorist's voice. As Henry Glassie asserts, theory is not exclusively the property of the educated elite (Glassie 1999:9). Rather, theory includes the abstract principles that creative individuals use in quotidian experience. Bringing the voice of vernacular theorists into the din of criticism that surrounds public folklore reveals the value of looking at ways in which folk artists interpret their own arts when presenting their cultural traditions on stage.

The festival stage is a site where spontaneous, even improvised, expressions of meaning emerge in the public sphere (Cantwell 1993: 247). Through fieldwork, the public folklorist works to ascertain a sense of the competence that supports a performance. Effective public presentations convey aspects of that understanding to an audience. What audience members learn from the presentation is often a highly individualized, even opaque, impression of the tradition because folklife festivals are what Robert Byington termed "low resolution media" (Kurin 1997:36 and 131). This low-resolution quality adds to the challenges of developing cultural interpretation within public folklore events.

Visitors attend festivals for a variety of reasons. Participants also have a variety of motives for displaying their arts, telling their stories, sharing their personal experiences, and performing their music and dances on the festival stage. Public folklorists must recognize this diversity and broker different understandings of the significance of the cultural traditions showcased in display events. The challenge of providing cultural interpretation at these events doesn't mean that academic training is moot. Rather, considering a display event, such as a folklife festival, as "festival" rather than a scholarly presentation opens up new opportunities for cultural interpretation (Kurin 1997:153). In this respect, the festival site becomes a fine space for placing what folklorists have learned into public discourse and broadening ideas about what constitutes cultural interpretation. The cultural interpretations at these events often emerge through conversations with the performers since the specialized vocabulary and theoretical orientation of the folklorist rarely resonates with the audience's interests. In this process, an important question emerges: How do the folk artists, musicians, dancers, cooks, storytellers, and other participants at a public display event convey the significance of their traditions to the audience?

There can be no one generalized answer to this broad question, but one virtuosic display of vernacular interpretation emerged on a folklife festival's workshop stage in a performance by three fiddlers from Florida. Bob Stone, a folklorist with the Florida Folklife Program mediated the First Coast Folklife Festival's presentation on April 3, 1993. His skill as a presenter anchored the interplay between the musicians. Together, the participants gave the audience a chance to understand how the musicians creatively blended experience, memory, music, and story to interpret their artistry vividly and in their own terms. Those who attended the event gained a better understanding of the importance of fiddling to three talented musicians by recognizing the value of interpersonal connections and aesthetic experience. Interacting with each other through their artistry, the fiddlers offered surprisingly unified views about history, community, spirituality, and artistry. Recognizing the value of their vernacular interpretation not only contributes to a wider understanding of America's fiddling tradition, but also opens up broader ways to analyze cultural traditions when we consider how artists themselves engage with vernacular theory.[1] By playing their music, telling their stories, and answering questions from a folklorist and each other, these fiddlers affirm the value of listening to performers' own interpretations of their own traditions.

The Players

The Saturday afternoon workshop was held at Jacksonville's Museum of Science and History's Carpenter-Gothic Church on the St. Johns River. Backed by Jim Quine, a guitarist with the bluegrass band Salt Run of St. Augustine, George Custer, Richard Seaman, and Robert "Chubby" Wise all shared their tunes and told their stories to an audience crowded into the small frame building. Although all were seasoned performers, this type of less formal workshop presentation was new to the musicians. To prepare them, the event's coordinator explained that the idea was to share their playing and answer questions posed by Stone. The three fiddlers were all highly skilled, and all were recognized with the Florida Department of State's "Florida Folk Heritage Award" for their contributions to the state's culture. This event was the only time all three fiddlers would ever perform together.

George Custer was born in Tift County, Georgia, into a musical family. Throughout his long career, Custer established himself as an important contributor to Florida's fiddle tradition by performing with bluegrass musicians, western swing bands, and classical musicians throughout the state. Richard Seaman was born in Kissimmee Park, Florida, in 1904. He learned to play old-time fiddle tunes by attending house parties as a boy, and his core repertory of tunes reaches back into the state's nineteenth-century musical traditions. Seaman moved to Jacksonville in the 1920s and played old-time and country music with local bands in the city through the 1950s. Wise was the most famous of the three fiddlers. Born in St. Augustine, Wise lived in many places in Florida as a young man (Noles 2002:53–62). During World War II, he launched a highly successful musical career as one of the first fiddlers with Bill Monroe's Bluegrass Boys, and he remained an active performer throughout his life.

The workshop's focus was to bring these musicians together to demonstrate styles of playing and discuss their music. Stone talked with the musicians prior to the event, telling them that this presentation would be different from a concert. The workshop would include playing tunes, but the more informal setting would also give them opportunities to answer questions and tell some stories about their experiences. This type of workshop setting is a familiar genre within folklife festivals, but it is not as commonly used in bluegrass festivals and country music shows. Nevertheless, all of the musicians were seasoned performers and had ample experience being interviewed. Stone developed his workshop questions from his own experience as a fiddler and through his extensive field research. The typical pattern he used to present the musicians in the workshop was to open with a musical selection and then offer an open-ended question or add a comment that invited a story.

History

Stone addressed his first question to Richard Seaman, asking him about his instrument. Seaman's answer shows how the specific question led to a wider connection between his own life and Florida's history. "Richard," Stone asked, "you've got a pretty good story on that fiddle of yours. Could you tell us that story?" He replied:

> Well, I come to Jacksonville from below Kissimmee, in 1926, and went to work for the railroads. While I was up here, my old fiddle was down home at my dad's place. When the '26 hurricane came, it destroyed Miami that time.
>
> It blowed the roof off of my daddy's house, and this old fiddle was laying on a table—up in the upstairs bedroom. Well, it got wet, naturally. So I drove down there to see how my folks were after the storm. Their house was roofless. Downed trees were everywhere. And I went up there and found my old fiddle all laying all over the floor. It was strung up, and when water got on it, I think it went off like a rattrap.
>
> Well, I gather it up, and I put it in an old shoebox. And I brought it up here. That was way back yonder during the Depression time, and I didn't have any money to have it fixed. So I kept it. So one day, I said, 'Why, I don't see why I can't fix this.'[2]
>
> I put it back together with clamps, and it looked pretty bad. It was rough, scratched, and beat up. I played it. One day, I think to myself, 'That looks terrible.' So I got myself a wood filler, and I went all over it. Sand it down, got me a three-dollar can of paint, and painted it black.
>
> So for three dollars and ten cents, I got it fixed!

Stone knew the basics of this story before he asked the question. He also recognized that musicians frequently have good stories about their instruments. His question employed a common fieldwork approach used in formal interviews. He began with a specific question about a cultural artifact. In the festival context, the meaning of the question shifted with the fiddler's answer. Rather than serving solely as a source of folkloristic data, Seaman transformed his answer into an artful narrative. He continued his narrative by linking his first fiddle to his home community's history of social dancing:

> I don't know how old it is. It was hanging up on the wall as far back as I can remember in the old house I was born in. It just hung there. My dad didn't play it. And after I got big enough to get around them woods they had square dances. It was the only means of entertainment we had: picnics and square dances. So I used to go around to the square dances, and I heard them old boys play. I liked that.
>
> I went home, and I was trying to learn it by ear. I wasn't doing too good, and one day one fellow says, "Say fellow, you've got to tune that fiddle before you play!"
>
> So I finally found out something about it and started playing along. And when I first started, my mother says, "I can't stand that. That's terrible. You can go outside."
>
> She made me go outside and sit on a stump. And one day she said, "Now the better you play, the closer you can get to the house."
>
> It was two years before I ever played a tune indoors!

Seaman's story has elements of the rich tall tale tradition that was also a major component of his artistic repertory. He used the story to elaborate on the significance of the fiddle within his family's history, and the tale's hyperbole shifts the story from the concrete particulars of his own experience in learning to play a challenging instrument. The shift from describing one historical event into crafting an artful narrative, however, opened up a greater historical truth, for his tale is resonant with experiences that both Chubby Wise and George Custer recounted in their stories. The stories and the interchange between artists also revealed wider patterns of culture that encompass the social context for the history. Chubby Wise's response to Seaman's story shows how this shift from individual experience to collective memory emerged in the presentation: "I know what you're talking about, though, because Ma didn't send me to that corncrib to shuck corn when I was learning there!"

George Custer directly confirmed this shift by contributing yet another story to the workshop's discussion:

This sounds almost like we've got the same script, but my dear little momma, a Georgia lady, just passed away here three or four years ago. It sounds like I'm telling an old story, but Granny Rutland, she started helping me, encouraging me to get started. I guess I was seven or eight years of age.[3]

Boy, I'd save up all my practicing for Saturday, and there's been many a time I'd go at it three and four hours, sometimes five and six. I remember now, little Momma very nicely saying, "Son, it sure is pretty weather outside. Don't you think you ought to play outside?"

Custer's story demonstrates how seeking out historical narratives, comparing them with other stories, and interpreting texts for meaning is a vibrant component of the musicians' artistry. He concluded, "Our stories are similar. I guess it just has to be part of your bloodstream or bone marrow to love to play the fiddle. It's the closest thing to the human voice, and it can communicate where words sometimes fail us."

Throughout the workshop, the process of vernacular cultural interpretation was embellished by the ways the musicians would play a tune, contextualize it within their life histories or the social history of their community, and often sharpen these earlier experiences by making comparisons between the past and the present. Their discussion of the social contexts for the early old-time square dance tunes played at Florida free-for-alls blended the modes of cultural interpretation used in living history programs with the ways of presenting contemporary culture used in folklife festivals (Kurin 1997:122). The history they captured in music, story, and memory became a vivid representation of folk culture, related in a way that is more immediate than can be conveyed solely through the printed page. Rather than talking or writing about history from second-hand accounts, the participants shared their own lived experiences of Florida's history.

Chubby Wise embodied one of the major shifts in the history of American fiddling. When Stone asked Wise to explain how he replaced Howdy Forrester as one of the early fiddlers in Bill Monroe's band, he explained:

I went to work for Bill either in '42 or '43. I was in Gainesville at the time with a group called Yulee's Hill-Billies, working out of WRUF. I heard Bill announce that Howdy was going into the Navy. That's how come I come to get the job.

He said, "I got to have a fiddler." He said, "My fiddler's going to the Navy, Big Howdy."

And I just caught a train and went to Nashville. And I walked in like a big dolt, and I said, "I'm from Florida and I play the fiddle and I want the job. I understand that you have it open."

And I'll never forget it. Bill was a very unconcerned type of fellow, you know. He was quick. He talked real fast—quick—there's just not any yes or no about it. He's just "that's it." So he said, "Do you know my stuff?"

And, of course, I didn't know too much. I had heard Howdy play a couple of things. And Howdy always played them double-stops on "Footprints in the Snow." Oh, it just slayed me. And I told Bill, I said, "Oh yeah, yes sir, I know them."

And I said, "How about 'Footprints in the Snow'? Let me play that one with you. I can play that one real good."

So I did it. And he said, "Well, play me a breakdown." And I knew I would be able to play "Katy Hill," and he said, "You got your clothes with you?"

And we were in the dressing room in Nashville at the Opry. I said, "No sir, they're at the hotel."

And he said, "Well go get them. We're leaving in three hours."

That's how I got my job with Bill Monroe. I was with him for about seven years, so I must have held out pretty well.

Stone knew that Wise's major contribution to bluegrass involved how he developed and refined the blues and jazz-inflected qualities of fiddling that helped make bluegrass different from the earlier old-time style. He asked Wise, "Well, you kind of put the 'blues' into bluegrass, didn't you?"

Well, I'll have to say this in all sincerity, Monroe taught me to play bluegrass. I had never played bluegrass. Many hours we spent in those hotels and motels, and he said, "Chubby, I want it this way."

Saying, "You take 'Footprints,'" Wise played the opening to "Footprints in the Snow" and commented, "Them long, bluesy notes, he was the man that showed me how to do that. I played more or less country when I went to work for him." As he noted, Chubby Wise wasn't Monroe's first fiddler. He grew up playing the old-time hoedowns and waltzes that Custer and Seaman first played. Although bluegrass fiddling is more prevalent today, all of the fiddlers throughout the workshop shared their earliest experiences in carrying on the early style of old-time fiddling. Wise showed how his unique instrumental techniques, musical ornamentation, and melodic phrasings contributed to bluegrass music. His live demonstration confirmed that his playing is a direct link between earlier styles of music-making and contemporary fiddling (Rosenberg 1985).

Community

In telling stories about history, the fiddlers often contrasted the past to the present. They compared what it was like to live without electricity with the luxuries of contemporary life. They reminisced about ten-cent taxi rides and quarter haircuts. They contrasted the older styles of music to contemporary genres. The place of music making within small-scale communities constituted a major theme in their tales about their musical roots. Although the three fiddlers grew up playing hoedown tunes for square dances in rural communities, they all went on to perform other kinds of music in new social contexts. The difference between the old communal social order and the current urban context is reflected in their stories, reminiscences, and fiddle tunes. When Stone asked Seaman to tell the audience about fiddling for dances in Kissimmee and Jacksonville, he replied with a classic "roll-back- the-rug" story about house parties:

> Well, really, square dancing and picnics were about the only thing we had for amusement. They have a picnic, and everybody would get together in the community. That night, they dance.
> Some would have to play, and there was only one or two down there that could play a fiddle. Some of them couldn't do very much at it, but if it wasn't for the fiddle beater, why they wouldn't have any tempo. But anyhow, they'd dance. I'd go hear them old fiddlers you know, and I'd practice on this.

Richard lifted his fiddle and bow to show the audience the instrument that he learned on seventy-five years ago and continued:

> And finally, I'd sit in there, in the corner, and I'd play too. But it stemmed from that. We didn't have much chance to learn tunes because we had no way to hear them unless somebody came through and played it. So we done it that way and then we sit up there almost the whole night playing. If you play some of them old-time fiddle tunes and if you put every note in there, you were going to work yourself to death. So you'd get them to dance, and you skip it, you see?

You'd just have to stomp, you know. And about ten or eleven o'clock, they'd all have a drink, and they'd get more stomped.[4]

Custer quipped, "And it wasn't always Coca-Cola, was it?" Seaman agreed:

No, there was no Coca-Cola. And then you'd have a scrap or two out there, and that made it even more interesting. But anyhow, it was the only fun we had, and we'd get out there in them woods. And I often wondered what it would sound like for the animals out there that heard all that going on out there. You actually could hear when you were going up where they were playing for a square dance. The first thing you could hear was the fiddler stomping his foot.

The presentation was polished off when Stone asked, "Richard, have you got a nice old tune from back in those days that you could play for us?"

Seaman lifted his fiddle and tucked it under his chin. Pulling his bow into a fast shuffle rhythm, he played a vibrant version of the old-time tune "Yellow Gals." Whereas the stories represent and describe an aural environment that existed in the early part of the twentieth century, the playing of this tune created an element of Florida's soundscape that stretches back well over a century.

It is important to remember that these old-time tunes are still played. Some fiddlers continue to perform for dances, and other fiddlers play the tunes publicly in contests and fiddlers' exhibitions. Many fiddlers also perform the tunes for their own enjoyment. But the old-time hoedowns and country waltzes that constitute the core of many old-time fiddlers' repertories are rarely heard. These tunes have a repetitive quality that doesn't have an appeal outside of the performances for dances or the short performances of show-stopping tunes in contests. The repetition in these tunes makes them perfect for dancers who must listen for the recurrent melody lines to complete their sets on the dance floor, but playing the same tune over and over does not hold the interest of audiences listening to the radio, or attending a country music show. Old-time fiddle tunes are still played today, but the older contexts of house parties and frolics in Florida have largely died out, taking many of the dance tunes with them into history's dustbin. Despite their faded popularity, however, the old-time music featured at the festival remains integral to the roots of contemporary acoustic music. Elements of the music's formal qualities, playing techniques, and performance style remain essential to two styles that are commonly performed today: bluegrass and western swing.

Chubby Wise's stories connected his bluegrass fiddling to the old-time style, but George Custer specialized more in western swing. He explained how his fiddling connects him to a family of professional musicians as well as with Bob Wills. Stone asked Custer to explain how his uncle, Georgia Slim Rutland, helped to popularize western fiddling. His answer developed the link between his uncle's playing and Custer's own artistry:

> Let's see. Slim was ten years older than me. He met Harold Good-man. Well, they wanted to break away from WSM, Grand Ole Opry. No problem, but they just wanted to see something new. So they formed The Saddle Mountain Roundup and went west to Oklahoma. But they were with KVOO, a big station there. They were more hard-driven. Wills was also on KVOO, and he was strictly western swing, even back in the later '30s. But that's where it got started.[5]

> So, anyhow, that was the taste. They liked what they heard in the Texas-style fiddling which many of you know as well as I do. It's a little bit slower and more ornate style than your bluegrass and the southeast-ern Appalachian style of fiddling.

George Custer was highly influenced by the new style of western swing. He performed with numerous bands during his own career and became a virtuoso musician. Stone asked him to play a tune in the western-swing style to demonstrate some of the differences he discussed. Custer and Wise played "Don't Let Your Deal Go Down." Taking a request from the audience, the three fiddlers then played another western swing classic, "Faded Love," backed by Jim Quine on guitar.

Custer's account of western-swing fiddling shared historical similari-ties with Wise's personal experiences in bluegrass. Both styles were devel-oped around the time of World War II. Both styles let fiddlers display their skills in short solos derived from the instrumental "breaks" prominently featured in blues and jazz. Both fiddle styles are amalgams of other styles but are rooted in the old-time fiddling that thrived in the nineteenth and early twentieth centuries in the southern United States. Both styles fea-ture tunes that are much more commonly known than the old-time tunes represented in Richard Seaman's playing. This popularity is related to new performance venues, such as the honky-tonks, dance halls, and festivals that came to replace the old house parties. Their popularity also is linked to their successful reception through new media. The repetitive qualities of hoedowns and waltzes did not make them commercially viable on the radio, but the innovations and variation inherent within bluegrass and western swing added to their wide popular appeal during radio's golden age. The social context for music changed remarkably during the 1940s. Prior to World War II, the old-time hoedowns were featured at square dances where the entire community could dance together on the floor. By the war's end, western swing had become much more popular as couples left their homes to dance together in an urban dance hall. Created during this transition period, bluegrass music was developed for a seated audience to enjoy as they attended a country music show or listened to the latest Monroe hit on the radio.

When the old-time fiddle tunes are compared to western swing and bluegrass, their form, ornamentation, and functions all support the stories told by the fiddlers; old-time music represents an earlier, rural configuration of community. The newer music reveals a shift toward an urbanized America. The new music distinctively features star performers playing for an audience gathered together by an interest rather than by the geographical associations of the old rural communities.

Fiddlers in the old community provided their music in the same way that picnickers would bring their goodies. Fiddlers in the new musical scene became more separated from the community's daily life, and a sharper line was drawn between audience and performer. They expected to be paid. Some hoped to become country music stars. The old, communal quality is relatively rare in the new media-driven soundscape, and it was the task of Stone and the musicians to interpret this significant element of historical change to an audience that was perhaps only vaguely familiar with the old-time style.

Spirituality

Although the performance was held in a small frame church, the building had been de-sanctified when it was purchased by the Jacksonville Museum of Science and History and relocated to its new grounds on the river's south bank. The old church is used now for educational activities and exhibit space. The acoustics are excellent, and it is a fine facility for lectures, panel discussions, and musical events. Given the symbolically charged location for the fiddlers' workshop, it is not surprising that the setting evoked discussion of music and spirituality. The fiddlers touched on the spiritual dimensions of their artistry by playing hymns from their repertories, by incorporating religious themes in the stories they told, and by reflecting on their music. One of the two hymns the musicians played that day was keyed when Stone asking Custer to demonstrate a little trick fiddling. Stone had seen Custer play a novelty version of an old hymn by loosening the horsehair on his bow and draping it over the fiddle's body to play all four strings together to complete a full chord. He began the demonstration by agreeing to show this aspect of trick fiddling. "Let's see if I can retune it." Custer began the demonstration by bringing his fiddle out of standard tuning into an open tuning in which all four strings resounded with a chord when played unstopped. He then provided a story to contextualize the trick fiddling:

> Sometimes when we might be playing a bluegrass show and the guitar would break a string—rather than just bringing things to a halt—I'd just use this as a little filler. But it's the truth. The background there is in Tift County. In the parlor in the front room of Granny's home, there was an old-time pump organ. Usually, hymns were played on it. But anyhow, this is what I hear in trying to imitate the old-time pump organ.[6]

When Custer began loosening the bow's hair to place it around the fiddle, he made a pun about the newly haggard appearance of his bow by quipping, "This is my 'broke' bow, for those of you who are into 'baroque' music."

He finished reworking the bow and introduced "What a Friend We Have in Jesus," by explaining how the new tuning and trick-playing technique worked. "This allows us to get three and four part harmony, and I hope that you can recognize the old-time hymn."

The unaccompanied hymn resounded through the church and clearly evoked the sound of an old pump organ. The melody, mood, and newly transformed soundscape were also resonant with a more direct invocation of the spiritual, offered by Chubby Wise in his introduction to another hymn:

> I think it's safe to say I never ever do anything for anybody unless I do a hymn. I'll tell you—I'm grateful. I'm not ashamed of this a bit: I am a born-again Christian. I love the Lord.
>
> About four years ago, He gave me the most precious thing a man could have. He gave me my life. There was three doctors. They told my wife, "It's just a matter of time for that man; there's no way for him to get well." But the good Lord had a different idea, and He spared me. And I'm just so grateful, I don't miss a chance to tell everybody about that.

And I don't do anything, anywhere—if I have a chance—to say a good word for our Lord and at least play one hymn. So, if you don't mind, let's do "Amazing Grace." It's one everyone knows and everyone loves. And I'll tell you what, if you could, join in and sing with us.

The three fiddlers and the guitarist began the tune. Lacking a song leader, the audience didn't quite know how to begin, and there was only scattered singing for the first verse. The singing grew with the second verse, and the little church once again filled with a song that was performed within the sanctuary when it was still a house of worship many years ago.

George Custer's demonstration of trick fiddling and his playing of "What a Friend We Have in Jesus," used religious content to demonstrate how spirituality is an element of context for the fiddling. His lyrical playing evoked the words to a well-known hymn. Wise's presentation was related to Custer's display, but there was a distinct difference. Like Custer, he followed a familiar pattern in country music shows by bringing sacred music into a secular performance venue, as bluegrass pioneer Bill Monroe did when he played hymns on the stage of the Grand Old Opry. What made Wise's performance different, however, was his use of a verbal genre common to southern religious culture. When Wise gave his personal testimony, he was no longer framing the performance as being "about spirituality." Instead, he offered the audience a chance to engage directly with the spiritual.

Scholars might shy away from religious expression, secularizing the sacred for academic inquiry, and missing the deepest dimensions of sacred expreience. But Chubby Wise got straight to the point and created an opening for religious experience, setting forth a story and a musical offering that invited the audience to participate in a singing ritual.

Artistry

When fiddlers play together, they explore their artistry. This exploration may be realized in the unspoken act of making music. It can involve listening as well as performing. The workshop setting provided the audience with a forum for hearing master fiddlers play in a range of genres and styles. It also opened up opportunities to hear how the musicians articulated key elements of the aesthetic qualities in their music. Despite the differences in their styles and experiences, they shared unified ideas about the aesthetic qualities of good fiddling.

Fiddlers often note that their musical tradition carries low-brow connotations that make it distinct from classical violin playing. George Custer posed a question about the old square dances that provided Richard Seaman an opportunity to reflect on the skills of musicians in his home community. Custer asked, "What would a band consist of back then in your parts in those early days? Just a fiddle and somebody beating straws?"

> Yeah, just a fiddler. That was all we had and somebody sitting there and beating the straws. We didn't have any accompaniment at all. But anyhow, it didn't make much difference. You could take two broom handles and dance by it.

Seaman tapped a shuffle rhythm on his chair to demonstrate the sound of two broom handles that could substitute for a fiddle and explained, "You'd hit one twice and one once, and they'd got to dancing. They had that tempo, and they'd go to dancing. They didn't care. So if you was playing and you got tired, you just sawed it that way, and they didn't know the difference."

Wise reflected on his similar experience and added, "As long as you kept the timing, it didn't matter, did it?"

Seaman's account, supported by Custer and Wise's comments, affirmed central elements of the aesthetic of old-time fiddling: a good dance fiddler did not need to be a virtuoso. What mattered more was the ability to keep good time and emphasize the bouncy qualities of bowing used to accompany the dance. In the early years, old-time fiddling served to accompany square dancers, and the square dance caller played a more important role in the dancing. A square dance could be held without a fiddler, but the patterns on the floor had to be directed by a skilled caller. In this respect, the fiddler's role in playing for dances could exhibit a self-deprecatory, even comical, view of musicianship. To play for a dance, he or she had to know how to play the tunes, but a fiddler knew that it would be possible to fake it by simply repeating easy bowing patterns, knowing full well that dancers would not necessarily hear the difference between a well-played tune and noodled rhythms. Even today, fiddlers sometimes describe playing for dances as good opportunities to practice tunes because the dancing upstages their musicianship. Although dancing is the featured activity at these events, the fiddlers often will pay much more attention to the music, perhaps even to the point of ignoring the dance. Fiddlers attending these events are quick to recognize talented fiddlers, and they look at the hoedowns as opportunities to learn new tunes.

Early in the workshop, Wise commented to Custer about his uncle's mastery of the instrument, "Well, I'll tell you George, and I mean this with all sincerity. There is fine fiddlers. There's great fiddlers. And then there was

Georgia Slim and Howdy Forrester. To me, they were just the top of about any field you'd want to put them in."

Wise's tribute invited listeners to reflect on what the musicians listen for when appreciating the talent of a highly skilled fiddler. Playing exciting melody lines accurately and at a fast tempo creates hot fiddling. By mastering instrumental techniques and using the performance space to display virtuosity, a hot fiddler allows the listener to experience the excitement of a flurry of intricate melody lines and complex variations on a theme. As expected, the audience that day burst into spontaneous applause when Wise ripped into the shuffle bowing in his showpiece rendition of "The Orange Blossom Special," a Florida tune that Wise helped to popularize. Fiddlers do appreciate the speed, timing, and intricate variations of fast playing, but these readily accessible elements comprise only a small facet of fine musicianship. Many call attention to the expert musicianship needed for playing waltzes, airs, and other tunes that emphasize melody and harmony over speed. They frequently say that it is harder to play a slow tune than a fast breakdown.

The musicians touched on this element of aesthetics when Wise led off an old waltz titled "Over the Waves." They first all played together in unison, but with each repetition each fiddler took turns playing the melody and then the accompaniment. Those who knew the melody line could recognize the beautiful variations. Those who knew fiddling could gain a greater appreciation for the intricate and tasteful harmonies provided by the fiddler backing up the melody line.

At the tune's completion, Custer touched on the spontaneous quality of improvisation that emerged in his playing that afternoon. "Don't ask me to do the same harmony again. That just spins off the top. I can't tell you what I do."

Wise complimented him by saying, "You must have done all right, George. That sounds good to me!"

On a tune they had played earlier, Custer's emphasis on harmony emerged when he asked Wise if he could back him on his rendition of "Down Yonder": "Would you mind if, on my turn, if I just have you play again and let me give you some harmony? I *love to play* harmony."

Wise responded, "Why I'd *love* it!"

Custer's favoring of harmony over lead was repeated in his commentary on Bob Wills's classic fiddle tune "Faded Love." He explained, "That was probably one of the finest numbers to go beyond its bounds. You'll find a few tunes like that. It's been recorded by some of the greatest pop singers.

That 'Faded Love,' it's one of my favorites. It's a chance to do some pretty, pretty, fiddle harmonies. Our good friend, Johnny Gimble, he's a master at that."[7]

Wise then added a name to his pantheon of fiddlers, "Oh, he is the master of the recording studio. Like I told them, there's fine fiddling, there's great fiddling, and then there's Johnny Gimble."

Discussing the aesthetics of fiddling is eased by paying tribute to the greatest players. Seaman extended approval to Chubby Wise and showed how articulating an appreciation for an individual's talent can reveal specific qualities that comprise great fiddling:

> I think Mr. Wise, here, has been a great inspiration to a lot of old-time fiddlers as well as country fiddlers because he had a way about it. And the way he played, you didn't have to see who is playing to know who played it. He has a touch, I guess, or just a way of making a fiddle talk. And he's been a great inspiration.

Graciously acknowledging Seaman's comment, Wise reflected on his own playing, "Well, I'm glad to hear you say that. Well, I'm lucky I guess. I have learned every style along with the rest of them. I've been playing so long, I'm afraid to change now."

Seaman's concluding comment revealed that, although fiddlers have unified ideas about the aesthetic system they use, they also appreciate the individual fiddler's ability to create a unique sound. "Just as soon as he goes to playing, I can tell that's Chubby's part right there. There's something, I don't know what it is, but you know it. Everybody has a little technique of his own." Custer seconded his observation, "Yes sir, they have their own style, yes sir."

The fiddlers valued their tradition and honored excellent musicianship. They revealed the elaborate relationship between the communal aesthetic that defines a particular style in relation to individual creativity. Seaman's comment about an ineffable quality in an individual's performance may be shared by other musicians, but, like academic theorists, fiddlers also work to identify the unique attributes of an individual artist's style. Unlike many academic theorists, however, the folk musician is often intent on creating an aesthetic experience and communicating the artistry to the audience without offering an in-depth analysis of specific techniques. Rather, the fiddlers' discussion of fiddling aesthetics opened up reflections on why they value the fiddler's art. Wise expressed his own passion for music: "I was just thinking now. And this is all kidding aside. The love of music, I think, begins at a very small age. And if you love it, you just hang in there. I don't care how rough it gets or how good it gets, you just don't seem to want to give up."

Regarding the music as a gift bequeathed to them from the past, the musicians agreed that there's a responsibility to preserve the art for future generations to understand, enjoy, and appreciate. George Custer summarized the value of preserving fiddling's aural tradition:

> The important thing we're talking about today. It applies to country music, fiddling, classical, jazz. The art of fiddling or violin playing is a perishable art. And it must be passed on from each generation. You can read all the books you want to about it, but unless you've got somebody to show you, or listen to, it will die.

Custer's summary was affirmed with Chubby Wise's interjection, "That's right!"

Custer continued, "I'm glad to see the resurgence of fiddling. It's come back. We just about lost it."

Wise enthusiastically echoed Custer's observation, by saying, "They're coming back. Yes. They are coming back. It will be a fiddle reunion again!"

Workshop Assessment

George Custer, Richard Seaman, and Chubby Wise created a successful workshop. Their stories and commentary conveyed significant elements of fiddling within its various contexts, and the workshop, itself, became a performance of history and artistry. In contrast to a main stage presentation, the workshop format was well suited to demonstrating the performance of history. It provided the participants with freedom to explain and explore the wider context of music. Bob Stone understood that, as the cultural interpreter, he had to provide a forum for the participants to explain aspects of the music that were unfamiliar to many in the audience. The people dancing in Kissimmee Park to Seaman's tunes in 1915 might have found the explication too obvious, but people at the end of the twentieth century were so removed from the original context that the fiddlers' stories became rich resources for understanding significant changes in Florida's history.

Important themes of history, community, spirituality, and artistry were opened up for presentation on the workshop stage. Individual experiences emerged in stories and tunes, but the cultural interpreter's mediation transformed quotidian experience into highly stylized artistic expression.

All the performers masterfully took the seemingly mundane questions of the folklorist and transformed them into more abstract and generalized articulations that expressed the central values they associated with their art. This process was perhaps most clearly evident in Richard Seaman's story of how he learned to play. Like the Irish bards from Ballymenone who took accounts from the past, organized them into historical narratives, and transformed them into ballads, Seaman used conventional genres to rework past experiences into verbal art (Glassie 1982:708). Instead of using the compositional techniques of the Irish ballad-maker, Seaman used the schemes and tropes of the tall tale genre to craft his story. He recalled the common experience of learning to play a challenging instrument, and then turned this account into a tall tale. His story wittily exemplifies how the social context of fiddling involves mastering a display of musicianship to meet an audience's expectations. Seaman's story articulated a deeper point about the need for patient perseverance when learning a new art. The seemingly simple tall tale symbolizes his creative engagement.

The event, itself, is now history, but when the musicians and folklorist met, the workshop created a lived experience of the central themes that unify history, community, and spirituality in artistic expression. Their fiddle playing, storytelling, and commentary all provided a surprisingly unified presentation of themes relevant to their experiences as fiddlers. These connections were most clearly revealed after the playing of "Amazing Grace." After the last notes of the fiddles rang out and the communal singing came to a close, George Custer's words celebrated the appeal of sharing experience through artistic performance.

"Three old Florida boys. We get along real well, don't we?"

Notes

1. The stories and quotations are from "Chapter 3: Workshop" in *A Florida Fiddler: The Life and Times of Richard Seaman* (Hansen 2007). I have reorganized the order in which the stories were told and slightly edited them for clarity. The focus on looking at music making and storytelling as a dynamic activity is derived from Henry Glassie's essay on the musical composition of Dorrance Weir in his article "Take That Night Train to Selma": An Excursion to the Outskirts of Scholarship in *Folksongs and Their Makers* (Glassie 1970). Ideas about studying history as a performance event are explored in *All Silver and No Brass: An Irish Christmas Mumming* (Glassie 1976), *Passing the Time in Ballymenone* (Glassie 1982), and *The Stars of Ballymenone* (Glassie 2006). In developing the workshop at the First Coast Folklife Exploration, I wanted to stage an event that would showcase this type

of performance of history. My ideas about looking at fiddling in relation to wide patterns of communal organization are inspired by Glassie's writing, especially *All Silver and No Brass* and *Folk Housing in Middle Virginia.*

2. This narrative has been edited due to space requirements. The full account can be found in Hansen (2007:37–38).

3. Custer's complete narrative can be found in Hansen (2007:38–39).

4. Seaman's complete description is on page 47 of Hansen (2007). He also provides additional accounts of house parties throughout the book.

5. Custer's full account can be found in Hansen (2007:43–44). His reference to "WSM" refers to the radio station that continues to broadcast the longest-running radio show of all time, "Grand Ole Opry."

6. Hansen (2007:50–51), contains the full description of Custer's demonstration of trick fiddling.

7. This portion of the workshop was presented early in the actual event, and it has been slightly edited to meet space requirements (Hansen 2007:6).

References

Abrahams, Roger. 1994. "Powerful Promises of Regeneration or Living Well with History." In *Conserving Culture: A New Discourse on Heritage,* ed. Mary Hufford, pp. 78–93. American Folklore Society Publication for the American Folklife Center at the Library of Congress. Chicago: University of Illinois Press.

Baron, Robert and Nicholas R. Spitzer, eds. 1992. *Public Folklore.* Washington, D.C.: Smithsonian Institution Press.

Bauman, Richard. 1992. "I Go into More Detail Now, To Be Sure": Narrative Variation and the Shifting Contexts of Traditional Storytelling." In *Story, Performance, and Event: Contextual Studies of Oral Narrative,* pp. 78–111. Cambridge Studies in Oral and Literate Culture 10, reprint ed. Cambridge: Cambridge University Press.

Bauman Richard, Patricia Sawin, and Inta Carpenter. 1992. *Reflections on the Folklife Festival: An Ethnography of Participant Experience.* Bloomington: Folklore Institute, Indiana University, Special Publications, No. 2.

Belanus, Betty, and Gregory Hansen, eds. 2000. Public Folklore, special issue of *Folklore Forum* 31.

Ben-Amos, Dan. 1998. The Name Is the Thing. *Journal of American Folklore* 111 (441): 256–80.

Cantwell, Robert. 1993. *Ethnomimesis: Folklife and the Representation of Culture.* Chapel Hill: University of North Carolina Press.

Feintuch, Burt, ed. 1988. *The Conservation of Culture: Folklorists and the Public Sector.* Lexington: University Press of Kentucky.

Glassie, Henry. 1970. 'Take That Night Train to Selma': An Excursion to the Outskirts of Scholarship. In Henry Glassie, Edward D. Ives, and John Szwed, *Folksongs and Their Makers,* pp. 1–68. Bowling Green: Bowling Green State Popular Press.

————. 1976. *All Silver and No Brass: An Irish Christmas Mumming*. Bloomington: Indiana University Press.

————. 1976. *Folk Housing in Middle Virginia: A Structural Analysis of Historic Artifacts*. Knoxville: University of Tennessee Press.

————. 1982. *Passing the Time in Ballymenone: History and Culture of an Ulster Community*. Philadelphia: University of Pennsylvania Press.

————. 1999. *Material Culture*. Bloomington: Indiana University Press.

————. 2006. *The Stars of Ballymenone*. Bloomington: Indiana University Press.

Green, Archie. 2001. *Torching the Fink Books and Other Essays on Vernacular Culture*. Chapel Hill: University of North Carolina Press.

Handler, Richard. 1988. *Nationalism and the Politics of Culture in Quebec*. Madison: University of Wisconsin Press.

Hansen, Gregory. 2007. *A Florida Fiddler: The Life and Times of Richard Seaman*. Tuscaloosa: University of Alabama Press.

Hawes, Bess Lomax. 2008. *Sing It Pretty: A Memoir*. Music in American Life. Chicago: University of Illinois Press.

Hufford, Mary. Ed. 1994. *Conserving Culture: A New Discourse on Heritage*. American Folklore Society Publication for the American Folklife Center at the Library of Congress. Chicago: University of Illinois Press.

Jones, Michael Own. 1994. Applying Folklore Studies: An Introduction. In *Putting Folklore to Use*, pp. 1–41. Lexington: University of Kentucky Press.

Kirshenblatt-Gimblett, Barbara. 1992. Mistaken Dichotomy. In *Public Folklore*, ed. Robert Baron and Nicholas Spitzer, pp. 29–48. Washington, D.C.: Smithsonian Institution Press.

Kurin, Richard. 1997. *Reflections of a Culture Broker: A View from the Smithsonian*. Washington D.C.: Smithsonian Institution Press.

Noles, Randy. 2002. *Orange Blossom Boys: The Untold Story of Ervin T. Rouse, Chubby Wise and the World's Most Famous Fiddle Tune*. Anaheim Hills: Centerstream Publications.

Rosenberg, Neil V. 1985. *Bluegrass: A History*. Chicago: University of Illinois Press.

Wilson, Joe and Lee Udall. 1982. *Folk Festivals: A Handbook for Organization and Management*. Knoxville: University of Tennessee Press.

Ernie Mills of Perry, Houston County, Georgia, shaping
a decoy body with his hatchet, 1993. Courtesy of Ernie Mills

Georgia Decoy Maker Ernie Mills: A Folk Artist Defines His Work

John A. Burrison

Written when in his mid-twenties, Henry Glassie's first of many books, *Pattern in the Material Folk Culture of the Eastern United States* (1969),[1] established a methodology that has helped those folklorists trained to study oral, musical, and customary traditions make sense of tangible traditions and embrace them as part of our discipline, thus effecting a major shift in the landscape of American folklore scholarship. In this essay I'd like to revisit Henry's pioneering work for its still-useful grasp of folk artifacts—in particular, his approach to folk art—and apply it to an individual practitioner to demonstrate its continuing relevance.

In *Pattern,* Henry first breaks down a human-made object into its components of form and construction in order to relate it to other examples and determine if it belongs to a tradition (1968:7–11). In later publications he actively pursues the individual maker's training in, and interpretation of, a tradition, but in that first book he does consider the importance of a traditional learning context: "a . . . wagon built by a person who does not have that . . . wagon as a part of his own tradition cannot be folk" (1968:5).[2]

Henry then tackles the concept of folk art, offering what may be the first folkloristic alternative to the art world's use of the term in vogue since the 1920s:

> [A] big piece of "folk art" is not folk because . . . it is not traditional; such would be the daubings of untutored [i.e., self-taught] geniuses. A problem harder to attack is determining how much of the material which is genuinely folk, is art. Art is the application of an aesthetic, . . . [so] art cannot

Carvings by Ernie Mills (left to right): fish decoys, 1998; miniature Canada goose, 2000; quarter-size canvasback "working" decoy, 2008; "roothead" shorebird decoy, 1995; Santa duckhead ornament, 2002. Author's collection; Christmas gifts from the artist

Wigeon hen, reduced-scale decoy by Ernie Mills, 2010

include things which the producer did not consider aesthetically, even when we [outside the tradition] find them pleasing. The bulk of folk material which is at all art is secondarily art—it is craft, that which is primarily practical and secondarily aesthetic in function. The decoy existed mainly to lure birds within shotgun range. In some instances the craftsman transcended necessity and carved and painted a decoy which pleased him; most of the time, though, the decoy was designed to please only the ducks. Recently some traditional makers of decoys, like Lem Ward of Crisfield, Maryland, have taken the pains to produce folk sculpture for the collector's shelf instead of stool to float in the gunner's rig. (1969:29–31)[3]

In this statement Henry uses decoys to suggest a sliding scale, with "art" (the application of imagination and aesthetic principles) at one end and "craft" (emphasis on hand-skills and the principle of practical utility) at the other, but with most traditional art positioned somewhere in between. As a folk artist, then, how does Georgia decoy maker Ernie Mills combine the notions of utility and beauty, and where does he see his work fitting on that sliding scale?

Only in America? A Bit of Wildfowl Decoy History

A hunter explained to me the basic purpose of decoys with this analogy: "When game birds see a bunch of decoys below, it's like seeing a lot of truckers parked at a diner: it means good eating." Talking about his art, Ernie Mills likes to echo what has often been stated in print by declaring, "Decoy making is considered one of the few original American folk arts," learned by European settlers from Native Americans.[4] The art form's history, however, is more complicated than that. In his 1653 book on hunting and trapping birds in Germany, *Kurtzer und einfältiger Bericht vom Vogelstellen,* Johann Conrad Aitinger wrote that some hunters placed carved and painted "images" of ducks, or duck skins stuffed with straw, along with live ducks, in net traps: "The wild ducks see a crowd of decoys and are attracted" (Engers 1990:296). Surviving wooden decoys are found in limited numbers throughout Europe, but they date mainly to the later nineteenth and twentieth centuries, suggesting the possibility of American influence (Engers 1990:294–99).[5]

Native American decoys, constructed of tule or other marsh reeds sometimes covered with bird skins, were concentrated in the Great Basin. A cache of eleven, recovered from western Nevada's Lovelock Cave in 1924, was radiocarbon-dated as more than 1500 years old, and that tradition has been practiced by some western tribes to recent times (Fowler 1990:93–111).

Duck decoy by Lacey Norwood of Savannah, Chatham County, Georgia, c. 1920. The body of this homely but serviceable decoy is of cork, recycled from surplus life jackets; the head and base are yellow pine. Photo by William F. Hull; courtesy of Atlanta History Center, gift of Malcolm Bell, Jr.

Canada goose decoy by Madison Mitchell. A master of the upper Chesapeake style, Mitchell was one of the carvers from whom Ernie Mills learned.

However, the earliest (late 1700s) reports of decoys by whites are from the East Coast, and there is no documentation of settlers learning to make them from Indian contact. One might therefore conclude that the North American tradition of carved wooden decoys arose independently of the Native American reed-based tradition and that, if there was an initial European impetus, circumstances here, including the demand created by commercial (market) hunters, sport hunters, and collectors, generated a "golden age"of decoy making from the mid-nineteenth to mid-twentieth centuries.[6]

The geographic distribution of traditional decoy making in the South is something of a puzzle with missing pieces. The tradition has been strong in tidewater Maryland, Virginia, and North Carolina, but does not pick up again until the Gulf coast, especially in Louisiana. It was thought that South Carolina had no such practice until the 1980s discovery of examples by, and information about, the five Georgetown-area Caines brothers (Engers 1990:184–85). And the only known maker in Georgia prior to Ernie Mills was Lacey Norwood, a market hunter who took his homemade boat and decoys up the Savannah River in the early 1900s when he wasn't working as a "squinch" (bill collector) in Savannah.[7] Georgia, as part of the Atlantic Flyway, is visited by migratory birds, but for reasons no one can satisfactorily explain, a decoy carving tradition did not develop here. Ducks certainly were hunted, but with mass-produced decoys shipped to the coast from northern factories. However, factory decoys were available and used elsewhere, so that in itself does not explain why Ernie is virtually the first traditional decoy maker in the state.

FINDING ERNIE

In my 1990 undergraduate American Folklore class at Georgia State University I mentioned that one tradition still to be discovered in Georgia was that of decoy carving. Student Gregory Ware took this as a personal challenge and pursued the subject for his term paper. A heroic search finally led him to Ernie Mills of Perry, Georgia (south of Macon). Gregory learned that Ernie, while not a native Georgian, was indeed a traditional artist, the third generation of carvers in his family. The resulting report prompted me to call Ernie immediately. A phone conversation with a stranger can be awkward, but Ernie and I quickly hit it off: we are both natives of Pennsylvania, and his Mid-Atlantic speech made me feel as if I were speaking to a neighbor back home. That shared identity became, in part, the basis of a friendship that continues to this day.

For my 1993 exhibit at the Atlanta History Museum, *Handed On: Folk Crafts in Southern Life*, I asked Ernie to make working decoys of a ring-necked duck and drake wood duck, birds often hunted in Georgia and reflecting his adaptation to the state. He subsequently donated a hen wood duck and a group of tools, patterns, and unfinished decoys to illustrate his process, all of which I used to feature him in the permanent exhibition, *Shaping Traditions: Folk Arts in a Changing South*, which opened in the same museum in 1996 (Burrison 2000:12–13, 112, 147–48). I chose Ernie for the subject of my contribution to this volume in part because Henry Glassie has met him, but also because it is one way I can honor a good friend and fine traditional craftsman who is now winding down his career, and because he raises some useful questions about folk artists in the modern world that I believe will support Henry's initial statement and subsequent international research on folk art.

Biographical Sketch

Ernest Mills Jr. was born in Bangor, Pennsylvania (north of Easton), in 1934. His father's jobs took the family there and to Delaware and Maryland; Ernie identifies himself as primarily from Delaware, where he graduated high school. However, his paternal grandfather, Henry Mills, was a tobacco farmer in Apex, North Carolina (west of Raleigh), and it was during one of his summer visits there, at age seven, that Ernie was given a pocket knife and taught the basics of carving by his granddad. Together in the farm woodshed they whittled little animals, boats, and airplanes. Both Henry and Ernie's father, Ernest Sr.—known by his middle name, Leon—hunted and made "real rough" decoys for their own use. At age nine Ernie started making decoys under the tutelage of his father:

> When I was big enough to start making decoys, it was kind of a chore: I helped to build up the rig [group of decoys for hunting]. They'd get all broken up, so each year they'd have to replace twenty-five or thirty at a time. We used to just take an eight-inch diameter tree (white cedar if you could find it), cut it with a saw in lengths—for a canvasback [duck] fourteen inches long—take a hatchet and split it right down the middle so you'd have two halves with the top part rounded. Then you take a hatchet and chop down the ends, shape 'em out. My family didn't have a bandsaw, we just couldn't afford it; we used hatchets. The heads were cut out of a flat piece of wood with a keyhole saw, just cut the profile; take a hatchet and knock the corners down, take a pocket knife and do

the best you could [to finish shaping it]. Screw or glue the head on there. Paint it with house paint—didn't have no fancy paints—and that was it. It made a good decoy.[8]

In about 1950 Leon left factory work and began to make his living "off the land" as a commercial fisherman on the Delaware and Chesapeake bays. He also hunted for his family's table and sometimes worked as a hunting guide. As pollution caused the Chesapeake's duck population to decline, the big hunting shifted to geese, for which Leon made hundreds of "shadow" (silhouette) decoys cut from scrap to be stuck up in the fields. But decoy making for him, and for Henry Mills back in North Carolina, was always part-time. As Ernie says,

Very few did it full time. In fact, the full-time decoy maker was known as the laziest bum in town! Nobody in his right mind would sit around and make decoys for a living. In the little town where we lived when I was a kid we didn't have a pool hall, but we'd go down to the local decoy maker's and hang out. That's where I learned to drink whiskey and tell dirty jokes! The ones that had a better reputation were a little more artistic: made a nicer-looking decoy, took time to put a little more carving, painting into it. Today *those* decoys are bringing in the big prices.

Ernie's work in Georgia, as we'll see, owes a big debt to his teenage visits with Mid-Atlantic decoy makers such as R. Madison Mitchell of Havre de Grace, Maryland, and brothers Steve and Lem Ward of Crisfield, Maryland. Those visits served as an informal apprenticeship beyond what Ernie learned from his dad and granddad. He recalls,

My father used to run a fishing boat; we'd do crabbing and oystering in the summers around Hooper's Island across Tangier Sound. Crisfield is where all the canneries and packers were; we'd bring the crabs there and sell 'em. That's where I got to meet the Ward brothers, who had a little shop on the water. They didn't *teach;* you'd just hang out. They'd make you run the bandsaw, tell stories. [Steve died in 1975, Lem in 1984.] They couldn't even pay their bills. My wife said [when Ernie took her to their vacant shop on a pilgrimage], "There you are: destitute!" They were selling decoys for $10 to $20, at the end $100 to $200, and customers would leave the shop and sell them for $1,000; their stuff now sells for $40,000 to $50,000. They're building a new Ward Museum at Salisbury, Maryland.[9]

Following a stint in the Navy as an aviation boatswain mate, Ernie entered a twenty-five-year career as an airline flight dispatcher, which, after frequent moves, landed him with Hawaiian Airlines at their cargo facility in Macon, Georgia, in 1978. After the company shut down that operation two years later, he displayed some of his decoys in the airport lobby. They sold quickly, planting in his mind the possibility of making a living with his art. So in January of 1981 Ernie launched his new career as a full-time carver, thinking he'd try it for six months, and hoping he wouldn't burn out on what had been a leisure-time activity: "If I'd stayed in the flight control business I'd probably be dead by now; it was giving me ulcers. Now I'm doing something I love with much less stress. If I had it to do over again I'd start in 1970 instead of 1980 to work at this."

Like his grandfather in central North Carolina, Ernie found himself in an atypical location to be making decoys—far inland. He likes to tell this story:

> When I started full time in middle Georgia, man, nobody knew what I was doing! I rented this little shop in town and went to get a city business license. The lady there could *not* understand what I was doing. She said, "You making bird houses, wooden bird houses?"
>
> I said, "No, I'm making wooden birds!" So anyway, they finally gave me a license for a *sculptor's studio* [laughs]. Perry is probably the most unlikeliest place in the whole United States I could be to make decoys! But it's picking up now. [As of 1991] eighteen percent of what I've made has sold in middle Georgia. Fifty percent [is divided] between Atlanta and the coast, and the rest out of the state. You can make decoys wherever you are, but if you're right there where people know 'em [i.e., the coast] it's a lot easier; you don't have to explain what you're doing to everybody.

Early in his carving career Ernie was commissioned by Ducks Unlimited, which has over a hundred chapters in Georgia, to make pieces for its fundraising events. His relationship with the conservation organization brought him steady business and a Life Sponsor award. Ernie was one of a dozen folk artists selected by the Southern Arts Federation and Smithsonian Institution to demonstrate in the Southern Crossroads Marketplace at the 1996 Atlanta Olympic Games, and that same year he was nominated for a National Endowment for the Arts National Heritage Fellowship. In the 1990s Ernie regularly demonstrated at the Havre de Grace Decoy Museum in Maryland, and at Hewell's Pottery Turning and Burning festival in Gillsville, Georgia; he also served as chairman of the carving competition at the Georgia National Fair in Perry. He still demonstrates at the Mossy Creek Barnyard Festival near Perry.

Georgia Duck Stamp painting by Herb Booth, 1994, showing hunters in a blind on Lake Seminole with a rig of ring-necked decoys made by Ernie Mills for Monty Lewis of Thomasville. Courtesy of Ernie Mills

Ring-necked duck decoy by Ernie Mills, 1990. This service-grade, hollow cypress decoy is popular with hunters on Lake Seminole. Photo by William F. Hull; courtesy of Atlanta History Center

Ernie's career as a folk artist has gained him national prominence and been personally rewarding—in every way but financial. At the ten-year mark he declared, "Making a living as a decoy maker—at any art or craft—is hard! The way things are today, you're fighting the whole way. . . . I've got more orders than I can keep up with, right now eight to twelve months backed up. I'm working seven days a week, but insurance and taxes keep going up and I can't really get nowheres, can't really make no money at it."

Now "officially" retired, Ernie no longer accepts orders but still carves: "I enjoy it more now, without the pressure of a deadline." His three children are not carrying on his tradition, but in 2001 he took on an apprentice (with support from the Georgia Council for the Arts Folk Arts Apprenticeship Program), Greg Balkcom of Fort Valley, the waterfowl biologist for the Georgia Department of Natural Resources. Starting with Ernie's patterns, Greg is developing his own stylistic features for working decoys, just as Ernie imbued his with his own personality. If others learn from Greg, a distinct Georgia decoy style may emerge.

Ernie's Brood

Ernie's carving falls into the following types: working decoys in two grades (service and premium); "mantel" (display) decoys, including quarter-size ones of the sort originally made as salesman's samples; decorative (natural-istic) bird carvings; and miscellaneous items made for his own satisfaction and as gifts, such as shorebird "rootheads," fishing lures, and Christmas tree ornaments.

His working decoys can be, and often are, "shot over"; they have a keel (for stability in choppy water) with a hole for an anchor line and a lead balance weight. Ernie's premium grade with its more detailed carving and painting, including the cutting-in of some feathers, requires several hours of extra work. He charged half the price for his more basic service grade, the type most often used for hunting. Hunters need a "rig" of at least a dozen, so at $75 (in 1991) for one of Ernie's service-grade decoys, this is no poor man's sport.

In the late 1980s a group of well-to-do sport hunters from Thomasville, Georgia, bought a clubhouse on Lake Seminole and ordered three hundred working decoys from Ernie. The lake, created in Georgia's southwest corner by damming the Chattahoochee and Flint rivers, was great for bass fishing until choking aquatic weeds crept up from Florida. What was bad for the fish proved to be good for the ducks that began feeding in large numbers on the plants, making Seminole one of the top duck-shooting lakes in the South. Ring-necked and wood (marsh) ducks are especially prevalent there so Ernie concentrated on those species, using southern timber from local lumber yards—cypress butt for his service grade and more expensive, easier-to-carve water tupelo for more decorative work.

That large order, for which Ernie bought a drum sander to save time, marked a watershed in his career:

> That's what's bringing me back to the working decoy. All of a sudden, they've got a need for them down there. You can buy a dozen plastic decoys for about forty bucks; mine sell for $720 a dozen, cut rate! But they got the money, and they're willing to buy 'em. The biggest reason is probably the prestige of shooting over a handmade wooden decoy. It's an investment for 'em, too: soon as that decoy's put in the water and shot over, it jumps in value, because it's been *used!*

Ernie elaborates on this aspect of the value system peculiar to connoisseurs: "A decoy that's actually been out there and used is real valuable to a collector—to a point. Now, the ones that have been used and still kept in decent-looking condition is worth more than ones that's all beat up. But being used makes it more valuable to a collector." In other words, beyond a decoy's artistic qualities and its creation by a known maker, it is the evidence of its inherent utilitarian function that adds a cachet of authenticity and increases its value in the collector subculture.

While acknowledging idiosyncrasies in the work of individual makers, publications on decoys emphasize their regional character. Ernie's working decoys clearly are rooted in the Mid-Atlantic tradition: "My style is lower Chesapeake style, the optimum decoy for performance. The wide, flat bottom will float more stable, won't rock back and forth; that sharp edge keeps 'em from cutting into the water." Referring to one of his signature details, the white, crescent-shaped "liner" he paints below the eyes of his ducks, he says, "That's something in that region where I was from, the lower end of Delaware and Maryland. Every [maker] around there did it."

Ernie's bodies start as two two-inch-thick planks; when using heavier wood he drills out the two sections and drops a metal bb in the cavity before joining the halves "so you can hear it's a hollow decoy." A technique common to New Jersey, hollowing reduces a decoy's weight and makes it ride higher in the water so it's more visible to the flying birds. The pebbled finish on Ernie's premium grade was inspired by that of Maryland's Ward brothers, but the technique for applying it is his own. He first lays on a coat of gesso (a mixture of plaster and glue) and lets it thicken, then "beats it up" with a paintbrush. Once it dries he can overlay his acrylic paints. The whole painting process for a premium bird takes four to six hours. The stippled surface "was not to make it look pretty, it was to cut the shine down. There's two things that'll scare the birds off: if the decoys are not sitting right, and shiny paint."

Ernie has some power tools in his shop, but his most important tools are his hatchets; he is one of the few traditional decoy makers still shaping by hand. "Carving," he says, "is nothing but rounding the corners off. I grew up with a hatchet; to me that's the fastest way of knocking all that wood off and controlling it. Some people use a motor-powered grinder, but that gets dust all over the place and can give a washboard effect with the harder and softer spots in the wood. I was taught to use a hatchet. Today there's very few people know how to use one. The secret is: you look at where you want to hit, not at the hatchet!" Some of the best are old Boy Scout hatchets, which have good steel in the blade and good balance; for decoy heads he uses his grandfather's narrow-blade lathing hatchet. Ernie especially cherishes a hatchet head said to have belonged to famed Maryland decoy maker Bob McGaw, which he uses to rough out his decoys. Making a decoy "from scratch" in the traditional manner, however slow (the woodworking alone takes about three hours), gives him "the gratification of reaching back in time and becoming part of that elite carving fellowship" (Grace 1998:14).

When demand for basic working decoys fell with the decline in market hunting as a result of the 1918 Migratory Bird Treaty Act, Ernie says, "They started making what they called mantel birds to put on your mantelpiece to display: fancy it up, add more carving and painting. . . . Later they wanted to get fancier yet, to make the birds more realistic: cutting feathers into it, putting texturing on it. Today if someone says, 'I'm a decoy carver,' more than likely he's making the realistic-looking birds, decorative-style." That trend in mantel decoys can overlap with the hobby (one that can be lucrative for winners of competitions) of carving naturalistic non-decoy birds and other wildlife—full-blown decorative carving.

Before Ernie could build a clientele for decoys he had to rely for part of his income on the decorative carving he'd developed as a pastime. In that branch of woodwork he is largely self-taught, except for a three-day class he took in 1982. He, in turn, then taught decoy and decorative carving classes at the University of Georgia, the John C. Campbell Folk School in Brasstown, North Carolina, and Glen Arden Camp for Girls in Tuxedo, North Carolina, as well as in the workshop he built at his home in Perry. He estimates that he's taught about 350 students, mostly females who, he says, had little interest in decoys.

Ernie declares, "There's basically two types of carvers: decoy makers and [decorative] bird carvers. I'm both." But he clearly has his preferences: "When you're doing these decorative carvings you're sitting there all day with those little burning pens and rotary tools, all crunched up. It would ruin my health, my eyesight, if I stayed with it. When I'm working on decoys I'm chopping here, and moving there; it'll keep me going longer. . . . I want to get to where it's all working decoys; that's what I enjoy doing. It's a family tradition; I just want to go back to where I started from."

In 1987 half of Ernie's business was in decoys, the other half in decoratives; by 1990 he had reduced the latter to twenty percent. His comparison of his decoy work to the nontraditional decorative carving he also practices is instructive:

People like the decorative birds, they're real impressive. But I can teach anybody how to make a decorative carving; I can guarantee that in three months they'd be winning blue ribbons! In decorative carving you're copying the actual bird, so you do research to be accurate. The ones who compete, they can spend up to a thousand hours on one carving. But you don't have any leeway to jazz it up, you have to make it look just like the real bird.

With a working decoy, you get the *essence* of the bird. You're free to do whatever you want; your style shows that way. That's why a collector can look at an old decoy and tell that it was made by a certain carver from a certain region. There's so much more that goes into a simple-looking working decoy, because I have to do a lot more "back-street" engineering. I know it's gonna be used hard; these things are not gently handled, they throw 'em out in the water with the anchor cords and they're banged on boats. I know the joints have got to be tight, got to be waterproof. The main thing in a good decoy is that it has to sit in the water and float just right. Each pattern I come up with is developed over half a dozen tries. Every one of these patterns is mine, I don't use nobody's patterns. So, it takes more brain power to make a good decoy.

Some of the best decorative carvers start out making decoys. I compare decorative carving to making a wedding cake: if you don't have that foundation underneath there, all that detail on top is fancy icing on a really bad cake. It looks beautiful, but when you cut into it there's nothing there.

Thus, Ernie regards decoys, with their suggestive interpretations of the real birds, as a creative art, and the highly ornamental decorative carving, with

Decorative pheasant
by Ernie Mills, 1989

Decorative wood duck family by Ernie Mills, 1988

a literal treatment of its subjects, as a technical craft—perhaps the opposite of how we might think of them. His former apprentice, Greg Balkcom, supports that philosophy: "[Ernie] showed me that working decoys can be even more artistic and expressive than a decorative piece. . . . [With] a working decoy, you can exaggerate some of the feathers, for example, or highlight your artistic strengths. Ernie taught me to be a little more creative" (Snyder 2008:43).

Conclusion: Artist or Artisan?

The issue with Ernie Mills is not whether he's a *folk* practitioner; from his life history it is clear that his work in Georgia draws on the North Carolina tradition he inherited from his grandfather and father and, more obviously, from the Mid-Atlantic tradition he absorbed in his visits to the workshops of decoy makers of that region. Some of his personal refinements result from creative experimentation, while others likely were influenced by his reading in the literature of wildfowl decoys and woodcarving. That he has an extensive library in those subjects should come as no surprise; few traditional artists in the modern world are so insular that they do not occasionally consult resources beyond their face-to-face contacts.

The question posed here, then, harks back to Henry Glassie's assertion that folk artists naturally combine in their work the notions of utility and beauty, and that the dichotomy of artist versus craftsman is artificial, at best confined to the elite perspective of the academic art world. For Ernie, the thing he loves to make—the decoy—is positioned on that sliding scale depending on whether it is truly a *working* decoy to be used for hunting or a more detailed bird intended primarily for display—his premium grade—that still embodies an essential decoy*ness*. To him, a good decoy is one that not only pleases the eye but one that can *do its job* effectively, and those two concepts are not mutually exclusive; functionality is a key component of its aesthetic value.[10] Ernie has his own way of addressing this issue:

> The ducks aren't art critics; what they're looking for is form. When they come in on a decoy it's the form that counts. So the main thing in making a good decoy is not worrying about the finished product, only the top side of it; it's the underneath part that counts: is it gonna sit on the water, or be cockeyed with the front end down—that'll scare the ducks off. Every working decoy I make I balance with a lead weight and test how it floats—in a bathtub!

A decoy with no paint on it'll work just as good as painted. In fact, when geese hunting became real big up on the Delaware, one of the best decoys we used was old car tires. Cut sections out of 'em about this big [a foot and a half], put out a piece of newspaper and lay that tire on top of it [to match the color contrast of a goose]. We also took old newspapers and dumped a shovelful of dirt on top; it'd look good. The fanciest goose decoys we used were silhouettes cut out of thin wood from landfills—old shipping crates, refrigerator boxes of thin plywood—slap paint on it and stick 'em up on a stake.[11]

That extremely utilitarian approach to decoys from Ernie's boyhood is in marked contrast to the meticulous care he has come to lavish on much of his work, as much to satisfy himself, I suspect, as his customers:

Decoys don't need eyes to work.[12] A lot were made with no eyes. . . . I wish I didn't have to use 'em; [the German-made glass eyes are] getting too expensive! But collectors want 'em. . . .

It takes me about an hour and a half to do a [working decoy] head, because there's a lot of carving goes into it. The [real] ducks don't look at these things, but the guy that buys it does. Like cutting little details into the bill [e.g., the nostrils and "nail" on the tip]; that's not necessary, it could be just plain. But it only takes a few minutes to cut that in, and it makes a little better-looking decoy. The [older decoys] that bring the big money are the ones that have a little more detail—a little more art— in them. The ducks could care less!

If signing one's creations indicates artistic self-consciousness, then Ernie's statements on this subject further reveal his self-image: "One thing about the old decoys: the guy who made it hardly ever put his name on it. It wasn't made as an art object, it was made to be used, like you go down to the hardware store and buy a rolling pin. It was a hunting tool." By contrast, Ernie adds a signature and date to virtually everything he makes, even his most serviceable products, suggesting pride in his work, concern about his legacy, and awareness of the future investment value of his creations: "I sign and date my working decoys in pencil inside; maybe in two hundred years it'll fall apart and you can see who made it." Further, he has produced a pair of mallards—drake and hen—to be kept in the family, their hollow bodies filled with his written thoughts about, and photographs of, his work and family, to be opened as "time capsules" long after he's gone.

When asked whether he considers himself an artist or a craftsman Ernie replied, "I never really thought about it. There is some art, I guess, to it. . . .

Drake and hen wood-duck decoys, 1990, 1993, made by Ernie Mills out of water tupelo. Though usable for hunting, these premium-grade "working" decoys are more suitable as "mantel-birds" for display.
Photo by William F. Hull; courtesy Atlanta History Center

A pair of mallard decoys by Ernie Mills, 1995, 2005, containing letters and pictures of his work and family "to be opened in 2095"

The carving part you get down after a while; the painting is something you might never be satisfied with."[13] Ernie accepts the label "folk artist," appreciating that it has brought him recognition and contributed to his livelihood. But when I asked the same question more recently, he felt "craftsman" was the best fit for him.[14] Neither term is the way he normally identifies himself, however. For that, we can turn to his letterhead and other promotional materials, which simply state, "Ernie Mills, Decoy Maker."

Notes

1. Henry wrote *Pattern* while still a doctoral student in the University of Pennsylvania's Department of Folklore and Folklife; the published book was accepted as his dissertation, and remains in print. He and I were fellow graduate students at Penn in 1965–66, marking the beginning of our friendship that continues to this day.

2. Henry later elaborated this initial statement on the nature of tradition (Glassie 1995).

3. This initial statement on folk art was expanded in many of Henry's subsequent publications (Glassie 1972; 1982; 1986; 1989; 1993; 1997; and 1999).

4. "Ernie Mills: Decoy Maker," in Inscoe (2004), video clip (http://www.georgiaencyclopedia.org/nge/Multimedia.jsp?id=m-1465). Robert Shaw, in his introduction to Engers (1990:12–13), says much the same thing: "The wildfowl decoy is the only folk art truly indigenous to North America. Unlike quilts, [etc.]—all of which have European precedents . . . The decoy is an Indian invention."

5. In England, "decoy" meant a tunnel of netting into which ducks were lured and trapped, for which see Payne-Gallwey (2008 [1886]) and Heaton (2001).

6. The Migratory Bird Treaty Act of 1918 essentially made it illegal to hunt wildfowl for sale, thus putting a serious damper on the market gunning for which decoys had been made in large numbers. Collectors' interest in decoys, first stimulated by Joel Barber's Long Island exhibition of 1923 and his subsequent book (1954 [1934]), roughly parallels, and sometimes intersects, the larger interest in American folk art, with Edith Halpert opening her American Folk Art Gallery in New York City in 1929 and Holger Cahill curating Abby Aldrich Rockefeller's collection for the seminal exhibit, *American Folk Art: The Art of the Common Man*, three years later.

7. Information from decoy collector Malcolm Bell Jr. of Savannah, Georgia, 1984.

8. I invited Ernie to Atlanta to speak to my Folk Crafts class on May 8, 1991, and the recording I made of his two-hour lecture-demonstration is the source, along with Gregory Ware's interview of November 3, 1990, of most of Ernie's quotations in this essay. This research is housed in the Georgia Folklore Archives at Georgia State University.

9. The Ward Museum of Wildfowl Art reopened on Schumaker Pond at Salisbury, Maryland in 1992 (http://www.wardmuseum.org/). Lem Ward was awarded

a National Heritage Fellowship by the National Endowment for the Arts in 1983, a year before his death. The Ward brothers are discussed by Jeff Williams in Engers (1990:144-50), and in other publications on decoys.

10. Herman and Orr (1979:28) state: "Questions of the decoy as art or tool are false in the sense that they imply the object must be one or the other; but the reality of the dilemma is simply that the decoy is both."

11. Forrest (1990:233) similarly quotes a North Carolina hunter as saying, "I've took cow manure—it was cold and dry—in the wintertime, and set 'em out on the edge of the ice, and had just as good shooting as I ever had in my life."

12. Forrest (1990:240) states: "[North Carolina hunters] speak of so-and-so as having a 'pretty rig,' that is, an attractive set of decoys. 'Prettiness' in this context refers to the elaborateness of carving and painting. . . . The eyes on a decoy, like all the other fine anatomical features, such as nostrils and pin feathers, are purely aesthetic. Decoys have eyes because [makers] paint them on, and they paint them on so that their decoys will be admired."

13. From a recorded interview with Ernie by Fred Mobley, October 8, 2008, housed in the Georgia Folklore Archives.

14. Author's conversation with Ernie, July 1, 2009.

References

Barber, Joel. 1954 [1934]. *Wild Fowl Decoys.* New York: Dover.

Burrison, John A. 2000. *Shaping Traditions: Folk Arts in a Changing South.* Athens: University of Georgia Press.

Engers, Joe, ed. 1990. *The Great Book of Wildfowl Decoys.* San Diego: Thunder Bay Press.

Forrest, John. 1990. Why Do Duck Decoys Have Eyes? In *Arts in Earnest: North Carolina Folklife,* eds. Daniel W. Patterson and Charles G. Zug III, pp. 232–40. Durham: Duke University Press.

Fowler, Catherine S. 1990. *Tule Technology: Northern Paiute Uses of Marsh Resources in Western Nevada.* Smithsonian Folklife Studies no. 6. Washington, D.C.: Smithsonian Institution Press.

Glassie, Henry. 1969. *Pattern in the Material Folk Culture of the Eastern United States.* Philadelphia: University of Pennsylvania Press.

———. 1972. Folk Art. In *Folklore and Folklife: An Introduction,* ed. Richard M. Dorson, pp. 253-80. Chicago: University of Chicago Press.

———. 1982. *Passing the Time in Ballymenone: Culture and History of an Ulster Community.* Philadelphia: University of Pennsylvania Press.

———. 1986. The Idea of Folk Art. In *Folk Art and Art Worlds,* eds. John Michael Vlach and Simon J. Bronner, pp. 269–74. Ann Arbor: UMI Research Press.

———. 1989. *The Spirit of Folk Art: The Girard Collection at the Museum of International Folk Art.* New York: Harry N. Abrams.

————. 1993. *Turkish Traditional Art Today.* Bloomington: Indiana University Press.

————. 1995. Tradition. *Journal of American Folklore* 108(430):395–412.

————. 1997. *Art and Life in Bangladesh.* Bloomington: Indiana University Press.

————. 1999. *Material Culture.* Bloomington: Indiana University Press.

Heaton, Andrew. 2001. *Duck Decoys.* Oxford: Shire Books.

Herman, Bernard, and David Orr. 1979. Decoys: A Cultural Interpretation. *Frontiers* (annual of the Academy of Natural Sciences of Philadelphia) 1:1–34.

Grace, Arlene. 1998. Ernie Mills: Georgia Decoys on My Mind. *The Canvasback* (periodical of the Havre de Grace Decoy Museum) 7(3):9–14.

Inscoe, John, gen. ed. 2004. *The New Georgia Encyclopedia* (online). Atlanta: Georgia Council for the Arts.

Payne-Gallwey, Ralph. 2008 [1886]. *The Book of Duck Decoys: Their Construction, Management, and History.* Whitefish: Kessinger Publishing.

Snyder, K. K. 2008. An Alluring Form of Art. *Southwest Georgia Living* 7(3):34–44.

Rapid Transportation

Lee Haring

In late 2008, the New York City Parks Department undertook a renova-
tion and remodeling of Henry James's precious Washington Square. Now
there are more plantings, which repel would-be sitters on the grass, and
more numerous, less comfortable benches (same purpose). The asymmetri-
cal placement of the fountain used to be a distinct, modernist enhance-
ment; now a smaller fountain plaza has been dropped into the very center of
the square and aligned with Washington Arch and Fifth Avenue. Thus dies
the cherished performance space of my youth, where young folkies gathered
on Sunday afternoons, to sing and play together songs they knew or learned
from one another. I often revisit the park, in its new sterilized version, and
think back to two friends from that time. Reading the autobiography Erik
Darling (1933–2008) left behind, exploring my 2001 interviews with Billy
Faier (1930–), and thinking back over my own musical life, my flood of
grateful remembrance reminds me of how Henry Glassie proclaims affection for his friends in every one of his prefaces. Erik, Billy, and I found
music to be "a means of rapid transportation to life," as John Cage once
said. Through music, Billy has told me, he learned to love himself: "Music
is the thread that keeps it all together." In the autobiography, Erik Darling
declares that through folk music, he found "feelings of personal hope and
ways to express them." For me too—dutiful piano pupil, exuberant folk-
singer, always indefatigable listener—music has kept life and self together. It
was what drew me first toward something called folklore. What perceptive
adult gave the teenaged me Alan Lomax's album *Listen To Our Story?* At
first, folk tradition seemed distant from me. Later, I found that when they
launched a discipline, Franz Boas, Francis James Child, and W. W. Newell
envisioned tradition impersonally, as if it were a collective anonymous force.
One of my mentors, Stanley Edgar Hyman, defended that vision all his life,

Lee Haring, Rajasthan, India, 2001

while field researchers were reconceiving tradition as human and identifi-able. It has been Henry Glassie's writings and friendship that have led me to appreciate how tradition is created and enacted by individuals. He has enabled me at last to see Erik, Billy, and myself as part of a long American habit of finding a path against mass culture. Perhaps this is our bit towards shaping American tradition, towards finding a place for individualism in the welter of demands, plans, duties, causes, and appeals.

The songs we called "folk," back then, were the heart of the tradition we affiliated ourselves with, or invented. Tom Paley, an occasional visitor from Yale, who was admired for his superlative skill as an instrumentalist and his unpredictable repertoire, observed that folkies sought and found in folksong an alternative to the popular commercial music of that time. Bill Haley's "Rock Around the Clock," Mickey and Sylvia's "Love Is Strange," Tommy Edwards's uncanny imitation of Nat "King" Cole in the song "It's All in the Game," Elvis Presley—these were alien to us. But the figure openly scorned was not Elvis; it was the actor Burl Ives, who, by his radio program from 1940 on, sired our tradition. There were two reasons to scorn Burl Ives: his commercial success, and his cooperation with the Red-baiting House Un-American Activities Committee. (Well, there was a third reason: he was our father.) So a song prohibited from our Washington Square repertoire and tradition was his most popular number, "The Blue-Tail Fly." For that crowd were all lefties; we all agreed to disdain mass culture and approve left-wing politics—which made it unnecessary ever to discuss politics overtly. Once in a while, a union representative would come around to the Square and invite us to a union meeting. Those meetings were not artistic moments.

The content of the tradition in which we improvised was a commercially distributed or broadcast pop-folk style, promulgated by Burl Ives and by Pete Seeger's group The Weavers. Style embraced the selection of instru-ments (mainly guitars, a few banjos, no drums or trumpets; the electric bass did not exist, period) and the repertoire. Songs were recognizably from America's country-music past, like "The Banks of the Ohio"; from incarcer-ated African-Americans, like Leadbelly's "Midnight Special"; from the labor movement in the South, like "Miner's Lifeguard." One song from black jazz, "When the Saints Go Marching In," would always call out youthful ener-gies into singing and playing loud. Style also embraced a shared concept of authenticity, which may have been informally articulated in conversation but was never referred to any authority except that of the group itself. What we did to traditionalize was to be loyal to one another, show up in the after-noon, not the morning, avoid arguments or disputes, keep learning from one

431

another, and focus primarily on performing, socializing only secondarily. All three of us young men came away from those years with a commitment to something we thought of as authenticity. Even now, returning to some Kingston Trio records after forty years, Billy Faier censures "twisted arrangements that not only obscure the true beauty of the folk songs from which they derive, but give them a meaning they never had" (http://archives. nodepression.com/2006/09/kingston-trio-the-essential/). Erik rationalized his joining The Weavers by feeling their authenticity, their "gritty, down-to-earth passion for the human condition which had drawn me to folk music in the first place" (Darling 2008:130). Plenty of listeners were drawn in by that same passion, that same authenticity, without being Communists.

Were we Communist dupes, as is repeatedly asserted by Red-baiting writers (Denisoff 1971)? Many of the admired mentors and teachers were involved in radical causes, yes, and the youngsters of the folksinging crowd were strongly sympathetic to what their masters believed. In those days, it was conventional for left-wingers not to admit openly to being a Communist (member of the party). After joining The Weavers, who were assuredly left-wingers, Erik Darling came to disagree with their political views. Near the end of his life, when he was called back to sing with them, "my old political differences with them seemed unimportant" (Darling 2008:267), but by that time, no one cared much if you were a Communist. For me, the politics shaped an orientation to nonmusical activities, but my politics were as much Quaker as they were left-wing. (It was at that time that I refused induction into the U. S. Army, in order to validate my position as a conscientious objector.) As to Billy, he readily admits, "My mother was a Communist, and I have some interesting memories of participating in Communist Party meetings with her." But he himself didn't participate in political activities. The three of us shaped divergent paths.

Billy Faier has always been a musician. One person who knew him well, without approving many of his actions or life decisions, once told him he admired the primary place of music in his life. He describes his young days: "The talk was constantly of anarchy and politics, and of art, and how horrible the world was and how wonderful the world was." But his website today declares:

> My real awakening to folk happened in Washington Square one Sunday afternoon in October of 1947. There I saw all sorts of people, kids like myself and adults, all singing the songs we came to know as folk songs. It was a weekly gathering which moved indoors to Gabe Katz's place when it got cold. This, for me, was the beginning of the so-called Urban Folk Revival. I started playing five string banjo at that time. (http://billyfaier.com/)

No one escaped the powerful influence of Pete Seeger, in both music and politics:

> I've often said, if I ever had heroes, Pete Seeger would be one. . . . He touched us in a certain way, made us sing. But a lot of people did that, but they weren't Pete Seeger, and the thing that made him different was that he really was true to his word. He refused to do that commercial. He really stood by and it was not a personal thing with him. . . . I was moved by him. I respect him. He's in my fantasies a lot. When I think about someone that I want to show something to, and of all the people that could have a good opinion of my music—he has a very high opinion of my banjo playing, and that is very marvelous to me. Like it means so much more than Burl Ives did.

But Billy, living in New York and Woodstock, was never absorbed into the Washington Square folkies. He fell in love with a West Coast woman and left New York.

> Because of my involvement with Barbara, I had missed some very, very important years in the folk music scene in New York. A lot had happened that I knew nothing about. I came back, I had a reputation because of tapes that I had made, people had heard me, and it was a really intense reputation.

Thenceforward he traveled as an itinerant musician to many parts of the country and the world: New Orleans, Peru, San Francisco, Mexico, Los Angeles, often with (or meeting up with) musical companions like Guy Carawan, Frank Hamilton, and Rambling Jack Elliott, who easily fit into the ancient tradition of wandering musicians:

> When I first met Frank and Jack, Guy had already gone to Mexico City to pick up his wife, and now he had come back and he wanted to continue on to New York. He had left Jack and Frank in New Orleans, where they spent a couple of weeks, or a month, whatever it was, until he picked them up. Now we're all going to New York and I'm going with them. Guy Carawan was such a horrible driver that I could not stand it. He let me drive once in a while, but he just did weird shit. . . . I finally said, "Guy, I'm going to get out and I'm going to hitchhike to New York." . . . So it was by the side of the road, I got out, got my stuff out, and it was all friendly. There was no animosity, no bad feelings, and Jack finally, he wants in the worst way, he doesn't want to leave me. He says, "Come on, man," he says, "well, how about if I go with you?" I said,

"Fine, let's go. Get out of the car." He gets out of the car, gets all his stuff out and we're about to say goodbye, when he changes his mind. Well, to make a long, long story short, we were there for two hours, maybe three . . . discussing this. Guy was just sitting at the driver's seat, dozing, sleeping through a lot of this. Frank was sitting in the back seat, listening, and every once in a while would nod his head very sagely. Never said a word. Guy and Frank and Jack and I are discussing whether he's going . . . and he finally did decide to go with me, and Guy and Frank drove off. And there was me and Jack. . . . So Jack and I hitchhiked the rest of the way to New York. And it was on that trip that I really got to know Jack, because at this point his great obsession was eighteen-wheelers, semis, trucks, and he knew everything about every truck. And every single person we met, he would start talking about trucks and he was going on and on. . . . I knew that I was witnessing something very profound and very important, I wasn't sure why. I knew that his obsession with trucks was something that was real and based on a lot of truth. He had seen the romance. . . . Rambling Jack Elliott was the first person I'd ever heard do something with a truck driver and trucks, and it was beautiful what he was doing and I knew it, despite my anger at him.

Jack Elliott at that time had already mastered Woody Guthrie's style and repertoire. His oft-performed narrative of the "912 Greens" (Billy's house number in New Orleans) is his contribution to Billy's growing reputation *(Ramblin' Jack Elliott, 1995)*. Ever after Jack began performing that song, people would come to Billy and say, "Did you ever live in New Orleans?" He did, but always his home base was Woodstock; always music was primary; always that reputation grew on its own.

Billy hardly uses the word *tradition,* but his stubborn individualism, a shaping characteristic of artists in Woodstock, places him in a tradition of street singing, which he practiced there.

How many people are around who claim to know Bob Dylan? Why? Because he became famous. If he hadn't, they would have forgotten him long ago. Many of them, not all of them. But you can't forget me because I'm here all the time, you know. The people in Woodstock, they see me playing on the street. Some people are, I feel, really embarrassed by it because they have preconceptions and assumptions about street musicians. They don't know what you and I know, that it's one of the most important channels of folk music. Certain kinds of folk music or street music, if it weren't for street musicians and street music, they'd probably be gone. . . . And so a lot of people around Woodstock were kind of weird because I didn't become the star that they thought I should become, or they thought I was becoming. . . . People invest emotional energy into this, and if you don't come through for them by living up to their expectations, they think that you've cheated them.

I never planned to become a street musician, but I am, and I really like it. But that's not all I am, though. So these people with their expectations, they don't know where my head is really at.

Today, having moved away from Woodstock, Billy has taken up another tradition. He gives away his music without charge, by way of his website. So he has joined the "sharing economy, where access to culture is regulated not by price, but by a complex set of social relations" (Lessig 2008:145). So he continues to shape his path against mass culture, as tradition-minded people do the world over. The complexities of those social relations, in Northern Ireland, Turkey, and Bangladesh, as well as in world folklore studies, are well known to Henry Glassie's readers. The sharing economy governed the ethos of the Washington Square folks.

Tradition enveloped us then, because we were creating it. As in early life the fashioning of things surrounded Henry Glassie, so music lay about me in my infancy. My earliest memory is of sitting under the baby grand Bechstein piano my mother had been given as a wedding present, wrapped in the resonances of the musical-comedy songs she sang to her own accompaniment. The songs that affected me, the way folksongs are supposed to affect a person, were by Richard Rodgers and Lorenz Hart: "There's a Small Hotel," in which Hart's lyric yearns for a getaway to a Bucks County, Pennsylvania, no one today would recognize; "Where or When," from the Broadway show *Babes in Arms,* for which my father was general business manager. The "authentic" folksongs in my mother's repertoire came from Herbert Hughes's *Irish Country Songs,* with his elegant piano arrangements. Folksinging with guitar came to me later. The piano lessons I had in childhood didn't do as much for me as the example of a schoolmate from Reno, who sang "Western songs" and played the guitar. That sounded and felt like the pleasurable music-making I'd heard from my mother.

Then, right out of high school, when I fell in love with Woodstock and made friends with Billy Faier, Pete Seeger's galvanic energy showed me a model of self-expression through music that I'd never known at the piano, as well as giving me all the political education I ever received. At college, I took up the banjo; after college, I discovered those people assembled in Washington Square Park on Sunday afternoons. That affiliation, that enthusiasm, that artistry drew me into an alternative social and artistic tradition to the one I'd been brought up in. My privileged upbringing should have oriented me to either Wall Street or Broadway, but my faithful dedication to the Sunday afternoons in the Square gave me an alternative affiliation. Though I never felt I had a place in *shaping* that tradition—you couldn't, it was something you entered into, the way Durkheim thought language was imposed on the person—I did take a nonartistic bit of responsibility. The New York City Department of Parks required us, every summer, to get and hold a permit for "singing with instruments" on Sundays. One year, I got and held the permit. I don't remember that any police officer ever asked to see it. That summer my father died; I spent as many weekends as I could at Pete Seeger's house in Beacon, New York, along with other folkies, who could stay, be fed, and join in music as long as they helped build that house. On Sundays I had to run back to New York to show up at the Square, holding the permit, so that my fellow folksingers would not be without authorization. How could I have also, at the same time, been holding an office job and studying for a master's degree in seventeenth-century English poetry? Youth thinks it can do anything. That was also the year when the power broker Robert Moses proposed thrusting Fifth Avenue through Washington Square, and was thwarted by majority opinion in Greenwich Village. The recent remodeling is not on the Robert Moses model; probably it is an accommodation to the overuse of the park.

My recollection of those Sundays is of an anonymous, collective swirl. Yet no more than any other traditional community did that crowd lack individualism (Glassie 1989:188–92). Roger Sprung, whom one historian singles out as New York's first bluegrass banjoist (Weissman 2005:94), sometimes acted like a leader to uphold musical standards ("If you don't know the song, don't play"). His brother George held the permit, long before I did. Despite succeeding him in that duty, I never felt like a leader (as indeed I hardly do anywhere), so the groupiness of the folksingers suited my expectation of being, well, not anonymous, but part of a crowd. At this distance, I can't identify any one person as having played a particular role in shaping that tradition.

For me as for Billy, the banjo was always a way of attracting young women (we called them girls in those days). "Why the banjo?" I once asked Billy. He said, "I'll tell you what I've told everybody else. I noticed that the banjo and the guitar players got all the girls first. They always had first choice. And I was very shy." I was shy too, and my rigid upbringing deterred me from noticing the magnetic power of the banjo. In time I got the idea.

The piano would never have done that for me. The masculine magnetism is the banjo's plangent sound and rapid run of notes; the feminine, as one friend recently suggested, is "the fact that the instrument can be held in its entirety by the musician, much as a woman could be held in one's arms and caressed." Instruments around the world attract the opposite sex; isn't it a cultural universal? Both Billy and I were seriously, aesthetically devoted to making music, but we both used our music as a means of attracting girls. Surely that's a traditional move for a musician. Folksinging never took me in, the way than the civil rights movement did for young people later. I was always an amateur, to whom music was central, but never the whole of life. Later, unlike Erik and Billy, I abandoned it in favor of the arts of the word. Several of my regular Sunday crowd, who acquired their own training in Washington Square, turned professional. That is Erik Darling's story.

Late in life, when Erik was listening inattentively to a car radio, "a song I had done with The Weavers came on. . . . In that subconscious, uncritical moment, a thought drifted up out of nowhere (I could even feel my lips move to the words in my head): 'I'd give my life to sing in a group like that'" (Darling 2008:253). He did give his life to sing in groups like that, in fact in that very group, and took that thought as a title for his autobiography. Erik was my closest friend in those Washington Square days. I appear in his book as a character in a sort of Tennessee Waltz. At a Christmas party in 1956, I introduced him to an actress I was going out with, and damn if they didn't move in together. Later they got married, then divorced, and she remained his most steadfast friend. Joan Darling had her own distinguished career, as a prominent teacher of actors in Los Angeles; Erik was committed to music as his means of rapid transportation through life. "If it wasna for the weavers, what would ye do?" asks a Scottish song popularized by Ewan MacColl. When Erik first heard The Weavers, that anti-McCarthy, pro-democracy group organized by Pete Seeger, he found the African song "Wimoweh" especially moving; later it would become one of his own specialties. Erik Darling is candid in answering the song's question: he modeled other groups on the work of The Weavers, in whose singing he heard a unique combination of individuality and community. "From then on, I would be trying to form my own group, modeled after The Weavers" (Darling 2008:65). Peak experiences followed, "beyond the idea of performing on a stage to an audience, more like a moment of having walked into a room of pure consciousness" (Darling 2008:109). The self he did not show in words, he revealed in music; but then, that was true for all three of us. Erik built his future as a person out of art inherited from the past.

He created and performed in one folksinging group after another. The folk revival was a collective phenomenon; stardom was not a goal. Although he doesn't mention Pete Seeger's group of high schoolers from Elisabeth Irwin High School, The Song Swappers (Folkways FW06912, FW07628, FW06911), he does recall The Tunetellers ("What a godawful name, I thought at the time, but . . . we had to call ourselves something" (Darling 2008:78). With the temporary addition of Karl Karlton, and then the more durable addition of the creative actor Alan Arkin, they became The Tarriers, who came to fame in the late 1950s by singing "The Banana Boat Song," made famous by Harry Belafonte. At that point in his book, Erik Darling tests the reader's credulity. He writes that when The Tarriers' version came on the charts, "I'd never heard his [Belafonte's] version," and anyway, "Harry Belafonte was an emoter/dramatizer of folk songs and was, therefore, not of great interest to me" (Darling 2008:97). How could a musician in such a closely related field have not heard Harry Belafonte's record? Anyway, the success of "Banana Boat" misled the agents and managers into publicizing The Tarriers as a calypso group. It is characteristic of Erik that he does not mention the group's biracial composition until his book reaches the point when The Tarriers were well established commercially. They lasted quite a while.

Pop-folk was becoming its own tradition. After more changes, the very Weavers themselves tapped Erik, who left The Tarriers and had to get past the intimidation of being a replacement for Pete Seeger. Then the phenomenal popularity of the Kingston Trio, the singer-songwriter movement launched by Bob Dylan, and the Beatles put an end to folk music as he understood it. He saw drugs take over the industry; soon he would watch that happen in a group of his own. Loyal to the sound of Leadbelly he still carried in his ears, Erik Darling left The Weavers and went out as a solo artist, then formed The Rooftop Singers. In 1962, no longer a Weaver, with a failed marriage to Joni and both parents dead, he reached a low point, after which he regained his strength. Music had not betrayed him, but the career was rocky.

In his book are many candid moments when he narrates romantic adventures—he was always attractive to women—but there are also puzzles. To form The Rooftop Singers, he called his old friend Bill Svanøe out of his past; adapting a jug band record by Gus Cannon, they recorded "Walk Right In," which became a hit. The back story is puzzling: his singing partner Bill married Joni, and thereafter, the pair never lived far away from him. In Santa Fe, they lived twelve minutes apart. What price the Tennessee Waltz now? Erik's solution to the puzzle is simple: "They were my family"

(Darling 2008:259). As his book shows, Erik Darling found a place in a world where, for a long time, he had felt at odds with himself.

Is his story, is my story, is Billy Faier's story "traditional"? These stories don't make big books. One reason folklore studies are ignored by the writers of big books, in history or anthropology, is that folklorists dedicate themselves to looking for tradition, the role of the individual, and the huge implications within them on a small scale. Hence the field is so often regarded as ancillary to other fields. A granting authority in Germany remarked, *"Volkskunde* is always threatened to be regarded as a subsidiary discipline, because it has not produced any big books." What sublime and willful ignorance it takes to look at *Volkskunde* without seeing the sociology in *Volkskultur in der technischen Welt* (Bausinger 1990), the social history in *Le conte populaire français* (Delarue 1976), or the revolutionary view of history in *Passing the Time in Ballymenone* (Glassie 1982). Privileging one individual or one tradition as a focus for study—as all of the contributors to this volume do—is not a matter of proceeding at too small a scale, where the stakes are too low. It's a matter of seeing great things in the small, as Blake and countless other sages have proclaimed. The books the folksingers of Washington Square produced aren't big: they are only precise accounts, with the power of any autobiography, of how an American situates himself in relation to tradition (Van Ronk and Wald 2005; Cohen 2001). Billy Faier, in fact, has written an autobiography, bits of which can be read on his website (http://www.billyfaier.com/memrabilia.html). My stories remain in my head. The lives the folksingers produced are as big as anyone's. As for societies, when they mold themselves into their relation to tradition, a full and sympathetic account of how they do it must be a big book (Glassie 1993; Glassie 1997; Glassie 2006). Those Sunday afternoon gatherings, always present in our memory, formed, transformed, and equipped the three of us, and many more, to respond to the demands of our existence. That amorphous band, those impassioned songs, that music gave our lives direction and beauty.

References

Bausinger, Hermann. 1990. *Folk Culture in a World of Technology.* Trans. Elke Dettmer. Bloomington: Indiana University Press.

Cohen, John. 2001. *There is no Eye: John Cohen Photographs.* Introduction by Greil Marcus. New York: PowerHouse Books.

Darling, Erik. 2008. *"I'd Give My Life": From Washington Square to Carnegie Hall.* Palo Alto: Science and Behavior Books.

Delarue, Paul. 1976. *Le Conte populaire français: catalogue raisonné des versions de France et des pays de langue française d'outre-mer. . . .* Paris: G.-P. Maisonneuve et Larose.

Denisoff, R. Serge. 1971. *Great Day Coming: Folk Music and the American Left.* Music in American Life. Urbana: University of Illinois Press.

Glassie, Henry. 1982. *Passing the Time in Ballymenone: Culture and History of an Ulster Community.* Philadelphia: University of Pennsylvania Press.

———. 1989. *The Spirit of Folk Art: The Girard Collection at the Museum of International Folk Art.* New York: Harry N. Abrams in association with the Museum of New Mexico, Santa Fe.

———. 1993. *Turkish Traditional Art Today.* Bloomington: Indiana University Press.

———. 1997. *Art and Life in Bangladesh.* Bloomington: Indiana University Press.

———. 2006. *The Stars of Ballymenone.* Bloomington: Indiana University Press.

Hughes, Herbert, arr. 1909. *Irish Country Songs.* London: Boosey & Co.

Lessig, Lawrence. 2008. *Remix: Making Art and Commerce Thrive in the Hybrid Economy.* New York: The Penguin Press.

Ramblin' Jack Elliott. 1995. Cambridge: Rounder Records.

Listen to Our Story—A Panorama of American Ballads. 1947. White Plains: Brunswick/Decca Records.

Van Ronk, Dave, In collaboration with Elijah Wald. 2005. *The Mayor of MacDougal Street, a Memoir.* New York: Da Capo Press.

Weissman, Dick. 2005. *Which Side Are You On? An Inside History of the Folk Music Revival in America.* New York: Continuum.

Working Through Tradition: Rug Farming In Anatolia

George Jevremović

The handmade carpet is one of the world's oldest traditional arts. In the sheepherding lands where it reached its fullest expressions in the past, its production was central to cultural life, a thread that cut across class and frequently connected the nomad to the official, the town to the court, the mountain to the valley. What we lack in records related to the production, art, and commerce of the "oriental carpet," is offset by an abundance of material: thousands upon thousands of antique carpets that are sometimes known by the names of the places where they were sold; sometimes by the tribal or ethnic groups that are believed to have woven them; sometimes by the name of a legendary workshop, or even the name of an importer.

If names are handles meant to clarify instead of obscure, they rely on consensus, our mutual agreement that we can tell the difference between a "Serapi" and a "Heriz," a "Mahal" and a "Ziegler," a "Tekke" and a "Salor." Much of our thinking and talk about antique carpets goes beyond attributes related to design, palette, materials, and technique; much of it goes back in fact, to terms we inherited. To call a rug a "Holbein," for example, or a "Lotto," names of European painters who depicted certain Anatolian carpets in their work, is not so much a weakness of scholarship as a statement of Western values: paintings matter. To name an Anatolian carpet after a European painter is an association meant to raise the value of that carpet to a Western audience. It is the work of scholars to research the evidence, publish articles, and deliver lectures; it is the prerogative of the market—dealers, collectors, consumers, producers—to find ways to fill the gap between the auction catalogue and the bookshelf, to find ways to communicate values.

Reflecting the explosion in world population, an unprecedented number of knots were tied in the twentieth century, a period during which
the reputation of the carpet as art was greatly diminished. The prescient
writings of William Morris, in the nineteenth century, along with his foray
into weaving a modern carpet rooted in the traditions of Turkey and Persia,
did relatively little to enhance the connoisseurship—or demand—for traditionally made decorative carpets into our time. The "mindless" work that
characterized the untold quantities of "hand-knotted" carpets—both in
terms of artistry and materials—commissioned during the greatest expansion in the history of the world's economy, was a rebuke to all that Morris
and the Arts and Crafts movement stood for. Beyond Morris, the fate of
the traditional carpet paralleled the fate of countless other species of art and
wildlife over the same period. To equate the fate of the world's environment
to the fate of a traditional art is not far-fetched, it is instructive: in contrast
to the "mixed-media values" of much of contemporary art and design, the
decidedly old-fashioned, utilitarian, craft values of the traditional carpet
are intimately tied to the equally old-fashioned technologies—considered
nearly "extinct" only three decades ago—of natural dyeing and handspin-
ning. Materials matter.

What does it mean to be a producer of traditional carpets in the first
decade of the twenty-first century? If the "oriental carpet," thousands of
years in development, survived modernization by returning to quality over
volume, then our work must be to continue to look hard and carefully at
the material that is our greatest resource: the carpets themselves. The traditional carpet is a marvel of engineering and its values are human to the core:
no other object produced in the world today has a greater potential to add
or subtract from the value of time itself, yet less is understood about it by
the public than is known about the contents in a box of cereal. As such, it
is a lightning rod for society's anxieties about all kinds of social, economic,
gender, labor, and development issues. To turn the "oriental carpet" into a
litmus test for what ails the "developing world" is to persist in a disconnect
the world can no longer afford. And to confuse design with tradition at the
expense of what it is that brings design to life, craft and materials, is also to
ignore the only "true" evidence at our disposal. Tradition matters.

It is not foolish now to invoke aesthetics as a basis for thinking about
the future, any more than it is romantic to say that unbridled industrial
development threatens the future of the planet. It is not even incongruous
for a business to say so in an advertisement. It is not too late to assert that
traditional art, to the degree that it responds to our common need to find

work rewarding, while also allowing us to take pleasure in the objects that fill our homes, may be the best option we have in bringing human needs and desire into balance with the rest of the world. Taste matters.

A Businessman's Thoughts on Production and Commerce in the Context of Tradition

The "Turkey" carpets of Williamsburg and the imperial thrones of Europe, geographically and historically linked to the West, have failed to persist into our era. But weavers still weave in remote villages, practicing their craft on imperfect looms. Mosques in the villages of northwest Turkey function as libraries of designs; they serve to anthologize those moments when a weaver, perhaps with great athletic ability, bore down on those famous types that we awkwardly call Holbein or Memling but which, in the weaver's language, pertain to things experienced. There are rug weaving villages in Turkey where an amateur photographer need only hold a camera to a house or yard to walk away with an image that evokes another century. Green hilly fields dotted with grazing sheep. Rooms that are like the displays I visited as a child, vaguely Balkan, vaguely like Iroquois interiors viewed at a cross-section through museum glass. But there is a world of difference. Real fire burns in the Anatolian stove.

One might, as a spoof, juxtapose two pictures: an early albumen photo, yellowed and creased, of sisters at a loom, say, in the stern, discomfiting pose of the nineteenth century; and the other photo, sharp and colorful, of the same women at the same loom in the same dress, staring straight into the lens of the camera, smiling. The joke is on those who would prefer the haze of the antiqued version, a picture of tribal women with no chance of testing our notions about their art. Such safe and sugar-coated distances we succumb to! It's a strange view that precludes the possibility of great weaving in our time, but less strange than the view that life has not changed. Indeed, what shouldn't be missed, what should come across clearly, are the photos of Madonna and various Turkish pop stars tacked to a loom in Nebiler, a village just south of Troy, within sight of the Aegean Sea, electrified eight years ago.

I can't speak for the great history of the Oriental rug, its tumultuous tale of rise and decline. And I can't pretend to understand a literature of footnotes, a hall of mirrors, called "rug studies," although I admire the illustrations of good catalogues. Caught in the midst of various rug productions, I'm in the wrong mood to argue the old dichotomy of antique versus

Hava Ergun and Gülüş Çelik. Değirmenbaşı, Balıkesir, Turkey, 1986

new, of pure versus purely commercial, terms better suited to conversation in elevators than the light of day. In relation to the opposite—but perilously close—poles of the rug world, those who declare great weaving a thing of the past and those who strive to perfect a product through "programming" in countries like China and India, I may as well be on the moon, waving slow, sad farewells to the dead and the dying.[1]

To make rugs really means to organize. To finance. To stay on top of things. My involvement is a culmination of thirty years of dealing in, at first, all manner of antique rugs and then, with the revival of natural dyeing in Çanakkale, new rugs. I like the equalizing way Turks describe it, dealing in *mal,* general material. The message is clear: it's all work. The analogy that fits best for me, recalling the seasonal quality of rug production, is farming. Rug farming. Like the farmer who is involved in the many tasks that define his singular endeavor, from the purchase of seeds to the marketing of his crops, you're always on call. One's farm is transformed, however, into a vast field that stretches between Philadelphia and Diyarbakır, filled with dark ocean, airports, warehouses full of wool and drying yarn, endless paperwork and formalities, muddy villages in midwinter, ateliers brimming with many looms. To make inventory of the activity, to list its needs and assets, is really to put it into a kind of perspective.

From this side, the American side, the starting point is the old: samples of old rugs, fragments, pictures of old rugs, old design ideas with which we are so familiar, they define the way we think about Oriental rugs. Like the Heriz carpet which, in its clunkiest (primitive) form, epitomizes the Oriental rug. It becomes a Serapi. Magic. An American tradition. But the Heriz is only a beginning, and a very modest one. In the world of free thought, no book or magazine is safe from scissors: borders are transplanted, flowers enlarged, colors rearranged, details added and taken away. A process of cross-fertilization takes root, informed by a world of similarities, between Thracian and ancient Peruvian textile designs, between Anatolian kilim motifs and the graffiti-like modernism of Kuban weavings. The Westerner, bulging with publications like so much baklava, has options, either to limp from the weight of his desk, in which the Serapi is a secure crutch, or to rummage, shift, combine, and invent. This latter view, however, confected out of a working library of diverse traditions and built from fragments, is in itself fragmentary. It risks falling apart; it risks losing meaning. To the extent that it moves away from the known, by rearranging it, it comes dangerously close to being a purely modern endeavor: the art of one—singular, unique, rootless, suspended in its own realm.

An idea for a new rug design begins as casually as a stroll. A bit of grass grows through the herringbone pattern of brick on Camac Street in Philadelphia. The brick is beautifully weathered, chipped in places, cracked, but holding together. I suppose it makes a kind of statement. What I like is its overall pattern of inconsistency, the way in which a thing as regular as brick becomes so irregular. The forces of nature have broken it down and given brick a peculiarly human face. Beneath the baked surface, its pure color is like broken yams, or like ground madder root. The connections multiply: brick and weed; birds that feed at the green borders of brick; Thracian birds picking Peruvian worms out of the rain; windswept maple leaves and urban dandelions. A piece of Americana in Pirot! The abstract beauty of an old brick sidewalk reminds me of the criss-crossing patterns in the corners of old Bijars.

But no one should begin with a design. Designs are ideas that spring from wool: the way wool looks when it is knotted. This is something that has taken a while to learn. It is a story about conflict and cooperation, and about the differences between village and workshop weaving, of rugs from Ayvacık and rugs from eastern Turkey named Azeri.

I think of the people who call themselves Turkmen, in northwest Turkey, who centuries ago settled next to the sea. They have almost no relation to the sea: they don't fish in it; they don't swim in it; they don't even look at it very much. The sea is a disappointment because it's where the land ends, an end to potential. The irony is heightened by the proximity of the Greek Isles, where culture is tied to the water. The rejection of the Aegean by people living so close to it is testimony to a deeply landlocked culture. I don't wish to offer a profound explanation, but merely to point this out as one of the salient features of Anatolia's most traditional weavers. Their backs to the sea, they work the rocky highlands where their sheep find sustenance.

Foreign designs, carried by hand from Istanbul to a village in Çanakkale, are filtered through a local design tradition. Gradually, knot by knot, an erasure (or replacement) of detail occurs, dashing the dealer's hopes for a convincing copy of an eagle Kazak. A photo says it's a Kazak, but close inspection reveals it for what it is: a "Bergama" rug with a strange design. But something significant is at work. As the village weaver integrates design elements outside her tradition, she brings them into the fold, altering them, mutilating them, until she feels comfortable with the result. The greatest compliment to a foreign design is for it to be incorporated, whole or in part, into a weaver's *çeyiz,* or dowry; as part of the dowry, it becomes a model for future carpets. I recall a weaver refusing to sell a rug I had commissioned from her on the grounds that it was destined for her betrothal, but insisting that I could have another one "exactly like this one." Its pattern was an older version of one she knew well, called *turnalı,* something like cranes flying. She had improved on the border by changing it from a leaf and chalice to a border of rosettes, with each flower uniquely colored. Bound to tradition, the village rug permits inter-marriage so long as it is conducted on its own ground, in control of its own destiny. Its credentials are paternal, and yet the true protectors of this paternalism are the women who weave.

Designs have a way of changing at about the speed of a bus crossing the Anatolian plain; but weave, the rug's structure, the way in which weft was passed through warp, and the manner in which the wool was spun, selvedge done, knots tied, has all the staying power in the world. It ties us into the greater concerns of the community, revealing rug making at its communal core; no child, man, or woman escapes participation at some level, whether as sheepherder, wool spinner, or weaver. Seen in this light, the act of sitting at a loom seems almost anticlimactic, an inevitability that follows the progression of seasons and exploits ecological potential.

When I say "weave," I most vividly mean the back of the rug, along with the selvedges and kilim ends. These are, I think, the most sensual parts of the body of the rug. They express, through a combination of materials and craft, the genuine signature of an anonymous art. Traditional patterning is secondary to the nuance of wefting; end braiding, the ribbon on the package, is a lovely expression of a girl's wish to be seen. The back of a rug is a better, more inclusive map of its making than its face, precisely because it expresses the work of many hands, busy in the many stages of production. Weave breaks the anonymous surface of tradition into a million pieces, and nothing is more traditional than weave.

The permanence of weave is obscured by the fickleness of palette. In 1982 I saw a few rugs enter the Istanbul market with colors unlike colors in any new rugs I had ever seen: good colors. They appeared to be natural. The designs were traditional Bergama patterns. By following the vendor back to the source, I became familiar with the DOBAG project and the revival of natural dyeing that was spreading throughout the villages that surround Ayvacık, a small town in the *vilayet* of Çanakkale.[2] Something akin to a gold rush swept through Ayvacık; a market returned to life. No amount of praise can do justice to the benefits brought by DOBAG, particularly to those it had no control over: the free dissemination of natural dyeing skills to a much greater weaving public.

What was astounding then, as it is now, was how the people of these villages never stopped weaving, never ceased filling dowries, albeit with

Rug hunting in Anatolia: George Jevremović (left) and Sait Bayhan (right) with their hosts in Çınarpınar, Çanakkale, 1986

Rug selling in Anatolia: the Friday market, Ayvacık, Çanakkale, 1990

synthetically dyed yarns, what they call *deli boya,* crazy dye. Compared to today, weaving in 1980 was low key. As if describing a deeply felt recession—or worse—people think of the 1970s as a bad period, when demand for their rugs reached a low point. Weaving with few exceptions became an almost entirely non-commercial activity. This was also the period when pickers began arriving from far and near to buy old rugs in any condition: grain bags, saddle bags, *cicims,* and pile carpets.

The demand for tribal rugs in Europe and America created a market for them in Turkey. The world-famous "Bergama" weavers, from Ezine in the north to Manisa in the south, without knowing they were world famous, began selling their old weavings instead of their new weavings. There is no real understanding among the people I have discussed it with that an antique rug should be more valuable than a new rug, especially since the old rug may be full of holes and without any real utility. There is nothing priceless about a rug that cannot be used. That someone, somewhere, should find a use for a worn-out rug merely reaffirmed the difference between *them* and *us.* Jokes were reciprocal: each side got the better of the other. Merchant and peasant were in harmony, as the peasant felt little remorse but merely held out for the best price as long as he could. Rugs that had previously been ignored, with names like Yüncü or Karakeçeli, became the rage among foreign buyers. Imagine the shock to the peasant who hears of prices being paid for an old rug that could buy a good house in his village, with a plot of land.

By 1982, the collectibles had nearly vanished. Those few pieces that occasionally surfaced brought prices that astounded those who were paying them, the Istanbul dealers. The marketing of these fragmented textiles created a massive service industry for their washing and repair. It's interesting to note that the migration of old rugs to Istanbul corresponded to the migration of peasants from countryside to city, and that many of the peasants who were selling their rugs found themselves soon in a position to master their restoration. This is particularly true of the Kurds of Malatya, who form a major part of the Istanbul carpet bazaar.

I have been having the same conversation for years in the Ayvacık villages. It is a conversation that begins in the morning, when I enter the first house that is weaving a rug I have commissioned, and continues throughout the day, house by house, village by village. Its repetition is a kind of comic relief against the seriousness I try to convey. After greetings, I check the yarn. I'm looking at color. The balls of yarn are usually in a basket or strewn on the floor just behind the weaving bench. The rug itself is only partly exposed because it is constantly being rolled as each section is completed. Only the weaver has a sense of where the rug is going. I focus on red and yellow, which tie for being the most problematic color. Madder, or *kök boya,* makes red, and in combination with other dye sources, it also makes yellow. But madder takes money out of the pocket of the weaver. We may be talking about pennies of difference between a deep russet and a light orange, but to the weaver this is a place to save. I lobby for the richest reds, knowing that the ground color of only about a third of all the rugs will satisfy me on this point.

Next comes abrash, what the weaver (who is usually the dyer) calls *dalga,* or waves. Abrash is to be avoided because it is the result of sloppy work and because, in the view of the weaver, it is not beautiful. This is not the time to talk about spontaneity and the depth of feeling created by an abrashed palette. The weaver strives for a perfect product, and any attempt to undermine her is viewed with skepticism, if not downright distrust. This is not to say that their rugs don't have abrash; they do, but abrash is never intended. I am from a culture where the customer is always right, but in the presence of the women of Ayvacık, I am humbled. This is not for lack of having tried. And it is not for lack of agreement; it is too easy to agree. We seem to be on a level where most efforts are half success and half failure, never bad enough to abandon and never good enough to relax.

Where I can exercise a degree of control is in the matter of payment. For all parties involved, the simplest and fairest method is paying by the knot, as opposed to a formula based on standard *çeyrek* (5 x 3 feet), *seccade* (7 x 4 feet), and *kele* (9 x 6 feet) sizes, a method that puts buyer and seller at odds and also limits the variety of sizes. Buying rugs by the square meter is counter-productive when there is no standard weave; its effect is to cheapen quality by underpaying good work and overpaying bad work. This is not always understood by the dealer accustomed to buying new rugs by the square foot, who enjoys the stability of a standard. And speaking of stability, I should add that few agreements with weavers are absolutely final, even when a rug has been commissioned in advance. It is not uncommon for dealers and pickers to scour the villages, eavesdropping on the "productions" of others, practicing a kind of commercial guerilla warfare. A slightly higher offer too often buys the rug.

My ambivalence about Ayvacık is tempered, however, by the attempts I have made to circumvent the difficulties there. I think of the tiny victories: projects to dye wool, to expand into long runner sizes, to add bits and pieces to the puzzle of a Bergama design tradition, to keep handspun wool not only in the pile of the carpet but in the warp and weft as well. The presence of a foreign dealer is practical and symbolic: tomorrow I will be gone; in six weeks I will return. The real work happens in my absence, as a middleman supplies the masculine link between a house in a remote village and a warehouse in Istanbul. Failure and frustration lead to other alternatives. One must take from the Ayvacık weaver what she does best: her own art. She neither rejects nor condones what you bring her. Her response is appropriate. This is the only conclusion. Your failure is not hers.

But the question remains: what is the option to good village weaving? There is a profusion of workshop carpets in Turkey. Some, called Bunyan, Ladik, Isparta, and Kayseri, have a market among middle-class urban Turks. Others, like Ushak, Kula, and Burdur, are more export-oriented. Wool Hereke carpets have a substantial market both inside and outside of Turkey. All of these types offer a similar approach to carpet weaving. They adhere strictly to graph paper cartoons, meaning that any failure to accurately interpret design risks being removed. "Mistakes" are taboo. Machine-like accuracy is the sign of the skillful weaver. The wool in these carpets is machine-spun, often in Balıkesir or Kula, where large factories spin and dye yarn destined for socks, sweaters, and three piece suits. While I have visited numerous wool factories in Turkey, and while I recognize the skill needed in combining different wools to produce a desired carpet yarn, the sad truth is that machine yarn is death for the rug. It comes apart like cotton in the hand.

Rescuing the workshop carpet from this fate means realigning the means of production with the aesthetics of the carpet. In a time of no options, when only hand spinning and natural dyeing existed, a competitive solution might have been to improve the selection of wool and the range of colors, within boundaries set by nature. But with the advent of modern technology came the logic of mass marketing. And yet, of all major weaving countries, only Turkey has failed to develop the continuity lines so favored by the modern Oriental rug dealer. Why?

The answer is both complex and simple. I will opt here for the simple answer. If I ask, as I often do, one of the major importers in New York why, with operations in so many places, he ignores Turkey, his answer is almost always the same. He cites the difficulty of getting the right product at the right time at the right price and on time, and doing so consistently. Continuity has not been achieved because the Turkish industry is dominated by small entrepreneurs. A major rug producer in Turkey is tiny by Indian standards, let alone the state-controlled productions of China and Romania.

Production of wool Hereke carpets is a good illustration. Hereke carpets aspire to fineness of weave and perfection of design, to flawless workmanship. For many years, however, Hereke carpets have not been connected to anyplace; the term Hereke is a vestige from Ottoman times, connoting high quality and a high degree of control. But the modern Hereke carpet is as portable as a loom, and what defines it is a set of designs, a gauge of warp and weft, an appropriate knot count, and a general quality of wool and color. A father can buy a loom, cartoon, ready yarn, and employ his daughters. He is a carpet producer. If he is motivated, he can create agreements with neighbors and purchase the looms and wool for production of additional carpets. By contracting fifty to one hundred looms in his community, he becomes a big producer, developing relations with Istanbul carpet dealers. Information flows back and forth, much as it does in Ayvacık, by visits to the looms by prospective buyers.

The paradox of this kind of carpet is that it strives for the perfection of a mass product while failing to organize along lines that would make it successful. The result is mediocre, neither easy to market to a large audience nor interesting enough to sell in the boutique atmosphere of an antique Oriental rug gallery. I can only hint at the complex nature of this issue by indicating that most of this weaving occurs at home, a cottage industry in the true sense. The tradition that abides in the hands of the women who weave is just too strong. Anyone attempting to replicate a Chinese-type rug industry in Turkey will meet with ignoble failure. This is why no one tries.

And yet, Turkey resonates with rug weaving. Whatever that means, it is a rug-weaving culture. It resuscitates the anemic term, authentic. The conditions are right, both economically and culturally, for a revival of weaving the likes of which the twentieth century did not see. It is a revival of good craft, founded on the informal partnership of many parties, from the village girls to the repairman-turned-entrepreneur, and from the fragment dealer to the rug farmer. Taken individually, its projects are on a small scale. Seen as a whole, it represents the single most important contribution to Oriental rug weaving in decades. It may be that I am talking about a small fraction of total production, but that may be enough. The partnership I speak of is like the conversation that swings between the possible and the impossible faster than one's mood can change, with the gray area in between left to God's will. It has nothing to do with one's faith in God. It has to do with habit, the habit of making difficult things impossible because experience taught us so. In this sense, revival means the rejection of rejections.

Rug farming in eastern Turkey has been an orchestrated effort, combining the skills of natural dyeing with the flexibility of young women who weave commercially. As if turning back time, we have devised a system to spin large amounts of wool by hand, employing hundreds of women in work that can be done at home. I call these carpets Azeri, after the Turks of Azerbaijan. It is a whimsical name, meant to recall the beautiful patterns of rugs vaguely called "north west Persian." As an idea, Azeri carpets are about the art of girls making pictures, using drawings and samples merely as a guide in their weaving. The room for interpretation is wide; its results could easily be mistaken for primitive, but nothing could be further from the truth. Rather, an organization has been fashioned around the notion that several weavers sitting on a bench, in a room with many other large looms, can use a hard, lustrous yarn to produce rugs that are as much the personal statement of an individual as they are a rich contribution to decoration.

NOTES

1. "Programming" or "Continuity" is a more recent rug trade practice. It is the production of a given design in a range of colors and sizes, allowing the sale of a wide range of rugs through a narrow range of samples, usually supported by a comprehensive catalogue.

2. DOBAG: An acronym drawn from *Doğal Boya Araştırme ve Geliştirme Projesi*, which translates as Natural Dye Research and Development Project. The DOBAG project was administered by the Faculty of Fine Arts, Marmara University, Istanbul, whose purpose is to provide technical expertise in the use of natural dyes and to foster the native weaving tradition in Anatolia. The project is headed by Professor Doctor Mustafa Aslier, dean of the Faculty of Fine Arts. Dr. Harald Böhmer, chemist, rug scholar, and co-author with Dr. Werner Brüggemann of *Rugs of the Peasants and Nomads of Anatolia,* is chief technical advisor to the project. The project provides expertise to two villager-owned and operated cooperatives, one in the Ayvacık area, the other in the Yuntdağ area of northwestern Anatolia. A DOBAG carpet is one that has been produced by either of the two cooperatives which receive technical assistance from the DOBAG Project and which has been certified by a University Project representative to meet the standards of the Project, that is, to be a traditional handwoven Turkish village rug dyed with natural dyes and indigo. All DOBAG carpets are registered by the University and have affixed to them a leather tag bearing the registration number.

Mark Hewitt, 2004. His pot exhibits an Asian form beneath
a Carolina surface of saltglaze and glass drips.

A Few of My Favorite Things about North Carolina Pottery

Mark Hewitt

As a British-born potter who has lived and worked in North Carolina since 1983, I have found myself increasingly captivated by the regional pottery traditions of both North and South Carolina. To me they are as significant a cultural expression as the better known musical traditions spawned in the American South. In particular I have found that the older nineteenth-century pots made here possess a beauty that is as compelling as the beauty inherent in any of the world's other great ceramic traditions. These Southern pots continue to provide me with guidance and inspiration.

Although I was born into an industrial pottery family in Stoke-on-Trent, England, and gained a deep understanding of industrial ceramics by osmosis during my childhood, my formal training as a potter didn't begin until I left university, in 1976, when I began an apprenticeship to the great English studio potter Michael Cardew.[1] Cardew, in turn, had been apprenticed to Bernard Leach[2] in the early 1920s. Leach was one of the founders of the Japanese Folk Art (Mingei) Movement[3] in Japan, and later the British Studio Pottery Movement. Both Leach and Cardew made functional pots inspired by folk pottery traditions from around the world, and advocated passionately about the beauty found in objects made by hand using locally available materials.

When I arrived in North Carolina, and began to see older Southern pots, they glowed with what my eyes had been trained to see, and ever since I have endeavored to understand what it is about these Southern pots that is so compelling. This paper, first presented as an address at the Catawba Valley Pottery Festival, in Hickory, North Carolina, in March 2009, is an attempt to decipher these pots both as discrete objects and as cultural manifestations.

Regional pottery traditions are extremely rare; they are like wild flowers that only grow in certain special soils and microclimates. A unique set of economic, historic, and cultural conditions have allowed the pottery tradition of the Catawba Valley to survive from the early nineteenth century until now. It is miraculous that alkaline-glazed pottery is still being made in the western Piedmont, and similarly miraculous that salt-glazed pottery is still being made in the Eastern Piedmont. The pottery culture of North Carolina is better developed than in any other state in America. Of course I know that pots are made elsewhere; they say that pots are made in Oklahoma and even Tennessee, no doubt in South Dakota, but no other state in the United States has such a rich ceramic heritage as North Carolina, and I'm going to discuss a few of the conditions that have allowed North Carolina to flourish as a place to make pots.

These are "A Few of My Favorite Things about North Carolina Pottery"

Well, it all starts with the materials. For those of us who enjoy the primal poetry of gathering local materials (an increasingly rare endeavor as the convenience of Big Clay dominates our psyches and supplies), North Carolina is a treasure trove for potters; we have good deposits of clay, any number of interesting glaze materials, and abundant wood. My apprenticeship with Michael Cardew in England showed me, among other things, the luxurious qualities of pots made with materials that potters gather locally and refine themselves.

When I first visited Burlon Craig, in 1981, I went straight to his clay pile. When visiting potteries, some people go straight to the showroom, others go straight to the kilns, I go to clay piles. I remember standing on top of his clay pile sensing the spirit of the earth, recognizing that the foundation of his pottery was sound, that his clay came from right there, close by, that his pots honored his place, they were part of it. My teacher, Michael Cardew, wrote that, "A good potter cannot treat his raw materials merely as a means of production; he treats them as they deserve to be treated, with love. He cannot make things merely as utensils; he makes them as they have a right to be, as things with a life of their own" (Cardew 1969:250).

Rather like stories of native peoples crawling on their knees the last few yards to sacred outcrops of hematite, or white clay, with which they adorn themselves, so too do I become ecstatic when I go to Lemon Springs, near Cameron, about thirty miles from my pottery, where at the bottom of a sand

and gravel pit, I get good clay for my pots. Though I confess that I succumb to the ease of ordering special materials from ceramic supply companies, it always feels, by contrast, as though I'm getting the ceramic equivalent of overly-processed junk food.

We all know the difference in taste between a home-grown tomato and one raised in a greenhouse far away and sent in February to our local Piggly Wiggly. Well, the same applies to the flavor of pots made from local materials. One of the greatest underlying pleasures of ceramic appreciation comes from our response to material quality. A pot is a record of a material process. You pick up a pot, you feel it, you look at it, and at some level, you know it.

There is interest these days in the concept of "food miles," or how far away the food on your table was grown, who grew it, and how much energy was consumed to get it from its source to you. This "locatarian" sensibility can be extrapolated to all the objects in your house, your furniture, your appliances, even your entertainment, and for us potters, to the materials that comprise our clay bodies and glazes. Where and under what conditions was that cobalt or copper mined? Where did the clay in those plastic bags originate? How far has that nephylene syenite traveled?

Alkaline-glazed pots, and salt-glazed pots, are among the simplest to make—which does not, however, make them easy to make. In the case of salt-glazed pots all you need is clay, a wheel (in fact, not even a wheel), a kiln, and a little salt. In the case of alkaline glazed pots all you need are clay, a wheel, a kiln, some wood ash, and a simple glass frit. Keeping things simple is very difficult, but if you do mine and refine materials locally, the flavor of that place and region is recorded in the pots you make, and, to me, the pots are healthier. The greens of South Carolina and Catawba Valley glazes are luminous; they have unfathomable depth and complexity. The clay quality underlying the salt glaze on Eastern Piedmont ware is like an intricate organic quilt, patterning the surface with unending pleasure.

In addition to these finely-tuned assessments of ceramic quality, economics is involved in the material equation too. For instance, as recently as the early 1980s, Burlon Craig spent a mere fifteen dollars to produce a large groundhog kiln load of pots. This was spent on gas for his pick-up to transport clay from old Rhodes clay holes near the Catawba River, and to go haul wood from a nearby saw mill. In a similar vein, my most recent twenty-ton truckload of Lemon Springs clay cost me a gallon pitcher and a gallon jar, including delivery.

My next favorite thing about North Carolina pottery is skill. I'd like to offer a quote from a member of one of the other branches of the Southern

Grace Nell Hewell, teaching her great-granddaughter, Susannah,
at the potter's wheel. Gillsville, Georgia, 2008

pottery tradition, taking the liberty of crossing state lines, and let Grace Nell Hewell, the wife of Harold Hewell, owner of Hewell's pottery in Gillsville, Georgia, talk about her skills. They make horticultural ware, which is often perceived as being at the very bottom of the hierarchy of ceramic practice. The Hewells specialize in making strawberry pots, flowerpots, beehives, and clay jack o'lanterns; their pots are ubiquitous in garden centers throughout the southeastern United States. Grace Nell Hewell was being interviewed in 1981 by Charles Mack, a folklore professor at the University of South Carolina, and quoted in his book, *Talking with the Turners: Conversations with Southern Folk Potters* (2006:99–100):

CHARLES R. MACK: How long have you been turning?

GRACE NELL HEWELL: Let's see, I got married in 1950, and I've been making pots ever since 1952.

CRM: Did you just decide that you wanted to do it, or did your husband ask you to do it?

GNH: No, he didn't ask me to do it. I just always said that, when I got married, whatever my husband done that was what I was going to do, whether he was a mechanic or a farmer or whatever, and he happened to be a potter, so I decided I wanted to make pottery.

CRM: Some people have said that women haven't done any turning. They may work around the shop a little bit, but they never do any turning. What do you think about that?

GNH: Well, I think women are missing out on the best part of the deal . . . cause, see what I do, I make a lot of pots and I finish pots for my son, Chester, my husband, Harold, every day, and for my brother-in-law, Carl. I finish pots for them every day—every pot they turn and when somebody is on vacation, I finish off pots for Henry and his son. I finished off 1,700 pots Monday, putting holes in them—strawberry jars—and turned 210 pieces myself.

CRM: How do you like doing it?

GNH: I love it. I'd have to like it as much as I do it. I made 735 pots in one day and done a lot of finishing, so one day I'm gonna break a record, one day when I haven't got a lot of finishing to do. I've been making 400 of these this morning, and then I'll have all the strawberries of Chester, Harold.

CRM: Are these the tops for the pumpkins?

GNH: Jack o'lanterns. I'll be turning 400 of these, and then this evening I'll finish every one of these strawberries. . . .

CRM: Do you do this everyday?

GNH: Every day. I even do all my housework, gardening, the yard, flowers. I do everything. I don't have no help. Don't want none.

CRM: It must sit pretty well with you.

GNH: It does. I enjoy it. There's a customer that comes here that said I never have done a day's work in my life. He said I liked it too good: it wasn't work.

What Grace Nell Hewell does daily is echoed by Black Mountain College poet Jonathan Williams, who said that one of the tasks of art is, "to raise 'the common' to grace; to pay close attention to the *earthy.*"[4] Grace Nell knows grace, just as surely as anyone else. Her strawberry pots help people raise strawberries out of the earth; they are placed on a porch, by a pathway, or in a garden, and tended carefully until you are able to pick a ripe, juicy berry as you pass by on a clear May day. That is grace.

Or, an echo from Charles Olson, another Black Mountain poet, "These days / whatever you have to say, leave / the roots on, let them / dangle // And the dirt // Just to make clear / Where they come from."[5]

Grace Nell Hewell is a rural minimalist; her production resembles a Steve Reich or Philip Glass composition, a dense tapestry of minor variations, an intricate, loving, daily ebb and flow.

Grace Nell Hewell's love of repetitive work is echoed across North Carolina, particularly in the workshops of the old guard folk potters, now sadly reduced in number, but including Neolia and Celia Cole, daughters of A. R. Cole, working in Sanford, who inscribe the bottoms of their pots with poems, homilies, and love notes, and whose mugs still cost four dollars, and Boyd and Nancy Owens, children of M. L. Owens, who make standard North Carolina domestic ware, simple, straightforward, inexpensive. Jugtown Pottery can also be considered part of this group.

All these potters learned their art, their craft, from family members; they did not go to art school, they went to work, learning as they went. Their motives for making pots may have been more financial than aesthetic, but not necessarily. Their range of expression is narrow, but their constraints do not preclude love, experimentation, imagination and change. On a trip

Mark at work, 2004

Mark Hewitt at work, 2010

Two-gallon jar by Mark Hewitt

through the South in 1981 with my wife, Carol, I remember watching Chester Hewell (son of Grace Nell Hewell) throw ten-gallon strawberry pots out of the sloppiest, coarsest clay I've ever seen, and, as he was making one, he looked up at me with a twinkle in his eye, and said, "You ain't seen nothin' cruder, have you?" At that moment he might just as well have been Peter Voulkos making an Abstract Expressionist ceramic sculpture. In fact if I close my eyes and think of the big stacks that Voulkos made, with their slashes and holes, I picture them as strawberry pots!

I've already mentioned Grace Nell Hewell and the pride she clearly has in her work. Whether or not you feel that she is engaged in the drudgery of factory work, or that she could be replaced by a Southeast-Asian press mold operator, she displays the passion, discipline, and skill common to all great artistic endeavors. Production potters like Grace Nell Hewell, and countless others throughout the South, have been invaluable models for me. I may not make as many pots, but I am quick, and can make a good variety of thinly-potted small pots, and generous big pots, with consistency and pride. I love every one, and my skills stand me in good stead in the marketplace, in fact they are vital.

The next item on my list of Favorite Things about North Carolina Pottery is style. Clearly making pottery is about more than technique and repetition. It matters what you make. Excessive quantity works to the detriment of quality, and quality is always the standard to which potters must be drawn. However, combine quantity and quality with innovation (whatever the schools of pottery you belong to), and you will most likely make work that is affordable and appreciated. In North Carolina our library of style is large, for in addition to our emblematic "roots" traditions, we also have the school and community of Penland and Black Mountain College. And I'll talk about them later.

In the case of the South Carolina alkaline-glaze tradition, the pots combine European vernacular forms with Asian ash and celadon glazes, and they also have an African-American inflection in both making and decorating. Together these elements combine to give South Carolina pots an epicurean melting pot of styles.

Not to be outdone, traditional Catawba Valley alkaline-glazed pots combine elements of the South Carolina tradition with a sophisticated formal refinement, peerless technical mastery, and the use of melted glass runs as an expressive decorative element.

Meanwhile, the North Carolina salt-glaze tradition combines European and New England forms with lively wood-fired surfaces produced in cross-draught groundhog kilns which correspond to the sophisticated surfaces found on Japanese *anagama* style wares (Hewitt and Sweezy 2005:19–20).

Together, pots from these Southern traditions have an underlying friendly soulfulness, and are, to me, as significant a cultural expression as the musical traditions of the South, like blues or bluegrass.

By grafting these pottery "roots" traditions together with what I learned as an apprentice in England I produce wares that have a regional aesthetic as well as a contemporary sensibility. My Iced Tea Ceremony Vessels, for instance, combine a tongue-in-cheek regional counterpoint to the Japanese Tea Ceremony with contemporary ceramic references. They are fun to look at, think about, and to use. Sometimes I like my pots to be spare and minimal, sometimes I like them to be elaborately ornamented. I am not root-bound, but choose to use these healthy Carolinian roots as the rootstock for my own hybrid growth.

Tradition can be new if its parameters are understood to be liberating, not confining, and if it is treated with imagination. It belongs now, just as much as the avant-garde belongs now. The one does not cancel out the other. One person's creativity is not at the expense of someone else's; individual creativity does not invalidate anyone else's creativity.

Josef Albers, the German émigré who taught at Black Mountain College for many years, objected to tradition only if it had moved from a "role of facilitation to one of inhibition" (Harris 2002:15). Tradition is not inhibiting if I decide to make 150 traditionally-inspired, alkaline-glazed mugs in a day, (not nearly as many as Grace Nell Hewell might make), endowing each one with all my attention, deliberately choosing to be restrained, allowing a single, pure note to be heard in each. Every one is an idea, and every one is a reality. Every one is a momentary bloom, with tradition facilitating the contemporary expression of a venerable root of American ceramic practice.

The title of my paper, "A Few of My Favorite Things about North Carolina Pottery," comes, as you know, from the Rogers and Hammerstein song in the "Sound of Music." You may also know the version of that song performed by the great jazz saxophone player, John Coltrane, who was born in Hamlet, North Carolina. He took a wonderful song and made something new out of it that is now, itself, a classic. Many contemporary North Carolina potters continue to do the same thing, taking a classic, and making it their own.

But North Carolina has more than just a "roots" tradition. We also claim the progressive, experimental, Black Mountain College, and its many distinguished alumni, including ceramic artists Robert Turner and Karen Karnes, as part of the rich tapestry of North Carolina's diversified ceramic heritage.

Pitchers by Mark Hewitt

The table set with Mark's stoneware in the home of
Mark and Carol Hewitt, Pittsboro, North Carolina

And, of course, we have Penland, and can only marvel at how it has fostered so many excellent craftspeople over the years, and how it has added an exciting range of new styles to contemporary North Carolina pottery. Indeed one of the tasks facing traditional North Carolina potters is figuring out how to absorb contemporary studio pottery practice without losing the essence of what has gone before.

It is all too easy to box ourselves into camps of potters, to be a "traditional North Carolina potter," or be a "Penland potter," or to favor the experimental legacy of Black Mountain pottery, to the exclusion of all else. How do we reconcile these differences? A recent documentary about Black Mountain College entitled, "Fully Awake," points to a way forward.[6] It is not difficult for potters to be "fully awake" to what is around them, gracefully acknowledging, if not necessarily embracing, all the varied approaches to pottery making. Let the words Black Mountain alumnus, composer John Cage, guide us, "The first question I ask myself when something doesn't seem to be beautiful is why do I think it's not beautiful. And very shortly you discover that there is no reason."[7]

Indeed I see the emergence of a new kind of melting pot, for some of my favorite contemporary North Carolina pots are being made at the place where Penland, Black Mountain and traditional North Carolina pottery intersect. This nexus of experimentation can perhaps be summarized by a quote from Josef Albers, when he said, "To experiment is at first more valuable than to produce; free play in the beginning develops courage" (Katz and Brody 2003:22).

My next Favorite Thing about North Carolina Pottery is the potters, of course. I would like to have known Daniel Seagle, his son James Franklin, Isaac Lefevers, the Hartzogs, Chester Webster, J. A. Craven, and all the other Cravens, Nicholas and Himer Fox, and Solomon Loy and Tom Boggs, and so many others. Their pots are so good, it is tempting to think that they were pretty interesting characters too. They all should, in my opinion, be given equal billing to Adelaide Alsop Robineau, Fergus Binns, and George Orr, when writing histories of American ceramics. However, these "country cousins" seem to irritate or embarrass art critics, and more often than not, it is the better-connected, urbane, and eccentric who end up in the national anthologies. Nonetheless the work of the great nineteenth-century North Carolina potters has been celebrated, and continues to be venerated for its fundamental aesthetic majesty.

Thanks to the remarkable transition from utilitarian to art ware pottery in North Carolina, the list of twentieth-century potters is also long and distinguished, including Ben Owen, J. B. Cole, A. R. Cole, the Reinhardts, Burlon Craig, Bachelder, the Aumans, and so many more.

Today you can wander the halls of this festival and enjoy contemporary North Carolina potters as much as their pots. This connection between maker and customer is at the heart of North Carolina's "Mud Love."

Another Favorite Thing about North Carolina is the market. North Carolina is not the only place with a reputation for being a good place to sell pots, but there are clear regional discrepancies throughout the United States in terms of potters' abilities to sell their wares locally. The market in North Carolina is strong partly as a result of the specific cultural history of North Carolina relating to its ceramic heritage, and partly because of the continued clustering of potters in Seagrove in the eastern Piedmont, the Catawba Valley in the western Piedmont, and up around Penland in the Mountains. These pods of potters provide an enhanced cumulative identity and a numerical economic advantage—like theaters on Broadway, or golf courses in Pinehurst, the more the merrier. Would that it were that simple, for wherever people cluster together as professionals, competition also produces tensions, jealousies, and rivalries that can all too easily muddy the waters. Notwithstanding occasional discord between potters, the market for pots in North Carolina remains healthy. This strength is also a function of the deliberate efforts of the state and a series of individuals who, in various capacities, actively promote pottery, in all its manifestations, through exhibitions, publications, conferences, schools, collector's guilds, and craft fairs.

Many of these advocates are able to float conceptually between traditional pottery made in Seagrove and the Catawba Valley, and contemporary work being made at Penland and elsewhere, without being ashamed of either, giving each aesthetic its day in the sun. They are equally happy in the company of ceramic sculptors like Michael Sherrill, whose sculptural work commands tens of thousands of dollars, as in the company of their "country cousins," like the fabulous eighty-year-old Cole sisters and their four-dollar mugs. A threshold of cultural acceptance has been crossed in North Carolina, and potters are well-received within the community at large, and are accorded a status that is more mainstream than marginal.

Of course, the healthy market is also a function of the healthy economy of the state (at least it was healthy up until 2009), not to mention the quality of pots being made here in North Carolina, and the confident entrepreneurial skills of many individual potters, who readily adapt to ever-changing marketing tools and conditions. For instance, many North Carolina potters are active bloggers, and use other social media like Facebook and Twitter.

Mark's pots on display,
Nasher Museum of Art,
Duke University, 2010

Mark Hewitt's pots on display beside his workshop, Pittsboro, 2010

All the talk, all the buzz about North Carolina pottery, is rooted in the tradition, and has extended along its many branches. Black Mountain poet, Robert Duncan, puts it nicely when he says, "We have come so far that all the old stories whisper once more."[8] The tradition whispers once more, but it wouldn't get far with only a whisper. Without people talking, or sometimes even shouting, about North Carolina pottery, what we see at the annual Catawba Valley Pottery and Antiques Festival would not be happening.

And so the last, but by no means least, of My Favorite Things about North Carolina Pottery is the advocacy performed by countless people across the state and elsewhere who have, over the years, boosted the profile of North Carolina pottery—talking it up, spreading the word. It is as though there were an unofficial Public Relations committee that has promoted North Carolina pottery ever since the Busbees began talking about Jugtown and Seagrove area pottery back in the 1920s—and it probably started well before then.

Essentially there is what amounts to an honor roll of North Carolina pottery advocates, who have been, and still are, responsible for putting on festivals, organizing guilds, sitting on pottery related boards, writing books, newsletters, and press releases about North Carolina pottery, organizing exhibitions and auctions and catalogues, giving talks to civic organizations, teaching at all different levels, volunteering to distribute fliers around the state, volunteering for all the thankless little tasks that keep the wheels turning. The entity, the phenomenon we know of as "North Carolina pottery," would be a shadow of what it is today without all these advocates.

We potters benefit more from this advocacy than you'll ever know, so, from the bottom of our collective hearts, thank you!

Notes

1. See Garth Clark, *Michael Cardew*.

2. See Bernard Leach, *A Potter's Book*.

3. See Soetsu Yanagi and Bernard Leach, *The Unknown Craftsman*.

4. Jonathan Williams, http://jargonbooks.com/JW_dossier_quotes.html.

5. Charles Olson, "These Days." http://www.harvardsquarelibrary.org/poets/olson.php

6. "Fully Awake—Black Mountain College," a documentary by Cathryn Davis and Neeley House. 2005. http://www.ibiblio.org/bmc/bmchomepage.html.

7. John Cage, http://www.writing.upenn.edu/~afilreis/88/cage-quotes.html.

8. Robert Duncan, "A Poem Beginning with a Line by Pindar," from *The Opening of the Field*.

References

Bridges, Daisy Wade. 1980. The Potters of the Catawba Valley. *Journal of the Ceramic Circle of Charlotte.*

Cardew, Michael. 1969. *Pioneer Pottery.* London: Longmans Publishing.

Clark, Garth. 1976. *Michael Cardew.* Tokyo: Kodansha International.

Duncan, Robert. 1960. *The Opening of the Field.* New York: New Directions Publishing Corporation.

Glassie. Henry Glassie. 1989. *The Spirit of Folk Art.* New York: Harry N. Abrams.

———. 1999. *The Potter's Art.* Bloomington: Indiana University Press.

Harris. Mary Emma. 2002. *The Arts at Black Mountain College.* Cambridge: MIT Press.

Hewitt, Mark, and Nancy Sweezy. 2005. *The Potter's Eye: Art and Tradition in North Carolina Pottery.* Chapel Hill: University of North Carolina Press.

Katz, Vincent and Martin Brody. 2003. *Black Mountain College: Experiment in Art.* Museo Nacional Centro de Arte Reina Sofía. Cambridge: MIT Press.

Leach. Bernard. 1940. *A Potter's Book.* London: Faber and Faber.

Mack. Charles. 2006. *Talking with the Turners: Conversations with Southern Folk Potters.* Columbia: University of South Carolina Press.

Scarborough Jr., Quincy. 1986. *North Carolina Decorated Stoneware: The Webster School of Folk Potters.* Fayetteville: Scarborough Press.

Yanagi, Soetsu, and Bernard Leach. 1972. *The Unknown Craftsman.* Tokyo: Kodansha International.

Zug, Charles G. III. 1986. *Turners and Burners: The Folk Potters of North Carolina.* Chapel Hill: University of North Carolina Press.

———. 1981. *The Traditional Pots of North Carolina.* Chapel Hill: University of North Carolina Press.

That's Where I Came In: Henry and His Teachers

Robert Cochran

"As a young professional," Henry Glassie wrote sometime around 1980, looking back a decade or so to the turbulent 1960s, "I had published a paper that conformed to academic norms and dutifully cleared a patch of intellectual new ground, but it offended the man I wrote about and lost me a friend."

There's a nuanced subtext here, a bit of tonal play, as in almost everything Henry writes—he's nothing if not an artful wordsmith. There's a gentle smile, for example, in "young professional," of course, harmonizing nicely with the conformity to "academic norms" and pride in the piece's "intellectual new ground." It takes a "young professional" to deploy such a phrase in unalloyed seriousness. It's the closing clause, however, and the opening one of the following sentence—"Friends are worth more than books"—that command a more lasting attention. A problem has by this point been posed: how might it be possible to "study people . . . without harming anyone?"

It is a crossroads moment. Determined to be faithful to a folklorist's version of the physician's traditional *"Primum Non Nocere"* motto, he turned from people to things: "Artifacts became my company." Keeping company with barns and houses, he could "question aggressively, push, rip, criticize" without fear of giving offense. On one level, this strategy worked spectacularly well—the groundbreaking *Pattern in the Material Folk Culture of the Eastern United States* appeared in 1969, followed by *Folk Housing in Middle Virginia* in 1976.

But somehow it wasn't wholly satisfactory, and by the time Henry went to Ireland, to the community of Ballymenone, in 1972, he was determined to do better: "I yearned for . . . conversation, live guidance" (1982:11). That

471

he found such guidance in abundance, followed it diligently, and did much better is clear from the books that resulted—*All Silver and No Brass* in 1976, *Passing the Time in Ballymenone* in 1982. Retrospect makes clear a pivotal change, already vividly clear in these works, but ever more prominent in the wide-ranging studies that appeared in the following decades, from the massive *Turkish Traditional Art Today* of 1993, to 1997's *Art and Life in Bangladesh*, 1999's *Material Culture*, and the 2006 volume marking a return to Ireland, *The Stars of Ballymenone*. It's wonderfully appropriate that Henry's latest effort is a biography, a move to a genre noted (especially when its subject lives) for the central role of "live guidance."

Even the most cursory glance reveals a fundamental shift. Pick up either of the earlier books and scan the pages. For all the wide range of the first and tight focus of the second, both are rich in illustration, packed with floor plans and photographs of houses, sketches of outbuildings and plows. But no people. In all of *Folk Housing in Middle Virginia*'s scores of photographs, only two contain people (pp. 127, 146), and one of these (p. 127) is an image not made by the author picturing a man with his back turned. Houses are viewed from the outside—there is but one interior sketch (p. 146). Doors are closed; windows are shuttered. The place looks deserted even when it isn't. Much the same practice is evident in *Pattern in the Material Folk Culture of the Eastern United States,* where a book studded with several hundred of the author's photographs and drawings includes only three human faces—New York basketmaker William Houck (p. 176) and West Philadelphia slingshot marksmen Piggy Becket and Lenny Divers (p. 219).

A striking emblem of this period in Henry's fieldwork would be an article-length piece from 1965, "The Old Barns of Appalachia." There are no photographs, but the fifteen drawings include five men, one cow, and one mule, each posed in isolation against a featured barn. The human figures are for the most part merely roughed out, viewed in the middle distance, clearly deployed as approximate indicators of scale. But the gent in figure 10, firmly at home next to his double-crib barn, is without question the author himself, a self-portrait of the folklorist as an old coot. He doesn't look truculent, or even especially wary, but he certainly projects an assured self-sufficiency. Lord of an emptied realm, posed by the artifact he has chosen for company, the scholar has projected himself into a world populated by no others.

In all this work, the "young professional" determined to do no harm has been true to his word. He's working hard, tramping through fields, taking pictures and making careful measurements and drawings. He's a really quite spectacular clearer of "intellectual new ground," already a bright star in the academy's firmament. But he's mostly by himself, a bit of a loner. No wonder he yearns for conversation, bestirs himself in search of "live guidance."

Turn now to the books from Ireland, Turkey, and Bangladesh—the work done during and after the trip to Ballymenone. The same wealth of illustration is present, but the focus has shifted markedly. Page after page flowers with people, old and young, male and female, at work and at rest. Artists display their work; housekeepers and shop owners stand at their doors. There's an obvious temptation to retrospective over-reading here, but I cannot resist locating a pivotal turning point in *Passing the Time in Ballymenone*'s first photograph of Ellen Cutler (p. 60). The volume's opening photographs, of countryside (pp. 3–10) and town (pp. 28–32) are very nearly as empty of humans as the earlier Virginia and Pennsylvania studies, though the reader is prepared for Mrs. Cutler's advent by a first glimpse of her open door (p. 10) as the concluding image of the opening countryside series. But mostly these are scenes a stranger sees, the new arrival's view of the community.

But then we meet Mrs. Cutler. She's standing in her doorway; she's smiling; her right hand is open in a gesture of welcome. She's a hostess; the scholar/photographer is being invited in. Other welcoming people are soon introduced—Joe and Peter Flanagan (pp. 93, 94), Hugh Nolan (p. 115), Michael Boyle (p. 130)—and the sought after "live guidance" begins in earnest. The student is more than ready. His analytic skills honed by the work of examining barns and houses, his appetite for conversation and patience with conversation's slow pace and oblique turns, perhaps augmented by the principled austerity of his long period of atonement, he's a very quick study. He sticks around, returns, evening after evening, for the deepening engagement of the ceili and the pub (and the hospital ward with Michael Boyle). The rewards are immense. Thirty years later he will remember Hugh Nolan as "the greatest teacher I have ever known" (2006:2) and Peter Flanagan as the first of "three completely realized artists" (2006:181) he would meet, the one who teaches him how to recognize the next two.

Passing the Time in Ballymenone and its successors are mostly big books, as rich in illustration as their predecessors. But here people are everywhere—rooking hay, clamping turf, thatching a roof, picnicking on a hillside. Sometimes they work in solitude, but just as often they labor in groups. And doors in addition to Mrs. Cutler's have been opened—interior views abound. Images of the hearth are especially common. The text includes the voices of women. The final image, place of honor, is a close-up of Hugh Nolan (p. 714), accompanying somber meditations on the deaths of teachers the student had come to love. Mr. Nolan was a childless man, but his photograph is balanced (one page earlier) by another of Ellen Cutler with her son and grandson. The "young professional" who had attempted to "atone for youthful misdeeds" by holding himself aloof from studying people has more than solved the problem that drove his Irish venture. He has learned more than how "to probe and write and learn without harming anyone," and has brought with him skills in addition to purely professional competencies and interests. He has achieved a deeper comprehension of ethnographic art's social responsibilities, has come to understand his own work as joining in the community's larger patterns.

Here, for example, is one among many lovely pictures of Ballymenone at work. The community's mason is Tommy Moore. When he helps his neighbor Paddy McBrien build a house, Paddy himself, by an outsider's perspective the "customer," and therefore assumed to be in charge, is in Ballymenone merely "one of the crew, a follower." But in the fields, when rain threatens and "hay lies on the spread," Paddy, the community's "agricultural expert," moves to the lead: "His neighbors submit to his direction and form a single force." Peter Flanagan, "an impoverished farm laborer" and Paddy's neighbor, joins in this effort, a follower here as Paddy was in the raising of his house. But in the pub, when day's work ends, "courtly Peter Flanagan opens his fiddle case and takes command" (1999a:253).

Only one thing is needed, for the reader to grasp what the writer had well in hand by the time he wrote this description. The lovely passage on the page, the book held in the hand, must be understood as analogous to the sturdy home, the successfully gathered hay, the expertly performed tune. It represents the moment when the scholar, a follower at the construction site, field, and pub, moves to the fore, understanding reciprocity's requirements, and repays the community's hospitality, makes his own contribution to the community's sustenance.

At the most basic level, the books made of the scholar's work are printed and sold, bringing in money. Distributed within the community, their royalties stand as the author's understanding of local standards of "engaged union," the "intense reciprocity" governing personal interactions. "When two men meet," we read by way of example, "a cigarette is offered." The recipient in turn offers a light, and soon he in turn "offers a cigarette and receives a light in return." Similarly, men "drinking together in a public house" will stick together for the evening, joining in "a tacit pact . . . so that each can take his turn buying drinks for the company" (1982:137). Understood in these local terms, the books' royalties are the scholar's round of drinks, his match struck in return for the offered cigarette. Ellen Cutler, we're told in passing (2006:204), used her share of the royalties from *All Silver and No Brass* to replace the thatch on her roof with metal.

But money, its importance recognized, is the least of the scholar's gifts. The scholar, enlarged by honorific titles and the gravity associated with institutional affiliation, carries upon her or his unimposing person an enhanced power of validation. When Henry Glassie's books heap praise upon Peter Flanagan, the familiar local musician gains additional stature in the eyes of his community by the outside authority's high estimate. When Mr. Flanagan died, the last of Henry's stars to go, the *Fermanagh Herald* eulogized him as "one of the great legends of our time" (2006:187). If there can be no doubt that Mr. Flanagan deserved every syllable of this tribute, there can also be no doubt that Henry Glassie's work helped guarantee he would receive it. Later, in Turkey, his scholar's clout is able to "arrange a belated award . . . from the Turkish government" for Ahmet Şahin, "the twentieth century's grand master of Islamic ceramics" (1999a:179, 178).

Henry's understanding of his work's valuable and appropriate role in local life is made vividly explicit in *The Stars of Ballymenone,* published almost a quarter century later. Speaking of an older generation of stars he came too late to know, Henry notes both their marginal economic status—"They failed as workers"—and their contributions to community life: "Their creations entertained the ceiliers and unified the community in their own days." When they died most of them left no children. But younger men in the neighborhood took up their stories and songs; they became in their turn the stars of Henry's time in Ballymenone: "Michael Boyle. Hugh Nolan, and Peter Flanagan— they, too, had no children. That is where I came in" (2006:111, 113).

There's a confidence in this brief phrase, made more resonant by our awareness of the scholar's former vow to remain outside. Ballymenone, at bottom, is the place where Henry "came in." Rooted in the lessons learned at Ballymenone's hearths, the student's mature work has long since proved itself a contribution to community life. In its opening pages, *The Stars of Ballymenone* puts into explicit and generalized terms the solutions Henry found to the disquiets that drove his quest a quarter century earlier. "No honest book can avoid all danger, all harm," the now matured professional admits, but there's a hard-won pride in the careful phrasing that follows: "but, in writing, injurious facts can be suppressed, compassionate explanation can muffle the shock, and balance is not impossible" (2006:4). Noting that he'd "slept in town to remained unaligned" during his initial visits, he adds that "neutrality can be sustained for only so long." Subsequent visits found him with neutrality explicitly abandoned, spending his nights with Joe and Peter Flanagan, "my pals P and Joe" (2006:5).

When he came to write about Ballymenone, he followed, in his search for "balance," the deep principles of neighborliness its people had taught him by their own example. The neighbors know, for example, that in most situations sociability appropriately trumps ideology. Asked what makes a good neighbor, Ellen Cutler responds not with abstract principle but with concrete instance: "I mind seein Tommy Lunny come up here in the middle of the night to help when the cow was goin to calve. Now that was a good neighbor." The scholar appreciates her point: "Though not a member of her religion, a man whose politics could not be more different from her own but who lives nearby came at a time inconvenient to himself to help in work on which her economic well-being depended without mention of repayment" (1982:291).

The key to everything, the heart of the saving solution to the problem that brought the scholar to Ballymenone, might seem to be this "live guidance" itself, to ethnography understood as "the ability to converse intimately" (1982:14). But this notion itself was hardly new—Henry as grateful student had already dedicated a book to his cherished teacher Fred Kniffen. He would remember his youthful collaborative work with students surveying log buildings in southwestern Pennsylvania as "my best experience as an educator" (2000:39). What does seem novel is the emphasis on "intense reciprocity" (1982:137), as a governing principle of human interaction, coupled with a dawning realization that the folklorist at work not only examines human communities but inevitably also joins them. Most central of all is a deeper understanding of the need for "compassionate explanation" and (more boldly) the occasional suppression of "injurious facts." There's a ranking implicit in this: whenever conformity to "academic norms" once privileged by the "young professional" urges publication of "injurious facts" potentially harmful to a friend, the mature scholar will present those facts indirectly, taking care to protect the friend. Ethnographers are at last not judges. The scholar who so esteems Ellen Cutler that he names a daughter for her will not in the service of ethnographic ends hang her out to dry.

No "young professional" is born knowing such things; few of any age learn so well, or find such superb teachers. My own "youthful misdeeds" were ameliorated by a patient spouse in Ellen Cutler's role as teacher: an invitation arrives in the mail, announcing a family festival involving several people featured in one of my books. "What are they inviting me for," I'm alleged to have asked, "the book's already out." "Because they actually LIKE you," Suzanne replied. "They think of you as a friend."

In later years this incident has been repeatedly cited as revealing previously unsuspected levels of cluelessness, calling for stepped up vigilance and pedagogical exertion by herself and the children.

Perhaps for me, the closest equivalent of Ellen Cutler's open door was a telephone call, not a posted invitation. On the line was a custodian, pictured and featured in a piece about a retirement party understood as a "folk festival." A single chapter, done at the request of the larger volume's editors, it was printed between hard covers and therefore expensive, but I'd bitten the bullet, purchased copies at my discounted rate for all eight partying custodians, and shipped one to each. The call was a thank you, and it included an extraordinary line. "This is the best thing that's ever happened to me," exclaimed the happy custodian. This was hyperbole, of course, the rhetoric of enthusiastic gratitude. But through that moment, out of my long-term pondering, I came to a better appreciation of the scholar's suprapersonal powers of validation. In the moment itself I was simply staggered, apprised as never before of the latent value in the work we do. I went off to think about it—and couldn't escape one thought: what if you hadn't done it? For Henry, such scenes have surely been recurrent—from Ballymenone to Kütahya, Dhaka to Arita, artists everywhere have had reason to rejoice over his arrival. In all these communities, he has been, in exactly the sense intended by my lone custodian, the best thing that ever happened to their "stars." He returned the gift of their hospitality with the reciprocal present of his listening and thinking and writing. He placed the books he made out of their meetings in their hands, allowed them to see for themselves the elevation of their accomplishments into a wider, more enduring light.

Taken together, all these lessons encapsulate the essential knowledge needed by the folklorist, the documentary filmmaker, the anthropologist— anyone, in fact, who for whatever mix of personal and professional motives intrudes upon the lives of others. Here then, in summary, are the three hearts of what I think Henry either learned or learned more deeply in Ireland and employed with spectacular success there and in three decades of fruitful labor in Turkey, Bangladesh, Japan, Nigeria, and elsewhere:

1. *The Exercise of Diligence*

This is the *sine qua non*. You take your work seriously, understand it as worthy, as participating in an honorable tradition, devote your best physical and intellectual energies to its accomplishment. Henry seems in full possession of this trait in even his earliest appearances. There's a wonderful story—did he write it somewhere or just tell me?—of a structure essential to study absolutely swathed in poison ivy. It must be measured; the scholar is acutely sensitive to *Toxicodendron radicans*. What to do? The structure measured, the scholar takes to his bed for a week of itchy recovery.

2. The Acceptance of Reciprocal Attachments

When you ask people to accept you, you must also accept them. Ethnography is not a one night stand—its interactions shape both parties, forge ties of mutual regard and obligation lasting as long as life. The distance of neutrality, of rigorous objectivity, is modified by affection, by loyalty. Perhaps the tersest personal sentence in all of *The Stars of Ballymenone* rises abruptly out of anecdote. A group of young men, worried about possible indiscretions dangerous to themselves in *Passing the Time in Ballymenone* but unwilling to undertake, even in tandem, a close perusal of its eight hundred pages, take the book to their priest for examination. No worries, he tells them when he's finished—"'This man knows everything about you, but he didn't say it.'" The next sentences are Henry's explanation of how and why, with why first: "I knew about moral lapses. I knew who made the bombs, but I talked about the present, as the old men did, through the indirection of historical analogy, leaving the living safe from reprisal" (2006:4). "I knew about moral lapses"—this is a chastened claim to lessons learned, to knowledge won. The scholar has found a way, after all, to study people and minimize harm. How? By "compassionate explanation," by the use of "the indirection of historical analogy" to keep the community that has opened its doors "safe from reprisal."

The scholar who grows into such praxis will of course be made to pay. New "young professionals" will not fail to both note the violations of "academic norms" and rise to their vigorous defense. I remember a drive with Pravina and Henry, me at the wheel, where conversation turned at one point to a colleague's address at a recent meeting. I had not been present, but I asked for a full account. In his work in Ireland, the speaker claimed, Henry had knowingly suppressed significant truths, had mistakenly allowed personal loyalties to interfere with the straightforward presentation of obvious facts. Henry seemed both resigned and not terribly put out, almost as if recognizing some vestige of himself as "young professional" in the rebuke.

His written rejoinder is a mild one, relegated to a footnote affirming the critique itself as "apt" and the critic as a "friend." Even with its "unusable" fraction, the additional information resulting from friendship's sustained and intimate conversations offers "a solid gain for science." The "unpublishable" component, moreover, "usefully conditions what gets written" (2006:421–42).

Several years back I reviewed Nolan Porterfield's superb biography of John Lomax, *Last Cavalier,* praising especially its careful parsing of the subject's complex mix of admirable and deplorable qualities. Its final pages report the reaction of Dock Reed, the great Alabama singer first recorded by Lomax in 1937, when he's told of the scholar's death by Ruby Pickens Tartt:

> Headed toward Reed's farm to give him the news, Mrs. Tartt saw Reed coming toward her in his wagon. When he stopped and got down, she told him of Lomax's death, and they stood together in the road and wept. "We can't hep it," Reed said. "I feels like a fatherless child. Mr. Lomac done gone to glory, and us here. What I'm going to do? He was such a friend, such a good man. I'm going to miss him bad." (1996:485)

Passing the Time in Ballymenone and the books that follow it have more than one such moment, though in them it's the singers who die and the scholar who mourns. The point could not be simpler: ethnography is a deeply social science, rooted in the engaged efforts of imperfect mortals. It is a privilege and an intimacy. There's elation and heartbreak in it.

3. *The Subordination of Ideology*

Just as Tommy Lunny, hauling himself from his bed in the middle of the night, ranked differences in religion and politics as less significant than the obligations of neighborliness, so the scholar learns, against the often shrill norms of academic discourse, to recognize that ideological differences rarely rank highest in the accomplishment of everyday life in other communities.

This doesn't mean the scholar is a ninny who checks her or his own convictions at the door, a spineless trimmer who kowtows to bigots in service to a credo calling for unruffled feelings at any cost. Neighborliness may in most instances trump ideology, but there are limits. Go for dinner at the Hitlers' and you'll rightly be suspected of being soft on National Socialism. Despite Henry's arsenal of Ballymenone-nurtured maneuvers designed to avoid giving offense, there remain moments where his own sense of right requires straightforward expression. When Ahmet and Nurten Şahin are twice left saddled with debt by their business partners, the account in *The Potter's Art* does not shy from harsh labels—they were, Henry wrote, "double-crossed" and "betrayed" (1999b:64). Dick Cutler, I'd guess, did not understand himself as complimented when Henry reports in detail his inheritor's disposition of the treasured "dresser of delph" his mother had polished and proudly displayed in her home. After her death, the son "took an axe, smashed the china to bits, and threw it out in the street" (1999a:273).

Folklorists, by their more frequent encounters, in the accomplishment of their chosen labors, with people outside the academy and outside their own class and regional communities, have opportunities to rid themselves of the academy's characteristic vices, or at least dilute them. University campuses have a reputation as wild places, hotbeds of disrespect for authority and convention, sinks of unbridled licentiousness. Wonderful spots, in short. But it's important to remember that this boisterous image attaches to the transient students, not the tenured faculty. Inside the walls, the academy is a mostly placid place, a club, sheltered and insular, a secular cloister obedient to the Rule of Saint Correcta. No group is more convinced of its own right thinking; few groups police their membership (and the society at large, when they can get its attention) more rigorously. We have a vigilant eye (and more especially a vigilant ear, since it is mostly by their unhip speech that we shall know and despise them), and we're always ready to send other folks off for consciousness raising. Every day these Yahoos offend with their silly bumper stickers, their bellicose flag waving, their obtuse use of language sedulously avoided by their right-thinking betters, their persistent elevation to high office of shameless demagogues who appeal to their basest selves. Even the best intentioned and most zealous among them can't hope to keep up with the dizzying pace of our shibboleth switches. Long before they learn a new lingo it's not only passé but downright retrograde, a sure sign of spiritual failing.

In *Material Culture,* Henry at one point devotes the better part of a page to lamenting just such tendencies in contemporary scholarship, studies that "focus on the petty sins and successes of the academy, composing tiny histories of disciplinary trends in order to chastise the ancestors and confirm their own superiority" (1999a:76). But as folklorists we more often than our colleagues in other disciplines actually leave the campus and the lab, encounter others on their home ground. Their haplessness soon drops away, and things get more complex. "Wisdom is too strong a word," the scholar concludes, "but living in connection, engaged on the one hand with nature, engaged on the other with the neighbors, people know what they know. . . . They might be ignorant about distant matters, but they know who they are. Identity is not a hot topic among them" (1999a:255).

Return for just a moment to Dock Reed and John Lomax. Porterfield's biography appeared at about the same time as a series of article-length studies devoted in large part to hammering its subject, specifically as a shameless exploiter of Huddie Ledbetter and generally as a holder of retrograde views on race. These critiques were not wrong—Porterfield's biography calls Lomax's financial dealings with Ledbetter "inequitable, even immoral" (1996:360). But they were tendentious, partial, finally jejune, almost wholly ideological and therefore lacking balance, good examples of pieces designed at last to "chastise the ancestors and confirm their own superiority." The Lomax who in whatever measure earned the respect and affection of Dock Reed is pictured with greater depth and incomparably greater balance in the lovely statement of Reed's grief at the news of his passing. In my own imagining of the scene I do not suppose Reed to be unaware of Lomax's limitations, any more than I imagine Tommy Lunny at midnight momentarily forgetful of his differences with Ellen Cutler. I credit both Reed and Lunny with fully informed insistence upon a larger picture, with subordinating the lesser value the better to support the greater. Of all the lessons learned at Ballymenone's hearths, this may have been the most valuable, the most fruitful for the scholar's subsequent work.

It's time to close. Chapters in a volume such as this end with backward glances appreciative of excellent work accomplished and with good wishes for a happy and productive future beyond the classroom. Here's to all that. But I'll actually close with a wonderful story I told myself I'd tell Henry even as it happened. For more than a decade now I've made my little contribution to my home town's cultural life by donning a tux and serving as a co-host at the annual Northwest Arkansas Music Awards event. "The envelope please," I say, every year. Last year, I told them, would be my last. I was sixty-five— too old for these late-night bashes.

Local bands, of course, entertain with brief sets between the various award categories. One of these last year was an outfit called Cletus Got Shot. They were terrific, five or six guys with traditional instruments played at full throttle speed and earsplitting volume. Bluegrass metal, I'd call it. The lyrics, when I could figure them out, were defiantly apocalyptic—"Tear up the Post Office," the singer screamed. "Burn down the school." Employed at the university, I could hardly endorse such sentiments, but I loved the scene, being the old guy sitting there in his tux, waiting to open more envelopes while the young guys wailed and the girls danced at the edge of the stage.

The next morning, opening email, I found a new message from a Nathan Miller with "Thanks for *Singing in Zion*" as the subject line. Nathan Miller, it turns out, plays mandolin in Cletus Got Shot. *Singing In Zion* is a book published nearly a decade ago. It features the music of Phydella

Hogan and Helen Fultz, Nathan's great aunt and grandmother. A teenager when the book was getting done, he appears there only as a kid singing in church whose rock-and-roll tastes worry his mother. "I didn't get a chance to introduce myself," Nathan wrote, "what with all the goings on. I just wanted to say thank you, ten years later, for writing the book *Singing in Zion*. Although Grandma and Aunt Phydella have passed on, our family still gets together quite often to play music, and Jeanie is still doing well."

Henry, you'll know out of your own wider experience how pleased I felt, sitting there in front of my computer screen. As you can also see, I've saved the message. Analogous scenes dot your books—the letters from Ellen Cutler, the desperate "For God's sake, tell the Yank I'm alive" from Peter Flanagan, the serenely accepting "I know" from Hugh Nolan. A sense of well-spent life, right? Right livelihood? Bread upon the waters? Well done. Every blessing, pal.

References

Cochran, Robert. 1999. *Singing in Zion: Music and Song in the Life of an Arkansas Family.* Fayetteville: University of Arkansas Press.

Glassie, Henry. 1964. The Old Barns of Appalachia. *Mountain Life and Work* 40:21–30.

———. 1969. *Pattern in the Material Folk Culture of the Eastern United States.* Philadelphia: University of Pennsylvania Press.

———. 1976a. *Folk Housing in Middle Virginia.* Knoxville: University of Tennessee Press.

———. 1976b. *All Silver and No Brass: An Irish Christmas Mumming.* Bloomington: Indiana University Press.

———. 1982. *Passing the Time in Ballymenone: Culture and History of an Ulster Community.* Philadelphia: University of Pennsylvania Press.

———. 1993. *Turkish Traditonal Art Today.* Bloomington: Indiana University Press.

———. 1997. *Art and Life in Bangladesh.* Bloomington: Indiana University Press.

———. 1999a. *Material Culture.* Bloomington: Indiana University Press.

———. 1999b. *The Potter's Art.* Bloomington: Indiana University Press.

———. 2000. *Vernacular Architecture.* Bloomington: Indiana University Press.

———. 2006. *The Stars of Ballymenone.* Bloomington: Indiana University Press.

———. 2010. *Prince Twins Seven-Seven: His Art, His Life in Nigeria, His Exile in America.* Bloomington: Indiana University Press.

Porterfield, Nolan. 1996. *Last Cavalier: The Life and Times of John A. Lomax, 1867–1948.* Urbana: University of Illinois Press.

At the Black Pig's Dyke and Other Writing: Crossing Borders of Art and Tradition

Vincent Woods

I

Born in a meadow of language and history. Born in a shining white hospital close to an ancient fortification between Ulster and the other Kingdoms of Ireland; close to the border between the counties of Leitrim and Fermanagh. Born in a gap of time, at the tail end of tradition.

I come into the world in August 1960, the last year they keep and kill a pig on our farm in Tarmon. The place name comes from Gaelic, most likely *Tearmann,* Place of Sanctuary. This duality of names and naming is everywhere, two languages side by side, within each other, twisting new sounds and new realities. Manorhamilton, where I'm born, may once have been *Cluain Maoldinn,* Sweet Meadow; its official Gaelic name now is *Cluainín Uí Ruairc,* the Meadow of the O'Rourkes, rulers of the old Kingdom of Breifne. The town was built and its English name given by Sir Frederick Hamilton, Presbyterian planter from Paisley in Scotland. Granted over three thousand acres of land by King James I in 1621; in the Irish rebellion of 1641 his soldiers destroy Sligo Abbey and the Franciscan abbey at Creevelea. On Christmas Eve that year they burn the nunnery at Gob, Cartronbeg, Tarmon, on the western shores of Lough Allen. *Teampeall na gCailleacha Dubha,* The Convent of the Black-veiled Women. They kill the sheltering nuns, burn the place.

I grow up with stories. My grandfather finding a book with a vellum cover in the ruins of the old convent, burning it for fear of bad luck. My grandmother seeing a mermaid combing her hair in a mirror on the lough

Vincent Woods. Enniskillen, County Fermanagh, 2003

Vincent Woods. Minneapolis, Minnesota, 2010

shore. Protestant landowner Sadlier drowning his Catholic manservant Trapp in the lake, putting him down with the oar. "His boast was there wasn't enough water in the lough to drown him." Because his servant can swim, when the boat overturns Sadlier downs his man with the oar, can't bear to see him survive. The searchers find Trapp's body first, are said to have put it back in the water so they'll have the honour, reward of taking Sadlier's body from the water before Trapp's.

That same year of my birth sees the last wedding with strawboys in Tarmon, in the townland of Faulthy up in the hills over the lough. My father and oldest brother Hugh go in straw; my uncle Michael Guihen too and Paddy Murray, whose father Myles was Captain of the Strawboys at a wedding in our townland of Aughamore in 1942. Fragments of his mock-heroic recitation on that occasion linger in memory as I listen, eager-eyed, a strange boy who crops his hair at the age of six in atonement for the sins of the world:

'We the Strawboys will light a fire
On an adjacent hill
To let them know in Ulster,
Munster
and Leinster
That an event of great significance
Has just happened in Connaught.'

Aughamore, the Big Space, our farm a universe of thirteen acres. I step the fields in memory and sometimes in sleep. The hilly, rushy ground, hedges, ditches, boundaries of hazel, white thorn, black thorn, sally, briar, holly. Banks of moss and primroses, bluebell, buttercup. The brow of the hill where you pause to drink in the view down over the lake and the blue Mountain of Iron where Fionn hunted with the Fianna. Here red cows and black graze and chew the cud, the sand-coloured donkey among them. By this dry bank my parents milk two cows in the evening, swish of warm milk into tin buckets.

Plenitude

"God bless the cows," the greeting from a neighbour on the path home.

The Co. Leitrim town of Manorhamilton, seven miles from the Fermanagh border was home to Gordon Wilson, whose daughter Marie was killed in the IRA bomb attack on the Poppy Day Remembrance ceremony in Enniskillen in November 1987. He worshipped in the Methodist church, now The Glens Arts Centre and where my play *At The Black Pig's Dyke* has been performed in English and Gaelic. His words of forgiveness after the Remembrance Day attack, and his profound, simple description of his daughter's death as he held her hand, her body trapped under rubble, were a turning point on the road to peace. They were also a deep inspiration for my play, set on the Leitrim-Fermanagh border, a play of swift violence and slow memory, of sectarian hate and human love, a play with mumming at its soul and centre.

At The Black Pig's Dyke, the play I could not have written without you, Henry. A play that would never have come to life without your miraculous work in Ballymenone; the world you captured and brought to life in the book *All Silver and No Brass.* A book I read first when I was in my early twenties, by grace of the brilliant folklorist and my then wife-to-be, Anne O'Connor. By her grace I meet you in Derry in April 2002 and life, love, literature, and tradition meet there too.

Step the farm path, across foot sticks, through gaps dusty-dry in summer, ploshed and hoof-holed-sodden in winter. Up the cobbled lane (pause to pick a fistful of redberries) to the old house, my father's mother's home, a ruin before I ever set eyes on it. My parents meet here for the first time, she is thirteen and carrying a setting of eggs in her apron, he eighteen or nineteen, just moved from Derrindangan to live with his bachelor uncles and inherit the place.

"I knew then and there she was the one for me," he tells us after her death. She's bringing the eggs to his uncles, Hugh and James, Hughie and Jimmy McPadden, his mother's brothers. Jimmy, who goes missing in June 1932, gone for days, a frantic search on, they walk field and lake shore. My father finds him hanging from the shaft of a cart in the pig house in the haggard behind the house. Hughie, great wit and caretaker of the graveyard where they all rest now: Curraghs, with the ruin of a monastery within it, the lap of water at its walls.

Both were great craftsmen, making baskets and creels from sally rods. Poll na Still, the hollow between the two meadows where they made poteen.

Another brother, Myles, emigrates to America, to Connecticut. He wants my parents to move there when they marry. They pay a photographer to take their picture, thinking they might go, thinking they'd need a formal photograph for travel. My father looks awkward in the photo, uncomfortable in suit and tie, my mother has a distant look in her eyes, serene, worldly. The photo is never put to use; they opt to stay in the place they love.

Myles McPadden was very close to Myles Murray, my father told me, as I am close to Michael, Myles Murray's grandson. There was a big night for my granduncle before he went off to the new world, a wake for the living who will vanish. The two friends said goodbye to each other at a place I knew well from my boyhood travels on the farm.

AFTER THE AMERICAN WAKE

for Michael

It is 1904 or 1905—we don't know the time of year
    but it's likely summer.
Two men are saying goodbye forever at a green gate
    over a stream.
They are both called Myles, both are tall and thin.
    One is going to America
    and will never return.

    One is staying here
    and will never leave.

They have watched the dawn rise over the lough,
    seen the last of the stragglers home.
They hear the jingle of the horse's harness, linger,
    clasp hands, hear the driver shout.
Remember, said the one leaving, Remember tonight.

The grass in summer falls to my father's scythe. Corncrake and hare are left in a sward uncut. We work and sweat and blister. My father stands on his head in the middle of the second meadow, comic acrobat when evening comes.

St. John's Eve: bonfires on the mountain and once on the roadside at our house. Always a fire at the bridge, boundary between two counties, Leitrim and Roscommon. Someone leaps over the flames.

St. Stephen's Day we straggle out on the Wren, put on old clothes, big jackets, false faces, walk miles and miles, singing badly, seeing into houses we didn't know existed.

The endless path to your neighbour's door.

As a young man my father had gone out with the wren boys, big groups, maybe forty, the leader carrying a wren, alive or dead. To bury a dead wren at a house was to bring bad luck. So always welcome them, treat them.

Nellie Redican in a panic, digging at the gate, fearful they'd buried the bird to curse her. To put a mí-ádh on the place.

2

My mother's mother believed in the fairies.
She'd say:

The Good People,
God bless them,
Our backs to them,
Our faces from them
And we wish them good luck
On their journey.

Bridget Flynn, small, swift, raven-haired. Could have been Spanish by her looks. Married James Guihen, Jim Curley, brought a dowry of five hundred pounds. Moved from the big two-storey farmhouse where Carolan had played music to the two-room thatched house where she lived till he died. Never much ease or comfort from the day she married. Seven children. My mother, Mary, the oldest. Gaelic still a living, breathing, warm language when she was a child. A coal wrapped in the tail of her skirt if she went abroad to a neighbour's house after nightfall. To keep her safe.

Before tea leaves were cast out the door, or a basin of dirty foot-water, the call:

Uisce Salach
Uisce Salach
Uisce Salach

So they wouldn't be splashed, dirtied, insulted.
The Good People.

Bridget Flynn, now B. Curley, sits vigil with her new-born grandchildren, the first five of my brothers and sisters, all born in the old house in Aughamore. Sits vigil until they're baptized, places a tongs across the cradle where they sleep.

Iron to keep them at bay.
So no Changeling will be left.

Terrified of storms, of lightening and thunder, holy water splashing. When the sun shines through rain she says, the Devil and his Mother are fighting.

The Devil: such a constant presence in language. The Devil take you, The Devil mend you, The Devil sweep them, The Devil is ridin that fella, The Devil is above on his back. The Devil is in that one.

Only 'Divil' and 'wan'—the sound broader, richer.

My father says, God is good and the Devil isn't bad either.

Such a turn out for B. Curley's wake and funeral. I'm eleven-almost-twelve when she dies, a July day, sunny, warm, still. I climb the hills with my collie to bring the news to my father shaking hay in the second meadow. He's talking to our neighbour, the shopkeeper, Eddie Guihen, who has been asking after the Old Woman. I gulp out my message. My father stops work, takes off his cap and blesses himself.

God rest the Dead.

In the long cortege of cars from our house the evening of her removal the sun simmers in a faint rain.

She had told my mother stories about The Black Pig's Dyke. How it was made by a black pig running beneath the ground and pushing the earth up. How it ran still and would run until the day of a Great Battle, when Protestant hordes would cross the Dyke from the north and would be defeated close to a chapel near the site of the Dyke, old fortification between the Kingdom of Ulster and the rest of Ireland.

My mother passed the stories on to me. I imagined the chapel was our chapel in Tarmon.

I make a play in the last nine months of my mother's life. Precious months spent with my parents, talking, listening, rereading *All Silver and No Brass,* Alan Gailey's *Irish Folk Drama.* Passing the time in my home place. I write on scraps of paper, type on an old typewriter in the cold back bedroom of the house in which I grew up. The house my father built in 1950, when they moved from the hills to live beside the main road. Built with stones from the lakeshore, the roof slated. That house gone now, a new one built on its footprint.

I write the mummers' plays first, drawing on the brilliant folk surrealism of Michael Boyle in Ballymenone. Mingling it with imagination. Making the old new:

The doctor's speech from the first mummers' play:

Here come I, a Doctor good, a Doctor pure,
There's no disease that I can't cure. (. . . with . . .)

The filicee fee of a bum bee
And the thunder nouns of creepie stool,
Boiled up in a wooden, leather, iron pot,
Poured into a ditch and left to rot.
Fishes' feathers, Lourdes water,
Babies rescued from the slaughter;
Spiders elbows, flags from graves,
Hearts fresh off the sharpest staves;
Certain hairs from randy goats,
Giblets out of overcoats.
Stir all up in a cat's behind—
Forty days to cure the blind.
The dead need certain extra measures,
This bottle here contains me treasures—
The broom's left foot, a midge's thigh,
A sparrow's fart, a graveyard's sigh.
Made into a mixture:
Hocus Pocus, Sally Campaign,
Rise up, dead Hero, and fight again.

I write a mock-heroic speech for Michael Flynn, Captain of the Straw-boys to recite at the fools' wedding in my unfolding drama. The words, the rhythm, the rhyme seem to float from air, arrive through me onto the page fully formed. I go to visit Paddy Murray, ask him about his father's speech back at the Aughamore wedding in 1942, read him some of mine. There's silence. Then he says, that's the exact pattern of rhyme my father used.

Paddy has prostate cancer; my mother has bladder cancer. Each sits at home, a mile away from one another. They will never see each other again. He had seen her parents go to church to be married, remembered the horse-shoes on the road for them as blessing and good luck.

My mother dies in July, two months before the play opens. A few weeks before her death I tell her the title I've settled on. *At The Black Pig's Dyke.* She smiles—a vast journey in that smile—says, that's a good name.

Paddy Murray dies the day after the play opens at Druid Theatre in Galway. His son Michael is there to see the past come alive through Ray McBride. See his grandfather remembered on stage, his words vivid through time and sacred space.

I have been blessed by grace of life to see what I have seen, to have known these people: farmers and miners and women in red headscarves

The Druid Theatre production of *At the Black Pig's Dyke*, 1992
Photograph by Amelia Stein

and bachelor men, their arms flailing like windmills as they march to Sunday mass. To have churned milk into butter, tasted the sweet slaking taste of buttermilk, stroked a black calf in a butterbox in our kitchen when I was seven or eight, poor sick calf and his long neck lolling and all the love that one living being can feel for another contained in that warm corner by the fire. To have made laps of hay and handshakings and cocks and ricks and pikes, to have twisted hay-ropes with my father letting out and me twisting and imagining an infinite journey in Africa as I walked away from him. The journeys too at the end of a pitchfork or rake as we shook the grass dry and raked it into rows for building. To have seen hay snigged into the haggard. To have cut seed potatoes and planted them, dug big tumbling white and red praties out of the earth, to have put out manure with the donkey and purdógs, cut sally rods to make a garden, to have sheltered with my mother and father in the dark, low byre, rain cascading down on the thatch, the three of us snug and embraced in the fresh hay scattered near the breathing animals. To have tasted boxty and pratie cake, soda bread and scone, nettle soup and wild strawberries. To have fished and caught eel and perch and bream—thecleancleartasteoflakelifewatersincetimebegan— to have gathered fossil stones on the lake shore.

The Good People, God bless them:

Flynns and Rynns and Lees and McKennas O'Brien and Gralton and Smith Travers, McPartland, Keavney, Gaffney, Gilhooley, Healy, Keane, McPadden, Murray, McMorrow, Lavin, McGoldrick, Harkin. McGovern, Rourke, McHugh Woods Guihen.

'What do ye see on the lake, Jack?'

Everything. All life, all lore, all the ways of being. Tradition being forged from time and repetitions. The splash of the oar and the hoofbeat of horse fade in the din of oncoming car, pit lorry, hearse. A small plane crashes and is lost in the deep water in dead of night. A white owl flies across the road near Cartron—spirit of a coal miner who spent forty years hoking coal in the pits of Arigna 'out of the light.'

3

From THIRTEEN ACRES

Babble pulls you down and back. The voices gabbling in the frozen thaw. All rush in one great meadow of scythed time. The men with flailing arms, the woman racing in impatient wake, a boy and girl who drowned and hanged, the seasons flow and flux of all that's gone. A tumbled pig house and an echoing gable ruin. All weeds and flowers shoot, trees fall, the summer stink of nettles and green rot. In this stone house a black tomcat did battle with a bride intruder into men's domain. He spat and arched and sprayed against her being; but lost and drowned or smoked to death inside a pot. In this white room five children slid to life; new afterbirth crackles in a blazing fire. A woman not-yet-old sits vigil with each child, iron tongs criss-crossed upon the cradle against fairy craft. One boy is dropped head first from her sleeping lap and bears a bruise to chapel for his christening. The first of many falls and risings up. Pink roses spatter the whitewashed wall. The cobbled way shines up a single stone through muck and mud. The hundreds who stepped here, the come and go of boots and winter feet, the shadows thronging wake and wedding, voices flinting the dark night. One man appears too late across the threshold, takes his whistle from his coat, asks the tall man Hugh how to turn the tune and plays a bar or two. "You'll turn straight round and out that door again, we'll turn the tune in daylight." Tall enough for any regiment, Hugh; his brother James is small and stout, wrapped in a cooper's apron in that brown photo of working men in Edinburgh. A dozen eggs thickyellowwhite fry perfect on the pan, the losset out for praties, cold buttermilk in the shaded churn. A wooden cup hooked up beside it for dipping deep, the cure for sunburnt thirst. This was the haggard where the donkey kicked in hayful dust, let loose from bands and harnesses, sweat lines smearing his grey belly and his sides. Rolling, snorting, the great brays of lonesome humanness, near-humanness, bonded, bound, all labouring, all fed now and thirsted in the shade. Gone the garden sanded from the blue lough shore and gone the path, well cowdunged from the dunkle at the byre door.

4

My father lived to see the play.

'Too much auld clatterin and bangin of sticks,' he said after.

He was upset when a performance was interrupted, disrupted in Derry, young republicans seeing it as pro-unionist.

'Draggin up the past, I knew them stories should be left to be forgotten.'

But I knew he didn't believe that. He had seen Tom Dennison laid out after he was shot in their shop in Drumkeeran. He had told that story over and over. I wove it into the heart's fabric of the play. Dennison becoming Boles.

My old love Elizabeth Fitzpatrick remembered in the double naming of Lizzie Flynn, sometimes Liz, and her granddaughter, Elizabeth, the surviving child of war and symbol of hope.

It was a long time ago, Elizabeth, and it was not a long time ago. . . . It was a time when to go east was go west, when to go south was to go north, when people sang songs at a wake and cried when a child was born. It was in a land where the sun never rose and the sun never set, where the dead prepared shrouds for the livin' and straw people walked the roads.

The moon was glorious and haunted over Tarmon in that winter of 1991. That November night when I walked back from Cartronbeg to Aughamore with Paddy Murray's slow, assured voice blessing the words I had written. I walked with a great lightness of step and an immense sense of connectedness to place and people, to the mystery and simplicity of time.

I was happy.

5

This from a short play for two people, *Broken Moon/Lune Brisée*. The story is inspired by Hugh Nolan's wonderful tale as told to you, Henry, and used to such effect on the back cover of *The Stars of Ballymenone*.

My uncle used to tell this. I don't know if he made it up or if it's older. Anyway—There was a man in a town. A very, very tall, very thin man and everyone said he was a fool. His arms were so long they almost reached his knees. He used to say he'd make a ladder to the moon, go and come back and tell them all what was on the moon, what it was made of, were there people there or not. And they all laughed at him and said he was a fool and the moon was the best place for him. He used to stand out in his small garden at night and watch the sky and say he was measuring the distance from earth to moon—and it varied depending on whether the moon was full or a half-moon or a crescent moon or just a sliver that you'd barely see.

He had a small workshop and he worked in there for years and years—people heard the sound of hammering and sawing and they'd laugh and say "listen to that, the mad fellow is building his ladder to the moon!" Then he vanished, one Sunday night, gone, not a trace. He was away for a month. When he came back he was even thinner and very pale and spent most of his time in bed. One woman used to look after him a bit and eventually he told her—he'd built his ladder, got the length and the angle just perfect, propped it up to the new moon and set off climbing.

Up he went and up and up and up and when he reached the top, he put his hand in on the moon—and what did he find but a whole pile of old moons, all shapes and sizes, thrown there like old bits of broken lamps—and nothing else, no people, no nothing. Only dust. And he didn't want to tell anyone because he knew they'd laugh at him and say it wasn't true. But he knew it was true: he lay there sighing and laughing, saying over and over: "And to think I was so foolish all these years, nothing but dust and a pile of old moons. . . ."

6

In the years after the Druid production of *At The Black Pig's Dyke* I often wondered, Henry, if you'd heard of the play, if you knew how central to it were your own work and words and images, and the older words and generous, surreal imaginations of the people of Ballymenone. Through reading your books these names and people had become familiar to me, alive, vital, like close friends of a close friend that one has heard about but never met. Peter Flanagan and Joe, Hugh Nolan, Michael Boyle, Ellen Cutler. They met and merged, somehow, with some of my own people from Tarmon: Mae Lee, Paddy Murray, Francie Flynn, my parents John Woods and Mary Guihen. I speak about those connections, those people that night we meet in Derry and I see your face in the gathering of people, alight with recognition, joyful that the words, the traditions, the lives you had been witness to, were remembered, made new, acknowledged.

After that meeting in Derry, and your talk in Enniskillen on the years, the people, the rich legacy of Ballymenone, I send you the published text of *At The Black Pig's Dyke*. You write back to say that the play and our meeting and conversations have given you more words and the ending for a chapter of a new book you are writing, *The Stars of Ballymenone*.

I don't remember if I told you about the play travelling to London, to Sydney, about how in Toronto George Seremba from Uganda says to me "But this play could be African." Did I tell you about the man who travelled from Montreal to Sydney to see it, and told me a sad story? From the Valley of the Black Pig, near Ballinamore, he had grown up with the tradition of mumming, with the beautiful straw costumes that were made for the performers. But the tradition of mumming was on the wane and there was only one old woman left who knew how to make the straw gear. So he asked her to make him a full set, tall mask, leggings, chest-piece to take back to his home in Montreal. She made it with a heart-and-a-half, proud and delighted when he went off with it, her work crossing the seas to a new home. He was stopped at customs on his way in to Canada, officials examined the straw suit and before he could protest or intervene, it was carted off to the incinerator and burned.

Every year when he went back to Leitrim the woman would ask about her mummer's costume and he would tell her that it had pride of place in his house and had had endless admirers.

A quarter of a century later the straw made it through Canadian customs and the besuited mummers danced to life on stage and the Leitrim man was happy and a little consoled.

Did I tell you, Henry that your drawings in *All Silver and No Brass* were the basis of the costume design and some of the set design for *At The Black Pig's Dyke?* And there's another story of life and art. I meet the designer, Monica Frawley, in the foyer of Druid Lane theatre on a Sunday evening in late August 1992. The play's director, Maelíosa Stafford says "She's the best."

So she was and so she is.

We have shared so much of life since then.

I can see the actress Stella McCusker as Lizzie Boles pull up a chair, settle herself for the arrival of the mummers, and that stage is transformed into the interior of one of your drawings, into the hearth of Ballymenone. Layer upon layer of life opens.

Light passes through.

When you greet me with Pravina in your home in Bloomington you pour me a glass of moonshine by way of welcome. Strong and mellow, the bounce of time in it, the power of transformation carried from the stills of Leitrim and Fermanagh to Indiana, Virginia.

Later that night the drift of your pipe smoke is another homecoming.

I sleep soundly, the journey over:

Tarmon, Ballymenone, Derry, Bloomington,

Henry.

7

In the hills of Tarmon, Aughamore in the 1940s an old woman waves a white sheet, calls out, jubilant to the houses around, "The Breifne Rourkes is saved!" A son has been born and all is well with the world. I spend days and nights of childhood in that house, watch early television, play cards, talk and listen; am saddened and a little lost when the Rourkes move to Dublin and the house is closed. Empty, it fades, goes to ruin, the vivacious glow of the rhododendron bushes a small reminder of what has been.

Here it is Henry, a little of my life, a fragment of tradition turning into language, into drama and the made gesture, into poetry. The first evening we meet we speak of Rumi, and a whole other world of eastern sensibility enters our discourse.

As fire shapes iron and the blacksmith beats out the shape for shoding, I beat at words . . .

As you, carpenter, shape wood for table, chair, bookcase, for roof beams I hew and hack at grain and knot of memory, tradition, what is given to construct—what? A chapel of bog-light. Small flares of language astray in the dark. A rick of words.

My father thatched the last of the thatched houses, my mother's home among them. It's a byre now. Jim Curley, her father, killed pigs for people around the area. As a child she'd hold the bowl for the pig's blood to pour into. When Jim was dying robins would come in to the bed to him, feed from his hand.

That July of 1992, my mother dying, I ask her if there's anything she would like: (the subtext "anything you would like before you die"). She thinks for a little, says "a drink of buttermilk." I ask around the place, only one woman in the area who churns fresh milk for butter. Teasie McMorrow, my old friend from boyhood, Teasie with the high, sweet voice and the gentleness and nobility of a saint. A bottle of buttermilk is sent to us and I pour a glass for my mother. She drinks deep, holding the glass firmly with both hands "No one," she says, "not you, no one could know what this means to me."

As she dies I hold a bottle of rose water perfume to her face so that she may breathe and smell life and nature. On the night of her funeral her soul returns, a butterfly, pink and black, lands on my hand, lands on my sister's hand, on the couch where she'd lie and rest in those last weeks. Settles on the fingernail of the little finger of my right hand and we sit together for a while before I release her, on the wind of my breath to the vast moon and the sky.

From these deep wells, these springs here is all. In Tarmon where I will return to dust. In Curraghs cemetery. By the lapping water of the lough.

Curraghs

When we are dust
And share the ground,
My prayer is that nights

When the moon is huge
And globed in water,
Lovers will listen
To the splash of lake
By the graveyard wall
And I pray they'll fuck,
Hard and joyful
And laugh and look up
At the sky and be happy.

A serene stone face stares east from a ruined church gable: Patrick or Bridget?

     Both
A man tramps a yellow daub floor
A hearth fire is set
Dancers hover at the edge of music
Swallows build on the new walls of my father's fallen house.
A nest tumbles   Eggs shatter

The birds return and build again

A Folklorist's Work: Henry Glassie's Life in the Field

Ray Cashman, Tom Mould, and Pravina Shukla

In November of 2009, Henry Glassie was awarded the Charles Homer Haskins Prize of the American Council of Learned Societies. The award honors "a scholarly career of distinctive importance." Previous recipients of the Haskins Prize include John Hope Franklin, Donald Meinig, Annemarie Schimmel, Helen Vendler, Clifford Geertz, and William Labov. Glassie is the first folklorist to be so honored.

In October of 2010, Glassie was given the award for a lifetime of scholarly achievement by the American Folklore Society. Glassie became a member of the AFS in 1964, when he was still an undergraduate. The next year he gave his first paper as part of the first AFS panel on material culture. Since then he has given twenty-two papers and chaired seven sessions at the annual meeting. Glassie was elected a Fellow in 1976, and he was elected President of the AFS for 1988–90, during the society's centennial era.

No living folklorist has reached wider for new experience, nor produced such a comprehensive scholarly oeuvre. He has done ethnographic work in New York, Pennsylvania, Virginia, North Carolina, Georgia, Louisiana, and New Mexico; and internationally in Fermanagh in Ireland, Devon in England, Dalarna in Sweden, and throughout Turkey, in Swat in Pakistan, in Rajasthan, Uttar Pradesh, and Tamil Nadu in India, and throughout Bangladesh, in Hagi and Seto in Japan, in Bahia and Pernambuco in Brazil, and in the Yorubaland of Nigeria. He has done fieldwork on dispersed rural landscapes in Virginia and Ireland, in agricultural villages in England and Sweden, in small industrial towns in Japan, and in two of the world's largest cities: Istanbul and Dhaka. He has written on architecture and the landscape, including *Folk Housing in Middle Virginia,* widely acknowledged as the most innovative book on American vernacular architecture. He has written on craft and art, including *Turkish Traditional Art Today,* the most complete ethnographic study ever produced of a single nation's folk art. He has written on folk drama, folksong, and folktale, including *The Stars of Ballymenone,* the most complete study ever written of a particular community's tradition of oral narrative.

This great spatial and topical breadth has consolidated as a single scholarly quest, guided by the folkloristic paradigm of performance, driven by an unrivaled intensity of long-term ethnographic endeavor, and motivated by a philosophical desire to democratize the ideas of history (human significance) and art (human excellence). Glassie's efforts, his method and its bountiful yield, have brought him transdisciplinary recognition—President Clinton nominated him for the National Council on the Humanities in 2000—and they have located his writings within the general cultural discourse: three of his books—*Passing the Time in Ballymenone, The Spirit of Folk Art,* and *Turkish Traditional Art Today*—were named among the notable books of the year by the *New York Times.*

Public Work

For most of Glassie's forty-one years of professional employment, he taught in the folklore departments at the University of Pennsylvania and Indiana University, but his career began as the state folklorist of Pennsylvania, and his work in the public sector continues to the present. For that work he was named a pioneer of public history, and his public work was described by Barbara Truesdell in an article in *The Public Historian* in 2008. Gregory Hansen's paper in the *Folklore Forum* in 2000 also stressed Glassie's public career.

Pennsylvania Folklorist

There had been a state folklorist in Pennsylvania before, Henry W. Shoemaker, but when the legislature established the position anew in 1967, MacEdward Leach, not wishing to live in Harrisburg, gave the job to Glassie, then a graduate student at Penn, and Glassie became the first in the new sequence of state folklorists. Glassie took the job, hoping he could work like the full-time collectors of the Irish Folklore Commission, for fieldwork is his love and skill, but he learned quickly that he had to labor within the institutional framework of state government. He co-authored a guide for collectors with Leach and visited the state's historical and ethnic societies, explaining field-work and gathering materials for the state archive. Concentrating on Polish, Italian, German, and African American traditions, he contributed to a massive bibliography on ethnic culture, used by high school teachers. He built the first Black History exhibits for the state museum. He was able to do some fieldwork in preparation for a series of folk festivals featuring Pennsylvania artists, the singer Ola Belle Reed, the fiddler Pop Hafler, the storytellers Lou Sesher and John Brendel. He organized the grandest of these festivals for the Girl Scouts of America. For folklorists, he edited the *Keystone Folklore Quarterly,* using it to advance study of folklife and material culture. He founded the Middle States Conference on Folk Culture to coordinate the efforts of folklorists in the region.

Working at the Pennsylvania Historical and Museum Commission, Glassie was at the time one of the few folklorists on a government payroll, so he was free to cooperate with other institutional entities. With Henry Douglas and Wilbur Zelinsky he founded the Pioneer America Society, organized to unify folklorists, geographers, and architectural historians in the study of the American landscape. The Society continues to thrive, and in 1993 Glassie was given the Douglas Award for his years of service.

Most important was Glassie's cooperation with Ralph Rinzler at the Smithsonian Institution. Glassie had worked with Rinzler at the Newport Folk Festival, organizing the craft demonstrations, and when Rinzler was planning the first Festival of American Folklife on the National Mall, Pennsylvania was the featured state because Glassie had found the people who could come to Washington to demonstrate their crafts and perform their music. The first Smithsonian festival was accompanied by a conference that drew scholars from Europe and the United States. Glassie, as chair of the conference, invited the scholars and directed the discussion that set the principles by which the Office of Folklife Programs—now the Center for Folklife and Cultural Heritage—continues to operate.

The year 1967 marked the beginning of Glassie's long association with the Smithsonian. In the next year, Glassie was seconded from the Pennsylvania Historical and Museum Commission to the Smithsonian in order to document the Poor People's Campaign. Dr. King had been murdered, but his plan was carried forward, and Glassie, accepted by the Southern Christian Leadership Conference as a writer of news releases, traveled with the

Western Caravan from Watts to Washington and lived in the encampment. His detailed notes were deposited in the Smithsonian's archive; from his thousands of photographs an exhibit of images of the fight for civil rights was mounted at the Smithsonian.

Over the years Glassie continued to cooperate with the Office of Folklife Programs, serving on the Smithsonian's Folklife Advisory Council from 1985 to 1992, recommending artists to appear at the festival, speaking there himself, and writing essays that were published in the program.

The high point of connection came in 2002 with Glassie's work on the organizing committee of the Silk Road Festival, the largest and most elaborate of the Smithsonian festivals on the Mall. The document Glassie wrote at the beginning became Yo-Yo Ma's guide; Glassie attended meetings in Washington, hosted a meeting at Indiana University, and, traveling to Asia, he selected for the festival four musicians, a sculptor, an engraver, and two weavers from Bangladesh, a goldsmith from India, five potters from Japan, and four potters from Turkey. All came to Washington, and during the festival Glassie served as a translator from Turkish and Bengali, and he stood with the potters in the heat, interpreting their art for the vast crowds of visitors. At the festival, on June 30, 2002, Glassie was the honoree of the Eighth Annual Rinzler Concert, thanked for his years of service to the Smithsonian.

Historic Preservation

After two years as a state folklorist, Glassie began teaching in the university, but his public career continued. Its first phase paralleled his research in architecture, and one aspect of his architectural interest had its public face in historic preservation. He spoke on the need for a more democratic historic preservation at the Point Park conference in Pittsburgh, the meeting at which public sector work was confirmed as basic to modern folkloristic practice. He lectured regularly for James Marston Fitch's pioneering historic preservation program at Columbia, and cooperated with Fitch in founding the historic preservation program at Penn.

Glassie's work in historic preservation has a private dimension. Using his professional knowledge of architecture and his amateur skills as a carpenter, he has restored six historic houses, one of which was featured in Marsh Davis's book on the most beautiful historic homes in Indiana. Glassie has been active locally. With his colleague Warren Roberts, he selected the historic houses that deserved protection in Bloomington; then, at the request of

Mayor Frank McCloskey, he drafted Bloomington's first historic preservation ordinance. At that time, early in the seventies, Bloomington had no society for historic preservation, but when Glassie returned to Indiana University after teaching at Penn, he joined Bloomington Restorations Incorporated. He is now in his fifth term as a member of the Board of Directors of BRI, a society that has won national acclaim for forging a connection between the historic preservation movement and governmental affordable housing initiatives, so that vernacular houses can be restored, neighborhoods brightened, and people of modest means can purchase lovely, refurbished homes. Twice Glassie has served as the President of BRI, both times being tasked to defend the city's historic fabric against the wishes of his employer, Indiana University. In 2000, Glassie was given the Roberts Award of BRI and a formal proclamation from Bloomington's City Council for his service to historic preservation. Recognized at the national level for his work in historic preservation, Glassie has given three keynote addresses at meetings of the National Trust. And his work became international with lectures for the Swedish National Housing Authority and his consultation with the architectural firm that designed the first mosque for Stockholm.

Outdoor Museums

The most important public consequence of Glassie's architectural research has been the subtle influence his writings have spread through the national historic preservation movement. Types identified, terms invented, and arguments advanced by Glassie and his beloved mentor Fred Kniffen have become basic to historic preservation practice. But the most conspicuous result of his public effort exists in the fabric of several outdoor museums. These museums, like his writing, are part of his scholarly achievement.

In 1971, Eli Lilly asked Glassie to advise in the restoration of an old log house he had bought. Soon Glassie was one of three, along with Myron Vourax and Sam Ritter, who designed and constructed Prairie Town, the first phase of the Conner Prairie Pioneer Settlement in Noblesville, Indiana; Prairie Town was called in the beginning "Henry's Heights." Glassie helped select the buildings; he guided their reconstruction, restoration, and siting. He traveled to North Carolina, beginning his work on Southern pottery that continues to this day, learning how to create the shop and kiln where the potter's art is demonstrated at Conner Prairie.

In 1973, he was invited to design more accurate housing for Plimoth Plantation in Plymouth, Massachusetts. Meshing James Deetz's archaeological discoveries with his own fieldwork in England, New England, and Virginia, Glassie not only designed a more accurate house that would influence future design at Plimoth, he put on period clothes, picked up period tools, and led a team in constructing the house that Anthony N. B. Garvan declared to be the most important experiment ever attempted in American architectural history. Continuing to work at Conner Prairie, Glassie became the conduit for ideas from Plimoth that continue to direct the interpretive style of the highly successful, much expanded and imitated museum in Indiana.

During the same period, Glassie was named the American consultant to the Ulster-American Folk Park in County Tyrone, Northern Ireland, which enabled him to continue his ethnographic project to the south in Ballymenone, County Fermanagh. For the museum in Ulster, he conducted fieldwork with a team of students—John Vlach, Howard Marshall, and Steve Ohrn—in southwestern Pennsylvania. Using the data they gathered, Glassie designed all the buildings in the museum's New World section and taught unemployed Ulster men how to build them.

The success of the Ulster-American Folk Park—where old Irish buildings have been reconstructed and old American buildings have been replicated to teach the story of Irish emigration—inspired Eric Montgomery, the museum's founder, to imagine a comparable museum in the United States. He located a site in the Valley of Virginia and asked Glassie to write *A Museum of American Frontier Culture: A Proposal,* which detailed the plan and rationale for the new museum. Once funding had been secured, Glassie took time away from his teaching at Penn to arrange the museum and help in selecting the American, Irish, and English buildings that were moved to the site. The Frontier Culture Museum invited the visitor to compare the complete American farmstead, moved from south in the Valley, with the complete farmsteads moved from England, Ireland, and Germany, learning how American culture was a synthesis of multiple sources, an innovation out of diverse traditions, and gaining from material evidence an understanding of the great American story of immigration, adjustment, and endurance.

To have been the creator of major segments of three large and successful outdoor museums—one in Indiana, one in Virginia, and one in Northern Ireland—would make a respectable career for many professionals. It has been a small and little-acknowledged facet of Glassie's work, though the time given to these projects is a clear expression of his sense of public responsibility, and the museums are the direct result of his scholarship in the field of vernacular architecture.

Indoor Museums

Work on outdoor museums was the logical consequence of the architectural phase of Glassie's scholarly endeavor. Work in roofed and temperature-controlled museums has been the logical consequence of his work with artists and art.

Glassie set the pattern in Ireland. He wrote a monumental scholarly book in *Passing the Time in Ballymenone,* but, aware of the ethical demands of ethnographic research, he also created two products for the community. One was a small book, *Irish Folk History,* that contained the key texts, and which he gave to every household in the community. The other was an exhibition at the Fermanagh County Museum in Enniskillen. He donated his photographs and drawings to the museum; they have proved useful in several exhibitions, most recently one entitled "Fermanagh Identity," and in local history projects for the schools. In 1983, they were first used in an exhibition at the museum to which Ballymenone's people, most of whom had never been in the museum, were invited. They all came, delighted by Glassie's slides that documented changes in their place, moved by the portraits of deceased elders on the walls, bursting into applause when Peter Flanagan, the last of the old stars, was asked to stand. It was a grand night.

Glassie elaborated that format in his next two ethnographic projects, both of them lasting, like his Irish work, for a full decade. The decade in Turkey, requiring him to master a new language, resulted in *Turkish Traditional Art Today.* In Ireland he made sure his books were published in Ireland as well as America, that they would be available to the native scholars, and his Turkish book was co-published by Indiana University Press and the Turkish Ministry of Culture in Ankara. As he did in Ireland, he also produced a small book. Translated as *Günümüzde Geleneksel Sanatı* and published in Istanbul, it outlined his project, and he sent copies to all who had helped him—well over a hundred people. While he was conducting his research, he was also buying objects for the permanent collection of the Museum of International Folk Art, which allowed him to get some money to the creators of the objects, and out of those things he assembled a major exhibition that was supported by the NEH and mounted by MOIFA. Ian Quimby, curator at Winterthur, said it was the best and most comprehensive exhibition of craft he had ever seen. Inspired by *Aditi,* the exhibition of Indian art at the Smithsonian, Glassie brought four artists from Turkey who demonstrated their skills amid the massive array of artifacts and photographs. It was, for the artists, their first time in America, and they enjoyed meeting their Native American colleagues. Fatma Balcı sat down to weave beside a Navajo woman. Mehmet Gürsoy and İbrahim Erdeyer traded ceramic insights, through Glassie's translation, with Wanda Aragon and Lilly Salvador at Acoma.

In its second incarnation, the Turkish exhibition was expanded at the Indiana University Art Museum, where Glassie designed the exhibition and his students installed hundreds of artifacts and hundreds of Glassie's photographs. The exhibition was accompanied by a film that Glassie made with Tom McCarthy and by a guide for high school students, relating the art to the precepts of Islam. Visitation was tremendous. With the support of the National Endowment for the Humanities and the Turkish Ministry of Culture, Glassie was able to bring from Turkey four potters, a weaver, a dyer, and two calligraphers to demonstrate their arts.

Both exhibitions were mounted for Americans who needed then, and need now, to understand more about Muslims, their culture and religion, but the positive impact on the artists was great. İbrahim Erdeyer said that the best moment of his life came when he stood at the opening in Indiana to receive the applause of the American people and the high officials of the Turkish government who were in attendance. Suddenly, İbrahim said, he understood the deep significance of the art to which he had devoted his life.

Glassie's next decade-long project took place in Bangladesh, resulting in *Art and Life in Bangladesh*. When Sheikh Hasina, the Prime Minister, asked what he wanted as a reward for his service to her people, he requested her to support him in the creation of a major exhibition at the National Museum in Dhaka. She agreed, commenting that only a foreigner who knew her country as well as Glassie could produce an adequately comprehensive exhibition. Knowing what she meant and what she wanted, Glassie produced a show of contemporary Bangladeshi traditional art that included equal numbers of Hindus and Muslims, equal numbers of women and men. He traveled the country, commissioning new creations that would become a well-documented permanent collection in the National Museum. From those objects, in cooperation with Bangladeshi colleagues, Glassie constructed a massive exhibition. All the artists came—some had never been to Dhaka, most had never seen a museum—and on the opening night they stood proudly beside their works to receive congratulations from officials of their government, and many of them remained to demonstrate their art during the show's first week.

For the exhibition, Glassie wrote a small, richly-illustrated catalog, *Contemporary Traditional Art of Bangladesh*, that became his gift of gratitude to the many who had helped. The potter Gauranga Chandra Pal told Glassie it was a wonder: he had lived a long time, had never owned a book, and now he owned a book and it had his picture in it. Glassie fills his books with his own fine photographs. They help the reader understand new places, but, in addition, he has learned it is important for the people, his subjects and collaborators, to receive books with their names and portraits in them. Glassie has never used pseudonyms, believing it is a crucial part of his work to bring new people—Hugh Nolan, Ahmet Şahin, Haripada Pal—into the permanent historical record.

Glassie feels it is important to give some lasting return to the people who help him, who teach him in the field, and that it is important to make sure the results of his research are available to the native scholars. *Art and Life in Bangladesh* was published by Indiana University Press, then in Dhaka by the Bangla Academy. Glassie began his work in Bangladesh by teaching workshops on folklore's methods and theories to young scholars in 1987. Twenty years later, the Asiatic Society of Bangladesh published *Living Traditions,* which Glassie co-authored with Firoz Mahmud, a Bangladeshi scholar whose master's thesis and doctoral dissertation Glassie directed at Indiana. In the third and fourth chapters of that book, Glassie used Bangladeshi examples to make clear the current methods and theories of American folkloristics for a Bengali scholarly audience.

Through his work at Conner Prairie (1971–76), the Ulster-American Folk Park (1972–82), and the Museum of Frontier Culture (1982–92), through his exhibition in Ireland (1983), his Turkish exhibitions (1991–94), and his exhibition at the Bangladesh National Museum (2000), Glassie has continued to bring his research to new audiences. His museum exhibitions, like his books, make his scholarship available. His latest book presents the life and art of the Nigerian painter Prince Twins Seven-Seven, and Glassie planned and hung an exhibition of the artist's works that opened at Material Culture in Philadelphia in April of 2010.

Academic Work

Glassie was on a fast track. After two years as a state folklorist and one year at the Capitol Campus of Penn State, Glassie joined the faculty of the Folklore Institute at Indiana in 1970. In 1972, he was awarded a Guggenheim Fellowship and went to Ireland. In 1975, he was invited to the National Humanities Institute at Yale to join colleagues in American Studies for discussion during the Bicentennial year. In 1976, when he was thirty-five, a

Fellow of the American Folklore Society with three major books published, he was a tenured full professor and chairman of the department of Folklore and Folklife at the University of Pennsylvania, where he had appointments in Folklore, American Civilization, and Architecture. In 1988, he returned to Indiana as a College Professor, a distinguished professorial rank, with appointments in Folklore and Ethnomusicology, American Studies, Near Eastern Languages and Cultures, Central Eurasian Studies, and India Studies. He retired, after a serious illness, in 2008.

Teaching was his delight. At Indiana, he was given the Trustees' Teaching Award, and the Department of Folklore and Ethnomusicology named its award for teaching excellence by a graduate student the Henry Glassie Award. For years at Indiana and Penn he taught a basic introduction to folklore for undergraduates, and from the beginning of his career to its end he taught the introduction to folklore practice for entering graduate students. His common topics for courses included folklore theory, folklore's history, ethnographic writing, vernacular architecture, folk art, American music, Irish literature, and Turkish art.

Most of Glassie's time as an educator was devoted to service on M.A. and Ph.D. committees; he was a great mentor when it came to planning and executing writing projects. He did not keep track of the number of theses and dissertations he directed, but when he retired in 2008, he was serving on forty-eight committees, and it seems likely that he served during his career on something like 180 committees. These were in anthropology, history, archeology, art history, and architecture, but most, of course, were in folklore, so he has had a hand in training a great many of today's professional folklorists, some of whom retired before he did, and with others he is continuing to work, refining their theories and sharpening their prose.

Teaching delights him, administration does not, but Glassie served a long term as the chair of folklore at Penn, and twice served as the chair of folklore at Indiana. At Indiana, he also served as the chair of Near Eastern Languages and Cultures. In his own estimation, he was not an effective chair in his thirties at Penn, but this modesty is belied by his success in holding Penn's superb department together while increasing its number of both students and faculty, and by his ability to forge a strong and lasting relationship with Penn's provost, Thomas Ehrlich, who later became president of Indiana University. He was equally effective a quarter of a century later, so successful as the chair of Near Eastern Languages and Cultures that a succession of deans gave him extraordinary administrative tasks: to write a report on the state of area studies, to chair the search for a director of India Studies, to chair difficult tenure and promotion cases in other departments. Throughout his time at Indiana, he served as the co-director of Turkish Studies.

From his professorial position, Glassie continued to reach across disciplinary boundaries by giving a steady stream of public lectures. Many of these were delivered at museums—the Met and Whitney in New York, the Smithsonian in Washington, the Victoria and Albert in London, the Louvre in Paris, the National Museum in Dhaka—and these, like his museum exhibitions, were oriented to the general public. More of Glassie's lectures, though, should be considered interdisciplinary, efforts to make the discipline of folklore better known within the academy. Glassie has lectured at Harvard, Yale, Princeton, Columbia, Brown, Berkeley, UCLA—at universities in forty of the United States, in departments of folklore, anthropology, geography, history, archaeology, art history, art, architecture, historic preservation, English, creative writing, popular culture, American studies, Irish studies, Middle Eastern studies, Turkish studies, South Asian studies, and East Asian studies. He has lectured as well at meetings of a variety of scholarly societies throughout the United States and Canada. Beyond North America, he has lectured at universities, museums, and academic meetings in Ireland, Wales, Scotland, England, Norway, Sweden, Finland, Denmark, France, Germany, Malta, Turkey, Israel, Kuwait, India, Bangladesh, China, and Japan. In addition to international lectures, he has given short courses on folklore method and theory at the Documentary Workshop, Jaisalmer, Rajasthan, India; at Kamaraj University, Madurai, Tamil Nadu, India; at the Bangla Academy, Dhaka, Bangladesh; in the Chinese Department, Peking University, Beijing, China. In some instances, connections made during these lectures led to jobs for young folklorists.

Writings

Glassie's scholarly reputation rests primarily on his publications. He published his first article, "The Appalachian Log Cabin," in 1963, when he was a senior at Tulane University. It gained praise from the poet and novelist Jesse Stuart, and it was sufficiently mature and original to be reprinted in later scholarly anthologies, in McNeill's *Appalachian Images* (1983) and Carney's *Baseball, Barns, and Bluegrass: A Geography of American Folklife* (1998). Since then he has published 110 articles and pamphlets, and there have been forty reprintings of his shorter writings, several of them translated into Turkish, Japanese, Swedish, or Finnish. Glassie's papers have become part of the general resource for folklorists. Many were written for festschrifts and encyclopedias, and original essays or reprints of articles by Glassie appear in these basic books: Dorson, *Folklore and Folklife;* Dorson, *Handbook of American Folklore;* Brunvand, *The Study of American Folklore;* Yoder, *American Folklife;* Feintuch, *Eight Words for the Study of Culture;* Ball, *Folklore and Folklife: A Teacher's Manual;* Schrempp and Hansen, *Myth: A New Symposium;* Brednich, Schneider, and Werner, *Natur-Kultur;* Fishwick and Browne, *Icons of Popular Culture;* Bronner, *American Material Culture and Folklife;* Vlach and Bronner, *Folk Art and Art Worlds;* Schlereth, *Material Culture Studies in America;* St. George, *Material Life in America;* Pocius, *Living in a Material World;* Ferguson, *Historical Archaeology and the Importance of Material Things;* Ingersoll and Bronitsky, *Mirror and Metaphor;* Upton, *America's Architectural Roots;* Upton and Vlach, *Common Places;* Turan, *Vernacular Architecture;* Brekke, *From Academic Art to Popular Pictures;* Klein and Widbom, *Swedish Folk Art;* Boström, *Folkkonsten;* Vena and Weinberg, *Frames of Reference: Looking at American Art;* Wyndham, *Re-imagining Ireland;* Cronin, Crosson, and Eastlake, *Orality and Modern Irish Culture;* Buckley, Ó Cathain, Mac Carthiagh, and MacMathuna, *Border-Crossing.*

Early in his career, Glassie co-authored two small books, the *Guide for Collectors* with Leach, *Folksongs and Their Makers* with Ives and Szwed. He co-edited *Forms upon the Frontier* with the Fifes, and co-edited, with Linda Dégh and Felix Oinas, Richard Dorson's festschrift. Later he created small books for his friends, teachers, and collaborators in Ireland, Turkey, and Bangladesh (though *Irish Folk History* has had an independent life, being reprinted by the University of Pennsylvania Press in a new edition in 1998). But, his major books are the mainstay of his legacy; they follow in chronological order, accompanied by a few quotations from the hundreds of reviews his works have received.

Pattern in the Material Folk Culture of the Eastern United States (1969)

From his college sophomore year forward, Glassie spent every free hour in fieldwork, recording singers at night, surveying architecture by day. He conducted this work in cooperation with Fred Kniffen, his master, who taught geography and anthropology at Louisiana State University, when Glassie was an undergraduate at Tulane. As a graduate student at Penn, Glassie wrote a book, an essay on the regions of the eastern United States, intending it as an invitation to the study of material culture for American folklorists. In the generation of Glassie and Michael Owen Jones, then in the generation of John Vlach and Simon Bronner, the book proved successful among folklorists. It was even more successful among American geographers who held a session at their annual meeting to celebrate the book's twenty-fifth anniversary. Published by the University of Pennsylvania Press in 1969, it has been reprinted eleven times, remaining continuously in print for more than forty years—a rarity among scholarly books.

When the book was published, the reviewers spread the news. In the *Geographical Review,* Wilbur Zelinsky informed geographers that it was "the first substantial effort to survey the fundamental facts of structure and process in the traditional (or 'folk') material culture of what is unquestionably the seminal zone of the country as a whole . . . a valiant attempt to build a much-needed bridge between the world of American folklore studies and that of human geography." The reviewer in *Choice* wrote, "Art historians will have to take notice of this new study of folklore as broad cultural patterns." Richard Candee, writing in the *Journal of the Society of Architectural Historians,* praised the book for providing "a theoretical framework" for vernacular architecture study. Ronald Brunskill in *Folk Life* and Alan Gailey in *Ulster Folklife* welcomed the book, for it brought North America at last into connection with European folklife research. Gailey called it "a major contribution," noting that "it has been exceptional in the history of material culture for students to attempt definition of culture areas and movements in the manner adopted in this book in the emergent stages of the subject . . . and it says much for the author's energy in the field and in the library that this book was written."

Folk Housing in Middle Virginia:
A Structural Analysis of Historic Artifacts (1976)

In 1972, Glassie used architectural data from his fieldwork, structural and phenomenological method, and performance theory to write a book about early Virginia. Intending to convince folklorists that material culture study could be theoretically sophisticated, he produced a book that was embraced and applied by archaeologists, historians, and architectural historians. In the second edition of his profoundly important *In Small Things Forgotten,* James Deetz stresses Glassie's general importance for historians and archaeologists, with this book as his text. Glassie's work was energetically applied in France and England, Matthew Johnson's *Housing Culture* providing an example of intelligent application and critique. Introducing *Common Places,* Upton and Vlach called the book "one of the key documents of vernacular architecture studies." Published after a long delay by the University of Tennessee Press in 1976, then reprinted six times in paperback, the book has remained continuously in press for thirty-six years, a testament to its importance, and Glassie has tested its basic theory of historical transformation in Ireland (*Passing the Time,* chapter 13), Turkey (*Turkish Traditional Art,* chapter 9), then summarized a quarter of a century of research in his award-winning *Vernacular Architecture* (2000).

Though the later history of *Folk Housing* confirmed its significance, its first reviewers, even when critical, acknowledged its originality. The geographer Peirce Lewis began his long review in *The Journal of Historical Geography* by saying, "For more than a decade Glassie has been a leader among the growing company of American scholars who are working to decipher the meaning of material artifacts in order to shed light on the pre-industrial vernacular history of the United States. . . . Glassie's most impressive quality is his insistence in asking hard and far-reaching questions about the large meanings of small objects, and on demanding rigorous answers to those questions. Few men are his equal when it comes to resolving the incessant tensions between fact and idea, between specific and general, between apparent chaos and underlying order." The geographer Peter O. Wacker concluded his review in *The Professional Geographer* by saying, "this book will stimulate endless debate. Geographers must read it. Henry Glassie has won a place for himself in the first rank of scholars concerned with material culture."

In *Western Folklore,* John Vlach began, "Henry Glassie has once again proved himself the leader in American studies of folk architecture. . . . With this book the nascent subject of material culture has achieved the threshold of maturity. Folklorists will long feel the impact of this book." Alan Gailey wrote comparably in *Ulster Folklife:* "This is an important book, with factual meatiness and freshness of approach sufficient to attract the attention of historians, anthropologists, folklorists, and students of vernacular architecture. . . . Here is a worthy demonstration of an approach to the study of material culture that takes the scholar away from a viewpoint that sees taxonomy as an end in itself, to consider the people represented by that material culture, how and why they designed their houses as they did, and the manner in which they accommodated change in their way of thinking. Glassie's approach will be followed by others in the years to come, turning their attention to other segments in the field of material culture."

All Silver and No Brass: An Irish Christmas Mumming (1976)

Glassie's Guggenheim Fellowship took him to Ireland in 1972. This book was the first yield of his Irish work. In it, people who had seen, and men who had performed, recalled the old mummers' play. It was a memory then, but, inspired by this book, Bryan Gallagher gathered his students and stimulated a robust revival of mumming in County Fermanagh. Vincent Woods found *All Silver and No Brass* helpful when he composed his magnificent play *At the Black Pig's Dyke*. Published first by the Dolmen Press in Dublin and the Indiana University Press, it was issued in paperback by Brandon in Ireland and the University of Pennsylvania Press in America. Reprinted six times, a text used in introductory folklore courses, it remains in print.

Roger Abrahams caught one of the book's virtues at the beginning of his review in *Contemporary Sociology*, saying, "This lovely book, ostensibly an ethnographic account of Christmas countryside amusements of the generation just passed, is really an essay on what folklorists are up to these days." The sociologist Howard Becker ended his review in the *American Journal of Sociology* by hoping that Glassie's book, in its combination of humanistic and social-scientific approaches, would be "part of a wave that is just beginning to sweep through sociology . . . a trend in which we will reclaim the possibilities of humanistic methods and styles from the present limbo."

The book shows how successful fieldwork can be when it is grounded on friendship, as Marshall Craig argued in *Western Folklore*. The book is also, as Cass, Preston, and Smith remark in *The English Mumming Play*, "a model of a synchronic study of the mumming play within a community." That is what Glassie set out to write, a study of folk drama, but looking back in an essay in *The Irish Times* in 1994, Fintan O'Toole, a leading scholar and critic of Irish drama, wrote, "*All Silver and No Brass* is still the most profound book on Irish theatre yet written."

Passing the Time in Ballymenone:
Culture and History of an Ulster Community (1982)

Glassie dealt with the festive in *All Silver and No Brass*, clearing the way for his major work on Ireland to be an existential ethnography, concentrated on the daily and commonplace, on farming and ceiliing. Inspired by anthropological studies in Mexico, he created a community study, but one that was connected to large historical forces. He settled in Northern Ireland in the bloodiest year of the Troubles to describe how people endure through newsworthy times. Published in the American Folklore Society Series by the University of Pennsylvania Press, and by the O'Brien Press in Dublin, it has been reprinted twice in paperback by Indiana and remains in print. *Passing the Time* won the Chicago Folklore Prize, the Haney Prize in the Social Sciences, and it was named a notable book of the year by the *New York Times.*

The book excited the reviewers. Both of the newspapers in Enniskillen, the county town of Fermanagh where Ballymenone is situated, greeted the book enthusiastically. P. J. O'Hare headlined his full page review in the *Fermanagh Herald,* "Fermanagh is honoured by the pen of a humble American genius: a marvellous book." Dennis Clark called it the "finest achievement in Irish folklore" in *The Irish Edition.* Michael Garvey called it "honorable, almost holy scholarship" in *Commonweal.* Emmet Larkin began his review in the *New York Times* by saying, "Henry Glassie's 'Passing the Time in Ballymenone' is an extraordinarily rich and rewarding book. It is about night and day, talk and work, man and nature, history and folklore, text and context, truth and order, art and culture, life and death, the ponderable and imponderable, but above all it is about the effort of one man to find for himself and us the life's breath of the people of Ballymenone." Writing in the *Geographical Review,* Wilbur Zelinsky said the book "is one of the most remarkable pieces of literature of the twentieth century. As such, the book merits the attention of all readers who care about great writing and important ideas. 'Passing the Time' is a many-layered masterpiece with the plenitude, ambiguities, allusiveness, multiple meanings, vitality, and spirit-stretching qualities of a great novel, one blessed with a language all its own."

In *International Folkloristics,* published in 1999, Alan Dundes described *Passing the Time* as a "remarkable tour de force" and "one of the finest examples of folklore fieldwork in Ireland, or, for that matter, anywhere in the world."

Irish Folktales (1985)

Glassie assembled this anthology, which included many tales he recorded, to accompany O'Sullivan's *Folktales of Ireland* and to meet Hymes' critique of anthologies by including different versions of single types and preserving a diversity of voices. Published by Pantheon in New York, reprinted as *The Penguin Book of Irish Folktales,* and translated into Italian, this book has been reprinted twenty-three times, and it has sold over one hundred thousand copies.

Irish Folktales was intended as a popular book. In the *Library Journal,* David Azzolina welcomed this addition to the Pantheon folktale series, saying the book "maintains and even exceeds the high standards of the previous ones." Alan Gailey called it "a significant contribution to Irish folk studies." Dell Hymes called it "a lovely blend of personal sensitivity and quiet scholarship." And the renowned Irish novelist Benedict Kiely wrote, "Henry Glassie is a scholarly and scientific folklorist . . . but he is also in breathing contact with the stories he relates, from literature and the living people. The result is a treasure cave of wonder."

The Spirit of Folk Art (1989)

At a time when the issue of folk art was a matter of emotional debate, Glassie set out to investigate the logic of the category at length, in detail, and in relation to his own international work in the field. He concluded that art is art and that such subdivisions as fine, folk, popular, and primitive, though handy in conversation, are intellectually flawed. John Burrison wrote that Glassie began the debate on folk art with his chapter, "Folk Art," in Dorson's *Folklore and Folklife* in 1972, then ended it with this comprehensive masterwork. Published by Abrams and the Museum of International Folk Art in 1989, it has been reprinted four times and remains in print. It won the Kniffen Prize of the Pioneer American Society, and it was named a notable book of the year by the *New York Times.* In the year of the book's publication, Glassie was awarded the American Folklore Society, Folk Art Section, Centennial Award.

Alan Gailey, writing in *Ulster Folklife,* said that *The Spirit of Folk Art* is "arguably the best book in English on the nature of folk art." In *The Clarion,* Randall Seth Morris wrote that this "rhapsodic essay is swept by purer breezes of discourse and philosophical import than we have seen on the folkloric front for a long time. I felt thrilled as I read the essay." The anthropologist Barbara Bode, intending a compliment, wrote in the *New York Times,* "In his encyclopedic coverage and his stress on the collective unifying power of sacred symbols, Mr. Glassie does for folk art what Joseph Campbell did for myth."

Turkish Traditional Art Today (1993)

At the invitation of Turkish colleagues and with the support of the United States government, Glassie went to Turkey in 1982 to lecture in schools of architecture. Excited by the vitality of Turkish folk art, he went home determined to learn Turkish and return for fieldwork. During a decade of research in the field, he got to every corner of the country, but concentrated his effort in the markets of Istanbul and in the Anatolian centers of production for ceramics and textiles. Co-published by the Indiana University Press and the Turkish Ministry of Culture in 1993, the book has been reprinted three times and remains in print. Named a notable book of the year by the *New York Times,* the book won for Glassie the Award for Superior Service to Turkish Culture from the Ministry of Culture of the Turkish Republic, the Outstanding Achievement in the Arts Award from the Assembly of Turkish American Associations, and the Fatih University Board of Trustees Recognition for Contributions to Turkish Cultural Life. In 2010, the municipal government named Glassie an honorary citizen of the city of Kütahya, Turkey, in recognition of his years of research on the city's ceramic tradition.

Writing in *Cornucopia,* the art historian John Carswell said that *Turkish Traditional Art Today* "is the most important book about everyday life in Turkey since Evliya Çelebi's in the seventeenth century." In the *MESA Bulletin,* Sarah Antis wrote, "An erudite exploration into the nature of art, this monumental tour de force draws on the disciplinary strengths of folklore, cultural geography, art history and anthropology . . . to provide a new foundation for the world of artistic production in Turkey today." In the *Oriental Rug Review,* Thomas Farnham said that "anyone interested in Oriental rug studies must regard it as a work of monumental significance." And in his review for the *New York Times,* the art historian Walter Denny wrote:

> It is Mr. Glassie's concern with the artist's view of truth, his complete indifference to the elegant pretension of word and thought that to one extent or another has plagued Western historians of art since Vasari, and above all his deep curiosity and willingness to learn and listen from the past and present, from the scholar and from the artist, that constitute the miraculous elements of "Turkish Traditional Art Today."

> Mr. Glassie's book has something revelatory and precious for the specialist in Turkish art with a 35-year experience of the country, its culture and language; it has something equally precious for the reader who has never been to Istanbul or Ankara, Sivas or Konya. Much of Mr. Glassie's commentary—especially in the general principles he sets forth in his four summaries of Turkish art . . . is as challenging to the traditions and accepted truths of scholarship as it is intoxicating to the reader encountering those traditions for the first time.

Art and Life in Bangladesh (1997)

Admiring Glassie's book on Turkey, Harunur Rashid, Director General of the Bangla Academy, asked Glassie to write a book on Bangladesh. Glassie's

Bengali is not as fluent as his Turkish, but he had begun fieldwork in Bangladesh in 1987, and, supported by the Bangla Academy, he stayed to do the fieldwork that led to this book. Published by Indiana in 1997, it was reprinted as *Traditional Art of Dhaka* by the Bangla Academy in 2000. For the book, Glassie was awarded the Certificate of Honour from the Ministry of Cultural Affairs of the People's Republic of Bangladesh, the Crest of Honour from the Islamic University of Kushtia, Bangladesh, and the Friend of Bangladesh Award from the Federation of Bangladeshi Association in North America.

In his review in the *New York Times,* Francis Robinson concluded, "This marvelous book is an outstanding introduction to a little-known land. A fine celebration of its people on the 50th anniversary of its freedom from British rule, it is worthy of the attention of all who value what it is to be creative and to be human." Godfrey Goodwin, writing in the *Journal of the Royal Asiatic Society,* said, "It is the strength of this book that it introduces a great many workers of all kinds. The author records their conversations and analyzes their thinking and has the uncanny gift of making the reader want to meet them. . . . This is a book that could have been written by no other scholar." After commenting that Glassie's interview with the sculptor Haripada Pal "is one of the most compelling accounts of aesthetic philosophy I have ever read," Lee Haring concluded his review in the *Journal of American Folklore* by saying the book "is a complete portrait of an artistic and cultural system by a master folklorist." Harunur Rashid ended his review in the *Dhaka Courier* by saying that Glassie "has given Bangladesh a book which is more of an ambassador to the outside world than all our chanceries put together. He eminently deserves the highest civil award of Bangladesh."

Material Culture (1999)

Thirty years after *Pattern in the Material Culture of the Eastern United States,* Glassie thought it was time for a new general statement on material culture. Unlike his other books, *Material Culture* is a collection of essays, though only one was reprinted with minor changes; the others were radically revised or wholly new. When Indiana published the book in 1999, the decision was not to offer a paperback, but to print two of its lengthy chapters in expanded versions as books. Both were comparative studies based on fieldwork in different locations. One, based on work in Bangladesh, Sweden, the U.S., Turkey, and Japan, became *The Potter's Art* (1999). The other, based on work in the U.S., Ireland, England, Sweden, Turkey, and Bangladesh, became

Vernacular Architecture (2000). *Vernacular Architecture,* widely used as a textbook in classes, has been reprinted twice, and it won the Abbott Lowell Cummings Award of the Vernacular Architecture Forum in 2001 for the best book on North American vernacular architecture.

Michael Brian Schiffer ended his review in *Technology and Culture* by writing, "Historians of technology seeking alternative explanatory frameworks and narrative structures should read *Material Culture* with care. . . . Glassie's perspective respects the individual while situating him or her in ever-widening sociocultural contexts of action and meaning. In contrast to postmodern perspectives, he offers an inclusive, artifact-based humanism that is richly empirical, theoretically informed, widely comparative, and engaged with sociocultural processes at many levels. In this beautiful, sometimes moving book, with its graceful prose and sensuous images, students of technology will find important ideas to ponder."

The noted archaeologist Mark Leone used the publication of *Material Culture* as an occasion to write an essay, "Henry Glassie and the General Meaning of Things," in *The Public Historian.* It begins, "Henry Glassie's *Material Culture* provides long-lasting definitions of material culture, the ethnographic technique for understanding it, the social context in which it exists, the kinds to be studied, what is to be studied against, and how to write about it." Leone praises in particular Glassie's writings on Turkish carpets and American architecture—"just about brilliant"—and asks and answers a question: "Will this book change scholarship? I hope so." Then after expanding on Glassie's studies of carpets and architecture, Leone explains why he hopes Glassie's work will change archeological scholarship: "It would add more of a point and return moral courage to our field."

The Stars of Ballymenone (2006)

In crafting this piece of experimental writing, Glassie returned to Ballymenone for two main reasons. He wanted to produce for the discipline of folklore a full study of a community's complete repertory of oral narrative to show that, if all the stories are gathered and thematically linked, a coherent worldview will emerge. He also wanted to employ technological advances to create, with Doug Boyd, a CD out of his old tapes, so the voices of Ballymenone could be at last heard. The CD came with the book when it was published by Indiana in 2006.

Writers in *The Irish Times* remembered Glassie's earlier writings on Ballymenone and they responded knowledgably to *The Stars.* Robert Roche complimented its "beautiful prose" and said, "This volume has rightly been described as a masterpiece. Can one say more?" Belinda McKeon found that the poet Louis de Paor listed it among the best books he had read during the year, and she wrote a feature piece on Glassie's research in Fermanagh, saying, "What Henry Glassie does is to observe. He traces patterns of behaviour, of belief; he takes note of customs and traditions, stories and superstitions; he spends time with habit, with custom, with the things that make a community and a people what and who they are. He listens and records . . . he captures the voices, the tunes, the jokes, and the gestures."

In America, Gregory Hansen wrote in the *Oral History Review,* "The book is a model for learning about the craft of fieldwork and the centrality of oral history research." Ray Cashman wrote in *Western Folklore* that Glassie's earlier works allowed him in this one "to bear down on verbal art. Here, Glassie set out to account for the entire repertory of verbal art among Ballymenone's circle of ceiliers, every story—the comic, the tragic, the sacred, and the absurd. . . . More generally, *Stars* offers us an unimpeachable case to set before anyone who should wonder out loud why folklore matters or why folklorists bother doing what we do. *Stars* performs a great service to our discipline by bearing witness to the absolute centrality of folklore in human experience. Very clear throughout is that all the stuff one might call folklore is not that which makes life quaint or colorful for the people of Ballymenone. Folklore is what makes life possible for them. . . . *The Stars of Ballymenone* demonstrates how people not so different from us—provoked by the very same issues—use folklore to carry on meaningfully, artfully, intelligently. Should anyone question the import of folklore, this book offers powerful, persuasive answers."

Robert Cochran ended his *Journal of Folklore Research Review* of *The Stars of Ballymenone* like this: "In Henry Glassie's many studies, read over forty years, I have found the best demonstration I have known of our discipline's capacity for intellectually rigorous right livelihood. This latest effort, this warm and wonderful book, at once an homage to his mentors and apologia for Glassie's own practice, enlivened by the voices he learned to love, measures up very nicely, for me, to the tall company of its predecessors."

Prince Twins Seven-Seven: His Art, His Life in Nigeria, His Exile in America (2010)

In this book, Glassie offers the first full monographic treatment of a contemporary African artist, and a model of the folkloristic study of the life and art of a singular individual. Conducting many interviews and traveling with Prince through Nigeria, Glassie was able to construct a biography, based on the artist's own words, and to analyze the art of Prince Twins Seven-Seven to exemplify his practice and outline his deeply spiritual worldview. Published by Indiana in 2010, the book received these comments by readers of the manuscript:

Phillip Peek, Africanist and folklorist, wrote, "The triumphs and sufferings, the complexities of a brilliant and bedeviled artist are given full voice with Glassie's usual perceptive and sympathetic flair. Glassie has given us yet another finely wrought work of art about artists and their works."

Roger Abrahams wrote, "Prince Twins Seven-Seven is a propulsive artist in many media, and this Miltonic book about him gives us an intricate and fascinating study of a Yoruba Big Man as he puts his life together and replays it in story. The wonder of it all is that he explained it to his friend Henry Glassie, and Glassie explains it then for us. There is no better description in the ethnographic literature of political and personal ascendancy. Glassie takes great chances, just as Prince does, giving us the mythic and legendary details we need to relate this man to art and artists throughout the world."

Robert Farris Thompson, chief among the historians of African art, wrote, "What happens when one of Nigeria's most powerful artists, Twins Seven-Seven, meets America's most distinguished folklorist, Henry Glassie? You get an all-time masterpiece of cultural portraiture. Twins Seven-Seven reveals and recounts his life and art, and Glassie translates all this into analytic gold. There were times when I did not know whether to cry (over Twins' career difficulties and the shock of Glassie being hospitalized in mid-book) or to shout (in celebration of the argument and its limitless beauty), but I can tell you this: I felt exalted at the end."

The historian Toyin Falola began his review in *Choice* by saying, "A product of extensive research presented in elegant sentences, beautifully illustrated and professionally printed, this book gives ethnography a good name, confers respect on a fine scholar, and turns Prince Seven-Seven into a larger-than-life figure."

In Conclusion

With the exception of *Material Culture,* Glassie's works are not collections of essays, but books, argued from the beginning to the end. Nor are they the slim volumes favored by academic publishers. Here are some page

Mehmet Gürsoy and Henry Glassie. *Çini* plate with portraits by Yıldırım Türkel and a border by Habib Bakılan. Kütahya, Turkey, 1994

Friendship in Colour. Henry Glassie and Prince Twins Seven-Seven, painted by Fattai, an artist in Osogbo, Nigeria, 2009

counts: *Pattern* (334 pages), *Passing the Time* (872 pages), *Turkish Tradition-al Art* (947 pages), *Art and Life in Bangladesh* (537 pages), *Material Culture* (413 pages), *The Stars of Ballymenone* (574 pages), *Prince Twins Seven-Seven* (488 pages). It takes time and space to answer the demands of performance theory with richness of empirical detail.

Reviewers regularly comment on the quality of Glassie's prose. It is "beau-tiful," "graceful," "lyrical," "poetic"; it is "clear" and free of fashionable jargon. As often they comment on the quality of his line drawings and photographs, and it should be noted that many of his drawings and photographs have been used or reused in publications of which he is not the author. Reviewers also frequently comment on the completeness of his notes, his mastery of a wide scholarly literature, and his astonishingly rich and interdisciplinary bibliographies. He is a voracious reader—two or three books a week—as well as an unstoppable fieldworker. Reviewers comment as well on the look of his books. Glassie not only writes and illustrates his books; he has de-signed eight of them, a difficult, time-consuming process that ensures that the words and images will cohere into an attractive, user-friendly whole.

The last thing to say is, though he is retired, he remains at work, still directing many dissertations. In May of 2010 he gave an address at the National Library in Dublin to celebrate the seventy-fifth anniversary of the founding of the Irish Folklore Commission. His lectures for 2011 in-clude the Haskins Prize Lecture at the annual meeting of the ACLS in Washington and keynote addresses at conferences in Malta, the Isle of Man, and Montreal. With his book on Prince Twins Seven–Seven done and the exhibition of the artist's work complete, he is looking forward to research and writing on Japanese figurative ceramics, with his colleague Takashi Takahara, and beyond that to continuing the fieldwork in Brazil with his wife and beloved fellow folklorist Pravina Shukla; the end in sight is a book on Brazilian imagery.

BIBLIOGRAPHY

Books by Henry Glassie

(with MacEdward Leach) *A Guide for Collectors of Oral Traditions and Folk Cultural Material in Pennsylvania*. Harrisburg: Pennsylvania Historical and Museum Commission, 1968.

Pattern in the Material Folk Culture of the Eastern United States. Philadel-phia: University of Pennsylvania Press, 1969.

(with Austin and Alta Fife, eds.) *Forms upon the Frontier: Folklife and Folk Arts in the United States*. Logan: Utah State University Press, 1969.

(with Edward D. Ives and John F. Szwed) *Folksongs and Their Makers*. Bowling Green: Bowling Green University Popular Press, 1970.

Folk Housing in Middle Virginia: A Structural Analysis of Historic Artifacts. Knoxville: University of Tennessee Press, 1976.

All Silver and No Brass: An Irish Christmas Mumming. Dublin: The Dolmen Press; Bloomington: Indiana University Press, 1976; Philadelphia: University of Pennsylvania Press; Dingle: Brandon Books, 1983.

(with Linda Dégh and Felix Oinas, eds.) *Folklore Today: A Festschrift for Richard M. Dorson*. Bloomington: Research Center for Language and Semiotic Studies, 1976.

Irish Folk History: Texts from the North. Philadelphia: University of Pennsylvania Press; Dublin: O'Brien Press, 1982.

Passing the Time in Ballymenone: Culture and History of an Ulster Community. Philadelphia: University of Pennsylvania Press; Dublin: O'Brien Press, 1982; Bloomington: Indiana University Press, 1995.

Irish Folktales. New York: Pantheon Press, 1985; *The Penguin Book of Irish Folktales*. Harmondsworth: Penguin, 1991; *Leggende Populari Irlandesi*. Milano: Arnoldo Mondadori, 1999.

The Spirit of Folk Art. New York: Harry N. Abrams, Museum of International Folk Art, 1989.

Günümüzde Geleneksel Türk Sanatı. Istanbul: Pan Yayıncılık, 1993.

Turkish Traditional Art Today. Bloomington: Indiana University Press; Ankara: Ministry of Culture of the Turkish Republic, 1993.

Art and Life in Bangladesh. Bloomington: Indiana University Press, 1997; *Traditional Art of Dhaka*. Dhaka: Bangla Academy, 2000.

Material Culture. Bloomington: Indiana University Press, 1999.

The Potter's Art. Bloomington: Indiana University Press; Philadelphia: Material Culture, 1999.

Vernacular Architecture. Bloomington: Indiana University Press; Philadelphia: Material Culture, 2000.

The Stars of Ballymenone. Bloomington: Indiana University Press, 2006.

(with Firoz Mahmud) *Living Traditions*. Cultural Survey of Bangladesh 11. Dhaka: Asiatic Society of Bangladesh, 2007.

Prince Twins Seven-Seven: His Art, His Life in Nigeria, His Exile in America. Bloomington: Indiana University Press, 2010.

A Selection of Shorter Writings by Henry Glassie

"The Appalachian Log Cabin," *Mountain Life and Work* 39:4 (1963): 5–14.

"The Smaller Outbuildings of the Southern Mountains," *Mountain Life and Work* 40:1 (1964): 21–25.

"Three Southern Mountain Jack Tales," *Tennessee Folklore Society Bulletin* 30:3 (1964): 88–102.

"The Old Barns of Appalachia," *Mountain Life and Work* 41:2 (1965): 21–30.

(with Fred B. Kniffen) "Building in Wood in the Eastern United States: A Time-Place Perspective," *The Geographical Review* 56:1 (1966): 40–66.

"The Pennsylvania Barn in the South," *Pennsylvania Folklife* 15:2 (1965): 8–19; 15:3 (1966): 12–25.

"The Wedderspoon Farm," *New York Folklore Quarterly* 22:3 (1966): 165–87.

"The Use of Folklore in *David Harum*," *New York Folklore Quarterly* 23:3 (1967): 163–85.

"William Houck, Maker of Pounded Ash Adirondack Pack-Baskets," *Keystone Folklore Quarterly* 12:1 (1967): 23–54.

"The Types of the Southern Mountain Cabin." In Jan H. Brunvand, ed., *The Study of American Folklore,* pp. 338–70. New York: W. W. Norton, 1968.

"The Double-Crib Barn in South-Central Pennsylvania," *Pioneer America* 1:1 (1969): 9–16; 1:2 (1969): 40–45; 2:1 (1970): 47–52; 2:2 (1970): 23–34.

"Eighteenth-Century Cultural Process in Delaware Valley Folk Building," *Winterthur Portfolio* 7 (1972): 29–57.

"Folk Art." In Richard M. Dorson, ed., *Folklore and Folklife: An Introduction,* pp. 253–80. Chicago: University of Chicago Press, 1972.

"A Folkoristic Thought on the Promise of Oral History." In Peter D. Olch and Forrest C. Pogue, eds., *Selections from the Fifth and Sixth National Colloquia on Oral History,* pp. 54–57. New York: The Oral History Association, 1972.

"Structure and Function, Folklore and the Artifact," *Semiotica* 7:4 (1973): 313–51.

"The Nature of the New World Artifact: The Instance of the Dugout Canoe." In Walter Escher, Theo Gantner, and Hans Trümpy, eds., *Festschrift für*

Robert Wildhaber, pp. 153–70. Basel: Schweizerische Gesellscaft für Volkskunde, 1973.

"The Variation of Concepts within Tradition: Barn Building in Otsego County, New York." In H. J. Walker and W. G. Haag, eds., *Man and Cultural Heritage: Papers in Honor of Fred B. Kniffen,* Geoscience and Man, pp. 177–235. Baton Rouge: Louisiana State University School of Geoscience, 1974.

"Barns Across Southern England: A Note on Transatlantic Comparison and Architectural Meanings," *Pioneer America* 7:1 (1975): 9–19.

"Source for a New Anthropology," *Book Forum* 2:1 (1976): 70–77.

"Folk Art," *Encyclopedia Americana* 11:486–92. New York: American Corporation, 1976.

"Archaeology and Folklore: Common Anxieties, Common Hopes." In Leland Ferguson, ed., *Historical Archaeology and the Importance of Material Things,* pp. 23–35. Columbia: Society for Historical Archaeology, 1977.

"Meaningful Things and Appropriate Myths: The Artifact's Place in American Studies," *Prospects: An Annual of American Cultural Studies* 3 (1977): 1–49.

A Museum of American Frontier Culture: A Proposal. New York: Scotch-Irish Trust of Ulster, 1978.

"The Moral Core of Folklore," *Folklore Forum* 16:2 (1983): 123–53.

"Folkloristic Study of the American Artifact: Objects and Objectives." In Richard M. Dorson, ed., *Handbook of American Folklore,* pp. 376–83. Bloomington: Indiana University Press, 1983.

"Vernacular Architecture and Society," *Material Culture* 16:1 (1984): 4–24.

"The Idea of Folk Art." In John Michael Vlach and Simon J. Bronner, eds., *Folk Art and Art Worlds,* pp. 269–74. Ann Arbor: U.M.I. Research Press, 1986.

"Irish." In Dell Upton, ed., *America's Architectural Roots: Ethnic Groups that Built America,* pp. 74–79 Washington, D.C.: The Preservation Press, 1986.

"Folklore and History," *Minnesota History* 50:5 (1987): 188–92.

"A Master of the Art of Carpet Repair: The Life of Hagop Barın," *Oriental Rug Review* 9:6 (1989): 32–38; 10:1 (1989): 16–22; 10:2 (1990): 38–49.

"Studying Material Culture Today." In Gerald L. Pocius, ed., *Living in a Material World: Canadian and American Approaches to Material Culture,* pp. 253–66. St. John's: Institute of Social and Economic Research, 1991.

"Turkish Traditional Art Today: Reflections of a Folklorist in the Field," *El Palacio* 96:3 (1991): 42–51.

"Epilogue: The Spirit of Swedish Folk Art." In Barbro Klein and Mats Widbom, eds., *Swedish Folk Art: All Tradition is Change*, pp. 247–55. New York: Harry N. Abrams, 1994.

"Values in Clay," *The Studio Potter* 22:2 (1994): 2–7.

"The Practice and Purpose of History," *Journal of American History* 81:3 (1994): 961–68.

"At Work in Bursa." In Roger D. Abrahams, ed., *Fields of Folklore: Essays in Honor of Kenneth S. Goldstein*, pp. 29–42. Bloomington: Trickster Press, 1995.

"Tradition," *Journal of American Folklore* 108: 430 (1995): 395–412.

"Turkish Folk Art and the Search for Meaning." In Yahya Aksoy, ed., *Ipek Yolu Uluslararası Halk Edebiatı Sempozyumu Bildirleri*, pp. 203–8. Ankara: T. C. Kültür Bakanlığı, 1995.

"The Word of God and the Song of the Soul: Calligraphic Art in Modern Turkey," *The American Muslim Council Report* 6:2 (1996):8.

"Prof. Evans." In E. Estyn Evans, *Ireland and the Atlantic Heritage: Selected Writings*, pp. ix–xiii. Dublin: Lilliput Press, 1996.

History's Dark Places. Distinguished Lecturer Series. Bloomington: Indiana University Institute of Advanced Studies, 1998.

"In Praise of Heroes at Work in the Clay," *NCECA Journal* 19 (1998): 17–27.

"Foreword." In Reha Günay, *Tradition of the Turkish House and Safranbolu Houses*, p. 6, Istanbul: Yapı-Endüstri Merkez Yayınları, 1998.

"Communication in the Twenty-First Century," *Civilization* 21 2 (1999): 16–27.

(with Firoz Mahmud) *Contemporary Traditional Art of Bangladesh*. Dhaka: Bangladesh National Museum, 2000.

"Style and Spirit in Representation." In Nils Georg Brekke, ed., *From Academic Art to Popular Pictures: Principles of Representation, Reproduction and Transformation*, pp. 9–20. Bergen: Bergen Museum, University of Bergen, 2000.

"The Builder's Art." In Carla M. Borden, ed., *Smithsonian Folklife Festival*, pp. 59–67. Washington, D.C.: Smithsonian Institution, 2001.

"Bengali Art in Metal." In Jean-Pierre Pichette, ed., *Entre Beauce et Acadie: Facettes d'un Parcours Ethnologique: Études Offertes au Professeur Jean-Claude Dupont*, pp. 21–27. Québec: Les Presses de l'Universite Laval, 2001.

"Performance Theory and the Documentary Act," *Indian Folklife* 1:5 (2001): 43–48.

"Nature, Culture, and Cosmological Interference." In Rolf Wilhelm Brednich, Annette Schneider, and Ute Werner, eds., *Natur-Kultur: Volkskundliche Perspectiven auf Mensch und Umwelt,* pp. 139–45 Munster: Waxmann, 2001.

"Keating Hero," *New Hibernia Review* 5:4 (2001): 43–48.

Mark Hewitt Outside. Wilmington: Louise Wells Cameron Art Museum, 2002.

(with Pravina Shukla) "Artists along the Silk Road." In Carla M. Borden, ed., *The Silk Road: Connecting Cultures, Creating Trust,* pp. 57–65. Washington, D.C.: Smithsonian Folklife Festival, 2002.

"Mud and Mythic Vision: Hindu Sculpture in Modern Bangladesh." In Gregory Schrempp and William Hansen, eds., *Myth: A New Symposium,* pp. 203–22. Bloomington: Indiana University Press, 2002.

"The Rural Landscape," *National Trust Forum Journal* 17:2 (2003): 32–37.

"Roberts, Warren Everett," *Enzyklopädie des Märchens* 11:2, pp. 742–43. Berlin: Walter de Gruyter, 2004.

"Protestant Identity in a Borderland Context." In Andrew Higgins Wyndham, ed., *Re-Imagining Ireland,* pp. 248–50. Charlottesville: University of Virginia Press, 2006.

"Mumming in Ballymenone." In Anthony D. Buckley, Seamas Ó Catháin, Criostoir Mac Carthiagh, and Seámus Mac Mathuna, eds., *Border-Crossing: Mumming in Cross-Border and Cross-Community Contexts,* pp. 91–101. Dundalk: Dundalgan Press, 2007.

"E. Estyn Evans and the Interpretation of the Irish Landscape." In Alvin Jackson and David N. Livingstone, eds., *Queen's Thinkers: Essays on the Intellectual Heritage of a University,* pp. 131–39. Belfast: Blackstaff Press, 2008.

"Virtuous Conventions: Thoughts on a Survey of Japanese Ceramics," *Museum Anthropology* 31:1 (2008): 47–50.

"The Beauties of Kütahya." In Iskender Işık and Uğur Kut, eds., *Ikinci Uluslararası Kütahya Çini Sempozyumu,* pp. 5–19. Kütahya: Dumlupınar Üniversitesi, 2010.

"A Foreword in Celebration." In John A. Burrison, *From Mud to Jug: The Folk Potters and Pottery of Northeast Georgia,* pp. vii–xi. Athens: University of Georgia Press, 2010.

"The Irish Folklore Commission: International Scholarship, National Purpose, Local Virtue," *Béaloideas* 78 (2010): 1–18.

Writings about Henry Glassie

Barefoot, Coy, "I Make Therefore I Am: A Profile of Folklorist Henry Glassie." *Gadfly Online* (2001).

Davis, Marsh, and Bill Shaw. *99 Historic Homes of Indiana: A Look Inside.* Bloomington: Indiana University Press, 2002. Pp. 95–97.

Hansen, Gregory, "An Interview with Henry Glassie," *Folklore Forum* 31:2 (2002): 91–113.

Joyner, Charles, "The Narrowing Gyre: Henry Glassie, Irish Folk Culture, and the American South." In Charles Joyner, *Shared Traditions: Southern History and Folk Culture,* pp. 166–73 Urbana: University of Illinois Press, 1999.

Leone, Mark, "Henry Glassie and the General Meaning of Things," *The Public Historian* 23:3 (2001): 83–87.

Truesdell, Barbara, "A Life in the Field: Henry Glassie and the Study of Material Culture," *The Public Historian* 30:4 (2008): 59–87.

Woods, Vincent, "An Irishman's Diary," *The Irish Times* (May 10, 2010): 15.

Acknowledgments

As editors of a book on the relationship between the individual and tradition, we are daunted by the task of acknowledging all the individuals who deserve recognition. On the one hand, the list is impossible to produce fully, when we consider the past and present impact of the individuals in our personal and professional lives. Add to that the individuals who populate the rich library of folklore research over the centuries—people we have never met but who have shaped the field of folklore broadly and the direction of our own research paths more particularly—and our task becomes insurmountable.

On the other hand, the nature of this book provides a viable solution: we encourage you to read it as an extended acknowledgement of the people who deserve credit for shaping our field, our careers, our interests, and our lives. Some of these individuals appear in photos, many appear in print, and many others will come to mind as you read, recalling the individuals in your own lives who compare and contrast with those you meet in these pages.

Of course, there are people in the immediate present who directly shaped this book. Their work, commitment, and support deserve recognition here. Our appreciation is deep, and no less so for its brevity.

First we thank the contributors to this volume; we are indebted to them for their excellent chapters. We also thank the many supporters whose names are listed in the Tabula Gratulatoria. Substantial institutional support came from the Department of Folklore and Ethnomusicology at Indiana University, particularly from John McDowell, Jason Jackson, Sheri Sherrill, Chris Roush, Michelle Melhouse, and Michelle Bright. Tim Lloyd and Lorraine Cashman at the American Folklore Society helped generate interest in the book and facilitated our AFS conference panels that explored the individual and tradition. We are grateful to many at Indiana University Press, especially to its director, Janet Rabinowitch, for her enthusiastic support of this project from its inception. Indebted to Janet for her advice and encouragement, we also thank Rebecca Tolen, sponsoring editor, for her help throughout the publication process. Mary Blizzard designed the beautiful cover. Dan Pyle and Bernadette Zoss provided invaluable help

529

with the production of the book. For copyediting and composition, we thank John McGuigan, who held to a high standard in creating the book's look. And for agreeing to read and respond before publication, we thank our colleagues Diane Goldstein and Dorry Noyes.

Finally, we owe our thanks to those individuals closest to us personally. To Lorraine, Brooke, and Henry we owe our gratitude and love. But most of all, we thank Henry Glassie—scholar, mentor, friend—for all that he has done to champion the serious study of individuals at work within their traditions. We dedicate our book to Henry in celebration of the contribution he has made to our discipline of folklore.

Photography Credits

Ackland Art Museum: 41 (bottom)
Acosta, Kimberlie: 226
Albee, L.: 46, 63 (bottom)
Bauman, Richard: 70, 76, 83
Beinecke Library, Yale University: 237, 242
British Museum: 288
Burrison, John A.: 410 (top), 422, 425 (bottom)
Cashman, Ray: 302
Cavanagh, Michael, and Kevin Montague: 521 (bottom)
Duffy, Karen M.: 194, 196 (bottom), 200, 206, 209, 212
Eilers, Charles: 92, 104 (bottom)
Ellington, Kim: 33 (top), 38, 41 (top), 42
Glassie, Henry: cover, frontispiece, xii, 146, 153, 170, 192 (bottom), 196 (top), 264, 360, 410 (bottom), 412 (bottom), 430, 444, 448, 454, 461, 465 (bottom), 468, 484
Glushko, Patricia: 337 (bottom)
Hansen, Gregory: 386
Hewitt, Mark: 462, 465 (top)
Holtzberg, Maggie: 112, 115, 116, 119 (bottom), 123

Hull, William F.: 412 (top), 417 (bottom), 425 (top)
Hunt, Marjorie: 49 (bottom), 58, 60
Joslyn, Lew: 119
Laudun, John: 267, 278, 281
Laurman, Robert C.: 63 (top)
McDowell, John Holmes: 326, 332, 337 (top)
Mills, Ernie: 408, 417 (top)
Mount, Marshall: 100 (bottom)
Palumbo, Vincent: 53
Peek, Philip M.: 99, 100 (top), 104 (top)
Schacker, Jennifer: 248
Shukla, Pravina: 144, 149, 164, 458, 521 (top)
Stein, Amelia: 491
Takahara, Takashi: 175, 180, 184, 190, 192 (top)
Vlach, John Michael: 345, 346, 350
Wagner, Paul: 49 (top), 65
Whyte, Allyson: 126, 131
Wiggs, Clara Ritchie: 28 (top)
Zug, Charles G.: 28 (bottom), 33 (bottom)

Tabula Gratulatoria

Jim Abrams
Amherst College Library
Jennifer Eastman Attebery
David S. Azzolina
Cristina Bacchilega
Ronald L. Baker
Robert Baron
Richard Bauman
Ruth B. Bottigheimer
Jan Harold Brunvand
Peggy A. Bulger
John Burrison
Canadian Museum of Civilization
    Library/Acquisitions
William M. Clements
Robert Cochran
Zsuzsanna Cselenyi
Susan G. Davis
Sandra K. Dolby
Karen Duffy
Department of Estonian and Com-
    parative Folklore, University of
    Tartu, Estonia
Bridget Edwards
Michael Robert Evans
Doris Devine Fanelli
Diamond Frandsen
Janice E. Frisch
Angus Kress Gillespie
Janet Gilmore
Diane Goldstein
Sylvia Grider
Grey Gundaker
Gregory Hansen
Lee Haring

Hannah Harvester
Anne F. Hatch
Elissa R. Henken
Carrie Hertz
Joe Hickerson
Maggie Holtzberg
Susan L. F. Isaacs
Jeanne Harrah Johnson
Thomas W. Johnson
Timothy J. Kloberdanz
Natalie Kononenko
Jim Leary
Outi Lehtipuro
Carl Lindahl
Jiang Lu
Jens Lund
Marion P. Martin
Material Culture
Ellen McHale
Joseph C. Miller
Ree Mobley
Eric Montenyohl
Dorothy Noyes
Beverly Patterson
Dan Patterson
Gerald Pocius
Thomas Grant Richardson
Ian Russell
Puja Sahney
Patricia Sawin
Steve Siporin
Moira Smith
Margaret Steiner
Beverly Stoeltje
Denise Stuempfle

531

Stephen Stuempfle
The Library of the Finnish
    Literature Society
Theresa Vaughan
John Vlach
Nicholas C. P. Vrooman
Stephen Wade
Marjut Wallin

Daniel Franklin Ward
Ward Museum of Wildfowl Art,
    Salisbury University
Anthony K. Webster
Mark E. Workman
Margaret R. Yocom
Charles Zug

Contributors

İlhan Başgöz is Professor Emeritus of Folklore and Central Eurasian Studies at Indiana University. He is a Guggenheim, Ford Foundation, and American Folklore Society Fellow. He served as president of the Turkish Studies Association (1978–1980), general editor of the Turkish Studies Series at Indiana University Press (1980–), member of the Governing Board of the American Research Institute in Turkey (1978–80), member of the Editorial Board of the *Journal of The Folklore Institute* (1973–78), and director of the Turkish Studies Program at Indiana University (1983–1997). His selected publications include: *Hikaye: Turkish Folk Romance as Performance Art* (2008), *Turkish Folklore and Oral Literature: Selected Essays of İlhan Başgöz,* (ed. Kemal Silay, 1998), *Bilmece: A Corpus of Turkish Riddles* (with Andreas Tietze, 1973), *Turkish Folklore Reader* (1971), and *Educational Problems in Turkey* (with Howard E. Wilson, 1967).

Richard Bauman is Distinguished Professor Emeritus of Folklore and Ethnomusicology, Communication and Culture, and Anthropology at Indiana University, Bloomington. He has served as President of the Society for Linguistic Anthropology and the Semiotic Society of America, and as editor of the *Journal of American Folklore.* Among his publications are *Verbal Art as Performance* (1977), *Story, Performance, and Event* (1986), *Voices of Modernity* (with Charles L. Briggs, 2003), which won the Edward Sapir Prize of the Society for Linguistic Anthropology, and *A World of Others' Words* (2004). In 2008, he received the Lifetime Scholarly Achievement Award of the American Folklore Society.

John A. Burrison received his Ph.D. in Folklore and Folklife at the University of Pennsylvania. He is Regents Professor of English and director of the Folklore Curriculum at Georgia State University, as well as curator of the Folk Pottery Museum of Northeast Georgia. His books include *Brothers in Clay: The Story of Georgia Folk Pottery* (1983), *Storytellers: Folktales and Legends from the South* (1989), *Shaping Traditions: Folk Arts in a Changing South* (2000), *From Mud to Jug: The Folk Potters and Pottery of Northeast*

Georgia (2010), all published by the University of Georgia Press, and *Roots of a Region: Southern Folk Culture* (2007), published by the University Press of Mississippi.

Ray Cashman is Associate Professor of Folklore in the English department at the Ohio State University, affiliated also with the departments of Anthropology and Comparative Studies. Having conducted most of his fieldwork in Ireland, north and south, he has published on outlaws and insurgents in folklore and popular literature; traditional customs, drama, and rites of passage; commemoration, nostalgia, and memory; and vernacular expressions of local, ethnic, sectarian, and political identities. His *Storytelling on the Northern Irish Border: Characters and Community* (2008) won the Donald Murphy Prize from the American Conference for Irish Studies and the Chicago Folklore Prize from the American Folklore Society.

Robert Cochran is Professor of English and Director of the Center for Arkansas and Regional Studies at the University of Arkansas, a Guggenheim Fellow (1989) and three-time Fulbright lecturer (Romania, Hungary, Korea). His book-length studies include two biographies (Vance Randolph, Louise Pound), two studies of Arkansas music, a portrait of a photographer (Geleve Grice), another portrait of a painter (Dorris Curtis), and a study of Samuel Beckett's short fiction. He has also directed three documentary videos and produced two CD collections devoted to Arkansas traditional life and music.

Karen M. Duffy, an independent folklorist based in Bloomington, Indiana, received her Ph.D. from Indiana University. A specialist in material culture and vernacular arts, she is particularly interested in how individual artists interpret and experience tradition. Her geographic areas of study are the U.S. Southwest (Native American pueblos) and Midwest; her articles have appeared in the *Journal of Folklore Research, Midwestern Folklore*, and *The Folklore Historian*. She has worked extensively in museums, taught folklore courses at Indiana State University and Indiana University, and consulted for a number of cultural institutions, most recently the Museum of International Folk Art in Santa Fe.

Michael Robert Evans is the Associate Dean for Undergraduate Studies at the Indiana University School of Journalism. He earned his Ph.D. in folklore from Indiana University in 1999, focusing his dissertation research on Inuit videography. He is the author of *Isuma: Inuit Video Art, The Fast*

Runner: Filming the Legend of Atanarjuat, *The Layers of Magazine Editing*, and *68 Knots*. He is currently working on a book about the events described in his chapter in this book.

Gregory Hansen is Associate Professor of Folklore and English at Arkansas State University, where he also teaches in the Heritage Studies graduate program. He received his graduate degrees in folklore from Western Kentucky University and Indiana University. He has completed public folklore projects for the Smithsonian Institution, Danish Immigrant Museum, Florida Folklife Program, Kentucky Center for the Arts, and other organizations. His research and publications center on folklore and education, public folklore, documentary media, and folk performances. He has produced a number of documentary videos and is the author of *A Florida Fiddler: The Life and Times of Richard Seaman.*

William Hansen is Professor Emeritus of Classical Studies and Folklore at Indiana University, Bloomington. He received his Ph.D. at the University of California, Berkeley, where he studied under Joseph Fontenrose (Classics) and Alan Dundes (Folklore). Among his books are *The Conference Sequence: Patterned Narration and Narrative Inconsistency in the Odyssey* (1972), *Saxo Grammaticus and the Life of Hamlet* (1983), *Phlegon of Tralles' Book of Marvels* (1996), *Anthology of Ancient Greek Popular Literature* (1998), *Ariadne's Thread: A Guide to International Tales Found in Classical Literature* (2002), and *Classical Mythology: A Guide to the Mythical World of the Greeks and Romans* (2005).

Lee Haring conducted research in the folklore of Madagascar, Mauritius, Reunion, Seychelles, and the Comoros for some thirty years, publishing his results in numerous scholarly articles and in the books *Stars and Keys: Folktales and Creolization in the Indian Ocean*, *Verbal Arts in Madagascar*, and the field manual *Collecting Folklore in Mauritius*. He has taught folklore at the University of Pennsylvania, University of Connecticut, and University of California at Berkeley.

Mark Hewitt was born in Stoke-on-Trent, England, and is the son and grandson of directors of Spode. After graduating from Bristol University in 1976, Mark apprenticed with Michael Cardew in Cornwall, then Todd Piker in Connecticut, where he met his wife, Carol. In 1983 they moved to Pittsboro, N.C., and established their pottery. He has written extensively in the ceramic press, and has exhibited in London, New York, and Tokyo, as well as throughout the United States. He co-authored *The Potter's Eye: Art and Tradition in North Carolina Pottery*, with Nancy Sweezy, and was featured in the nationwide PBS television series "Craft in America." His website is www.hewittpottery.com.

Maggie Holtzberg is Manager of the Folk Arts & Heritage Program at the Massachusetts Cultural Council (1999 to the present). As a folklorist, she works closely with traditional artists and communities through documentary fieldwork, grant programs, presenting, and technical assistance. She is author of *Keepers of Tradition: Art and Folk Heritage in Massachusetts* (2008), *The Lost World of the Craft Printer* (1992), *Portrait of Spirit: One Story at a Time* (1996), producer of the sound recording *Georgia Folk: A Sampler of Traditional Sound* (1990), and co-director/producer of the documentary film *Gandy Dancers* (1994). Holtzberg holds a Ph.D. in Folklore and Folklife from the University of Pennsylvania and served as Folklife Program Director of the Georgia Council for the Arts before coming to Massachusetts.

Marjorie Hunt is a folklorist and curator with the Center for Folklife and Cultural Heritage at the Smithsonian Institution. She received her Ph.D. in Folklore and Folklife from the University of Pennsylvania in 1995. Her extensive work in the area of traditional art includes her Academy- and Emmy-Award winning documentary film *The Stone Carvers* and her book *The Stone Carvers: Master Craftsmen of Washington National Cathedral*. She was the curator of the "Masters of the Building Arts" program for the 2001 Smithsonian Folklife Festival and is currently working to complete a documentary film on master artisans in the building trades.

George Jevremović is an entrepreneur, business owner, lecturer, occasional writer, editor, designer, and wide-ranging supporter of artists and the arts. In 1979, bitten by the "tribal rug bug" during a brief stint teaching at Uskudar Girls College in Istanbul, he started dealing and trading antique oriental carpets. In 1982, convinced that a return to the lost crafts of natural dyeing and hand spinning would be a catalyst for a revival of the art of the traditional Oriental carpet, his company, Woven Legends (founded 1980), provided the vision and strategy, the investment in training and infrastructure, and the research and development necessary to recover knowledge and skills lost in the wake of the Industrial Revolution. What resulted was the creation of a successful cottage industry centered in Eastern Turkey, employing thousands, followed by similar projects in India, Romania, and China; Woven Legends Restoration, a state of the art antique carpet and textile restoration facility in Izmir, Turkey; and Material Culture in Philadelphia, a vast emporium of art and commerce, and an ever-evolving stage for exhibitions, lectures, and celebrations.

Greg Kelley holds a Ph.D. in Folklore from Indiana University. Former president of the Hoosier Folklore Society and editor of the journals *Folklore Forum* and *Midwestern Folklore*, he also served as coordinating publisher for Trickster Press, where he was Associate editor (with Michael Evans and John McGuigan) of Dell Hymes' *Reading Takelma Texts*, Warren Roberts's *Log Buildings of Southern Indiana*, and *Fields of Folklore: Essays in Honor of Kenneth S. Goldstein* (Roger D. Abrahams, ed.). He has published broadly on folklore, folklore and literary relations, and humor. Currently, he teaches in the School of English and Theatre Studies at the University of Guelph and in Media Studies at the University of Guelph-Humber.

John Laudun is a folklorist and essayist living in Lafayette, Louisiana where he is Associate Professor of English at the University of Louisiana. His essay is drawn from a larger research program focusing on the nature of creativity within a community, *The Makers of Things: Creativity on a Human Scale*. He has published widely on verbal art, material culture, and folkways in scholarly articles, public essays, CDs, films, radio and television programming, as well as the web. More information can be found at http://johnlaudun.org/.

John Holmes McDowell is professor of Folklore and Ethnomusicology at Indiana University, working primarily in Mexico and the Andes of Colombia and Ecuador where he focuses on traditional expressive forms, especially songs and stories, as they enter into the life of individuals and their communities and as they are processed to represent these communities to the outside world. His most recent monograph is *Poetry and Violence: The Ballad Tradition of Mexico's Costa Chica*, published in 2000 by the University of Illinois Press and released as a paperback in 2008.

Tom Mould is Associate Professor of Anthropology at Elon University and director of PERCS, Elon's Program for Ethnographic Research and Community Studies. He is the author of two books on Choctaw narrative—*Choctaw Prophecy: A Legacy of the Future* and *Choctaw Tales*—and has published on issues of generic boundaries and constructed identities, particularly in the study of oral narrative. He has also produced numerous video documentaries for public television on folk art and culture in Indiana, Kentucky and North Carolina. His current research explores prophecy and revelation among Latter-day Saints, with a book *Still, the Small Voice: Revelation, Oral Narrative and the Mormon Folk Tradition* due out in 2011.

Elliott Oring received his M.A. and Ph.D. degrees in Folklore from Indiana University. He was Professor of Anthropology at California State University, Los Angeles and served as the chair of the department. He has written extensively on folklore, humor, and cultural symbolism. Professor Oring was editor of *Western Folklore* and currently serves on the editorial boards of *Humor: International Journal for Humor Research* and *Journal of Folklore Research*. He also has served on the executive boards of the American Folklore Society and the International Society for Humor Research. He is a Fellow of the American Folklore Society and a Folklore Fellow of the Finnish Academy of Arts and Sciences.

Philip M. Peek has recently retired from the department of Anthropology, Drew University. He was a Peace Corps teacher in Nigeria, 1964–66, after which he earned his M.A. in Folklore at the University of California, Berkeley, and his Ph.D. at Indiana University. In addition to over thirty articles on African divination systems and verbal and visual arts, his publications include *African Divination Systems, Ways of the River: Arts and Environment in the Niger Delta* (co-edited with Martha Anderson), *African Folklore: An Encyclopedia* (co-edited with Kwesi Yankah). Current work has focused on the soon to be published anthology, *Double Trouble or Twice Blessed: Twins in African Cultures and the Diaspora*.

Jennifer Schacker is Associate Professor of English at the University of Guelph, Ontario, Canada. Her research interests include the histories of British folklore study, children's literature, and the fairy tale. She is author of *National Dreams: The Remaking of Fairy Tales in Nineteenth-Century England* (University of Pennsylvania Press), awarded the 2006 Mythopoeic Scholarship Award in Myth and Fantasy Studies. Schacker is currently working with Christine Jones on an anthology of tales and new critical perspectives, and completing a study of sexual and sartorial subversion in fairy-tale pantomime, entitled "Cross-Dressed Tales: French Fairy Tales and the British Pantomime Tradition."

Pravina Shukla is Associate Professor in the Department of Folklore and Ethnomusicology, Indiana University, where she teaches courses on American folklore, dress and adornment, museums, food, and material culture, and is a three-time winner of the Indiana University Trustees Teaching Award. She is the author of *The Grace of Four Moons: Dress, Adornment, and the Art of the Body in Modern India,* winner of the Milia Davenport Award of the Costume Society of America and of the A. K. Coomaraswamy Book Prize by the South Asia Council of the Association for Asian Studies. She has lectured on material culture, dress, and adornment within the United States, and also in India, Bangladesh, Canada, Israel, and Germany.

Takashi Takahara received his Ph.D. in folklore from Indiana University. Currently he is a professor in the Department of Comparative Cultures, Faculty of International Communication, Aichi University, Toyohashi, Japan. His primary research interests are *Oniitashi* (ogre-tile makers) and Japanese figurative ceramics, which are closely related to each other in the Japanese ceramic tradition. This interest began with the fieldwork for Henry Glassie's study of world traditional art. In 2010, he published a book in Japanese, entitled *Oniitashi: The People Who Have Been Making Oni (Ogres).*

John Michael Vlach is Professor of American Studies and Anthropology at The George Washington University in Washington, D.C. Over the course of his thirty-four years as a scholar and museum curator he has developed numerous exhibitions and authored many books and catalogues including: *The Afro-American Tradition in Decorative Arts, Back of the Big House: The Architecture of Plantation Slavery, Charleston Blacksmith: The Work of Philip Simmons, Plain Painters: Making Sense of American Folk Art, The Planter's Prospect: Privilege and Slavery in Plantation Paintings,* and he initiated a series of architectural monographs published by the Library of Congress with *Barns*—a book that received the Kniffen Prize for best book on American material culture. He has served as guest curator for numerous museums, historic sites, and art galleries across the country and also works to upgrade the skills of high school teachers all across the United States through the "Teacher Serve" program operated by the National Humanities Center in Research Triangle, North Carolina.

Vincent Woods is a Dublin playwright, poet and broadcaster. He presents/hosts arts programmes, including Arts Tonight, on RTÉ Radio 1. His plays include *At the Black Pig's Dyke, A Cry from Heaven,* and *Song of the Yellow*

Bittern. His poetry collections are *The Colour of Language* and *Lives and Miracles.* He co-edited *The Turning Wave,* an anthology of the poetry and song of Irish Australia. He received the Stewart Parker award for Drama and the Ted McNulty poetry award. He is a member of Aosdána, the Irish Academy of distinguished artists.

Charles G. (Terry) Zug retired from the University of North Carolina at Chapel Hill in 2001 after teaching for thirty-three years in the Department of English and the Curriculum in Folklore. His major research interest has been the material culture of the South. He has written exhibition catalogues, articles, and books, including *Turners and Burners: The Folk Potters of North Carolina* (University of North Carolina Press, 1986). He also helped lead the citizens' committee that designed, funded, and constructed the North Carolina Pottery Center, the first state pottery center in the nation, and in his "retirement" has served as Director of the Center.

American Folklore Society, panels on The Individual and Tradition, Nashville, Tennessee, 2010
Back row, from left: Karen Duffy, Ray Cashman, Michael Evans, John Burrison, John Vlach, Gregory Hansen, Phil Peek, Bill Hansen, Dick Bauman, Lee Haring, Tom Mould.
Front row: Bob Cochran, Pravina Shukla, John Laudun, Henry Glassie, Takashi Takahara, Jennifer Schacker.

Index

Abshire, Jimmy, 19, 268, 247, 282
Acoma, 18, 95, 194–218
Adams, D. J., 254
African art, 94, 92–111
African-American, 343–52
Ahojeobe, 132
Akenzua II, Oba, 96–97, 101–2, 105
Albers, Josef, 464, 466
Alm, Albert, 150–51, 162
Alver, Brynjulf, 195
American Folklore Society, 499
American Indian Movement, (AIM) 223, 228, 230
Amos, Billy, 18, 130–33
Amos, Wagoner, 130
Anagama Japanese kiln, 31, 39
Ankara, 13
Ankarcrona, Gustaf, 150, 158, 162–63, 165
Anyichie, J. A. Okeke, 93
Appalachia, 10
Aragon, Marvis, 202
Aragon, Wanda, 18, 194–218, 506
Arkansas, 481–82
Armstrong, Robert Plant, 50
Aronsson, Knis Karl, 147, 163
At the Black Pig's Dyke, 486, 490–91, 493, 495–96, 513
Atlanta History Center, 414
attribution, 8–10

Bakhtin, Mikhail, 5
Ballymenone, 13–14, 71, 95, 114, 127, 266, 405, 471–76, 478–79, 481, 489–90, 495–96, 505, 512–15, 518–19
Bangladesh, 20, 506–7, 516–17
Banks, Dennis, 230
Başgöz, İlhan, 21, 353–64
Basso, Ellen, 324

Bauman, Richard, 3, 16, 18, 70–91, 127–28, 220–21, 315
Beier, Georgina, 96, 103, 105, 108
Beier, Ulli, 93, 96, 101, 103, 105, 108–9
Belafonte, Harry, 438
Ben-Amos, Dan, 5, 98
Ben-Amos, Paula Girshick, 96, 98
Bendix, Regina, 163
Benin City, Nigeria, 17, 93, 95–98, 105–8
Benoit, Harold, 19, 268, 273–74, 278, 280
Bernstein, Basil, 323
Bishop, Petie, 134
Björklöf, Sune, 149
Björklöf, Ulla, 161, 163
Black Mountain College, 460, 463–64, 466, 469
Blamires, David, 250, 255
Boas, Franz, 48, 61, 138, 429
boats, 17, 113–25, 265–86
body art, 10, 144–69
Bolter, David, 71
Boruff, Virgil, 15
Boston, 113, 117
Boyle, Michael, 473, 475, 489–90, 495
bricolage, 4–5, 17, 93–94, 108–9, 303–5, 315
Brown, Pamela Allen, 255, 258
Bunzel, Ruth, 205
Burke, Kenneth, 323, 341
Burnham, Harold A., 17–18, 113–25
Burrison, John, 21, 408–28
Bush, George W., 222
Byington, Robert, 389

Cage, John, 429, 466
Cajuns, 268–69
Canada, 224–25
Çanakkale, 360, 445–48
Cardew, Michael, 9–10, 455–56

Carroll, Noël, 381
Casey, Thomas, 14
Cashman, Ray, 20, 219, 303–22
Catawba Valley, 16, 27, 29–31, 34–37,
    39–40, 43–45, 455–57, 463, 467
Çelebioğlu, Amil, 353, 361
Cephas, John, 15
Chartres Cathedral, 59, 62
Chicunque, Mariano, 20, 325–26, 328,
    334–36, 341
Child, Francis James, 429
Choctaw, 9, 17, 126, 129, 130–34, 140
Cochran, Robert, 23, 471–82
Colombia, 20, 324–25, 328–35, 340
Comby, Olman, 132
commedia dell'arte, 251
Concho, Lolita, 198
Conner Prairie Museum, 503–4
Coomaraswamy, Ananda K., 220
Cormier, Henry, 19, 268, 281–82
Cornett, Chester, 15
Courville, Clayton, 19, 268, 274, 280
Craig, Burlon, 15–16, 29–37, 39, 40, 43,
    44, 456–57, 467
Craig, Don, 37
Crisfield, MD, 415
Crow Dog, Leonard, 230
Cultee, Charles, 324
Cunningham, Robert Hays, 259
Custer, George, 21, 386, 390, 392–405
Cutler, Ellen, 473, 474–77, 481–82, 495

D'Azevedo, Warren, 94
Dalarna, Sweden, 146–69
Darling, Erik, 22, 429–40
Deetz, James, 503
Defoe, Daniel, 236
Dégh, Linda, 5, 133, 137, 241, 304
DeMain, Paul, 19, 226–32
Devon, 9
Dickerson, Sara Jane Hollis, 96, 101, 107
Dior, Christian, 158
Dixon, Jim, 132

Dolby, Sandra, 307
Donegal, 302–22
Dorson, Richard M., 365
Drake, David, 21, 343–52
Druid Theatre, 490–91, 495
Dubois, Thomas, 163
duck decoys, 21, 408–28
Duffy, Karen, 18, 195–218
Duncan, Robert, 469
Dylan, Bob, 434, 438

Eboigbe, Felix, 98
Ecuador, 324–25, 327, 335–41
Edgefield District, 343–44, 347–50
Edwards, Archie, 15
Egbedi, Eture, 105
Eilers, Charles, 103
Eliot, T. S., 3
Ellington, Betsy, 32, 34
Ellington, Kim, 16, 18, 27–45
Elliott, Jack, 433–34
Ellis, Bill, 240
Ellis, Captain Tom, 117, 122
engineering, 20, 265–86
England, 9, 10, 249–52, 254–61, 455,
    464, 504
Enniskillen, 486, 495, 505
epic, 7, 20, 287–301
Erdeyer, İbrahim, 13, 506
Essex Shipbuilding Museum, 118
Essex, MA, 17, 116–18
Evans, Michael, 18, 219–34
Eweka, Oba, 95

Fagg, William, 102
Faier, Billy, 22, 429–40
fairies, 312–19
fairy tales, 19, 249–63
Fermanagh, 8, 114, 165, 483, 486, 495,
    505, 512–15, 518–19
festival, 388–407
fieldwork, 2, 5, 11–12, 14, 22–23, 113,
    471–82

First Coast Folklife Festival, 21, 386, 389–407
Fitch, James Marston, 502
Flanagan, Joe, 473, 476, 495
Flanagan, Peter, 473–76, 482, 495, 505
Florida, 21, 386–407
Foley, John Miles, 289
folk art, 22, 124, 409–28, 515
folk costume, 18, 144–69
folklore, 5, 10, 23, 128–29, 232
folksong revival, 22, 429–40
folktale, 75, 514–15
Forssell, C., 154
France, 19, 249–54, 256–59
Frawley, Monica, 496
Frost, Robert, 306
Frugé, Greg, 19, 268, 274, 280
Frykman, Jonas, 162
Fultz, Helen, 482

Gailey, Alan, 165, 489
Gallagher, Bryan, 165
Garland, Joseph, 122
Gates, Irene Reinhardt, 3
Georgia, 244, 408–28, 458–60, 463, 464
Germany, 356, 411, 439, 464, 504
Gilman, Lisa, 132
Glassie, Henry, 1–4, 7, 10–15, 20, 22–23, 27, 51, 54, 61, 64, 66, 71, 93–95, 106–07, 113, 127, 137, 165, 219–20, 222, 232, 243, 265–66, 305, 319, 365, 388, 409, 411, 414, 423, 429, 435, 471–82, 489, 494–97, 499–527
Gloucester, MA, 115, 117–18, 122
Goldstein, Diane, 136
Goldstein, Kenneth, 11–13
Gomme, George Laurence, 259, 323
Gradén, Lizette, 161
Grimm Brothers, 71, 254
Grusin, Richard, 71
Gummere, Francis, 5, 141
Gürsoy, Mehmet, 12, 13, 506, 521
Guthrie, Woody, 434

Habetz, Tedmon, 19, 268, 273–74, 280
Hainsworth, J. B., 293
Halvares, Anna, 161
Hamada, Shoji, 10
Handler, Richard, 388
Hansen, Gregory, 21, 386–407
Hansen, William, 20, 287–301
Haring, Lee, 22, 429–40
Harries, Elizabeth, 249, 255
Hart, Bob, 32, 34
Hartland, Edwin Sidney, 1
Hartzog, David, 40
Havre de Grace Decoy Museum, 416
Havre de Grace, MD, 415
Hawkins, Jim, 19, 235, 236, 238–39
Hazelius, Artur, 145, 147, 154, 162–63, 165
Hazlitt, William, 259
Heaney, Seamus, 219
Heleema, 132
Hellspong, Mats, 161
Henley, W. E., 245
Henry, Inez, 132
Henson, Dana C., 124
heritage, 145, 147, 161, 163
Hewell, Chester, 459, 463
Hewell, Grace Nell, 458, 459–60, 463–64
Hewell's Pottery, 416, 459
Hewitt, Carol, 463, 465
Hewitt, Mark, 9–10, 22, 39, 454–70
Hickory, NC, 29, 30, 32, 455
Hogan, Phydella, 481–82
Holland, Peter, 251
Holtzberg, Maggie, 17, 112–25
Homer, 7, 20, 288–301
Houck, William, 15
Hughes, Dale, 19, 268, 281–82
Hunt, Marjorie, 16, 46–69
Hyman, Stanley Edgar, 429
Hymes, Dell, 128, 130, 132, 145, 324

Idah, Chief Ovia, 17, 18, 92–111
Idah, George, 101, 107
Idah, Henshaw, 107

Idah, Omere, 107
Idah, Samuel, 107–8
Idah, Thomas, 107
Idehen, Festes, 98
India, 10
Indiana University Museum of Art, 13
individual, 4–6, 6–11, 14–23, 128, 140, 303–4, 306–7
intermediality, 220–22
intertextuality, 10
Ireland, 2, 8, 13–14, 20, 23, 71, 95, 114, 127, 165, 266, 302–22, 405, 471–76, 478–79, 481, 483–98, 504–5, 512–15, 518–19
Irish Folklore Commission, 501, 522
Istanbul, 13, 447, 449
Italy, 46–69
Ives, Burl, 431
Ives, Edward D., 5

Jacob, Joseph, 5
James, John, 57, 59, 62
Japan, 10, 18, 31, 39, 170–93, 455, 464
Jevremović, George, 22, 441–53
Jobs, Karin, 151, 156, 163
Jobs, Verner, 147
Jobs-Björklöf, Kersti, 18, 144–69
Johnson, Captain Charles, 236
jokes, 8, 21, 134, 365–85
Jones, Christine A., 254–55
Jörgensen, Märta, 158, 162
journalism, 219–34
Juajibioy, María, 20, 325–26, 329–32, 334–36, 341
Jugtown, NC, 469

Kağıtçıbası, Çiğdem, 354, 362
Kajikawa, Hyakutaro, 178–80, 189, 191
Kajikawa, Kenichi, 179, 181–82, 185–86, 189, 191
Kajikawa, Morio, 179, 181, 185–86, 189
Kajikawa, Ryoji, 170, 175, 179, 184, 185–89, 192
Kajikawa, Shunichiro, 188–90

Kajikawa, Tsutomu, 179, 181–87, 189
Kato, Chōko, 179, 182–83, 185, 187
Kelley, Greg, 19, 235–47
Kennedy, Jean, 101
Kimball, J. Golden, 133
King, Don, 15
King, Dr. Martin Luther, 501
Kingston Trio, 432, 438
Kirshenblatt, Mayer, 15
Klein, Barbro, 147, 161, 163
Kniffen, Fred, 476, 503, 510
Kobayashi, Akio, 173–74, 183
Korea, 171, 175
Kramer, Louis, 273–74
Kröger, Elis, 164
Kütahya, Turkey, 12–13, 127

Lagos, Nigeria, 96–98, 101, 108
Landrum, Abner, 343
Lang, Mabel, 291–93
Larsson, Carl, 154, 158, 162, 165
Larsson, Karin, 158, 162
Latter-day Saints, 129, 133–37, 139, 140
Laudun, John, 19, 264–86
Leach, Bernard, 10, 455
Leach, MacEdward, 500
Ledbetter, Huddie, 431, 481
legend, 8, 19, 221, 235, 238, 240, 244–45
Leitrim, 483–98
Lévi-Strauss, Claude, 4, 94–95, 109, 303, 323
life stories, 20, 306–12, 318–19
Linde, Charlotte, 222, 306
Linnaeus, Carl, 162
Löfgren, Orvar, 154, 162
Lomax, Alan, 268, 429
Lomax, John A., 479–81
Lord, Albert, 7, 20, 287, 289–90, 293, 298
Louden, Bruce, 292–94
Louisiana, 19, 265–86, 348
Lowenstam, Steven, 219, 294
Luck, Sid, 11
lullabies, 21, 353–64

Lum, Ray, 14
Lynn, Jim, 37

Ma, Yo-Yo, 502
Mack, Charles, 459–60
Madame d'Aulnoy, 19, 248–63
Maguire, John, 15
Malinowski, Bronislaw, 323
Maryland, 412–16, 419–20
Massachusetts, 17, 113–25
material culture, 9, 15, 17, 21, 27–45,
    46–69, 92–111, 113–25, 144–69,
    170–93, 195–218, 343–52, 408–28,
    441–70, 510, 517–18
Matsson, Britta, 161
Matthiessen, Peter, 228
Mbari Mbayo, 105
McDowell, John, 20, 323–42
McGiveney, Hughie, 13
McGrath, Packy Jim, 20, 302–22
Meaders, Cheever, 15
Meaders, Lanier, 15
Means, Russell, 230
Meko, Duga of, 15
Memorate, 20, 134, 327, 336
Middleton, Richard, 239
Miller, D. Gary, 291, 294
Miller, Nathan, 481–82
Mills, Ernie, 21, 408–28
Mingei Japanese Folk Art Movement, 455
Mint Museum, 45
Mississippi, 17, 126, 129, 130–33
Misueda, Sotaro, 179, 191
Mitchell, Madison R., 412, 415
Monroe, Bill, 390, 393–94, 400
Monson, Thomas S., 133–34
Morigi, Roger, 16, 18, 46–48, 50–66
Morris, William, 162, 442
Mother Bunch, 19, 249–50, 255–61
Mother Goose, 255, 260
Mould, Tom, 17, 126–40
Mount, Marshall, 96–97
Müller, Max, 323

mumming, 165, 489–90, 512–13
Murphy, Seamus, 50, 57, 62
Murray, Kenneth, 96
museum exhibitions, 505
music, 21, 386–407, 429–40
Mystic Seaport Museum, 124
Myths, 20, 138, 312, 323–42

narrative, 8, 10, 13, 16–17, 19–21, 70–91,
    127–43, 221–22, 235, 238, 240–41,
    244–45, 249–63, 287–342
National Council on the Humanities, 500
National Heritage Museum, Lexing-
    ton, MA, 121
Native Americans, 194–218, 219–34, 411
Navajo, 138
Nevadomsky, Joseph, 98, 107
New Mexico, 196–218
New York City, 22, 429–40
Newell, W. W., 429
Nigeria, 2, 17, 20, 92–111, 519–20
Nolan, Hugh, 8, 13–14, 71, 304, 473–75,
    482, 494–95, 507
Nordiska Museet, 154–55, 157, 162
North Carolina, 10–11, 15–17, 22, 27–45,
    127, 129, 135, 413–16, 423, 454–70
North Carolina Museum of Art, 45
North Carolina Pottery Center, 45
Noyes, Dorothy, 3, 163

Ó Conaill, Seán, 14
Ó Duilearga, Séamus, 306–7
Ó Súilleabháin, Seán, 311
Oglala, South Dakota, 223
ogre-tile makers, 18, 170–93
Ohihyaku family, 18, 177–82, 185, 191
Ojibwe Nation, 225, 227
Ojo, John, 103
Olinger, Dale, 265
Olinger, Gerard, 19, 265, 268, 274–83
Olson, Charles, 460
Omogbai, Colette, 105

Oring, Elliott, 21, 219, 221, 231, 238, 240, 365–85
Ortiz, Mamie, 198
Ortutay, Gyula, 137
Oshogbo, Nigeria, 108
Osudi, Chief, 97
Owen III, Ben, 11
Owens, Pamela, 11
Ozolua, Oba, 97

Pal, Haripada, 15, 305, 507
Palkó, Zsuzsanna, 14, 137, 304
Palumbo, Vincent, 16, 18, 47–66
pantomime, 19, 250–52, 256–57, 260–61
Parry, Milman, 7, 20, 287, 289, 293, 298
Peace Corps, 93, 98, 102
Peek, Pat, 109
Peek, Philip, 17, 92–111
Peltier, Leonard, 223–25, 227–31
Penland, 463, 466–67
Pennsylvania, 413, 414, 476, 500–501, 504
Pentikäinen, Juha, 5
performance, 3–4, 6–9, 16, 21, 51, 75, 79, 80, 127, 128, 130, 135, 163, 195, 220, 353, 365–66
Perrault, Charles, 252–53, 255–57
Philadelphia, 445–46
Pickens, Ruby, 479
Picuasi, Maruja, 20, 325, 327, 336–41
Pierce, Elijah, 15
Pioneer America Society, 501
Pirous, A. D., 15
Plimoth Plantation, 503–4
Porterfield, Nolan, 479, 480
pottery, 9–10, 12–13, 15–16, 18, 21–22, 27–45, 54, 61, 94, 127, 170–218, 343–52, 454–70
Poulsen, Richard C., 136
preservation, 154–57, 161, 502
Pritchett, David, 102
prophecy, 9, 129, 130, 132, 134
Propst, Sam, 37, 39
public folklore, 387–90, 500–507

Pye, David, 59, 66

Quirk, Michael, 19, 268, 281–82

Redford, Robert, 228
Reed, Dock, 479–81
Reinhardt, Enoch, 31
Reinhardt, Harvey, 29
remediation, 16–17, 71–72, 85
revitalization, 14, 17, 27
revival, 18, 27, 145, 158–59, 163, 195, 197, 208, 214
Richard, Mike, 19, 268, 274–77, 279, 281–83
Riddle, Almeda, 15
Rinzler, Ralph, 501–2
Robbie, William, 15
Roberts, Warren, 502
Rodin, Auguste, 179
Ronnberg, Erik Jr., 120
Roos, Sven, 154, 163
rug weaving, 22, 441–53

Şahin, Ahmet, 12, 475, 479, 507
Salisbury, MD, 415
Salvador, Lilly, 204, 506
Savannah, Georgia, 244
Sawin, Patricia, 306–7
Schacker, Jennifer, 19, 249–63
Seagle, Daniel, 40, 43, 466
Seagrove, NC, 11, 27, 127, 467, 469
Seaman, Richard, 21, 386, 390–405
Seeger, Pete, 431, 433, 435–38
Seferlis, Constantine, 65–66
Seifert, Lewis, 253
Seven-Seven, Prince Twins, 2, 11, 15, 22, 232, 305, 507, 519–22
Shopes, Linda, 308
Shukla, Pravina, 18, 144–169
Shuman, Amy, 306
Sibundoy Valley, 20, 324–25, 328–35, 340
Silver, Long John, 19, 238–40, 245
Simmons, Philip, 15

Skansen Open Air Museum, 145, 154, 162
Smith, Georgina, 240
Smithsonian Institution, 107, 203–04, 416, 501–02
South Carolina, 21, 343–52, 455, 457, 463
Spufford, Margaret, 255
Stanley, Keith, 135
star informant, 11–14, 23, 71
star performer, 12–14, 16–19, 22–23, 79–80, 87, 93, 95, 114, 127–30, 132–34, 137, 140–41, 266, 304
Starkweather, Frank, 102
Steve, Rosalie, 18, 130–31
Stevenson, Robert Louis, 19, 235–47
Stewart, Cal, 16–18, 70–91
Stewart, Susan, 44
Stoke-on-Trent, 455
stone carving, 16, 46–69
Stone, Bob, 389–404
storytelling, 70–91, 222, 235
Stump, Dwight, 15
Sweden, 18, 144–69

Tägtström, David, 151
Takahara, Takashi, 18, 171–93
tall tales, 72, 134
Tandioy, Francisco, 20, 325, 331–34
Thompson, John Hunter, 132
Thompson, Stith, 2
Thoreau, Henry David, 304
Tingle, Tom, 130
Tokugawa, Yoshimune, 172, 177
Torivio, Frances, 197–98, 200, 202, 206
Torivio, Frank, 197
tradition, 2–4, 5–23, 27, 51, 145, 161, 195, 303–4
traditionalization, 14, 145
Treasure Island, 19, 235–47
Trimbach, John M., 228
Trimbach, Joseph H., 228
Troy, Jack, 27
Trudell, John, 231
Tubby, Estelline, 9, 18, 127, 130, 132–33

Tubby, Simpson, 132
Turkey, 2–4, 12–13, 21–22, 54, 61, 107, 127, 353–64, 441–53, 475, 505–6, 515–16

UNESCO 13

Vázsonyi, Andrew, 133
Venable, Kurt, 19, 268, 274–77, 279–83
verbal art, 365
vernacular architecture, 7, 8, 472, 503–4, 511–12
Viehmann, Frau, 71
Vinokurova, Natal'ia Osupovna, 14
Virginia, 7, 413, 504, 511–12
Vlach, John Michael, 21, 343–52

Walker, Carson, 228
Wallin, Lee, 10
Walsh, Jim, 85
Ward Museum of Wildfowl Art, 415
Ward, Lem, 415, 419
Ward, Steve, 415, 419
Warner, Mariana, 255, 258
Washington National Cathedral, 46–48, 57–59, 63, 65
Washington Square Park, NY, 22, 429–40
Williams, Jonathan, 460
Williams, Raymond, 51
Wise, Robert "Chubby", 21, 386, 390, 392–405
Woods, Vincent, 23, 165, 483–98
Woodstock, NY, 433, 435

Yamamoto, Kichibei, 178
Yamamoto, Otake, 178–79, 191
Yamberla, Luis Alberto, 20, 325, 327, 336–38, 340–41
York, Baxter, 132
Yoruba, 11

Zic, Frank, 47, 62, 64–66
Zorn, Anders, 154
Zug, Charles C., 15–16, 27–45